Social Work Practice with a Difference

SOCIAL WORK PRACTICE WITH A DIFFERENCE:

Stories, Essays, Cases, and Commentaries

Alice A. Lieberman
(University of Kansas)

and

Cheryl B. Lester
(University of Kansas)

Boston   Burr Ridge, IL   Dubuque, IA   Madison, WI   New York
San Francisco   St. Louis   Bangkok   Bogotá   Caracas   Kuala Lumpur
Lisbon   London   Madrid   Mexico City   Milan   Montreal   New Delhi
Santiago   Seoul   Singapore   Sydney   Taipei   Toronto

Higher Education

SOCIAL WORK PRACTICE WITH A DIFFERENCE

Published by McGraw-Hill, a business unit of The McGraw-Hill Companies, Inc., 1221 Avenue of the Americas, New York, NY 10020. Copyright © 2004 by The McGraw-Hill Companies, Inc. All rights reserved. No part of this publication may be reproduced or distributed in any form or by any means, or stored in a database or retrieval system, without the prior written consent of The McGraw-Hill Companies, Inc., including, but not limited to, in any network or other electronic storage or transmission, or broadcast for distance learning.

Some ancillaries, including electronic and print components, may not be available to customers outside the United States.

This book is printed on acid-free paper.

Domestic   1 2 3 4 5 6 7 8 9 0 DOC/DOC 0 9 8 7 6 5 4 3

ISBN 0-07-283547-8

Vice president and editor-in-chief: *Thalia Dorwick*
Publisher: *Stephen D. Rutter*
Special projects editor: *Rebecca Smith*
Editorial assistant: *Ann Helgerson*
Marketing manager: *Courtney Cooney*
Project manager: *Mary Lee Harms*
Production supervisor: *Enboge Chong*
Design coordinator: *Gino Cieslik*
Cover image: *Mike McPheeters*
Associate art editor: *Cristin Yancey*
Senior supplement producer: *David A. Welsh*
Compositor: *GAC/Indianapolis*
Typeface: *Palatino*
Printer: *R. R. Donnelley/Crawfordsville, IN*

The credits section of this book begins on page 533 and is considered an extension of the copyright page.

All artistic products for this book were produced by the children of Van Go Mobile Arts, Inc., Lawrence, KS, who have participated in the JAMS (Jobs in the Arts Makes Sense) Program. This "earn while you learn" program employs area teens year-round. Under the direction of professional teaching artists, the apprentice artists are paid minimum wages to create commissioned art benches, murals, and a variety of 2-and 3-D pieces sold in the JAMS gallery. All proceeds are used to support Van Go. Using art as the vehicle, the JAMS program teaches jobs and life skills that translate into the "real world."

Library of Congress Cataloging-in-Publication Data

Social work practice with a difference: stories, essays, cases, and commentaries / [edited by] Alice A. Lieberman and Cheryl B. Lester.
   p. cm.
Includes bibliographical references and index.
ISBN 0-07-283547-8 (softcover)
   1. Social service—United States. 2. Social work with minorities—United States.
   3. Marginality, Social—United States. I. Lieberman, Alice A. II. Lester, Cheryl B.
HV91.S6255 2003
361.3'0973—dc22   2003059398

The Internet addresses listed in the text were accurate at the time of publication. The inclusion of a website does not indicate an endorsement by the authors or McGraw-Hill, and McGraw-Hill does not guarantee the accuracy of the information presented at these sites.

www.mhhe.com

Table of Contents

Unit 4:   Building Interventions in Cases Where Gender or Sexuality Is at Issue

Unit 5: Accessing Resources for Persons Affected by Relocation and Dislocation   227

Social Institutions and Diversity

Unit 6: Negotiating Multiple Systems on Behalf of Children and Families   305

Unit 9: Advocating on Behalf of Clients in Poverty

Preface

ABOUT THIS BOOK

This textbook is decidedly different from others you may have used in the past. Rather than trying to "give" students the skills and tools needed for successful social work practice, this text invites the reader to "take" the stories (both fiction and non-fiction), essays, case studies, and commentaries we offer, and from them to fashion a more expansive, generous view of our diverse humanity. We think this, in turn, will contribute to the development of a more effective, more conscious, social work practitioner.

We intend our selections to offer different perspectives on a variety of personal and social circumstances that set individuals apart from—and give them less social power or cultural capital than—individuals more securely positioned as members of the mainstream or dominant culture. Almost by definition, the purpose of social work is to act on behalf of such individuals and groups who are determined by society to have less access to its rewards and benefits, resources and services. Yet the social worker, if only in function of her professional status, has privileged access to the very resources and services that are out of reach to her clients. To fulfill the mandate of the profession, it is imperative that social workers find a way to bridge the distance between their own privileges and their clients' obstacles, just as we must learn to acknowledge our weaknesses and their strengths.

We believe that knowledge of the beliefs, feelings, and past and present circumstances of others can help social workers develop greater understanding and more effective practice. At the same time, we are aware that such understanding requires lifelong dedication, learning, and application. Our book was put together in the hope that it could initiate processes indispensable to working with diverse people in diverse circumstances: self-knowledge, multicultural education, and empathy (Jenkins 1993). With the important addition of practice itself, these are the vital aspects of what we are calling "social work practice with a difference," i.e., a generalist social work practice sensitized to and transformed by the demands of working with the full range of human diversity. Only through practice are the crucial knowledges of self and other fully developed. The stories, essays, cases, and commentaries offered in this book can serve as windows into the experiences, thoughts, feelings, and challenges other people face. The questions at the end of each unit are meant to help the reader mine these texts for their relevance to practice. We focus each unit on diversity issues as well as social work knowledge, values, and skills in order to emphasize our belief that transformation is action-based and grounded in practice.

As you may have noticed, we, the co-editors of this book, have very different academic backgrounds. Alice Lieberman is a social worker and a social work professor. Cheryl Lester is an English and American Studies professor, who has also studied extensively at the Bowen Center for the Study of the Family in Washington, D.C. This combination of training and experience has facilitated an unusual opportunity: Cheryl's broad knowledge of literary narratives and multicultural theory, and her skills as a writer and academic who has spent her life in words, and Alice's experience in social work practice, teaching, and research, gave us an opportunity to find points of convergence between social work practice and the narrative tradition from a very broad canvas. In social work education, we often note that our professional foundation rests on a liberal arts base. This book provides a very clear operationalization of that concept.

We bring up our diverse backgrounds for another reason as well: throughout the book, you will note that, when referring to social workers, we sometimes use the pronoun "we." This is a pronoun of convenience and is used to reflect the fact that the production of this book was a partnership, rather than the fact that "we" are both social workers.

ORGANIZATION OF THIS BOOK

This book is divided into two sections: the first, *Social Identities and Power*, contains five discrete units focused upon increasing our understanding of race, class, gender, national identity, ability, and age as sources of vulnerability and disempowerment for social work's populations of concern. The second, *Social Institutions and Diversity*, is composed of four units that parallel the knowledge, values, and skills of social work practice and the means by which at-risk clients (who often come from diverse backgrounds) may be at increased risk in the absence of culturally competent helping systems (cf. Hoffman and Sallee 1994). Each of these nine units, consisting of four narratives and a related case study, is linked with some aspect of the knowledge, values, and skills of social work practice.

We articulate the links between the narratives and case study that comprise each unit with a two-pronged editorial device: an Editors' Introduction that precedes each unit and an Invited Commentary that follows each unit. In a text devoted to making social workers more mindful of diversity, we felt it was imperative to offer a multiplicity of both narratives and interpretive voices. It is precisely the limitations of our knowledge, familiarity, and responsiveness to others that compelled us to seek diverse commentators, i.e., social workers grounded in different standpoints, varying with race or ethnicity, gender or sexual orientation, age or ability, national identity, or class.

UNIT SUMMARIES

Our first section, *Social Identities and Power*, consists of five units, each of which focuses upon a social work skill element and its application to persons from diverse backgrounds.

Unit 1: Building Relationships across Social Class examines the difficulties imposed by class differences on the skill of building relationships. None of the readings explicitly involves a social worker; rather, the readings illustrate relationship difficulties that one is likely to encounter with clients owing to class differences. We open our volume with this issue because of the basic structural difference that separates social workers from their clients, namely, the power and authority of the social worker. Although the social worker may know intellectually that he or she has some authority over clients, he or she may not be aware of how it affects the work with them. We urge the reader to approach these pieces with the goal of discovering how power and authority function in social work relationships and how that power can be used to benefit others.

Unit 2: Assessing Clients with Attention to Race asks the reader to think about the social work skill of assessment in the context of the predicaments and social situations that are depicted in these literary selections. Without multicultural education and practice, a social worker is likely to be unaware of experiences that are everyday occurrences in racial and ethnic communities. In the face of persistent racialized injustice, individuals struggle to assert their rights and maintain their dignity. Assessments should be ever mindful of this struggle.

Unit 3: Reframing Client Issues in Aging and Ability combines the themes of aging and the broad concept of ability—which, in the parlance of helping professionals, is a more empowering, strengths-focused notion than its converse, disability. In keeping with this perspective, we chose to examine issues of aging and ability through the application of the skill of reframing, or working with clients to develop more positive and productive outlooks on their potentials. By examining the themes of aging and ability in the same unit, we are not implying that the central theme of aging is diminishing abilities or that the experience of differently abled people is one of unmitigated decline. We do believe, however, that both populations are forced to confront issues of dependency that social workers can help them reframe.

Unit 4: Building Interventions in Cases Where Gender or Sexuality Is an Issue offers readings that highlight gender and sexuality as social institutions and sometimes ill-fitting identities. These readings invite consideration of how social workers might be sensitive to the interconnections of sexuality and gender as they develop a plan of action or an intervention. What particular issues and resources should you consider when you are seeking to help a gay man, a lesbian couple, a pair of interlocking straight and gay families, or someone whose cultural identity renders his or her gender identity ambiguous or contradictory?

Unit 5: Accessing Resources for Persons Affected by Relocation and Dislocation explores the immigrant experience, as well as the phenomenon of being a stranger in one's own land. Because such populations are often unaware of the resources to which they are entitled, we believe that this unit lends itself particularly well to an application of the social work skill of resource acquisition. Specifically, we ask readers to consider what kinds of resources are most important for indigenous people and for immigrants to a new land and what are the most appropriate means of securing them.

The second section, *Social Institutions and Diversity,* focuses upon the application of a variety of social work knowledge, value, and skill elements with persons often identified as "at risk." Inevitably, there is overlap between persons so identified and the many conceptualizations of diversity that social workers recognize.

Unit 6: Negotiating Multiple Systems on Behalf of Children and Families provides four stories of very different families. All could have benefited from the assistance of a skilled social worker; in some stories, the actions of those in the social welfare system were deleterious. We can learn from these stories how the skill of a social worker in negotiating multiple systems, and surrounding families with the supports needed to be successful, might have averted some of the tragedies recounted here.

Unit 7: Invoking our Code of Ethics with Clients in the Criminal Justice System explores the lives of clients who enter our correctional systems and facilities and discloses potential minefields that social workers face as they practice in these systems with our particular Code of Ethics. How is it possible, for example, to foster self-determination in systems built to reduce choice? What are the parameters of ethical practice with other professionals who are not bound by this code?

Unit 8: Using Our Social Work Knowledge Base to Help Clients Attain Health examines how our knowledge of the relationships among health, health behavior, the effects of expectancy, and social support—in other words, *biopsychosocial knowledge*—is crucial to our work with clients with physical and mental illness. The selections that comprise this section of the book—about a Southeast Asian child, a young First Nations woman, two brothers in the throes of addiction, and a lesbian woman battling mental illness—were chosen for their stark illustration of these concepts. Furthermore, the case study offered here generously illustrates the resistance of entrenched systems to the accommodation of persons with serious illness—and invites thought about how committed social workers can help.

Unit 9: Advocating on Behalf of Clients in Poverty emphasizes our profession's traditional focus of concern with persons who have little or no financial resources. How they manage, and how we might effectively advocate in their behalf, is the primary focus of our last unit. We are specifically concerned with the questions that social workers have asked since our earliest beginnings: specifically, how do we help to enable those rendered voiceless in our society to amplify their voices loudly and effectively enough to be heard in the dialogues of our communities? How and when do we engage in case vs.

class advocacy? And why are these questions so important to social workers, as opposed to those in other helping professions?

CULTURAL COMPETENCE: A SOCIAL WORK PRACTICE IMPERATIVE

This book cannot provide the exhaustive knowledge required for culturally competent practice. No book can. We do hope, however, that this book provides our readers with a model for mining narratives in a way that opens a wide window on the experiences, feelings, and histories that clients may have. Such privileged access to the thoughts and feelings of others is not always available in face-to-face relationships, yet more knowledge of the values and feelings of others can create a better basis for understanding, respect, and empathy. This is not just a prerequisite for competent practice, but our Code of Ethics requires it.

We also believe that this book provides a strong link between the liberal arts foundation and the social work education curriculum. Reading these texts will, we hope, clarify for students the reason they were required to take all of those English, sociology, and anthropology courses! We want the student experience with this book to be an enjoyable one, but we are very serious in our desire to create a bridge between the liberal arts and professional learning, as well as general college learning, and the "andragogic," adult-learning experience.

ACKNOWLEDGEMENTS

This book has had an extraordinarily long gestation period. As with all such developmental processes, we have encountered the usual trials and tribulations of too much work, too little time, minor editorial disagreements, broken work appointments, and copyright permission delays. We have also received a great deal of support and encouragement along the way, and we wish to recognize all the individuals who have made this book possible:

First and foremost, we want to thank our editor at McGraw-Hill, Steve Rutter, who is the most patient person we know. He is also one of the smartest people in the college text publishing business, and a very astute observer of the social work profession. His insights, especially in the early development of this text, have survived every critical vetting this book has undergone. We are grateful for his unwavering encouragement, intellectual curiosity, adventurousness, and sense of humor. We also wish to thank Kirsten Stoller, Marty Granahan, and Mary Lee Harms, also at McGraw-Hill, for their contributions to the production of this book and for their good humor throughout the process.

Our invited essayists and interlocutors are a critical and unique element of this text. Each was asked because their life history, life work, or area of scholarship, gives them each a standpoint that is different from ours as middle-class, middle-aged Jewish women (we even went to elementary school in Detroit together!), and we are in their debt, not only for agreeing to participate, but for teaching us so much. We cannot overstate our admiration and respect for each of them. At the same time, and as insistent as we are that diverse voices must be brought to the table, we want to note that, for all of our apparent similarities, we remain divided by many facets of ourselves that are profoundly different. As our friendship, trust, and respect for one another grows, we will continue to broach if not always to explain the differences that sometimes cloud our understanding and other times just amaze and delight us.

Five anonymous readers gave this text a critical going-over at several stages in the process, and their feedback made this book better than we could have hoped for. To all of them, feel free to self-identify, so that we can thank you personally for your careful consideration and thoughtfulness. Developmental Editor Becky Smith also read the manuscript, and provided wonderful suggestions and great encouragement. Lynn Porter of the

College Word Processing Center at the University of Kansas provided us with emergency support and helped us to prepare the manuscript for submission to McGraw-Hill.

Our colleagues and students in the School of Social Welfare and the Department of English and the American Studies Program in the College of Liberal Arts and Sciences have been exceptionally supportive. David Anthony Tyeeme Clark and Ray Pence made early contributions that have resulted in a better book. Lea Currie, the cultural diversity biographer at Watson Library at the University of Kansas, performed invaluable search-and-recovery missions on lost texts and helped us discover some of the readings included here.

Philip and Julia Barnard, and Tom, Jared, and Ethan McDonald provided daily support and humor, as well as restraint, when it came to questioning whether this project would ever be done. Alice thinks it is unbelievable luck that she and Cheryl found each other again, forty years after their last birthday party and class picture together. Cheryl remains unspeakably grateful to Alice's mother not only for preserving birthday party and grade school photographs, but also for her amazing memories of Cheryl's extraordinarily large childhood vocabulary—a harbinger of her life as the English professor that she is today!

Finally, we wish to thank each other. In many ways, this project has brought us home.

A SPECIAL MESSAGE TO STUDENTS

You have chosen an extraordinary career path. And while we wish you all the best of luck, we also wish you knowledge, values, skill, and high ethical standards. These are the core elements of social work practice; we hope this book will contribute to yours.

We want to hear from you! Specifically, what stories, cases, or commentaries did you find most compelling? Which readings were less useful or appealing? Do you think that this method of learning about diversity in social work is an effective one? Why or why not?

Please contact us, via email, at the University of Kansas, at alice1@ku.edu or chlester@ku.edu. Emails will be shared and your feedback taken seriously. And if you have a question, you will get an answer.

Alice A. Lieberman

Cheryl B. Lester

The University of Kansas

February, 2003

REFERENCES

Hoffman, K. S. and Sallee, A. L. (1994). *Social Work Practice: Bridges to Change*. Boston: Allyn & Bacon.

Jenkins, Y. M. (1993) "Diversity and Social Esteem." In *Diversity in Psychotherapy: The Politics of Race, Ethnicity, and Gender*, eds., J. L. Chin, V. De La Cancela, and Y. M. Jenkins, 45–63 Westport, CT: Praeger.

Unit 1   BUILDING RELATIONSHIPS ACROSS SOCIAL CLASS

Editors' Introduction

All social workers, by virtue of their professional education and status, and regardless of their personal histories, occupy a privileged social position. Social workers are members of the elite, managerial class, with professional credentials that grant them authority to make important decisions about others. As advocates of people who often lack such membership and its concomitant authority and privileges, social workers have a responsibility to critically examine the impact of this difference upon their ability to build effective relationships with their clients, the basis of all good practice.

We note here that the concept of social class, which emerged with capitalism, modernization, and the related phenomena of industrialization, urbanization, and bureaucratization, was developed in the nineteenth century by Karl Marx to explain the impact of political and economic structures on social life. Today, we recognize that there are many factors besides social class that determine which people gain access to wealth, power, and privilege. Subsequent units in this book examine

1

various social identities (i.e., race and ethnicity, national identity, gender) as social constructions that invest or withhold social capital from individuals and groups.

We have selected the readings for this unit in the belief that they will provoke reflection and discussion about the inequality inherent in the relationship between social workers and the people they serve. As is evident from Nocona Pewewardy's "Invited Commentary," the role and reach of relationships in the interest of advocating for social justice is arguable and complex. While Pewewardy emphasizes the primary importance of redressing structural inequalities and unjust institutional practices, family psychologist Nancy Boyd-Franklin emphasizes in her case study her use of methods aimed at enhancing the resourcefulness and reducing the conflicts in her clients' most significant relationships. Through her effort to enhance personal strengths and resources, Boyd-Franklin also works to narrow the gap between her own functional capacities as a helping professional and the functioning abilities of her clients.

In "Intersection of History and Biography: My Intellectual Journey," from *Maid in the U.S.A.*, Latina academic Mary Romero explains how her personal experience as a domestic worker, from a family of domestic workers, impelled her to redress the circumstances of Latina women working as domestics in the homes of her colleagues and others like them. Of special interest is the relationship she formed with Juanita, the young woman she met while a guest of a colleague. Clearly, Romero's past experience as a domestic provided her with a basis for empathy, and thus a starting point for the development of a relationship.[1]

In the excerpt from *Restavec: From Haitian Slave Child to Middle-Class American*, Jean-Robert Cadet, the son of a black Haitian woman and a white man, demonstrates how his childhood sufferings as the poor servant of a wealthy family (a *restavec*, meaning, literally, "to stay with") confused and inhibited his ultimately fulfilled desire to rise to the American middle-class.[2] We specifically focus upon his relationship with Pfc. Kelly, and the pain and confusion experienced by both Cadet and the Kelly family during a weekend Thanksgiving visit to the Kelly home. Cadet's inability to explain, and the Kelly's lack of knowledge of his circumstances, resulted in the slow death of this relationship. This story allows us to consider how such a divide can work against the formation of relationships and to think about ways of mitigating these barriers in social work practice.

If Cadet provides the insider perspective on one type of Haitian immigrant experience, then Dreyfuss provides a broader, outsider perspective, even though he too is a Haitian immigrant. In his article, "The Invisible Immigrants: Haitians in America Are Industrious, Upwardly Mobile, and Vastly Misunderstood," Dreyfuss points out that immigrants to the United States often lose the distinctions that mark them as high or low in social class in their nation of origin. Building relationships with clients from different countries, with different markers of social distinction, requires a social worker to recognize gaps in his or her own knowledge about those distinctions as well as the clients' struggle to adjust to shifts in their own cultural capital and social affiliations. Social workers trying to help immigrants need to make cautious assumptions about the social status of their clients and, furthermore, need to encourage their clients to build relationships across class divisions. As Dreyfuss notes, Haitians developed resources as immigrants by identifying with each other as Haitians and as immigrants and by putting class differences aside.

We also include an excerpt from *Rivethead: Tales from the Assembly Line*, in which author Ben Hamper writes of his life working on the General Motors assembly line in Flint, Michigan, in the shadow of deindustrialization. One of the few autobiographical narratives of life on an assembly line, Hamper captures with both humor and accuracy the stress, monotony, and impact of this work on one's physical and mental health. Of particular note is the way in which his low-status job allows him little say in making vital decisions about his own life, such as what job he performs in the workplace and even where he works and lives. Building a relationship with someone in Hamper's position would require sensitivity not only to his entrenched passivity, but also to the anger that accompanies his diminished power and self-responsibility. Furthermore, it would demand that a social worker become more informed about and engaged with the labor and economic issues and policies—from downsizing to globalization—with which a client like Hamper would be struggling.

Our case study, by Nancy Boyd-Franklin, "Therapy with African-American Inner City Families," demonstrates the necessity of working not only on the social worker's relationships with clients but also on clients' relationships with others important or potentially important to their well-being. By understanding the centrality of extended family to the support systems of African Americans and by recognizing the source of the fear that was driving conflict among three generations of women in a family, Boyd-Franklin was able to mobilize the strengths and guide the family to more cooperative solutions to some of its problems. Boyd-Franklin concludes that nothing is more important in diversity training than the acquisition of concrete knowledge and the development of cultural sensitivity. "Paradoxically," she notes, "the most profound and powerful way to learn about the culture of others is to start with one's own."

In her guest commentary, Nocona Pewewardy discusses the influences in her life—both the people and events—that shaped her goals as a social worker and an activist for social justice. Her observations, particularly following her marriage to a First Nations man,[3] led her to examine her own privilege and to loudly and actively point to its source. Her understanding of the inequities in the lives of First Nations peoples created a point of identification and thus the basis of strong intercultural relationships.

Points of personal identification with clients will tend to increase a social worker's cultural sensitivity and competence. The challenge to which all people in helping professions must rise is to begin with their own culture in order to develop and then enlarge a broadening and deepening range of cultural sensitivities and competencies, cross-cultural relationships, and potentials for social action. Although class is just one factor governing relationships, social workers should be mindful of its impact on clients and on the relationships they build and encourage in their social work practice.

NOTES

[1]In their new book, *Global Woman: Nannies, Maids, and Sex Workers in the New Economy* (New York: Metropolitan Books, 2003), Barbara Ehrenreich and Arlie Russell

Hochschild (eds.) present a series of articles that explore the consequences of the employment of immigrant domestic labor on both the poorer countries from which these women emigrate and the more prosperous nations in which they become employed. In this book, Ehrenreich's "Maid to Order" argues that this transfer of skills from the country of origin to more prosperous countries has disastrous consequences for both countries and that the employment of domestics is immoral and should be stopped.

[2]At the core of this volume is the belief that racial identities are socially and culturally constructed. If we use the terms "black" and "white" without typographically marking them off in any way, it is not because we believe that racial or other identities are real or essential categories, even if they have real material effects. A central aim of this volume is to persuade our readers to interrogate the impacts of racial and other identity markers on the opportunities and challenges of the people that they as social workers hope to serve.

[3]Throughout this book, we will use the term "First Nations" rather than the terms Native Americans, American Indians, or Indians. The preference for this term is explained by our colleague Michael Yellow Bird. In a footnote to his essay in Unit 5, he writes: "The substitution of labels is necessary because the labels Indians, American Indians, and Native Americans are 'counterfeit identities' resulting from the hegemony of European American colonialism and linguistic imperialism (Yellow Bird 1999a, p. 86). Indigenous Peoples are 'not Indians or American Indians because they are not from India. They are not Native Americans because Indigenous Peoples did not refer to these lands as American until Europeans arrived and imposed this name' (Yellow Bird 2001, p. 61). The change in terminology is a matter of social justice because Indigenous Peoples have struggled and continue to struggle against the oppressive paradigms of American linguistic colonialism. Terms like Native Americans or American Indians ignore individual tribal identities and falsely name Indigenous Peoples to serve the needs and history of the colonizer. Counterfeit labels are dangerous because 'they are historically entangled in American racist discourses that claim Europeans discovered a new world that needed to be settled, claimed, and civilized. This myth-making has promoted the notion that the original inhabitants were unable to settle, claim, and civilize these lands because they were nomadic, unsettled, savage peoples' (Yellow Bird 1999a, p. 86)."

Intersection of Biography and History: My Intellectual Journey

MARY ROMERO

When I was growing up many of the women whom I knew worked cleaning other people's houses. Domestic service was part of my taken-for-granted reality. Later, when I had my own place, I considered housework something you did before company came over. My first thought that domestic service and housework might be a serious research interest came as a result of a chance encounter with live-in domestics along the U. S.-Mexican border. Before beginning a teaching position at the University of Texas in El Paso, I stayed with a colleague while apartment hunting. My colleague had a live-in domestic to assist with housecleaning and cooking. Asking around, I learned that live-in maids were common in El Paso, even among apartment and condominium dwellers. The hiring of maids from Mexico was so common that locals referred to Monday as the border patrol's day off because the agents ignored the women crossing the border to return to their employers' homes after their weekend off. The practice of hiring undocumented Mexican women as domestics, many of whom were no older than fifteen, seemed strange to me. It was this strangeness that raised the topic of domestic service as a question and made problematic what had previously been taken for granted.

I must admit that I was shocked at my colleague's treatment of the sixteen-year-old domestic whom I will call Juanita. Only recently hired, Juanita was still adjusting to her new environment. She was extremely shy, and her timidity was made even worse by constant flirting from her employer. As far as I could see, every attempt Juanita made to converse was met with teasing so that the conversation could never evolve into a serious discussion. Her employer's sexist, paternalistic banter effectively silenced the domestic, kept her constantly on guard, and made it impossible for her to feel comfortable at work. For instance, when she informed the employer of a leaky faucet, he shot her a look of disdain, making it clear that she was overstepping her boundaries. I observed other encounters that clearly served to remind Juanita of her subservient place in her employer's home.

Although Juanita was of the same age as my colleague's oldest daughter and but a few years older than his two sons, she was treated differently from the other teenagers in the house. She was expected to share her bedroom with the ironing board, sewing machine, and other spare-room types of objects.[1] More

5

importantly, she was assumed to have different wants and needs. I witnessed the following revealing exchange. Juanita was poor. She had not brought toiletries with her from Mexico. Since she had not yet been paid, she had to depend on her employer for necessities. Yet instead of offering her a small advance in her pay so she could purchase the items herself and giving her a ride to the nearby supermarket to select her own toiletries, the employer handled Juanita's request for toothbrush, toothpaste, shampoo, soap, and the like in the following manner. In the presence of all the family and the house guest, he made a list of the things she needed. Much teasing and joking accompanied the encounter. The employer shopped for her and purchased only generic brand items, which were a far cry from the brand-name products that filled the bathroom of his sixteen-year-old daughter. Juanita looked at the toothpaste, shampoo, and soap with confusion; she may never have seen generic products before, but she obviously knew that a distinction had been made.

One evening I walked into the kitchen as the employer's young sons were shouting orders at Juanita. They pointed to the dirty dishes on the table and pans in the sink and yelled "WASH!" "CLEAN!" Juanita stood frozen next to the kitchen door, angry and humiliated. Aware of possible repercussions for Juanita if I reprimanded my colleague's sons, I responded awkwardly by reallocating chores to everyone present. I announced that I would wash the dishes and the boys would clear the table. Juanita washed and dried dishes alongside me, and together we finished cleaning the kitchen. My colleague returned from his meeting to find us in the kitchen washing the last pan. The look on his face was more than enough to tell me that he was shocked to find his houseguest—the future colleague—washing dishes with the maid. His embarrassment at my behavior confirmed my suspicion that I had violated the normative expectations of class behavior within the home. He attempted to break the tension with a flirtatious and sexist remark to Juanita which served to excuse her from the kitchen and from any further discussion.

The conversation that followed revealed how my colleague chose to interpret my behavior. Immediately after Juanita's departure from the kitchen, he initiated a discussion about "Chicano radicals" and the Chicano movement. Although he was a foreign-born Latino, he expressed sympathy for *la causa*. Recalling the one Chicano graduate student he had known to obtain a Ph.D. in sociology, he gave several accounts of how the student's political behavior had disrupted the normal flow of university activity. Lowering his voice to a confidential whisper, he confessed to understanding why Marxist theory has become so popular among Chicano students. The tone of his comments and the examples that he chose made me realize that my "outrageous" behavior was explained, and thus excused, on the basis of my being one of those "Chicano radicals." He interpreted my washing dishes with his maid as a symbolic act; that is, I was affiliated with *los de abajo*.

My behavior had been comfortably defined without addressing the specific issue of maids. My colleague then further subsumed the topic under the rubric of "the servant problem" along the border. (His reaction was not unlike the attitude employers have displayed toward domestic service in the United States for the last hundred years.)[2] He began by providing me with chapter and verse about how he had aided Mexican women from Juarez by helping them cross the border and employing them in his home. He took further credit for introducing them to the appliances found in an American middle class home. He shared several funny accounts about teaching country women from Mexico to use the vacuum cleaner, electric mixer, and microwave (remember the maid scene in the movie *El Norte*?) and implicitly blamed them for their inability to work comfortably around modern conveniences. For this "on-the-job training" and introduction to American culture, he complained, his generosity and good-will had been rewarded by a high turnover rate. As his account continued, he assured me that most maids were simply working until they found a husband. In his experience they worked for a few months or less and then did not return to work on Monday morning after their first weekend off. Of course it never dawned on him that they may simply have found a job with better working conditions.

The following day, Juanita and I were alone in the house. As I mustered up my best Spanish, we shared information about our homes and families. After a few minutes of laughter about my simple sentence structure, Juanita lowered her head and in a sad, quiet voice told me how isolated and lonely she felt in this middle-class suburb literally within sight of Juarez. Her feelings were not the consequence of the work or of frustrations with modern appliances, nor did she complain about the absence of Mexican people in the neighborhood; her isolation and loneliness were in response to the norms and values surrounding domestic service. She described the situation quite clearly in expressing puzzle-ment over the social interactions she had with her employer's family: why didn't her employer's children talk to her or include her in any of their activi-ties when she wasn't working? Her reaction was not unlike that of Lillian Pet-tengill, who wrote about her two-year experience as a domestic in Philadelphia households at the turn of the century: "I feel my isolation alone in a big house full of people."[3]

Earlier in the day, Juanita had unsuccessfully tried to initiate a conversation with the sixteen-year-old daughter while she cleaned her room. She was of the same age as the daughter (who at that moment was in bed reading and watch-ing TV because of menstrual cramps—a luxury the maid was not able to claim). She was rebuffed and ignored and felt that she became visible only when an or-der was given. Unable to live with this social isolation, she had already made up her mind not to return after her day off in Juarez. I observed the total im-possibility of communication. The employer would never know why she left, and Juanita would not know that she would be considered simply another un-grateful Mexican whom he had tried to help.

After I returned to Denver, I thought a lot about the situations of Juanita and the other young undocumented Mexican women living in country club areas along the border. They worked long days in the intimacy of American middle class homes but were starved for respect and positive social interaction.

Curiously, the employers did not treat the domestics as "one of the family," nor did they consider themselves employers. Hiring a domestic was likely to be presented within the context of charity and good works; it was considered a matter of helping "these Mexican women" rather than recognized as a work issue.

I was bothered by my encounter along the border, not simply for the obvious humanitarian reasons, but because I too had once worked as a domestic, just as my mother, sister, relatives, and neighbors had. As a teenager, I cleaned houses with my mother on weekends and vacations. My own working experience as a domestic was limited because I had always been accompanied by my mother or sister instead of working alone. Since I was a day worker, my time in the employer's home was limited and I was able to return to my family and community each day. In Juanita's situation as a live-in domestic, there was no distinction between the time on and off work. I wondered whether domestic service had similarly affected my mother, sister, and neighbors. Had they too worked beyond the agreed upon time? Did they have difficulty managing relationships with employers? I never worked alone and was spared the direct negotiations with employers. Instead, I cooperated with my mother or sister in completing the housecleaning as efficiently and quickly as possible.

I could not recall being yelled at by employers or their children, but I did remember anger, resentment, and the humiliation I had felt at kneeling to scrub other people's toilets while they gave step-by-step cleaning instructions. I remember feeling uncomfortable around employers' children who never acknowledged my presence except to question where I had placed their belongings after I had picked them up off the floor to vacuum. After all, my experience was foreign to them; at the age of fourteen I worked as a domestic while they ran off to swimming, tennis, and piano lessons. Unlike Juanita, I preferred to remain invisible as I moved around the employer's house cleaning. Much later, I learned that the invisibility of workers in domestic service is a common characteristic of the occupation. Ruth Schwartz Cowan has commented on the historical aspect of invisibility:

> The history of domestic service in the United States is a vast, unresolved puzzle, because the social role "servant" so frequently carries with it the unspoken adjective *invisible*. In diaries and letters, the "invisible" servant becomes visible only when she departs employment ("Mary left today"). In statistical series, she appears only when she is employed full-time, on a live-in basis; or when she is willing to confess the nature of her employment to a census taker, and (especially since the Second World War) there have frequently been good reasons for such confessions to go unmade.[4]

Although I remained invisible to most of the employers' family members, the mothers, curiously enough, seldom let me move around the house invisibly, dusting the woodwork and vacuuming carpets. Instead, I was subjected to constant supervision and condescending observations about "what a good little girl I was, helping my mother clean house." After I had moved and cleaned behind a hide-a-bed and lazy-boy chair, vacuumed three floors including two sets of stairs, and carried the vacuum cleaner up and downstairs twice because "little

Johnny" was napping when I was cleaning the bedrooms—I certainly didn't feel like a "little girl helping mother." I felt like a domestic worker!

There were employers who attempted to draw parallels between my adolescent experience and their teenagers' behavior: they'd point to the messy bedrooms and claim, "Well, you're a teenager, you understand clothes, books, papers, and records on the floor." Even at fourteen, I knew that being sloppy and not picking up after yourself was a privilege. I had two brothers and three sisters. I didn't have my own bedroom but shared a room with my sisters. Not one of us would think of leaving our panties on the floor for the others to pick up. I didn't bother to set such employers straight but continued to clean in silence, knowing that at the end of day I would get cash and confident that I would soon be old enough to work elsewhere.

Many years later, while attending graduate school, I returned to domestic service as an "off-the-record" means to supplement my income. Graduate fellowships and teaching assistantships locked me into a fixed income that frequently was not enough to cover my expenses.[5] So once again I worked alongside my mother for seven hours as we cleaned two houses. I earned about fifty dollars for the day. Housecleaning is strenuous work, and I returned home exhausted from climbing up and down stairs, bending over, rubbing, and scrubbing.

Returning to domestic service as a graduate student was awkward. I tried to reduce the status inconsistency in my life by electing to work only in houses from which families were absent during the day. If someone appeared while I worked, I ignored their presence as they did mine. Since working arrangements had been previously negotiated by my mother, I had limited face-to-face interactions with employers. Most of the employers knew I was a graduate student, and fortunately, most seemed reluctant to ask me too many questions. Our mutual silence served as a way to deal with the status inconsistency of a housewife with a B.A. hiring an ABD to clean her house.

I came to El Paso with all of these experiences unquestioned in my memory. My presuppositions about domestic service were called into question only after observing the more obviously exploitative situation in the border town. I saw how vulnerable undocumented women employed as live-in domestics are and what little recourse they have to improve their situation, short of finding another job. Experiencing Juanita's shame and disgust at my colleague's sons' behavior brought back a flood of memories that eventually influenced me to study the paid housework that I had once taken-for-granted. I began to wonder professionally about the Chicanas employed as domestics that I had known throughout my own life: how vulnerable were they to exploitation, racism, and sexism? Did their day work status and U.S. citizenship provide protection against degradation and humiliation? How did Chicanas go about establishing a labor arrangement within a society that marked them as racial and cultural inferiors? How did they deal with racial slurs and sexist remarks within their employers' homes? How did Chicanas attempt to negotiate social interactions and informal labor arrangements with employers and their families?

NOTES

[1]The conditions I observed in El Paso were not much different from those described by D. Thompson in her 1960 article, "Are Women Bad Employers of Other Women," *Ladies Home Journal:* "Quarters for domestic help are usually ill placed for quiet. Almost invariably they open from pantry or kitchen, so that if a member of the family goes to get a snack at night he wakes up the occupant. And the live-in maid has nowhere to receive a caller except in the kitchen or one of those tiny rooms." As a general rule anything was good enough for a maid's room. It became a catchall for furniture discarded from other parts of the house. One room was a cubicle too small for a regular-sized bed." Cited in Linda Martin and Kerry Segrave, *The Servant Problem: Domestic Workers in North America,* p. 25.

[2]David Katzman addresses the "servant problem" in his historical study of domestic service, *Seven Days a Week: Women and Domestic Service in Industrializing America.* Defined by middle-class housewives, the problem includes both the shortage of servants available and the competency of women willing to enter domestic service. Employers' attitudes about domestics have been well documented in women's magazines. Katzman described the topic as "the bread and butter of women's magazines between the Civil War and World War I"; moreover, Linda Martin and Kerry Segrave, *The Servant Problem,* illustrate the continuing presence of articles on the servant problem in women's magazines today.

[3]Lillian Pettengill's account *Toilers of the Home: The Record of a College Woman's Experience as a Domestic Servant* is based on two years of employment in Philadelphia households.

[4]Ruth Schwartz Cowan, *More Work for Mother: The Ironies of Household Technology from the Open Hearth to the Microwave,* p. 228.

[5]Earning money as domestic workers to pay college expenses not covered by scholarships is not that uncommon among other women of color in the United States. Trudier Harris interviewed several African American women public school and university college teachers about their college day experiences in domestic service. *From Mammies to Militants: Domestics in Black American Literature,* pp. 5–6.

Restavec: From Haitian Slave Child to Middle-Class American

JEAN-ROBERT CADET

At Fort Lewis, Washington, I reported to a non-airborne unit, or a "leg unit."

"I see that you've been to clerical school," said the first sergeant, looking at my personnel file.

"Yes, First Sergeant," I answered.

"Battalion Headquarters needs an S-2 clerk. Report to Lieutenant McKay," he said. I went to headquarters.

"Corporal Cadet reporting for duty, sir," I said, saluting the lieutenant. Lieutenant McKay returned the salute.

"You look sharp, Corporal," he said.

"Thank you, sir," I replied.

In the S-2 office were two desks and a big safe. The lieutenant assigned me the desk closer to the safe, opened it, and handed me a stack of documents stamped "Secret."

"I'll show you how to log and sort," said the lieutenant. After the first week, I learned the office's routine and was in charge whenever the lieutenant was absent.

One day after chow, a colonel walked in to inspect the office. I snapped to attention.

"At ease, Corporal. Show me your log," said the colonel.

"May I see your identification card, sir?" I asked.

"You're very sharp, Corporal," said the colonel, handing me his ID card.

"Thank you, sir," I answered, feeling proud.

"I detect an accent. 'Where are you from, Corporal?" asked the colonel.

"I am from Haiti, sir," I answered, feeling embarrassed.

"I assume you are a naturalized citizen," said the colonel.

"No, sir, I am not a citizen, but I intend to be," I answered.

"Are you telling me that you're not an American citizen and you're handling military secrets?" asked the colonel with a concerned look on his face.

"I did not know that I had to be an American citizen to work in S-2, sir," I replied.

"How long have you been handling military secrets, soldier?" asked the colonel.

"About two months, sir," I answered.

"I am afraid you can't work here any more," said the colonel, whose face was now turning red. He went to see the battalion commander and I returned to the barracks.

"Why didn't you tell me that you were not a U.S. citizen?" asked the first sergeant.

"I never thought about it," I answered.

"The colonel told the general, who called Immigration and a federal judge. I think you're about to become a U.S. citizen sooner than you think," said the first sergeant.

"I want to become a U.S. citizen, Sarge," I said.

"In the meantime, report to the platoon sergeant," said the first sergeant. Life in the barracks at Fort Lewis was no different from that of Fort Bragg. Every night after work and every weekend a few soldiers got together to smoke marijuana. I found myself saying constantly, "No, man, I don't smoke."

While at the PX one Friday afternoon, I noticed a sharply dressed white soldier with glass-shined boots. His black beret rested neatly the right side of his crew cut. I approached him.

"Excuse me, are you stationed here?" I asked.

"Yea, I am with the 75th Rangers," answered the corporal.

"How can I join your unit?" I asked.

"Call the first sergeant and tell him that you want to be a Ranger. He might call you in for an interview. If he likes you, he'll tell the CO, and you'll get your orders to join," explained the Ranger. First thing Monday morning, I told my platoon sergeant.

"Sarge, I want to join the Rangers. I'd like permission to call their first sergeant," I said.

"You don't wanna join the Rangers. They spend more time in the woods than fuckin' snakes. Those guys are nuts, they train in the swamps," explained the platoon sergeant.

"I don't care; they look good," I said.

That morning I called the Ranger unit, and their first sergeant invited me in for an interview.

"Why do you want to be a Ranger?" asked the first sergeant.

"I am a paratrooper in a leg unit, and I miss jumping." I answered.

"What's your GT score?" he asked.

"It's 122," I answered. The first sergeant smiled.

"Do you smoke dope and use drugs?" he asked.

"Never," I answered.

"Congratulations, welcome to the 75th Rangers," he said, shaking my hand.

The Rangers were different from other units. They looked sharp, walked tall, and seemed proud of themselves. They treated each other with a kind of respect that seemed to solidify their esprit de corps, and their company commander always congratulated them for performance beyond the call of duty. The compound and the barracks reflected their attitudes about themselves. The walkways were lined with two columns of freshly painted white rocks. Not a single piece of debris could be found anywhere on the ground. The floor in the barracks was shined enough to shave on. A faint smell of wax was always noticeable in the air. In the mess hall, the cooks treated everyone like familiar paying customers.

Since I was the only black Ranger in the barracks, I never heard the word "nigga" again.[1]

The following week, I was driven to a government building in Seattle, Washington, where a federal judge was waiting for me.

"Raise your right hand and repeat after me," said the judge. I complied with his request and repeated after him.

"Congratulations, you're now an American citizen," he said. I suddenly realized that I had inadvertently met half of the requirements to become an officer in the United States Army.

I went to the library for the first time, to inquire about colleges. I looked at the ranks of people in uniform and noticed that they were all officers. The librarian looked at me inquisitively.

"I would like to know what I need to do in order to get accepted to college," I said.

"Have you taken the SAT?" she asked.

"I am not familiar with it. What is it?" I asked.

"It's called the Scholastic Aptitude Test," she said slowly as if I were deaf and dumb.

"How can I study for it?" I asked. The librarian handed me a few booklets to read.

"These have sample questions and information about the SAT," she said. I began to visit the library regularly during my free time to prepare for the SAT. I was determined to become an army officer.

Around this time, my three years in the army were coming to an end. I was called into the first sergeant's office for a reenlistment talk.

"If you reenlist for four more years, Uncle Sam will give you a ten thousand dollar bonus and you'll make sergeant," said the first sergeant. I had no idea who Uncle Sam was and I didn't care to know.

"I want to go to college to become an officer," I said.

"Are you gonna try for ROTC?" asked the first sergeant.

"Yes," I answered, not knowing what ROTC stood for.

In the barracks I was sometimes teased because I had not taken any furlough, not even on holidays.

"Hey, Frenchy, you wanna go home with me for Thanksgiving? My mom's a great cook. You'll get a chance to meet my family," said Pfc Kelly, his voice full of pride. I accepted the invitation and we drove off to Oregon on a cool Wednesday afternoon. I wasn't worried about going to someone's house and staying overnight because I hadn't wet my bed in a very long time.

At the Kellys', I slept in a spare bunk in Pfc Kelly's room. His family was warm and friendly. Mrs. Kelly had been busy cooking and baking. The smell of pumpkin pie and cloves lingered in the house. The radio was playing country music. Every time Mrs. Kelly walked by her son, she made contact with him. A pat on the head, a shoulder rub, a friendly headlock, or a bright smile that seemed to say, "I love you. Welcome home, my son." Mr. Kelly, on the other hand, was busy showing his son the work he had done on the house and keeping him up to date on local events. Betty, Pfc Kelly's little sister, jumped on her brother's back for piggyback rides. The sight of all this affection made me feel uncomfortable, causing the void in my chest to feel even bigger. If there had been a gun available, I would have blown my head off while sitting in the family room. Whenever I found myself away from people, I would disappear deep into the backyard and sit on a tree stump behind the tool shed.

When dinner was about ready, the house was full of relatives. Pfc Kelly called me in to join his family and friends. At the dinner table, my hands began to shake. I kept my head down.

"Are you okay?" someone asked.

"I have a headache," I answered.

"Would you like to lie down?" asked Mrs. Kelly.

"Yes, please," I answered, excusing myself from the table. Everyone seemed concerned. I went into Pfc Kelly's room and then slipped through the back door. I went back behind the shed where I felt most comfortable.

I heard Pfc Kelly calling me. "Hey, Cadet, where are you?" I pretended not to hear him. He yelled again and louder.

"Over here," I finally answered.

"What's the matter with you? You're acting a little strange," he said.

"I'm okay now," I answered. Pfc Kelly seemed disappointed.

"My mom saved some dinner for you. Why don't you go eat?" he said. I went back in the dining room and ate alone as fast as I could. While the men watched football in the living room, the women were in the family room talking and preparing dessert. When I finished eating, I slipped back out again. Pfc Kelly called me back inside for the third time.

"Why can't you stay inside with us?" he asked.

"I don't know, I like to be outside," I answered.

"Come on, let's go inside. We're gonna have dessert now," he said. When I entered the family room, my presence seemed to transform the festivity into a wake. Mrs. Kelly tried to break the silence by passing around the family albums. I felt like I was sitting naked in front of all those people. I was trembling and sweat was running down my back. Someone passed an album to me and I kept it in my lap without opening it. I thought about Denis's and Florence's albums where I never saw a picture of myself. I thought about the mulatto taking pictures of Emilie with her dog.[2] As Mr. Kelly took pictures of his son, daughter, and wife among the guests, I went to the bathroom so as not to have my picture taken.

Later, when Betty accidentally dropped a piece of pie on the floor, I sprang forward like a cat and picked it up. I then cleaned the spot on the carpet with a napkin. For a brief moment, I saw myself as the little restavec I once was, keeping the floor clean whenever there was a reception. Everyone seemed surprised.

"Thank you," said Betty. As I carried the dirty napkin out of the room, I let out a sigh of relief. I tried to remain in the kitchen as long as I could, but Mrs. Kelly coaxed me back into the family room.

"Well, Corporal, are you gonna make the army a career?" asked Mr. Kelly, trying to breath life back into the room.

"I want to become an officer," I answered glumly.

"That's a good move," replied Mr. Kelly. I nodded yes.

Mr. Kelly left the room and some people turned their attention to the small portable television set on the breakfast bar.

By late evening the guests were saying good-bye. Before bedtime, Pfc Kelly suggested leaving after breakfast in the morning.

Mr. and Mrs. Kelly came by the door of the bedroom and said goodnight. Everyone seemed awkward. Mrs. Kelly slowly closed the door. Pfc Kelly lay in bed facing the wall. I took a T-shirt from my bag and stuffed it in my underwear to absorb urine in case of an accident. I was awakened by the soaked T-shirt. The mattress was dry. I ate breakfast with the Kellys in silence and awkwardness.

During the drive back to Fort Lewis, Washington, the humming of the engine was the only sound in the car. The friendship between Pfc Kelly and me died a slow death.

NOTES

[1]In an earlier passage, Cadet describes how the troops at Fort Bragg self-segregate in the barracks according to race. He notes with discomfort that the blacks call each other "nigga." The whites call him "Frenchy" because of his accent (124).

[2]In this passage, Cadet refers to an incident in which he is holding Emilie, the child of Florence's son and daughter-in-law Denis and Lisa, members of the household in which he is a domestic servant. This is the day of Emilie's baptism, and her mulatto godfather is about to take a photograph when Denis intervenes, proclaiming that it is a waste of time to take a photo of Cadet. He takes the baby into his own arms and, with the family dog in the background, poses for the photo.

The Invisible Immigrants: Haitians in America Are Industrious, Upwardly Mobile and Vastly Misunderstood

JOEL DREYFUSS

"Where are you from?" In multiethnic America, the question is a way to classify you: to embrace or dismiss you. For those of us who came to America from Haiti 20 or 30 years ago, the question is usually a signal to brace ourselves. If our interrogators knew anything about our native land just a few hundred miles south of Miami, it was not likely to be very positive. "Aha!" people would say once we had answered, "Voodoo. Poverty. Papa Doc." It was a snapshot that, denying the complexity of our country, imprisoned us in a stereotype. Today the response is "Aha! AIDS. Boat People."

For 12 years, the news media have dutifully reported the thousands of black people packed to the gunwales of leaky boats trying to make their way to Florida or, once there, quarantined because they are H.I.V. positive.

Despite the stereotypes and our having come from the poorest country in the Western Hemisphere, we Haitians have established ourselves in the United States as an industrious, upwardly mobile immigrant group with a strong work ethic. We are cabdrivers and college professors, schoolteachers and police officers, stockbrokers and baby sitters, soldiers and politicians, bankers and factory workers. "By and large, one can compare the Haitian immigration experience in the United States to that of other, more celebrated, immigrant groups," says Michel S. Laguerre, an anthropologist of Haitian origin who teaches at the University of California at Berkeley. "They are young, aggressive, even pushy, and to that extent, not very different from other immigrants."

There are about 290,000 who claimed Haitian ancestry in the 1990 census, but that does not include the tens of thousands who are here illegally or second- and third-generation Haitian-Americans who simply identify themselves as black, Laguerre explains. Even legal immigrants may not want to admit to roots that go back to a Caribbean nation so often associated with superstition and poverty. Laguerre, who has written extensively about Haitians in America, estimates that as many as 1.2 million people in the United States are of Haitian ancestry.

The two largest communities are in Southern Florida (300,000) and the New York metropolitan area (500,000), with smaller communities in Boston and Chicago. Yet, for the most part, Haitians are invisible immigrants, hidden by the banality of success. Detailed data from the 1990 census has not yet been released, but experts say that few Haitian immigrants are on welfare. And police say that even fewer get in trouble with the law.

This is not to suggest that all is wonderful for Haitians in America. Many are undocumented, trapped in fear and dead-end jobs. Behind the facade of pride and achievement, there is a litany of social problems: battered women, homeless families, economic exploitation. But like most immigrants, Haitians busy themselves in the pursuit of the American dream.

"Even some of those who came on boats are homeowners now," says the Rev. Thomas Wenski, director of the Pierre Toussaint Haitian Catholic Center in the Little Haiti district of Miami. "It's a tribute to the Haitians' resourcefulness and their self-discipline."

My own family settled in New York in the 1950's. The Haitian community was small, consisting mostly of mixed-race members of the so-called elite. Many could be mistaken easily for white or Hispanic. Back then, when New Yorkers learned we were Haitian, the reaction was mostly bewilderment. Most had never heard of Haiti, and they knew even less about it. "Tahiti?" I was asked more than once. We were proud to tell them about the world's first black republic, about our own struggle for independence and about Alexandre Dumas, the author of "The Three Musketeers" and the son of a Haitian general.

We had to explain that Haiti's middle and upper middle classes had their unique melting pot: Africans, Europeans, Arabs, Asians, Jews. That yes, most light-skinned Haitians were members of the elite, but so were some very dark-skinned Haitians. Status back home was a matter of history and family and circumstance, much more complex than the simplistic racial definitions in the United States. But we had no easy explanation for the sharp disparities of power and income back home, of the even sharper division among social classes—and of the treacherous politics that had forced us to America.

My family was typical of the ethnic stew that prevailed in Haiti's middle class. Emmanuel Dreyfuss, a Jew from Amiens, France who had served in the French Army in Indochina, sailed west in the 1880's in a wave of European emigrants and landed in Haiti. He would never confirm any relation to Capt. Alfred Dreyfus, the French officer whose anti-Semitic persecution had outraged the world and bitterly divided France, but my father remembered that mere mention of the case was enough to set his father's pince-nez quivering and his hands shaking. Dreyfuss married into a fair-skinned and class-conscious family of South American and French origin, which traced its roots in Haiti back to the 1700's.

My mother came from an equally haughty black family in Haiti's north, where Henri Christophe, one of the three leaders of the struggle for independence, had ruled. In fact, one of my great-great-grandfathers had helped build the Citadelle, Christophe's mountaintop fortress in the early 1800's, and another,

Jean-Baptiste Riché, who had been a general in Christophe's army, served as a president of Haiti in the 1840's. But all that history and all that pride counted for naught in America. I remember well as a 7- or 8-year-old my bewilderment when my mother tried to explain why a cab wouldn't pick us up at the Miami airport because we were "colored." America—at least on matters of race—was a great social leveler.

Our community was centered on the West Side of Manhattan, mostly around 86th Street along Broadway and Amsterdam Avenue (West End Avenue and Riverside Drive landlords would not often rent to blacks—even exotic, light-skinned foreigners with French accents). A number of families managed to congregate at the Bretton Hall on 86th and Broadway and the Oxford Hotel at 88th and Amsterdam. My sisters and I went to the local Catholic schools. As in most families, our parents spoke French to us, Creole to each other, and did their best to preserve the memories of home. The nostalgia was most obvious at the loud Sunday dinners with steaming dishes of our savory foods from home—spicy chicken and goat, rice and djondjon, a dried mushroom—Haitian music, loud arguments in Creole and French and much laughter.

Some of our neighbors came from other highly respected Haitian families, but in New York, they were just blacks who took care of other people's children, cleaned other people's apartments, worked in the garment factories around 34th Street or drove cabs. The weekend gatherings were an opportunity to regain self-respect, to cast off the burden of being black in a white world and to recall what they had lost: privilege, status, servants, warm weather. Few from that old middle and upper class had plans to set down roots in America.

The first hint that our stay might be long came when the nature of the Haitian community began to change in the 1960's. Since François Duvalier had taken power in 1957, many of my parents' friends had expected him to be ousted in a matter of weeks or months. After all, that was the pattern for Haitian presidents. But his regime, swept into office on a vague platform of "black power," became unusually tenacious. Duvalier instituted a reign of terror uncommon even for Haiti. Schoolchildren were bused to public executions. Opponents, real or imagined, were beaten or killed with impunity. Those who had stayed behind lived in daily fear of arbitrary arrest. The Tontons Macoutes, Duvalier's vicious militia, swaggered through the towns and villages in dark glasses and denim suits, with pistols tucked in their belts.

New arrivals to our community from Haiti were now politicians and professionals who had finally grasped the scope of Duvalier's brutality. One frequent Sunday guest was a former Senator who had been forced to flee after running afoul of the regime. He came from a prominent political family and he lived for politics. He and his cronies crowded the benches on a Broadway traffic island on weekends, naming each other to hypothetical cabinets and reading position papers out loud in flawless French, waiting for the change of Government. But on weekdays, the Senator pushed a hand truck through the bustling traffic of the garment district. Sharp-tongued Haitians were merciless. "Make way for the Senator," they shouted as he maneuvered down Seventh Avenue. "Make way for Senator Broadway."

After "Papa Doc" Duvalier died in 1971 and his 19-year-old son, Jean-Claude, was placed at the head of the government as "President-for-Life," the exodus accelerated. Many of the new arrivals were working-class Haitians, chased out by the realization that no improvement in their lives was likely under a regime led by a boy more interested in fast cars and women than in public works and budgets. The stream of refugees became a flood, many of them illegals who came on tourist visas. They were not "people we know," the elite sniffed.

The West Side was no longer the Haitian haven. Gentrification had priced the neighborhood out of reach. People began moving to Flushing and Elmhurst, in Queens. The new, poorer arrivals settled around Nostrand and Flatbush avenues in Crown Heights. Florida, with employment opportunities at Miami Beach resorts and weather reminiscent of Haiti's, became a new center of Haitian activity.

"The boat people are a tragic aspect of Haitian life," says one Haitian immigrant. "But most of us are not boat people and we hate being lumped with them." I can understand his anger. The majority of Haitians arrive in the United States by plane. The daily American Airlines Flight No. 658 between Port-au-Prince and Kennedy Airport disgorges passengers who reflect the range of Haitians living in the United States. There are those who are returning from visiting relatives back home: the prosperous upper-middle-class Haitians are deliberately casual in their designer jeans and resort wear; the working-class immigrants wear their Sunday best and carry the bags of food from home that they hope to slip by alert customs officials. Then there are the new arrivals, often shivering in their thin suits and dresses and glancing about with open anxiety for the relatives and friends who are supposed to meet them.

In the Haitian enclaves of New York and Miami, a strong entrepreneurial spirit has spawned grocery stores, barbershops, restaurants, real-estate firms and medical clinics. Bustling shopping districts have taken on a strong Caribbean flavor, laced with Haiti's African-inflected Creole and driven by the beat of merengues and compas. Haitian weekly papers report the minutiae of political maneuverings back home. Radio and cable television programs air heated political debates and, increasingly, instructions on coping with life in America. Farther north, the computer boom along Route 128 in Massachusetts has created plenty of factory jobs for Haitians.

The latest wave of Haitian immigrants comes on the bicentennial of the first. Haiti, then called St. Domingue, was the richest of the French colonies. In the 1790's, the black population of the island revolted against slavery and there was a panicked exodus. Thousands of whites, free blacks and slaves fled to American seaports, contributing to large French-speaking communities in New Orleans, Norfolk, Va., Baltimore, New York and Boston.

Immigrants from Haiti who made their mark in the United States during the 18th and 19th centuries include Jean Baptiste Point du Sable, a trapper who settled on the shore of Lake Michigan and became the founder of the city of Chicago. There was also Pierre Toussaint, whom the Vatican is considering naming the first black saint from the United States. Toussaint, a devout

Catholic, came to New York as the slave of a French family in 1787. He became a prominent hairdresser to New York's rich, and a major fund-raiser who helped the sick and the destitute.

France remained the center of the universe for most educated Haitians. Only a few middle-class Haitians chose the United States, which the elite saw through Francophile eyes as a nation bursting with energy but lacking in civilization. My own father was considered something of a rebel when he decided to come to America in 1927 to accept a scholarship to graduate school at Yale. During World War II, with access to Europe cut off by the war, growing numbers of Haitian scholars came here. Felix Morisseau-Leroy, a renowned poet and playwright, lived at the International House on Riverside Drive with a half-dozen men and women who would be Haiti's brightest literary stars in the postwar years. Morisseau-Leroy recalls few racial incidents. "We were treated well," he says. "We had the feeling that the Americans had been told to be nice to us."

The slow migration of Haitians to the United States might have remained unnoticed by most Americans had not the first bodies washed up on the Florida coast in 1979. The very poor were now determined to escape the dictatorship of Baby Doc, which had changed the emphasis of Government from terror to just plain larceny. Blaise Augustin, a native of St. Louis-du-Nord, an impoverished town in Haiti's northwest, saved enough money to take a boat to the Bahamas in 1977. When the newly independent island began expelling Haitians, Augustin headed for Florida. He was one of several dozen Haitians pushed off an overcrowded boat by a panicked smuggler. A woman and her four children drowned. Augustin managed to make it to the Florida shore. The son of peasant farmers, Augustin is a small-boned slim man with an uncanny resemblance to exiled President Jean-Bertrand Aristide. Like many boat people, he has unusual energy.

Policy makers argue about whether the Haitians are economic or political refugees. Augustin's description of the obstacles he faced back home explain why a simple answer is difficult. "If you saved some money and bought some cement blocks to add to your house or opened a small grocery story, everyone noticed," he says. "Sooner or later, the local Tontons Macoutes or chef de section (a regional military chieftain) approached you for a loan. If you refused, he might denounce you as an opponent of the Government and have you arrested.

"In Haiti, it's very hard to move up," says Augustin. "The U.S. is a country with a lot of complications, but if you're smart, you can get ahead."

Today, Augustin is an outreach worker for a Catholic church in Pompano Beach, 20 miles north of Miami. He owns his home and a car. He and his wife have opened a small variety store to serve the town's growing Haitian population. He has taken a course in photography and now takes pictures at weddings and baptisms. The store shares a tiny mall with a sleepy Haitian restaurant and a Haitian doctor's office. It stocks Haitian foods, records and tapes. An employee helps Augustin's wife with the store while he is engaged in church business. "I have a vision of becoming a business man," says Augustin, modestly.

Augustin's story—and his ambition—are repeated again and again in south Florida. Dr. David Abellard, who lives a few miles farther north along the Florida coast, is a fine example of the immigrant success story Americans like to celebrate. As a boy growing up in a hilltop village, he woke before dawn and walked miles in bare feet to attend school. On Saturdays, he helped his peasant mother sell vegetables in the market. Today, he has a profitable medical practice in Lake Worth, 60 miles north of Miami. A steady stream of affluent patients passes through his waiting room. Abellard has no nostalgia about home. "I had influential friends," he says, citing connections made in high school and at the University of Haiti, where he earned degrees in law and medicine. "I could have been a minister. But it would have been very unstable. I might have been shot."

Little Haiti, which tourist-conscious Miami officials have touted as an example of immigrant entrepreneurship, may have passed its peak. The several blocks of shops, restaurants, travel agencies, community centers, law offices and doctors' clinics that display signs in French, Creole and English seem worse for wear. A bad imitation of Port-au-Prince's famous Iron Market sits seedy and half-empty.

Haitians in New York have also begun to abandon their traditional enclaves in Manhattan, Queens and Brooklyn. The ads in Haiti-Observateur, the largest Haitian paper in the United States, with a circulation of 30,000, are directed to Haitians in northern New Jersey, Spring Valley, N.Y., Nassau and Suffolk counties in New York, Boston and Montreal.

Radio and television are the glue that holds these geographically dispersed communities together. Programs like "Moment Creole," which airs every Sunday on WLIB-AM from 10 A.M. to 4 P.M., and "Eddy Publicité" on WNWK-FM, offer a mix of Haitian music, news and a discussion of community issues. There is even a radio "underground," subcarrier stations that require a special radio, but offer freewheeling discussion, call-in shows, news, gossip and nuts-and-bolts services like death announcements. Radio Tropical (50,000 subscribers) and Radio Soleil d'Haiti (10,000 subscribers) both broadcast 24 hours a day over special radios that the stations sell to listeners for between $75 and $120. Several cable television programs have also begun to target Haitian audiences. Some focus on community or health issues—or politics. Others simply show videos made by Haitian performers.

The ability of broadcast media to reach an audience of a half a million interests Wilner Boucicault, 43, whose A&B Furniture & Appliances in Brooklyn is one of the largest Haitian-owned businesses in New York.

He has ambitions to help propel Haitian immigrants to the next important stage in their Americanization—politics. "Haitians are ready," says Boucicault, who came to New York from Haiti at age 19, attended New York University and eventually opened the store with a partner. "Since Aristide, Haitians have developed a political consciousness. They have to organize themselves here." He and other Haitians trace their American political awakening to April 20, 1990. That was the day more than 50,000 Haitians marched across the Brooklyn Bridge to City Hall. They were protesting the most damaging label yet attached to Haitians. The Centers for Disease Control and the American Red Cross had ruled that no Haitians could give blood because all Haitians were AIDS risks. That ruling, the only one ever applied to one nationality, was later rescinded.

The size of the march, and the ability of Haitian leaders to organize it, stunned New York's political establishment—and the organizers themselves. "We told the police we expected 5,000 people, but we hoped 25,000 would turn up," says Fritz Martial, a vice president at Inner City Broadcasting. "When we saw the size of the crowd, we ran to the front of the line in panic." Now Martial, Boucicault and others are looking for a Haitian candidate to back for City Council from Brooklyn, which has the highest concentration of Haitians in New York.

Bringing no historical baggage to their American relationships, Haitians tend to get along with neighbors from different ethnic backgrounds. In Crown Heights, where American-born blacks and Hasidic Jews have been at odds, Haitians mention Jews as a model of effective political organization. Haitian stores sit side by side with shops owned by Dominicans and British West Indians. On Sundays, neatly dressed Jamaicans and Trinidadians, flow out of Methodist and Evangelical churches, shouting to their children in English patois. On the same streets, Haitians pour out of the Catholic churches, shouting caution in French and Creole to their suited and ribboned children.

Even Haitians like me, who have been in America far longer than in Haiti, retain a close identification with our native land. We agonize over the political turmoil there, and we rage over United States inaction. But while we look for ways to help, we have no plans to go back. Ghislain Gouraiges Jr., 34, and his family left Haiti when he was 8 years old. Gouraiges grew up in Albany, where his father taught at the State University. Today Gouraiges works for Citibank in Miami, where he manages the accounts of multimillionaires and looks the part: well-tailored pinstripes, suspenders, two-tone shirts and gold cufflinks. There is no trace of Haiti in his English and he has no ambition to return there. Yet, "I feel Haitian," he says. "One of the reasons I moved here was to be closer to Haiti."

For those who have difficulties grabbing the first rung of the ladder of American success, a group of self-help programs and social agencies is evolving. Haitian-Americans United for Progress sits in a nondescript storefront on a section of Linden Boulevard in Queens dominated by Haitian businesses. On a Saturday morning, the Haitian-American Women's Advocacy Network is meeting. They have contacted American feminist groups for advice and are drawing up a constitution and a charter. "Many Haitian women need help integrating themselves into American society," says Marie Thérèse Guilloteau, one of the organizers. "They have a different role here."

In Brooklyn, a community organizer, Lola Poisson, just won a $400,000 New York City grant to provide mental health services to Haitians and other Caribbean immigrants. Poisson says she wants to provide an "extended family" for Haitians, who often feel emotionally lost in New York.

At the Haitian Information Center on Flatbush Avenue, the entire staff is unpaid. Daniel Huttinot, one of the founders, says the organization was started to counter misinformation about Haiti and Haitians, but its staff soon learned that Haitians had more pressing needs. They switched gears and now offer help with immigration problems, teaching language classes and courses in computers. In Miami, the Pierre Toussaint Haitian Catholic Center offers literacy classes, Sunday school, preparation for the high-school equivalency exam and help in job placement.

Getting these services is hardly unusual for new immigrants. What is remarkable is the involvement of Haitians, who came from a country where social services and philanthropy are usually left to foreign missionaries. In a way, this charity is a sign of their Americanization.

A subject of ambiguity for Haitians is race. Most are eager to talk about their country's role as the first independent black nation in the modern era. Even middle-class Haitians are now willing to acknowledge the deep African roots of Haitian culture. But they are less sure about the value of being categorized with African-Americans. Most will acknowledge that many of the obstacles they face are racial. "They want to force us to live in black neighborhoods by pricing us out of the white areas," complains Augustin, the young entrepreneur in Pompano Beach. "We need the help of black Americans to help save Haiti, and to help against what whites do to us here."

Yet, almost as quickly, he begins to delineate the differences he perceives between African-Americans and Haitians. "We have a different culture. We are completely different," says Augustin, echoing comments I hear frequently in discussions with Haitians. What these perceived differences are depends on what experience the Haitians have had with black Americans. Those in Miami's Little Haiti, which abuts impoverished Liberty City, often talk in stereotypes. "The blacks" are not clean, they say. They do not work. They don't care about their homes. When pressed, Haitians acknowledge that they have heard about the black middle class. But living near poor black neighborhoods that most successful blacks escaped long ago, many Haitians say they don't know any "good blacks."

Most Haitian-Americans seek a middle ground between assimilation and ethnic isolation. Edeline Léger, 15, and her sister Edna, 13, live in Lincroft, a New Jersey suburb. They were both born in the United States. Their father, Eddy, is a settlements manager for the brokerage firm of Kidder Peabody. Although the two girls have never been to Haiti, they are its staunch defenders. They write book reports in school on Haitian topics and don't hesitate to speak in defense of the country they've never seen. "We're not ashamed of Haiti," Edeline says. "We tell everybody we're Haitian."

I suspect that being Haitian teen-agers in a predominantly white suburb makes them exotic, as we were decades earlier. But I find myself comforted by their self-assertion. Haitians will change in America and they will learn to flex their new economic and political muscle. They are now moving more deeply into the mainstream, away from Little Haiti to the Miami suburbs, from Brooklyn to Westchester, from the West Side to Long Island and New Jersey, from Boston to Newton and Brookline. But they seem in no danger of losing their identity. No one says "Tahiti?" any more when we say Haiti, and even the boat people label and the AIDS label will pass too. Someday the other Americans will even appreciate our role as a new link in the long chain of hyphenated Americans.

Rivethead: Tales from the Assembly Line

BEN HAMPER

One of the guys from the plant called me up one morning. It was just after 11:00 A.M. and I was still tryin' to snooze off a hangover.

"Get outta bed and switch on Channel 5," the voice demanded. "Your damn bowling buddy is holding a press conference. They broke right in on *Hour Magazine!*"

"Why?" I mumbled.

My informer wasn't sure. Something to do with plant closings and little pink slips fluttering down on the heads of the working class. There had been rumors of such. I went in and turned on the television.

It was him all right. Roger B. Smith, my elusive bowling foe, GM's resident reducing plan guru. Perhaps the only fella in the entire Western Hemisphere to possess eight million freckles and yet absolutely no sense of humor whatsoever. He looked like Howdy Doody presiding over a hangin' party—a fiendish combination of power, dread, panic and too much rouge.

Evidently, I had tuned in just after Rog had revealed his roll call of plants headed for extermination. The walking papers having been served, it was now time for the heavy Q & A. The media swarmed in on The Boss, a great sea of gnats luggin' minicams and mic cables. The ultimate American game show squirming to life with 30,000 potential urchins lined up behind Door Number One.

I sat there in my underwear wondering if I would be among them. I wondered what else I could possibly do for a living. I had no training, no skills, no degrees, no connections. I drank too much to fit into most occupations and I wasn't ambitious enough to have a shot at the rest. Above all, I didn't like poking my head into society. People bothered me. That was the best part of my factory job: never really having to relate to anyone or anything other than the awkward-lookin' rivet apparatus that hung from the rafters next to my job. We understood each other. We got along just fine.

While I was reflecting on all of this, Roger was doing his best to explain everything to the media. It was very apparent that as far as public speakers went, Smith rated far down the dais, say, right behind a garden hoe or a doorknob. I could sympathize a bit. I'd be a nervous wreck too if I had his lousy job. Shredding people's livelihoods to bits before it was time for lunch had to jangle one's nerves.

What I found most alarming was that Smitty appeared totally confused with the subject matter itself. Specifics like when, where, who, WHY? Jesus, spit it out, boss. Your ass is covered. You ain't one of the gang bein' upchucked curbside.

Befuddled, Smith began to deflect most of the questions over to his side-kick, GM President Jim McDonald. Now here was a guy who ate decimals and divisors for breakfast, lunch and dinner. A real chatterbox in banker's blue. Jimbo babbled on in the kinda cool-daddy corporate jumble-thump that plain old numbskulls like you and me and the owl in the tree could never hope to untangle. If he was clarifying anything, it still managed to sail about ten feet over my head. (I remember a year or so later, during GM's angry brawl with EDS, it suddenly dawned on me why these stiffs ached so bad in their urge to rid themselves of Ross Perot. It had nothing to do with his loud criticisms or his uppity swagger or even his beguiling hickoid funkiness. Pure and simple, THAT SON-OF-A-BITCHIN' BILLIONAIRE DARED SPEAK PLAIN OLD ENGLISH! Show that goofball the gate!)

I went into the kitchen and opened a can of beer. On the way back, I overheard what had to be the unquestioned highlight of the entire press conference.

A reporter in the back of the room leaned forward and, quoting Smith, hollered: "How can the elimination of 30,000 jobs IMPROVE job security?" Hey, this hack was on the beam. Even the Rivethead hadn't caught how hopelessly inane this statement had been. Remaining completely stone-faced, Roger Smith glanced at the reporter and reasoned: "For those who are left, their jobs will become that much more secure." Ouch.

That cinched it. The guy in charge of the largest corporation in America had a brain the size of a fuckin' lima bean. Not that he was lyin'. It only figured that *anytime* you were able to dispose of 30,000 workers you were going to be able to provide a more secure base for "those who are left." What had me rockin' in my recliner was Smith's casual infusion of flat-out genocide as a harmless means of streamlining the roster. He launched this verbal septic log so nonchalantly, one was left with the distinct impression that Smith actually believed that what he was saying would send a soothin' gush of relief through the rattled wits of the blue-collars. Man, some guys had balls large enough to use on a demolition crane.

For those who are left. That sounded awful damn grim for a solution that was intended to come off as some form of reassurance. It was entirely possible that Roger Smith had missed his calling in life. He could have been our ambassador to Ethiopia: "A food shortage, you say? Nooo problem. Simply exterminate a vast portion of your population, stack 'em out of view where they won't upset anyone's appetite and, PRESTO!, vittles aplenty for THOSE WHO ARE LEFT."

I swear somedays it just doesn't pay to get outta bed.

As it turned out, one of the ten targeted plants for elimination was Flint Truck & Bus. The plan was to close down Line One, the Pickup Line, and move it down south to a new facility in Pontiac, Michigan. Tastes great, less workers! New robots, less filling! The end result would mean the eventual slashing of 3,500 jobs at our plant.

This disclosure tended to fall in step with GM's stubborn desire to keep its work force forever herding southward. Consider this scenario: at least half of the guys around me on the Rivet Line were refugees from closed plants in Saginaw or Bay City. They had to drive south forty or fifty miles a day to barely hang on in Flint. Now, from the information I was receiving, in order to retain my job I would have to sign some transfer sheet and steer my nose fifty miles to the south to the plant they were constructing in Pontiac. The people in Pontiac were probably headed for the plant in Fort Wayne, Indiana. The folks in Fort Wayne were no doubt being packed off for new jobs at the factory in Shreveport, Louisiana. Meanwhile, these Cajuns were being prepared to duck under the border and tinker for a while in Mexico. Notice a trend here? Precisely! Sooner or later, we were all gonna scrape our heads playin' limbo with the Equator.

And I bet it wouldn't end there. Nope, GM would have us all down there by the mid-nineties and the robots would be working out just fine. They'd have some massive burial pit ready and, before any of us could whip off a letter back home, we'd all be fifty feet under some godforsaken desert, laid out elbow to elbow with absolutely no recall rights to anywhere but the bottom of a dusty plaque hangin' over the middle urinal inside Mark's Lounge.

One thing was for certain. I had absolutely zero interest in signing up to work at this newfangled gulag in Pontiac. I felt by doing so I'd be bailing out on my ancestral destiny as the last in a long line of kin who had spent their entire earning years in the factories of Flint. If they were bringing down the curtain, so be it. I simply felt I had to be there when it ended.

Naturally, Dave Steel thought I was nuts. "Forget this town," he told me. "GM is movin' us south and anyone who chooses to remain behind will be freezin' their ass off waitin' in line for food stamps and government cheese."

Tony, our repairman on the Rivet Line, was of the same opinion. He talked constantly about the supposed benefits of transferring to Pontiac. Tony: "With our seniority, we should be able to land gravy jobs. I hear the place is supposed to be climate-controlled. On top of everything else, they won't even have a Rivet Line down there!"

Hold on a second. No Rivet Line? Jesus Christ, what kind of alien broomshack were they building down in Ponti-yuk? NO RIVET LINE? No Rivetheads? No Rivetettes? Don't tell me those damn robotics had finally eaten away at the one and only profession I'd ever been able to nurture, conquer and dominate? It was like tellin' a pollywog there was no such thing as frogs.

To hell with resettling. I'd been at GM long enough to grow accustomed to their habit of hollerin' "Earthquake!" at every little speed bump on the road. It only made perfect sense that if General Motors was offering me a rubber raft in one hand, chances were way more than likely that they had to be packin' a harpoon in their other paw. I would call their bluff and stay put. Go ahead and bring on that World Van you've been whisperin' about. I know you frauds are hidin' something up your sleeves. I won't be taken in. Furthermore, I won't be taken away.

The day arrived when we were scheduled to accept or refuse our transfers to the upcoming plant in Pontiac. Group by group, they called us down to the small conference room adjacent to the workers' cafeteria. I walked down with Tony and Kirk, who were heatedly debating which was the better option. I found myself beginning to flit from one line of thinking to the next. The plain truth was that I was a complete wuss at decision making. Maybe that was one of the reasons I chose to become a shoprat in the first place. GM always made your decisions for you.

Inside the conference room, union reps and recruiters from Pontiac were seated behind long rows of tables. They all wore large name tags as if we really gave a shit who they were. Kirk, Tony and I stood in line waiting to be popped the offer. I spoke with Kirk. He was starting to vacillate as crazily as I was. Stay put or venture south? It was an enormous decision, one that would affect the rest of our careers. We both were able to agree on one thing. The only prospect more dreadful than having a job at GM was *not* having one.

My name was called and I slid into a chair across from some stern-lookin' union shill. I told him I had severe reservations about leaving my hometown and forfeiting all rights to ever return to Flint in the future. He asked for my seniority date. "Seven nine seventy-seven," I replied.

The union man shook his head. "If you stay here, you'll be out of a job within two years."

"That's a long time off," I said. "Things could turn around in that span."

He seemed angry that I would quibble with his assessment of the situation. "Anything's possible, but your safest bet would be to transfer down to Pontiac."

I looked down the tables at Kirk. Further down, I could see Tony. Both of them were scrawling their signatures to the transfer contracts. Reluctantly, I followed suit. Though the Plant wasn't even entirely built yet, though it would be another two years before I ever set foot inside that cretin farm—I was now signed, sealed and delivered as sole property of the Pontiac Truck & Bus division, Union Local 594. I walked back to the Rivet Line feeling like a rotten Judas.

That very same night, I found that I couldn't sleep. I felt as though I had made a terrible blunder. I turned out all the lights in my apartment and stood at the window drinking bourbon from a plastic mug emblazoned with the motto: WE MAKE OUR OWN HISTORY—50 YEARS, UAW. I stared at the apartment building across from me. Nothing was going on. Just a bunch of self-assured Americans tucked beneath the sheets with three hours to go before the alarms started to ring and it would all unwind again. The meetings. The deadlines. The parking spot. The boss. They were truly amazing specimens. They adapted to everything.

The next afternoon, I got to the plant early. I was a man on a mission. I had changed my mind. I would not go south. I stormed through the lobby and into the workers' cafeteria. I fixed my gaze on the little conference room that held my treasonous contract with the poachers from Pontiac. I would resolve this matter quickly. I would rant and rave until they fetched that fraudulent contract and let me rip it apart. I would declare myself a loyal domestic, a devoted Flintoid, a rock-solid pillar on the listing hull. I would throw the doors open and . . .

HUH? The room was totally dark. I flipped on a light switch and peered around. The room was entirely empty. No tables, no chairs, no files, no ashtrays—NO CONTRACT! I went back into the cafeteria and pulled one of the servers aside. "Could you tell me where all of the transfer people have gone? It seems they've stepped out somewhere."

"What transfer people?" replied the moron in the hair net.

"The transfer people who've inhabited that back room all week! Where'd they go?"

"How should I know. I just work the grill. I don't know any transfer people."

This had a bad aroma to it. One day ado, the next day adieu. It was spooky. Where in the hell did those cradle-lootin' nomads disappear to? I wandered out of the cafeteria perplexed as to my next move. As I did, I half expected to turn around and catch a glimpse of Rod Serling ducking out of one of the phone booths, his hands knotted at groin level, his mocking sneer poking out of the plume of his eternal Winston. I could almost hear him:

"Witness if you will an enigma, a frustrated punster besieged by his lack of an appropriate punchline. We may call him the Rivethead, a self-designation currently on very tenuous footing, obscured amongst the nervous shuttle of those who would waver between embarkation and a fostered urge to remain. For here amidst the impossible din, amongst the sooty backdrop of this macabre garden, nothing is a sure bet. Nostalgia is as worthless as a slug nickel. A reconsideration only an old key prying hopelessly against an exchanged lock. However, a contract remains a contract, a coward still a coward. Now witness if you will a man's desperate attempt to undo that which is done, a man in need of what is known, a man's march through darkness into the Transfer Zone."

I raced upstairs to the Rivet Line looking for Gino. I found him in his office going over a stack of paperwork. I didn't bother to knock.

"Tell me something, Gino," I blurted. "Where in the fuck did those transfer people from Pontiac, go? Their office has simply vanished."

"Yesterday was their last day," Gino answered. "They won't be back until next spring or summer. What happened, did you miss the boat or something?"

"No, the damn boat ran my ass right over! I signed their rotten transfer contract and—"

"You've changed your mind," Gino finished for me.

I told Gino about how I had panicked. About how the union had claimed I'd be out of a job in two years if I didn't sign on. I told Gino that I'd been struck with this vision of myself cramming sugar paste into the butt end of cream sticks for three bucks an hour while the repo men tap-danced down the boulevard with my end tables and record collection in tow. I told him I was possibly the biggest fuckup either of us had ever met.

"Did they mention to you that, once you signed on, the contract was irreversible?"

"Yeah," I moped, "they stuck that right in at the top."

"I'm afraid you're locked in. Let me ask around and see what I can come up with."

"I'd appreciate it."

Gino wasn't able to find a single loophole. Nor was I. For weeks, I went around shaking down every union rep and boss-type I could find. Their only response was to ask me if I had inked the transfer sheet. Once I admitted that I had, they simply shook their heads and wished me luck. GM wasn't in the habit of lettin' a sucker off the leash.

Pontiac was in the offing. I had a couple of years before I shipped out. Two years of Rivet Line mania. Two years of the spectacular and the absurd. I didn't intend to waste a minute of what was left on the meter. All aboard for clown time. The mayhem was only beginning.

Therapy with African American Inner-City Families

NANCY BOYD-FRANKLIN

The treatment of African American inner-city families is a critical component in family psychology. Clinical training programs, however, frequently do not train students to work with these families. This [case study] presents key areas that family psychologists must address in order to provide effective treatment.

Although families of African descent come from many different countries and backgrounds, such as Afro-Caribbean, Haitian, African, and Afro-Latino, the emphasis here will be on African American families whose ancestors were brought to this country as slaves. This chapter will highlight the treatment issues for African American families living in poverty, even though many similarities exist with middle-class African American families.

In the first half of this [study], a background for therapists working with poor, inner-city, African American families is provided. The class-not-race myth, the opinions many of these families have of therapy, and the importance of the therapist's use of self are emphasized. Some of the multiple family structures often found within these families are described, and the importance of spirituality to this population is stressed. Next the effects of racism on gender roles are examined, and treatment-relevant issues related to poverty are highlighted. In each of these areas, implications for practice are described.

In the second part of the [study] a multisystem intervention model for working with these families is introduced. Multisystemic issues, tools to assess multisystems, and use of the model to organize treatment are explained. To see the model in action, an extended case example of work with an African American extended family, living in poverty in the inner city, is provided. The [study] concludes by examining some of the implications of this model for training and supervising professionals.

INITIAL CULTURAL AND THERAPEUTIC CONSIDERATIONS

To understand the complex therapeutic relationships that family psychologists may encounter in the treatment of African Americans, professionals first need to be cautioned against stereotyping, to realize the shortcomings of the class-not-race theory, to comprehend the expected responses of African American families to therapy, and to understand the importance of the therapist's use of self with these families.

There is tremendous variability among African American families in terms of geographic region, spiritual or religious orientation, class and socioeconomic level, education, skin color, and family structure. The material in this [study] should be used as a cultural lens through which African American inner-city families can be viewed, or as a set of guidelines that must be readjusted and sometimes discarded, depending on the particular family with which the therapist is working.

To understand fully the complex interplay of issues affecting African American families, one must consider both social class and racial issues (Boyd-Franklin 1989). Poor African American families are affected daily by unemployment, violence, crime, drugs, and homelessness. Furthermore, the intrusiveness of outside systems, such as the welfare department, child protective services, and various agencies, clinics, and hospitals engenders a profound suspicion. In addition, unlike other ethnic groups, they must cope with the burdens of racism, discrimination, and oppression as a consequence of the legacy of slavery in the United States.

There is a tendency on the part of some clinicians to dismiss racial differences. Many Caucasian clinicians tend to minimize these differences as "class-not-race" issues (Boyd 1977). This dismissal is unfortunate because the issues of race and racism persist even as the individual and family rises to middle class and a higher income and educational level. Therapists must be aware of the complex interplay of racial, cultural, and class themes in order to work effectively with these clients.

The clinician needs to understand the suspicion toward therapy that exists in many African American communities, which derives from the class and race issues just discussed. Grier and Cobbs (1968) have called this "healthy cultural paranoia." I prefer "healthy cultural suspicion," because of the pejorative nature of the word *paranoia*.

Therapy is also viewed by many African Americans as being appropriate only for others—sick, crazy, or weak people, or for Caucasians. African Americans may also distrust therapy because they see it as being anti-spiritual. Because of these unfavorable predispositions, family psychologists must first take the time to join with all family members and to build trust. This is particularly important with clients who feel coerced into therapy, as is common with inner-city African American families. Too often, African American clients are mislabeled as "resistant" and may be dismissed by therapists because many training programs prepare clinicians to work only with clients who want therapy. However, the majority of these families can and do benefit from therapy once their fears and concerns are addressed. This process will be discussed in more detail later in the [study].

The most important component in the treatment of inner-city African American families is the therapist's use of self. Indeed, this is the most important part of the therapeutic process with any family. It is particularly crucial in work with African American families because of the healthy cultural suspicion with which they may approach therapy. Therapists must especially take the time to connect with these families and help them understand the process of therapy.

Because of the legacy of racism and discrimination in this country, African Americans are particularly sensitive to the way in which they are approached by therapists. This is not only an issue in cross-racial therapy. A therapist who is of the same race as the family may still be perceived by family members as different—either as a result of social class or because the therapist is identified as being part of the system.

African Americans are very conscious of "vibes"—verbal and nonverbal clues that indicate whether the therapist respects them, is judgmental of their lives or family circumstances, and is "for real" (Boyd-Franklin 1989). It is very important during supervisory sessions that therapists be helped to be themselves and to take the time to connect as people with each family member. It is often very helpful, for example, for the therapist in a cross-racial therapeutic situation to ask the family how they feel about working with a Caucasian therapist. This gives a message that even the difficult subject of race can be raised in therapy. This should not be done in the first session but should be raised only at points where the therapist is encountering resistance from the family.

MULTIPLE FAMILY STRUCTURES

Although the stereotype in the literature is of single-parent families (Deutsch and Brown 1964; Moynihan 1965), many family structures are represented within African American inner-city communities. Families may be traditional two-parent nuclear families, they may consist of a single parent and a boyfriend or girlfriend, or they may form a complex extended family that includes members from both inside and outside the household, as well as blood and nonblood relatives (Billingsley 1968; Boyd-Franklin 1989; Hill 1972, 1977). Clinicians must be aware of this diversity because African American families who are suspicious about therapy may send in an "expeditionary force" to "check out" the therapist.

As was just mentioned, African American families may include complex extended family kinship systems. Stack (1974) discussed the reciprocity inherent in these systems in which very poor family members assist each other with child care, finances, emotional support, housing, counseling, and so forth, particularly in times of trouble or stress. Blood family members might include mothers, fathers, grandmothers, grandfathers, aunts, uncles, cousins, or siblings. In addition, African American families, particularly when moving to new communities, may create bonds with nonblood relatives, such as neighbors, babysitters, friends, ministers, ministers' wives, and church family, that are as strong as those with family members (Boyd-Franklin 1989; Billingsley 1968; Hill 1972, 1977; Hines and Boyd-Franklin 1982; McAdoo 1981; McAdoo and McAdoo 1985).

In addition, because of the legacy of slavery in which family systems were pulled apart, and the segregated nature of child welfare and adoption systems prior to 1950, African Americans have developed their own informal systems to take in children (and sometimes the elderly) in times of loss, separation, or crisis—a process called *informal adoption* by Hill (1977). This concept, often confusing for family psychologists when first encountered, is also complicated by the reluctance of African Americans to air family business in public (Boyd-Franklin 1989; Hines and Boyd-Franklin 1982). Also, because of a cultural admonition not to discuss these issues with children (irrespective of age), family secrets may result. The exploration of such secrets requires a great deal of sensitivity and timing on the part of the therapist (Boyd-Franklin 1989).

When family systems are very complex, therapists may spend hours treating the "wrong" family or a small subsystem of the family (e.g., mothers and children). Far too often powerful family members—blood as well as non-blood—are overlooked because they are not the initial patients. However, these members can undermine or sabotage treatment if they are not engaged.

Families may not reveal the true, complex nature of the family support system to the therapist until trust is established. As trust develops, constructing a genogram may be of great help. Because of the family's potential suspicion, therapists are cautioned against using a genogram in a first session (Boyd-Franklin 1989). The process of gathering this information should evolve over time: As trust in the therapist grows, more family members will be revealed.

Although many family psychologists have been trained to expect a family to come in for treatment, effective therapy with African Americans often involves outreach in the form of home visits, letters, or phone calls. Fathers or boyfriends are often particularly difficult to engage. The following is an example of a letter that might be sent to a father in order to reach out to him initially. This direct communication in a letter or a phone call is often more effective than working through mothers:

> Dear _____:
>
> My name is _____, and I am working with your son Johnny in family counseling to try to resolve his school problems. As you know, things are very serious right now, and the school has threatened to leave him back if his behavior does not improve. Your wife and I have been working with him on doing his homework after school, but we need your help. Can you give me a call at (telephone number) so that I can get your ideas on how best to help him? You are a very important person in his life, and I would not treat your son without asking for your input and advice.
>
> We have been meeting on Wednesday nights at 7:00 P.M. If you can join us next week, it would be very helpful. Let me know if the time is a problem and we can reschedule.
>
> Sincerely yours,
>
> _____

The extended family kinship system is a cultural legacy and testament to the survival skills of those of African heritage. However, therapists must distinguish between functional kinship networks and conflictual support systems. In functional systems, there is a great deal of reciprocity between extended family members; in conflictual systems there often tends to be one central (Aponte 1976a, 1976b), overburdened family member—typically a grandmother, mother, or aunt—who constantly provides support to others but receives little in return. This person has been termed a "switchboard" by Boyd-Franklin (1989), because all communication runs through her.

Whereas such a style of family organization may be very rewarding for the switchboard, it is also a prescription for burnout. Often grandmothers or great-aunts, who may have held this role for generations, must be helped to ask for support from other family members and to delegate tasks. This is not easy for African American women who have been given cultural messages to be strong. An extended family system that is functioning well may deteriorate when key family supports die or move away.

Lindblad-Goldberg and Dukes (1985), Lindblad-Goldberg et al. (1988), and Boyd-Franklin (1989) have explored the differences between functional and conflictual support systems in single-parent African American families, and provide models of functional extended family interactions that can be utilized by family psychologists to restructure and reframe extended family involvement.

Families with conflictual supports often lack structure, suffer from "underorganization" (Aponte 1976b), and are particularly susceptible to boundary and role confusion. Reframing and clarifying roles is often necessary when extended family members give diverse and confusing mixed messages to children (Boyd-Franklin 1989). Family psychologists must be trained to identify the key members of the extended family and to involve them in the process of boundary and role clarification. This is particularly important when different family members are involved in discipline and child rearing.

In addition to overcentralization, some families are also very susceptible to isolation. Individuals and family subsystems who become cut off or isolated are particularly vulnerable to mental health problems. Patients often experience isolation either through cutoffs that are due to drug and alcohol histories or chronic mental illness or through deaths, losses, diseases such as HIV/AIDS, homelessness, and relocation. Isolation can also, ironically, be the result of upward mobility.

Therapists can often help those in isolated situations to reconstruct their original family genogram and heal cutoffs (Bowen 1976; Carter and Orfanides-McGoldrick 1976). It was pointed out earlier that when functional African American families move to a new community, they build a nonblood family network of friends, neighbors, and church family members. Therapists must empower their clients to build these networks also. When this is not possible, families can be helped to form "families of choice" by becoming involved in multiple family groups (Boyd-Franklin, Steiner, and Boland, 1995).

SPIRITUALITY

Another extremely important strength derived from the African heritage of African American families is that of spirituality. In some families, this may mean a formal expression of religious orientation and church membership; in others, it is part of a pervasive belief system that is more spiritual than religious.

Many African Americans, particularly older ones, describe "psychological" pain in spiritual terms. For example, a grandmother, when asked how she had tried to change her grandson's behavior, responded that she had "prayed to the Lord." Without training, therapists mislabel or misdiagnose such expressions as evidence of religiosity or grandiosity. This, in turn, gives rise to the suspicion by African Americans that therapy is antispiritual. Therapists must be trained to inquire further and explore the person's actual belief system. For example, an adolescent may express rebellion through conflict with familial religious values.

Unresolved mourning issues, related to complex cultural and spiritual belief systems, can also be a source of psychological and spiritual pain for African American families. The ritual of the funeral assumes special significance in African American families (Hines, as cited in McGoldrick et al. 1991; Boyd-Franklin et al. 1995). For many religious groups, the *whole* family comes together at a funeral, so it is often postponed for a week after the death to give extended family members time to travel from distant areas. Because the funeral is a time when deep emotions can be expressed, it is not uncommon to see tears, weeping, moaning, and fainting. The problem, however, is that these emotions are expected to "seal over" after the spiritual and emotional release of the funeral. Family members are expected to be strong, and tears subsequent to the funeral may be viewed as a sign of weakness.

When therapists are attuned to these beliefs they can help African American families with serious losses to share their grief and complete the mourning process. Therapists working with inner-city families should also be aware of the repercussions of violent deaths and losses on the family. This is often expressed through acting-out behavior in children and adolescents, depression in one or more family members, and/or increased somatic complaints, particularly in older adults.

It is important for therapists to inquire with care and sensitivity about losses that may have occurred at the time that symptoms began to appear. These may include deaths or anticipated losses of, for example, a terminally ill family member. Losses frequently are not fully processed or discussed with the children and can inadvertently become secrets in the family (Boyd-Franklin 1993).

THE EFFECTS OF RACISM ON GENDER ROLES

The Invisibility Syndrome and African American Men

One of the most misunderstood areas in the treatment of African Americans is the impact of racism on gender roles and male–female relationships. This complex interplay requires therapists to be familiar with the concept of the "invisibility syndrome" and its impact on African American men (Franklin 1993).

Invisibility is both a racial and cultural paradox. High skin color visibility, as well as the fears and guilt associated with slavery and continuing experiences of racism, have caused American society to treat African American men as if they are invisible. African American children (particularly males) are overrepresented in special education programs and are frequently subject to the expectation of teachers that they will fail (Kunjufu 1985; Rosenthal and Jacobson 1968).

Media images have ingrained a stereotype of violent African American men in the psyche of many Americans, so that when African American male children grow taller and stronger they are often responded to with fear. The welfare system has also contributed to the invisibility of Black men because the mother's representation as a single parent is often a condition for the family's ability to receive benefits. Because researchers have often used intactness (a two-parent nuclear family) as a measure of family strength (Moynihan 1965), family therapists may play into the invisibility myth by dismissing a boyfriend in an African American family because he is not married to the mother.

African American mothers have responded with fear to the legacy of racism (and often violence) in society against their male children and often compensate for the invisibility syndrome in their socialization and child-rearing practices. For example, a commonly held cultural belief is that many African Americans "raise their daughters but love their sons." African American mothers are in a dilemma: They struggle with the desire to raise strong, assertive children, but they fear society will punish their children for this assertiveness, particularly if they are male.

Double Jeopardy for African American Women

African American women experience the double burdens of racism and sexism in society, the workplace, and the family As a survival mechanism they have learned to be strong. However, this strength can become a burden in some families when African American women are able to find jobs when African American men are not. This has often created power struggles for African American couples. The dilemma for therapists treating such families and couples is that they are often confused when clients conceptualize these issues in terms of racism. Therapists are often surprised at the degree of rage they experience in African American couples when this issue is discussed, but it is important for therapists to accept this formulation and not attempt to impose gender role expectations based on a Caucasian middle-class orientation (Boyd-Franklin 1989).

A very helpful reframe with couples such as these, who may be experiencing intense conflicts around the husband or boyfriend's job loss, can be to help them in their struggle against a common enemy, such as racism, unemployment, discrimination, or last hired, first fired practices. It should be noted, however, that this reframe should be applied only if it is appropriate to the situation. Contrary to many popularly held stereotypes (Moynihan 1965), even chronically unemployed African Americans want to work (Hill 1972) and feel defeated by their inability to gain and keep employment (Wilson 1987).

ISSUES RELATED TO POVERTY

When issues surrounding the extreme poverty in which many African American and other minority families live in this country are not explored in training programs, psychologists are often unprepared for and overwhelmed by these realities. One staff member at the Community Mental Health Center in Newark, NJ on a school visit discovered that the ground outside the building was littered with crack vials and exposed needles. He was horrified that children played in an area that had served as a shooting gallery and crack den the night before.

Inner-city families may live in housing projects or tenements in which rats and roaches are everywhere and where hallways and elevators can be the scene of violent crimes. Because of the incidence of drug traffic there, children have frequently experienced random violence against close friends and family. The development of psychiatric symptoms in a child, adolescent, or family member can often be traced to a chronic posttraumatic stress disorder following experiences of violence.

Many parents struggle desperately to protect their children and raise them right against tremendous odds. A "60 Minutes" episode on television depicted a school in inner-city Los Angeles in which kindergarten children had found a dead body in the yard outside their classroom. The program portrayed the therapeutic support and group intervention for these children and their families created by the principal, the school psychologist, and the social worker.

African American inner-city families may be victims of arson, eviction, or homelessness. It is not uncommon to see families huddled together in a shelter or "welfare motel" or an abandoned building. These families are confronted with basic issues of survival: hunger and illness and lack of housing, resources, and money. Faced with chronic unemployment, they struggle to survive with the barest necessities of life. Often these are the first psychological issues that they want to address in therapy.

It is incorrect to assume that all African Americans living in the inner city are on welfare. These areas contain many families considered working-class or the working poor. Such families may be overlooked because of the stereotypes with which the mental health profession has often approached poor families (Parnel and Vanderkloot 1989).

The status of these working families, however, is tenuous. If the key provider is laid off or becomes sick, the family often has no choice but to seek public assistance, because minimum-wage jobs frequently do not offer health benefits. Family members may also work "off the books" but choose not to inform their therapists for fear of being reported to the welfare department.

In many inner-city, poor African American neighborhoods, the impact of the drug culture is profound. In African American poor communities, parents frequently fear that they are fighting a losing battle against the lure of drugs. Parents are afraid not only that their children will use drugs, but also that they will begin dealing drugs at a young age or become runners for drug dealers. Injecting drug use has exacerbated the spread of HIV/AIDS in African American communities, and the crack epidemic has resulted in many more reports of violent drug reactions.

Inner-city African American parents are eager to help their children. In fact, the education of children is one of the issues that will bring an African American family into treatment. These families need therapists who will work with them to "take their children back from the streets"—a very powerful reframe with African Americans.

Pervasive fear of the drug culture has led many African American families to resist placing children or adolescents or adults on medication (e.g., ritalin or psychotropic drugs). For example, at a pediatric AIDS unit in a large inner-city area, medical staff had to build a great deal of trust with families before they would even consider the use of AZT (a drug used in treating AIDS). These families need therapists who understand and are realistic about the survival issues they face and who are willing to address these issues in treatment.

Inner-city, poor families are often vulnerable to the intrusion of outside systems and agencies, such as schools, hospitals, mental health clinics, courts, police, juvenile authorities, welfare departments, housing authorities, and child protective services. For example, when there is a report of neglect or abuse, child protective services is far more likely to remove a child from an inner-city home than from a more affluent home. Paradoxically, clinicians who work with African American inner-city families have also found it more difficult to get systems to intervene in truly dangerous situations because the current economic situation has caused agencies to lay off personnel.

Poor families may have a welfare case worker, a child protective worker, teachers, a school social worker, hospital and medical staff, and a probation officer involved with them, so that a therapist may be viewed as just one more intrusive person or agency. Family psychologists thus need to distinguish themselves from other agencies and to explain the concept of confidentiality because of families' concerns that the therapist will "tell their business" to another agency. These fears must be addressed early in treatment.

A MULTISYSTEM INTERVENTION MODEL

As was discussed in the last section, outside agencies have a tremendous amount of power in the lives of poor families. Child protective services has the power to remove a child, the welfare department can take away the family's livelihood, the family can be evicted from public housing, and so on. Many family psychologists, however, have been trained to consider problems with agencies to be the province of the agencies' social workers. This is unfortunate because these issues often bring families into treatment and provide the entree into a family and the means of joining and building therapeutic credibility.

Discussing multisystems issues with a family allows communication between family members to be explored and facilitated, and it gives a therapist a means of joining and an initial vehicle for exploring the family's structure,

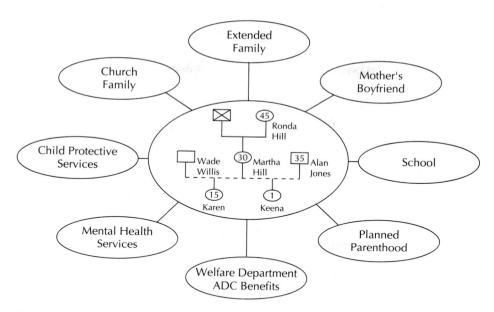

FIGURE 1 The Hill family ecomap.

resiliency, executive or parental system, and the important "powerful figures" in the family. Empowerment must be a very important theme in therapy. The therapist's role is to mobilize the strengths and the strong individuals in the family and extended family to work together efficiently to solve their problems.

In order to work effectively with the complex issues and problems facing these families, the therapist must take into account different systems levels, including the individual, family and extended family, nonblood kin and friend supports, church and community services, social service agencies, and outside systems. Boyd-Franklin (1989) and Boyd-Franklin and Shenouda (1990) described in detail and gave case examples to illustrate the utility of such a multi-system model.

Hartman and Laird (1983) provided another tool known as the ecomap (see Figure 1), which allows the therapist to depict the family at the center of a complex system and to diagram through a series of circles the outside agencies that are involved. The therapist can then work with the family to prioritize each problem and to identify the agencies needed to be involved or disengaged from overinvolvement. A genogram or family tree (see Figure 2) can also be constructed to help diagram the family structure (Carter and Orfanidis-McGoldrick 1976; McGoldrick and Gerson 1985; McGoldrick, Pearce, and Giordano 1982).

By empowering the family to decide on their own priorities and by facilitating rather than helping, the therapist can begin to put the adults in the

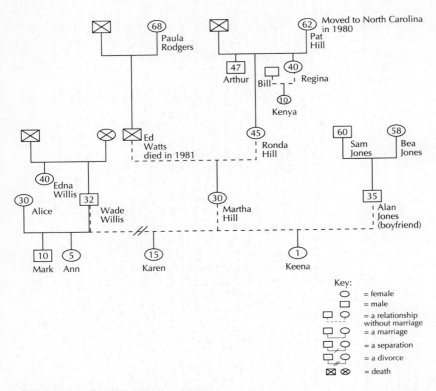

FIGURE 2 The Hill family genogram.

family in charge of these interventions. For example, it is not unusual for these families to have workers and case managers in different systems working at cross-purposes. The therapist may empower a family to call a meeting of these key agency representatives and facilitate discussion and problem resolution.

Family therapists often find working with such complex systems to be overwhelming. A clear model helps the therapist to structure useful interventions. The problem-solving focus that has evolved from the structural school of family systems theory is helpful (Haley 1975; Minuchin and Fishman 1981; Minuchin 1974). Axis 1 of the multisystems model incorporates these guidelines. The treatment process involves the following steps:

Step 1. Joining and engaging new family members and subsystems
Step 2. Initial assessment
Step 3. Problem solving (establishing credibility)
Step 4. Use of family enactment prescriptions and tasks
Step 5. Information gathering: the genogram
Step 6. Restructuring the family and the multisystems

(Boyd-Franklin 1989, p. 35)

The following case illustrates these processes, as well as the involvement of multisystems including an extended family member (the grandmother), the mother's boyfriend, the school, Planned Parenthood, and the church family.

Case Example: The Hill Family

The Hill family was referred for therapy by the high school counselor, who was concerned about the behavior of Karen (15). The initial call to my office was made by Ronda Hill (45), her grandmother. On the day of the first interview, Karen, her grandmother, and her mother, Martha Hill (30), arrived for the session.

In the first session, I joined with each member of the family and learned that Karen's mother, Martha Hill, had given birth to Karen when she was 15 and Karen's grandmother, Ronda Hill, and her great-grandmother, Pat Hill (62), had raised her when she was very young. Pat Hill, the great-grandmother, subsequently moved in 1980 to North Carolina to live with her extended family. The mother, Martha Hill, returned to high school and lived as a sibling with her daughter in the grandmother's house. There had been no contact since Karen's birth with her father or his family. When Karen was 10 years old, her mother had become involved in a relationship with a boyfriend, moved out of her mother's house, and went on public assistance (welfare, ADC benefits). Approximately one year later, Martha was reported to the child protective agency by a neighbor for "neglecting" Karen and leaving her alone in the apartment. The child protective agency then made a kinship placement to the grandmother.

Subsequently, Martha became pregnant by her boyfriend (Alan, age 35) and had a second child Keena (now 1). She then returned to live in Ronda Hill's home. The Hill family household then consisted of the grandmother, Martha, Karen, and Keena. Both Karen's grandmother and mother were very concerned about her acting out behavior. She had been a very good student when she was younger but had become "boy crazy" (by her grandmother's description) in the past year and was now failing two subjects in school. She had also stayed out late and returned home after her curfew on a number of occasions. After joining with this family and learning their concerns, we began to discuss these issues further.

In the problem stage of the first session, it was clear that Ronda Hill, the grandmother, was the spokesperson for the family and appeared to be very much in charge. However, when each family member was asked what they thought the problems were in the family, the grandmother stated that she felt that Karen's mother was "too easy on her." Karen defiantly mumbled that she felt that her grandmother was "too hard on her." Martha Hill agreed with her daughter and appeared to be in a cross-generational alliance with her against the grandmother.

In an attempt to further explore the mother–daughter relationship, I asked Martha to talk to Karen about her behavior in missing curfew. As mother and daughter began to talk, the grandmother interrupted a number of times. Finally, I asked her to please sit near me so that we could observe the daughter and granddaughter's interaction and give them some suggestions for improving their communication.

From the discussion, it was obvious that Martha had not set limits for her daughter and was often inconsistent about consequences for her daughter's misbehavior. After a short period of interaction, it became clear that a large part of the problem was related to arguments between the grandmother and mother regarding how Karen should be raised. The grandmother attempted to interrupt a number of times to point out how incompetent Martha was as a mother.

Therefore, I asked the mother and grandmother to talk to each other about the issue of Karen's curfew and to come to some agreement on the time they would expect her in this Saturday night. *After a number of false starts in which they each attempted to talk to me instead of each other and each assured me that they could never agree, they decided that she had to be home by 11:00 P.M. I asked them to discuss the consequences if she arrived home later than the designated time. They agreed that she would be "grounded" for the following week and would not be allowed to go out with her friends on the next Saturday.*

Because the family was new to the concept of therapy, I explained that we would need to meet once per week to work on these issues with the family. At the end of the session, I gave the family a task and asked the mother and grandmother to discuss Karen's curfew with her when she arrived home on Saturday. If she was on time, they were to praise her; if not, they were to ground her for the week. Grandmother, mother, and Karen all agreed to try this plan and to let me know in the next session how things had gone.

In the second session, mother and grandmother reported that Karen had acted out and come in late on Saturday and that they had grounded her for that week. She therefore had to come straight home from school and would not be able to go out with her friends the following Saturday night. Karen came into the second session very angry and refused to speak. I praised the teamwork of the mother and grandmother and asked if Karen had talked to them about how she would begin to earn back her privileges. Karen immediately sat up in her chair, and all three family members looked very surprised: The concept of earning or returning privileges was a new one for them. Karen reported that in the past, her grandmother would punish her "for life," and her mother would let her off in a day or so. I asked the three members of the family to discuss what would happen after the following Saturday. After some initial arguments about Karen's misbehavior in the past, her mother proposed that if Karen came straight home every day after school this week and stayed in on Saturday, that she could start over on Sunday and earn the right to go out the next Saturday. I asked the mother to discuss this idea with the grandmother, who raised the question of "What if she messes up one day?" She and the mother were able to agree that they would "tighten up" on Karen and not let her off if she misbehaved. I turned to Karen and asked if she thought that her mother or her grandmother would really be able to "tighten up" on her, or did she think, "they'd let her off"? Karen replied that she thought they would be able to keep to the plan.

In the third session, Karen had kept to the after-school rules and had stayed home on Saturday and was working on earning the right to go out the next Saturday. I asked the family to continue the task for the next week. In this third session, I also felt that I had a strong enough relationship with the family to help them to construct a family genogram (see Figure 1) and find out more of the details of their history. We also constructed an ecomap (Hartman and Laird 1983) to explore the family's support systems with other systems and agencies (see Figure 2).

The genogram revealed that there was a multigenerational pattern of teenage pregnancy in this family. Both mother and grandmother had become pregnant and had had a child at 15, and the great grandmother had had her first child at 17. This is a common pattern in many inner-city African American families. This created two multigenerational transmission processes (Bowen 1976) in this family: (1) the "nonevolved grandmother" (Hines 1988), and (2) the increased anxiety within the family and concerns about teenage pregnancy as the adolescent approaches the age at which her mother first became pregnant.

Ronda (at age 45) was in fact a nonevolved grandmother (Hines 1988). When she had become pregnant at 15 and given birth to Martha, her mother Pat had raised

Martha. Ronda, therefore, had never had an opportunity to be a mother. When Martha also became pregnant at 15 and had Karen, Ronda technically became a grandmother but, in fact, had her first opportunity to actually mother a child. Therefore, her investment in Karen was really that of a mother. However, she was very ambivalent about this and gave Martha very mixed messages about her mothering role.

As Karen had entered adolescence, her family had become very anxious about the fear of her repeating the family pattern of teenage pregnancy. They had never discussed this openly. Her grandmother became preoccupied with her boy crazy behavior and had tightened up on her because, as she said, she did not want her to "have a baby before she was grown." When this happens with no explanation, adolescents typically act out even more. In some cases, acting out and teenage pregnancy become a self-fulfilling prophecy. I therefore decided to use this pattern and to discuss it openly with the family. Although on some level, the issue of multigenerational teenage pregnancy was known in this family, it had become a "toxic secret" that was never discussed.

I shared with the family that I sensed that they were all concerned about Karen becoming sexually active and that they were worried about the possibility of her becoming pregnant. Both grandmother and mother agreed. Karen seemed surprised. I asked her why, and she told me that no one had ever discussed this with her before. I told Karen that I had a feeling that her mother and her grandmother had both had a very difficult time with their mothers when they were adolescents. She was intrigued by this idea and asked each of them. Both told a very similar tale of family members who had tightened up but been inconsistent with them in adolescence and described situations that led to more staying out late with boyfriends.

I told the mother and grandmother that I felt that they had discovered a very important factor, and I asked the grandmother if she would support her daughter in explaining to Karen why they were concerned about her staying out late and becoming involved with boys, and their concerns about pregnancy. Martha explained that her whole life had changed when she had Karen. She loved her, but she could not go out with her friends any more because she had to stay home and help out with her care, and she reported that she began to resent the additional responsibility. The grandmother added that they both wanted more for Karen than they had had. I asked her to tell her granddaughter what their hopes and dreams were for her. She told Karen that no one in the family had ever gone to college and they hoped that she would go. I asked the grandmother to check that out with Martha also. They both agreed, and Karen stated that she wanted to go to college. The dream of an education for their children is often expressed by African American families.

As I underscored how important that goal was, I used that opportunity to help the grandmother and the mother see that they had to work together if they were going to break the cycle of acting out and teenage pregnancy in their family and help Karen to succeed and go on to college. For the next five sessions, this issue was focused on in many different ways. One of these sessions was a subsystem meeting with just the mother and grandmother to discuss their issues with each other, particularly Martha's anger at her mother for allowing her grandmother to raise her. This allowed an opening for me to empower Martha to tell her mother that she wanted more of a role in raising her daughter. Although the grandmother agreed, this was a very difficult process for her.

Karen provided them with a crisis at school in which to test their fragile alliance. After a period of good school behavior and better grades, she had been cutting classes and was again in danger of failing one of her classes. I spoke with the mother and the grandmother and Karen together and asked the grandmother if she would be willing to *allow the mother to call the school herself this time and arrange for a family session at the school. They both agreed. Martha called and made the appointment. At the school meeting, both the mother and the grandmother were able to express their concerns about Karen. The school counselor supported their plans to tighten up on Karen and offered to check in with her teachers regularly and let them know how she was doing. She talked with Karen about arranging regular meetings with her at the school. I underscored the theme of teamwork between the mother and grandmother as a parenting team and their teamwork with the school and their support of Karen. This multisystems intervention at the school was another important turning point.*

This theme of teamwork and clarifying roles continued over the next 3 months. In one session, a visit by Karen and her mother to Planned Parenthood to obtain birth control information was discussed. The grandmother objected at first on religious grounds, but was able to understand the mother, Martha's, pragmatic concerns about pregnancy. By the end of the session, the grandmother encouraged the mother to take Karen to the local Planned Parenthood office. Increasingly, I also discussed the need for both the mother and the grandmother to have a life of their own.

About 2 months later, Martha reported that she and her boyfriend, Alan, wanted to move out and "become a family" with Karen and Keena. The grandmother at first was very opposed. Although she worked as a teacher's aide, I sensed that their moving would leave a large void in her life. I said as much to her in a family session and began to discuss with her the idea that she was still a young woman who was entitled also to a life of her own. She seemed surprised until I shared with her that she and I were close to the same age. This seemed to make the concept more acceptable to her. Martha and Karen encouraged Ronda to, as they put it, "get a life." This was actually a surprisingly light and humorous session, which occurred about a year into the therapy. In subsequent sessions, we discussed many different facets of Ronda's life. It was clear that she was a very spiritual person and that her church was a very important part of her world. Although she was a regular churchgoer, she reported that she had "never had time" to get more involved. Over the next few months, she discussed more and more involvement. She had joined the senior choir and had gotten very involved in a parenting project for teenage mothers.

She was finally able to let Martha, Karen, and Keena go, and they moved into their own apartment in September. A session was held with the mother, her boyfriend, Karen, Keena, and the grandmother. At the end, Martha and her boyfriend were seen alone briefly to draw a boundary around their relationship and to encourage and support their couple bond. The following December, after a year and a half, they completed treatment. Karen was doing well in school, and she, Martha, and Keena maintained close contact with the grandmother through regular visits.

SUPERVISION AND TRAINING

Supervision, within the multisystems model, requires a very active, hands-on approach. Trainees need the opportunity to work with African American inner-city families during their training. The supervisor must provide a supportive environment that is easily accessed by the supervisee. This is especially true during crisis intervention periods, when therapists must feel their supervisors are available to them, at least by phone. Furthermore, the supervisory process provides trainees with the opportunity to develop their most important therapeutic tool—

themselves. It can become a time when the therapist's countertransference issues with African American families living in poverty can be discussed (Hunt 1987). Because this is very demanding work, supervision can become a lifeline and an important antidote to staff burnout.

Training in the area of racial and cultural diversity requires two levels of intervention: increasing awareness and developing sensitivity. The first level requires concrete knowledge about different racial, cultural, and class groups that include African Americans. Students who have never experienced these cultures need a starting point. Once again, caution must be applied to avoid using this material in a stereotypical manner. Movies, videotapes of interviews with families from different cultural backgrounds, and the inclusion of faculty and students of diverse cultural backgrounds into the training program can all facilitate the level of cultural diversity and awareness within a program.

The most important issue in training, however, is the development of cultural sensitivity. Paradoxically, the most profound and powerful way to learn about the culture of others is to start with one's own. The most significant part of any course on cultural diversity must involve students sharing their own family genograms and cultural backgrounds, as well as their own experiences of feeling different and the things they like and do not like about their own cultural group(s). This is often a very moving experience for students and promotes a degree of sharing and sensitivity that can become the true basis for the exploration of families from another culture.

In conclusion, as clinicians become more sensitive to the issues facing African American inner-city families, the quality of psychotherapeutic and family therapy services will become more effective. This [study] has addressed how a culturally sensitive multisystems model can meet the needs of this population.

REFERENCES

Aponte, H. (1976a). The family-school interview: An ecostructural approach. *Family Process, 15*(3), 303–311.

Aponte, H. (1976b). Underorganization in the poor family. In P. J. Guerin (Ed.), *Family therapy: Theory and practice* (pp. 432–448). New York: Gardner Press.

Billingsley, A. (1968). *Black families in white America.* Englewood Cliffs, NJ: Prentice-Hall.

Bowen, M. (1976). Theory in the practice of psychotherapy. In P. J. Guerin (Ed.), *Family therapy: Theory and practice* (pp. 42–90). New York: Gardner Press.

Boyd, N. (1977). *Clinicians' perceptions of Black families in therapy.* Unpublished doctoral dissertation, Teachers College, Columbia University, New York.

Boyd-Franklin, N. (1989). *Black families in therapy: A multisystems approach.* New York: Guilford Press.

Boyd-Franklin, N. (1993). Racism, secret-keeping, and African-American families. In E. Imber-Black (Ed.), *Secrets in families and family therapy* (pp. 331–354). New York: Norton.

Boyd-Franklin, N., and Shenouda, N. (1990). A multisystems approach to the treatment of a Black family with a schizophrenic mother. *American Journal of Orthopsychiatry, 60*(2), 186–195.

Boyd-Franklin, N., Steiner, G., and Boland, M. (Eds.), (1995). *Children, families and AIDS/HIV: Psychosocial and psychotherapeutic issues*. New York: Guilford Press.

Carter, E., and Orfandis-McGoldrick, M. (1976). Family therapy with one person and the family therapist's own family. In P J. Guerin (Ed.), *Family therapy: Theory and practice* (pp. 193–219). New York: Gardner Press.

Deutsch, M., and Brown, B. (1964). Social influences in Negro–white intellectual differences. *Social Issues*, 27–36.

Franklin, A. J. (1993, July/August). The invisibility syndrome. *Family Therapy Networker*, 33–39.

Grier, W., and Cobbs, P. (1968). *Black rage*. New York: Basic Books.

Hartman, A., and Laird, J. (1983). *Family centered social work practice*. New York: Free Press.

Haley, J. (1976). *Problem-solving therapy*. San Francisco: Jossey-Bass.

Hill, R. (1972). *The strengths of black families*. New York: Emerson-Hall.

Hill, R. (1977). *Informal adoption among Black families*. Washington, DC: National Urban League Research Department.

Hines, P. M. (1988). The family life cycle of poor Black families. In B. Carter and M. McGoldrick (Eds.), *The changing family cycle: A framework for family therapy* (2nd ed., pp. 513–542). New York: Gardner Press.

Hines, P. M., and Boyd-Franklin, N. (1982). Black families. In M. McGoldrick, J. K. Pearce, and J. Giordano (Eds.), *Ethnicity and family therapy* (pp. 84–107). New York: Guilford Press.

Hunt, P. (1987). Black clients: Implications for supervision of trainees. *Psychotherapy* 24(1), 114–119.

Kunjufu, J. (1985). *Countering the conspiracy to destroy Black boys* (Vol. 1). Chicago: African-American Images.

Lindblad-Goldberg, M., and Dukes, J. (1985). Social support in black, low-income, single-parent families: Normative and dysfunctional patterns. *American Journal of Orthopsychiatry*, 55, 42–58.

Lindblad-Goldberg, M., Dukes, J., and Lasley, J. (1988). Stress in Black, low-income, single-parent families: Normative and dysfunctional patterns. *American Journal of Orthopsychiatry* 58(1), 104–120.

McAdoo, H. P. (Ed.). (1981). *Black families*. Beverly Hills, CA: Sage.

McAdoo, H. P., and McAdoo, J. L. (Eds.). (1985). *Black children: Social, educational and parental environments*. Beverly Hills, CA: Sage.

McGoldrick, M., and Gerson, R. (1985). *Genograms in family assessment*. New York: Norton.

McGoldrick, M., Moore Hines, P., Garcia-Preto, N., Almeida, R., Rosen, E. and Lee, E. (1991). Mourning in different cultures. In F. Walsh and M. McGoldrick (Eds.) *Living beyond loss: Death in the family* (pp. 176–206). New York: Norton.

McGoldrick, M., Pearce, J., and Giordano, J. (Eds.). (1982). *Ethnicity and family therapy*. New York: Guilford Press.

Minuchin, S. (1974). *Families and family therapy*. Cambridge, MA: Harvard University Press.

Minuchin, S., and Fishman, C. (1981). *Family therapy techniques*. Cambridge, MA: Harvard University Press.

Moynihan, D. P. (1965). *The Negro family: The case for national action*. Washington, DC: U.S. Department of Labor, Office of Policy Planning and Research.

Parnell, M., and Vanderkloot, J. (1989). Ghetto children. In L. Combrinck-Graham (Ed.), *Children in family contexts: Perspectives on treatment* (pp. 437–462). New York: Beacon Press.

Rosenthal, R., and Jacobson, L. (1968). *Pygmalion in the classroom: Teacher expectation and pupil intellectual development.* New York: Holt, Rinehart & Winston.

Stack, C. (1974). *All our kin: Strategies for survival in a black community.* New York: Harper & Row.

Wilson, W. (1987). *The truly disadvantaged: The inner city, the underclass and public policy.* Chicago: The University of Chicago Press.

Questions for Further Study

1. In the excerpt from her book *Maid in the USA*, Mary Romero describes the experience of her identification with the young domestic worker in her colleague's employ. This anecdote illuminates how such identification can assist in the development of a working relationship. However, it is also important to note that Romero's actions might just as well have had negative consequences. For example, it is possible that Juanita might have been very uncomfortable with Romero's assistance, and fearful for her job. We point this out because it is as important for social workers to avoid the hazard of over-identification as it is for them to avoid the hazard of identifying with one client at the expense of another (for a discussion of the two-client concept, see Shulman 1999).

   Had Juanita been your client, and had she reported her working conditions to you, what strategies for change might you have discussed with her? Are there other actions that Romero might have taken, had she been a social worker?

2. Jean-Robert Cadet's early experiences in Haiti profoundly shape the way he responds to other people. Nowhere is this clearer than in his description of the trip to the home of Pfc Kelly's family. Cadet himself understands this, but at this point in his journey, he is unable to shake the powerful forces that inhibit his relationship-building abilities. What personal strengths can Cadet bring to bear on his ability to form relationships? How could a social worker assist him in this regard?

3. As we noted in our introduction, Dreyfuss points out that immigrants to the United States often lose the distinctions that marked them as high or low in social class in their nation of origin. Such information, however, would be crucial to understanding the issues people confront in adjusting to a new life. With this in mind, how might a social worker be helpful to both "the Senator," as well as to those living in U.S. communities who originally came to this country as "boat people?" How does a social worker help these two groups recognize the mutualities in their condition, so that they can share resources with each other?

4. Building a relationship with someone in Hamper's position would require sensitivity not only to his entrenched passivity but also to the anger that accompanies his relinquishment of power and responsibility for self—what some might call his "learned helplessness" (Seligman 1999). It would also demand that a social worker become more informed about the structural conditions governing Hamper's work life.

   What specific actions might you undertake as a social worker that would have the dual impact of building a relationship with Mr. Hamper, as well as acting to move those environmental structures that maintain the working conditions he describes (hint: it need not be revolutionary!)?

5. Boyd-Franklin, in her description of her clinical work with an African American family, offers a model of cultural competence for social workers. Despite the class differences that separate her from her clients, Boyd-Franklin makes use of her own African American heritage and experience as a female to develop open relationships with clients. Similarly, the challenge for social workers is to find a basis of common ground with their clients despite differences in social class. Think about the clients at your field placement. On what bases might you find common ground with those who are most different from you, particularly with regard to social class?

Invited Commentary

NOCONA PEWEWARDY

I was asked by one of the editors of this book to read the excerpts in this section and write a summary about the barriers to building social work relationships through class differences. In responding to this request I have interspersed descriptions of some of my own experiences and beliefs in order to establish my standpoint for interpreting the pieces in this collection. Every person that reads this collection of stories will have a standpoint for interpreting what he or she reads. However, readers will vary with regard to how much their socio-political standpoint is part of his or her self-awareness.

A great deal has been written in the social work discourse about the importance of self-awareness. According to Cournoyer (as cited in Carrillo, Holzhalb, and Thyer 1993), competent social workers make a lifelong commitment to the development of self-awareness, knowing that effectiveness in practice requires extensive knowledge of the attitudes, values, feelings, and experiences that combine to produce reactions. This is the type of writing about self-awareness that I have grown accustomed to over the past 15 years. I find these types of conversations about self-awareness to be lacking because they fail to address the political nature of social work. Where is the recognition that at the end of the work day, most social workers are fully functional members of society who drive our kids to soccer practice or participate in other functions that reflect our community membership, while the people we work with as clients are often isolated, unsafe, and lacking adequate resources? How many white social workers consider the differences in the neighborhoods they work in and the neighborhoods they live in? Integrating these types of questions into the contemporary social work discourse about self-awareness is one way to ensure that the political nature of social work isn't overlooked.

I knew that I would become a social worker very early in my life, and I graduated with a bachelor of social work degree at 22 years of age. Following school, I worked for three years in entry-level social work positions, primarily case-management positions. After three years, I realized that I was only qualified for case management type positions with a BSW, so I returned for a master's degree in social work, and three years later began pursuing a doctorate in social work. My entry into both of my graduate programs was inspired by a frustration born out of the limitations of my own influence. Prior to entering my doctoral program, I felt that I was being paid to be an agent of social control. In the positions I held with my BSW and later my MSW, critical thinking was discouraged. My frustration manifested in anger that I channeled through constant challenges to agency practices that perpetuated consumer marginalization, and in every position, I was inevitably labeled as "an angry white woman." Following my marriage to an Indigenous man, a human being whose father was born into the Comanche Nation and whose mother was born into the Kiowa Nation, my colleagues and supervisors viewed my perspectives as even more suspect, because following my marriage to Cornel, I was labeled as an "angry white woman married to a minority." The thing I found most appalling about the way that I was perceived after my marriage to Cornel was that he was labeled as a "minority" rather than as an accomplished man with two master's degrees and a doctorate in educational administration.

Cornel lives a commitment to social justice and was doing more to promote social justice in one day than the people who labeled him would do in their whole careers—in fact, even labeling him, or anyone else, as a "minority" flies in the face of social justice. So through these experiences I became conscious of some of the manifestations of white privilege, and my socio-political awareness and my commitment to work for social justice increased.

I hope the reader will think critically about the way that other peoples' labels for me served to deflect attention away from my standpoint and to marginalize my point of view in such a way that I was rendered impotent as a social worker committed to social change—this tactic is closely related to the method that Dr. Romero's colleague employed when he marginalized Dr. Romero's attempt to intervene with his sons who were shouting orders to "WASH!" "CLEAN!" at Juanita.

When Dr. Romero's host/colleague returned home to find her washing dishes with Juanita, he marginalized Juanita by making a sexist remark and marginalized Dr. Romero's intervention with his sons by associating her with "Chicano radicals." His privileged perspective afforded him and his family the luxury to externalize the behavior of other people in order that they could wrap themselves in a cocoon of superiority. This is evident in the way he described his attempts to introduce poor women from Mexico to American culture and how his generosity and goodwill had been returned by a high turnover rate. I wonder what it would take for this man to experience a shift in consciousness that would liberate him and the women he employed from a worldview shaped by colonialism?

My own worldview has also been shaped by colonialism. I feel I have experienced some degree of liberation from my hegemonic beliefs by pursuing a doctorate in social work. For the first time in my life, I have been exposed to the theories and techniques needed in order to engage in discourse about my ideas without being dismissed out of hand. But a very small number of social workers in the United States will actually pursue doctoral degrees. A 1995 survey of NASW members revealed that only 4.1% of respondents reported having earned a doctorate (Gibelman and Schervish 1997). If a social worker has to pursue a doctorate before his or her colleagues, supervisors, and peers will acknowledge expressions of critical consciousness, then critical conversations will remain a very limited part of the professional discourse. Social workers must be vigilant to guard against practices that perpetuate hierarchical structures that place higher value on educational status than on a commitment to critical thinking. Doctoral education does not automatically translate into critical thinking.

However, it can be a vehicle for critical thinkers to develop the skills and competence to be more effective advocates, and I am living proof that it increases a person's human capital.

Perhaps the personal capital afforded through education is what made pursuit of a four-year degree so important to Jean-Robert Cadet. The small excerpt from his book communicates volumes about the value of a four-year college degree. Even though he did not have a four-year college degree, his superiors obviously recognized his value—this is evidenced in the way they facilitated the process for him to become a naturalized citizen. His characteristics and skills were valued enough to help him attain citizenship, which made him eligible to oversee "secret" documents, but where was the Army's commitment to helping him achieve his college education in order that he could cross the gulf between being an enlisted soldier or a non-commissioned officer and a commissioned officer? His initiative and abilities were sufficient to join the Rangers, but his ambitions were smothered when he went to the library to pursue a college degree. This is one way that classism is maintained and perpetuated. Education is a vehicle to transcending socio-economic class status but as Mr. Cadet's story illustrates, first generation college students face tremendous challenges even getting through the doors to higher education, let alone finishing a four year degree.

Certainly, there must be more to Mr. Cadet's story than the excerpt I read. After all, the name of the book is *Restavec: From Haitian Slave Child to Middle-Class American*. I can't help but wonder what the rest of the book will reveal. What does it mean to achieve Middle-Class American Status? If I read the rest of the book will I find that Mr. Cadet got his college degree, got a secure job, has a permanent address, and found a loving partner and established a warm, fulfilling bond? What is middle-class status, and should social workers buy into the fiction that middle-class status translates into health and well being for people in the United States?

Is Mr. Hamper, the man who calls himself Rivethead, a middle-class American? Is he healthy, and does he have well-being? If all I saw was his external appearance, the apartment he lived in, the vehicle he drove, would I think he had achieved the "American dream"? Mr. Hamper's story, his sense of himself that he had no training, no skills, no degrees, no connections, that he drank too much, lacked ambition, and was bothered by people in society, is the story in this group that most resonates with the experiences of my family. As I read this man's description of himself, I was taken back to living with my father, a truck driver with chronic depression who died of heart disease at 50 years of age. I remember my father's insecurities, which everyone in my family referred to as his inferiority complex, that kept him in the social margins, even in our small Oklahoma town where the bourgeoisie class is nothing more than a smattering of doctors, lawyers, and the owners of farm implement dealerships and horse-trailer manufacturers. My dad couldn't hear out of his right ear as a result of being beaten by an adult male who said my dad cheated him on the sale of a watch when my dad was 13 years of age. This was one of many experiences that shaped my dad's self-image. My dad's victimization resulted in internalized guilt and family secrets. I think my family expected me to guard those secrets, but in keeping with my own self-interest and wanting liberation for myself I questioned everything around me instead.

I knew I was going to be a social worker from a very early age. One night as my mom and I drove home from my grandmother's house, we passed a yard where a mother was chasing a terrified child. When she grabbed the child, she slapped him and began yelling at him. It was obvious that he was in pain and he was terrified. Seeing that I was visibly upset, my mother told me not to worry about this little boy because there were people called social workers and that it was their job to intervene in those types of situations. That was the critical moment when I decided I was going to be a social worker, and I solidified my commitment in the fourth grade when I wrote a paper about what I was going to be when I grew up. So I feel like I had a linear journey into the social work profession, but my social work career has been more like a maze. A series of straight lines to dead ends that caused me to turn around and start over again.

In every job I have had, working in the Aid to Families with Dependent Children program (AFDC), the public assistance program that preceded Temporary Assistance for Needy Families (TANF); being a case manager at a geriatric rehabilitation center and then a pediatric rehabilitation center; working with people with HIV and AIDS; and working as a home-based family therapist, I have come to the same conclusion: conventional social work interventions in the human suffering that comes from oppression and exploitation are inadequate and ineffective. Contemporary social workers that espouse a commitment to social justice have a professional obligation to intervene to deconstruct structural inequalities rather than only engaging in work designed to enhance the individual capacities of the poor. According to Currie (1996), working with people to enhance their capacities is not the same as insuring opportunities, and the first without the second cannot be other than limited.

While Boyd-Franklin's case study did address some of the barriers to effective interventions with contemporary African American families, I found the action steps toward ensuring that Karen would have access to the information and resources to fulfill her dream of a college education to be lacking. What Boyd-Franklin described as a multisystem intervention approach, I would call a psycho-dynamic approach with community features. I did not see one aspect of Boyd-Franklin's intervention that was directed at social transformation. How about taking this idea that "families need therapists who understand and are realistic about the survival issues they face and who are willing to address these issues in treatment" a step or two further? Why doesn't Boyd-Franklin feel compelled to intervene in the societal structures and institutional practices that result in the "extreme poverty in which many African American and other minority families live"? How about doing more than acknowledging the "invisibility syndrome" of African American males and the "double jeopardy" for African American women? Given that Karen is going to be a first generation college student, and Boyd-Franklin has a history of success navigating admission to higher education, why doesn't she inquire about the kind of help the family will need to help Karen get into college and secure the resources she will need once she is admitted? Where's the part of the conversation related to the types of barriers people of color face at predominantly white institutions and what Karen's options might be?

In an attempt to be fair about Boyd-Franklin's article, she does state in the first paragraph that the "chapter presents key areas that family psychologists must address in order to provide effective treatment," and therefore, a commitment to social justice and structural change may not be as critical as it is supposed to be to social workers. Therefore, social workers whose practice will be influenced by Boyd-Franklin's work have a professional obligation to critique this piece for its strengths and limitations. Structural inequalities and unjust institutional practices result in oppressive conditions that affect individual human beings. However, social work interventions that are only directed at individuals' problems do not extend far enough to eradicate the oppressive conditions that caused the problems and are, therefore, incomplete. By adopting an individualistic approach, social workers unwittingly blame the victims and ignore the ecological perspective and person-in-environment configuration (McMahon and Allen-Meares 1992). Indeed, working with clients while ignoring the sociopolitical influences that result in oppression supports the dominant value system (McGoldrick 1994).

Every social worker has the privilege that comes from professional sanction, and each social worker must make decisions about spending his or her professional privilege. In my experience, social workers spend a great deal more time analyzing and critiquing consumers of social services than they do looking at themselves, their profession, or the society that sanctions them. For me, I intend to spend my privilege, status, and professional license challenging conventional social work practices. I want to spend my time in the profession asking my colleagues how social workers can achieve social justice in an unjust society, and how they can rationalize working with people to improve their human capital in a society that is built on exploitation and that is not designed to offer meaningful and adequate work to most, let alone all, members.

According to Currie (1996), there is in too much of the thinking about poverty, crime, and social policy, from the 1960s to the present, a largely unexamined presumption that the problems of the persistently poor that breed crime and delinquency are ones of mismatch and individual insufficiency rather than of structure and opportunity. As long as social workers operate under that presumption, we are complicit in the injustices and exploitation on which the United States economy is based. We all have choices about where to spend the privilege that comes from being a professional social worker. Each person must consider whether he or she will operate on the basis of pervasive norms and values and engage in uncritical social work practice or if he or she will apply critical thought to each situation and intervene in as broad a way as is possible by challenging the institutions and structures that marginalize so many people in the United States.

I have provided readers with descriptions of the memories that commingled with my thoughts as I read the excerpts in this section as a way to establish my standpoint. A person's standpoint is influenced by his or her experiences and constantly evolves. Social workers must, therefore, engage in continuous reflexivity in order to be aware of how his or her standpoint is changing. According to Danielewicz (2001), reflexivity involves a person's active analysis of past situations, events, and procedures with the inherent goals of critique and revision for the purpose of achieving an understanding that can lead to change in thought or behavior. Social workers that operate without reflexivity miss an opportunity to learn from their experiences and uncover inadequacies in their knowledge and thinking. Perkinson (2002) suggested that human beings are fallible, and the knowledge and behaviors we create are always imperfect in some way. However, because our knowledge is imperfect it can always get better, improve, and grow (Perkinson 2002).

Professional growth and development require persistent reflexivity. Personal and professional relationships provide opportunities to learn about ourselves when we purposefully reflect on and evaluate the perceptions we have about other people as a result of our values and expectations. As a result of my relationship with my father and my relationship with my husband I learned to look beyond superficial characteristics and find human beings who are often wrapped in layers of defense mechanisms that enable them to persist through adversity. For example, my father was very cautious (and somewhat suspicious) in his personal relationships as a result of the depth and severity of the physical and emotional abuses he experienced as a child. I developed acute interpretation skills by learning to traverse his insecurities and defense mechanisms to find his love. As a social worker, I often find myself in relationships with people who are healthily skeptical about trusting me, because I represent institutions that perpetuate social control. For instance, in my current position where I oversee mental health data collection, people have concern about how the data will be used. I often find myself generalizing what I learned through my relationship with my father to interpret peoples' behaviors in order to try to address their concerns.

Whereas my relationship with my father provided the foundation for the skills I use to develop interpersonal relationships, my marriage to Cornel has informed my political orientation. Living with Cornel influenced me to begin interrogating the interaction between privilege and oppression and the nature of structural inequalities. My life with Cornel illuminated the fact that race, racism, and white privilege are among the most potently destructive myths in my white culture. As a white woman living with an Indigenous man, I realized that I could spend my life working for gender equality, and things would perhaps get better for me. But all of my brothers and sisters who are viewed through the cataracts of racism would be excluded from my life's journey. The other thing I realized was that being white gives me insider knowledge and status and that if I share those resources with my brothers and sisters from all walks of life we collectively have more power to work for liberation.

REFERENCES

Carrillo, D. F., Holzhalb, C. M., and Thyer, B. A. (1993). Assessing social work students'
    attitudes related to cultural diversity: A review of selected measures. *Journal of Social
    Work Education, 29*(3), 263–268.

Currie, E. (1996). Missing pieces: Notes on crime, poverty, and social policy. *Critical Crim-
    inology, 7*(1), 37–52.

Danielewicz, J. (2001). *Teachingselves: Identity, pedagogy, and teacher education.* Albany, NY:
    State University of New York Press.

Gibelman, M. and Schervish, P. H. (1997). *Who we are: A second look* (2d ed.). Washington,
    DC: NASW Press.

McGoldrick, M. (1994). Culture, class, race, and gender. *Human Systems: The Journal of
    Systemic Consultation & Management, 5,* 131–153.

McMahon, A., and Allen-Meares, P. (1992). Is social work racist? A content analysis of re-
    cent literature. *Social Work, 37*(6), 533–539.

Perkinson, H. J. (2002). The critical approach to social work. *Journal of Social Work Educa-
    tion, 38*(3), 365–368.

Unit 2   ASSESSING CLIENTS WITH ATTENTION TO RACE AND ETHNICITY

Editors' Introduction

Client assessment—the process of coming to an understanding of a problem, its causes, and possible methods for ameliorating it—is a central task of the social work process. Although social workers operate from many diverse theories and models of practice, they all share one common theme: without an adequate assessment, constructed from a combination of client input, clinical judgment, and all relevant data from environmental sources, the social work process becomes a house of cards, inevitably undermined by a shaky foundation of false assumptions, lack of information, or failure to collaborate with the client. In this unit, we focus on the impact of race, broadly defined, in the assessment of individuals, families, and communities.

What does it mean to "broadly define" race? We wish to acknowledge here that three categories are offered to define the term "race" in *The Social Work Dictionary*: traditional, geographical, and legal. Under a traditional definition, three basic groups—the Negroid, Mongoloid, and Caucasoid—are recognized worldwide. However, racial groups are also distinguished geographically, according to where they historically reside (e.g. African, American Indian, Indian, Asian), as well as by national ancestry, tribe, or family. According to this definition, race becomes a consideration not only of genetic traits but of culture as well. Finally, legal considerations of race have been adjudicated in the United States throughout our history, resulting in prohibitions against discrimination on the basis of race for groups not traditionally thought of as racially distinct, such as people of Jewish and Arab ancestry (Barker 1991).[1]

We define race broadly because of our professional commitment to the entitlement of dignity for all persons, and to the all-encompassing prohibition against discrimination on the basis of race, color, or national origin, among other characteristics in the Code of Ethics. However, we have also chosen this broad definition because it allows us to better demonstrate the contribution of race in all its complexity to our understanding of client problems and strengths that are at the heart of the assessment process.

We noted in Unit 1, "Building Relationships across Social Class," that social workers are members of the elite, managerial class, with professional credentials and positions that grant them authority over the lives of others. This privileged status becomes compounded, and decidedly more complex, when race is factored into the mix. For example, "The American Invasion of Macun," from Esmeralda Santiago's *When I Was Puerto Rican*, offers the reader a view of colonial subjugation of Hispanic peoples by the government of the United States. In a light and even humorous manner, the author is making serious points. As a child in Puerto Rico in the 1950s, she was both witness to, and a target of, efforts to replace indigenous culture with mainland culture. Those efforts, which included teaching nutrition to the citizens of Macun, produced laughable chaos, because the American cultural ambassadors assigned to illustrate food groups and a healthy diet failed to select foods that are produced and consumed in Puerto Rico. They furthermore failed to acquire enough cultural information to recommend appropriate substitutes. Clearly, the educators in this story would have been well advised to conduct a comprehensive assessment of this community before jumping in with the intervention. Note too, that the result of these efforts by the U.S. was a kind of subterranean resistance, best exemplified by the query and response between young Negi and her father at the end of the story: "If we eat all that American food they give us at the Centro communal, will we become Americanos?" Negi asks her father, who wryly answers: "Only if you like it better than our Puerto Rican food."

At the same time, Maxine Clair's story, "Creation," from her novel *Rattlebone*, allows us to underscore the point that any community assessment must guard against the risk of missing differences within racial groups. Within the African-American community in 1950s Kansas City, the Red Quanders offer a stark contrast to the values, aspirations, and traditions that organize the life of the protagonist Irene's family. Their rejection of European and Western traditions and values stands as a powerful alternative to the more mainstream beliefs and goals of Irene's family. The Red Quanders' imperviousness to the attitudes of others towards them is, quite possibly, a very effective strategy for mitigating the soul-scarring effects of racism, and a strength to be noted in any assessment of this community. However, Irene cannot become a Red Quander; she must struggle to engage the opportunities and disappointments that arise from her membership in a more mainstream community, whose values and hopes are to assimilate and accede to the good life promised to the American middle-class.

In "The Death of the Profane (A Commentary on the Genre of Legal Writing)," in *The Alchemy of Race and Rights,* Harvard law professor Patricia Williams offers the reader a story about racial injustice. The essay details the failure of Williams, who is black, to gain entrance into a Benetton store, and her subsequent efforts to publish an article about this incident in a law review. Williams' story may seem trivial beside the story offered us in Clair's "Creation." However, her testimony reminds us of the persistence of racism in contemporary American life. Moreover, the two tales together draw attention to the problem of reporting incidents of racial discrimination in the hope of some redress, for in a racist society, to whom can you turn? As Williams points out, you cannot expect understanding or apologies or even acknowledgement from those who wronged you. In fact, there is no forum available for simply reporting everyday racial wrongdoings, let alone for expressing the hurt and rage that accompany them. In the context of making assessments of individuals and communities, social workers confront narratives that they question, doubt, or even disbelieve. A failure to acknowledge the truth of a client's experience, by omitting details, substituting alternative explanations, or in any way protecting racist perpetrators, is unethical. This essay highlights the necessity of incorporating the client's narrative in an assessment, even when the social worker has difficulty making sense of it. Our Code of Ethics demands that we treat individuals with dignity and respect.

Wilma Mankiller's "Child of the Sixties," from her autobiography *Mankiller,* offers the reader an opportunity to witness how this woman came to an understanding of herself and her family by looking at her life through the prism of history and community, two essential elements of Native life. Her childhood experience of relocating to San Francisco with her family must be read as a crucible that influenced her path to becoming an activist and Cherokee chief. Mankiller places her family's relocation—and the Bureau of Indian Affairs (BIA) removal program of the 1950s—in the context of the harsher and more painful relocation experience of the Cherokee people on the Trail of Tears in 1830. To properly assess the problems of First Nations peoples today—which include unemployment, lack of education, low self-esteem, and alcoholism—Mankiller argues that we must look to history. Seeing her own experience in historical context enables Mankiller not only to better assess it, but also to see herself as having common cause with other Cherokees in an ongoing struggle that is deeply rooted in the past. Noting her opposition to the family's decision to relocate, Mankiller remembers their suffering in the face of ethnic and racial intolerance, which she also locates in the context of California's history. It is important to note that Mankiller is able to so articulately link her peoples' history to her own life path precisely because this history is an indispensable building block in the identity of the Cherokee people. Her attunement to historical forces is also reflective of the importance of the group as a whole over the individual in Cherokee culture. This knowledge and understanding of the people to whom she belongs, and her position in their historical struggle, would be crucial information in an assessment, particularly a strengths-based assessment.

When James Wahlberg became responsible for a satellite center on a reservation, he brought with him years of study of First Nations culture and experience as a white social worker living and practicing among First Nations people. Even his description of his surroundings—noting the juxtaposition of a buffalo herd, and the lost way of life that buffalo signify, with the hundreds of military tankers produced and stored in the area—reveals knowledge and awareness of First Nations history and the struggles of their peoples. The social worker's ability to assess the situation accurately depends on the knowledge and skills he has developed and brought to his position. Approaching an environment dominated by First Nations culture, Wahlberg imagines that his disorientation might be similar to those typically experienced by non-white people when they are in predominantly white environments. His efforts to immerse himself in the community—to immerse himself as much as possible in the life experience of his clients—is exemplary. From his interactions, he learns that acceptable patterns of "helping" on the reservation are neither intrusive nor coercive but are rather based on values of mutual respect and trust. He also draws on his relationship with his mentor Frank Running Deer.

Wahlberg's assessment of the case of John and Mary does not appear to bring race and ethnicity especially to bear. However, the problems he identifies—alcohol, a history of physical and sexual abuse, poverty, marital discord, hyperactive children, and poor access to services—are framed by his discussion as problems particular to First Nations people (see Michael Yellow Bird's essay in Unit 5). He is non-judgmental about John and Mary's alcoholism, living conditions, marital conflict, low level of education and professional training, etc., and sensitive to Mary's silence on the topic of her stepbrother's abuse of both her and her children. Perhaps the most important aspect of Wahlberg's assessment is his conclusion that neither he nor traditional social service agencies are likely to help John and Mary and his belief that his clients will be best served if he can help them and their children develop stronger connections with traditional First Nations beliefs and culture.

Finally, as Debora Ortega notes, we must all recognize that as social workers, we make assessments in the context of our own experiences, and from a privileged standpoint. A large proportion of social workers are white, for example, while many of our clients are not. Inevitably, we bring our own values, biases, and race consciousness to the table. The goal must always be an effort to transcend our biases, understanding that we will often fail. The process of trying, however, will inevitably open us up, allowing us to better connect with our clients, and ultimately result in better practice.

NOTES

[1]For us, race is most significant because, whatever its basis in tradition, geography, or law, it serves in our racist social order as a decisive factor in the inequitable distribution of resources, privileges, and opportunities.

The Creation

MAXINE CLAIR

If I had not seen my life sinking in the unhip backwater of high school, I would not have prayed night after night for something big to happen to me, the way it seemed to be happening to everyone else. By everyone else I meant Carol Walker who had to be "stabilized" at the hospital after eating crackers and water for two weeks because her boyfriend quit her. And Wanda. She had become one of the exalted. A senior, and crowned by the entire school when the police caught her drinking liquor at Shady Maurice's, where she placed second in the Friday-night talent show. Not a month went by that I didn't observe Jewel Hicks's wan return to school after being stupefied with morphine her doctor gave her for the cramps. If such events shook up their existences to make those girls aware of living, not a single event disrupted mine. I spent my time walking around looking for something I could not describe, until I found it in the Red Quanders.

I was only six or seven when Dottie, my play aunt from church, first took Wanda and me to the colored lights strung around the pony rides, tubs of cotton candy, and stalls of hit-the-target games we called the carnival. Instead of taking us the long way down Tenth and across Walrond, she walked us along the railroad tracks to the trestle high over the open sewer of Skagg Creek.

"Don't look down at the water or you'll fall in," she yelled, then ran off and left us.

The trestle, higher than Union Hall in Rattlebone, might as well have been a tightrope. Dizzy above the leaden, gray stream, I had nothing to hold on to. I knelt down. Wanda kept walking ahead of me. Then when neither of them would come back, I crawled on hands and knees, afraid to keep my eyes shut, afraid to open them. That's how I got across. That's how I remember the first time I saw Red Quanders.

I passed their strange district as I lagged behind alone. The dozen or so shotgun shacks and outhouses pushed up close to the railroad tracks reminded me of how scared I had been of spiders and daddy longlegs in the outhouse we used before we were hooked up to the city. Long before the day Obadele Quander first knocked on our door selling fresh-dressed chickens, I was passing near his house looking at chicken coops, goat stalls, and gardens, wondering who were all these people living between the tracks and the woods. At the time, nothing was as puzzling as the way all of them had their heads covered in fire-red satin, the men in a do-rag style, and the women in a kind of wrapped gèle.

Finally, my play aunt came back for me.

"Who are they?" I asked her.

"Red Quanders," she said. "This is Redtown and those obeah women will get you if they catch you looking at them, so stop staring and come on."

None of the dark men with braided beards, and none of the dark women cooking over wash-tub fires seemed to notice us.

YEARS WENT BY. Redtown was there, a part of our part of the city. I was familiar with Folami and Akin, the Red Quanders everybody knew because they went to our high school. They were twins, not identical, but you could tell they were related. Aside from them, I seldom saw any of the others, they seldom came over our way. So what led Obadele Quander to my house that September? And on a Saturday morning, too, when I looked like Hooty Coot in my mother's faded sack dress and my hair not even combed. Of all the doors he could have knocked on, why did ours stand out to him? And when I opened it and he saw my face, did he think of cinnamon, or tobacco juice? With that hair I must have resembled a picked chicken.

"Is your mamma home?"

"Yes," I said, holding down my hair with both hands.

"Can you go get her? I got only two corn-fed chickens left. Fresh-dressed this morning. I got a few brown eggs on the truck too."

"Just a minute," I said and went to get my mother. I thought, This boy doesn't go to our school, I won't have to see him, what do I care. I wondered why they wore white shirts when white was the hardest to keep clean. Was he Folami and Akin's brother? Because by then I knew that all of the Reds were Quanders, and few of them ever went to our schools.

At first my curiosity about Obadele, Folami, and Akin was casual. Other matters concerned me more. For instance, why I had never heard about squaring a corner until my turn in the tryouts for the Drill Team. Why, after a month of school, no boy except the doofus Alvin Kidd had ever called me up. And the school's upcoming speech competition. The way I saw it, the competition was the only imminent thing whose outcome I could influence in the least. I hoped that Mrs. Welche, our new white teacher, would select me to represent our class.

Mrs. Welche had made *The Kansan* the spring before with her insistence that as an exercise "for all involved," she and one of our English teachers at Douglass should exchange schools. It would be a "first." At that point we had two white students at Douglass and no white teachers. The two students were sisters who had come by choice and with much fanfare. A reluctant superintendent had made it clear that a few more years would pass before the new desegregation law would take effect districtwide.

But Mrs. Welche was having none of it. At one time her husband had been a member of the Board of Education, and people said she must have known something damaging to hold over the superintendent's head. People said the school would go to pot, that there would be no discipline with a white woman coming in and changing the rules. Others thought it was a show of good faith.

I didn't mind that she had come. Her blue eyes and brown hair didn't seem to matter to anybody, and I was flattered by the fact that she noticed my small talent for public speaking. I liked her even more when she suggested I learn "Annabel Lee" by Edgar Allan Poe, and represent our class in the competition.

Wanda was a convenient, if reluctant, practice audience. Her mother, eager for Wanda's interest in anything other than her "Annie Had a Baby" record, encouraged me to come and recite for them some evenings. And one of those evenings she brought out a slim volume of poems called *God's Trombones*.

"This belongs to Reverend's wife," she said. "It's a nice book, but Wanda isn't ever going to make use of it." She said that if I wanted I could keep it for a while.

I took the book home. The more I read, the more excited I became about the poems. They reminded me of spirituals. I wouldn't have been surprised to find that Reverend had borrowed some of these lines to use in his sermons. Any one of these poems was sure to make an audience sit up and take notice.

"If you really feel that strongly about it," Mrs. Welche said, "then I'm willing to let you switch. Choose one poem and we'll see how it goes."

And God stepped out on space,
And He looked around and said:
I'm lonely—I'll make Me a world.

That was it. "The Creation." I was set.

"We'll try it tomorrow after school," Mrs. Welche said.

PERHAPS I THOUGHT Folami would make an exotic critic. True, I wanted her to hear my recitation, but that wasn't all. I was curious. She had attracted me and everyone else precisely because of our superstition, based on hearsay, that she had powers. Her face was no different from any of our faces—moon-round, dark as Karo syrup, with big black eyes, nothing unusual. She was a little stout, but she didn't have to worry, Red Quander women never wore store-bought clothes. We all wondered why they made no effort at being stylish.

"Don't you feel funny being the only girl with wraparound skirts down to your ankles?" I asked her.

"It's all I've ever worn. All of my friends at home wear them too, you all just don't get to see them."

"But your skirts are too straight, you can't walk that good, let alone run in them."

"Yes I can," she said.

I didn't know how to ask her about those sloppy-looking blouses that didn't match the skirts. Why didn't they wear them tucked in? And what kind of hairstyle was up under that gèle?

We had physical education, English, and algebra together. Wanda claimed that Folami smelled, but that was after Folami showed us the stone she rubbed under her arms instead of using baking soda or Mum.

"You're smelling your upper lip," I told Wanda. "I'm around her a lot and I never smell anything."

"Well, she doesn't ever take showers after gym."

"At her house they probably still have to heat water for a bath. Maybe she isn't ready for showers. She always looks clean."

Folami was careful always to slip into her one-piece gym suit beneath her long skirt, then go through contortions getting the top part on under her long-sleeved blouses, all the while holding on to her gèle. And after gym she reversed the careful plan so that no one would ever see any part of her without clothes, except of course her arms and legs. We all hated the common shower too. Granted, the rest of us didn't have to worry about headwraps, but we couldn't afford to get *our* hair wet either. We managed by putting on shower caps and running through. I thought Folami was silly to risk getting an F for the semester just because she was modest. Anyhow, I couldn't reconcile her modesty with her powers. Finally, though, Folami stopped getting dressed at all for gym, and when we suited up, she went to Study Hall with the girls who were on their periods.

"Why don't you ever suit up anymore?" I asked her.

"Too much trouble," she said.

I thought about those hideous scars on the bodies of young African girls pictured in the encyclopedia.

"It's only twice a week," I said. "Why don't you take your gym suit home every day and wear it to school under your dress?"

She didn't seem moved by my idea, but she thanked me. No one else had bothered to notice her problem.

I wouldn't say we were friends after that, but we were okay. Since Wanda usually talked to, walked with, or hid from some boy every morning, Folami and I began meeting on the corner in front of Doll's Market to walk to school. Generally she had little to say, but she waited there each morning with her brother—Akin of the white shirt and flimsy brown trousers. I never saw either of them eating in the cafeteria, yet every morning they had delicious-smelling, paper-wrapped lunches that disappeared before they walked to Redtown in the evening.

I knew in my heart that Folami didn't want to bring me home with her. I considered myself clever enough, though, to talk her into it.

"That's okay, my mother is a little peculiar too," I told her. And when she mentioned dinner, I told her, "Don't worry about that. I'll wait until I go home to eat dinner."

"How long is this poem?" she asked me. I assured her that it wouldn't take more than five or ten minutes. I didn't want her to think I was going to bore her with some dry speech.

"Are you sure you want to hear me do my poem?" I said. I didn't think that she would refuse me. She told me that it was usually the old people who recited things to them in Redtown. I let her know that I wouldn't be too embarrassed if somebody else listened.

And so, for the first time, I went to Redtown and into a Red Quander house. What was so different there? The strangely heady, earth-oil smell. The glow from a kerosene lamp. The cloth on the wall, the circle of chairs. The shiny coal of an old woman, her skinny white braids sprouting like a fringe from her red gèle. The carved stool in the corner of the first room where she sat. The snuff she packed into her lower lip. The second room and the low table with no chairs. Akin in gray overalls. And Folami's mother, with a figure and a gèle fuller and more regal than Folami's.

"Who is this girl?" her mother asked Folami.

Folami answered that I was a friend who had helped her at school.

"What is she doing here?"

"I'm helping her learn a poem."

"Hi, Mrs. Quander," I said.

At that greeting she flashed a mouthful of square white teeth, then burst out with laughter so deep that at first I started to laugh too. Softening it a bit, she shook her head and went back to the kitchen.

Akin brought a plate of strange candy. "Crystal ginger," Folami said. "Take one, it's good. It's rolled in sugar."

Folami sat down in the first room on one of the wooden, straight-back chairs. I stood before her.

And as far as the eye of God could see,
Darkness covered everything . . .

"Wait," Folami said. "You look dead. You ought to move around. When we tell stories, we move our arms and look at people. We make faces and jump around. Don't just stand there. Do something!"

And the light that was left from making the sun
God gathered it up in a shining ball
And flung it against the darkness,
Spangling the night with the moon and stars.

When Folami's mother came to sit and listen, I hesitated.

"Keep going. Suppose somebody at school walks in while you're up there. Are you going to stop?" Folami asked.

Then down between
The darkness and the light
He hurled the world;
Then He stopped and looked and saw
That the earth was hot and barren.
So God stepped over to the edge of the world
And He spat out the seven seas—

Another woman, stout and wearing a robe affair, came walking from the kitchen through the eating room to stand outside the circle of chairs and listen. Then still another woman. Then a girl about Folami's age entered, and they sat in the circle of chairs.

And the waters above the earth came down,
The cooling waters came down.

They held themselves, listening intently, rocked and looked at the floor. Now and again someone hummed. When finally I finished, they were quiet.

"They tell you this story at school?" Folami's mother asked, casually.

"Irene is going to say this poem in front of the whole school," Folami said.

"You like this story too?" her mother asked Folami.

"It's just a poem out of a book. It doesn't mean anything," Folami said.

Her mother stood abruptly, and pointed a long finger nearly touching my chest. "Don't come back here to our place with stories," she said. "When you talk, you talk to them that understands you. Not us."

Immediately I was out the door. And there he was, the boy with the chickens. The lean, smooth boy, taller this time, white teeth, ripe lips, sloe eyes.

"Scared you, didn't she?" he said. I ignored him. He walked at my heels, teasing.

"What you scared of, somebody gonna sprinkle dust? Take some of your hair? Turn you into a dog? Guess you won't be coming around here singing your sweet little songs."

That broke the spell. I surely wasn't going to let some boy, Red Quander or not, make fun of me.

"If you have the nerve to come over to Tenth Street trying to sell those puny guinea hens and sorry brown eggs, I can come over in Redtown to see my friend."

"What you mean guineas? Your mother sure doesn't mind giving me a dollar every Saturday."

I turned around and looked at him. "Those women in there would just as soon bawl me out as look at me. At least my mother is nice to you."

That caught him off guard.

"What was that you were telling them, anyway?" he asked.

"It was a poem I have to memorize for school."

"Oh. Well, you better be careful about what you do in Redtown, especially in that house," he said, and he smiled. "My name is Obadele."

Every Saturday my mother bought her usual chickens and eggs and teased with Wanda about our Red Quander eggman. She watched me, though. By the way I washed and braided my hair late Friday nights to get up straightening it early Saturdays before Dele came with the eggs, she knew. She knew by the school clothes I put on just to have on. I was at least fascinated.

"Who's that egg boy and how you know them Red Quanders?" she asked me.

"I've been to one of their houses," I said. "And his name is Obadele Quander. He's some kin to Folami, the one who goes to our school."

"I see he got a funny name too, but you know all of them is Quanders. Every last one of them."

"That's just like us. All of us are Wilsons."

"In *this* house," my mother said. "Not in the whole city. Don't make no sense one man having so many women. You stay away from there."

I saw Folami every day at school. She was apologetic about her mother's ways, but until I pressed her, she didn't say any more.

"Who is your father?" I asked.

"His name is Oba Quander," she said. "Why?"

"I don't know. Curious, I guess. And what's your mother's name?"

She told me that her mother had died when she and Akin were born, but the woman I saw—her Mamma Mandisa—had raised them. Those other women were all sort of aunts of hers.

No mystery there. I thought about the play aunt I once had. I told Folami what my mother had said about their unusual ways, especially about how men could have several wives. She said it was true, but she said,

"So what? To us every father is Oba—that means king. We're just a family that keeps to itself. Only bigger."

I didn't quite get it. If so many had the same father and every father had the same name, how would I know one Oba Quander from another?

"*You* wouldn't," she said. "*I* would."

The evening Obadele first walked with Folami, Akin, and me down by the creek, he itched to tell me how pure the Quanders were, how, across generations, their blood had seldom been mixed.

"Who cares?" I said. "Besides, lots of people say that, but how do you know?"

"I know because I'm my father's son, and my father came from his pure-blooded father, and we go on back just like that to the time we were first brought here. Same is true with my mother."

"Why don't you speak African, then? You all sound just like us to me. Like you're from around here."

"I do, a little," he said. "Anyway, we can use the same words you use, but it doesn't mean we speak the same language. We don't want to be like you," he said.

"Well, you sure do go through a lot of trouble trying to be different," I said.

"Us? What about you? You can't be what you really are at your school," Obadele said.

"I knew you'd say that, but it's not true." I tried to sell him on the advantages of common knowledge, but he wasn't interested.

"Look," he said. And he untied his red satin. I think I expected a conk because the red cloth fit his head as closely as the do-rags my father sometimes wore. I wasn't prepared for the way Dele's naps grew in perfect swirls around his head, like a cap.

He said to me, "Cut off all your hair and let it be, then see what happens. I dare you."

No wonder Folami had held on to her gèle at school. Was he crazy? The last thing I wanted was hair shorter than mine already was. Who wanted to look like an African, even a civilized one?

I didn't want to look like him, but I wouldn't have minded having his gift for storytelling. He knew he was good.

"This is the way it was," he would say. And then he would become quiet as if he were recalling all the details of a life he once knew. This set a certain mood. Then he would begin:

"At first there was no solid land. There were only two kingdoms. There was the sky, the domain of the *orisha* Olorun, the Sky God. And far below that, the watery mists, the domain of Olukun, a female *orisha*. The two kingdoms existed separately, and they let each other alone. Back then, all of life was in the sky, where Olorun lived with many other powerful *orishas*.

"There was Ifa, who could see the future and who was in charge of Fate; Eshu, who was made of chance and whim, and who causes the unforeseen troubles and pleasures in our lives. There was Agemo, the chameleon, and many others, but the most important was Obatala, the Sky God's son."

Obadele went on to tell how it was Obatala who formed the earth. How he hooked a gold chain onto the edge of the sky and descended to the water below, carrying with him a snail's shell filled with sand, a pouch of palm nuts, and the egg that contained the essence of all the *orishas*. The story explained how, when he reached the end of the golden chain, Obatala poured out the sand and dropped the egg, releasing an exquisite bird who scattered the sand, along with the traits of the *orishas*, throughout the mists. In this way he created solid land with hills and valleys. And when he planted his palm nuts, vegetation sprang up on all the earth. Then he saw a reflection of himself in a shallow pool, and began to make figures from the clay, human figures imbued with the personalities of all the *orishas*. He made them carefully and set them in the sun to dry while he quenched his thirst on palm wine. When he resumed his work, because he was intoxicated he made mistakes—the disfigured, the blind, the lame, the deaf. Then the Sky God's breath set the earth spinning, and washed across the figures drying in the sun, bringing them to life. One by one, they rose from the earth and began to do all the things people do. And Obatala, the Sky God's son, became the chief of all the earth.

But every so often, the *orisha* of the watery mists casts powerful juju on the earth, which once was her domain.

I liked Obadele's story, but I was even more fascinated with his version of the mystery of Folami and Akin and their Mamma Mandisa. According to Dele, the twins were not ordinary people. All twins, he said, have the power to bring good fortune into the lives of those who treat them well. Whatever they want, they get. The wise do everything they can to make twins happy.

Obadele said that Akin, the second born, sent Folami into the world first to see if life was worth living. Their mother was suffering great pains at that moment and Folami made this known to Akin. A whole day later, the reluctant Akin arrived, and sure enough, their mother died.

Mandisa was another of their father's wives. Apparently she was always a mean woman. Dele said only that she "used to be troublesome." At any rate, she was hard to get along with and she made an enemy of a neighbor woman, inviting that other woman's juju. And powerful it was. The woman, whose name Dele would not say, caused what he called an *abiku* child to enter Mandisa's womb. This was a child that was born over and over again, a child that died shortly after each birth just to torment Mandisa. But Mandisa was more clever. She took the newborn twins into her house and succeeded in nullifying all of the obeah woman's power.

Week after week, Dele mesmerized me with stories of *orishas*, of lost kingdoms and ancient rulers, and of people—Hausas and Zulus—he claimed I had to thank for more than my black skin. Squat on his haunches on the bank of the creek, he talked about how his father's father's father was the end-all, be-all keeper of the secrets of life, how the old man could recite, for days, every event since the beginning of time without one mistaken word. I was convinced that at least *he* believed what he was saying.

And when Folami gave me an amulet, I pinned it to my brassiere. For an unbeliever, an amulet has no charm. But I liked the idea of it, and maybe it worked because a certain kind of luck followed me to school, right to the stage of our auditorium. Whoever won the competition would represent Douglass in the state competition at KU that next month. Thanks to Mrs. Welche, it was the first year our school would participate. The reading, a kind of oratorical talent show, would be judged by several teachers.

I had decided to wear my navy blue chemise dress with the white collar because I would be standing, and it would show off what I hoped was my slinky-but-not-skinny figure. On the stage, we sat facing the student body and the scattered teacher-judges with their tablets and pens poised. According to their lottery, I was to go third. The Girls' Ensemble sang two selections, we were introduced, and the contest was on.

First the one white student who was competing, Ann Marie Cooper, walked to the podium. I was immediately struck by how confident she seemed. She threw her golden hair back over her shoulder and said good morning to the audience, then turned to greet her fellow schoolmates on the stage. Though brief, her background comments, in which she explained why she had chosen the Gettysburg Address, were more successful than her overheated rendition of Lincoln's speech. I was heartened, but also frustrated. I had not prepared an introduction. Were we expected to follow her example?

John Goodson went next. He towered over the podium. He clutched it, preacher-like, rolled up on the balls of his feet, and in his sonorous best, all but shook the place. *Out of the night that covers me, Black as the Pit from pole to pole!* The assembly sat entirely still. Not once did John let up until he had built to the final *I am the master of my fate; I am the captain of my soul!* with such power that half the students jumped to their feet in applause. Well, okay, I hadn't prepared a nice introduction to put everybody at ease. And "The Creation" certainly couldn't begin on a loud note.

When I stood up, I smoothed the lap creases of my dress and walked deliberately to the podium. I felt the sweat on my palms. Despite my three-inch, pointed-toe shoes, I was short. Nevertheless, in a sudden inspired moment I stepped to the side of the podium and gently opened my arms. Unhurried, I looked from one side of the auditorium to the other, then began. *And God stepped out on space, and He looked around and said: I'm lonely—I'll make Me a world.* I swept out an arm. *And as far as the eye of God could see, darkness covered everything, blacker,* I said "blacker" with a rasp: . . . *blacker than a hundred midnights down in a cypress swamp.* I paused, dropped my arms, turned my head away from the audience, and walked a few steps across the stage. I faced them again, loosely folded my hands in a prayer stance and smiled, nodding my head. *Then God smiled, and the light broke, and the darkness rolled up on one side* . . . and when I said "rolled up," I sang the O sound made grand loops in the air with one hand, then finished: . . . *and the light stood shining on the other.* I sang "shining" and flung up my other hand. With my entire being bent on heaven, the rest was automatic. *And God said: That's good!*

Some other, bolder Irene had taken over, and batted her eyes hard when she came to *batted His eyes and the lightning flashed* . . . and she clapped the thunder and toiled with her hands until anyone watching would be hard put to deny that she held an actual lump of clay. As that Irene *blew into it the breath of life* . . . six hundred souls in the auditorium held their breath, quiet, until Mr. Harris's "Amen!" released them to clap hard and long.

Donald South closed with Tennyson's "Ulysses," potentially a good choice, since the last line, *To strive, to seek, to find, and not to yield,* had been selected for the senior class motto. Unfortunately for Donald, that fact contributed to his undoing when several seniors shouted out the line a beat ahead of him, destroying his delivery of the final words.

I won. Obadele was not impressed, What was the point? What did it mean to win? So I could recite a poem—was it an important poem? Why would I want to do that for a school that taught me nothing relevant? Why was I so bent on impressing a white woman teacher?

He's jealous, I thought. I realized that in some ways he was smarter than he knew. He could discuss a simple story with a depth no one in my class would attempt. The Red Quander men and women mainly taught their children at home. I suppose they had books to augment all of that reciting the old folks did. But wasn't I the one who watched John Cameron Swayze explain the world several times a week on our new television, something Dele could see only if he dared to take his Red Quander self into the Montgomery Ward store on the avenue? Didn't I know the facts he dismissed outright about the girl ironically named Brown who lived in Topeka, just fifty miles away, and who had been named in the Supreme Court case that was changing everything? Ours was the school that had maps and literature. Mine was the mother who saw to it that I went there every day. I knew more facts. He was jealous. I knew more.

The next time he knew more. He knew that if he carried a load of chicken wire and rags in his Oba-fixed truck, the state patrol would not stop a Red Quander riding out in the county on a Friday night. He knew the place in the hills at Wyandotte Lake where, if you stood on the edge of a boulder, you could see the whole of the winding water. He knew that the moon affects everything it shines on. He knew that I was afraid to be with him and the dark trees, and how a scent is a charm, how the nose can catch what the eye misses. He was the one who explained the rot of Skagg Creek as something to get beyond. That in it I could discover the wonder of everything turning to dust, and my hunger for the smell of earth's dark life. Obadele knew the effect that smell would have on me as he oiled it into his pores.

I had never talked the talk for hours on the telephone with him, never drank a single Nehi with him at Nettie's Dinette. He had never been past the front door of my house, or seen me dressed up at church, never even heard of Al Hibbler and "Unchained Melody." We had never slow-danced.

"It's all right," he said. Inside his truck, on a bed of soft rags, we took off our clothes. Without light to see by, he touched me as if, slowly and gently, he were shaping my body into a woman. He opened door after door. This was the slow dance I had wanted to learn. I found the steps awkward, but he was a born dancer. Instinctively, he set a rhythm and unchained us both.

FOR SOMEONE WHO loved school, I became a slouch. I ignored poetry and logarithms. My mind busied itself with logistics. Meeting Dele. At first it didn't matter that he had no telephone, I saw him every morning and every evening unless he had to go hauling or selling in his father's truck too early and too late. Or unless Mrs. Welche pressed me about staying after school to practice my speech. Or unless Folami stuck to me like warm mush and asked too many questions, unless Akin spied, unless Wanda used her sixth sense.

"Hope you know you can get pregnant," Wanda said. "Red Quanders don't play. They'll be workin hoodoo on you, and you won't even know it."

Then it mattered that he had no phone. Even when I came early and stayed late, I couldn't be sure he would be under the trestle. He said that people like us who were forced to hide had to be careful. We were to act as if nothing had changed. But it was impossible. I lived to see Dele, and looked for him every chance I got, despite his father and my schedule and my friends. I didn't care what time I got home, or what time I got to school.

Once, I even met him after the morning classes had already begun. The crisp November air was filled with him. In the truck we drove right past the school, out to the highway and up through Olathe. To Leavenworth to see anything we had never seen, which turned out to be the prison and the army base. I wished for a gèle and long skirt so that people could see that we belonged together.

"It's more than the clothes," Dele said. "You have to *be* one of us, or at least see yourself as we do."

"Who knows," I told him, "maybe someday I will."

As we rode out Highway 40, the designation "great" came easily to my mind when I looked at the plains. Fields of winter wheat, undulant and green, surged to recede into pale seas of corn, or plowed black acreage, or loam as brown as the bread it supported. It seemed that if we could rise high enough above those vast stretches, we would see that they formed the very center of a continent. And if we focused closely, a certain symmetry would emerge with our highway as the dividing line, and a boy who was Obadele and a girl who was my very self as the axis from which it all sprang.

We drove on to Topeka that afternoon, licking his salt fish from our fingers. I wanted to show him the streets where history had begun to unfold.

"It isn't going to make any difference," Dele said. "White people don't want you all in their schools, and no court can change that. You should keep to your own, forget about them."

He didn't understand, but I was in no mood to spoil our adventure. When we got home, I saw no reason for him to drop me off anywhere but in front of my house. Of course I didn't expect to see my mother watching for me out the front door. My mother was never tempted to mince words. I knew what was coming when she yelled, "Just a minute," and came out to the truck.

"I know what you're doing and I'm not going to allow it," she said to Dele. "Irene is not one of y'all and I don't want her around y'all. Don't make me come over to Redtown looking for your people, because that's just what I'm going to do if I catch you around here again. You can consider that a promise," she told Dele.

"You can't do that!" I said.

"Don't try me, Irene. Get your hind parts out of that truck." Given my opinion on how little my mother knew about love, I was furious. As soon as Dele left I told her I loved him. "I'm not going to stop just because you don't understand him."

She attempted to pull rank with "You ain't too grown yet for me to whip."

"I don't care," I told her. "You can't stop me.

"I can tell your daddy," she said. She was losing ground.

"I don't care. Tell him."

My love for a Red Quander had made me my own woman.

Later that same week, I missed seeing Folami and noted that she had been absent for several days. I asked Dele about her.

"I don't know. I'm not her keeper," he said. "Maybe she's had enough of y'all's school."

And I asked Akin about her.

"She's at home," he said.

"What's the matter with her?"

"Nothing," Akin said. "She's just not coming back to school anymore."

At the first glimmer of a realization, it's hard to distinguish titillation from dread. I wondered if Folami's absence had anything to do with Obadele and me. Friday of that week my mother and I stood in the door waving Wanda on, when who else but Dele rode by in his truck. I remember clearly that it was a Friday evening because I had decided against going to the football game with Wanda.

Since the confrontation with my mother, Dele had made me promise that we would be more careful. Although I had missed him under the trestle that morning, I was shocked that he would provoke my mother by coming to our street, and thrilled that he would defy her to see me. His truck didn't stop, though. Just rattled on by.

"He can drive on any street he wants to," my mother said. "It's a free country. But he better not be looking for you." She had already heard me tell Wanda that I wasn't going to the game, and so I couldn't get out to talk to him that night.

Wanda did, however. First thing Saturday morning she came over to get me.

"Come on, we got to walk to the store. Mamma needs some milk," she said. Wanda never got up early on Saturday mornings. I hurried to finish curling my hair, just in case. Once we were outside my house, walking fast, our breath disappearing in the fog, I urged her, "Tell me what's up."

"Nothing, why?"

"I know something is up. Your mother probably doesn't even know you're out of bed."

"Okay, I just want us to talk," Wanda said.

"About what? Did you see Dele last night? Did he ask you to get me out of the house this morning?"

"Yeah, I saw him last night. Let's go over to my house. It's too cold out here."

Appeal moved toward alarm. I dismissed the fantasy of seeing the truck in the alley behind her house and went quickly with her up to her attic bedroom.

"Sit down," she said. I sat down. She looked out her window and shook her head. Then she sat down beside me and surrendered.

"You know Folami, right?"

"Yeah."

"Well, she's pregnant."

"What?"

"Yeah," Wanda said, letting it register.

"So that's why she can't come back to school. How did you find out?"

"How do you think? Obadele told me."

"I just asked him—why would he tell *you?*" My stomach began to float up.

"So I could tell you what he didn't have the guts to tell you himself. He's about to become a little king in Redtown. Full-fledged man. No more nigger girls."

I didn't want to hear any more from Wanda.

"Look, don't blame me," she said. "I wasn't there to hold the light while he did it to her. I just told him I'd tell you."

I understood the words, but it didn't make sense to me. There had to be something Wanda missed. That, or Obadele must have told Wanda a half-truth because of the pressure from the world.

It took a Monday morning under the trestle waiting in the cold, and a Monday afternoon in gym class hearing about Folami, and a Monday evening walking around outside Redtown with Wanda, hoping to see Dele's truck—it took all that for me to allow that it could even be possible. On Wednesday, after Wanda left me under the trestle in the cold morning, cursed me out in the evening, and threatened to go get my mother, I was only slightly more convinced that Dele could have done this.

By Friday it became clear that it would take a lot more than Wanda's word or my mother's threats to bring the fullness of it home. Why go to school when what I needed to know was in Redtown? I fastened my car coat, tied my scarf, collected my books, and left the house.

So what if I didn't have the slightest clue to where Dele lived? I would look for the truck.

Instead, when I got to Redtown, I headed for the only familiar place, Folami's house. My father used to say, when somebody burns down a house, he can't hide the smoke. I had to see her with my own eyes first. As I tramped up to the door, her Mamma Mandisa opened it, filling the doorway, hands on her hips, superiority beaming on her face.

"What you want, girl?"

"Can I speak to Folami?"

"Nothing around here for you. She's not coming back to the school, so you may as well get on away from here." She didn't wait for me to respond before she closed the door.

I found the truck parked in front of a house covered in brown tar-paper siding. I knocked loudly on the front door. When that didn't rouse anyone,

I knocked again, with both fists, and when that didn't do it, I went to the back of the house and knocked on the door with my feet. When that didn't bring Dele outside to tell me that I had it all wrong, I got into the truck and laid on the horn. Surely he would hear, surely he would see me sitting out there. The horn blasted a minute or two, then gave up in a hoarse bleat. I got out of the truck, with its cracked window and wrong-color fender and its smell of kerosene and earth.

Where could I go? I wanted to be some other place, anywhere except this red town where I was certain that red eyes watched my foolish misery and cackled their red pleasure. I followed the railroad tracks, where I could be lost without losing my way.

For hours I walked. Through the woods, outside other neighborhoods, along the river, and into the outskirts of Rattlebone. I was one with the fallow fields I passed through, and with the harvested ones too, where sheaves stood like empty spools. How could he? How could this be happening to me?

I got home after dark that night. Through the window in the front door I could see the kitchen and Wanda at the table with my mother and father, chattering to distract them. I could have been a ghost the way my mother flinched when she saw me.

Wanda said, "Girl, we were really worried—weren't we, Miss Wilson?" I knew it was her attempt to diffuse the tightness in the air.

"You ain't got no business wandering around by yourself this late," my father said. "I was waiting till nine. You better be glad you got some sense and came on home before I had to come after you." His speech sounded rehearsed.

My mother went to the stove and dipped up a bowl of oxtail stew. She unbuttoned my car coat for me and touched her fingers to my cheek.

"Too cold for you to be out with nothing on," she said. "Sit down and eat." I obeyed.

Days later, Wanda broached the subject again. "Welcome to the club," she said. "I could have told you. They're all alike. Dogs, all of them. Forget him. You have to tell yourself nothing happened. Nothing at all happened. After all," she said, "I'm the only one at school who knows the whole story, and I know how to keep it to myself. There's nothing else to do unless you plan to jump in the river.

I tried following Wanda's expert advice, act as if nothing had happened. Forget Obadele Quander. He wasn't anyone, anyway. If my life was going to be a mess, it wasn't going to show.

I HAD MISSED several rehearsals with Mrs. Welche. I frightened myself with the possibility that I had ruined my chances for the competition.

"I understand you've been having some problems at home," she said. I wondered who she had been talking to.

"I hope whatever is going on, you won't miss any more days of school or we may have to reconsider the tournament," she said.

That short-circuited my cure. What I needed now was a victory. Mrs. Welche was offering that possibility, and I would focus all my energy on claiming it.

"I'm fine now," I said. I wanted to give the right slant to what she had heard. "I won't have to miss any more days of school."

"You know," she said, "those students of ours that live in Redtown, from what I understand, you've been spending a lot of time with them. I'm not so sure they're the kind of influence you should be exposed to. Most of them aren't even interested in school."

"Yes, ma'am, I know," I said. I could not look at her.

"They have strange ideas," she said.

"Yes ma'am," I said.

"They don't believe in God, and they don't believe in washing themselves," she said.

I didn't say anything.

"They're all related, yet they marry each other."

"I'm having a little trouble with the last part of my introduction," I said.

The tournament was to be held on the Saturday after Thanksgiving. Mrs. Welche had already arranged for me to ride with her and a student from her old school. Of the twenty-five contestants, I suspected, few to none would look like me. I considered it an initiation into the world I would move through if and when I went to college.

Usually I rehearsed twice a week in the auditorium after school with Mrs. Welche sitting at various places to see how well I projected. Occasionally another teacher would sit in, or a student would sneak in to watch. About ten days before Thanksgiving, Mrs. Welche asked me to meet her in her classroom instead of going to the auditorium. When I got there she sat on her desk with her arms folded.

"I received some bad news a couple of days ago," she said. "I've been wondering how to tell you. Why don't you sit down."

She picked up the letter from her desk. "I want you to know that if I had known this, I would have never even mentioned the state competition to you. I've been involved with it for years. I just didn't think."

She was looking at the letter, but of course, I already knew.

"They won't let me be in it, will they?" I said.

"I'm sorry," she said. "The contest has never been open to you all. They say in the future . . ."

"But isn't that against the law now?"

"Well, sort of," she said. "But things take time."

This was not news. I told myself that perhaps it had happened this way for a good reason. Maybe I would have frozen up on that stage. Those people probably had never even heard of James Weldon Johnson. From the way Mrs. Welche had responded at first, I believed she had never heard of him herself.

"Then Mrs. Welche said, "I was just thinking, you've done all this work for nothing. Wouldn't it be wonderful if we could salvage some of it, put it to good use?"

"Yes, but how?" I asked her.

"Well, you know, Ann Marie Cooper is a pretty good speaker. She has poise and she can project. I had her read "The Creation" for me yesterday, and she wasn't nearly as good as you are, but she could probably learn to do it your way. I thought if you would teach it to her, you know, teach her your inflections and gestures, all the drama you put into it, she could take it to state."

I gathered my books without answering. Outside, November trees had lost their leaves, and their branches showed crooked against the clouds. I took the shortcut along the tracks past Redtown. Without looking down, I crossed the narrow trestle and went home.

Reading

The Death of the Profane
(A Commentary on the Genre of Legal Writing)

PATRICIA WILLIAMS

Buzzers are big in New York City. Favored particularly by smaller stores and boutiques, merchants throughout the city have installed them as screening devices to reduce the incidence of robbery: if the face at the door looks desirable, the buzzer is pressed and the door is unlocked. If the face is that of an undesirable, the door stays locked. Predictably, the issue of undesirability has revealed itself to be a racial determination. While controversial enough at first, even civil-rights organizations backed down eventually in the face of arguments that the buzzer system is a "necessary evil," that it is a "mere inconvenience" in comparison to the risks of being murdered, that suffering discrimination is not as bad as being assaulted, and that in any event it is not all blacks who are barred, just "17-year-old black males wearing running shoes and hooded sweatshirts."[1]

The installation of these buzzers happened swiftly in New York; stores that had always had their doors wide open suddenly became exclusive or received people by appointment only. I discovered them and their meaning one Saturday in 1986. I was shopping in Soho and saw in a store window a sweater that I wanted to buy for my mother. I pressed my round brown face to the window and my finger to the buzzer, seeking admittance. A narrow-eyed, white teenager wearing running shoes and feasting on bubble gum glared out, evaluating me for signs that would pit me against the limits of his social understanding. After about five seconds, he mouthed "We're closed," and blew pink rubber at me. It was two Saturdays before Christmas, at one o'clock in the afternoon;

there were several white people in the store who appeared to be shopping for things for *their* mothers.

I was enraged. At that moment I literally wanted to break all the windows of the store and *take* lots of sweaters for my mother. In the flicker of his judgmental gray eyes, that saleschild had transformed my brightly sentimental, joy-to-the-world, pre-Christmas spree to a shambles. He snuffed my sense of humanitarian catholicity, and there was nothing I could do to snuff his, without making a spectacle of myself.

I am still struck by the structure of power that drove me into such a blizzard of rage. There was almost nothing I could do, short of physically intruding upon him, that would humiliate him the way he humiliated me. No words, no gestures, no prejudices of my own would make a bit of difference to him; his refusal to let me into the store—it was Benetton's, whose colorfully punnish ad campaign is premised on wrapping every one of the world's peoples in its cottons and woolens—was an outward manifestation of his never having let someone like me into the realm of his reality. He had no compassion, no remorse, no reference to me; and no desire to acknowledge me even at the estranged level of arm's-length transactor. He saw me only as one who would take his money and therefore could not conceive that I was there to give him money.

In this weird ontological imbalance, I realized that buying something in that store was like bestowing a gift, the gift of my commerce, the lucre of my patronage. In the wake of my outrage, I wanted to take back the gift of appreciation that my peering in the window must have appeared to be. I wanted to take it back in the form of unappreciation, disrespect, defilement. I wanted to work so hard at wishing he could feel what I felt that he would never again mistake my hatred for some sort of plaintive wish to be included. I was quite willing to disenfranchise myself, in the heat of my need to revoke the flattery of my purchasing power. I was willing to boycott Benetton's, random white-owned businesses, and anyone who ever blew bubble gum in my face again.

My rage was admittedly diffuse, even self-destructive, but it was symmetrical. The perhaps loose-ended but utter propriety of that rage is no doubt lost not just to the young man who actually barred me, but to those who would appreciate my being barred only as an abstract precaution, who approve of those who would bar even as they deny that they would bar *me*.

The violence of my desire to burst into Benetton's is probably quite apparent. I often wonder if the violence, the exclusionary hatred, is equally apparent in the repeated public urgings that blacks understand the buzzer system by putting themselves in the shoes of white storeowners—that, in effect, blacks look into the mirror of frightened white faces for the reality of their undesirability; and that then blacks would "just as surely conclude that [they] would not let [themselves] in under similar circumstances."[2] (That some blacks might agree merely shows that some of us have learned too well the lessons of privatized intimacies of self-hatred and rationalized away the fullness of our public, participatory selves.)

On the same day I was barred from Benetton's, I went home and wrote the above impassioned account in my journal. On the day after that, I found I was still brooding, so I turned to a form of catharsis I have always found healing. I typed up as much of the story as I have just told, made a big poster of it, put a nice colorful border around it, and, after Benetton's was truly closed, stuck it to their big sweater-filled window. I exercised my first-amendment right to place my business with them right out in the street.

So that was the first telling of this story. The second telling came a few months later, for a symposium on Excluded Voices sponsored by a law review. I wrote an essay summing up my feelings about being excluded from Benetton's and analyzing "how the rhetoric of increased privatization, in response to racial issues, functions as the rationalizing agent of public unaccountability and, ultimately, irresponsibility." Weeks later, I received the first edit. From the first page to the last, my fury had been carefully cut out. My rushing, run-on-rage had been reduced to simple declarative sentences. The active personal had been inverted in favor of the passive impersonal. My words were different; they spoke to me upside down. I was afraid to read too much of it at a time—meanings rose up at me oddly, stolen and strange.

A week and a half later, I received the second edit. All reference to Benetton's had been deleted because, according to the editors and the faculty adviser, it was defamatory; they feared harassment and liability; they said printing it would be irresponsible. I called them and offered to supply a footnote attesting to this as my personal experience at one particular location and of a buzzer system not limited to Benetton's; the editors told me that they were not in the habit of publishing things that were unverifiable. I could not but wonder, in this refusal even to let me file an affidavit, what it would take to make my experience verifiable. The testimony of an independent white bystander? (a requirement in fact imposed in U.S. Supreme Court holdings through the first part of the century[3]).

Two days *after* the piece was sent to press, I received copies of the final page proofs. All reference to my race had been eliminated because it was against "editorial policy" to permit descriptions of physiognomy. "I realize," wrote one editor, "that this was a very personal experience, but any reader will know what you must have looked like when standing at that window" In a telephone conversation to them, I ranted wildly about the significance of such an omission. "It's irrelevant," another editor explained in a voice gummy with soothing and patience; "It's nice and poetic," but it doesn't "advance the discussion of any principle . . . This is a law review, after all." Frustrated, I accused him of censorship; calmly he assured me it was not. "This is just a matter of style," he said with firmness and finality.

Ultimately I did convince the editors that mention of my race was central to the whole sense of the subsequent text; that my story became one of extreme paranoia without the information that I am black; or that it became one in which the reader had to fill in the gap by assumption, presumption, prejudgment, or prejudice. What was most interesting to me in this experience was how the blind application of principles of neutrality, through the device of omission, acted either to make me look crazy or to make the reader participate in old habits of cultural bias.

That was the second telling of my story. The third telling came last April, when I was invited to participate in a law-school conference on Equality and Difference. I retold my sad tale of exclusion from Soho's most glitzy boutique, focusing in this version on the law-review editing process as a consequence of an ideology of style rooted in a social text of neutrality. I opined:

> Law and legal writing aspire to formalized, color-blind, liberal ideals. Neutrality is the standard for assuring these ideals; yet the adherence to it is often determined by reference to an aesthetic of uniformity, in which difference is simply omitted. For example, when segregation was eradicated from the American lexicon, its omission led many to actually believe that racism therefore no longer existed. Race-neutrality in law has become the presumed antidote for race bias in real life. With the entrenchment of the notion of race-neutrality came attacks on the concept of affirmative action and the rise of reverse discrimination suits. Blacks, for so many generations deprived of jobs based on the color of our skin, are now told that we ought to find it demeaning to be hired, based on the color of our skin. Such is the silliness of simplistic either-or inversions as remedies to complex problems.

What is truly demeaning in this era of double-speak-no-evil is going on interviews and not getting hired because someone doesn't think we'll be comfortable. It is demeaning not to get promoted because we're judged "too weak," then putting in a lot of energy the next time and getting fired because we're "too strong." It is demeaning to be told what we find demeaning. It is very demeaning to stand on street corners unemployed and begging. It is downright demeaning to have to explain why we haven't been employed for months and then watch the job go to someone who is "more experienced." It is outrageously demeaning that none of this can be called racism, even if it happens only to, or to large numbers of, black people; as long as it's done with a smile, a handshake and a shrug; as long as the phantom-word "race" is never used.

The image of race as a phantom-word came to me after I moved into my late godmother's home. In an attempt to make it my own, I cleared the bedroom for painting. The following morning the room asserted itself, came rushing and raging at me through the emptiness, exactly as it had been for twenty-five years. One day filled with profuse and overwhelming complexity, the next day filled with persistently recurring memories. The shape of the past came to haunt me, the shape of the emptiness confronted me each time I was about to enter the room. The force of its spirit still drifts like an odor throughout the house.

The power of that room, I have thought since, is very like the power of racism as status quo: it is deep, angry, eradicated from view, but strong enough to make everyone who enters the room walk around the bed that isn't there, avoiding the phantom as they did the substance, for fear of bodily harm. They do not even know they are avoiding; they defer to the unseen shapes of things with subtle responsiveness, guided by an impulsive awareness of nothingness, and the deep knowledge and denial of witchcraft at work.

The phantom room is to me symbolic of the emptiness of formal equal opportunity, particularly as propounded by President Reagan, the Reagan Civil Rights Commission and the Reagan Supreme Court. Blindly formalized constructions of equal opportunity are the creation of a space that is filled in by a meandering stream of unguided hopes, dreams, fantasies, fears, recollections. They are the presence of the past in imaginary, imagistic form—the phantom-roomed exile of our longing.

> It is thus that I strongly believe in the efficacy of programs and paradigms like affir-mative action. Blacks are the objects of a constitutional omission which has been in-corporated into a theory of neutrality. It is thus that omission is really a form of expression, as oxymoronic as that sounds: racial omission is a literal part of original intent; it is the fixed, reiterated prophecy of the Founding Fathers. It is thus that af-firmative action is an affirmation; the affirmative act of hiring—or hearing—blacks is a recognition of individuality that re-places blacks as a social statistic, that is pro-foundly interconnective to the fate of blacks and whites either as sub-groups or as one group. In this sense, affirmative action is as mystical and beyond-the-self as an initiation ceremony. It is an act of verification and of vision. It is an act of social as well as professional responsibility.

The following morning I opened the local newspaper, to find that the event of my speech had commanded two columns on the front page of the Metro sec-tion. I quote only the opening lines: "Affirmative action promotes prejudice by denying the status of women and blacks, instead of affirming them as its name suggests. So said New York City attorney Patricia Williams to an audience Wednesday."[4]

I clipped out the article and put it in my journal. In the margin there is a note to myself: eventually, it says, I should try to pull all these threads together into yet another law-review article. The problem, of course, will be that in the hierarchy of law-review citation, the article in the newspaper will have more au-thoritative weight about me, as a so-called "primary resource," than I will have; it will take precedence over my own citation of the unverifiable testimony of my speech.

I have used the Benetton's story a lot, in speaking engagements at various schools. I tell it whenever I am too tired to whip up an original speech from scratch. Here are some of the questions I have been asked in the wake of its telling:

Am I not privileging a racial perspective, by considering only the black point of view? Don't I have an obligation to include the "salesman's side" of the story?

Am I not putting the salesman on trial and finding him guilty of racism without giving him a chance to respond to or cross-examine me?

Am I not using the store window as a "metaphorical fence" against the po-tential of his explanation in order to represent my side as "authentic"?

How can I be sure I'm right?

What makes my experience the real black one anyway?

Isn't it possible that another black person would disagree with my experi-ence? If so, doesn't that render my story too unempirical and subjective to pay any attention to?

Always a major objection is to my having put the poster on Benetton's win-dow. As one law professor put it: "It's one thing to publish this in a law review, where no one can take it personally, but it's another thing altogether to put your own interpretation right out there, just like that, uncontested, I mean, with nothing to counter it."[5]

NOTES

1. "When 'By Appointment' Means Keep Out," *New York Times*, December 17, 1986, p. B1. Letter to the Editor from Michael Levin and Marguerita Levin, *New York Times*, January 11, 1987, p. E32.
2. *New York Times*, January 11, 1987, p. E32.
3. See generally *Blyew v. U.S.*, 80 U.S. 581 (1871), upholding a state's right to forbid blacks to testify against whites.
4. "Attorney Says Affirmative Action Denies Racism, Sexism," *Dominion Post;* (Morgantown, West Virginia), April 8, 1988, p. B1.
5. These questions put me on trial—an imaginary trial where it is I who have the burden of proof—and proof being nothing less than the testimony of the salesman actually confessing yes yes I am a racist. These questions question my own ability to know, to assess, to be objective. And of course, since anything that happens to me is inherently subjective, they take away my power to know what happens to me in the world. Others, by this standard, will always know better than I. And my insistence on recounting stories from my own perspective will be treated as presumption, slander, paranoid hallucination, or just plain lies.

   Recently I got an urgent call from Thomas Grey of Stanford Law School. He had used this piece in his jurisprudence class, and a rumor got started that the Benetton's story wasn't true, that I had made it up, that it was a fantasy, a lie that was probably the product of a diseased mind trying to make all white people feel guilty. At this point I realized it almost didn't make any difference whether I was telling the truth or not—that the greater issue I had to face was the overwhelming weight of a disbelief that goes beyond mere disinclination to believe and becomes active suppression of anything I might have to say. The greater problem is a powerfully oppressive mechanism for denial of black self-knowledge and expression. And this denial cannot be separated from the simultaneously pathological willingness to believe certain things about blacks—not to believe them, but things about them.

   When students in Grey's class believed and then claimed that I had made it all up, they put me in a position like that of Tawana Brawley. I mean that specifically: the social consequence of concluding that we are liars operates as a kind of public absolution of racism—the conclusion is not merely that we are troubled or that I am eccentric, but that we, as liars, are the norm. Therefore, the nonbelievers can believe, things of this sort really don't happen (even in the face of statistics to the contrary). Racism or rape is all a big fantasy concocted by troublesome minorities and women. It is interesting to recall the outcry in every national medium, from the *New York Post* to the *Times* to the major networks, in the wake of the Brawley case: who will ever again believe a black woman who cries rape by a white man?

Now shift the frame a bit, and imagine a white male facing a consensus that he lied. Would there be a difference? Consider Charles Stuart, for example, the white Bostonian who accused a black man of murdering his pregnant wife and whose brother later alleged that in fact the brothers had conspired to murder her. Most people and the media not only did not claim but actively resisted believing that Stuart represented any kind of "white male" norm. Instead he was written off as a troubled weirdo, a deviant—again even in the face of spousal-abuse statistics to the contrary. There was not a story I could find that carried on about "who will ever believe" the next white man who cries murder.

Reading

The American Invasion of Macún

ESMERALDA SANTIAGO

Lo que no mata, engorda.

What doesn't kill you, makes you fat.
Pollito, chicken
Gallina, hen
Lápiz, pencil
y Pluma, pen
Ventana, window
Puerta, door
Maestra, teacher
y Piso, floor

Miss Jimènez stood in front of the class as we sang and, with her ruler, pointed at the chicks scratching the dirt outside the classroom, at the hen leading them, at the pencil on Juanita's desk, at the pen on her own desk, at the window that looked out into the playground, at the door leading to the yard, at herself, and at the shiny tile floor. We sang along, pointing as she did with our sharpened pencils, rubber end out.

"¡*Muy* bien!" She pulled down the map rolled into a tube at the front of the room. In English she told us, "Now gwee estody about de Jun-ited Estates gee-o-graphee."

It was the daily English class. Miss Jiménez, the second- and third-grade teacher, was new to the school in Macún. She looked like a grown-up doll, with high rounded cheekbones, a freckled *café con leche* complexion, black lashes, black curly hair pulled into a bun at the nape of her neck, and the prettiest legs in the whole *barrio*. Doña Ana said Miss Jiménez had the most beautiful legs she'd ever seen, and the next day, while Miss Jiménez wrote the multiplication table on the blackboard, I stared at them.

She wore skirts to just below the knees, but from there down, her legs were shaped like chicken drumsticks, rounded and full at the top, narrow at the bottom. She had long straight hair on her legs, which everyone said made them even prettier, and small feet encased in plain brown shoes with a low square heel. That night I wished on a star that someday my scrawny legs would fill out into that lovely shape and that the hair on them would be as long and straight and black.

Miss Jiménez came to Macún at the same time as the community center. She told us that starting the following week, we were all to go to the *centro comunal* before school to get breakfast, provided by the Estado Libre Asociado, or Free Associated State, which was the official name for Puerto Rico in the Estados Unidos, or in English, the Jun-ited Estates of America. Our parents, Miss Jiménez told us, should come to a meeting that Saturday, where experts from San Juan and the Jun-ited Estates would teach our mothers all about proper nutrition and hygiene, so that we would grow up as tall and strong as Dick, Jane, and Sally, the *Americanitos* in our primers.

"And Mami," I said as I sipped my afternoon *café con leche*, "Miss Jiménez said the experts will give us free food and toothbrushes and things . . . and we can get breakfast every day except Sunday . . ."

"Calm down," she told me. "We'll go, don't worry."

On Saturday morning the yard in front of the *centro comunal* filled with parents and their children. You could tell the experts from San Juan from the ones that came from the Junited Estates because the *Americanos* wore ties with their white shirts and tugged at their collars and wiped their foreheads with crumpled handkerchiefs. They hadn't planned for children, and the men from San Juan convinced a few older girls to watch the little ones outside so that the meeting could proceed with the least amount of disruption. Small children refused to leave their mothers' sides and screeched the minute one of the white-shirted men came near them. Some women sat on the folding chairs at the rear of the room nursing, a cloth draped over their baby's face so that the experts would not be upset at the sight of a bare breast. There were no fathers. Most of them worked seven days a week, and anyway, children and food were woman's work.

"Negi, take the kids outside and keep them busy until this is over."

"But Mami . . ."

"Do as I say."

She pressed her way to a chair in the middle of the room and sat facing the experts. I hoisted Edna on my shoulder and grabbed Alicia's hand. Delsa pushed Norma out in front of her. They ran into the yard and within minutes had blended into a group of children their age. Hector found a boy to chase him around a tree, and Alicia crawled to a sand puddle where she and other toddlers smeared one another with the fine red dirt. I sat at the door, Edna on my lap, and tried to keep one eye on my sisters and brother and another on what went on inside.

The experts had colorful charts on portable easels. They introduced each other to the group, thanked the Estado Libre Asociado for the privilege of being there, and then took turns speaking. The first expert opened a large suitcase. Inside there as a huge set of teeth with pink gums.

"*Ay Dios Santo, qué cosa tan fea,*" said a woman as she crossed herself. The mothers laughed and mumbled among themselves that yes, it was ugly. The expert stretched his lips into a smile and pulled a large toothbrush from under the table. He used ornate Spanish words that we assumed were scientific talk for teeth, gums, and tongue. With his giant brush, he polished each tooth on the model, pointing out the proper path of the bristles on the teeth.

"If I have to spend that much time on my teeth," a woman whispered loud enough for everyone to hear, "I won't get anything done around the house." The room buzzed with giggles, and the expert again spread his lips, took a breath, and continued his demonstration.

"At the conclusion of the meeting," he said, "you will each receive a toothbrush and a tube of paste for every member of your family."

"*¿Hasta pa' los mellaos?*" a woman in the back of the room asked, and everyone laughed.

"If they have no teeth, it's too late for them, isn't it," the expert said through his own clenched teeth. The mothers shrieked with laughter, and the expert sat down so that an *Americano* with red hair and thick glasses could tell us about food.

He wiped his forehead and upper lip as he pulled up the cloth covering one of the easels to reveal a colorful chart the major food groups.

"*La buena* nutrition is *muy importante para los niños.*" In heavily accented, hard to understand Castilian Spanish he described the necessity of eating portions of each of the foods on his chart every day. There were carrots and broccoli, iceberg lettuce, apples, pears, and peaches. The bread was sliced into a perfect square, unlike the long loaves Papi brought home from a bakery in San Juan, or the round *pan de manteca* Mami bought at Vitín's store. There was no rice on the chart, no beans, no salted codfish. There were big white eggs, not at all like the small round ones our hens gave us. There was a tall glass of milk, but no coffee. There were wedges of yellow cheese, but no balls of cheese like the white *queso del país* wrapped in banana leaves sold in bakeries all over Puerto Rico. There were bananas but no plantains, potatoes but no *batatas,* cereal flakes but no oatmeal, bacon but no sausages.

"But, *señor,*" said Doña Lola from the back of the room, "none of the fruits or vegetables on your chart grow in Puerto Rico."

"Then you must substitute our recommendations with your native foods."

"Is an apple the same as a mango?" asked Cirila, whose yard was shaded by mango trees.

"*Sí*," said the expert, "a mango can be substituted for an apple."

"What about breadfruit?"

"I'm not sure . . ." The *Americano* looked at an expert from San Juan who stood up, pulled the front of his *guayabera* down over his ample stomach, and spoke in a voice as deep and resonant as a radio announcer's.

"Breadfruit," he said, "would be equivalent to potatoes."

"Even the ones with seeds?" asked Doña Lola, who roasted them on the coals of her *fogón.*

"Well, I believe so," he said, "but it is best not to make substitutions for the recommended foods. That would throw the whole thing off."

He sat down and stared at the ceiling, his hands crossed under his belly as if he had to hold it up. The mothers asked each other where they could get carrots and broccoli, iceberg lettuce, apples, peaches, or pears.

"At the conclusion of the meeting," the *Americano* said, "you will all receive a sack full of groceries with samples from the major food groups." He flipped the chart closed and moved his chair near the window, amid the hum of women asking one another what he'd just said.

The next expert uncovered another easel on which there was a picture of a big black bug. A child screamed, and a woman got the hiccups.

"This," the expert said scratching the top of his head, "is the magnified image of a head louse."

Following him, another *Americano* who spoke good Spanish discussed intestinal parasites. He told all the mothers to boil their water several times and to wash their hands frequently.

"Children love to put their hands in their mouths," he said, making it sound like fun, "but each time they do, they run the risk of infection." He flipped the chart to show an enlargement of a dirty hand, the tips of the fingernails encrusted with dirt.

"Ugh! That's disgusting!" whispered Mami to the woman next to her. I curled my fingers inside my palms.

"When children play outside," the expert continued, "their hands pick up dirt, and with it, hundreds of microscopic parasites that enter their bodies through their mouths to live and thrive in their intestinal tract."

He flipped the chart again. A long flat snake curled from the corner at the top of the chart to the opposite corner at the bottom. Mami shivered and rubbed her arms to keep the goose bumps down.

"This," the *Americano* said, "is a tapeworm, and it is not uncommon in this part of the world."

Mami had joked many times that the reason I was so skinny was that I had a *solitaria*, a tapeworm, in my belly. But I don't think she ever knew what a tapeworm looked like, nor did I. I imagined something like the earthworms that crawled out of the ground when it rained, but never anything so ugly as the snake on the chart, its flat body like a deck of cards strung together.

"Tapeworms," the expert continued, "can reach lengths of nine feet." I rubbed my belly, trying to imagine how long nine feet was and whether I had that much room in me. Just thinking about it made my insides itchy.

When they finished their speeches, the experts had all the mothers line up and come to the side of the room, where each was given samples according to the number of people in their household. Mami got two sacks of groceries, so Delsa had to carry Edna all the way home while I dragged one of the bags full of cans, jars, and bright cartons.

At home Mami gave each of us a toothbrush and told us we were to clean our teeth every morning and every evening. She set a tube of paste and a cup by the door, next to Papi's shaving things. Then she emptied the bags.

"I don't understand why they didn't just give us a sack of rice and a bag of beans. It would keep this family fed for a month."

She took out a five-pound tin of peanut butter, two boxes of cornflakes, cans of fruit cocktail, peaches in heavy syrup, beets, and tuna fish, jars of grape jelly and pickles and put everything on a high shelf.

"We'll save this," she said, "so that we can eat like *Americanos cuando el hambre apriete.*" She kept them there for a long time but took them down one by one so that, as she promised, we ate like Americans when hunger cramped our bellies.

One morning I woke up with something wiggling inside my panties. When I looked, there was a long worm inside. I screamed, and Mami came running. I pointed to my bottom, and she pulled down my panties and saw. She sat me in a basin of warm water with salt, because she thought that might draw more worms out. I squatted, my bottom half in, half out, expecting that a *solitaria* would crawl out of my body and swim around and when it realized it had come out, try to bite me down there and crawl back in. I kept looking into the basin, but nothing happened, and after a long time, Mami let me get up. That night she gave us only a thin broth for supper.

"Tonight you all get a *purgante,*" she said.

"But why," Delsa whined. "I'm not the one with worms."

"If one of you has worms, you all have worms," Mami said, and we knew better than to argue with her logic. "Now go wash up, and come get your medicine."

The *purgante* was her own concoction, a mixture of cod liver oil and mugwort, milk of magnesia, and green papaya juice, sweetened to disguise the fishy, bitter, chalky taste. It worked on our bellies overnight, and in the morning, Delsa, Norma, Héctor, and I woke up with cramps and took turns at the latrine, joining the end of the line almost as soon as we'd finished. Mami fed us broths, and in the evening, a bland, watery boiled rice that at least stuck to our bellies and calmed the roiling inside.

"Today," Miss Jiménez said, "you will be vaccinated by the school nurse."

There had never been a school nurse at Macún Elementary School, but lately a woman dressed in white, with a tall, stiff cap atop her short cropped hair, had set up an infirmary in a corner of the lunchroom. Forms had been sent home, and Mami had told me and Delsa that we would be receiving polio vaccines.

"What's polio?" I asked, imagining another parasite in my belly.

"It's a very bad disease that makes you crippled," she said.

"Is it like meningitis?" Delsa asked. A brother of one of her friends had that disease; his arms and hands were twisted into his body, his legs splayed out at the knees, so that he walked as if he were about to kneel.

"No," Mami said, "it's worse. If you get polio, you die, or you spend the rest of your life in a wheelchair or inside an iron lung."

"An iron lung!?!?" It was impossible. There could not be such a thing.

"It's not like a real lung, silly," Mami laughed. "It's a machine that breathes for you."

"¡Ay Dios Mío!" Polio was worse than *solitaria*.

"But how can it do that?" Delsa's eyes opened and shut as if she were testing to see whether she was asleep or awake.

"I don't know how it works," Mami said. "Ask your father."

Delsa and I puzzled over how you could have an iron lung, and that night, when Papi came home from work, we made him draw one for us and show us how a machine could do what people couldn't. He drew a long tube and at one end made a stick figure face.

"It looks like a can," Delsa said, and Papi laughed.

"Yes," he said, "it does. Just like a can."

Miss Jiménez sent us out to see the nurse two at a time, in alphabetical order. By the time she got to the *S*'s, I was shaky, because every one of the children who had gone before me had come back crying, pressing a wad of cotton against their arm. Ignacio Sepúlveda walked next to me, and even though he was as scared as I was, he pretended he wasn't.

"What crybabies!" he said. "I've had shots before and they don't hurt that much."

"When?"

"Last year. They gave us shots for tuberculosis." We were nearing the lunchroom, and Ignacio slowed down, tugged on my arm, and whispered, "It's all because of politics."

"What are you talking about? Politics isn't a disease like polio. It's something men talk about at the bus stop." I'd heard Papi tell Mami when he was late that he'd missed the bus because he'd been discussing politics.

Ignacio kept his voice to a whisper, as if he were telling me something no one else knew. "My Papá says the government's doing all this stuff for us because it's an election year."

"What does that have to do with it?"

"They give kids shots and free breakfast, stuff like that, so that our dads will vote for them."

"So?"

"Don't you know anything?"

"I know a lot of things."

"You don't know anything about politics."

"Do so."

"Do not."

"Do so."

"Who's the governor of Puerto Rico, then?"

"Oh, you could have asked something really hard! . . . Everyone knows it's Don Luis Muñoz Marín."

"Yeah, well, who's *el presidente* of the Jun-ited Estates?

"Ay-sen-hou-err."

"I bet you don't know his first name."

I knew then I had him. I scanned Papi's newspaper daily, and I had seen pictures of *el presidente* on the golf course, and of his wife's funny hairdo.

"His first name is Eekeh," I said, puffed with knowledge. And his wife's name is Mami."

"Well, he's an imperialist, just like all the other *gringos!*" Ignacio said, and I was speechless because Mami and Papi never let us say things like that about grown-ups, even if they were true.

When we came into the lunchroom, Ignacio presented his arm to the nurse as if instead of a shot he were getting a medal. He winced as the nurse stuck the needle into him and blinked a few times to push back tears. But he didn't cry, and I didn't either, though I wanted to. There was no way I'd have Ignacio Sepúlveda calling me a crybaby.

"Papi, what's an imperialist?"

He stopped the hammer in midstrike and looked at me.

"Where did you hear that word?"

"Ignacio Sepúlveda said Eekeh Aysenhouerr is an imperialist. He said all *gringos* are."

Papi looked around as if someone were hiding behind a bush and listening in. "I don't want you repeating those words to anybody . . ."

"I know that Papi. . . . I just want to know what it means. Are *gringos* the same as *Americanos*?"

"You should never call an *Americano* a gringo. It's a very bad insult."

"But why?"

"It just is." It wasn't like Papi not to give a real answer to my questions. "Besides, *el presidente's* name is pronounced Ayk, not Eekeh." He went back to his hammering.

I handed him a nail from the can at his feet. "How come it's a bad insult?"

He stopped banging the wall and looked at me. I stared back, and he put his hammer down, took off his hat, brushed his hand across his forehead, wiped it on his pants, sat on the stoop, and leaned his elbows back, stretching his legs out in front of him. This was the response I expected. Now I would hear all about *gringos* and imperialists.

"Puerto Rico was a colony of Spain after Columbus landed here," he began, like a schoolteacher.

"I know that."

"Don't interrupt."

"Sorry."

"In 1898, *los Estados Unidos* invaded Puerto Rico, and we became their colony. A lot of Puerto Ricans don't think that's right. They call *Americanos* imperialists, which means they want to change our country and our culture to be like theirs."

"Is that why they teach us English in school, so we can speak like them?"

"Yes."

"Well, I'm not going to learn English so I don't become American."

He chuckled. "Being American is not just a language, *Negrita*, it's a lot of other things."

"Like what?"

He scratched his head. "Like the food you eat . . . the music you listen to . . . the things you believe in."

"Do they believe in God?"

"Some of them do."

"Do they believe in phantasms and witches?"

"Yes, some Americans believe in that."

"Mami doesn't believe any of that stuff."

"I know. I don't either."

"Why not?"

"I just . . . I believe in things I can see."

"Why do people call *Americanos gringos*?"

"We call them *gringos*, they call us spiks."

"What does that mean?"

"Well," he sat up, leaned his elbows on his knees and looked at the ground, as if he were embarrassed. "There are many Puerto Ricans in New York, and when someone asks them a question they say, 'I don spik inglish' instead of 'I don't speak English.' They make fun of our accent."

"*Americanos* talk funny when they speak Spanish."

"Yes, they do. The ones who don't take the trouble to learn it well." He pushed his hat back, and the sun burned into his already brown face, making him squint. "That's part of being an imperialist. They expect us to do things their way, even in our country."

"That's not fair."

"No, it isn't." He stood up and picked up his hammer. "Well, I'd better get back to work, *Negrita*. Do you want to help?"

"Okay." I followed him, holding the can of nails up so he wouldn't have to bend over to pick them up. "Papi?"

"Yes."

"If we eat all that American food they give us at the *centro comunal*, will be become *Americanos*?"

He banged a nail hard into the wall then turned to me, and, with a broad smile on his face said, "Only if you like it better than our Puerto Rican food."

Child of the Sixties

WILMA (PEARL) MANKILLER

A hunter was in the woods one day in winter when suddenly he saw a panther coming toward him and at once prepared to defend himself. The panther continued to approach, and the hunter was just about to shoot when the animal spoke. Suddenly it seemed to the man as if there were no difference between them, that they were both of the same nature. The panther asked the man where he was going, and the man said he was looking for a deer. "Well," said the panther, "we are getting ready for a green-corn dance, and there are seven of us out after a buck, so we may as well hunt together."

The hunter agreed, and they went on together. They started up one deer and another, but the panther made no sign, and said only, "Those are too small, we want something better." So the hunter did not shoot, and they went on. They started up another deer, a larger one, and the panther sprang on it and tore its throat, and finally killed it after a hard struggle. The hunter got out his knife to skin it, but the panther said the skin was too much torn to be used, and they must try again. They started up another large deer, and this the panther killed without trouble. Then, wrapping his tail around it, he threw it across his back. "Now, come to our town house," he said to the hunter.

The panther led the way, carrying the captured deer on his back, up a little stream branch until they came to the head spring. It seemed as if a door opened in the side of the hill, and they went in. The hunter found himself in front of a large town house, with the finest detsanunli *(ceremonial ground) he had ever seen. The trees around were green, and the air was warm, as in summer. There was a great company there getting ready for the dance, and they were all panthers, but somehow it all seemed natural to the hunter. After a while, the others who had been out came in with the deer they had taken, and the dance began. The hunter danced several rounds, and then said it was growing late and he must be getting home. So the panthers opened the door and the hunter went out, and at once found himself alone in the woods again. It was winter and very cold, with snow on the ground and on all the trees. When he reached the settlement, he found a party just starting out to search for him. They asked him where he had been so long, and he told them the story. Then he found that he had been in the panther town house for several days instead of only a very short time as he had thought.*

He died within seven days after his return, because he had already begun to take on the nature of the panther, and so could not live again with men. If he had stayed with the panthers, he would have lived.

My family's relocation experience in San Francisco was disturbing in many ways. But in retrospect, our ordeal was not nearly as harsh or painful as the problems encountered by the Cherokee people who had been forced to take the Trail of Tears in the late 1830s. At least we did not have to walk hundreds of miles through snow and sleet. We did not worry about getting bayoneted or shot by some soldier or bushwhacker. Our relocation was voluntary and not by federal mandate. There were some parallels, however. For instance, even after we had settled down in our two-family flat in the Potrero District, we still felt as alienated as our ancestors must have felt when they finally arrived in those unfamiliar surroundings that became their new home. Despite the decades that separated us, we shared a feeling of detachment with the Cherokees who had come before us.

I know that many native people who turned up in San Francisco as part of the BIA's removal program in the 1950s considered California to be the land of new beginnings. At least that was their hope. They wanted to believe the promotional literature that spoke of good jobs and happy homes waiting for those who had relocated. I was only a youngster, but I did not accept the government propaganda. Instead, I was convinced that my parents had made the wrong decision when they bought the BIA's bill of goods.

At first, nothing about the city was very appealing. The overt discrimination we encountered is what got to me the most. It became obvious that ethnic intolerance was a fact of life in California, even in the urbane and sophisticated world of San Francisco. Not only did African and Hispanic Americans feel the sting of racism, so did Native Americans.

I recall an incident that drove home for me the concept of racial bias. Soon after we moved to California, a woman came up to my mother and told her straight out that we were all "nigger children." Then she called my mother a "nigger lover." The woman said those things because of my father's dark complexion. Mother was outraged by that repulsive word of contempt. Prompted by blind hatred and ignorance, it was intended to inflict pain. It must have stung like a hard slap on the face. My soft-spoken mother was so distraught by such a blatant display of malice that she jumped the woman!

Most of the time, however, people who had a problem with our being different did not say what they thought about us to our faces. They made snide remarks behind our backs. It was then that we found out the place where we lived was hardly exempt from racial prejudice.

All ethnic minorities in California have suffered from various kinds of unjust treatment and bigotry over the years. The abuse of Native Americans began with the white settlement of California and was the worst kind of oppression that any minority group has experienced there. Except for the cessation of violent acts in recent years, the shoddy treatment of California's original inhabitants still continues.

At one time, the state sustained a much larger number of Native Americans than any other region of comparable size on the continent north of Mexico. Native people hunted, fished, gathered food, and generally learned to get along without killing one another. By the time the first Spanish settlement was founded in the mid-1700s, there were at least 275,000 Indians living in present California. That changed very quickly. By 1900, less than sixteen thousand native people remained.

Throughout history, beginning with the Spanish conquerors and continuing with the white settlers, the Indians of California endured genocide, disease, starvation, and overt oppression. In many instances, widespread violence became wholesale murder. While the Cherokees and the other Five Tribes adjusted to their new homes in Indian Territory, in California the white settlers, miners, and armed posses had a field day indiscriminately slaughtering native people. The law of the white man was, in fact, no law at all.

In many ways, California in the middle to late 1800s was much like violence-plagued Bosnia, where "ethnic cleansing" in the 1990s has become the norm. Wholesale genocide and rape became standard in California. According to a study conducted by the University of California, at least one thousand Indian women in the 1850s alone were raped so brutally that most of them died. Thousands of other native women were forced to become white men's concubines. During that same period, almost four thousand Indian children were kidnapped and sold into slavery. Considered to be obstacles to white men's progress, Native Americans were hunted like wild game. As late as 1870, there were communities in California actually paying bounties for Indian scalps or severed heads.

The only good Indians I ever saw were dead.

General Philip Henry Sheridan, January 1869

Some whites tried to halt the carnage. In the early 1880s, New England author Helen Hunt Jackson, noted for her espousal of the Native American cause, distributed to every member of Congress a copy of *A Century of Dishonor,* her book about governmental mistreatment of Indians. It set the standard for muckraking books that followed two decades later, and it became one of the most influential books of the late nineteenth century. Jackson was made a member of a special commission to study the problems of native people in California. The report that resulted had little impact on Congress, but by serving on the commission, Jackson came up with enough material to write *Ramona.* Some critics labeled this 1884 novel about the criminal abuse of the Mission Indians as the "*Uncle Tom's Cabin* of California."

Other whites also made attempts to help Native Americans. In 1901, a group in Los Angeles led by Charles F. Lummis founded the Sequoya League, named for our noted Cherokee linguist. Incorporated to "make better Indians"—whatever that meant—the organization had as its main objective giving aid to native people in obtaining food and clothing, or financial and legal assistance.

California Indians faced difficulties that most tribes elsewhere in the United States did not always encounter, because only a small number of the California Indians were ever placed on reservations. Treaties proposed in the nineteenth century that provided for reservations were never ratified, so the majority of California Indians were left without any land. They were forced to get along to the best of their abilities and wits. A great number of native people did not survive. Of those who did pull through, many of them became agricultural workers in the vast California growing fields. Others ended up destitute and homeless. They were shoved aside and written off as burdens to society.

I know what the misfortune of the tribes is. Their misfortune is not that they are red men, not that they are semi-civilized, not that they are a dwindling race. Their misfortune is that they hold great bodies of rich lands, which have aroused the cupidity of powerful corporations and of powerful individuals. . . . I greatly fear that the adoption of this provision to discontinue treaty-making is the beginning of the end in respect to Indian Lands. It is the first step in a great scheme of spoliation, in which the Indians will be plundered, corporations and individuals enriched, and the American name dishonored in history.

California Senator Eugene Casserly, 1871

Some of the questions I am asked most frequently today include what happened to native people, such as those in California? Why do native people have so many problems? How is it that they ended up facing high unemployment, low educational attainment, low self-esteem, and problems with alcohol abuse? I answer that all one needs to do is look at our history. History clearly shows all the external factors that have played a part in our people being where we are today.

Regardless of all the problems Native Americans faced, they became the fastest-growing minority group in California in the twentieth century. This took place without their reaping much of California's extraordinary affluence. From fewer than sixteen thousand in 1900, at least forty thousand native people lived in the state by 1960, just a few years after my family arrived. Some sources claim that the 1960 population count could have been as high as seventy-five thousand, because census takers did not identify as Indians all native persons who were using Anglo or Hispanic surnames. Only a small percentage of those native people lived on reservations or *rancherias;* most had homes in the Los Angeles or San Francisco areas.

Several factors account for the dramatic rise in the Indian population in California, especially since World War II. First of all, native people were starting to be treated a little better. Numerous social and economic troubles remained, but an awakening of consciousness began among some whites in the late 1920s and continued to gain momentum. About the time our family moved west, California was attempting to abolish barriers separating Indians from non-Indians in terms of education, welfare assistance, and other public services. The substantial Indian immigration from Oklahoma, the Dakotas, and the Southwest throughout the postwar years helped to boost the Native American population in California. The BIA's removal program accounted for a great many Native American individuals and families moving to California, including the Charley Mankiller brood, direct from Mankiller Flats in Oklahoma.

Nonetheless, our troubles did not disappear, even though the old days of exterminating Indians had ceased and California's Native American population was increasing. There were still problems to solve and predicaments to face.

Besides the poverty and prejudice we encountered, I was continually struggling with the adjustment to a big city that seemed so foreign and cold to me.

The San Francisco I experienced as a young girl in the late 1950s and early 1960s was not the sophisticated city of palatial Nob Hill mansions, picturesque cable cars, fancy restaurants, and elegant hotels. My family did not lunch amid the tourists at Fisherman's Wharf or dine at Trader Vic's. We did not meet friends to watch from the Crown Room high atop the Fairmont Hotel as the mists rolled in on the bay. Folks who did those things were on a much higher rung of the economic and social ladder than we were. Our family was more familiar—and comfortable—with the crowd that shopped for bargains at Goodwill or St. Vincent de Paul. We ate simple meals at home, wore hand-me-down clothes, and got by from paycheck to paycheck. Our family's meager budget could not handle any nonessentials or luxuries.

After we had lived in San Francisco for a little more than a year, my father, with help from my older brother Don's salary contributions, was able to scrape together enough money for a down payment on a small house. So we left the crowded flat in the Potrero Hill District and moved into a new home in Daly City, just south of San Francisco on the southern peninsula in San Mateo County. Daly City had come into being as a result of the earthquake and fire of 1906, when many San Franciscans fled to John Daly's dairy ranch. It grew into a residential area that mushroomed during the boom years after World War II, when it became one of California's fifty most populous communities.

Our new residence looked as if it had come straight out of a cookie-cutter mold. There were three small bedrooms, a full basement, and not many frills. My sisters and I shared bunk beds. I would describe it as modest, just like the hundreds of other ticky-tacky houses in endless rows that climbed up and down the landlocked hills flanked by the Pacific Ocean and San Francisco Bay.

For our family as a whole, the move to Daly City was a good one. It represented a marked improvement over our first dwelling. We were moving up in the world. At about that same time, my father started to become active at the San Francisco Indian Center, where we met and spent time with other native people living in the area. That had a positive impact on the family. But for me, nothing had changed. I still loathed being in California, and I particularly despised school.

I was uncomfortable. I felt stigmatized. I continually found myself alienated from the other students, who mostly treated me as though I had come from outer space. I was insecure, and the least little remark or glance would leave me mortified. That was especially true whenever people had to teach me something basic or elementary, such as how to use a telephone. I was convinced that they must think it odd to be teaching an eleven- or twelve-year-old how to pick up a phone, listen for a tone, and then dial a number.

In Daly City, I was getting ready to enter the seventh grade. The thought of that depressed me a great deal. That meant having to meet more new kids. Not only did I speak differently than they did, but I had an unfamiliar name that the others ridiculed. We were teased unmercifully about our Oklahoma accents. My sister Linda and I still read out loud to each other every night to lose our accents. Like most young people everywhere, we wanted to belong.

Also, there were changes going on inside me that I could not account for, and that troubled me very much. I was experiencing all the problems girls face when approaching the beginning of womanhood. I was afraid and did not know what to do. Besides having to deal with the internal changes, I was also growing like a weed and had almost reached my full adult height. People thought I was much older than twelve. I hated what was happening. I hated my body. I hated school. I hated the teachers. I hated the other students. Most of all, I hated the city.

I did not hate my parents or the rest of the family. I always loved them very much. But it was a time of great confusion for me. I was silently crying out for attention, but nobody heard me. My dad was constantly busy trying to make a living and, at the same time, deal with his own frustrations and confusion about city life in California. My mother was doing her best to help all of us with our problems while she kept us fed and clothed. Then on top of everything, my oldest brother, Don, announced that he was going to get married. He had met a nice young Choctaw woman named LaVena at the Indian Center. They had fallen in love. Everyone was very happy about the news, but there were long discussions about Don leaving home with his bride and how that loss of income would affect the rest of the family.

With so much going on, I felt like nobody had any time for me. I felt there was not one single person I could confide in or turn to who truly understood me. My self-esteem was at rock bottom. That is when I decided to escape from all of it. I would run away from home. At the time, that seemed my best and only option.

I ran off to Grandma Sitton, who, lived at Riverbank. She was an independent woman. I had gotten to know her better since our move to the West Coast, and I liked her very much. I thought perhaps my grandmother would understand and comfort me and help with my problems. Also, I liked Riverbank because Oklahoma families who had come out during the Dust Bowl period were living in the area. I felt more comfortable around them.

My younger sister Linda and I had stashed away a little bit of money saved from baby-sitting jobs we had gotten through meeting other families at the Indian Center. We did not have much, but it was enough to buy a bus ticket. Of course, as soon as I got to her house, my grandma called my folks and said, "Pearl's here, you better come get her." My parents were upset—very upset—and my dad drove out and took me back. But that did not end it. That first time was just the start of a pattern of behavior that lasted until I became a teenager.

I waited a little while, and then I ran away a second time and went straight to my grandmother's house. My parents and I went through the same routine. But I did not stop. I did it again. Once more, my dad drove to Riverbank and took me back to Daly City. One time my sister Linda ran away, too. She took off for somewhere on her own. I am not sure where she went. My folks found her and brought her home. But I kept running away. Every single time, I went to

Grandma Sitton's. Over a year or so, I guess I ran away from home at least five times, maybe more.

My parents could not control me. Eventually, they decided that I had become incorrigible. They saw that I truly did not want to live in the city. I wanted no part of it. So they gave in and let me stay with my grandmother. By then, she had outlived another husband. She sold her home and gave the money to her son and his wife—my Uncle Floyd Sitton and Aunt Frauline. They had moved to California after Uncle Floyd's return from World War II and his discharge from the service. He used the money my grandmother gave them to buy a dairy ranch north of Riverbank, near the town of Escalon. In exchange for helping them buy their "dream place," Grandma Sitton moved in with my uncle and aunt and their four children, Tommy, Mary Louise, and twins about my age, Eddie and Teddie.

I was preparing to begin the eighth grade when I joined my grandmother and the other Sitton relatives at their ranch. The agreement was for me to stay with them for one year. Ultimately, it turned out to be a very positive experience, but at first there were difficulties. There was a fair amount of conflict between my cousins and me, but they finally got used to my living there. Our problems sprang not from my Native American blood, but from a rivalry between the four of them and me. In a nutshell, we were all competitive kids. We were pure country, too, and that meant we would not run from a fight. When I arrived, it took only the slightest agitation to provoke me. I was highly sensitive and self-conscious.

One time in particular, I recall, several of us were walking back from the fields following Uncle Floyd. My cousin Teddie kept taunting and teasing me until I could not take any more. When he pulled my hair again, I whirled around and punched him in the jaw so hard that he dropped to the ground. I got into trouble over that incident, and there was some talk about shipping me back home to the city. That finally passed. I settled down, and the teasing stopped. The conflict faded. My life seemed to improve.

I began to gain some confidence. As I felt better about myself, I felt better about others. My grandmother deserves much of the credit. Even though she was strict, she was never judgmental. At a very critical point in my life, she helped me learn to accept myself and to confront my problems.

School even seemed more palatable. When I moved to the farm, I did not have one single friend my age at school. I relied on my tough demeanor to protect myself, and I found that this really turned off people. My cousins had told all the other kids at the small community school we attended that my parents had sent me to live with them because they could not handle me. That was not a good way for me to begin. During lunch and recess, I was usually by myself. Although I got off to a bumpy start, I had made some friends and had developed a routine by the close of the school year. I got along better with my cousins and enjoyed the work on the farm.

All in all, the year I spent on the dairy farm was just what I needed. I slept in the same bed with my grandmother, and we all got up every day at 5:00 A.M. to milk the cows and take care of chores. My main job was to help keep the barn clean. Besides the dairy cows, my uncle and aunt had some pigs and a horse. There was a big vegetable garden. I even helped my Aunt Frauline deliver a calf during a difficult birth. The hard work and fresh air at the farm were so good. We also found time to explore the fields and swim in the creeks.

During our year together, my grandmother helped shape much of my adolescent thinking. I spent much of my time with her, and never considered a single moment wasted. Although she was small, only about four feet ten inches tall, she was solidly built. She also was opinionated, outspoken, tough, and very independent. She was deeply religious and sang from her hymnbook every day. Her favorite song was "Rock of Ages." My grandmother also loved to garden, raise chickens, and pick peaches. Grandmother Sitton and my father—two of the people I most admired as a young woman—valued hard work. I believe it was their examples more than anything else that contributed to my own work ethic.

I continued to visit the farm every summer during my high school years. Some of my brothers and sisters usually came too, and we would help tend the crops or pick fruit to earn money for new school clothes. We worked alongside some white people in the fields, and my mistrust of whites certainly did not apply to them. The people whom some Californians derisively called Okies or Arkies were great friends—hardworking people, close to the land, and quick to share what little they had with others who had even less. The farm work was demanding, but those were summers of freedom. We swam in the canals, went to drive-in movies, and sipped cherry Cokes or limeades at the local Dairy Queen. Sometimes we headed to the nearby town of Modesto to cruise the streets. Later, Modesto was the setting for *American Graffiti,* the film about teenage life in small-town America directed by George Lucas, a native son.

I looked forward to those visits with my grandmother. After I was married, I still went to see her. I would sit on her lap, and we teased each other and laughed. Full of spirit and energy, my grandmother married her third and last husband when she was in her eighties. During their courtship, she had me dye her hair black because she believed it would make her look her best. I obliged. Later, I helped her get all prettied up before they went to Reno, Nevada, for a quick wedding. Pearl Halady Sitton never stopped enjoying life. She canned vegetables and fruit, kept chickens, worked in the garden, and sang those hymns until shortly before she died. I am inspired whenever I think about her and all those good times we had.

> *Guided by my heritage of a love of beauty and a respect for strength—in search of my mother's garden, I found my own.*
>
> Alice Walker
> In Search of Our Mothers' Gardens, 1974

At the end of the year I spent with my mother's family, I returned to the Bay area, but not to our house in Daly City. My family no longer lived there. While I was gone, my brother Don and his girlfriend, LaVena, had married. LaVena got a job with the telephone company, and Don went to work for Pacific Gas and Electric. They set up housekeeping at their own place not far from Candlestick Park. As was expected, the loss of Don's income meant my parents were forced to make budgetary adjustments. That meant giving up the house in Daly City. I came home to a more affordable residence my father had found for us, in southeastern San Francisco on a spit of land projecting into the bay. It was a place known as Hunter's Point.

Named for Robert E. Hunter, a forty-niner from the last century who had planned to create a city on the site, Hunter's Point eventually had become the home of a huge U.S. Navy shipyard and dry docks. It flourished during World War II and continued to thrive for some years afterward when a severe housing shortage occurred. Ironically, Japanese-Americans returned to the Bay area after their long confinement in Dillon Myer's camps only to find that black workers, attracted by plenty of jobs at the shipyards and defense plants, had moved into the "Little Tokyos" of the city. But thousands of black families also occupied the housing built on tidelands adjoining the shipyard at Hunter's Point. Many of those black families had migrated from Oklahoma, Texas, and other states that whites also had fled during the Dust Bowl years.

Hunter's Point may sound like the name of an affluent residential development where polo players and stockbrokers lived, but it was far from that. The only thing fancy about it was the name. Shipyard employees and hourly wage earners made their homes there. Although the shipyard did not close until 1974, jobs started to become more and more scarce in the 1960s. The workers who resided at Hunter's Point fell into financial difficulties, and the housing area became little more than a ghetto.

We found a few Native Americans living at Hunter's Point, including another Cherokee family. They had come to California from Locust Grove, an old Cherokee Nation town in eastern Oklahoma and the home of the late Willard Stone, the wood sculptor whose claim of Cherokee ancestry recently created a great deal of controversy. That other Cherokee family at Hunter's Point was also part of the relocation program masterminded by the BIA.

At Hunter's Point, my perceptions of the world around me began to take shape. Most police, teachers, political leaders, and others in positions of power and authority were whites. There were a few white people living at Hunter's Point, perhaps a few Asians, and several Samoan families. Regardless of the ethnic sprinkling, Hunter's Point was primarily a community of black families. Black culture had a profound impact on my development. When the rest of America was listening to Pat Boone, the Beach Boys, or Elvis, my friends and I listened to Etta James, Dinah Washington, Sarah Vaughan, B. B. King, and others. I talked endlessly with my best friends, Johnnie Lee and LaVada, about things which girls our age were obsessed with—music, boys, parents, and growing up. We sometimes put on makeup, fixed our hair, played records, and danced, pretending we were at a party far away from Hunter's Point. Even today, more than thirty years later, the sisterly company of black women is especially enjoyable to me.

My mother also became good friends with people from different backgrounds. She developed a close relationship with a Filipina woman who lived next door. This neighborhood of diverse cultures was where we remained for several years. Those outside our community called our new home "Harlem West."

We lived in one of the typical little houses, but to everyone's amazement, it had a surprisingly pleasant interior. The rooms were small, but the house had two stories and was not as tiny as some of the other places we had lived More important, there was not a rat in sight. The kitchen and bathroom were satisfactory, and the wooden floors were in fairly decent shape.

Outside was another story. There was a great deal of animosity between the black youths and Samoan youths of Hunter's Point. Sometimes it seemed like a war zone when rival gangs clashed on the streets. Now and then there were enormous battles. Upstairs, in the bedroom I shared with my sister Linda, we could gaze out the window at the beauty of the sky and water, or we could lower our eyes to the streets where the gangs fought furiously.

I was taught invaluable lessons on those mean streets. They were part of our continuing education in the world of urban poverty and violence.

In many ways, Hunter's Point appeared to be like everywhere else we had been, yet it was also a very different world. Most of the differences, I found, were a matter of perception. I learned that in the "hood," there is a constant fight against racial prejudice. There is a struggle to keep the children off the streets and away from drugs. This takes place in an environment of overwhelming frustration among many diverse people who are alienated from the rest of America in many ways other than by simple geography. Living there was really like one long, hot, boring, lazy afternoon—nothing to do, no place to go, and no promise of anything better in the future.

I will not forget the time I was choking on something, and I became so distraught that my father called an ambulance. It was late at night, and when my father gave our address to the person on the telephone, he was told that no ambulance would come to Hunter's Point after sundown. My father finally cleared my throat and I was fine. We never discussed what would have happened to me if he had not been successful. Another time, I recall a police car driving around our neighborhood. When the officers stopped to make a call and left their car unattended, every window was shattered. That was standard procedure. All of the police, across the board, were considered to be "the enemy." They were never looked upon as concerned individuals who could help. Hunter's Point was like a "no man's land" that was constantly under siege.

Still, Hunter's Point was my home. I would not trade my experiences there for any amount of money. We were living there when my brother Bob died in Washington, when I decided to get married, and when my father made the decision to leave San Francisco for Castroville in Monterey Bay. Many important moments in my life took place there.

Living in Hunter's Point also gave me an insight into cultures I otherwise might not have ever known. In 1991, when I saw the film *Boyz N the Hood*, I was struck by how familiar the families in the film seemed to me, even though more than thirty years had passed since I had lived in a similar place.

Whenever I hear or read about inner-city crime, drugs, and gangs, I filter it through my own experiences at Hunter's Point. Although communities such as Hunter's Point have tremendous problems, they also have strengths that few outsiders ever recognize or acknowledge. The women are especially strong.

Each day, they face daunting problems as they struggle just to survive. They are mothers not only of their own children but of the entire community. Poverty is not just a word to describe a social condition, it is the hard reality of everyday life. It takes a certain tenacity, a toughness, to continue on when there is an ever-present worry about whether the old car will work, and if it does, whether there will be gas money, digging through piles of old clothes at St. Vincent de Paul's to find clothing for the children to wear to school without being ridiculed; wondering if there will be enough to eat. But always, there is hope that the children will receive a good education and have a better life.

> *There are tens of millions of Americans who are beyond the welfare state. Taken as a whole there is a culture of poverty . . . bad health, poor housing, low levels of aspiration and high levels of mental distress.*
>
> Michael Harrington
> The Culture of Poverty, 1962

By the time we moved to Hunter's Point, in 1960, my father had left the rope factory and was working as a longshoreman on the docks. He began to augment his income by playing poker. People used to come to our house for big poker games that lasted well into the night. Before they left, my dad usually had picked up a little money. He had a lot of confidence. That was important. Some of those who played cards with him were men he worked with, but many were other native people he had met at the San Francisco Indian Center.

Located upstairs in an old frame building on Sixteenth Street on the edge of the very rough and tough Mission District, the Indian Center became a sanctuary for me. It was my safe place for many years. At last, the mythical Rabbit had finally found a hollow stump the Wolves were not able to penetrate.

In many ways, the Indian Center became even more important to me than the junior high and various high schools I attended. During my teen years, I transferred from an inner-city school dominated by violence to another public high school with a predominantly Asian student body, because it offered a calmer atmosphere. However, changing schools did not help me very much. I had made some headway in gaining self-esteem, but like many teens, I remained unsettled as far as goals, with no sense of direction. I was not sure what I wanted to do once I finished school and had to make my own way in the world. But a moody and self-absorbed teenager could count on one thing—at the end of the day, everything seemed brighter at the Indian Center. For me, it became an oasis where I could share my feelings and frustrations with kids from similar backgrounds.

There was something at the center for everyone. It was a safe place to go, even if we only wanted to hang out or watch television. For the younger children, the center provided socialization with other native people through organized events such as picnics and supervised outings. Older kids went there for dances, sports programs, and an occasional chance to work behind the snack bar to earn a little money. Adults played bingo, took part in intertribal pow-wows and, most important, discussed pertinent issues and concerns with other

BIA relocatees from all across the country. We would jump on a city bus and head for the Indian Center the way some kids today flock to shopping malls.

The Indian Center was important to everyone in my family, including my father. Always a determined person who stuck to his principles, even if they turned out to be lost causes, Dad ultimately quit working as a longshoreman to become a shop steward and union organizer with a spice company based in San Francisco. Besides his union activities, he also became more involved with projects at the Indian Center. For instance, when the question arose about the need for a free health clinic for Indians living in the Bay area, he rallied the forces at the Indian Center to get behind the issue. In an effort to heighten public awareness, he appeared on a television panel discussion about the urban clinic. Perhaps at that time, he influenced my life in ways I could not imagine then.

When he believed in something, he worked around the clock to get the job done. He was always dragging home somebody he had met, someone who was down on his luck and needed a meal and a place to stay. It was a tight fit, but we made room. My dad never gave up on people. I think my father's tenacity is a characteristic I inherited. Once I set my mind to do something, I never give up. I was raised in a household where no one ever said to me, "You can't do this because you're a woman, Indian, or poor." No one told me there were limitations. Of course, I would not have listened to them if they had tried

The exception would have been my father. I always listened to him, even if I did not agree with what he had to say. From the time I was a little girl, we discussed all the topics of the day. Our very best debates concerned politics. Sometimes those conversations would get a bit heated. After my political awakening as a teenager, I became aligned with the party of Franklin Roosevelt, Harry Truman, and a rising young star of the sixties—John F. Kennedy. My father, on the other hand, was a registered Republican, which was not unusual among older members of the Five Tribes, especially the Cherokees. Folks who know our people's past can usually figure out why so many of the older Cherokees belonged to the Republican party. The story goes that a historian once asked an Oklahoma Cherokee why so few of the old-timers became Democrats. The Cherokee supposedly replied, "Do you think we would help the party that damned ol' Andy Jackson belonged to?" For the elders, the choice was obvious—Republicans were the lesser of two evils.

Despite our political differences, my father and I enjoyed our discussions, and especially our time spent at the Indian Center. Throughout the sixties, my entire family considered the Indian Center to be a stronghold. At the center, we could talk to other native people about shared problems and frustrations. Many families we met there were like us. They had come to the realization that the BIA's promises were empty. We all seemed to have reached that same terrible conclusion—the government's relocation program was a disaster that robbed us of our vitality and sense of place. That is why the Indian Center was so immensely important. It was always there for us. It was a constant. During the turmoil and anguish of the 1960s, it was where we turned.

In 1960, when my brother Robert was killed, we went to the Indian Center for solace. Bob was only twenty years old when he died. He had joined the National Guard, boxed a little bit, and worked at various odd jobs. He did not seem to have any real plans. My dad wanted him to settle down and find steady employment. But Bob was restless. He and his pal, Louie Cole, a quarter Choctaw, decided to leave the city. Louie was nineteen, and I thought of him as my first real boyfriend. He and my brother took off one morning, intent on making money for a grubstake. Then they planned to go off on their great adventure and discover the rest of the country.

Bob and Louie had been gone for two or three weeks and were up the coast in Washington state when they found work as apple pickers. The boys lived in sharecroppers' cabins near the orchards. When they got up early in the morning, it was still cold and dark outside, so they would start a fire in a wood stove using a little kerosene to get the flames going. One morning, my brother was still groggy with sleep when he lit the fire. Instead of the kerosene, he mistakenly picked up a can of gasoline. The cabin exploded in flames. The door was locked with a dead bolt, so by the time the boys got outside, they were severely burned Louie was burned over much of his body, but Bob was in far worse condition.

My parents, my brother Don and my oldest sister, Frieda, who still lived in Oklahoma, went to Washington to be with Bob. The doctor told them that if Bob lived for seven days, he would probably survive. Among Cherokees, the number seven is considered sacred. We have seven clans, our sacred fire is kindled from seven types of wood, and there are seven directions—north, south, east, west, up, down, and "where one is at." We thought maybe the seven days would bring luck to Bob.

Attractive and charming, Bob always had been the best looking of all of us. He was tall and athletic, a happy-go-lucky type. I looked up to my big brother Don, but for my carefree role model, I had Bob. I think all of us wondered what his life would be like if he survived. It was clear that he would never be the same.

When it seemed that there was a slim chance Bob might pull through, my father, who had to return to his job, left my mother in Washington to stay with Bob through his long recovery. But as it turned out, Bob could not be saved. He lived for seven days and no more. On the seventh day, he died. I am not so sure the number failed him.

When they brought him home to California, he was buried at Oakdale, a community on the Stanislaus River not far from my grandmother's place. Bob's death stunned all of us. It left me in a state of shock. I cannot remember who told me that Bob had died. Probably it was one of my older sisters. All I know is, I just stood there and screamed. I screamed as loud as I could, hoping that my screams would drown out those awful words. I did not want to hear. I was fifteen years old, and the loss of Bob was the closest I had ever been to death up to that point.

My parents, of course, were devastated. The loss of a child is the worst kind of death experience. You never expect to outlive your offspring. But after that tragic event, something very good happened to our family. My mother, who was forty years old, became pregnant the same month my brother Bob died. Everyone was quite surprised. Nine months later, my brother William was born. No one can take someone else's place, but after losing Bob as we had, all of us were happy when Bill arrived.

Louie Cole remained hospitalized in Washington for several months before he was allowed to return to California. He lived near Riverbank, where I had first met him when I stayed with my grandmother. We stayed in touch after he came home to recover, but we were never girlfriend and boyfriend again. Every so often, we wrote to each other, and then finally that stopped.

Many years later, long after I had come home to Oklahoma and had became involved in tribal politics, Louie came to visit me. He had been married several times, and he still collected disability because of the injuries he had received in that fire so many years before. I was not totally comfortable seeing Louie again. There was something brooding about him, and he wanted only to focus on the past, especially the bad times. About a year after his visit, I received a letter from Louie's mother informing me that he had been shot and killed by one of his former wives during a quarrel.

Louie was my first boyfriend, but it was not as if I had a whole string of them. In fact, I was basically shy with boys. However, I did meet several young men at the Indian Center who interested me. One of them was Ray Billy. I was about sixteen when I started to date him. He was Pomo, a California tribe, and was a little older than I was. He had his own apartment. I dated him for about a year. My dad liked him, and that counted for something. Occasionally, Ray got the use of a car, and he would come to our house at Hunter's Point and ask my dad if he could take me for a ride. Other times, my dad let us go for rides in our family car. Everyone liked Ray. He was a gentleman—most of the time.

He was also crafty, and I had to watch my step. One night we were down on the beach. I was getting cold, so he suggested that we go to his place to get a jacket and warm up. It was a classic trick, and I almost fell for it! When we got to his apartment, he said he was tired and we ought to rest on his bed for a while. I came to my senses. I put my foot down and would not cooperate. He thought I was stupid for reacting as I did. A short time later, he dropped me for a girl who had just been crowned Miss Indian San Francisco, or some such title. Ray and I did not see each other again. I was hurt by his treatment, but I pulled through. I learned that most first crushes—even second or third crushes—can be survived.

Friends and family helped me mend my broken heart and get over Ray Billy. Our music was also a big help. My girlfriends and I listened to rock and roll and to soul music. "Hit the Road, Jack" and "I Found my Thrill on Blueberry Hill" were popular then. We listened to two soul stations, KDIA and KSAN. We dreamed of the time we would be out of school and free.

Most of the time, I was only going through the motions of attending classes. I was never much of a scholar, and I do not have many memories from my years in high school. Those I do have are not of much consequence. My grades ranged from A to F, depending on the subject and my level of interest. Science and math were my downfalls, but I had an affinity for English and literature courses.

None of my teachers left enough impact for me even to remember their names. I was not much of a joiner. I did not go in for glee club or the yearbook staff or sports or any of the organizations except Junior Achievement. I did participate in that for a while, and I liked it.

Mostly, I went to the Indian Center. That is still my best teenage memory. Much more was going on at the center besides pingpong games and dance parties. It was the early 1960s, and change was in the air. A person could almost touch it. During that time, many people, including my friends and siblings and I, were aware of the currents of restlessness. The new decade promised to be a time of momentous social movements and open rebellion. There would be sweeping legislation and great achievements, as well as devastating war and senseless tragedies.

Even before the 1960s, the entire Bay area had become a magnet for artists and rebels who were ready and willing to act as the merchants of change. Now a new generation was getting its voice, testing its wings. I was part of that generation. San Francisco was the place to be. We were ready to proceed with the decade and with our lives.

Case Study

Personal Growth and Self-Esteem through Cultural Spiritualism: A Native American Experience

JAMES WAHLBERG

INTRODUCTION: MY FIRST IMPRESSIONS

This was my first trip to the reservation under these new circumstances. I had traveled through on a number of occasions, but only to "get someplace else." After earning my MSW degree, I came to live among Native Americans and have been practicing social work there ever since.

Because of a restructuring of the regional human service network, I became responsible for a satellite clinic located adjacent to the reservation. The clinic was part of a regional service center located in both the urban and rural parts of the state. Several Indian reservations are part of these regional operations. In an effort to provide services in the most rural environments of the state, satellite centers such as mine were mostly staffed by local people.

As I approached the reservation carrying a responsibility other than tourism, I was struck by an apparent over-sensitivity to the different stimuli I was receiving. Perhaps this was partly attributable to a generalized fear I identified within myself. I was very concerned about being so clearly "white" and so obviously "different" from the population I was approaching. I had considerable exposure to academic content relative to cultural diversity and the Native American experience, and I had been studying the spiritual lessons of the culture with a Native American mentor. I had worked with Native Americans in urban areas, but this seemed somehow quite different, inasmuch as I was going to them rather than they coming to me.

I clearly remember my first impressions as I arrived at the reservation border on this rather crisp February morning. The trip took about two hours. The temperature was ten degrees below zero, without the windchill factor. A recently fallen three-inch blanket of snow covered the landscape. As I approached the reservation, I was struck by the beauty of the rolling forested area with its heavenly blanket of snow. I noticed a herd of buffalo, unfenced and roving to my right, and I was struck by the historical impact buffalo herds had in this region. Adjacent to the buffalo range was a modern looking industrial complex with hundreds of camouflage-covered gas, water, and oil tankers manufactured for use in the Gulf War. The corporation responsible for these survived primarily through government contracts and was a major employer of Native Americans.

As I proceeded further onto the reservation, I was impressed with the extremely colorful grounds of a local Catholic cemetery immediately to my left. Although it was the dead of winter, the plastic flowers and other ornamentation provided a colorful contrast to the white environment. This colorful symbolism exemplifies the paradox of religious syncretism involving Native American spirituality and white Christendom.

The reservation was characterized by a wide diversity of housing types, ranging from modern, new and beautiful homes to Bureau of Indian Affairs (BIA) housing projects similar to public housing development projects in urban areas. I was also impressed with the variety of buildings associated with the properties. Stereotypical or not, many properties had sheds, lumber, additional vehicles, and horse trailers adjacent to the dwellings. The evidence of domestic and farm animals was also noticed as dogs, cats, horses, and cattle seemed attentive to my visit.

It was difficult to define the borders of the "city" or to describe "downtown." There were a number of gas stations, convenience stores, fast food outlets, as well as a tiny mall. In addition to the dwellings, a community college and other government buildings dominated the city landscape. If the structures that were government-connected were removed from this landscape, there would be few major buildings in this community.

ENGAGEMENT: MAPPING THE ENVIRONMENT

It was not difficult to assume where the offices might be located, since I spotted a large (obviously government) complex between a convenience store and the mini-mall. After parking my car and walking toward the entrance, it became obvious that people were staring at me. I expected to be viewed as a newcomer but was unaware of how communications about my coming had been transmitted throughout the community. I was later informed that almost immediately the local police had verified my identity by checking my license plate with the state Department of Motor Vehicles. This had become a regular procedure because of the increase in drug trafficking on the reservation. I also learned that since many people on the reservation own scanners to monitor law enforcement and other communications, my arrival had been duly noted. Approaching a new job situation is at best uncomfortable and sometimes traumatic. Recalling that I was a white person moving into the Native American community, issues of comfort, ethnocentrism, and stereotypes came to mind. Perhaps my thoughts and feelings were similar to those of minority persons functioning in the environment of a majority. Most of the individuals working in the office were Native Americans, since the Bureau of Indian Affairs, Public Health Service (PHS), and other government agencies had instituted policies of recruiting underrepresented populations, especially Native Americans. I wondered how I would be viewed and whether my authority and legitimacy would be questioned because I might be seen as another "white" person intruding on "their territory."

There were many new issues to settle. I had to set up an office, hire a secretary, check out the cafeteria, arrange for coffee, locate restrooms, and countless other details to get started. I also had to carry out other activities on my first day, including meeting my colleagues, reading policy manuals, and finding housing for myself. The satellite operation was new and would suffer growing pains, as any new operation might. Developing and maintaining relationships with the tribe and the tribal government, with other governmental units, and with members of the service delivery network would certainly keep me busy. I learned that many of these agencies had a history of serving at cross purposes, and this would make my job more challenging.

I was looking forward to my first contacts with clients. As I began to familiarize myself with information about my clients, a colleague gave me several books, and I was encouraged to do some reading to help me understand the context of the people I would be serving. I was cautioned by my literary benefactor that while many Native Americans have some characteristics in common, there are often more differences than similarities among people of differing tribes.

In my orientation to the reservation, I met several interesting people. It was suggested that I spend some time with the tribal police to better understand some of the problems people on the reservation experienced. A visit to the Tribal Law Enforcement Center might otherwise have been somewhat threatening. However, as part of my orientation to the reservation, I was able to connect with people who knew other people who knew people with the tribal police, and I was authorized to participate in a "ride-along" program. I was granted permission to ride with law enforcement officers as they patrolled the reservation. Participating with the officers on a day-to-day basis provided considerable insight into not only their personalities but the personality of the whole community. The awareness and understanding law enforcement officers had was enhanced by their roots in the community, especially through family, extended family, and clan. Because of the size of the reservation community, it was not unusual for law enforcement officers to know almost everyone on the reservation. They knew about various situations and social problems people were experiencing, and they seemed particularly wise when it came to predicting people's behaviors such as child neglect and abuse, spouse abuse, unemployment, and alcoholism.

On one particular Friday evening ride-along, the law enforcement officer I was with really didn't do any "law enforcement." Rather, he was mostly involved in a series of domestic events, spending his full shift working with individuals and personal problems. In essence, he used some of the same skills I use as a social worker. He used the strength of his personal relationship with his clients, and this seemed to be appreciated by those with whom he worked that night. I realized there was a lot to learn about relating to people on the reservation, including the importance of noninterference, avoidance of manipulation and coercion, and the values of mutual respect, consideration, and sharing. I was appreciative of the lessons I learned on my ride-alongs.

DATA COLLECTION: MY FIRST CASE

I received a referral from the Tribal Law Enforcement Center concerning a 27-year-old man who was in custody because of suspected spouse abuse. The report indicated that John Red Fox was drinking and had apparently threatened his wife. The law enforcement authorities were called to investigate, and it was discovered that John had been drinking and was verbally abusive, although there was no evidence of his physically attacking his wife or children. It was decided that he should be incarcerated for his own protection. Although the incident took place two days prior to receiving this referral, John was still in jail. It was decided that a visit to the correctional facility would be an appropriate plan.

I knew the officer who made the arrest and was able to talk to him prior to entering the cell to talk to John. Apparently, John Red Fox was recently discharged from the state hospital for alcohol treatment and had started drinking just prior to his arrest. It was reported that he had been fighting with his wife, but there was no evidence of physical abuse.

As I entered the cell, I was surprised to see a very handsome, well-built, young man with braided long black hair, wearing blue jeans, tennis shoes, and a red and black flannel shirt. He was also wearing a beautiful beaded necklace. John seemed rather subdued and sullen and volunteered little information. His expression was almost blank, and his voice expressed little inflection or affect. He seldom looked up while we communicated and spoke rather softly. John was aware of the referral to my agency and, consequently, did not question my approach to him. Although I needed to prompt him with specific questioning, John was able to provide a good deal of information.

John stated he was 27 years old and was a high school dropout at age 14. He and his wife Mary, age 22, have three children. Two of the children, age 7 and 5, are from two different fathers, and the couple have a 3-year-old son from their marriage. They have been married for approximately two and one-half years. Mary also dropped out of high school at a young age. John and Mary survive by getting part-time jobs on the reservation and are also involved in seasonal work. John admitted to having a drinking problem, and he described his most recent admission to the state hospital for alcoholism.

John's mother and father were alive and also lived on the reservation. John has six brothers and three sisters. In general, Mary's mother takes primary responsibility for caring for John and Mary's children, as Mary also has a problem with alcohol.

John suggested that there were serious troubles with the children. He described all three children as being unmanageable, easily distracted, hyperactive, and difficult to communicate with, even under the best of circumstances. John said that both he and Mary had been drinking since their teens, and I wondered if fetal alcohol syndrome (FAS) might play some part in the children's behaviors.

When I asked him about why he had dropped out of school, John said he didn't particularly dislike school but that studying was difficult for him. He often found it difficult to concentrate and, consequently, got poor grades. He said he was never tested for any learning disabilities but admitted to having difficulty transferring numbers and letters. He also finds it difficult to read basic material. He did say that he was interested in sports and enjoyed participating in baseball and basketball in grade school and junior high. He also admitted to being involved in a peer group that did not complete high school and was involved in parties, drinking, smoking, and some petty theft. At the time he quit school, there were good paying jobs on the reservation, mostly in construction of BIA funded housing projects. The money he earned from these jobs helped him support himself and contribute to his family. He considered taking care of himself and helping his family more important than the frustrating experience of completing high school.

When we discussed the event leading to this arrest, John related that a brother and a friend who were living in Minneapolis had recently returned to the reservation. The brother had just lost his job but had considerable money and decided to move in with John and Mary. While Mary was disappointed about this decision, she accepted John's brother as a matter of tradition and respect for John's family. Since John's brother had the necessary money, the three were able to party almost day and night for about a week. John had been released from the state hospital about three weeks prior to this and had remained sober. However, this latest incident of drinking had an immediate effect on his functioning. Mary became more and more agitated about John and experienced difficulty with the children. As a result, a fight broke out between the two, causing the police to be involved. John admitted to being very angry and threatening, but he denied striking Mary or the children.

Both John and Mary had been involved in periodic counseling since their marriage. Although Mary did not participate often, both were involved in counseling while John was in treatment at the state hospital. It was recommended that John and Mary become involved in Alcoholics Anonymous and Al-Anon, but they only sporadically participated. The reservation community provided little support for individuals struggling with maintaining sobriety. The amount of alcohol consumption and its visibility and acceptance on the reservation were strong motivators for individuals to abuse alcohol.

After my discussion with John, I thought it might be important to talk with Mary, with the children, and with members of the extended family. Perhaps they would add their insights about the overall situation with John. The family didn't have a telephone, and because of the urgency of the situation I made an unscheduled home visit.

The family lived three miles north of the agency on a rural, unmarked gravel road. I had to ask for directions from some of the neighbors, but I finally located it. When I arrived, I was curious about the scene I viewed. The residence included three dwellings, two of which were connected, suggesting that the living arrangement had been built in sections over time. There were a number of exposed roof areas, as shingles had apparently blown off. Tar paper was visible through the siding, most of the windows had no screens, and a few windows were broken. Four automobiles in various stages of repair and disrepair were in the front yard. There were two dogs, three horses, and other farm animals around the living area, including chickens, ducks, geese, and goats. There were a number of old appliances outside the home. There were also some fallen trees and some firewood stacked in neat rows. In addition, I saw a number of tools and other woodworking items. I was somewhat surprised at the overall appearance of John and Mary's home.

I was again surprised as I entered their home. An elderly woman answered the door and, without hesitation, invited me in. I was impressed with the colorful wallpaper, drapes, fixtures, and furniture in the home. There were some beautiful Native American arts and crafts throughout the home, and overall it appeared orderly and tidy. I was impressed with the small size of the quarters relative to the number of people living there.

I identified myself, and the woman responded by saying, "I figured someone would be out. I suppose you want to see Mary?" Mary came from a back bedroom, and after I introduced myself we settled ourselves at the kitchen table. Mary was an attractive young woman with features distinct to her tribal heritage. She had long dark hair, a pleasant smile, and intense dark eyes.

Mary was gracious and hospitable during the visit. She said that she knew the reasons for my visit and appeared interested in volunteering information about her husband. Throughout the interview, Mary's three children and four other children were continually in and out of the kitchen. Although not specifically disruptive, their presence was obvious. They jumped on and off Mary's lap, and eventually they paid attention to me, climbing on my lap and looking through my attaché case and other effects. They appeared curious about our conversation but would appear and disappear frequently.

Mary volunteered a good deal of information about herself. She described her childhood as a difficult one. She faced a lot of pressure as a teenager, and had difficulties attending and performing in school. She mentioned, "I became a mother way too early." When I asked her to clarify her statement, she said she had gotten pregnant at a young age. She also said that she was the second oldest of four children and had to care for her brothers and sisters in her parents' absence. According to Mary, her father disappeared from the family when she was rather young. Her mother spent considerable time away from home participating in part-time and seasonal work, and she had a drinking problem. Mary described a series of unstable relationships she had with boyfriends, and she said that her parents sent her away to an Indian boarding school. Mary said she dropped out of high school because she became pregnant and had difficulty making good grades.

Mary told me that she and John had been having problems with their marriage. She felt that her relationship with John was made difficult by their mutual drinking problems, but she felt that their relationship was salvageable. In general, the information she provided was similar to the information John and others had provided.

I appreciated Mary's spontaneity. However, when I asked her about her children, she was much more guarded. Although she said that each of the children had different fathers, she refused to talk any more about her children's behaviors. It appeared that Mary was motivated and willing to be further involved in some form of counseling relationship, although I was unsure of what that might be. In retrospect, I wondered if Mary "had all the right things to say," since she had been in and out of counseling with multiple human service providers for many years. Additionally, I wondered if she said what she thought I might want to hear so I would leave her, her children, and her relatives alone.

After a week had passed since John's arrest, he was released and returned to Mary. Knowing this, I decided to review their situation more closely by examining their existing case records and making contact with other providers who were involved with this family over time. Having received written permission from John and Mary to obtain information from other service providers, I discovered that as a child Mary had apparently been abused by her older stepbrother and had possibly been physically and sexually abused by her stepfather. In addition, there was some suspicion raised by the school system relative to sexual abuse of Mary's two oldest children, ironically, by that same stepbrother. Having obtained this new information, I realized why Mary might have been reluctant to share information about herself and her children.

ASSESSMENT: DEFINING THE ISSUES

It seemed important to me to review all the information I had in this case to establish some priorities and possible intervention plans and strategies. It was obvious that the Red Fox family had multiple problems. John and Mary, and both of their parents and grandparents, had continuously lived on the reservation. There was a history of unemployment, alcoholism, divorce, desertion, and parent-child relationship issues throughout both families. Most family members had survived by taking odd jobs and seasonal work, utilizing the food allotment and subsidy received through Tribal Social Services, and benefiting from monies distributed from treaty renegotiation resettlement for enrolled tribal members. Several family members had been involved with various counseling services that were arranged by Public Health Service workers. While the Red Fox clan had benefited from several programs to which they were entitled, such as medical and dental services, most of the counseling services to which they were referred were deemed ineffective.

I decided to sort out the different components of the Red Fox situation. My preliminary assessment led to identifying the following problems:

1. John's drinking and threatening behavior to Mary and the children often brought the family into crisis.
2. Mary's drinking contributed to the overall instability of the family situation. Mary also had a family history in which she might have experienced physical and sexual abuse as a child.
3. Lack of employment opportunities on the reservation made the family at risk for poverty. This was exacerbated by John and Mary's lack of educational credentials and employment skills.

4. John and Mary suffered frequent marital discord. This was due, in part, to their inability to deal with their children and their difficulties resulting from alcohol abuse.

5. There were significant issues with the children's behavior, perhaps owing to fetal alcohol syndrome and physical/sexual abuse. The children were hyperactive, and could have learning deficits or disabilities.

6. Although living arrangements were not identified as being unusual, the family's ability to access services, such as employment and education, was limited. The distance from the reservation and the family's lack of adequate transportation contributed to the isolating experience of living on the reservation.

While I was able to identify a number of interrelated problems in the Red Fox case, I was somewhat pessimistic about whether I could help John and Mary solve any of them. I thought of all the services available to them, both on and off the reservation, and realized that these traditional services had all been tried, with little success. I was not sure whether the ineffectiveness of the services was due to the Red Foxes' lack of motivation or whether the services themselves were ineffective or culturally inappropriate. It seemed obvious that I was going to have to be pretty creative to involve John and Mary in any kind of treatment plan.

GOAL PLANNING: FINDING A POINT OF INTERVENTION

As I sat alone in my office, I tried to decide how to reach the Red Fox family. Work had been done before with John and Mary, and more of the same didn't seem appropriate. I thought that if only I could reach the children and explore their situation, a point of intervention might present itself.

As luck would have it, I remembered a staff presentation I had attended during my first week at the agency. A number of individuals from Montana, Arizona, and New Mexico had presented a program about efforts to revitalize traditional Indian beliefs and culture. There were several social workers involved in the presentation, and this rather impressed me. The presentation, entitled "The Red Road," had to do with the traditional Native American spiritual orientation, which stressed a holistic unification of people and the environment. As I thought back to the presentation, I realized I had neglected to consider helping the Red Fox family with any strategy other than a traditional, agency-oriented intervention. As a social worker, I had been trained to think of the human condition in a holistic way but not in the same sense as is stressed in traditional Native American beliefs.

I made contact with a number of the presenters and intensified my study in this whole area. I decided to look up a friend who was also my Native American mentor, Frank Running Deer, and ask him how to connect with people like John and Mary. Frank, who held the honored tribal role of "Pipe Carrier," had been authorized by tribal leaders to conduct the Sweat Lodge ceremony, and

I had been granted the privilege of learning and participating in this and other ceremonies since coming to the reservation. Although I didn't identify the Red Fox family by name, I discussed my concerns about engaging them and other families with traditional social services. Frank agreed to work with me on my concerns. As we shared intervention strategies and goal planning relative to my assessment of the family situation, we agreed it might be good to begin by working with the children.

Frank told me of a new program developed by private and public sponsorship. including religious groups, spiritual leaders, and a number of funding agencies. It was a unique combination of "white religion and native spiritualism" in which the traditional involvement of people in their cultural environment was stressed. I agreed to make an on-site visit to the program and assess its possibilities.

The program was located in beautiful surroundings halfway between the reservation and the city. It included, among other things, a lovely beach, canoes, and all associated water and outdoor camp activities. In addition, authentic Native American structures were constructed, including the traditional wigwam, tepee, and earth lodge, used for ceremonial and educational purposes by such tribes as the Ojibwa, Mandan, and Plains Apache. Children were instructed in Native culture and spiritualism, and they were able to sleep outdoors in a tepee. I was told by the camp staff that a critical part of the experience was involvement of the parents, which stressed their contribution to educating the children in Native American cultural ways. As I listened to the camp staff, I realized why Frank had suggested the program as an intervention. For one thing, by involving the children in this culturally appropriate activity, it was unnecessary to "label" the parents as the "identified patients." I also realized that the program might help identify the strengths I believed existed within this family, including the relationship between John and Mary. Frank and I later agreed that the program had possibilities and might help John and Mary use their innate capacities, which we believed were considerable.

INTERVENTION: USING CULTURALLY APPROPRIATE PROGRAMMING

I had some second thoughts about how to approach this situation. I realized that I had been doing a lot of planning without involving John and Mary, and they had the right to participate in the planning process. I also wondered about the ethical implications of "getting to" John and Mary by involving their children in programming, even though the program seemed innovative and worthwhile.

My strategy included asking the school system to refer all three children to the camp program. I worked with the staff and consulted with Frank Running Deer as I sought ways to encourage John and Mary to enroll the children in the program. Although they appeared hesitant at first, John and Mary agreed that the program would be appropriate for the children. They appeared to welcome the respite from the demands of the children and even expressed interest in participating in their children's experiences. I considered this to be my first victory and a marvelous point of entry into the helping relationship.

The children's experience with the program was quite positive. I discussed their progress with John and Mary, hoping to reinforce their involvement with their children's camp activities. I also worked with the camp director, urging him to write notes home with the children and asking him to seek ways to involve John and Mary. As I recalled my first contact with Mary, I remembered the beautiful Native American art projects she had completed and displayed in her home. I suggested to the camp director that Mary be invited to come to camp and help teach children some of the native art. While several of the camp activities were recreational, many had cultural implications. For example, children participated in native dances and "talking circles" and were encouraged to study about their heritage. I felt Mary's special talents would fit well with the mission of the camp, would increase her feelings of connection to her community, and could enhance her self-esteem.

After further discussion with the camp director, I learned that there was a continued need for adults to supervise children as they designed and constructed authentic Indian dance outfits. This involved the traditional tanning of hides as well as making Indian costuming. Later, the children would learn to dance and would attend various powwows throughout the area. I suggested that the camp director contact Mary about involving her in these activities. Mary was delighted at the camp director's suggestion and said she was interested in helping children with bead work and especially with work in leather and birch bark. Her involvement in camp programming developed and increased over time.

My friend Frank Running Deer, who seemed to have a particular interest in this case, suggested that while we were encouraging Mary's involvement we should think of a way to ensure John's participation. He offered to help John become involved, suggesting that John and he might plan a children's powwow, including constructing a Sweat Lodge and other important components of the powwow. As luck would have it, John took up Frank's invitation. As we later found out, John was somewhat frustrated by Mary's increased involvement in the program and saw this as a good way to keep in touch with his family.

Mary, John, and the children remained involved with these activities through the summer months. There was no further indication of marital discord, abuse, or alcohol consumption, although I was not sure why, given their stormy history. As summer ended and fall neared, activities diminished on our rural, northern reservation. With the changing climate and with the restrictions of winter, Frank and I were puzzled about how we might continue to work with this family. Frank suggested that at the closing ceremonies of the camp he and I should approach Mary and John and talk with them about their participation. He suggested that we stress their positive involvement and suggest that they continue to stay involved in the future.

After the ceremony, there was an opportunity, although brief, for Frank and me and Mary and John to walk through the camp and chat about the experience. Frank was first to approach the subject and suggest there might be ways to continue involvement throughout the winter in anticipation of more involvement in next summer's program. Frank's way of broaching this suggestion to John and Mary was very nondirect, and I realized this to be his cultural style of communicating. Although Frank's intent was clear, his way of making the suggestion seemed less judgmental and intrusive and allowed John and Mary to accept his suggestion by exercising their own self-determination. Frank also suggested that John and he needed to continue their activity with Native spiritualism, which included involvement with the Sweat Lodge. John and Mary seemed to hold Frank in very high regard, and they tended to follow his suggestions. I later found out that as a result of Frank's suggestion, both John and Mary rejoined Alcoholics Anonymous.

Frank and I continued to work with the family, and we were able to arrange for diagnostic services for the three children and educational testing for Mary and John. Because the family became more involved in activities in town, they were more accessible to the available diagnostic services. I developed an excellent relationship with the school social worker who helped secure thorough medical, physical and emotional exams for the children. In addition, Frank convinced John and Mary to check out the adult education program at the community college and to consider enrolling.

It would certainly be unrealistic and unfair to suggest that all was smooth throughout the process of my involvement with the Red Fox family. I was proud for them, since they seemed to find a way to help themselves. The goals that John and Mary eventually set for themselves included participating in the Sweat Lodge ceremony and the Sun Dance, which would help them reach their potential as individuals.

EVALUATION

Throughout the process of working with this family, I attempted to define what might constitute success. It seemed to me that I evaluated the family, evaluated the effectiveness of the various treatment strategies that had been used with this family in the past, and evaluated my own efforts. From the beginning of my involvement with the Red Fox family, it was obvious that many others had tried to reach this family, so I wasn't very optimistic about my chances of reaching them.

I also evaluated the effect of the workshop on me and the others in attendance. Assessing and analyzing the outcome of that experience lead me to believe that there might be other interventions available. I concluded that I was not going to be able to reach this family, nor was I going to create an immediate link between the family and traditional social service agencies. Involving another person in the intervention helped engage this family and helped suggest a creative and culturally appropriate treatment plan.

The ending of this story is a positive one. John and Mary continue to participate. John has been involved in many sweats. He is not yet a pipe carrier and has not yet been authorized to dance in this year's Sun Dance; however, he continues to struggle with his lessons to achieve that distinction, honor, and responsibility. Mary continues to work throughout the winter months and has worked with several children and parents to produce beautiful costumes for many of the traditional dances. She and John have been involved in several powwows.

Both John and Mary successfully completed their GED and are beginning college studies. Although the studies are very difficult and frustrating, they have received good support from the instructional and counseling staff at the community college. They remain living at home with their extended family, and while this continues to cause a certain degree of difficulty, it appears manageable. The children are less of a problem in school this year but will require continued observation and attention as we continue to learn more about fetal alcohol syndrome, its consequences, and its treatment.

I encountered some interesting variables in this situation: mapping the service terrain of the reservation, using traditional and nontraditional interventions, assessing and intervening in the "spiritual" aspects of people's lives, and a holistic understanding of people in their environment. Additionally, working together with a "veteran" helped this to be a positive experience for me. The idea that my clients in this situation were somewhat "manipulated" into a process of "treatment" raised some ethical questions for me. I'm still not sure how to answer them.

READINGS

Berthold, S. (1989). Spiritism as a form of psychotherapy: Implications for social work practice. *Social Casework, 70*(8), 502–509.

Black Elk and Brown, J. (1975). *The sacred pipe: Black Elk's account of the seven rites of the Oglala Sioux.* Norman, OK: University of Oklahoma Press.

Black Elk and Neihardt, J. (1979). *Black Elks speaks: Being the life story of a holy man of the Oglala Sioux.* Lincoln, NE: University of Nebraska Press.

Deloria, V., Jr. (1969). *Custer died for your sins: An Indian manifesto.* New York: Macmillan.

Erdoes, R. (1972). *The Sun Dance people: The Plains Indians. their past and present.* New York: Knopf.

Hogan, L. (1992). All my relations (Indian sweat lodge ceremony). *Parabola, 17,* 33–35.

Sheridan, M., Bullis, R., Adcock, C., Berlin, S., and Miller, P. (1992). Practitioners' personal and professional attitudes and behaviors toward religion and spirituality: Issues for education and practice. *Journal of Social Work Education, 28*(2), 190–203.

Questions for Further Study

1. In "The American Invasion of Macún," from *When I Was Puerto Rican*, Santiago recalls how "experts" from the United States come to the village of Macún to educate the townspeople about the "proper" diet, hygiene, etc. In the parlance of the social work profession, they seem to be intervening without having made a proper assessment. Assume you are a social worker whose job it is to work with the townspeople. Assume also that there is, in the town, an expressed desire to reduce hunger, to have easier access to food, and to have healthier families. How would you proceed with an assessment?

2. In "The Death of the Profane," Patricia Williams forcefully tells a personal story of disenfranchisement, followed by several failures with several audiences (legal, journalistic, and school) to be honestly heard. When clients speak to social workers across cultural divides, the risk that they will not be heard often results in a shutting down, a truncation of their stories. How would you take this risk into account in an assessment process with a client from another race or culture? Based upon the facts presented by Williams here, how would you have responded to her?

3. What approach to race and ethnicity made James Wahlberg successful in his work in the Native American community? How could you apply his model in your practice of the assessment process in communities different from your own?

4. In "The Creation," from *Rattlebone*, we read about the adolescent attraction of Irene to a young man, Obadele, who is racially the same, but culturally different. It is this cultural difference that fosters suspicion and hostility between the two communities. How would you assess the community of the Red Quanders, in terms of both its strengths and weaknesses, in a way that is both honest and fair to its inhabitants?

5. In "Child of the Sixties," from *Mankiller*, Wilma Mankiller uses the history of the Indigenous peoples in nineteenth-century California to help explain the

circumstances she grew up in during the fifties and sixties in that state. Should such a history be included in a biopsychosocial assessment of an individual or family? Community? What are some historical precedents in your background that you might include in a self or family assessment?

Invited Commentary

DEBORA M. ORTEGA

INTRODUCTION

Assessment is a fundamental piece of social work practice. Too often assessment of clients occurs without an understanding of the context within which clients live. The five readings associated with this section highlight the importance of context through the lens of race, ethnicity, culture, privilege, power, and strength. The context is personal to the main figures in each reading, and we glimpse their experience of the context through their eyes. These readings allow us exposure to an understanding of the main figure's thoughts, beliefs, feelings, environment, and self-defined opportunities and barriers—information that might otherwise be inaccessible in a typical assessment.

The first step in assessing the five readings is to recognize each (for lack of a better term) "client's" understanding of his or her situation rather than imposing our preconceived beliefs and values on them. Second, since assessments would ideally lead to collaborating with clients, assessment includes eliciting the client's beliefs and ideas about the areas amenable to change to improve their present situation. Lastly, assessment needs to identify the "tools" that will be used to create change (Cowger 2002). The client's personal and environmental strengths are those "tools" that will, more than likely, be available to them on consistent bases. These strengths are used to procure other transient resources or combat situational and environmental barriers.

ASSESSING THE CLIENT CONTEXT: RACE, ETHNICITY, AND CULTURE

The five writers present five unique and individual perspectives about race, ethnicity, and culture. These perspectives allow us to entertain a range of possibilities about client s' experiences of themselves in a multicultural environment fraught with misunderstanding, inequality, complex reaction, and hope.

Claire's character Irene strongly identifies with the African American community. Her identity as a young black woman is not the point of interest but rather her relationship with a community that is culturally different yet racially the same (Red Quanders). Mankiller's poignant story of colonization provides a second view. Her identity as a First Nations woman is unwavering despite the hostile response from the white community to her race and culture. Her cultural identity becomes her lifesaver. Santiago's Negi is a member of the dominant cultural group in Macún. Her experience of race, ethnic, and cultural difference

119

is from foreign "experts." In part, because Negi's culture has not been devalued, she is not inclined to adopt a foreign culture as superior to her own. Her consumption of "Americano" culture in lieu of her own literally makes her vomit. African-American law professor Patricia Williams is taken by surprise when she encounters the hostility of the dominant culture in the midst of her Christmas shopping. Barred from entering a shop by a clerk, Williams confronts the contradiction between her racial and class status and the difficulties of seeking any redress. Lastly, Wahlberg's experience as a social worker assisting First Nations people reveals two aspects of culture. First, the clients' success through culturally specific interventions is reminiscent of Mankiller's experience of culture as a lifesaver. Second is his experience as a white social worker who is an outsider in a different culture. His identity as a white social worker could interfere with his ability to aid his client because of his own bias, unfamiliarity with their culture, and the "client's" distrust based on historical experiences of deceit. These five perspectives highlight the unique and personal experience of race, ethnicity, and culture experienced by people whose history includes enslavement, colonization, occupation, or domination.

DISCOVERING THE AREAS OF CHANGE: CLIENT AS EXPERT ON CHANGE

Our view as readers/observers of the lives represented in these readings is expansive. Although we cannot always utilize our relationship to clients to elicit their expertise about the problems affecting their lives, we can observe from the readings the consequences that occur when the "professional" determines the problem and area of change while disengaged from the client. Similarly, we can see what occurs when the client is not only included but is the primary and loudest voice identifying areas of needed change.

The clearest example of imposed change to solve a (perceived) problem is in *The American Invasion of Macún*. Arguably, the purpose of the "Gringo" experts was to provide an intervention that would improve the quality of life in the region. The Americans' confidence in their assessment of and solution to the problem destined the intervention to fail. The over-confidence and absolute reliance on their knowledge (gained through professional training in a dominant culture) prohibited them from looking beyond their "cookie cutter" answer to poor health problems in Macún. At one level, the misunderstanding between the Puerto Rican women and the American professionals is comical. Yet at another level, we are shown that the real needs of the community go unmet, as evidenced by Negi's tapeworm and the resulting home remedy. The loss resulting from the failed mode of "help" is not solely that of the women of Macún but is also that of the Americans. Tangibly, the Americans lost time, funds, and energy. Intangibly, they removed themselves from the possibility of enrichment based on an exchange and instead shaped an interaction based on domination or invasion.

Wahlberg provides an alternative to the imposition of an intervention devoid of client input. Wahlberg engages John and Mary Red Fox in identifying the areas that they view as problematic. The selection of an intervention that is focused on the children directly responds to John Red Fox's initial concern about the "serious troubles with the children being . . . unmanageable, easily distracted, hyperactive, and difficult to communicate with, even under the best of circumstances." Responding to Mr. Red Fox's initial concern and bringing about a successful result strengthened the relationship between the social worker and clients, provided the opportunity for accomplishment (for both the client and the social worker), and laid the foundation for trust in the future. Interestingly, early on, Wahlberg struggles with his own tendency to plan *for* John and Mary Red Fox rather than to plan *with* them. His willingness to be open to an exchange with Mr. and Mrs. Red Fox or his cultural guide Frank Running Deer allowed his effort to be fruitful, allowed the family to begin feeling powerful over their troubles, and allowed the Red Fox family to contribute to community life.

RECOGNIZING THE TOOLS OF CHANGE: CLIENT AND ENVIRONMENTAL STRENGTHS

Individuals possess a variety of personal and environmental strengths that can be utilized to create change and maintain the fulfilling aspects of their lives. Claire's Irene demonstrates the possibilities of using a personal strength to shift the focus away from personal pain and disappointment. Upon learning of Obadele's sexual relationship and resulting pregnancy with Folami, Irene utilizes her personal strengths to keep herself from being paralyzed with disappointment and grief. Irene's strengths are her magnetism, openness to diverse experiences, and her intelligence. These strengths are the foundation for her relationships with her friend Wanda and with her teacher Mrs. Welche, and they are the basis of her success as a public speaker. Choosing to focus on the resources that emerge from her strengths permit her to utilize her personal power to overcome her sadness. This moves her to be constructive rather than destructive in her choices. Her environmental resources (Wanda, Wanda's mother, Mrs. Welch, Irene's parents, and other community relationships) support her choices.

Mankiller's story is a complex web of historical and contemporary loss. Her troubles are interwoven with her strengths. She utilizes her resources to change those areas of her life that are painful. At times, these choices do not seem helpful, but ultimately they enable her to be part of an environment that is a better fit. For instance, running away to her grandmother's house five times over a one-year period demonstrated her strength and resourcefulness. Her running away was like a scream about the distress she felt in her city environment. The dominant culture's reaction to her First Nations culture, coupled with the unfamiliar physical environment, eroded her confidence and feelings of worth. Mankiller attributes her survival to her family's "intervention" (sending her to her grandmother). Mankiller's connection to her extended family and her connection to her culture vis-a-vis the community center supported her development as a youth and ultimately as a tribal leader.

Patricia Williams, in "Death of the Profane," exemplifies the importance of personal power as a client strength. Her response to being denied entrance to the store is rage. This rage is born from the shock of exclusion and the initial powerlessness she experiences in her effort to combat the store clerk's authority to judge, discriminate, and eliminate her from his world. The barred entrance feeds her rage until she reaches a crossroads. One road is to allow the power of her rage to lead her to destruction. The other is to mobilize her feelings to tell her story, as she did when she posted the sign on the store window and told her story through her writings and presentations.

PRIVILEGE AND POWER: FACILITATING AND IMPEDING CHANGE

The figures in these readings provide a unique view of privilege and power. Each story conveys the power of privilege granted to people based on their color, socioeconomic class, gender, position, and education. The readings relate a tale of privilege, earned and unearned, which interacts with the racial, ethnic, and cultural aspects of individuals.

Claire's character, Mrs. Welche, and her involvement with Irene illustrate two aspects of privilege. Mrs. Welche uses her privilege to facilitate change by choosing to be at Irene's school. She uses her relationship to a school board member to gain entry to the mostly racially segregated school. Potentially, Mrs. Welch's involvement with the children provides access to resources that might not be otherwise available. Specifically, for Irene, Mrs. Welche recognized, encouraged, and developed Irene's public speaking skills.

Conversely, Mrs. Welche's privilege potentially became a barrier to change. Mrs. Welche's suggestion that a white student deliver Irene's speech so that "all the work" would not be wasted, highlights the gap between Irene's world and Mrs. Welche's experience of privilege.

Williams describes another aspect of privilege—the censorship, the revision, and the diluting of her experience. The editors' and students' response to the telling of her story is "whitewashing." In other words, the listeners cover up content that is distasteful or emotional. It is Williams' own privilege gained (in part) through education, which allows her multiple opportunities to tell her story. For Williams, the healing is in the telling of the story.

THE MORAL OF THE STORY: A SOCIAL WORKER'S RESPONSE.

What can we learn from these readings about social work with diverse people? There are several possible answers to this question. One possible answer is that every client's racial, ethnic, and cultural identity will be unique to his or her experience. These unique experiences may include the characteristics of their community, family history, cultural history, phenotype, and geographical location. These experiences are part of the "goodness of fit" that plays a part in the troubles and solutions for clients.

Another possible response, based on Mrs. Welche's experience, is that even in our most enlightened moments we can be dim. While we may think of ourselves as combating racism or "spending" our privilege to move to an equitable system for vulnerable people, there are ways that our participation in an inequitable system and the benefits we receive from this system are injurious to vulnerable people. When we fail to realize the power behind privilege, we devalue the painful experiences of racism and oppression (and heterosexism, and sexism, et al.).

Finally, the "moral of the story" is that as social workers, assessment is not just about clients. Assessment is about evaluating our own position, which includes our own personal and professional values, bias, and privilege, when we join with clients to work toward the amelioration of societal and personal "troubles."

REFERENCE

Cowger, C. D., and Snively, C. A. (2002). Assessing client strengths: Individual, family, and community empowerment. In D. Saleebey (ed.), *The Strengths Perspective in Social Work Practice* (3d ed., pp. 106–123). Boston: Allyn and Bacon.

Unit 3   REFRAMING CLIENT ISSUES IN AGING AND ABILITY

Editors' Introduction

Dazed and Confused   1/3

Reframing is an indispensable skill set of the well-trained social worker. First defined and described by therapists at the Mental Health Research Institute some thirty years ago (Watzlawick, et al. 1974), reframing is a technique in which a presenting problem is recontextualized, so that the client(s) may view that problem in a new and hopefully more constructive way. As Ona Bregman suggests in her Invited Commentary at the end of this unit, reframing moves the focus of a problem from a narrowly identified perspective or target to a broader, more comprehensive framework (a "systems perspective"), thus redistributing the pressure for change and support across a wider system of people and services. Similarly, in the case study "On Being Different: Sophie's Story," by Jeanne Matich-Maroney, we read of a middle-aged woman, labeled as mentally retarded nearly all of her life, enabled

by a series of interventions and the collection of additional data to reframe her potential, forge a new self-concept, and pursue a more productive life.

The skill of reframing seems to be an adaptive response to the struggles faced
by otherwise healthy people as they age and/or face disabilities and impairments
that place quality of life at risk. Thus, we offer the following literary selections and
meditations on aging and ability as exemplars: two offer triumphant narratives of
individuals who have developed positive relationships to their own abilities and
limitations (e.g. a successful reframing), while two emphasize the difficulties of
overcoming the despair and helplessness that can arise and persist as a consequence of unfair and inhumane treatment on the bases of age or ability.

We begin with a chapter by Temple Grandin called "Learning Empathy," from
Thinking in Pictures (and Other Reports from My Life with Autism). In attempting
to explain to those of us not similarly afflicted what it means to be autistic, she reframes her eschewing of physical contact with others as an "allergy": for those of
us who are allergic to substances, we know that exposure to that substance results
in irritation and stress, just as human contact does for her. Ultimately, Grandin
was able to reframe her condition as one in which contact was integral but of a
very restricted type. Her "squeeze machine," designed to soothe cattle as they are
led to slaughter, proves to be a vehicle for offering her comfort without human
contact. The calm state that she was able to obtain from the squeeze machine not
only lessened her irritability, but enabled her to see what others seek in the human
touch. Thus, Grandin's insights, in conjunction with her ability to reframe this element of her condition, allow us to better understand what it means to be autistic,
and what enabled her to develop empathy with others.

Of course, the fundamental ways in which autism separates its victims from
those who do not suffer from autism are a source of great despair as well. Battling
despair is something Nancy Mairs discusses openly in her piece, "Freeing
Choices," from *Waist-High in the World: A Life among the Disabled*. Like
Grandin, she depends upon anti-depressants to sustain herself. To give a sense of
the negative perceptions that affect her opportunities in the world and that diminish her integrity and self-confidence, Mairs examines attitudes toward pregnancy
and death that reveal the everyday devaluation of people with disabilities. As she
points out, the commonplace consideration that it would be better to abort a fetus
than give birth to an infant with spina bifida, for example, is dehumanizing to her
and to other people with disabilities. Although people without such disabilities
find it difficult to imagine adjusting to life without all their present abilities and
freedoms, Mairs points out that, over the course of a debilitating illness, she discovered that she was indeed able to make such adjustments. From her perspective, the unwillingness in our society to accommodate people who have needs
that are unusual or "special" is merely selfish and greedy. She recommends a massive reframing of our view of the disabled from severely limited, or "defective," to
full human beings, having agency, dignity, and abilities. If we fail to support those
with disabilities with our personal attention and our tax monies, we will never
know the talents and skills lost to us because of our indifference.

Aging gracefully, as described by Leonard Kriegel in "Falling into Life" from
Falling into Life: Essays by Leonard Kriegel appears to be much like Mairs' con-
ception of coming to terms with the increasing physical limitations of illness.
Both, according to these authors, require us to reframe our feelings about depen-

dency and to work at strengthening our ability to accept help. Kriegel approaches the experience of aging with the benefit of lessons learned with the onset of polio and the loss of the use of his legs when he was eleven years old. As his essay suggests, aging confronts everyone with firsthand experience of a loss of ability formerly taken for granted. When Kriegel lost the use of his legs and had to learn to walk with braces and crutches, he was unable to draw on prior experience. For him, this change in life circumstances felt like a complete rupture with the past. As he describes it, the hardest adjustment he had to make was learning how to fall, something crucial to the process of becoming proficient at walking with braces and crutches. With this rich metaphor that we are left to explore for further meanings, Kriegel suggests that he could not succeed in walking once again without accepting the fact that failure and success, independence and need, glory and defeat, go hand in hand. As he faces the diminution in ability that comes with age, Kriegel takes the idea of falling even further. As a young person, he was able to fall and, however ashamed or humiliated, pick himself up again. As an older person, however, he would require help from others to get back up after a fall. It is this reframing of (dis)ability, in the context of aging, that helps Kriegel view his experience as normative when, for so much of his life, the effects of polio separated him and made him feel so different.

The selection from *Storyteller*, by Leslie Marmon Silko, called "Lullaby," with its theme of unmitigated sorrow and despair permeating, might seem an unlikely choice as a vehicle to look at the skill of reframing. Silko suggests that the history of the Navajo people and the age and life experiences of Ayah have shaped the way she relates to the white community. Consider the admonition by the "old ones" to Ayah that learning any of the white man's language or their ways was dangerous. For example, after doing the one thing she knew how to do according to the ways of the whites, i.e., signing her name, Ayah loses her children. Consider also the death of her son, Jimmie, in the white man's war, her husband Chato's dismissal from his job of many years, and Ayah and Chato's resulting eviction. Her negative experiences with white people mark her as she makes her way through the world; Ayah sees herself, for example, when she searches for Chato in Azzie's bar, not as a helpless or broken old woman but as a frightening presence who engenders anxiety in those who have oppressed her. While Ayah gains a stubborn satisfaction by reframing her isolation from others as a form of personal power, we are troubled by her isolation from sustaining relationships. We wonder how Ayah and Chato became so isolated from the Navajo community and how more connection to their people might have enabled them to reframe and survive their ordeals more successfully?

These readings, taken in their entirety, allow us to see that reframing can be utilized to help us see problems in new ways at all levels, from the most personal to large-system. And we hope that you, the reader, will find opportunities for the reframing of problems and issues in these readings that we do not discuss here.

REFERENCE

Watzlawick, P., Weakland, J. H. and Fisch, R. (1974). *Change: Principles of Problem Formation and Problem Resolution*. New York: W. W. Norton.

Reading

Learning Empathy: Emotion and Autism

TEMPLE GRANDIN

TO HAVE FEELINGS of gentleness, one must experience gentle bodily comfort. As my nervous system learned to tolerate the soothing pressure from my squeeze machine, I discovered that the comforting feeling made me a kinder and gentler person. It was difficult for me to understand the idea of kindness until I had been soothed myself. It wasn't until after I had used the modified squeeze machine that I learned how to pet our cat gently. He used to run away from me because I held him too tightly. Many autistic children hold pets too tightly, and they have a disproportionate sense of how to approach other people or be approached. After I experienced the soothing feeling of being held, I was able to transfer that good feeling to the cat. As I became gentler, the cat began to stay with me and this helped me understand the ideas of reciprocity and gentleness.

From the time I started using my squeeze machine, I understood that the feeling it gave me was one that I needed to cultivate toward other people. It was clear that the pleasurable feelings were those associated with love for other people. I built a machine that would apply the soothing, comforting contact that I craved as well as the physical affection I couldn't tolerate when I was young. I would have been as hard and as unfeeling as a rock if I had not built my squeeze machine and followed through with its use. The relaxing feeling of being held washes negative thoughts away. I believe that the brain needs to receive comforting sensory input. Gentle touching teaches kindness.

I always thought about cattle intellectually until I started touching them. I was able to remain the neutral scientist until I placed my hands on them at the Swift plant and feedlots in 1974. When I pressed my hand against the side of a steer, I could feel whether he was nervous, angry, or relaxed. The cattle flinched unless I firmly put my hand on them, but then touching had a calming effect. Sometimes touching the cattle relaxed them, but it always brought me closer to the reality of their being.

People have a need to touch animals in order to connect with them. I still vividly remember an experience I had while handling cattle at the Arlington feedlot in Arizona. We were working them through a squeeze chute to give them vaccinations. I was operating the chute and giving the animals their vaccinations. When I gave an injection, I always placed my hand on the animal's back, which had a calming effect on me. This calmness seemed to be reciprocal, because when I was calm, the cattle remained calm. I think they sensed this, and

129

each animal walked quietly into the chute. I mentally asked him to relax so he would not get hit by the head restraint. Everything remained calm until the side of the squeeze chute broke and knocked over a bucket. This got me and all the cattle completely rattled for the rest of the afternoon. The spell had been broken.

The application of physical pressure has similar effects on people and animals. Pressure reduces touch sensitivity. For instance, gentle pressure on the sides of a piglet will cause it to fall asleep, and trainers have found that massaging horses relaxes them. The reactions of an autistic child and a scared, flighty horse are similar. Both will lash out and kick anything that touches them. Wild horses can be desensitized and relaxed by pressure. Recently I watched a demonstration of a pressure device for breaking them. The horse used in the demonstration had been sold by a rancher because he was unrideable, and he kicked and reared when people approached. The effect of the pressure device on his nervous system was similar to that of my squeeze machine. Pressure helped this frightened horse to overcome his intense fear of being touched.

The machine was built by Robert Richardson of Prescott, Arizona, and it used sand to immobilize the horse gently as it applied pressure. The wild horse was placed in a narrow stall similar to a horse trailer, with two gentle horses in adjacent stalls to keep it company because wild horses will panic when they are alone. The horse's head protruded through a padded opening in the front of the stall, and a rear pusher gate prevented him from backing up and pulling his head inside. Sand from an overhead hopper flowed down the stall walls and slowly filled up the stall so that the horse hardly felt it until he was buried up to his back. Slow application of pressure is the most calming. It wasn't until the sand came up to his belly that he jerked slightly, but then he appeared to relax. He seldom put his ears back, which is a sign of fear or aggression, and he never tried to bite anybody. He was alert and curious about his surroundings, and he acted like a normal horse in a stall, even though his body was now completely buried. He was free to move his head, and eventually he allowed people to touch his face and rub his ears and mouth. Touching that had been intolerable was now being tolerated.

After fifteen minutes, the sand was removed from the stall by draining through a grating in the floor. The horse now tolerated being touched on the rest of his body. The effect of the pressure lasted for thirty minutes to one hour. During that time the horse learned to trust people a little more and to experience touch as a positive sensation.

The effects of gentle touching work at a basic biological level. Barry Keverne and his colleague at the University of Cambridge in England found that grooming in monkeys stimulated increased levels of endorphins, which are the brain's own opiates. Japanese researchers have found that pressure on the skin produces a relaxed muscle tone and makes animals drowsy. Pigs will roll over and solicit scratching on their bellies when rubbed. The drive for contact comfort is great. Harry Harlow's famous monkey experiments showed that baby monkeys that had been separated from their mother needed a soft surface to cling to. If a baby monkey was deprived of contact with either a real mother or a mother substitute such as the soft fluffy paint roller Harlow gave them, then its capacity for future affection was weakened. Baby animals need to feel contact and comfort and to have normal sensory experiences to develop normally. Harlow also found that gentle rocking helped prevent abnormal, autistic-like behavior in baby monkeys who were separated from their mothers. Every parent knows that rocking calms a cranky baby, and both children and adults enjoy rocking. That's why rocking horses and rocking chairs continue to sell well.

The old theory of autism, popular until the 1970s, placed blame on the "refrigerator mother," whose supposed rejection of the child caused the autism. The psychologist Bruno Bettelheim's theories, popularized in his book *The Empty Fortress*, held that psychological difficulties caused autism. We now know that autism is caused by neurological abnormalities that shut the child off from normal touching and hugging. It is the baby's abnormal nervous system that rejects the mother and causes it to pull away when touched. There is the further possibility that secondary damage to the brain, caused by a defective nervous system, adds to the child's further retreat from normal comforting touch.

Studies of the brain show that sensory problems have a neurological basis. Abnormalities of the cerebellum and the limbic system may cause sensory problems and abnormal emotional responses. Margaret Bauman and her colleagues at Massachusetts General Hospital autopsied the brains of people with autism and found that both the cerebellum and the limbic system had immature neuron development. Eric Courchesne also found abnormalities in the cerebellum on MRI brain scans. Research on rats and cats has shown that the center part of the cerebellum, the vermis, acts as a volume control for the senses. As early as 1947, Dr. William Chambers wrote an article in the *American Journal of Anatomy* reporting that stimulating a cat's vermis with an electrode caused the cat to become supersensitive to sound and touch. A series of abnormalities in lower brain centers probably causes sensory oversensitivity, jumbling, and mixing.

Tests done in many different laboratories around the world clearly indicate that people with autism have abnormal results on brain stem function tests, and that nonverbal people with severe impairments have the most abnormal results. Neurological problems occur during fetal development and are not caused by psychological factors. However, it's possible that if a baby does not receive comforting touch, the feeling and kindness circuits in the brain shrivel up.

AUTISM AND ANIMAL BEHAVIOR

Zoo animals kept in barren concrete cages become bored and often develop abnormal behavior such as rocking, pacing, and weaving. Young animals placed alone in such environments become permanently damaged and exhibit strange, autistic-like behavior, becoming overly excitable and engaging in stereotypical behaviors such as self-mutilation, hyperactivity, and disturbed social relations. The effects of sensory deprivation are very bad for their nervous systems. Total rehabilitation of these animals is extremely difficult.

Animal and human studies show that restriction of sensory experiences causes the central nervous system to become hypersensitive to sound and touch. The effects of early sensory restriction are often long-lasting. Puppies reared in empty concrete kennels become very excited when they hear a noise. Their brain waves still show signs of excessive excitability six months after they are removed from the kennel and housed on a farm. The brain waves of autistic children show similar signs of excessive arousal. Further experiments with rats have illustrated the damaging effects of restricting normal sensory experiences. Trimming the whiskers on baby rats causes the parts of the brain that receive sensations from the whiskers to become oversensitive, because there are no incoming touch sensations. This abnormality is relatively permanent; the brain areas are still abnormal after the whiskers grow back. It may be that the autistic child's abnormal sensory functioning causes his or her brain to develop secondary abnormalities because of distorted sensory input or a lack of such input. And these distortions may affect what are considered normal emotions.

The environment a young animal is raised in will affect the structural development of its brain. Research by Bill Greenough, at the University of Illinois, indicated that rearing rats in cages with toys and ladders to play with increased the number of dendrites, or nerve endings, in the visual and auditory parts of their brains. I conducted research as part of my Ph.D. dissertation that indicated that pigs engaging in abnormal rooting, owing to being raised in a barren plastic pen, grew extra dendrites in the part of the brain that received sensations from the snout. Construction of this abnormal "dendrite highway" may explain why it is so difficult to rehabilitate zoo animals that have engaged in years of stereotypical pacing. This is why it is so important to start therapy and education when an autistic child is young, so that developing nerve endings can connect in the right places.

AUTISTIC EMOTIONS

Some people believe that people with autism do not have emotions. I definitely do have them, but they are more like the emotions of a child than of an adult. My childhood temper tantrums were not really expressions of emotion so much as circuit overloads. When I calmed down, the emotion was all over. When I get angry, it is like an afternoon thunderstorm; the anger is intense, but once I get over it, the emotion quickly dissipates. I become very angry when I see people abusing cattle, but if they change their behavior and stop abusing the animals, the emotion quickly passes.

Both as a child and as an adult, I have felt a happy glee. The happiness I feel when a client likes one of my projects is the same kind of glee I felt as a child when I jumped off the diving board. When one of my scientific papers is accepted for publication, I feel the same happiness I experienced one summer when I ran home to show my mother the message I had found in a wine bottle on the beach. I feel a deep satisfaction when I make use of my intellect to design a challenging project. It is the kind of satisfied feeling one gets after finishing a difficult crossword puzzle or playing a challenging game of chess or bridge; it's not an emotional experience so much as an intellectual satisfaction.

At puberty, fear became my main emotion. When the hormones hit, my life revolved around trying to avoid a fear-inducing panic attack. Teasing from other kids was very painful, and I responded with anger. I eventually learned to control my temper, but the teasing persisted, and I would sometimes cry. Just the threat of teasing made me fearful; I was afraid to walk across the parking lot because I was afraid somebody would call me a name. Any change in my school schedule caused intense anxiety and fear of a panic attack. I worked overtime on my door symbols because I believed that I could make the fear go away if I could figure out the secrets of my psyche.

The writings of Tom McKean and Therese Joliffe indicate that fear is also a dominant emotion in their autism. Therese stated that trying to keep everything the same helped her avoid some of the terrible fear. Tony W., another man with autism, wrote in the *Journal of Autism and Developmental Disorders* that he lived in a world of daydreaming and fear and that he was afraid of everything. In my case the terrible fear did not begin until puberty, but for some autistic people it starts in early childhood. Sean Barron reported that he felt pure terror during the first five or six years of his life. The highly structured environment of the classroom reduced some of his fear, but he was often afraid and anxious in the hallways.

The intense fear and anxiety I used to experience has been almost eliminated by the antidepressant medication I've been on for the last thirteen years. The elimination of most of my fears and panic attacks has also attenuated many of my emotions. The strongest feeling I have today is one of intense calm and serenity as I handle cattle and feel them relax under my care. The feeling of peacefulness and bliss does not dissipate quickly like my other emotions. It is like floating on clouds. I get a similar but milder feeling from the squeeze machine. I get great satisfaction out of doing clever things with my mind, but I don't know what it is like to feel rapturous joy. I know I am missing something when other people swoon over a beautiful sunset. Intellectually I know it is beautiful, but I don't feel it. The closest thing I have to joy is the excited pleasure I feel when I have solved a design problem. When I get this feeling, I just want to kick up my heels. I'm like a calf gamboling about on a spring day.

My emotions are simpler than those of most people. I don't know what complex emotion in a human relationship is. I only understand simple emotions, such as fear, anger, happiness, and sadness. I cry during sad movies, and sometimes I cry when I see something that really moves me. But complex emotional relationships are beyond my comprehension. I don't understand how a person can love someone one minute and then want to kill him in a jealous rage the next. I don't understand being happy and sad at the same time. Donna Williams succinctly summarizes autistic emotions in *Nobody Nowhere:* "I believe that autism results when some sort of mechanism that controls emotions does not function properly, leaving an otherwise relatively normal body and mind unable to express themselves with the depth that they would otherwise be capable of." As far as I can figure out, complex emotion occurs when a person feels two opposite emotions at once. Samuel Clemens, the author of *Tom Sawyer,* wrote that "the secret source of humor is not joy but sorrow," and Virginia

Woolf wrote, "The beauty of the world has two edges, one of laughter, one of anguish, cutting the heart asunder." I can understand these ideas, but I don't experience emotion this way.

I am like the lady referred to as S. M. in a recent paper by Antonio Damasio in *Nature.* She has a damaged amygdala. This part of the brain is immature in autism. S. M. has difficulty judging the intentions of others, and she makes poor social judgments. She is unable to recognize subtle changes in facial expression, which is common in people with autism. In developing many varied, complex ways to operate the squeeze machine on myself, I keep discovering that slight changes in the way I manipulate the control lever affect how it feels. When I slowly increase the pressure, I make very small variations in the rate and timing of the increase. It is like a language of pressure, and I keep finding new variations with slightly different sensations. For me, this is the tactile equivalent of a complex emotion and this has helped me to understand complexity of feelings.

I have learned how to understand simple emotional relationships that occur with clients. These relationships are usually straightforward; however, emotional nuances are still incomprehensible to me, and I value concrete evidence of accomplishment and appreciation. It pleases me to look at my collection of hats that clients have given me, because they are physical evidence that the clients liked my work. I am motivated by tangible accomplishment, and I want to make a positive contribution to society.

I still have difficulty understanding and having a relationship with people whose primary motivation in life is governed by complex emotions, as my actions are guided by intellect. This has caused friction between me and some family members when I have failed to read subtle emotional cues. For instance, it was difficult for my younger sister to have a weird sister. She felt she always had to tiptoe around me. I had no idea that she felt this way until years later, when she told me about her childhood feelings toward me. Motivated by love, my mother worked with me and kept me out of institutions. Yet sometimes she feels that I don't love her.

She is a person for whom emotional relationships are more important than intellect and logic. It pains her that I kicked like a wild animal when I was a baby and that I had to use the squeeze machine to get the feeling of love and kindness. The irony is that if I had given up the machine, I would have been a cold, hard rock. Without the machine, I would have had no kind feelings toward her. I had to feel physical comfort in order to feel love. Unfortunately, it is difficult for my mother and other highly emotional people to understand that people with autism think differently. For her, it is like dealing with somebody from another planet. I relate better to scientists and engineers, who are less motivated by emotion.

At a conference a man with autism told me that he feels only three emotions, fear, sadness, and anger. He has no joy. He also has problems with the intensity of his emotions, which both fluctuate and get mixed up, similar to sensory jumbling. My emotions don't get mixed up, but they are reduced and simplified in some areas. The emotional jumbling described by this man may be like the sudden emotional changes that normally occur in two-year-old children. They can be laughing one minute and having a tantrum the next. The tendency to shift emotional states rapidly often occurs in autistic children at a later age, whereas older autistic children may have the emotional patterns of a younger child.

During the last couple of years, I have become more aware of a kind of electricity that goes on between people which is much subtler than overt anger, happiness, or fear. I have observed that when several people are together and having a good time, their speech and laughter follow a rhythm. They will all laugh together and then talk quietly until the next laughing cycle. I have always had a hard time fitting in with this rhythm, and I usually interrupt conversations without realizing my mistake. The problem is that I can't follow the rhythm. Twenty years ago, Dr. Condon, a Boston physician, observed that babies with autism and other developmental disorders failed to move in synchrony with adult speech. Normal infants will tune into adult speech and get in synch with it.

The work I do is emotionally difficult for many people, and I am often asked how I can care about animals and be involved in slaughtering them. Perhaps because I am less emotional than other people, it is easier for me to face the idea of death. I live each day as if I will die tomorrow. This motivates me to accomplish many worthwhile things, because I have learned not to fear death and have accepted my own mortality. This has enabled me to look at slaughtering objectively and perceive it the way the cattle do. However, I am not just an objective, unfeeling observer; I have a sensory empathy for the cattle. When they remain calm I feel calm, and when something goes wrong that causes pain, I also feel their pain. I tune in to what the actual sensations are like to the cattle rather than having the idea of death rile up my emotions. My goal is to reduce suffering and improve the way farm animals are treated.

People with autism are capable of forming very strong emotional bonds. Hans Asperger, the German doctor after whom the syndrome is named, states that the commonly held assumption of poverty of emotion in autism is inaccurate. However, my strong emotional bonds are tied up with places more than people. Sometimes I think my emotional life may appear more similar to those of animals than humans, because my feelings are simpler and more overt, and like cattle, I have emotional memories that are place-specific. For instance, I am not aware of a subconscious full of memories that are too painful to think about, and my emotional memory is very weak. It is highly doubtful that cattle become emotionally aroused when they think about a cowboy who whipped them, but they will have a measurable fear response, such as increased heart rate or stress hormone release, when they see that particular cowboy or return to the place where they were whipped. They often associate danger with a specific place. People with autism also have place- or object-specific memories. Going back to the place where something good happened or looking at an object associated with good feelings helps us reexperience the pleasure. Just thinking about it is not enough.

I have emotional reactions to places where I've stayed for a number of days or weeks while working on designing a livestock system. One of my clients told me that I fussed over a project for two weeks like a mother with a new baby. Places where I invest a lot of time become emotionally special. When I return to one of these spots, I am often overwhelmed with fear as I approach. I panic, thinking that I will be denied entry to my special place. Even though I know it's irrational, I always survey each place I work in to make sure I can get back in. Large meat-packing plants have security guards, but in almost every plant I have figured out how to evade security, just in case it becomes one of my special places and I need to get back in. Driving by, I will see every hole in the fence and every unlocked gate and imprint them in my memory forever. My fear of blocked passages feels very primal, as though I were an animal that has been trapped.

For me, finding these holes and gaps is similar to the way a wary animal surveys new territory to make sure it has safe escape routes and passages, or crosses an open plain that may be full of predators. Will the people try to stop me? Some of the surveying is automatic and unconscious. I'll find the unlocked gate even when I am not looking for it. I can't help but see it. And when I spot an opening, I get a rush of happy excitement. Finding all the holes in the fence also reduces fear. I know I am emotionally safe if I can get through the fence. My fear of blocked passages is one of the few emotions that is so great that it's not fully suppressed by my antidepressant medication.

I had similar fearful reactions when I approached my symbolic doors. I was partly afraid that the door would be locked, like the blocked burrow of a tunneling animal. It was as if an antipredator system deep in my brain was activated. Basic instincts that we share with animals may be triggered by certain stimuli. This idea has been suggested by respected scientists such as Carl Sagan in his book *The Dragons of Eden* and Melvin Konner in *The Tangled Wing*. Judith Rapoport suggests in *The Boy Who Couldn't Stop Washing* that obsessive-compulsive disorders, where people wash their hands for hours or repeatedly check whether the stove is off, may be the result of an activation of old animal instincts for safety and grooming.

The fear of blocked passages persisted in both my visual symbolic world of doors and in the real world long after I stopped using door symbols. In my early days I would find the doors that opened up to the roofs of the highest buildings on the school campus. From a high vantage point I could survey the danger that lurked in the next stage of my life. Emotionally I was like an animal surveying the plains for lions, but symbolically the high place signified striving to find the meaning of life. My intellect was trying to make sense of the world, but it was being driven by an engine of animal fears.

Nearly thirty years ago, when I was navigating my visual symbolic world of doors, I recognized that fear was my great motivator. At that time I didn't realize that other people experience other major emotions. Since fear was my major emotion, it spilled over into all events that had any emotional significance. The following diary entry shows very clearly how I attempted to deal with fear in my symbolic world.

October 4, 1968
I opened the little door and went through tonight. To lift up the door and see the wide expanse of the moonlight roof before me. I have put all my fears anxieties

about other people on the door. Using the trap door is risky because if it were sealed shut I would have no emotional outlet. Intellectually the door is just a symbol but on the emotional level the physical act of opening the door brings on the fears. The act of going through is my overcoming my fears and anxiety towards other people.

The intellectual side of me always knew that making changes in my life would be a challenge, and I deliberately chose symbolic doors to help me get through after the first door almost magically appeared. Sometimes I had massive activation of my sympathetic nervous system—the system that enables an animal or person to flee from danger—when I went through a door. It was like facing a lion. My heart would race and I would sweat profusely. These reactions are now controlled with antidepressant drugs. In conjunction with vast amounts of stored information in my memory, the drugs have enabled me to leave the visual symbolic world behind and venture out into the so-called real world.

Yet, it has only been during the last two or three years that I have discovered that I do not experience the full range of emotions. My first inkling that my emotions were different came in high school, when my roommate swooned over the science teacher. Whatever it was she was feeling, I knew I didn't feel that way toward anyone. But it was years before I realized that other people are guided by their emotions during most social interactions. For me, the proper behavior during all social interactions had to be learned by intellect. I became more skilled at social interactions as I became more experienced. Throughout my life I have been helped by understanding teachers and mentors. People with autism desperately need guides to instruct and educate them so they will survive in the social jungle.

Reading   # Freeing Choices

NANCY MAIRS

A September Sunday morning, still and hot. George and I munch our ritual scones with strawberry jam as we leaf through the *New York Times* and half listen to Weekend Edition on NPR. An interview comes on that I begin to heed more closely: a discussion of the increasingly common practice of using amniocentesis to determine the sex of a fetus, followed by abortion if the parents don't want the sort they've begun. What they generally want, as parents have done from time immemorial, is a boy.

The person being interviewed plainly shares my distaste for sexual selectivity. But the way she articulates it brings me up short. "Sex," she tells her interlocuter emphatically, "is not a birth defect."

"That sort of statement strikes a chill straight through my heart," I say to George, who has begun to listen more closely, too. He looks puzzled for a moment and then responds: "Oh Yes. I can see how it might. I never thought of it that way."

Not very many people would. The implicit argument appears self-evident: the use of abortion to fulfill the desire for a male (or female) child is impermissible, but the same use to prevent an imperfect one is not merely legitimate but, many would argue, socially responsible. As a defective myself, however, I have some doubts.

Although mine was not a birth defect, some evidence suggests a genetic predisposition toward MS, and one day—perhaps even quite soon—this may be detectable. What then? What if, I find myself wondering, such a test had been devised more than half a century ago? Suppose a genetic counselor had said to my mother, "Your baby will be born healthy, and she will probably remain so throughout childhood. But at some point, perhaps in her twenties, she is likely to develop a chronic incurable degenerative disease of the central nervous system. She may go blind. She may not be able to speak. Her bladder and bowels may cease to function normally. She may become incapable of walking or even of moving at all. She could experience tingling, numbness, or intractable pain. In the end, she might have to be fed, bathed, dressed and undressed, turned over in bed, as helpless as an infant." What would Mother have done then? What should she have done?

I don't know. Morally, I feel a lot more confident asking questions than answering them. What I do know, from my own circumstances, is that I am glad Mother never faced the option to "spare" me my fate, as she might have felt obliged to do. I simply cannot say—have never been able to say, even at my most depressed, when I have easily enough wished myself dead—that I wish I had never been born. Nor do I believe that MS has poisoned my existence. Plenty of people find my life unappealing, I know. To be truthful, it doesn't altogether appeal to me. But a good scone with a cup of hot coffee does much to set things right.

I know I am lucky. There are conditions crueler than MS, including many birth defects, and some of these are already detectable by amniocentesis and ultrasound. Suppose—and I'm being far less speculative here than I was in imagining my own mother—that a woman learns that her fetus has spina bifida. The degree of disability may be impossible to predict, but the risks, she is told, include intellectual impairment, bladder and bowel dysfunction, repeated infections, and the inability to walk. Bright, healthy, and active herself, the woman strains to imagine what quality a life thus impaired might possess. Such a child can adapt to her circumstances, of course, and grow into an energetic and resourceful woman like my friend Martha, now in her sixties, married, the moderator of her own radio show.

Even if persuaded of this potentiality, the mother still must decide whether she is emotionally and financially equipped for such an undertaking, with access to medical care and educational programs, reliable assistance from the child's father, a supportive community, a flexible attitude toward surprises and obstacles, and an indefatigable sense of humor. You can't decide that you're in the middle of a great book, and anyway you're sick unto death of the four-hour catheterization schedule, and the kid's bladder can damned well wait a couple of hours till you're more in the mood. Caring for children, even undamaged ones, never ceases, and in our society mothers are customarily expected to provide or arrange it. Much as I admire the mothers of variously disabled children I have known—and much as I believe their extraordinary qualities to derive, at least in part, from the rigors of their lives—I could not blame a woman who chose not to test her mettle in this way.

If I make her appear to be choosing in a social vacuum, I do so because, in a society where the rearing of even a healthy child is not viewed as a community undertaking, where much-touted "family values" are always ascribed to the nuclear and not the human family, the parents of a disabled child will find themselves pretty much on their own. If they are lucky enough to have health insurance, the insurer, whose goal is to maximize shareholders' profits rather than the well-being of patients, is not about to spring for a $7,000 power wheelchair that would enable a child with muscular dystrophy to mingle independently with his classmates on an almost equal "footing," though it might provide $425 for a manual wheelchair to be pushed by an attendant (which it would not pay for). A school system, underfunded by screaming taxpayers, is not likely to procure a Kurtzweil machine that would permit its blind students to "read" their own textbooks. Unless they are wealthy, Mom and Dad do the pushing, the reading, and whatever other extra duties are required, on top of their jobs and their care for any other children in the family.

"Eric and I plan to have only a couple of children," my daughter tells me, contemplating the start of a family. "Why should we expend our resources on a damaged one?" A plausible point, as I have come to expect from this most clearheaded of young women. And in fact, as she knows, her father and I took great care to avoid conceiving another child after her younger brother was born in distress because of Rh incompatibility. After a couple of blood exchanges, he recovered, but we were told that another baby would likely be damaged, perhaps gravely, by the antibodies in my blood. I was no more eager to raise a deformed or retarded child than Anne is. I might have chosen an abortion if contraception had failed.

But then I think of my godson, the product of contraceptive failure, who shares with his sister a possibly unique genetic condition that has caused severe visual impairment in them both. Many seeing people have a dread of blindness so overwhelming that they might well consider abortion if such a defect could be detected (as it could not in this case). But these are otherwise ideal children—healthy, smart, funny, confident, affectionate—and I think they're going to become terrific adults. The problem is that if you eliminate one flaw, you throw out the whole complicated creature, and my world would be a poorer place without Michael and Megan.

Obviously, I don't have an unambiguous answer to this dilemma. I don't think one exists. I do feel certain, in view of the human propensity for exploiting whatever techniques we can devise with virtually no regard for consequences, that more and more people will choose, either for their own reasons or in response to the social pressure not to produce "unnecessary" burdens, to terminate pregnancies so as to avoid birth defects (and to select for sex as well). This development won't eradicate people with disabilities, of course: birth trauma, accidental injury, and disease will continue to create them from those who started out as even the healthiest fetuses. What it will do is to make their social position even more marginal by emphasizing that no one with the power to choose would ever have permitted them to exist. Their own choice to survive will seem suspect. *We're doing everything we can to exterminate your kind*, the social message will read, *and we'd get rid of you too if only we knew how.* No one will ever say this. No one will have to.

This mute message—that one is an accident that ought not to have happened—is communicated again, in the issues surrounding the other end of life, by the current movement to legally protect the "right to die." This phrase always strikes me as a little odd, since the right to do a thing presupposes the option not to do it. Although one's conception and birth are chancy at best (will a sperm reach the egg, and if so, which one? will the egg implant? will the fetus reach viability?), one's death is absolutely not; and legislation in such matters seems wildly inappropriate. Human beings have never been able to leave one another's bodies alone, however, but seem compelled to regulate even their most private moments, and so I suppose it is inevitable that some of them are going to set out to protect one's legal right to do what one can't help doing anyway.

The phrase "right to die" is shorthand, of course, and seems considerably less reductive when spelled out: what is generally being called for by right-to-die advocates is the protection of one's freedom to choose the time and circumstances of one's own death and to receive assistance from willing accomplices if necessary. I am as adamantly pro-choice in this matter as I am with regard to abortion; but as with abortion, the question of "choice" here is vastly more complex than politicians, legislators, and religious fundamentalists make it. Their (self-)delegated task is to reduce the rich ambiguities of life to a set of binaries—us/them, law/transgression, right/wrong. The labels vary but the underlying aim is constant—so that we can all stretch out on the couch every Saturday afternoon in front of some quintessentially binary sports contest rather than on a moral rack. Just as your team wins or loses, you either vote for a candidate or you don't, who upon election either does or does not enact certain promised laws, which you either break or obey, and in the end, depending on the choices made, both you and your representative go to Heaven or to Hell.

For absolutists, the "right to die" issue is as indisputable as abortion: killing oneself, or helping another to die, is murder; although the first act is humanly unpunishable, the second ought to be penalized to the full extent of the law, which, in most states, requires that the perpetrator receive assistance in dying by electrocution, suffocation, or lethal injection. Oh well, "a foolish consistency is the hobgoblin of little minds," and all that. Absolutists come in more than one stripe, however (though such a pluralistic view would be repudiated by absolutists themselves), and some of those who crusade to pass legislation permitting assisted suicide seem just as scarily single-minded as their opponents: Jack Kevorkian, "Dr. Death," the principal figure among them.

My own relationship to suicide renders this an unusually vexed topic for me. I have suffered from clinical depression for several decades now, and although not all depressives become suicidal during an episode, I do. I have tried to kill myself more than once, and the last time I so nearly succeeded, taking an overdose of antidepressant medication, that I am unlikely to fail another time. Thus, I must monitor myself ceaselessly for symptoms that signal a downward spiral in order to seek timely treatment. I have spent a good deal of my life struggling to deny myself the death to which activists would like to guarantee me the right.

To complicate matters, I am as vulnerable as the next person to the ordinary situational depression that surges in response to painful life events. The triggers vary from person to person—a broken friendship, a miscarriage, divorce, the departure of children, even a failed exam or the death of a pet—but almost all of us have endured at least brief periods of sleeplessness, loss of appetite, panic attacks, distractability, or ill-defined malaise following some personal catastrophe. Although my own situation gladdens more than it pains me, it does contain some grimmish elements, especially the threat of my husband's death. And because I am a suicidal depressive, I respond to this threat by wanting to kill myself.

A couple of years ago, George began to experience severe bowel problems, and because his melanoma had last recurred in his small bowel, these strongly suggested a relapse. Although I have always known that this may happen at some point, knowledge is no proof against terror, and I went instantly into a tailspin that very nearly carried me over the precipice of panic into the eternal abyss. I procured twice the amount of the medication that had nearly killed me the last time, and I began to plan: "Some afternoon while George is still teaching, so as to have plenty of time," I wrote in my journal. "Drink a beer to relax. Spread out an underpad to avoid soiling the bed. Lie down on it. That way I can't chicken out—once down, I can't get up again. Put on the white-noise machine. Go to sleep forever." Fortunately, I've been in the depression business long enough now to remain a little skeptical about my urges. "It would be stupid to die for no reason," I noted, "so I suppose I should wait until the tumor has been located." That shred of rationality held me back long enough to learn that this time George had not cancer but an antibiotic-induced colitis, and we have both lived to tell the tale.

My intimacy with self-destructive urges leads me to question the term "rational" suicide, which right-to-die proponents use supposedly to distinguish the death they have in mind from the one I have approached so closely. Suicide appears imperative only when one loses sight of all other alternatives (and there is always at least one other). Since hopelessness is a distinctive symptom of depression, which is an emotional disorder, actions carried out in a despairing state seem to me intrinsically irrational. This last time I clung to some shreds of reason, which saved me.

I also remembered my son-in-law's words during a family discussion of the precarious future, his voice flat and slightly muffled as it can get with strong feeling: "I think it would be very inconsiderate of you to kill yourself." If there's anything that chagrins me, it's acting stupid or inconsiderate. Better I should stay alive.

Seriously, consideration for others is one of the motives often expressed by people who argue for the license to end their own lives: the desire, sometimes quite desperate, not to be a "burden" on others. Perhaps as a legacy of the rugged individualism that fueled colonial settlement, our society has developed a peculiar structure, in which we create small units that, after a certain amount of time, break and expel even smaller fragments who will form their own similarly friable units: children can't wait to escape their parents, who sometimes can't wait to be escaped, and have families of their "own." The parent who becomes more than a peripheral part of the new constellation, especially one who because of incapacity requires a child's assistance, is considered an intrusion.

Shucking the previous generation in this way doesn't appear to have a practical basis. I mean, we hardly live under the conditions that forced the Eskimos to float their aged and ill off on ice floes in order to conserve scarce resources. The hardships entailed in keeping three or even four generations under one roof are, I think, psychological rather than material. And, as our staggering divorce rate makes clear, we are not, as a society, tolerant of the kind of psychological hardship I have in mind, caused by the tensions that inevitably arise between people living in intimacy. Our notion of satisfactory relationships is incurably romantic in the least wholesome sense of the phrase. We are so bombarded in the media by various and garbled messages about intimate interactions—from the pictorial rapture of a perfume advertisement to the pop-psych-speak of experts on television talk shows to horrific newspaper accounts of domestic abuse—that instead of accepting ordinary conflict as one of the fixed, though less agreeable features, of the human condition, we label it "bad," "sick," and damp it down as best we can, sticking the latest Arnold Schwarzenegger movie into the VCR, pouring a drink or popping a Prozac, heading out for a day at the mall, filing for divorce, whatever it takes to disengage from the maddening other. Or we explode, savaging or even killing the source of irritation.

No wonder the presence of another can seem a burden. No wonder some people would rather die than play such a role.

Many years ago, when I first became active in securing low-income housing for my community, I asked a friend from Israel, whose descriptions of various social programs there had impressed me, about housing for the elderly. He looked a little puzzled, and thinking he didn't understand the term, though his English was excellent, I explained the concept.

"Yes, I understand," he said. "We don't have any."

"What do you do with your old people, then?"

"They live with their families."

This notion was hardly foreign to me, since my grandmother had lived with us from the time I was nine; but the idea that an entire society could accept such an arrangement seemed strange indeed. Even though my own experience proved the contrary, I assumed that each generation naturally desired to be quit of the other, except perhaps at holidays, as soon as possible.

The horror of functioning as one of Job's afflictions can be so overwhelming that it obscures the needs and desires of others. That day years back when, panic-stricken at George's impending death, I told my neurologist that I didn't want my children to take care of me because "that's not who I want to be in their lives," Dr. Johnson merely nodded, and we went on to discuss home help, Meals on Wheels, assisted-living arrangements in retirement communities, and other alternatives to the nursing home that evokes dread in just about all of us. I had then, and still have, no idea whether Anne (and now her husband) would consider taking me into their lives, and how burdensome they would find me if they did, but that's just the point: *I have no idea.* Anne was sitting right there, but I blurted what I thought she'd be relieved to hear—that she'd never be saddled with me—without taking the time to ask. At that moment, in the presence of a woman we scarcely knew, both of us distraught over George's illness, we could hardly have delved into the matter. But I could have said, should have said, something open-ended: "I don't know about living with my children. We haven't yet talked about it." Instead, I played Boss Mom, as I have done all too often, decreeing that only what I wanted could be done.

What I wanted—and what I think all of us want who demand the right to die on our own terms—was to maintain a sense of control. Even more than the dread of becoming a burden, helplessness triggers in us a manic terror that things are slipping from our grasp, and I was feeling more impotent than I had ever felt before. A few months earlier, a severe fall had signaled the dreaded end of my walking days. Since then, I had watched George's flesh melt mysteriously away, and now the bony remains huddled like jetsam on a hospital bed, tubes in his arms, his nose, his penis, and nothing I could do would bring him back. These circumstances struck me as intolerable, and I wanted the right to refuse them permanently and irreversibly.

I still do. I want to be the one in charge of my life, including its end, and I want to be able to enlist someone to help me terminate it if I choose "rational" suicide. I have a friend, a doctor whom I admire deeply, who has told me about assisting a patient, irreversibly ill and on a ventilator, to die: listening carefully to the man's clear and repeated requests, calling together his family for their last goodbyes, administering a shot of morphine to ease his passage, turning off the ventilator, remaining with him until he had gone. I would hope to find someone as brave and compassionate if I were to make a similar appeal.

But I would not seek out Dr. Kevorkian or any other crusader for euthanasia, because people who act on principle are likely to sacrifice the individual for the agenda, which is frequently shaped by their own, often deeply buried, presuppositions about what constitutes an acceptable life. Doctors despise disease, or else they wouldn't become doctors, and I have heard of those who couldn't bring themselves to tell a patient she or he had multiple sclerosis because the diagnosis seemed too horrible to bear. Isn't a doctor suffering from this kind of anxiety all too likely to tell me: "You have MS? Of course you want to die! Here, let me write you a prescription so you can peacefully end it all."

In other words, the social construction of disability which makes me uneasy about urging abortion to prevent defective children disturbs me here, too. Behind the view of death as a "right" to be seized and defended lurks the hidden assumption that some lives are not worth living and that damaged creatures may be put out of their misery. True, all kinds of safeguards would be put into place to ensure that only the person doing the dying could make the ultimate decision; but no amount of regulation can eliminate the subtle pressure to end a life perceived by others to be insufferable. If, ideally, I ought never to have been born, and if my dependent existence creates a burden on those who must care for me, then don't I have not merely the right but the obligation to die? How can I honorably choose otherwise?

My purpose in raising questions about abortion and euthanasia is not to condemn these procedures, which I believe ought to be freely available, in strict privacy, to any fully informed person who elects them. In fact, I would educate doctors more, and regulate them less, so that they and their patients could explore options, reach decisions, and take action without intrusion. My concern is that these issues be confronted in such a way as to create a social climate in which people with disabilities perceive life to be an honorable choice. And that means sending the social message that disabled people are valued and valuable, precious even, by investing, financially and emotionally, in institutions and practices that help them out.

Everybody, well or ill, disabled or not, imagines a boundary of suffering and loss beyond which, she or he is certain, life will no longer be worth living. I know that I do. I also know that my line, far from being scored in stone, has inched across the sands of my life: at various times, I could not possibly do without long walks on the beach or rambles through the woods; use a cane, a brace, a wheelchair; stop teaching; give up driving; let someone else put on and take off my underwear. One at a time, with the encouragement of others, I have taken each of these (highly figurative) steps. Now I believe my limit to lie at George's death, but I am prepared to let it move if it will. When I reach the wall, I think I'll know. Meanwhile, I go on being, now more than ever, the woman I once thought I could never bear to be.

I cannot excuse or condemn those women with MS, less crippled than I, who sought out Dr. Kevorkian's services. They had their lines. They may have lacked adequate support: familial, medical, psychological, spiritual. I can, however, defend the human right to choose actions that the nondisabled find unfathomable and perhaps even indecent. If a woman, upon learning that her fetus has spina bifida, may choose abortion, then she ought also to feel free to decide, without apology, to bear and rear the child, certain that she will have the same access to medical care and educational programs that a nondisabled child enjoys. If, after consulting with family, spiritual counselors, and medical personnel, a diabetic with gangrenous legs may ask for an easeful death, he should also be fully supported in his decision to live on as an amputee, confident that he can continue to work, shop, attend church, take his wife out for dinner and a movie, just as he has always done. Only in a society that respects, and enables, these choices are atrocities against the disabled truly unthinkable.

"But provisions for these people cost *money*," fiscal conservatives squeal, "and why should *I* pay for someone else's misfortune?" Because that's what human beings do: take care of one another. "But we can't *afford* it." In my experience, this argument is most commonly made by those who mean they can't afford both high taxes or charitable donations and membership in the country club or a winter home in Florida, but never mind. The perception of scarcity is highly subjective and if you believe yourself on the doorsill of the poorhouse, nothing I say can comfort your fears (though, as Thomas Friedman once pointed out in an editorial in the *New York Times,* a short trip to Africa might have a salutory effect).

Let me point out, instead, being something of a fiscal conservative myself, that we're not talking huge amounts here, nothing like the billions squandered on Star Wars and the B-2 stealth bomber, which plenty of people believed we could afford. If the money is spent wisely, it will constitute not a drain but an investment. Thousands of people with disabilities are already productive citizens; with adequate funds for medical care and research into preventable and treatable conditions, education, structural modifications, and adaptive equipment, we can create thousands more. They will support themselves! They will pay taxes! They will make charitable donations! Their potential contributions to culture are impossible to gauge. (Alexander Pope and Toulouse-Lautrec were hunchbacks, after all; Milton went blind; Beethoven, deaf, and so on, and so on. We can ill afford to kill off our geniuses, and every live birth holds such promise.) They will weave into the social fabric important strands of tenacity, patience, and ingenuity. We will all be glad they were born, I think. We will be glad they chose to live on.

Reading   # Falling into Life

LEONARD KRIEGEL

It is not the actual death a man is doomed to die but the deaths his imagination anticipates that claim attention as he grows older. We are constantly being reminded that the prospect of death forcefully concentrates the mind. While that may be so, it is not a prospect that does very much else for the imagination—other than to make us aware of its limitations and imbalances.

Over the past five years, as I have moved into the solidity of middle age, my own most formidable imaginative limitation has turned out to be a surprising need for symmetry. I am possessed by a peculiar passion: I want to believe that my life has been balanced out. And because I once had to learn to fall in order to keep that life mine, I now seem to have convinced myself that I must also learn to fall into death.

Falling into life wasn't easy, and I suspect that is why I hunger for such awkward symmetry today. Having lost the use of my legs during the polio epidemic that swept across the eastern United States during the summer of 1944, I was soon immersed in a process of rehabilitation that was, at least when looked at in retrospect, as much spiritual as physical.

That was a full decade before the discovery of the Salk vaccine ended polio's reign as the disease most dreaded by America's parents and their children. Treatment of the disease had been standardized by 1944: following the initial onslaught of the virus, patients were kept in isolation for a period of ten days to two weeks. Following that, orthodox medical opinion was content to subject patients to as much heat as they could stand. Stiff, paralyzed limbs were swathed in heated, coarse woolen towels known as "hot packs." (The towels were the same greenish brown as the blankets issued to American GIs, and they reinforced a boy's sense of being at war.) As soon as the hot packs had baked enough pain and stiffness out of a patient's body that he could be moved on and off a stretcher, the treatment was ended, and the patient faced a series of daily immersions in a heated pool.

I was ultimately to spend two full years at the appropriately named New York State Reconstruction Home in West Haverstraw. But what I remember most vividly about my stay there was, in the first three months, being submerged in a hot pool six times a day for periods of between fifteen and twenty minutes. I would lie on a stainless steel slab, only my face out of the water, while the wet heat rolled against my dead legs and the physical therapist at my side worked at a series of manipulations intended to bring my useless muscles back to health.

Each immersion was a baptism by fire in the water. While my mind pitched and reeled with memories of the "normal" boy I had been a few weeks earlier, I would close my eyes and focus not, as my therapist urged, on bringing dead legs back to life but on my strange fall from the childhood grace of the physical. Like all eleven-year-old boys, I had a spent a good deal of time thinking about my body. Before the attack of the virus, however, I thought about it only in connection with my own lunge toward adolescence. Never before had my body seemed an object in itself. Now it was. And like the twenty-one other boys in the ward— all of us between the ages of nine and twelve—I sensed I would never move beyond that fall from grace, even as I played with memories of the way I once had been.

Each time I was removed from the hot water and placed on a stretcher by the side of the pool, there to await the next immersion, I was fed salt tablets. These were simply intended to make up for the sweat we lost, but salt tablets seemed to me the cruelest confirmation of my new status as spiritual debtor. Even today, more than four decades later, I still shiver at the mere thought of those salt tablets. Sometimes the hospital orderly would literally have to pry my mouth open to force me to swallow them. I dreaded the nausea the taste of salt inspired in me. Each time I was resubmerged in the hot pool, I would grit my teeth—not from the flush of heat sweeping over my body but from the thought of what I would have to face when I would again be taken out of the water. To be an eater of salt was far more humiliating than to endure pain. Nor was I alone in feeling this way. After lights-out had quieted the ward, we boys would furtively whisper from cubicle to cubicle of how we dreaded being forced to swallow salt tablets. It was that, rather than the pain we endured, that anchored our sense of loss and dread.

Any recovery of muscle use in a polio patient usually took place within three months of the disease's onset. We all knew that. But as time passed, every boy in the ward learned to recite stories of those who, like Lazarus, had witnessed their own bodily resurrection. Having fallen from physical grace, we also chose to fall away from the reality in front of us. Our therapists were skilled and dedicated, but they weren't wonder-working saints. Paralyzed legs and arms rarely responded to their manipulations. We could not admit to ourselves, or to them, that we were permanently crippled. But each of us knew without knowing that his future was tied to the body that floated on the stainless steel slab.

We sweated out the hot pool and we choked on the salt tablets, and through it all we looked forward to the promise of rehabilitation. For, once the stiffness and pain had been baked and boiled out of us, we would no longer be eaters of salt. We would not be what we once had been, but at least we would be candidates for reentry into the world, admittedly made over to face its demands encased in leather and steel.

I suppose we might have been told that our fall from grace was permanent. But I am still grateful that no one—neither doctors nor nurses nor therapists, not even that sadistic orderly, himself a former polio patient, who limped through our lives and through our pain like some vengeful presence—told me that my chances of regaining the use of my legs were nonexistent. Like every other boy in the ward, I organized my needs around whatever illusions were available. And the illusion I needed above any other was that one morning I would simply wake up and rediscover the "normal" boy of memory, once again playing baseball in French Charley's Field in Bronx Park rather than roaming the fields of his own imagination. At the age of eleven, I needed to weather reality, not face it. And to this very day I silently thank those who were concerned enough about me, or indifferent enough to my fate, not to tell me what they knew.

Like most boys, sick or well, I was an adaptable creature—and rehabilitation demanded adaptability. The fall from bodily grace transformed each of us into an acolyte of the possible, a pragmatic American for whom survival was method and strategy. We would learn, during our days in the New York State Reconstruction Home, to confront the world that was. We would learn to survive the way we were, with whatever the virus had left intact.

I had fallen away from the body's prowess, but I was being led toward a life measured by different standards. Even as I fantasized about the past, it disappeared. Rehabilitation, I was to learn, was ahistorical, a future devoid of any significant claim on the past. Rehabilitation was a thief's primer of compensation and deception: its purpose was to teach one how to steal a touch of the normal from an existence that would be striking in its abnormality.

When I think back to those two years in the ward, the boy who made his rehabilitation most memorable was Joey Tomashevski. Joey was the son of an upstate dairy farmer, a Polish immigrant who had come to America before the Depression and whose English was even poorer than the English of my own *shtetl*-bred father. The virus had left both of Joey's arms so lifeless and atrophied that with pinky and thumb I could circle where his bicep should have been and still stick the forefinger of my other hand through. And yet Joey assumed that he would make do with whatever had been left him. He accepted without question the task of making his toes and feet into fingers and hands. With lifeless arms encased in a canvas sling that looked like the breadbasket a European peasant might carry to market, Joey would sit up in bed and demonstrate how he could maneuver fork and spoon with his toes.

I would never have dreamed of placing such confidence in my fingers, let alone my toes. I found, as most of the other boys in the ward did, Joey's unabashed pride in the flexibility and control with which he could maneuver a forkful of mashed potatoes into his mouth a continuous indictment of my sense of the world's natural order. We boys with dead legs would gather round his bed in our wheelchairs and silently watch Joey display his dexterity with a vanity so open and naked that it seemed an invitation to being struck down yet again. But Joey's was a vanity already tested by experience. For he was more than willing to accept whatever challenges the virus threw his way. For the sake of demonstrating his skill to us, he kicked a basketball from the auditorium stage through the hoop attached to a balcony some fifty feet away. When one of our number derisively called him "lucky," he proceeded to kick five of seven more balls through that same hoop.

I suspect that Joey's pride in his ability to compensate for what had been taken away from him irritated me because I knew that, before I could pursue my own rehabilitation with such singular passion, I had to surrender myself to what was being demanded of me. And that meant I had to learn to fall. It meant that I had to learn, as Joey Tomashevski had already learned, how to transform absence into opportunity. Even though I still lacked Joey's instinctive willingness to live with the legacy of the virus, I found myself being overhauled, recreated in much the same way as a car engine is rebuilt. Nine months after I arrived in the ward, a few weeks before my twelfth birthday, I was fitted for double long-legged braces bound together by a steel pelvic band circling my waist. Lifeless or not, my legs were precisely measured, the steel carefully molded to form, screws and locks and leather joined to one another for my customized benefit. It was technology that would hold me up—another offering on the altar of compensation. "You get what you give," said Jackie Lyons, my closest friend in the ward. For he, too, was now a novitiate of the possible. He, too, now had to learn how to choose the road back.

Falling into life was not a metaphor; it was real, a process learned only through doing, the way a baby learns to crawl, to stand, and then to walk. After the steel bands around calves and thighs and pelvis had been covered over by the rich-smelling leather, after the braces had been precisely fitted to allow my fear-ridden imagination the surety of their holding presence, I was pulled to my feet. For the first time in ten months, I stood. Two middle-aged craftsmen, the hospital bracemakers who worked in a machine shop deep in the basement, held me in place as my therapist wedged two wooden crutches beneath my shoulders.

They stepped back, first making certain that my grip on the crutches was firm. Filled with pride in their technological prowess, the three of them stood in front of me, admiring their skill. Had I been created in the laboratory of Mary Shelley's Dr. Frankenstein, I could not have felt myself any more the creature of scientific pride. I stood on the braces, crutches beneath my shoulders slanting outward like twin towers of Pisa. I flushed, swallowed hard, struggled to keep from crying, struggled not to be overwhelmed by my fear of falling.

My future had arrived. The leather had been fitted, the screws had been turned to the precise millimeter, the locks at the knees and the bushings at the ankles had been properly tested and retested. That very afternoon I was taken for the first time to a cavernous room filled with barbells and Indian clubs and crutches and walkers. I would spend an hour each day there for the next six months. In the rehab room I would learn how to mount two large wooden steps made to the exact measure of a New York City bus's. I would swing on parallel bars from one side to the other, my arms learning how they would have to hurl me through the world. I balanced Indian clubs like a circus juggler because my therapist insisted it would help my coordination. And I was expected to learn to fall.

I was a dutiful patient. I did as I was told, because I could see no advantage to doing anything else. I hungered for the approval of those in authority—doctors, nurses, therapists, the two brace-makers. Again and again, my therapist demonstrated how I was to throw my legs from the hip. Again and again, I did as I was told. Grabbing the banister with my left hand, I threw my leg from the hip while pushing off my right crutch. Like some baby elephant (despite the sweat lost in the heated pool, the months of inactivity in bed had fattened me up considerably), I dangled from side to side on the parallel bars. Grunting with effort, I did everything demanded of me. I did it with an unabashed eagerness to please those who had power over my life. I wanted to put myself at risk. I wanted to do whatever was supposed to be "good" for me. I believed as absolutely as I have ever believed in anything that rehabilitation would finally placate the hunger of the virus.

But when my therapist commanded me to fall, I cringed. The prospect of falling terrified me. Every afternoon, as I worked through my prescribed activities, I prayed that I would be able to fall when the session ended. Falling was the most essential "good" of all the "goods" held out for my consideration by my therapist. I believed that. I believed it so intensely that the belief itself was painful. Everything else asked of me was given, and given gladly. I mounted the bus stairs, pushed across the parallel bars until my arms ached with the effort, allowed the medicine ball to pummel me, flailed away at the empty air with my fists because my therapist wanted me to rid myself of the tension within. The slightest sign of approval from those in authority was enough to make me puff with pleasure. Other boys in the ward might not have taken rehabilitation seriously, but I was an eager servant cringing before the promise of approval.

Only I couldn't fall. As each session ended, I would be led to the mats that took up a full third of the huge room. "It's time," the therapist would say. Dutifully, I would follow her, step after step. Just as dutifully, I would stand on the edge of those two-inch-thick mats, staring down at them until I could feel my body quiver.

"All you have to do is let go," my therapist assured me. "The other boys do it. Just let go and fall."

But the prospect of letting go was precisely what terrified me. That the other boys in the ward had no trouble in falling added to my shame and terror. I didn't need my therapist to tell me the two-inch-thick mats would keep me from hurting myself. I knew there was virtually no chance of injury when I fell, but that knowledge simply made me more ashamed of a cowardice that was as monumental as it was unexplainable. Had it been able to rid me of my sense of my own cowardice, I would happily have settled for bodily harm. But I was being asked to surrender myself to the emptiness of space, to let go and crash down to the mats below, to feel myself suspended in air when nothing stood between me and the vacuum of the world. *That* was the prospect that overwhelmed me. *That* was what left me sweating with rage and humiliation. The contempt I felt was for my own weakness.

I tried to justify what I sensed could never be justified. Why should I be expected to throw myself into emptiness? Was this sullen terror the price of compensation, the badge of normality? Maybe my refusal to fall embodied some deeper thrust than I could then understand. Maybe I had unconsciously seized upon some fundamental resistance to the forces that threatened to overwhelm me. What did it matter that the ground was covered with the thick mats? The tremors I feared were in my heart and soul.

Shame plagued me—and shame is the older brother to disease. Flushing with shame, I would stare down at the mats. I could feel myself wanting to cry out. But I shriveled at the thought of calling more attention to my cowardice. I would finally hear myself whimper, "I'm sorry. But I can't. I can't let go."

Formless emptiness. A rush of air through which I would plummet toward obliteration. As my "normal" past grew more and more distant, I reached for it more and more desperately, recalling it like some movie whose plot has long since been forgotten but whose scenes continue to comfort through images disconnected from anything but themselves. I remembered that there had been a time when the prospect of falling evoked not terror but joy: football games on the rain-softened autumn turf of Mosholu Parkway, belly-flopping on an American Flyer down its snow-covered slopes in winter, rolling with a pack of friends down one of the steep hills in Bronx Park. Free-falls from the past, testifying not to a loss of the self but to an absence of barriers.

My therapist pleaded, ridiculed, cajoled, threatened, bullied. I was sighed over and railed at. But I couldn't let go and fall. I couldn't sell my terror off so cheaply. Ashamed as I was, I wouldn't allow myself to be bullied out of terror.

A month passed—a month of struggle between me and my therapist. Daily excursions to the rehab room, daily practice runs through the future that was awaiting me. The daily humiliation of discovering that one's own fear had been transformed into a public issue, a subject of discussion among the other boys in the ward, seemed unending.

And then terror simply evaporated. It was as if I had served enough time in that prison. I was ready to move on. One Tuesday afternoon, as my session ended, the therapist walked resignedly alongside me toward the mats. "All right. Leonard. It's time again. All you have to do is let go and fall." Again I stood above the mats. Only this time it was as if something beyond my control or understanding had decided to let my body's fall from grace take me down for good. I was not seized by the usual paroxysm of fear. I didn't feel myself break out in a terrified sweat. It was over.

I don't mean that I suddenly felt myself spring into courage. That wasn't what happened at all. The truth was I had simply been worn down into letting go, like a boxer in whose eyes one recognizes not the flicker of defeat—that issue never having been in doubt—but the acceptance of defeat. Letting go no longer held my imagination captive. I found myself quite suddenly faced with a necessary fall—a fall into life.

So it was that I stood above the mat and heard myself sigh and then felt myself let go, dropping through the quiet air, crutches slipping off to the sides. What I didn't feel this time was the threat of my body slipping into emptiness, so mummified by the terror before it that the touch of air preempted even death. I dropped. I did not crash. I dropped. I did not collapse. I dropped. I did not plummet. I felt myself enveloped by a curiously gentle moment in my life. In that sliver of time before I hit the mat, I was kissed by space.

My body absorbed the slight shock and I rolled onto my back, braced legs swinging like unguided missiles into the free air, crutches dropping away to the sides. Even as I fell through the air, I could sense the shame and fear drain from my soul, and I knew that my sense of my own cowardice would soon follow. In falling, I had given myself a new start, a new life.

"That's it!" my therapist shouted triumphantly. "You let go! And there it is!"

You let go! And there it is! Yes, and you discover not terror but the only self you are going to be allowed to claim anyhow. You fall free, and then you learn that those padded mats hold not courage but the unclaimed self. And if it turned out to be not the most difficult of tasks, did that make my sense of jubilation any less?

From that moment, I gloried in my ability to fall. Falling became an end in itself. I lost sight of what my therapist had desperately been trying to demonstrate for me—that there was a purpose in learning how to fall. She wanted to teach me through the fall what I would have to face in the future. She wanted to give me a wholeness I could not give myself. For she knew that mine would be a future so different from what confronts the "normal" that I had to learn to fall into life in order not to be overwhelmed.

From that day, she urged me to practice falling as if I were a religious disciple being urged by a master to practice spiritual discipline. Letting go meant allowing my body to float into space, to turn at the direction of the fall and follow the urgings of emptiness. For her, learning to fall was learning that most essential of American lessons: How to turn incapacity into capacity.

"You were afraid of hurting yourself," she explained to me. "But that's the beauty of it. When you let go, you can't hurt yourself."

An echo of the streets and playgrounds I called home until I met the virus. American slogans: Go with the flow, roll with the punch, slide with the threat until it is no longer a threat. They were simple slogans, and they were all intended to create strength from weakness, a veritable world's fair of compensation.

I returned to the city a year later. By that time I was a willing convert, one who now secretly enjoyed demonstrating his ability to fall. I enjoyed the surprise that would greet me as I got to my feet, unscathed. However perverse it may seem, I felt a certain pleasure when, as I walked with a friend, I felt a crutch slip out of my grasp. Watching the thrust of concern darken his features, I felt myself in control of my own capacity. For falling had become the way my body sought out its proper home. It was an earthbound body, and mine would be an earthbound life. My quest would be for the solid ground beneath me. Falling with confidence, I fell away from terror and fear.

Of course, some falls took me unawares, and I found myself letting go too late or too early. Bruised in ego and sometimes in body, I would pull myself to my feet to consider what had gone wrong. Yet I was essentially untroubled. Such defeats were part of the game, even when they confined me to bed for a day or two afterward. I was an accountant of pain, and sometimes heavier payment was demanded. In my mid-thirties, I walked my two-year-old son's babysitter home, tripped on the curbstone, and broke my wrist. At forty-eight, an awkward fall triggered by a carelessly unlocked brace sent me smashing against the bathtub and into surgery for a broken femur. It took four months for me to learn to walk with the crutches all over again. But I learned. I already knew how to fall.

I knew such accidents could be handled. After all, pain was not synonymous with mortality. In fact, pain was insurance against an excessive consciousness of mortality. Pain might validate the specific moment in time, but it didn't have much to do with the future. I did not yet believe that falling into life had anything to do with falling into death. It was simply a way for me to exercise control over my own existence.

It seems to me today that when I first let my body fall to those mats, I was somehow giving myself the endurance I would need to survive in this world. In a curious way, falling became a way of celebrating what I had lost. My legs were lifeless, useless, but their loss had created a dancing image in whose shadowy gyrations I recognized a strange but potentially interesting new self. I would survive. I knew that now. I could let go, I could fall, and, best of all, I could get up.

To create an independent self, a man had to rid himself both of the myths that nurtured him and the myths that held him back. Learning to fall had been the first lesson in how I yet might live successfully as a cripple. Even disease had its inviolate principles. I understood that the most dangerous threat to the sense of self I needed was an inflated belief in my own capacity. Falling rid a man of excess baggage; it taught him how each of us is dependent on balance.

But what really gave falling legitimacy was the knowledge that I could get to my feet again. That was what made letting go a fall into life. That was what taught me the rules of survival. As long as I could pick myself up and stand on my own two feet, bracebound and crutch-propped as I was, the fall testified to my ability to live in the here and now, to stake my claim as an American who had turned incapacity into capacity. For such a man, falling might well be considered the language of everyday achievement.

But the day came, as I knew it must come, when I could no longer pick myself up. It was then that my passion for symmetry in endings began. On that day, spurred on by another fall, I found myself spinning into the inevitable future.

The day was actually a rainy night in November of 1983. I had just finished teaching at the City College Center for Worker Education, an off-campus degree program for working adults, and had joined some friends for dinner. All of us, I remember, were in a jovial, celebratory mood, although I no longer remember what it was we were celebrating. Perhaps it was simply the satisfaction of being good friends and colleagues at dinner together.

We ate in a Spanish restaurant on 14th Street in Manhattan. It was a dinner that took on, for me at least, the intensity of a time that would assume greater and greater significance as I grew older, one of those watershed moments writers are so fond of. In the dark, rainswept New York night, change and possibility seemed to drift like a thick fog all around us.

Our mood was still convivial when we left the restaurant around eleven o'clock. The rain had slackened off to a soft drizzle and the streetlights glistened on the wet black creosote. At night, rain in the city has a way of transforming proportion into optimism. The five of us stood around on the slicked-down sidewalk, none of us willing to be the first to break the richness of the mood by leaving.

Suddenly the crutch in my left hand began to slip out from under me, slowly, almost deliberately, as if the crutch had a mind of its own and had not yet made the commitment that would send me down. I had apparently hit a slick patch of city sidewalk, some nub of concrete worn smooth as medieval stone by thousands of shoppers and panhandlers and tourists and students who daily pounded the bargain hustlings of 14th Street.

Instinctively, I at first tried to fight the fall, to seek for balance by pushing off from the crutch in my right hand. But as I recognized that the fall was inevitable, I simply went slack—and for the thousandth time my body sought vindication in its ability to let go and drop. These good friends had seen me fall before. They knew my childish vanities, understood that I still thought of falling as a way to demonstrate my control of the traps and uncertainties that lay in wait for us all.

Thirty-eight years earlier, I had discovered that I could fall into life simply by letting go. Now I made a different discovery—that I could no longer get to my feet by myself. I hit the wet ground and quickly turned over and pushed up, trying to use one of the crutches as a prop to boost myself to my feet, as I had been taught to do as a boy of twelve.

But try as hard as I could, I couldn't get to my feet. It wasn't that I lacked physical strength. I knew that my arms were as powerful as ever as I pushed down on the wet concrete. It had nothing to do with the fact that the street was wet, as my friends insisted later. No, it had to do with a subtle, mysterious change in my own sense of rhythm and balance. My body had decided—*and decided on its own, autonomously*—that the moment had come for me to face the question of endings. It was the body that chose its time of recognition.

It was, it seems to me now, a distinctively American moment. It left me pondering limitations and endings and summations. It left me with the curiously buoyant sense that mortality had quite suddenly made itself a felt presence rather than the rhetorical strategy used by the poets and novelists I taught to my students. This was what writers had in mind when they spoke of the truly common fate, this sense of ending coming to one unbidden. This had brought with it my impassioned quest for symmetry. As I lay on the wet ground—no more than a minute or two—all I could think of was how much I wanted my life to balance out. It was as if I were staring into a future in which time itself had evaporated.

Here was a clear, simple perception, and there was nothing mystical about it. There are limitations we recognize and those that recognize us. My friends, who had been standing around nervously while I tried to get to my feet, finally asked if they could help me up. "You'll have to," I said. "I can't get up any other way."

Two of them pulled me to my feet while another jammed the crutches beneath my arms, as the therapist and the two brace-makers had done almost four decades earlier. When I was standing, they proceeded to joke about my sudden incapacity in that age-old way men of all ages have, as if words might codify loss and change and time's betrayal. I joined in the joking. But what I really wanted was to go home and contemplate this latest fall, in the privacy of my apartment. The implications were clear: I would never again be an eater of salt; I would also never again get to my feet on my own. A part of my life had ended. But that didn't depress me. In fact, I felt almost as exhilarated as I had thirty-eight years earlier, when my body surrendered to the need to let go and I fell into life.

Almost four years have passed since I fell on the wet sidewalk of 14th Street. I suppose it wasn't a particularly memorable fall. It wasn't even particularly significant to anyone who had not once fallen into life. But it was inevitable, the first time I had let go into a time when it would no longer even be necessary to let go.

It was a fall that left me with the knowledge that I could longer pick myself up. That meant I now needed the help of others as I had not needed their help before. It was a fall that left me burning with this strange passion for symmetry, this desire to balance my existence out. When the day comes, I want to be able to fall into my death as nakedly as I once had to fall into my life.

Do not misunderstand me. I am not seeking a way out of mortality, for I believe in nothing more strongly than I believe in the permanency of endings. I am not looking for a way out of this life, a life I continue to find immensely enjoyable—even if I can no longer pull myself to my own two feet. Of course, a good deal in my life has changed. For one thing, I am increasingly impatient with those who claim to have no use for endings of any sort. I am also increasingly embarrassed by the thought of the harshly critical adolescent I was, self-righteously convinced that the only way for a man to go to his end was kicking and screaming.

But these are, I suppose, the kinds of changes any man or woman of forty or fifty would feel. Middle-aged skepticism is as natural as adolescent acne. In my clearer, less passionate moments I can even laugh at my need for symmetry in beginnings and endings as well as my desire to see my own eventual death as a line running parallel to my life. Even in mathematics, let alone life, symmetry is sometimes too neat, too closed off from the way things actually work. After all, it took me a full month before I could bring myself to let go and fall into life.

I no longer talk about how to seize a doctrine of compensation from disease. I don't talk about it, but it still haunts me. In my heart, I believe it offers the only philosophy by which anyone can actually live. It is the only philosophy that strips away both spiritual mumbo jumbo and the procrustean weight of existential anxiety. In the final analysis, a man really is what he does.

Believing as I do, I wonder why I so often find myself trying to frame a perspective that will prove adequate to a proper sense of ending. Perhaps that is why I find myself sitting in a bar with a friend, trying to explain to him all I have learned from falling.

"There must be a time," I hear myself tell him, "when a man has the right to stop thinking about falling."

"Sure," my friend laughs. "Four seconds before he dies."

Reading   # Lullaby

LESLIE MARMON SILKO

The sun had gone down but the snow in the wind gave off its own light. It came in thick tufts like new wool—washed before the weaver spins it. Ayah reached out for it like her own babies had, and she smiled when she remembered how she had laughed at them. She was an old woman now, and her life had become memories. She sat down with her back against the wide cottonwood tree, feeling the rough bark on her back bones; she faced east and listened to the wind and snow sing a high-pitched Yeibechei song. Out of the wind she felt warmer, and she could watch the wide fluffy snow fill in her tracks, steadily, until the direction she had come from was gone. By the light of the snow she could see the dark outline of the big arroyo a few feet away. She was sitting on the edge of Cebolleta Creek, where in the springtime the thin cows would graze on grass already chewed flat to the ground. In the wide deep creek bed where only a trickle of water flowed in the summer, the skinny cows would wander, looking for new grass along winding paths splashed with manure.

Ayah pulled the old Army blanket over her head like a shawl. Jimmie's blanket—the one he had sent to her. That was a long time ago and the green wool was faded, and it was unraveling on the edges. She did not want to think about Jimmie. So she thought about the weaving and the way her mother had done it. On the tall wooden loom set into the sand under a tamarack tree for shade. She could see it clearly. She had been only a little girl when her grandma gave her the wooden combs to pull the twigs and burrs from the raw, freshly washed wool. And while she combed the wool, her grandma sat beside her, spinning a silvery strand of yarn around the smooth cedar spindle. Her mother worked at the loom with yarns dyed bright yellow and red and gold. She watched them dye the yarn in boiling black pots full of beeweed petals, juniper berries, and sage. The blankets her mother made were soft and woven so tight that rain rolled off them like birds' feathers. Ayah remembered sleeping warm on cold windy nights, wrapped in her mother's blankets on the hogan's sandy floor.

The snow drifted now, with the northwest wind hurling it in gusts. It drifted up around her black overshoes—old ones with little metal buckles. She smiled at the snow which was trying to cover her little by little. She could remember when they had no black rubber overshoes; only the high buckskin leggings that they wrapped over their elkhide moccasins. If the snow was dry or frozen, a person could walk all day and not get wet; and in the evenings the beams of the ceiling would hang with lengths of pale buckskin leggings, drying out slowly.

She felt peaceful remembering. She didn't feel cold any more. Jimmie's blanket seemed warmer than it had ever been. And she could remember the morning he was born. She could remember whispering to her mother, who was sleeping on the other side of the hogan, to tell her it was time now. She did not want to wake the others. The second time she called to her, her mother stood up and pulled on her shoes; she knew. They walked to the old stone hogan together, Ayah walking a step behind her mother. She waited alone, learning the rhythms of the pains while her mother went to call the old woman to help them. The morning was already warm even before dawn and Ayah smelled the bee flowers blooming and the young willow growing at the springs. She could remember that so clearly, but his birth merged into the births of the other children and to her it became all the same birth. They named him for the summer morning and in English they called him Jimmie.

It wasn't like Jimmie died. He just never came back, and one day a dark blue sedan with white writing on its doors pulled up in front of the boxcar shack where the rancher let the Indians live. A man in a khaki uniform trimmed in gold gave them a yellow piece of paper and told them that Jimmie was dead. He said the Army would try to get the body back and then it would be shipped to them; but it wasn't likely because the helicopter had burned after it crashed. All of this was told to Chato because he could understand English. She stood inside the doorway holding the baby while Chato listened. Chato spoke English like a white man and he spoke Spanish too. He was taller than the white man and he stood straighter too. Chato didn't explain why; he just told the military man they could keep the body if they found it. The white man looked bewildered; he nodded his head and he left. Then Chato looked at her and shook his head, and then he told her, "Jimmie isn't coming home anymore," and when he spoke, he used the words to speak of the dead. She didn't cry then, but she hurt inside with anger. And she mourned him as the years passed, when a horse fell with Chato and broke his leg, and the white rancher told them he wouldn't pay Chato until he could work again. She mourned Jimmie because he would have worked for his father then; he would have saddled the big bay horse and ridden the fence lines each day, with wire cutters and heavy gloves, fixing the breaks in the barbed wire and putting the stray cattle back inside again.

She mourned him after the white doctors came to take Danny and Ella away. She was at the shack alone that day they came. It was back in the days before they hired Navajo women to go with them as interpreters. She recognized one of the doctors. She had seen him at the children's clinic at Cañoncito about a month ago. They were wearing khaki uniforms and they waved papers at her and a black ball-point pen, trying to make her understand their English words. She was frightened by the way they looked at the children, like the lizard watches the fly. Danny was swinging on the tire swing on the elm tree behind the rancher's house, and Ella was toddling around the front door, dragging the broomstick horse Chato made for her. Ayah could see they wanted her to sign the papers, and Chato had taught her to sign her name. It was something she was proud of. She only wanted them to go, and to take their eyes away from her children.

She took the pen from the man without looking at his face and she signed the papers in three different places he pointed to. She stared at the ground by their feet and waited for them to leave. But they stood there and began to point and gesture at the children. Danny stopped swinging. Ayah could see his fear. She moved suddenly and grabbed Ella into her arms; the child squirmed, trying to get back to her toys. Ayah ran with the baby toward Danny; she screamed for him to run and then she grabbed him around his chest and carried him too. She ran south into the foothills of juniper trees and black lava rock. Behind her she heard the doctors running, but they had been taken by surprise, and as the hills became steeper and the cholla cactus were thicker, they stopped. When she reached the top of the hill, she stopped to listen in case they were circling around her. But in a few minutes she heard a car engine start and they drove away. The children had been too surprised to cry while she ran with them. Danny was shaking and Ella's little fingers were gripping Ayah's blouse.

She stayed up in the hills for the rest of the day, sitting on a black lava boulder in the sunshine where she could see for miles all around her. The sky was light blue and cloudless, and it was warm for late April. The sun warmth relaxed her and took the fear and anger away. She lay back on the rock and watched the sky. It seemed to her that she could walk into the sky, stepping through clouds endlessly. Danny played with little pebbles and stones, pretending they were birds eggs and then little rabbits. Ella sat at her feet and dropped fistfuls of dirt into the breeze, watching the dust and particles of sand intently. Ayah watched a hawk soar high above them, dark wings gliding; hunting or only watching, she did not know. The hawk was patient and he circled all afternoon before he disappeared around the high volcanic peak the Mexicans called Guadalupe.

Late in the afternoon, Ayah looked down at the gray boxcar shack with the paint all peeled from the wood; the stove pipe on the roof was rusted and crooked. The fire she had built that morning in the oil drum stove had burned out. Ella was asleep in her lap now and Danny sat close to her, complaining that he was hungry; he asked when they would go to the house. "We will stay up here until your father comes," she told him, "because those white men were chasing us." The boy remembered then and he nodded at her silently.

If Jimmie had been there he could have read those papers and explained to her what they said. Ayah would have known then, never to sign them. The doctors came back the next day and they brought a BIA policeman with them. They told Chato they had her signature and that was all they needed. Except for the kids. She listened to Chato sullenly; she hated him when he told her it was the old woman who died in the winter, spitting blood; it was her old grandma who had given the children this disease. "They don't spit blood," she said coldly. "The whites lie." She held Ella and Danny close to her, ready to run to the hills again. "I want a medicine man first," she said to Chato, not looking at him. He shook his head. "It's too late now. The policeman is with them. You signed the paper." His voice was gentle.

It was worse than if they had died: to lose the children and to know that somewhere, in a place called Colorado, in a place full of sick and dying strangers, her children were without her. There had been babies that died soon after they were born, and one that died before he could walk. She had carried them herself, up to the boulders and great pieces of the cliff that long ago crashed down from Long Mesa; she laid them in the crevices of sandstone and buried them in fine brown sand with round quartz pebbles that washed down the hills in the rain. She had endured it because they had been with her. But she could not bear this pain. She did not sleep for a long time after they took her children. She stayed on the hill where they had fled the first time, and she slept rolled up in the blanket Jimmie had sent her. She carried the pain in her belly and it was fed by everything she saw: the blue sky of their last day together and the dust and pebbles they played with; the swing in the elm tree and broomstick horse choked life from her. The pain filled her stomach and there was no room for food or for her lungs to fill with air. The air and the food would have been theirs.

She hated Chato, not because he let the policeman and doctors put the screaming children in the government car, but because he had taught her to sign her name. Because it was like the old ones always told her about learning their language or any of their ways: it endangered you. She slept alone on the hill until the middle of November when the first snows came. Then she made a bed for herself where the children had slept. She did not lie down beside Chato again until many years later, when he was sick and shivering and only her body could keep him warm. The illness came after the white rancher told Chato he was too old to work for him anymore, and Chato and his old woman should be out of the shack by the next afternoon because the rancher had hired new people to work there. That had satisfied her. To see how the white man repaid Chato's years of loyalty and work. All of Chato's fine-sounding English talk didn't change things.

It snowed steadily and the luminous light from the snow gradually diminished into the darkness. Somewhere in Cebolleta a dog barked and other village dogs joined with it. Ayah looked in the direction she had come, from the bar where Chato was buying the wine. Sometimes he told her to go on ahead and wait; and then he never came. And when she finally went back looking for him, she would find him passed out at the bottom of the wooden steps to Azzie's Bar. All the wine would be gone and most of the money too, from the pale blue check that came to them once a month in a government envelope. It was then that she would look at his face and his hands, scarred by ropes and the barbed wire of all those years, and she would think, this man is a stranger; for forty years she had smiled at him and cooked his food, but he remained a stranger. She stood up again, with the snow almost to her knees, and she walked back to find Chato.

It was hard to walk in the deep snow and she felt the air burn in her lungs. She stopped a short distance from the bar to rest and readjust the blanket. But this time he wasn't waiting for her on the bottom step with his old Stetson hat pulled down and his shoulders hunched up in his long wool overcoat.

She was careful not to slip on the wooden steps. When she pushed the door open, warm air and cigarette smoke hit her face. She look around slowly and deliberately, in every corner, in every dark place that the old man might find to sleep. The bar owner didn't like Indians in there, especially Navajos, but he let Chato come in because he could talk Spanish like he was one of them. The men at the bar stared at her, and the bartender saw that she left the door open wide. Snowflakes were flying inside like moths and melting into a puddle on the oiled wood floor. He motioned to her to close the door, but she did not see him. She held herself straight and walked across the room slowly, searching the room with every step. The snow in her hair melted and she could feel it on her forehead. At the far corner of the room, she saw red flames at the mica window of the old stove door; she looked behind the stove just to make sure. The bar got quiet except for the Spanish polka music playing on the jukebox. She stood by the stove and shook the snow from her blanket and held it near the stove to dry. The wet wool smell reminded her of new-born goats in early March, brought inside to warm near the fire. She felt calm.

In past years they would have told her to get out. But her hair was white now and her face was wrinkled. They looked at her like she was a spider crawling slowly across the room. They were afraid; she could feel the fear. She looked at their faces steadily. They reminded her of the first time the white people brought her children back to her that winter. Danny had been shy and hid behind the thin white woman who brought them. And the baby had not known her until Ayah took her into her arms, and then Ella had nuzzled close to her as she had when she was nursing. The blonde woman was nervous and kept looking at a dainty gold watch on her wrist. She sat on the bench near the small window and watched the dark snow clouds gather around the mountains; she was worrying about the unpaved road. She was frightened by what she saw inside too: the strips of venison drying on a rope across the ceiling and the children jabbering excitedly in a language she did not know. So they stayed for only a few hours. Ayah watched the government car disappear down the road and she knew they were already being weaned from these lava hills and from this sky. The last time they came was in early June, and Ella stared at her the way the men in the bar were now staring. Ayah did not try to pick her up; she smiled at her instead and spoke cheerfully to Danny. When he tried to answer her, he could not seem to remember and he spoke English words with the Navajo. But he gave her a scrap of paper that he had found somewhere and carried in his pocket; it was folded in half, and he shyly looked up at her and said it was a bird. She asked Chato if they were home for good this time. He spoke to the white woman and she shook her head. "How much longer?" he asked, and she said she didn't know; but Chato saw how she stared at the boxcar shack. Ayah turned away then. She did not say good-bye.

She felt satisfied that the men in the bar feared her. Maybe it was her face and the way she held her mouth with teeth clenched tight, like there was nothing anyone could do to her now. She walked north down the road, searching for the old man. She did this because she had the blanket, and there would be no place for him except with her and the blanket in the old adobe barn near the arroyo. They always slept there when they came to Cebolleta. If the money and the wine were gone, she would be relieved because then they could go home again; back to the old hogan with a dirt roof and rock walls where she herself had been born. And the next day the old man could go back to the few sheep they still had, to follow along behind them, guiding them, into dry sandy arroyos where sparse grass grew. She knew he did not like walking behind old ewes when for so many years he rode big quarter horses and worked with cattle. But she wasn't sorry for him; he should have known all along what would happen.

There had not been enough rain for their garden in five years; and that was when Chato finally hitched a ride into the town and brought back brown boxes of rice and sugar and big tin cans of welfare peaches. After that, at the first of the month they went to Cebolleta to ask the postmaster for the check; and then Chato would go to the bar and cash it. They did this as they planted the garden every May, not because anything would survive the summer dust, but because it was time to do this. The journey passed the days that smelled silent and dry like the caves above the canyon with yellow painted buffaloes on their walls.

He was walking along the pavement when she found him. He did not stop or turn around when he heard her behind him. She walked beside him and she noticed how slowly he moved now. He smelled strong of woodsmoke and urine. Lately he had been forgetting. Sometimes he called her by his sister's name and she had been gone for a long time. Once she had found him wandering on the road to the white man's ranch, and she asked him why he was going that way; he laughed at her and said, "You know they can't run that ranch without me," and he walked on determined, limping on the leg that had been crushed many years before. Now he looked at her curiously, as if for the first time, but he kept shuffling along, moving slowly along the side of the highway. His gray hair had grown long and spread out on the shoulders of the long overcoat. He wore the old felt hat pulled down over his ears. His boots were worn out at the toes and he had stuffed pieces of an old red shirt in the holes. The rags made his feet look like little animals up to their ears in snow. She laughed at his feet; the snow muffled the sound of her laugh. He stopped and looked at her again. The wind had quit blowing and the snow was falling straight down; the southeast sky was beginning to clear and Ayah could see a star.

"Let's rest awhile," she said to him. They walked away from the road and up the slope to the giant boulders that had tumbled down from the red sandrock mesa throughout the centuries of rainstorms and earth tremors. In a place where the boulders shut out the wind, they sat down with their backs against the rock. She offered half of the blanket to him and they sat wrapped together.

The storm passed swiftly. The clouds moved east. They were massive and full, crowding together across the sky. She watched them with the feeling of horses—steely blue-gray horses startled across the sky. The powerful haunches pushed into the distances and the tail hairs streamed white mist behind them.

The sky cleared. Ayah saw that there was nothing between her and the stars. The light was crystalline. There was no shimmer, no distortion through earth haze. She breathed the clarity of the night sky; she smelled the purity of the half moon and the stars. He was lying on his side with his knees pulled up near his belly for warmth. His eyes were closed now, and in the light from the stars and the moon, looked young again.

She could see it descend out of the night sky: an icy stillness from the edge of the thin moon. She recognized the freezing. It came gradually, sinking snowflake by snowflake until the crust was heavy and deep. It had the strength of the stars in Orion, and its journey was endless. Ayah knew that with the wine he would sleep. He would not feel it. She tucked the blanket around him, re-membering how it was when Ella had been with her; and she felt the rush so big inside her heart for the babies. And she sang the only song she knew to sing for babies. She could not remember if she had ever sung it to her children, but she knew that her grandmother had sung it and her mother had sung it:

> *The earth is your mother,*
> *   she holds you.*
> *The sky is your father,*
> *   he protects you.*
> *Sleep,*
> *sleep.*
> *Rainbow is your sister,*
> *   she loves you.*
> *The winds are your brothers,*
> *   they sing to you.*
> *Sleep,*
> *sleep.*
> *We are together always*
> *We are together always*
> *There never was a time*
> *when this*
> *was not so.*

On Being Different: Sophie's Story

JEANNE MATICH-MARONEY

INTRODUCTION

The Admissions Review Committee had gathered to hear the intake assessment of a woman named Sophie. This was not the typical case referred to the Agency for People with Mental Retardation/Developmental Disabilities. The psychiatrist cautioned the prospective treatment team that the part-time nature of the program might not be sufficient to meet her evidently strong dependency needs. Furthermore, her long history of psychiatric involvement seemed to indicate the need for service delivery within the mental health system, vs. the Office of Mental Retardation/Developmental Disabilities (OMRDD) system. The psychologist reminded the team that her high level of cognitive functioning and the fact that she was not employed technically placed her outside the realm of program eligibility. The social worker emphasized the fact that Sophie had been socialized as a person with a developmental disability through her placement in special education classes at a point in time when no distinctions were made about the nature of a child's disability. Furthermore, despite years of service, the chronic depression persisted, suggesting that perhaps the approach of the mental health system was not adequately designed to meet the needs of this woman who was clearly dually diagnosed (Developmental Disability/Psychiatric Impairment). Discussion continued until the team felt there was sufficient justification to admit Sophie to the Agency's Intensive Clinic Treatment Program. And so it was that the Agency became an integral part of Sophie's story.

REASON FOR REFERRAL

Sophie was a 43-year-old, Caucasian woman of Italian heritage. At the time of intake, she was found to be functioning in the "borderline" (classification does not technically exist) range of intellectual capability with a WAIS-R Full Scale I.Q. of 70. She self-reports experiencing chronic depression since the death of her father in 1967. The depression has been characterized by episodes of anhedonia, lethargy, decreased appetite, reports of suicidal ideation and gestures.

For many years, Sophie received services through programs sponsored by the Office of Mental Health (OMH). These services included traditional weekly psychotherapy, monthly pharmacotherapy and residential placement in an OMH sponsored "supervised" apartment. Sophie was unemployed and spent the majority of her time alone in the apartment out of fear of being harmed in the neighborhood (she had been mugged three times in the lobby of her building). A series of frantic phone calls to a paternal aunt led to the aunt's dissatisfaction with the quality of services Sophie was receiving and the initiation of contact with the OMRDD through its local Developmental Disabilities Service Office (DDSO).

The outcome of the DDSO assessment led to referral for an OMRDD sponsored milieu treatment program (i.e. three days per week, 6 hours per day). Reasons for the referral cited by the case manager were social isolation, deflated self-esteem, and chronic depression. Additionally, the worker was seeking to secure clinical services for Sophie in closer proximity to her home as it had been discovered that she had been traveling via taxi to a mental health clinic in Brooklyn incurring a $50.00 per week unreimbursed transportation expense.

Upon admission, Sophie was prescribed a variety of drugs as treatment for her numerous "conditions" (as she described them). Meprobamate, tofranil, and valium were all prescribed by the treating psychiatrist at the mental health clinic. Dilantin, phenobarbitol, and clonopin were prescribed by a private neurologist to address a seizure disorder. Dyazide and nitroglycerin were prescribed by yet another physician as treatment for hypertension and cardiac arrhythmia respectively. From the outset, this menu of medications had presented as an issue of great concern to the clinic treatment team, and initial efforts at coordination of service proved futile as Sophie was invested in maintaining each of her prescribing physicians. It should be noted that Sophie had requested continuation of her individual psychotherapy services at the previous mental health clinic. She was therefore initially admitted for group, collaborative, and "as needed" crisis services through the clinic while the individual psychotherapy and pharmacological services continued at the mental health clinic.

Within six months of admission, the "as needed" crisis services had escalated to near daily individual sessions as Sophie appeared to be in perpetual crisis. These crises peaked when Sophie verbalized some suicidal ideation and detailed a plan which could easily be implemented within her home. An emergency room visit resulted in a recommendation for hospitalization which Sophie vehemently opposed. Not wishing to seek involuntary status, the psychiatrist discharged her to the care of her aunt. Shortly thereafter, all of Sophie's therapeutic services were assumed by the OMRDD sponsored clinic (the Agency); group and collaborative efforts continued while individual and psychiatric services were initiated. She became connected to the outpatient medical clinic of the hospital where she had been seen for emergency services. And, finally, she took up "permanent" residence with her aunt.

BACKGROUND INFORMATION

Through individual supportive therapy sessions, the social worker came to learn a great deal more about Sophie, her life story and her experience of the world. Sophie was born prematurely at seven months gestation. According to her, the premature birth was due to a fall her mother incurred. Sophie held great contempt for her mother's seeming ineptitude as she is acutely aware of the part it played in her resultant neurological impairment. Sophie further described the occasion of her mother's pregnancy and her subsequent birth as an "accident." On numerous occasions Sophie has referred to herself as an "accident," and one which should never have occurred.

As she grew up, Sophie reported feeling "different" than the other children at school and recalled being taunted for being "stupid." She was able to sustain herself in the educational system through the eighth grade (regular classes through the fifth grade, Children with Retarded Mental Development (CRMD) classes beginning in sixth) at which time she left school to care for her father who had become chronically ill with the debilitating effects of a complicated diabetic condition. Despite Sophie's valiant efforts (inclusive of insulin administration, bathing, and changing), his physical and emotional deterioration continued until his death in 1967. Sophie acknowledged an "empty" feeling since the time of his death and was even aware that her mourning was protracted, but she felt powerless to overcome it.

Following her father's death, Sophie continued to reside with her mother (who, though undiagnosed and untreated, was believed by surviving relatives to have been schizophrenic). Sophie recalled frequent hostile arguments that occasionally involved violence directed toward her by her mother. Six years later, Sophie's mother died.

This marked a new life phase for Sophie, who made attempts to secure employment and was finally placed in a sheltered workshop through the (then) Office of Vocational Rehabilitation. This placement proved quite stressful for her. Altercations with peers ensued, and she was soon referred for psychotherapy services (through the Office of Mental Health). She subsequently discontinued her involvement with the sheltered workshop, and at the time of admission it had been more than a decade since she had last worked.

For a number of years prior to her move to the OMH sponsored supervised apartment, Sophie resided with the same aunt in whose home she was now residing. The return to her aunt's home apparently triggered some repressed recollections, and Sophie disclosed to the social worker that she had been sexually abused by her uncle (this aunt's husband) but had never shared this information with anyone out of respect for her aunt. The shame and guilt associated with this experience further exacerbated her lifelong sense of "differentness."

SOCIAL WORK INTERVENTION

Having now consolidated her services, Sophie began her work in earnest. She became quite engaged with the social worker and appeared motivated to make some changes in her life. The first order of business was to tend to the stabilization of her medication. With Sophie's consent, the social worker initiated and maintained close contact with both Sophie's medical doctor and treating psychiatrist. Based upon careful medical, neurological, and psychiatric reassessment, informed by observations of both the social worker and her aunt, Sophie's medication regimen was gradually altered. Dosages were decreased, meprobamate (an antiquated psychotropic medication) was discontinued, Xanax was introduced, and Sophie was closely monitored.

During this period of relative medical stabilization, Sophie used her supportive therapy sessions to explore her chronic depression and the obstacles it had placed upon her life. She expressed a strong desire to feel better. Yet the struggle with her fragile mental state continued.

In the late Spring following her full admission to the program, the need for a second psychiatric E.R. visit surfaced. Sophie had taken three times her usual dose of Xanax and then took a cab to the Agency looking for her social worker. In exploring the circumstances surrounding this suicidal gesture, it was discovered that her aunt had gone away on a very brief vacation, an overnight stay, leaving Sophie alone at home. She had responded to the separation as if her aunt had abandoned her. Conjointly, the need for an emergency psychiatric consultation was determined. The worker once again accompanied Sophie to the E.R., and hospitalization was recommended. This time Sophie did not refuse but inquired instead, "Do you think it will help?"

This hospitalization actually served as a turning point for Sophie. It was determined that the interactive effects of the medications she had been taking at the dosages prescribed had actually reached a level of toxicity. All medications needed to be discontinued. A comprehensive re-evaluation of her physical and mental status was conducted and ultimately, a new medication regimen established.

Though living with her aunt at the time, the temporary nature of this arrangement weighed heavily upon Sophie. She was once again able to acknowledge the need to seek residential placement. However, one of the prerequisites for residential placement in the OMRDD system was that the individual be gainfully employed or otherwise committed to a full-time day program. Sophie was not either.

Thus, preparation for eventual residential referral and placement necessitated preparation for vocational placement. As on so many prior occasions, Sophie struggled with her perceived sense of inadequacy and lack of marketable skill. She adamantly refused the option of sheltered workshop placement as a stepping-stone to eventual competitive employment; her prior experience in this type of setting told her that it was not a good match, even if it was the only available option. She refused to be pigeonholed into a work placement that didn't afford the opportunity for her to realize her true work potential. Alternative work options were limited, particularly in light of the fact that Sophie had never traveled via mass transportation independently. The social worker recognized the need to shift the focus of intervention and became very actively engaged in the process of seeking resources that would be responsive to Sophie's unique set of needs.

Fortunately, the social worker was able to link Sophie to a local organization with a solid reputation for vocational training and supported work placement.

This organization was able to accommodate both Sophie's transportation limitations and her desire to become engaged in productive, meaningful work. She entered their vocational training program and was placed as a volunteer at a local children's hospital where she worked in the laundry room. Sophie experienced tremendous personal satisfaction and a sense of competence working in this capacity. The work itself held significant meaning for her as she recognized the contribution it made to helping ill children to feel clean and comfortable. She formed close relationships with co-workers who were impressed with the care and dedication she demonstrated. The supervisor was eager to hire her and move her from a volunteer to an employee status. The vocational training program was thrilled with the apparent match and the prospect of moving yet another one of their job-training candidates to full-time paid employment. Furthermore, the stability of her vocational status positioned her well for residential applications.

Then the economic recession of the early 1990s hit. With unemployment rates soaring among the general population and organizations forced to downsize, supported work and competitive employment "slots" for people with developmental disabilities began to shrink. And in short order, the promising prospect of employment with the children's hospital evaporated. Sophie continued in the vocational training program but had lost much of the confidence and momentum gained through her experience at the children's hospital. She missed her work and her co-workers a great deal and was forced to negotiate yet another significant loss in her life.

Yet Sophie persevered. She continued in her clinical work, attended her vocational program, participated in her socialization program, and pursued the residential applications that had already been filed. With the coordinated support of her family and vocational and clinical staff, Sophie was able to manage the symptoms of her chronic depression without a major crisis. In the interim, she was accepted for admission to a community residence.

Again, with the network of support provided by her family and by vocational, socialization and clinical programs, Sophie handled the transition from her aunt's home to the community residence with remarkable ease. She adjusted well to residential life and soon was held in high esteem by both her housemates and the residential staff. The experience of "being different" and being a guest in the home of a family member began to dissipate and for the first time in her life she felt at home.

PROLOGUE

Over the years of involvement with the Agency, Sophie was seen for psychological re-evaluations (standard protocol for service continuation within an OMRDD sponsored agency). As the haze of her chronic depression began to lift and she became productively engaged in vocational as well as academic activity, a concomitant increase in her cognitive abilities was noted. Each re-evaluation resulted in the addition of several points to her full-scale IQ score.

On last testing, Sophie's cognitive ability was assessed to fall within the low-average range of intelligence (IQ in the lower 80s). Though socialized throughout her 50 years as a person with mental retardation, she, in fact, was not. Her specific learning disability had not been detected, and her unique abilities/ potential had not been nurtured. Her perceived sense of "differentness" premised on the belief that she was a person with mental retardation was ever so gently dismantled by the team of professionals who had worked so closely with her over a period of 8 years. Emancipated by this knowledge and supported by experiences facilitated by the work of the Agency, Sophie came to the realization that she was indeed unique and special, but in a way that no longer taunted and tormented her.

Questions for Further Study

1. In the essay "Learning Empathy," taken from her book, *Thinking in Pictures*, Temple Grandin makes the point that, while empathy is an instinctive quality, it can also be learned. The feelings she had when she used the squeeze machine enabled her to access her own feelings of physical comfort and to understand what "love" felt like. What are the implications of this knowledge for social work practice with persons with disabilities, and for older persons as well?

2. Nancy Mairs, in this selection from *Waist High in the World*, writes about a prevailing attitude toward pregnancy and death that reveals a devaluation of people with disabilities. Specifically, she is concerned with the disposability of life when that life is likely to be one of pain, great expense, and inconvenience to others. Hers is a thoughtful reflection on this issue, and the ideas are important for a profession that holds the dignity and worth of every human being as a cardinal principle. What is your own view on the question of how best to discuss the question of life and death with clients (e.g., prospective parents of a fetus with serious deformities, or clients with progressive illnesses, like Mairs') in a way that honors our professional principles and allows for maximum self-determination for the client?

3. Leonard Kriegel, in his essay "Falling into Life," from his book of the same name, examines the sorrows of a child who must face the fact of lifelong disability, and uses one of the goals of his rehabilitation—learning how to fall—as an analogy for the necessity of learning to accept it. What are some of the ways that social workers can help clients with disabilities learn "how to fall"? What lessons can social workers draw from the story of Joey Tomashevski?

4. In "Lullaby," from Leslie Marmon Silko's *Storyteller*, Silko emphasizes Ayah's perception of the fear and nervousness of the non-Navajo people assembled in the bar where she searches for Chato. Conversely, she describes the disempowered Ayah as "satisfied" with the fear she has engendered. It would seem that this knowledge is a slender, but real, source of empowerment for Ayah. This is a rather small moment in the story, but important because it underscores that the empowerment that we seek for all of our clients can emerge from unlikely places. At what other points in the story might Ayah

have benefited from the assistance of a social worker oriented towards the empowerment of clients? What might an empowerment-oriented intervention have looked like?

5. In Jean Matich-Maroney's case study, "On Being Different: Sophie's Story," what were the most significant contributions of the social worker(s) to Sophie's transformation from a person with "mental retardation" to a person who was not only not retarded, but "unique and special"?

Invited Commentary

ONA BREGMAN

Teaching about diversity is a priority in the education of social workers. Practicing with respect for diversity is a core value in social work practice. What do social workers actually mean when they introduce the notion of diversity? Are they able to move beyond a linear, politically correct position to a systems view of diversity? This would incorporate appreciation and respect for difference in ideas and thinking. It would include appreciation and respect for those people who don't fit the categories implicit in the word "diversity" as it is currently used. It would include people whose approach to life may be quite different from their own. Recognizing that responsibility and accountability are an essential part of all relationship transactions, it is nevertheless important to keep in mind that most behavior makes sense in context. Diversity is about being different from the accepted norm, distinct from what is expected and anticipated as the norm. It is about the rich tapestry that makes up the whole. The expected norm may vary depending on who is doing the expecting. Understanding diversity from a systems perspective involves using a lens large enough to encompass the entire gestalt, representing an integrated pattern of observable data that cannot exist when reduced to its parts. It is difficult for many people to see from this broad view, as they have difficulty with difference, finding it threatening. In such situations, people sometimes inflate themselves and feel as if they are above those who are different, often without realizing it. Even for those with a clearer sense of self and an appreciation for difference, situations arise that are challenging to their comfort and sense of what is right. It is critically important for social workers to be aware of, appreciate and respect diversity in order to come to the client/social worker relationship with integrity and respect.

How can social workers contribute to others' becoming more thoughtful about their problems? How can they contribute to others' developing broader and more thoughtful perspectives for understanding themselves and setting their goals and course of action? How does one keep from focusing on other people and their problems? How does one not do too much for others? What appear to be good intentions on the part of some may represent the need to feel competent—or one up—or filled up—or less anxious. Is there an implicit message in doing too much for someone that the recipient of one's efforts is incapable, unworthy, hopeless, or helpless? By maintaining a focus on others, is one actually defining the problem for them and labeling their difference, often with negative implication? A "helper" who is able to be more aware of and more focused on himself or herself and less eager to be helpful contributes to a context where all parties involved can discover new ideas and new parts of themselves. In order to focus on self, however, one has to recognize his or her own discomfort, vulnerability, and need to fix, achieve, perform, rescue, or control. This recognition makes it possible to appreciate whatever ability is present in the other. It is important to recognize that all people have resources that can be tapped. From the perspective of this commentator, the job of the social worker is not to fix or do something to someone. It is to provide an opportunity and context for movement, led by the client. This way of thinking and experiencing will be a shift for some social workers and their clients and is, in part, a reframing of the helping process.

The readings in this section demonstrate how powerful it is when the person viewed as needing help finds a way to mobilize personal resources in order to move on. In some cases the stories demonstrate the complexity of different forms of diversity intersecting in one person. The stories also demonstrate on some occasions the possibilities for developing new and creative perspectives through "reframing," which has been implicit in social work practice for many years. It was specifically defined and named, however, in the 1970s, by the so-called brief therapists at the Mental Research Institute in Palo Alto (Watzlawick et al. 1974). Reframing can be understood as an attempt to change the meaning of a particular situation by providing alternative ways to perceive it. It is one piece of what can be useful to a person seeking a broader range of choices, both in perceiving and acting upon a given situation. Whether the social worker uses reframing as an intervention technique with a client or as an attitude with which to approach a client would depend upon the theoretical framework being used. This commentator uses Bowen theory as a foundation for her thinking and, by coaching and questioning, attempts to provide a space in which the client is able to do the reframing. One piece of this would be the possibility for the client to recognize himself or herself as a member of a system. This can lead to a different view of responsibility for self and to others. Let us consider the readings in this section.

There were several things that facilitated Temple Grandin's ability to understand her own autism differently from the usual understanding. By seeking out current research in neuroscience and on "sensory problems associated with a diagnosis of autism," she was able to reframe her own diagnosis. Understanding the neurological implications rather than focusing on the psychological left space for Grandin to discover new and creative ways to understand and manage herself.

Describing herself as a person who feels as though she is driven by an engine of animal fears, Dr. Grandin proceeds to define herself to those who are different and inclined to provide definitions for her. It is interesting to observe that Bowen theory (Bowen 1978, Kerr and Bowen 1988, Papero 1990) suggests that human beings respond to life through automatic, instinctual patterns that reach back into the human's legacy from evolution. This connects human beings to other living systems. A distinct feature of humans, however, is the ability to be aware of emotional reactions and think about them. This provides the opportunity to observe and manage oneself. Temple Grandin seems to have done just that, a masterful job of reframing for herself.

If one thinks about the assumptions that have been made about people who are autistic and the blame that has been placed on those considered "responsible" for them, we have an excellent example of the focus on other described earlier. Conversely, had Dr. Grandin chosen to focus on others, blaming and judging, she would have deprived herself of the opportunity to learn about herself, develop, and take charge of her life.

In the section called "Freeing Choices" by Nancy Mairs, we watch the author reframe the idea of a disability as only one part of the person, not the whole or essence of the person. Ms. Mairs is brutally honest in her examination of her daily struggles with life, the ratio of dependence to independence, and bouts of depression leading to serious suicide attempts.

She is equally honest in her discussion of the moral issues involved in one's assessment of whether or not to bring a "damaged" child into the world. Clearly this is a complex issue with no simple answers, and Ms. Mairs does not pretend to have answers, only pointed questions.

She abhors generalizations and a one-size-fits-all approach to individuals. She is an eloquent spokesperson for the individual with a disability, and she proclaims the inherent dignity for all human beings of being in charge of their own lives. Implicit in what she presents is the criticism that those who intervene and make both decisions and policy for the disabled do so out of their own need and focus on the other. They are not able to see the volume of contributions made to the world by those whom they would label. Could this connect to those peoples' inability to appreciate their own contribution and to their corresponding need to create the opportunity to do something for the other in order to do something for themselves? If so, the people being focused on pay a heavy price.

Once again, in this series of essays we are privileged to witness what can emerge from a concerted effort to think about one's feelings and to work hard to think about them differently as one manages oneself. Ms. Mairs is often able to find much value in her life and in her relationships. It is only when a sense of hopelessness overcomes her that she loses the ability to do this and slides into depression. Aware of this emotional process (and she labels this emotional state as "intrinsically irrational"), she devised an approach of clinging to reason in order to survive. Not entirely ruling out the choice to die under certain circumstances, her emphasis is on a thinking decision. Her approach to the act of suicide reframes it from an act of desperate helplessness to a thoughtful act of choice during a time of reason.

Leonard Kriegel, in "Falling into Life," describes his rehabilitation following his bout with polio during 1944. Learning to fall in order to avoid hurting himself was preliminary to learning to stand on his own two feet. The reader is reminded of the importance of both hope and the conscious effort to be in charge of one's life.

In this essay, aging and disability merge as an issue as Mr. Kriegel deals with the process of aging and becoming even less physically competent as he moves toward the ending phase of his life. Confronting mortality can throw a curve into life's course. By reframing the possibility of falling from something feared as a danger to something learned as a lesson, he shifts his entire approach to living with a disability. Later in his life, he applies this approach to aging. In trying to learn from his lesson in falling, Mr. Kriegel attempts to imagine what he would consider a proper ending to his life. Perhaps in learning not to be afraid of falling he was preparing to confront mortality a bit differently. By not being afraid to fall, he was able to move forward. Perhaps by not being afraid to die, he will be able to die well—a lesson for all.

In "Lullaby," by Leslie Marmon Silko, we listen to the story of a woman who spends most of her life responding and reacting to others. It is a sad story as we watch Ayah lose her children, her husband Chato lose his job, and her life, empty and full of pain, lose direction and hope. Ayah is a Navajo woman, with little standing in mainstream culture. Due to poverty and lack of connection to the larger culture, she had little opportunity to become literate or to learn the ways of the whites. This renders her helpless in dealing with this society as it imposes its standards and expectations on her. Blaming Chato for much of what has happened, she distances from him emotionally and physically until he is in the process of dying. Depriving herself of any gratification in the relationship with Chato, she lives a lonely and deprived life. She feels hopeless and victimized by those who deal with her from a one-up position. On a larger scale, this can evolve into social oppression, where the people in the targeted group can easily fall into the victim position. How might this story have been different had the government authorities who seized her children engaged Ayah in a mutual process of problem-solving and decision-making? How different if Ayah had acknowledged to herself that she didn't know what she was signing, taken a position about that, and refused to sign until she knew what she was signing? How different if instead of blaming Chato she had sought comfort in this relationship? Is there a way Ayah might have approached life differently in spite of the deck being so stacked against her? Could she have defined herself as a less willing victim, challenging authority and asking questions?

In "Sophie's Story," we have the opportunity to observe a wide continuum of behavior among those involved in Sophie's life. In particular, the so-called human service people, some of whom early on assumed the worst in dealing with Sophie, are contrasted with those who later appreciated her potential. The difference in outcome of these two positions is dramatic. In the first instance, everyone is doing for and to Sophie as well as defining and labeling her. In addition to the events in her life which may have contributed to her depression, being the target of so many others' determining and limiting her options may have contributed to her depression as well. Later as her potential is recognized and she is given the opportunity to take some responsibility for herself, Sophie blossoms. As her strengths and abilities become the focus of the work, she is able to move toward more independence and competence. Here we have the same person, at first viewing herself as an "accident" with little or no value or competence, transforming herself into a person with the ability to appreciate herself and develop.

Each story in this section demonstrates the difference between two approaches to living and to providing service. The first focuses on the other person and doing something to or presumably for them. The second focuses on taking responsibility for oneself and one's choices. When focusing on the other, one labels differences and defines the problem for the other person, usually with negative implications. When focusing on self, one is pushed to recognize one's own discomfort with difference and vulnerability. In the first instance one is pushed to fix, rescue, perform, restrict and/or control. In the second, by staying with oneself, there is an implicit assumption that the other has abilities to deal.

Can one actually "help" someone or does one provide an opportunity for others to help themselves? This writer operates on the assumption that if a person is going to change, he must do that for himself. A focus on the other appears to leave the person who is the object of that focus in a position to continue whatever theme or role he has inherited from his family system. If a social worker reframes the view of "other" to a focus on "self," for both the social worker and the client, the person being focused on is then free to revise his view of self and to use whatever potential is available.

It appears to this discussant that oppression of people from any group grows out of the inability of those who consider themselves "helpers" to define self in relation to oppression except by seeking to move to the one-up position. Concurrently, as the people in any oppressed group define self as victim, they too perpetuate the cycle. These factors set up a polarization of victim/victimizer, needy one/provider and/or helpless one/helper. Dr. Murray Bowen said, "A universal target of the projection process is the scapegoating of vulnerable minority groups. . . . Just as the least adequate child in a family can become more impaired when he becomes an object of pity and over-sympathetic help from the family, so can the lowest segment of society be chronically impaired by the very attention designed to help. No matter how good the principle behind such programs, it is essentially impossible to implement them without the built-in complications of the projection process. Such programs attract workers who are over-sympathetic with less fortunate people. They automatically put the recipients in a "one down" inferior position, and they either keep them there, or get angry at them." (Bowen 1978, p. 445).

In another chapter, Bowen discusses the focus on rights in a similar context, suggesting that this tends to minimize the taking of responsibility. He says "There can be no rights without a responsible majority to guarantee the rights. The more a person focuses on rights for himself, the less he is aware of the rights of others, and the more he becomes irresponsible in violation of the rights of others. The focus on rights destroys the goal it was designed to attain" (Bowen 1978, pp. 279–81). It is, of course, possible to be a member of an oppressed group without adopting a victim stance. It is equally possible to be a member of the responsible majority without patronizing the oppressed or aggrandizing oneself.

In a recent personal experience, this author has confronted the challenge of supporting the acquisition of human services for her mentally competent but somewhat physically limited 92-year-old mother without taking over. This is indeed a challenge that is often difficult and sometimes impossible to meet. With mother being entirely mentally competent but with limited ability to circumvent the complex physical and administrative tasks of seeking service, how does daughter facilitate this process without making decisions or contributing to a loss of independence and dignity on the part of mother? It is a difficult balance and a miniscule version of the challenge to society in providing service.

Several questions arise from this discussion.

1. How does one contribute to the ability of human beings who are aging and/or disabled (or any other targeted difference) to access services without a focus that strips them of dignity and self worth?
2. How does a service provider or one who sets policy construct service delivery that doesn't reflect her own need to focus on the other, rescue, and pass judgment?
3. How might advocates for human rights shift the focus from blaming others to taking responsibility and providing opportunity?
4. How can those with unmet needs define these needs without falling into other-focus and blaming?

REFERENCES

Bowen, M. (1978). *Family Therapy in Clinical Practice*. New York: Jason Aronson.

Kerr, M. E. and Bowen, M. (1988). *Family Evaluation*. New York: W. W. Norton.

Papero, D. (1990). *Bowen Family Systems Theory*. Needham Heights, Mass.: Allyn and Bacon.

Watzlawick, P., Weakland, J. H., and Fisch, R. (1974). *Change: Principles of Problem Formation and Problem Resolution*. New York: W. W. Norton.

Unit 4   BUILDING INTERVENTIONS IN CASES WHERE GENDER OR SEXUAL IDENTITY IS AT ISSUE

Editors' Introduction

Intervention in social work practice refers to the action phase of the helping process. After one has engaged the client, listened to his/her story, and used professional expertise to frame the issues and the possible means for addressing them, the worker moves to enable the client to solve or prevent problems. Sometimes called "treatment," we prefer the term intervention because it encompasses *any* activity undertaken in the service of reaching client goals. These activities may include psychotherapy, resource development and acquisition, mediation, advocacy, social planning, community organization or development, and many others

(Barker 1999). Some of these interventions are discussed further in subsequent units.

We have chosen to look at this step in the process through the eyes of people, both real and fictional, whose navigation of the world has been made more complex because they occupy oppositional and multiple identities. Such persons must sift and sort through conflict, contradiction, and a dearth of positive self-representations and images in popular culture. Where gender and sexuality are at issue, building effective interventions must take into account a complex and shifting tangle of identifications, self-scrutiny, and public censure.

"In Search of Bruce Lee's Grave," by Shanlon Wu, describes Wu's disconnection from both his Chinese culture of origin and the Western culture of his birth. Perceiving himself as neither fully Chinese nor fully American, he struggles to formulate a Chinese-American male ideal. Going to law school and becoming a successful litigator earned Wu some of the trappings of American male achievement, yet he still feels like an outsider because of his Chinese background and appearance. To bolster his power and authority as a Chinese-American male in a predominantly white professional environment, Wu turns for models of strength to Chinese kung fu actor Bruce Lee and even to the general who masterminded the attack on Pearl Harbor, the few images he finds in mainstream American popular culture. In college, he learned about the all-Japanese U.S. army unit that defended the same country that interned these soldiers' families.

Wu's story draws our attention to the difficulty of forging identities that are not culturally normative. People whose identities are not widely represented in mainstream American society and culture are *de facto* excluded from gaining authority and access to equal opportunities. Popular culture gives us our cultural icons, models of adoration, authority, and respect. For the majority of people, whose identities do not in actuality correspond to those of iconic figures, looking to popular culture for a remedy is futile. Social workers can assist clients who are suffering because they fall short of an iconic ideal—of whiteness, manliness, female beauty, wealth, physical strength, power, etc.—by providing alternative sources for the development of appropriate ideals of selfhood. Such resources might include mentoring programs (e.g., Big Brothers, Big Sisters, youth groups), affinity groups, opportunities for cultural study (history, language, art, music, etc.), and psychotherapy.

Shani Mootoo's "Out on Main Street" offers us a fictionalized portrayal of a person who is Indian by ethnicity, Canadian by geography, Trinidadian by culture, and lesbian. The story is about a series of encounters that illuminate the main characters' difficulties in establishing the credentials needed to claim the identities they assume. They are "inauthentic" Indians, challenged when they cannot correctly identify Indian pastries that they eat. They are also "inauthentic" women, challenged when they express their lack of interest in male sex partners. They are not even altogether reliable lesbian lovers, as illustrated when the sexual overtures of males strike jealousy and fear in our narrator's heart. Mootoo seems to be suggesting that the task of maintaining multiple and oppositional identities, whether diasporic or sexual, is exhausting, because such identities are subjected to constant self and public scrutiny and provocation.

Whereas Wu's story drew our attention to the difficulty of formulating ideals for identities that differ from the cultural norms, Mootoo's story illustrates the confusions and conflicts—both humorous and threatening—faced in everyday social encounters by people conscious of multiple and alternative identities. At such a narrow intersection of race, ethnicity, culture, and gender, it is difficult to find a larger community of interest. However, Mootoo's story illustrates the hypersensitivity of a woman with plenty of social interaction, who is actively discovering, studying, and evaluating models of identity out on the street.

"Cartography," by Karl Woelz, brings into sharp relief the ambiguous role of what we call the "parent-proxy." Bryan, the homosexual partner of Trevor, has assumed a parental role in the life of Philip, a young man on his way to adulthood. As the story progresses, you, the reader, may be persuaded that Bryan, in many ways, has been a more effective parent than either of the biological parents. Yet, in view of Philip's imminent flight from the nest, Bryan's sadness, envy, and insecurity are palpable. Thus, an intervention aimed at helping Bryan establish a sense of legitimacy in this family, from his own point of view and the view of the others, might enable him to adapt more easily to an empty nest.

In writing this introduction, we debated our responses to Bryan's awareness of Philip's body, which teeters between parental affection and sexual eroticism. Woelz deliberately forces us to recognize that, in our society, the affection of a gay parent for his same-sex offspring is frequently the object of suspicion. Legal interventions in many child custody cases have been based on this suspicion, with less evidence to support it than is presented here. Although Philip is, at this point, too old, and his biological parents clearly congenial enough to work things out on their own, child custody cases where the parental circumstances are similar often require the input of a social worker. How might you intervene in such a case?

Gloria Anzaldua's piece, "*Movimentos de rebeldia y las culturas que traicionan* " [Rebel movements and cultures that betray] from *Borderlands La Frontera: (The New Mestiza),* speaks powerfully of the contradictions between the cultural expectations of her community of origin, the gender roles prescribed therein, and her sexual orientation. With recourse to terrifying but compelling cultural myths, she frames her sexual orientation as a conscious choice, demanded of her by her "Shadow Beast," that part of herself that chooses to rebel. Although she has chosen to repudiate the notions about sex and gender that emerge from her Mexican, Catholic origins, she nevertheless kept major elements, such as language, as the ground of her own being. Having *lo mexicano* in her system, as she notes, gave Anzaldua personal strengths and resources unavailable to Shanlon Wu and less available to Shani Mootoo. Both Anzaldua and Mootoo use a mixture of languages to foreground their differences and opacity to outsiders.

Anzaldua's work weaves the theme of "*los intersticios,*" the crevices, or interfaces, among sexual orientation, sex roles, and culture, that she occupies, into her work. The theme of multiple, contradictory identities could be aptly applied to all the readings in this volume. We point it out here because of the way in which Anzaldua has used this theme to empower and to enable a sense of fidelity to all of those contradictory aspects of her being. Her ability to frame who she is in this manner is in itself an intervention.

Once again, all of these pieces have fixed our focus on the interface among sexual orientation, gender roles, and culture, and the problems that lie within. It is notable that Colleen Reed, our guest essayist, and Ona Bregman, our case study author, disagree so fundamentally on the theoretical problems for assessing the women profiled in Bregman's case study, "Three Women." Clearly, these disparate interpretations inevitably will result in the development of different interventions. However, while Bregman frames the exchange of self within relationships in almost market terms of borrowing and lending, and argues for some self-correction, Reed argues that the problem lies in the larger terrain of gender expectations and enforcements. The former requires a change in behavior, while the latter requires a change in societal norms. In our view, both are necessary and correct. Their respective points of origin into the presenting problems of these women point to the need for social workers to be mindful of the action on both sides of *los intersticios* of person and environment.

REFERENCES

Barker, R. (1991). *The Social Work Dictionary.* Washington, D.C.: National Association of Social Workers.

Watzlawick, P., Weakland, J. H. and Fisch, R. (1974). *Change: Principles of Problem Formation and Problem Resolution.* New York: W. W. Norton.

Movimientos de rebeldía y las culturas que traicionan

GLORIA ANZALDUA

Esos movimientos de rebeldía que tenemos en la sangre nosotros los mexicanos surgen como ríos desbocanados en mis venas. Y como mi raza que cada en cuando deja caer esa esclavitud de obedecer, de callarse y aceptar, en mi está la rebeldía encimita de mi carne. Debajo de mi humillada mirada está una cara insolente lista para explotar. Me costó muy caro mi rebeldía—acalambrada con desvelos y dudas, sintiéndome inútil, estúpida, e impotente.

Me entra una rabia cuando alguien—sea mi mamá, la Iglesia, la cultura de los anglos— me dice haz esto, haz eso sin considerar mis deseos.

Repele. Hable pa' 'tras. Fui muy hocicona. Era indiferente a muchos valores de mi cultura. No me dejé de los hombres. No fui buena ni obediente.

Pero he crecido. Ya no sólo paso toda mi vida botando las costumbres y los valores de mi cultura que me traicionan. También recojo las costumbres que por el tiempo se han probado y las costumbres de respeto a las mujeres. But despite my growing tolerance, for this Chicana *la guerra de independencia* is a constant.

THE STRENGTH OF MY REBELLION

I have a vivid memory of an old photograph: I am six years old. I stand between my father and mother, head cocked to the right, the toes of my flat feet gripping the ground. I hold my mother's hand.

To this day I'm not sure where I found the strength to leave the source, the mother, disengage from my family, *mi tierra, mi gente,* and all that picture stood for. I had to leave home so I could find myself, find my own intrinsic nature buried under the personality that had been imposed on me.

I was the first in six generations to leave the Valley, the only one in my family to ever leave home. But I didn't leave all the parts of me: I kept the ground of my own being. On it I walked away, taking with me the land, the Valley, Texas. *Gané mi camino y me largué. Muy andariega mi hija.* Because I left of my own accord *me dicen, "¿Cómo te gusta la mala vida?"*

At a very early age I had a strong sense of who I was and what I was about and what was fair. I had a stubborn will. It tried constantly to mobilize my soul under my own regime, to live life on my own terms no matter how unsuitable to others they were. *Terca.* Even as a child I would not obey. I was "lazy." Instead of ironing my younger brothers' shirts or cleaning the cupboards, I would pass many hours studying, reading, painting, writing. Every bit of self-faith I'd painstakingly gathered took a beating daily. Nothing in my culture approved of me. *Había agarrado malos pasos.* Something was "wrong" with me. *Estaba más allá de la tradición.*

There is a rebel in me—the Shadow-Beast. It is a part of me that refuses to take orders from outside authorities. It refuses to take orders from my conscious will, it threatens the sovereignty of my rulership. It is that part of me that hates constraints of any kind, even those self-imposed. At the least hint of limitations on my time or space by others, it kicks out with both feet. Bolts.

CULTURAL TYRANNY

Culture forms our beliefs. We perceive the version of reality that it communicates. Dominant paradigms, predefined concepts that exist as unquestionable, unchallengeable, are transmitted to us through the culture. Culture is made by those in power—men. Males make the rules and laws; women transmit them. How many times have I heard mothers and mothers-in-law tell their sons to beat their wives for not obeying them, for being *hociconas* (big mouths), for being *callajeras* (going to visit and gossip with neighbors), for expecting their husbands to help with the rearing of children and the housework, for wanting to be something other than housewives?

The culture expects women to show greater acceptance of, and commitment to, the value system than men. The culture and the Church insist that women are subservient to males. If a woman rebels she is a *mujer mala.* If a woman doesn't renounce herself in favor of the male, she is selfish. If a woman remains a *virgen* until she marries, she is a good woman. For a woman of my culture there used to be only three directions she could turn: to the Church as a nun, to the streets as a prostitute, or to the home as a mother. Today some of us have a fourth choice: entering the world by way of education and career and becoming self-autonomous persons. A very few of us. As a working class people our chief activity is to put food in our mouths, a roof over our heads and clothes on our backs. Educating our children is out of reach for most of us. Educated or not, the onus is still on women to be a wife/mother—only the nun can escape motherhood. Women are made to feel total failures if they don't marry and have children. "*¿Y cuándo te casas, Gloria? Se te va a pasar el tren.*" Y yo les digo, "*Pos si me caso, no va ser con un hombre.*" *Se quedan calladitas. Sí, soy hija de la Chingada.* I've always been her daughter. *No 'tés chingando.*

Humans fear the supernatural, both the undivine (the animal impulses such as sexuality, the unconscious, the unknown, the alien) and the divine (the superhuman, the god in us). Culture and religion seek to protect us from these two forces. The female, by virtue of creating entities of flesh and blood in her stomach (she bleeds every month but does not die), by virtue of being in tune with nature's cycles, is feared. Because, according to Christianity and most other major religions, woman is carnal, animal, and closer to the undivine, she must be protected. Protected from herself. Woman is the stranger, the other. She is man's recognized nightmarish pieces, his Shadow-Beast. The sight of her sends him into a frenzy of anger and fear.

La gorra, el rebozo, la mantilla are symbols of my culture's "protection" of women. Culture (read males) professes to protect women. Actually it keeps women in rigidly defined roles. It keeps the girlchild from other men—don't poach on my preserves, only I can touch my child's body. Our mothers taught us well, *"Los hombres nomás quieren una cosa"*; men aren't to be trusted, they are selfish and are like children. Mothers made sure we didn't walk into a room of brothers or fathers or uncles in nightgowns or shorts. We were never alone with men, not even those of our own family.

Through our mothers, the culture gave us mixed messages: *No voy a dejar que ningún pelado desgraciado maltrate a mis hijos.* And in the next breath it would say, *La mujer tiene que hacer lo que le diga el hombre.* Which was it to be—strong, or submissive, rebellious or conforming?

Tribal rights over those of the individual insured the survival of the tribe and were necessary then, and, as in the case of all indigenous peoples in the world who are still fighting off intentional, premeditated murder (genocide), they are still necessary.

Much of what the culture condemns focuses on kinship relationships. The welfare of the family, the community, and the tribe is more important than the welfare of the individual. The individual exists first as kin—as sister, as father, as *padrino*—and last as self.

In my culture, selfishness is condemned, especially in women; humility and selflessness, the absence of selfishness, is considered a virtue. In the past, acting humble with members outside the family ensured that you would make no one *envidioso* (envious); therefore he or she would not use witchcraft against you. If you get above yourself, you're an *envidiosa*. If you don't behave like everyone else, *la gente* will say that you think you're better than others, *que te crees grande*. With ambition (condemned in the Mexican culture and valued in the Anglo) comes envy. *Respeto* carries with it a set of rules so that social categories and hierarchies will be kept in order: respect is reserved for *la abuela, papá, el patrón,* those with power in the community. Women are at the bottom of the ladder one rung above the deviants. The Chicano, *mexicano,* and some Indian cultures have no tolerance for deviance. Deviance is whatever is condemned by the community. Most societies try to get rid of their deviants. Most cultures have burned and beaten their homosexuals and others who deviate from the sexual common.[1] The queer are the mirror reflecting the heterosexual tribe's fear: being different, being other and therefore lesser, therefore sub-human, inhuman, non-human.

HALF AND HALF

There was a *muchacha* who lived near my house. *La gente del pueblo* talked about her being *una de las otras,* "of the Others." They said that for six months she was a woman who had a vagina that bled once a month, and that for the other six months she was a man, had a penis and she peed standing up. They called her half and half, *mita' y mita'*, neither one nor the other but a strange doubling, a deviation of nature that horrified, a work of nature inverted. But there is a magic aspect in abnormality and so-called deformity. Maimed, mad, and sexually different people were believed to possess supernatural powers by primal cultures' magico-religious thinking. For them, abnormality was the price a person had to pay for her or his inborn extraordinary gift.

There is something compelling about being both male and female, about having an entry into both worlds. Contrary to some psychiatric tenets, half and halfs are not suffering from a confusion of sexual identity, or even from a confusion of gender. What we are suffering from is an absolute despot duality that says we are able to be only one or the other. It claims that human nature is limited and cannot evolve into something better. But I, like other queer people, am two in one body, both male and female. I am the embodiment of the *hieros gamos:* the coming together of opposite qualities within.

FEAR OF GOING HOME: HOMOPHOBIA

For the lesbian of color, the ultimate rebellion she can make against her native culture is through her sexual behavior. She goes against two moral prohibitions: sexuality and homosexuality. Being lesbian and raised Catholic, indoctrinated as straight, I *made the choice to be queer* (for some it is genetically inherent). It's an interesting path, one that continually slips in and out of the white, the Catholic, the Mexican, the indigenous, the instincts. In and out of my head. It makes for *loquería*, the crazies. It is a path of knowledge—one of knowing (and of learning) the history of oppression of our *raza*. It is a way of balancing, of mitigating duality.

In a New England college where I taught, the presence of a few lesbians threw the more conservative heterosexual students and faculty into a panic. The two lesbian students and we two lesbian instructors met with them to discuss their fears. One of the students said, "I thought homophobia meant fear of going home after a residency."

And I thought, how apt. Fear of going home. And of not being taken in. We're afraid of being abandoned by the mother, the culture, *la Raza*, for being unacceptable, faulty, damaged. Most of us unconsciously believe that if we reveal this unacceptable aspect of the self our mother/culture/race will totally reject us. To avoid rejection, some of us conform to the values of the culture, push the unacceptable parts into the shadows. Which leaves only one fear—that we will be found out and that the Shadow-Beast will break out of its cage. Some of us take another route. We try to make ourselves conscious of the Shadow-Beast, stare at the sexual lust and lust for power and destruction we see on its face, discern among its features the undershadow that the reigning order of heterosexual males project on our Beast. Yet still others of us take it another step: we try to waken the Shadow-Beast inside us. Not many jump at the chance to confront the Shadow-Beast in the mirror without flinching at her lidless serpent eyes, her cold clammy moist hand dragging us underground, fangs barred and hissing. How does one put feathers on this particular serpent? But a few of us have been lucky—on the face of the Shadow-Beast we have seen not lust but tenderness; on its face we have uncovered the lie.

INTIMATE TERRORISM: LIFE IN THE BORDERLANDS

The world is not a safe place to live in. We shiver in separate cells in enclosed cities, shoulders hunched, barely keeping the panic below the surface of the skin, daily drinking shock along with our morning coffee, fearing the torches being set to our buildings, the attacks in the streets. Shutting down. Woman does not feel safe when her own culture, and white culture, are critical of her; when the males of all races hunt her as prey.

Alienated from her mother culture, "alien" in the dominant culture, the woman of color does not feel safe within the inner life of her Self. Petrified, she can't respond, her face caught between *los intersticios*, the spaces between the different worlds she inhabits.

The ability to respond is what is meant by responsibility, yet our cultures take away our ability to act—shackle us in the name of protection. Blocked, immobilized, we can't move forward, can't move backwards. That writhing serpent movement, the very movement of life, swifter than lightning, frozen.

We do not engage fully. We do not make full use of our faculties. We abnegate. And there in front of us is the crossroads and choice: to feel a victim where someone else is in control and therefore responsible and to blame (being a victim and transferring the blame on culture, mother, father, ex-lover, friend, absolves me of responsibility), or to feel strong, and, for the most part, in control.

My Chicana identity is grounded in the Indian woman's history of resistance. The Aztec female rites of mourning were rites of defiance protesting the cultural changes which disrupted the equality and balance between female and male, and protesting their demotion to a lesser status, their denigration. Like *la Llorona*, the Indian woman's only means of protest was wailing.

So *mamá, Raza,* how wonderful, *no tener que rendir cuentas a nadie.* I feel perfectly free to rebel and to rail against my culture. I fear no betrayal on my part because, unlike Chicanas and other women of color who grew up white or who have only recently returned to their native cultural roots, I was totally immersed in mine. It wasn't until I went to high school that I "saw" whites. Until I worked on my master's degree I had not gotten within an arm's distance of them. I was totally immersed *en lo mexicano,* a rural, peasant, isolated, *mexican-ismo.* To separate from my culture (as from my family) I had to feel competent enough on the outside and secure enough inside to live life on my own. Yet in leaving home I did not lose touch with my origins because *lo mexicano* is in my system. I am a turtle, wherever I go I carry "home" on my back.

Not me sold out my people but they me. So yes, though "home" permeates every sinew and cartilage in my body, I too am afraid of going home. Though I'll defend my race and culture when they are attacked by non-*mexicanos, conozco el malestar de mi cultura.* I abhor some of my culture's ways, how it cripples its women, *como burras,* our strengths used against us, lowly *burras* bearing humility with dignity. The ability to serve, claim the males, is our highest virtue. I abhor how my culture makes *macho* caricatures of its men. No, I do not buy all the myths of the tribe into which I was born. I can understand why the more tinged with Anglo blood, the more adamantly my colored and colorless sisters glorify their colored culture's values—to offset the extreme devaluation of it by the white culture. It's a legitimate reaction. But I will not glorify those aspects of my culture which have injured me and which have injured me in the name of protecting me.

So, don't give me your tenets and your laws. Don't give me your lukewarm gods. What I want is an accounting with all three cultures—white, Mexican, Indian. I want the freedom to carve and chisel my own face, to staunch the bleeding with ashes, to fashion my own gods out of my entrails. And if going home is denied me then I will have to stand and claim my space, making a new culture—*una cultura mestiza*—with my own lumber, my own bricks and mortar and my own feminist architecture.

THE WOUNDING OF THE *INDIA*-MESTIZA

Estas carnes indias que despreciamos nosotros los mexicanos así como despreciamos y con-
denamos a nuestra madre, Malinali. Nos condenamos a nosotros mismos. Esta raza vencida,
enemigo cuerpo.

Not me sold out my people but they me. *Malinali Tenepat,* or *Malintzin,* has become known as *la Chingada*—the fucked one. She has become the bad word that passes a dozen times a day from the lips of Chicanos. Whore, prostitute, the woman who sold out her people to the Spaniards are epithets Chicanos spit out with contempt.

The worst kind of betrayal lies in making us believe that the Indian woman in us is the betrayer. *We, indias y mestizas,* police the Indian in us, brutalize and condemn her. Male culture has done a good job on us. *Son las costumbres que traicionan. La india en mí es la sombra: La Chingada, Tlazolteotl, Coatlicue. Son ellas que oyemos lamentando a sus hijas perdidas.*

Not me sold out my people but they me. Because of the color of my skin they betrayed me. The dark-skinned woman has been silenced, gagged, caged, bound into servitude with marriage, bludgeoned for 300 years, sterilized and castrated in the twentieth century. For 300 years she has been a slave, a force of cheap labor, colonized by the Spaniard, the Anglo, by her own people (and in Mesoamerica her lot under the Indian patriarchs was not free of wounding). For 300 years she was invisible, she was not heard. Many times she wished to speak, to act, to protest, to challenge. The odds were heavily against her. She hid her feelings; she hid her truths; she concealed her fire; but she kept stoking the inner flame. She remained faceless and voiceless, but a light shone through her veil of silence. And though she was unable to spread her limbs and though for her right now the sun has sunk under the earth and there is no moon, she continues to tend the flame. The spirit of the fire spurs her to fight for her own skin and a piece of ground to stand on, a ground from which to view the world—a perspective, a homeground where she can plumb the rich ancestral roots into her own ample *mestiza* heart. She waits till the waters are not so turbulent and the mountains not so slippery with sleet. Battered and bruised she waits, her bruises throwing her back upon herself and the rhythmic pulse of the feminine. *Coatlalopeuh* waits with her.

Aquí en la soledad prospera su rebeldía.
En la soledad Ella prospera.

NOTES

1. Francisco Guerra, *The Pre-Columbian Mind: A study into the aberrant nature of sexual drives, drugs affecting behaviour, and the attitude towards life and death, with a survey of psychotherapy in pre-Columbian America* (New York, NY: Seminar Press, 1971).

Reading

In Search of Bruce Lee's Grave

SHANLON WU

It's Saturday morning in Seattle, and I am driving to visit Bruce Lee's grave. I have been in the city for only a couple of weeks and so drive two blocks past the cemetery before realizing that I've passed it. I double back and turn through the large wrought-iron gate, past a sign that reads: "Open to 9 P.M. or dusk, whichever comes first.'"

It's a sprawling cemetery, with winding roads leading in all directions. I feel silly trying to find his grave with no guidance. I think that my search for his grave is similar to my search for Asian heroes in America.

I was born in 1959, an Asian-American in Westchester County, N.Y. During my childhood there were no Asian sports stars. On television, I can recall only that most pathetic of Asian characters, Hop Sing, the Cartwright family house-boy on "Bonanza." But in my adolescence there was Bruce.

I was 14 years old when I first saw "Enter the Dragon," the granddaddy of martial-arts movies. Bruce had died suddenly at the age of 32 of cerebral edema, an excess of fluid in the brain, just weeks before the release of the film. Between the ages of 14 and 17, I saw "Enter the Dragon" 22 times before I stopped counting. During those years I collected Bruce Lee posters, putting them up at all angles in my bedroom. I took up Chinese martial arts and spent hours comparing my physique with his.

I learned all I could about Bruce: that he had married a Caucasian, Linda; that he had sparred with Kareem Abdul-Jabbar; that he was a buddy of Steve McQueen and James Coburn, both of whom were his pallbearers.

My parents, who immigrated to America and had become professors at Hunter College, tolerated my behavior, but seemed puzzled at my admiration of an "entertainer." My father jokingly tried to compare my obsession with Bruce to his boyhood worship of Chinese folk-tale heroes.

"I read them just like you read American comic books," he said.

But my father's heroes could not be mine; they came from an ancient literary tradition, not comic books. He and my mother had grown up in a land where they belonged to the majority. I could not adopt their childhood and they were wise enough not to impose it upon me.

Although I never again experienced the kind of blind hero worship I felt for Bruce, my need to find heroes remained strong.

In college, I discovered the men of the 442d Regimental Combat Team, a United States Army all-Japanese unit in World War II. Allowed to fight only against Europeans, they suffered heavy casualties while their families were put in internment camps. Their motto was "Go for Broke."

I saw them as Asians in a Homeric epic, the protagonists of a Shakespearean tragedy; I knew no Eastern myths to infuse them with. They embodied my own need to prove myself in the Caucasian world. I imagined how their American-born flesh and muscle must have resembled mine: epicanthic folds set in strong faces nourished on milk and beef. I thought how much they had proved where there was so little to prove.

After college, I competed as an amateur boxer in an attempt to find my self-image in the ring. It didn't work. My fighting was only an attempt to copy Bruce's movies. What I needed was instruction on how to live. I quit boxing after a year and went to law school.

I was an anomaly there: a would-be Asian litigator. I had always liked to argue and found I liked doing it in front of people even more. When I won the first-year moot court competition in law school, I asked an Asian classmate if he thought I was the first Asian to win. He laughed and told me I was probably the only Asian to even compete.

The law-firm interviewers always seemed surprised that I wanted to litigate.

"Aren't you interested in Pacific Rim trade?" they asked.

"My Chinese isn't good enough," I quipped.

My pat response seemed to please them. It certainly pleased me. I thought I'd found a place of my own—a place where the law would insulate me from the pressure of defining my Asian maleness. I sensed the possibility of merely being myself.

But the pressure reasserted itself. One morning, the year after graduating from law school, I read the obituary of Gen. Minoru Genda—the man who planned the Pearl Harbor attack. I'd never heard of him and had assumed that whoever did that planning was long since dead. But the general had been alive all those years—rising at 4 every morning to do his exercises and retiring every night by 8. An advocate of animal rights, the obituary said.

I found myself drawn to the general's life despite his association with the Axis powers. He seemed a forthright, graceful man who died unhumbled. The same paper carried a front-page story about Congress's failure to pay the Japanese-American internees their promised reparation money. The general, at least, had not died waiting for reparations.

I was surprised and frightened by my admiration for General Genda, by my still-strong hunger for images of powerful Asian men. That hunger was my vulnerability manifested, a reminder of my lack of place.

The hunger is eased this gray morning in Seattle. After asking directions from a policeman—Japanese—I easily locate Bruce's grave. The headstone is red granite with a small picture etched into it. The picture is very Hollywood—Bruce wears dark glasses—and I think the calligraphy looks a bit sloppy. Two tourists stop but leave quickly after glancing at me.

I realize I am crying. Bruce's grave seems very small in comparison to his place in my boyhood. So small in comparison to my need for heroes. Seeing his grave, I understand how large the hole in my life has been and how desperately I'd sought to fill it.

I had sought an Asian hero to emulate. But none of my choices quite fit me. Their lives were defined through heroic tasks—they had villains to defeat and wars to fight—while my life seemed merely a struggle to define myself.

But now I see how that very struggle has defined me. I must be my own hero even as I learn to treasure those who have gone before.

I have had my powerful Asian male images: Bruce, the men of the 442d and General Genda; I may yet discover others. Their lives beckon like fireflies on a moonless night, and I know that they—like me—may have been flawed by foolhardiness and even cruelty. Still, their lives were real. They were not house-boys on "Bonanza."

Reading ## Out on Main Street

SHANI MOOTOO

I.

Janet and me? We does go Main Street to see pretty pretty sari and bangle, and to eat we belly full a burfi and gulub jamoon, but we doh go too often because, yuh see, is dem sweets self what does give people like we a presupposition for untameable hip and thigh.

Another reason we shy to frequent dere is dat we is watered-down Indians—we ain't good grade A Indians. We skin brown, is true, but we doh even think 'bout India unless something happen over dere and it come on de news. Mih family remain Hindu ever since mih ancestors leave India behind, but nowadays dey doh believe in praying unless things real bad, because, as mih father always singing, like if is a mantra: "Do good and good will be bestowed unto you." So he is a veritable saint cause he always doing good by his women friends and dey chilren. I sure some a dem must be mih half sister and brother, oui!

Mostly, back home, we is kitchen Indians: some kind a Indian food every day, at least once a day, but we doh get cardamom and other fancy spice down dere so de food not spicy like Indian food I eat in restaurants up here. But it have one thing we doh make joke 'bout down dere: we like we meethai and sweetrice too much, and it remain overly authentic, like de day Naana and Naani step off de boat in Port of Spain harbour over a hundred and sixty years ago. Check out dese hips here nah, dey is pure sugar and condensed milk, pure sweetness!

But Janet family different. In de ole days when Canadian missionaries land in Trinidad dey used to make a bee-line straight for Indians from down South. And Janet great grandparents is one a de first South families dat exchange over from Indian to Presbyterian. Dat was a long time ago.

When Janet born, she father, one Mr. John Mahase, insist on asking de Reverend MacDougal from Trace Settlement Church, a leftover from de Canadian Mission, to name de baby girl. De good Reverend choose de name Constance cause dat was his mother name. But de mother a de child, Mrs. Savitri Mahase, wanted to name de child sheself. Ever since Savitri was a lil girl she like de yellow hair, fair skin and pretty pretty clothes Janet and John used to wear in de primary school reader—since she lil she want to change she name from Savitri to Janet but she own father get vex and say how Savitri was his mother name and how she will insult his mother if she gone and change it. So Savitri get she own way once by marrying this fella name John, and she do a encore, by calling she daughter Janet, even doh husband John upset for days at she for insulting de good Reverend by throwing out de name a de Reverend mother.

So dat is how my girlfriend, a darkskin Indian girl with thick black hair (pretty fuh so!) get a name like Janet.

She come from a long line a Presbyterian school teacher, headmaster and headmistress. Savitri still teaching from de same Janet and John reader in a primary school in San Fernando, and John, getting more and more obtuse in his ole age, is headmaster more dan twenty years now in Princes Town Boys' Presbyterian High School. Everybody back home know dat family good good. Dat is why Janet leave in two twos. Soon as A Level finish she pack up and take off like a jet plane so she could live without people only shoo-shooing behind she back . . . "But A A! Yuh ain't hear de goods 'bout John Mahase daughter, gyul? How yuh mean yuh ain't hear? Is a big thing! Everybody talking 'bout she. Hear dis, nah! Yuh ever see she wear a dress? Yes! Doh look at mih so. Yuh reading mih right!"

Is only recentish I realize Mahase is a Hindu last name. In de ole days every Mahase in de country turn Presbyterian and now de name doh have no association with Hindu or Indian whatsoever. I used to think of it as a Presbyterian Church name until some days ago when we meet a Hindu fella fresh from India name Yogdesh Mahase who never even hear of Presbyterian.

De other day I ask Janet what she know 'bout Divali. She say, "It's the Hindu festival of lights, isn't it?" like a line straight out a dictionary. Yuh think she know anything 'bout how lord Rama get himself exile in a forest for fourteen years, and how when it come time for him to go back home his followers light up a pathway to help him make his way out, and dat is what Divali lights is all about? All Janet know is 'bout going for drive in de country to see light, and she could remember looking forward, around Divali time, to the lil brown paper-bag packages full a burfi and parasad that she father Hindu students used to bring for him.

One time in a Indian restaurant she ask for parasad for dessert. Well! Since den I never go back in dat restaurant, I embarrass fuh so!

I used to think I was a Hindu *par excellence* until I come up here and see real flesh and blood Indian from India. Up here, I learning 'bout all kind a custom and food and music and clothes dat we never see or hear 'bout in good ole Trinidad. Is de next best thing to going to India, in truth, oui! But Indian store clerk on Main Street doh have no patience with us, specially when we talking English to dem. Yuh ask dem a question in English and dey insist on giving de answer in Hindi or Punjabi or Urdu or Gujarati. How I suppose to know de difference even! And den dey look at yuh disdainful disdainful—like yuh disloyal, like yuh is a traitor.

But yuh know, it have one other reason I real reluctant to go Main Street. Yuh see, Janet pretty fuh so! And I doh like de way men does look at she, as if because she wearing jeans and T-shirt and high-heel shoe and make-up and have long hair loose and flying about like she is a walking-talking shampoo ad, dat she easy. And de women always looking at she beady eye, like she loose and going to thief dey man. Dat kind a thing always make me want to put mih arm round she waist like, she is my woman, take yuh eyes off she! and shock de false teeth right out dey mouth. And den is a whole other story when dey see me with mih crew cut and mih blue jeans tuck inside mih jim-boots. Walking next to Janet, who so femme dat she redundant, tend to make me look like a gender dey forget to classify. Before going Main Street I does parade in front de mirror practicing a jiggly-wiggly kind a walk. But if I ain't walking like a strong-man monkey I doh exactly feel right and I always revert back to mih true colours. De men dem does look at me like if dey is exactly what I need a taste of to cure me good and proper. I could see dey eyes watching Janet and me, dey face growing dark as dey imagining all kind a situation and position. And de women dem embarrass fuh so to watch me in mih eye, like dey fraid I will jump up and try to kiss dem, or make pass at dem. Yuh know, sometimes I wonder if I ain't mad enough to do it just for a little bacchanal, nah!

Going for a outing with mih Janet on Main Street ain't easy! If only it wasn't for burfi and gulub jamoon! If only I had a learned how to cook dem kind a thing before I leave home and come up here to live!

2.

In large deep-orange Sanskrit-style letters, de sign on de saffron-colour awning above de door read "Kush Valley Sweets." Underneath in smaller red letters it had "Desserts Fit For The Gods." It was a corner building. The front and side was one big glass wall. Inside was big. Big like a gymnasium. Yuh could see in through de brown tint windows: dark brown plastic chair, and brown table, each one de length of a door, line up stiff and straight in row after row like if is a school room.

Before entering de restaurant I ask Janet to wait one minute outside with me while I rumfle up mih memory, pulling out all de sweet names I know from home, besides burfi and gulub jamoon: meethai, jilebi, sweetrice (but dey call dat kheer up here), and ladhoo. By now, of course, mih mouth watering fuh so! When I feel confident enough dat I wouldn't make a fool a mih Brown self by asking what dis one name? and what dat one name? we went in de restaurant. In two twos all de spice in de place take a flying leap in our direction and give us one big welcome hug up, tight fuh so! Since den dey take up permanent residence in de jacket I wear dat day!

Mostly it had women customers sitting at de tables, chatting and laughing, eating sweets and sipping masala tea. De only men in de place was de waiters, and all six waiters was men. I figure dat dey was brothers, not too hard to conclude, because all a dem had de same full round chin, round as if de chin stretch tight over a ping-pong ball, and dey had de same big roving eyes. I know better dan to think dey was mere waiters in de employ of a owner who chook up in a office in de back. I sure dat dat was dey own family business, dey stomach proudly preceeding dem and dey shoulders throw back in de confidence of dey ownership.

It ain't dat I paranoid, yuh understand, but from de moment we enter de fellas dem get over-animated, even armorously agitated. Janet again! All six pair a eyes land up on she, following she every move and body part. Dat in itself is something dat does madden me, oui! but also a kind a irrational envy have a tendency to manifest in me. It was like I didn't exist. Sometimes it could be a real problem going out with a good-looker, yes! While I ain't remotely interested in having a squeak of a flirtation with a man, it doh hurt a ego to have a man notice yuh once in a very long while. But with Janet at mih side, I doh have de chance of a penny shave-ice in de hot sun. I tuck mih elbows in as close to mih sides as I could so I wouldn't look like a strong man next to she, and over to de l-o-n-g glass case jam up with sweets I jiggle and wiggle in mih best imitation a some a dem gay fellas dat I see downtown Vancouver, de ones who more femme dan even Janet. I tell she not to pay de brothers no attention, because if any a dem flirt with she I could start a fight right dere and den. And I didn't feel to mess up mih crew cut in a fight.

De case had sweets in every nuance of colour in a rainbow. Sweets I never before see and doh know de names of. But dat was alright because I wasn't going to order dose ones anyway.

Since before we leave home Janet have she mind set on a nice thick syrupy curl a jilebi and a piece a plain burfi so I order dose for she and den I ask de waiter-fella, resplendent with thick thick bright-yellow gold chain and ID bracelet, for a stick a meethai for mihself. I stand up waiting by de glass case for it but de waiter/owner lean up on de back wall behind de counter watching me like he ain't hear me. So I say loud enough for him, and every body else in de room to hear, "I would like to have one piece a meethai please," and den he smile and lift up his hands, palms open-out motioning across de vast expanse a glass case, and he say, "Your choice! Whichever you want, Miss." But he still lean up against de back wall grinning. So I stick mih head out and up like a turtle and say louder, and slowly, "One piece a meethai—dis one!" and I point sharp to de stick a flour mix with ghee, deep fry and den roll up in sugar. He say, "That is koorma, Miss. One piece only?"

Mih voice drop low all by itself. "Oh ho! Yes, one piece. Where I come from we does call dat meethai." And den I add, but only loud enough for Janet to hear, "And mih name ain't 'Miss.' "

He open his palms out and indicate de entire panorama a sweets and he say, "These are all meethai, Miss. Meethai is Sweets. Where are you from?"

I ignore his question and to show him I undaunted, I point to a round pink ball and say, "I'll have one a dese sugarcakes too please." He start grinning broad broad like if he half-pitying, half-laughing at dis Indian-in-skin-colour-only, and den he tell me, "That is called chum-chum, Miss." I snap back at him, "Yeh, well back home we does call dat sugarcake, Mr. Chum-chum."

At de table Janet say, "You know, Pud [Pud, short for Pudding; is dat she does call me when she feeling close to me, or sorry for me], it's true that we call that 'meethai' back home. Just like how we call 'siu mai' 'tim sam.' As if 'dim sum' is just one little piece a food. What did he call that sweet again?"

"Cultural bastards, Janet, cultural bastards. Dat is what we is. Yuh know, one time a fella from India who living up here call me a bastardized Indian because I didn't know Hindi. And now look at dis, nah! De thing is: all a we in Trinidad is cultural bastards, Janet, all a we. *Toutes bagailles!* Chinese people, Black people, White people. Syrian. Lebanese. I looking forward to de day I find out dat place inside me where I am nothing else but Trinidadian, whatever dat could turn out to be."

I take a bite a de chum-chum, de texture was like grind-up coconut but it had no coconut, not even a hint a coconut taste in it. De thing was juicy with sweet rose water oozing out a it. De rose water perfume enter mih nose and get trap in mih cranium. Ah drink two cup a masala tea and a lassi and still de rose water perfume was on mih tongue like if I had a overdosed on Butchart Gardens.

Suddenly de door a de restaurant spring open wide with a strong force and two big burly fellas stumble in, almost rolling over on to de ground. Dey get up, eyes red and slow and dey skin burning pink with booze. Dey straighten up so much to overcompensate for falling forward, dat dey find deyself leaning backward. Everybody stop talking and was watching dem. De guy in front put his hand up to his forehead and take a deep Walter Raleigh bow, bringing de hand down to his waist in a rolling circular movement. Out loud he greet everybody with "Alarm o salay koom." A part a me wanted to bust out laughing. Another part make mih jaw drop open in disbelief. De calm in de place get rumfle up. De two fellas dem, feeling chupid now because nobody reply to dey greeting, gone up to de counter to Chum-chum trying to make a little conversation with him. De same booze-pink alarm-o-salay-koom-fella say to Chum-chum, "Hey, howaryah?"

Chum-chum give a lil nod and de fella carry right on, "Are you Sikh?"

Chum-chum brothers converge near de counter, busying deyselves in de vicinity. Chum-chum look at his brothers kind a quizzical, and he touch his cheek and feel his forehead with de back a his palm. He say, "No, I think I am fine, thank you. But I am sorry if I look sick, Sir."

De burly fella confuse now, so he try again.

"Where are you from?"

Chum-chum say, "Fiji, Sir."

"Oh! Fiji, eh! Lotsa palm trees and beautiful women, eh! Is it true that you guys can have more than one wife?"

De exchange make mih blood rise up in a boiling froth. De restaurant suddenly get a gruff quietness 'bout it except for a woman I hear whispering angrily to another woman at de table behind us, "I hate this! I just hate it! I can't stand to see our men humiliated by them, right in front of us. He should refuse to serve them, he should throw them out. Who on earth do they think they are? The awful fools!" And de friend whisper back, "If he throws them out all of us will suffer in the long run."

I could discern de hair on de back a de neck a Chum-chum brothers standing up, annoyed, and at de same time de brothers look like dey was shrinking in stature. Chum-chum get serious, and he politely say, "What can I get for you?"

Pinko get de message and he point to a few items in de case and say, "One of each, to go please."

Holding de white take-out box in one hand he extend de other to Chum-chum and say, "How do you say 'Excuse me, I'm sorry' in Fiji?"

Chum-chum shake his head and say, "It's okay. Have a good day."

Pinko insist, "No, tell me please. I think I just behaved badly, and I want to apologize. How do you say 'I'm sorry' in Fiji?"

Chum-chum say, "Your apology is accepted. Everything is okay." And he discreetly turn away to serve a person who had just entered de restaurant. De fellas take de hint dat was broad like daylight, and back out de restaurant like two little mouse.

Everybody was feeling sorry for Chum-chum and Brothers. One a dem come up to de table across from us to take a order from a woman with a giraffe-long neck who say, "Brother, we mustn't accept how these people think they can treat us. You men really put up with too many insults and abuse over here. I really felt for you."

Another woman gone up to de counter to converse with Chum-chum in she language. She reach out and touch his hand, sympathy-like. Chum-chum hold the one hand in his two and make a verbose speech to her as she nod she head in agreement generously. To italicize her support, she buy a take-out box a two burfi, or rather, dat's what I think dey was.

De door a de restaurant open again, and a bevy of Indian-looking women saunter in, dress up to weaken a person's decorum. De Miss Universe pageant traipse across de room to a table. Chum-chum and Brothers start smoothing dey hair back, and pushing de front a dey shirts neatly into dey pants. One brother take out a pack a Dentyne from his shirt pocket and pop one in his mouth. One take out a comb from his back pocket and smooth down his hair. All a dem den converge on dat single table to take orders. Dey begin to behave like young pups in mating season. Only, de women dem wasn't impress by all this tra-la-la at all and ignore dem except to make dey order, straight to de point. Well, it look like Brothers' egos were having a rough day and dey start roving 'bout de room, dey egos and de crotch a dey pants leading far in front dem. One brother gone over to Giraffebai to see if she want anything more. He call she "dear" and put his hand on she back. Giraffebai straighten she back in surprise and reply in a not-too-friendly way. When he gone to write up de bill she see me looking at she and she say to me, "Whoever does he think he is! Calling me dear and touching me like that! Why do these men always think that they have permission to touch whatever and wherever they want! And you can't make a fuss about it in public, because it is exactly what those people out there want to hear about so that they can say how sexist and uncivilized our culture is."

I shake mih head in understanding and say, "Yeah. I know. Yuh right!"

De atmosphere in de room take a hairpin turn, and it was man aggressing on woman, woman warding off a herd a man who just had dey pride publicly cut up a couple a times in just a few minutes.

One brother walk over to Janet and me and he stand up facing me with his hands clasp in front a his crotch, like if he protecting it. Stiff stiff, looking at me, he say, "Will that be all?"

Mih crew cut start to tingle, so I put on mih femmest smile and say, "Yes, that's it, thank you. Just the bill please." De smart-ass turn to face Janet and he remove his hands from in front a his crotch and slip his thumbs inside his pants like a cowboy 'bout to do a square dance. He smile, looking down at her attentive fuh so, and he say, "Can I do anything for you?"

I didn't give Janet time fuh his intent to even register before I bulldoze in mih most un-femmest manner, "She have everything she need, man, thank you. The bill please." Yuh think he hear me? It was like I was talking to thin air. He remain smiling at Janet, but she, looking at me, not at him, say, "You heard her. The bill please."

Before he could even leave de table proper, I start mih tirade. "But A A! Yuh see dat? Yuh could believe dat! De effing so-and-so! One minute yuh feel sorry fuh dem and next minute dey harassing de heck out a you. Janet, he crazy to mess with my woman, yes!" Janet get vex with me and say I overreacting, and is not fuh me to be vex, but fuh she to be vex. Is she he insult, and she could take good enough care a sheself.

I tell she I don't know why she don't cut off all dat long hair, and stop wearing lipstick and eyeliner. Well, who tell me to say dat! She get real vex and say dat nobody will tell she how to dress and how not to dress, not me and not any man. Well I could see de potential dat dis fight had coming, and when Janet get fighting vex, watch out! It hard to get a word in edgewise, yes! And she does bring up incidents from years back dat have no bearing on de current situation. So I draw back quick quick but she don't waste time; she was already off to a good start. It was best to leave right dere and den.

Just when I stand up to leave, de doors dem open up and in walk Sandy and Lise, coming for dey weekly hit a Indian sweets. Well, with Sandy and Lise is a dead giveaway dat dey not dressing fuh any man, it have no place in dey life fuh man-vibes, and dat in fact dey have a blatant penchant fuh women. Soon as dey enter de room yuh could see de brothers and de couple men customers dat had come in minutes before stare dem down from head to Birkenstocks, dey eyes bulging with disgust. And de women in de room start shoo-shooing, and putting dey hand in front dey mouth to stop dey surprise, and false teeth, too, from falling out. Sandy and Lise spot us instantly and dey call out to us, shameless, loud and affectionate. Dey leap over to us, eager to hug up and kiss like if dey hadn't seen us for years, but it was really only since two nights aback when we went out to dey favourite Indian restaurant for dinner. I figure dat de display was a genuine happiness to be seen wit us in dat place. While we stand up dere chatting, Sandy insist on rubbing she hand up and down Janet back—wit friendly intent, mind you, and same time Lise have she arm round Sandy waist. Well, all cover get blown. If it was even remotely possible dat I wasn't noticeable before, now Janet and I were over-exposed. We could a easily suffer from hypothermia, specially since it suddenly get cold cold in dere. We say goodbye, not soon enough, and as we were leaving I turn to acknowledge Giraffebai, but instead a any recognition of our buddiness against de fresh brothers, I get a face dat look like it was in de presence of a very foul smell.

De good thing, doh, is dat Janet had become so incensed 'bout how we get scorned, dat she forgot I tell she to cut she hair and to ease up on de make-up, and so I get save from hearing 'bout how I too jealous, and how much I inhibit she, and how she would prefer if I would grow *my* hair, and wear lipstick and put on a dress sometimes. I so glad, oui! dat I didn't have to go through hearing how I too demanding a she, like de time, she say, I prevent she from seeing a ole boyfriend when he was in town for a couple hours *en route* to live in Australia with his new bride (because, she say, I was jealous dat ten years ago dey sleep together.) Well, look at mih crosses, nah! Like if I really so possessive and jealous!

So tell me, what yuh think 'bout dis nah, girl?

Cartography

KARL WOELZ

Trees sway gold and green and rust leaves in the brisk wind that whistles around the corner of the squat gray house with the carefully trimmed shrubs and forest-green shutters beside windows cleaned to sparkling. The seasonal wreath on the front door encircles a gleaming brass knocker and nameplate upon which, dead center, the deeply engraved *Hargrove* beckons like the heart of a target.

Bryan traces circles on the top of the kitchen table with the hard white end of his ballpoint pen, his mind settled on nothing in particular. The neat stack of bills on the table before him. The patch of sunlight in which a squirrel sits in the backyard, head tilted to one side as if listening to the quiet hum of the refrigerator. The occasional clunk of the ice-maker. *Mr. and Mrs. Richard VanHoffstatt request the honor of your presence* peeks out from beneath a sky-blue envelope from the orthodontist, a bill yet unpaid. The invitation, its elegant, looping script printed on heavy cardstock, has been addressed to Trevor and Philip Hargrove and Bryan Lefflin, the third name by itself on a line of its own, separate from the others.

Bryan looks at the small, cream-colored envelope which rests on top of his bills, addressed to a young woman he barely knows whose name will soon change, and examines the stamp unlike those he has just used—*Love 29¢*—in the upper right-hand corner of this delicate square of cream-colored paper. He can see the girl, leaning over the dark-brown counter of the post office, her hand, soon to be ringed, gracefully tucking a swath of hair behind her ear as she pores over a laminated sheet of brightly colored stamps while her mother pulls a crisp, twenty-dollar bill from the back of her thick, black leather checkbook.

Weddings. Bryan thinks. Smiling glassy-eyed women. Self-satisfied men, husbands or boyfriends or lovers, their arms resting on the backs of oiled wooden pews, casually marking off territory. Pastors or priests or reverends, talking always of the sanctity of Union. *Does Philip own an appropriate pair of shoes?* Bryan taps his pen on top of the checkbook. *Which card can hold a pair of shoes?*

It's unlikely that Philip will allow himself to be seen in a pair of loafers, although one never knows. Bryan remembers shopping with his mother. *Is it too tight? Do you have enough room? Are you sure you like that color? What about this one?* He tries to avoid saying things like this when out with Philip, but he hears the words coming out of his mouth all the same, as if the words have a will all their own. He's one of the few men he knows who hates to shop. His friends, and Trevor too, can spend hours rummaging through antique shops, men's furnishings or housewares departments, record stores. "Are you *sure* you're a fag?"

they ask, as he hangs back, bored silent, listening to them compare and argue and haggle. "Can we see your membership card, please?"

He hasn't even thought about a gift. Shoes and a wedding present. *Might as well get both out of the way at the same time. Maybe Philip will have some ideas; he's closer to the girl's age anyway.*

Bryan hears the Mustang pull into the driveway and looks at his watch: 4:20.

"I'm home," Philip calls as he opens the front door.

"Kitchen," Bryan answers, hearing the heavy click of the lock as the door swings shut.

"You know, I leave in the morning," Philip says as he comes into the kitchen, a rush of cool air in his path, "and you're sitting at the table. I come home and you're still sitting here." He puts his books down on the island countertop and opens the refrigerator.

"I'm turning into Ann-Margaret in *Carnal Knowledge,*" Bryan says.

"Yeah, but she stayed in *bed.*"

"I'm working up to that."

Philip takes a glass out of a cabinet next to the refrigerator and pours himself a glass of Coke. "You want some more coffee?"

"Sure."

Philip returns Bryan's coffee mug to its place beside the stack of bills, pulls out a chair, and sits down at the table. "So how was your day? You didn't go in to the shop?"

"No. I left Melisse in charge. It's pretty slow this week."

"Man of leisure."

"And how was your day?"

"The usual. A high-pressure trough of boredom with scattered showers of enlightenment in the low-lying areas."

"When was the fall of Constantinople?"

"You're a funny man. World History was last year, anyway. Do we have anything sweet to eat?"

"I think there's a couple brownies left in the bread-saver, unless your father finished them off."

Philip gets up from the table again. Bryan listens to him rummaging through the pantry, hears the lid of the Tupperware bread-saver being popped off and placed on the counter.

"Hey, he actually left me more than a crumb. For once."

"Your mother dropped some stuff off for you," Bryan says over his shoulder.

"Oh yeah? What'd she leave?"

"Brochures, mostly."

"Europe stuff?"

Philip returns to the table, half a brownie in his mouth, the rest wrapped in a napkin in his hand. Bryan slides a thick gray envelope across the surface of the table, the logo of a nearby travel agency stamped along its left edge, but Philip only glances at it and pushes it aside.

"Aren't you going to open it?" Bryan asks.

"Later," Philip says. He looks at the stack of bills next to Bryan's hand. "Is that Heather's wedding thing there?"

"Yep."

"I don't really have to go, do I?"

"Uh, *yes*"

"Oh come on, Bryan. You're not really going to make me go to that pud-fest are you?"

"Don't look at me. It's not *my* decision." Philip grimaces. "And don't use the term 'pud-fest,' please."

"But why do I have to go? Heather Van is the lamest piece of crap around," Philip says, popping a chunk of brownie into his mouth. "Just because her mom and my mom were in the same prehistoric sorority, I have to have my whole Saturday night ruined? Can't you talk to Dad about it?"

"It's one Saturday night in the grand scheme of the universe. Six weeks away, at that."

"You're a big help."

"You could bring a date."

"Yeah, right."

"I'll sneak you a beer or two."

"Philip rolls his eyes. "*That* is pretty lame bribery, Bryan. Can't you *please* convince Dad that I don't need to go?"

"Hey," Bryan offers, "you can get a new pair of shoes out of it."

Philip looks at Bryan, the image of his father, an eyebrow raised and his head cocked to one side. "You are *joking*."

"Do your toes have enough room?" Bryan asks.

Philip glares at him. "I feel like I'm on my way to a sockhop."

"But are they comfortable?"

Like a temperamental fashion model, Philip walks away from Bryan and the salesclerk, the heels of the loafers clicking sharply on the parquet floor that surrounds the carpeted island of the men's shoe department. He turns and walks back toward the two men, his head lowered either in embarrassment or examination of the denim bunched around his ankles.

"I hate them."

"They'll look better when you're wearing the right pants," Bryan offers.

"They hurt across the top of my foot."

Bryan looks at the salesclerk, a thin blond not much older than Philip, who wears too much gold. Several rings, a tie clip, a delicate bracelet. His perfectly clipped fingernails look as if they've been painted with a layer of clear polish.

"How about a wing tip?" Bryan asks the young man.

"Do you really think so?" he replies, giving Bryan a look not unlike that of a mother trying to explain why a cookie before dinner is not a good idea.

Philip sits down heavily in the chair beside Bryan and immediately removes the offending shoes. The salesclerk gently places them back in their box, folding a sheet of tissue paper over the shoes like a baby blanket, tucking it around them, carefully placing the lid back on the box.

I'm too young for this, thinks Bryan. *This is Trevor's job.* As an adolescent, he had always resented being dragged from store to store like a life-sized doll, living proof of his mother's control over the universe. He realizes now that those excursions had been as humiliating for her as they had been for him.

"So," the salesclerk says, looking at Bryan. "Wing tips?"

Philip looks at Bryan. Bryan looks at the salesclerk. The salesclerk looks at Philip's white-socked feet.

"Just bring us a pair of your plainest black shoes," Bryan says. "Lace-ups." The salesclerk disappears into the stockroom, a rush of lemony cologne in his wake.

"We are buying this pair of shoes," Bryan says, "even if, in the ten seconds they're on your feet, they turn your toes into bleeding stubs."

"Whatever you say."

"I should have made your father do this."

"He hates shopping with me."

"No small wonder."

"Here we are," the salesclerk says as he reseats himself on the ottoman in front of them. He holds up an ugly shoe free of all ornament. "Plain black lace-ups."

"We'll take them," Bryan says, offering his credit card to the young man. "Could you put the sneakers in a bag? He'll wear these out of the store."

"You know what I was thinking?" Philip says, looking out the passenger window of the Cherokee on the way home.

"About the Europe thing?"

"No, Bryan." Philip shakes his head. "I wasn't thinking about *that.*"

"It's just that your mother—"

"I *know* what my mother thinks."

Bryan wants to look at Philip but doesn't, the boy's silence a reprimand to which the older man cannot respond.

"I was thinking," Philip says slowly, "that you and Dad could have some kind of ceremony. They do things like that now."

"I don't think so." Bryan keeps his eyes on the road ahead, squinting slightly at the headlights of cars in the other lane. "Can you see your father in front of an altar?"

Philip fiddles with his shoulder restraint. "You don't have to do it in a church or anything. You could do it in the backyard. Casual."

"It's not exactly our style, Philip."

"But people do that kind of thing after ten years, don't they."

"Some people."

"We could invite some of your friends. Melisse. Art and Charles. The Murphs. Maybe a couple of my friends."

"Right."

"The cooler ones."

"Uh-huh . . ." Bryan says.

"Mom."

Bryan can't help but let out a laugh. "Your mother?"

"Just because her new husband's kind of a dweebus doesn't mean *she's* so bad. She's cool. She likes you, Bryan."

"Now she does."

"What are you always saying about water under bridges?"

"Thank you for throwing that back in my face. A natural ability you've obviously inherited from your father. Should we play 'Three Times a Lady' as I walk down the aisle?"

"Har. I'm sure we could find an appropriate k.d. lang song or something."

"Your father and I aren't *lesbians,* Philip."

"I don't know," he says, shrugging his shoulders and looking at the large hands resting in his lap, trying to make light of it all. "I just thought it might be something to do."

Bryan looks over at this handsome teenage boy, his responsibility by default, now staring out the window at the quiet, tree-lined neighborhood in which he has lived for the past ten years of his life. He sees the boy's face, mostly shadow, reflected by the dashboard light in the glass of the passenger window; a face he has washed and held and kissed and taught to shave. A face as familiar as his own. A face he will miss when Philip leaves for college in a few months.

"I'll talk to your father," Bryan says, knowing as he says it that he has already let the moment slip through his fingers.

"Forget it," Philip says, still looking out at the passing houses and their soft, golden squares of light from kitchen and living- and dining-room windows. "It was just an idea."

Bryan and Trevor lie in bed, each in his own pool of soft white light cast by a lamp on the nightstand by his head. Bryan flips through the pages of a large, glossy magazine. Trevor reads, glasses low on the bridge of his nose, from a thick, hardcover book.

"I wish you wouldn't open those cologne ads," Trevor says without looking up.

"I didn't," Bryan replies, glancing over at his partner. "Imagine how strong it would be if I had."

Trevor turns a page loudly.

"Will June be at the VanHoffstatt wedding?" Bryan asks.

"I suppose."

"You realize that Philip doesn't want to go."

"Because of June?"

"Because he's seventeen. Did you want to go to weddings at his age?"

"It wasn't a question of what I wanted to do at his age."

Don't pull that Father Knows Best *shit with me.* Bryan flips through several pages of his magazine at once. "I bought him a pair of shoes for the wedding today."

"I'm sure that was a pleasant experience."

"I can always use them for work."

"How much?"

"Eighty-something."

"Cheaper than sneakers."

Silence falls again. Bryan closes the magazine and puts it on the nightstand. He rolls over on his side, facing Trevor.

"You know what he said to me in the car on the way home tonight?"

"No" Trevor says, eyes trained on the page of his book.

"What?"

"He thinks we should have some kind of commitment ceremony."

"You and I?" Trevor looks up from his book.

"A renewal-of-vows thing."

"What did you say?"

"I said I didn't think it was our style."

"Where did he get an idea like that?"

"God only knows. I thought it was kind of sweet. Misguided, of course, but sweet."

Trevor closes his book, removes his glasses, and places both carefully on the night table. He switches off the light, leaving the two men in the glow from Bryan's lone lamp. He takes Bryan's hand and holds it in his own.

"What's with the sudden romanticism, do you think?"

"I don't know," Bryan says. "Maybe he's tired of us living in sin. Maybe he wants to make an honest woman of me."

"That's my job, I think," Trevor replies, still holding Bryan's hand as he slides into a position from which he can face his lover. He kisses Bryan's forehead.

"He even mentioned some of his friends coming."

"God, what kind of postmodern *Brady Bunch* episode is this thing supposed to *be?*"

"Do you think Robert Reed ever sucked off Greg? That was the oldest one's name, wasn't it?"

"You're disgusting," Trevor says, pinching at Bryan's nipple.

Bryan reaches across the bed, turns off the light, and slides back into Trevor's arms. "Maybe we should do it."

"No," Trevor stage-whispers into Bryan's ear, wrapping his arms and legs around him, pulling him tight against his body.

"No? We could wear white linen and play a tasteful k.d. lang ballad or something."

Trevor slaps the flat of his palm against Bryan's rump. "For Christ's sake, honey, we're not *lesbians.*"

Philip was eight years old when Bryan first met Trevor, a little boy whose new front teeth were too big for his face. He was a quiet child, watchful of the adults around him. His parents had divorced two years earlier, and he had spent those many months shuttling back and forth between the homes of his estranged parents—four days here, three days there; two tastefully quiet neighborhoods separated by a twenty-minute drive past Methodist churches, awninged dry cleaners, refurbished one-screen movie theaters with espresso bars in the lobby, and charming boutiques with heavy wooden doors in rich shades of cranberry and slate and forest green.

There are times, even now, when Bryan can still see that little boy. He stands in the open doorway of Philip's bathroom, watching him shave with a deliberateness—his brow creased in concentration—that reminds him of the boy with the tip of his tongue peeking out from between thin lips as he shades, so intent on keeping within the lines, the pages of his *Goofy and Friends* coloring book. Philip stands in front of the sink, a thick turquoise towel wrapped around his waist, unaware, Bryan thinks, of his beauty, of the handsome grace of skin and bone and muscle that defines his manhood.

"You know we're leaving in twenty-five minutes . . ." Bryan says.

"Yes," Philips answers, not taking his eyes off the mirror.

"And you still have to get dressed."

"Yes."

"And you know what your father's like about being on time."

"Bryan, you're not helping me move any faster by trying to chat right now."

"Sorry," Bryan says, turning away and walking over to the bed, where Philip's clothes are laid out, as if waiting to come to life. "Just trying to avoid catastrophe."

Philip grunts.

The box of shoes, bought weeks ago, sits unopened at the bottom of the bed. Bryan removes the lid and unfolds the tissue paper. He takes the shoes out of the box and places them next to a stack of school books on Philip's desk. He runs the fingers of his right hand across the dull, black leather. These aren't Philip at all, Bryan thinks, struck, as he sometimes is, by the idea that there is someone—a son, no less—whose existence is so intimately connected to his own and yet, at the same time, so completely independent of it.

But I'm not his father, Bryan thinks, barely registering the feel of leather beneath his fingertips. There is no doubt that Philip loves him, that Philip accepts as part of "family" this man who cooks breakfast and demands chores be done and checks homework and sleeps in his father's bed. But where in his heart is the place for such a man? *What claim do I have to all this?* Perhaps there is no place, Bryan thinks, even though he knows better, even though he knows the flash of panic in his gut is unfounded.

"What are you doing?"

Startled by Philip's voice, Bryan's hand jumps, knocking the shoe beneath his fingers off the desk. Behind him, he can hear the gentle rustle of cotton pulled over skin, the crisp snap of elastic as Philip puts on underwear. "I was just thinking," he says to the floor as he bends over to retrieve the shoe.

"Well, try not to wreck the whole desk while you're thinking so hard," Philip says as he sits on the edge of the bed and pulls on his socks.

"No, I won't," he says, placing the fallen shoe back on the desk, his voice quiet.

"Bryan, please don't get all glassy-eyed on me, okay? I thought weddings didn't make you go all goopy?"

"They don't. It was just a momentary out-of-body experience."

"What do you think of this tie?" Philip holds up a bright red tie with suns on it; suns that look like the kind you find on old maps. Maps with faded-ink drawings of sea dragons. Archaic, Bryan thinks, enjoying the word's hard vowel and the sharp click of the final "c." He sees bearded men hunched over tables lit by candles, coloring the boundaries of human experience.

"Mom got it for me," Philip says, laying the tie on the bed and picking up his navy blue pants. "For the wedding."

"Nice. Hurry up and get dressed. Dry your hair. I don't want to give your father an excuse for giving us any grief."

"Yes, O Perennial Peace-Maker."

"Smart-ass."

"Can I borrow some cologne?"

"Yeah, but I want it back," Bryan says as he begins to walk out of the bedroom.

"Smart-ass," Philip answers, throwing the tie at Bryan's back. "May I *have* some cologne?"

"What kind?" Bryan asks, stopping to lean against the frame of the bedroom door.

"I don't care. Whatever will make me smell irresistible." Philip grins.

Bryan tosses the tie back to his half-dressed son. "Dry your hair."

"Well," Trevor says, taking a sip from his wineglass, "the Van H's certainly know how to put on a good spread."

Bryan nods, fingering the stem of his own glass, which stands before him on the round table, presently empty, at which they're seated. "Are you surprised?"

"No. Grateful I'm never going to be father-of-the-bride, though."

Bryan lets out a barely audible "hmmm."

"Did you talk to June?" Trevor asks.

"Yes. And new husband."

"What did you think?"

"Philip's right: he is kind of a dweeb. Pleasant." Trevor nods in agreement. "But still a dweeb."

"Did she talk to you about the trip to Europe?"

"Of course she did," Bryan says, a little too quickly. "Why do you ask such a ridiculous question?"

"Why do you say it like that?"

"I thought the whole idea was that he was going with the Peterson boy."

"June is hardly going to pay for a friend to go *with* him."

"I'm not *suggesting* that—"

"What's the matter with you?"

"Forget it."

"Why are you upset about this? Philip shouldn't go abroad just because Jason Peterson got an internship with the *Tribune?*"

"You think it's a good idea to send Philip off to Europe by himself?"

"Don't you?" Trevor sounds surprised. "He's capable of handling a EurRail pass and youth hostels."

"I guess." Bryan sounds unconvinced.

The small band at the front of the long, tastefully decorated banquet room is playing a slow, romantic song. Bryan looks at the couples dancing; delicate heads resting on broad shoulders.

"I think it would be a good experience for him. Help him grow up."

"You take it for granted," Bryan mutters under his breath.

"What?"

"Nothing."

"Trevor!" a deep voice booms from several feet away. A tall, ruddy-faced man, one of Trevor's lawyer friends, approaches the table.

"Jack," Trevor says as he stands up to shake the man's hand. "What have you been up to?"

"Too damn much." He laughs, smiling widely and pumping Trevor's hand. "Hello Bryan. How are you?"

"Fine thanks, Jack," Bryan says, nodding and remaining seated.

"Mind if I steal this man away for a few minutes?" he asks.

"Be my guest," Bryan answers, hearing Jack say something about "that frigging Landers job" as he and Trevor head off in the direction of the bar at the back of the room.

Looking past the table's floral centerpiece, a carefully orchestrated explosion of green and white and peach, Bryan sees the bride on the other side of the dance floor, talking to a group of middle-aged women whose faces beam as if they'd just witnessed the Annunciation. The groom, an athletically handsome blond, stands jacketless at her side, holding a tall glass of beer from which he occasionally takes small sips. Pacing himself, Bryan thinks. He can see the groom's biceps straining against the sleeves of his crisp white shirt. *Solid.*

Philip in Europe, Bryan thinks. He sees Philip, a large duffel bag slung over one shoulder, standing in some dusty Spanish street with a half-folded train schedule in one hand, an obvious *turista.* Target. A gaggle of street urchins brandishing homemade weapons chase him down an alley á la Sebastian Venable.

Listen to me, Bryan thinks. *Molly Melodrama.* He takes a drink from his wineglass, clears his head of this vision, thinks briefly of the groom standing naked beneath a waterfall, an advertisement for some Hawaiian honeymoon paradise. *Philip is not an adventurous child.*

He can see the reflection of Philip's face in the windows of third-class train compartments as he hurtles across plains and over mountains, maybe meeting other American students along the way. Or not. Standing in front of paintings at the Louvre, by himself, without companions, thinking of the houses he calls home, eating at McDonald's because it's easier, doing what he must out of some sense of duty, some sense of keeping those who care for him happy.

"Are you having another out-of-body experience?" Philip asks, appearing out of nowhere, sitting in his father's vacated seat. "You are such a liar about weddings, Bryan. You have been funky all night."

"Have I?"

"Pensive is the word," Philip says, smiling. His eyes are bright. "Lighten up. Think of Heather naked, that should make you laugh."

"She's really quite pretty," Bryan says. "I don't know why you're always ragging on her."

"We go way back." Philip holds the rim of the table with one hand as he balances his chair on its rear legs. "To before you, even. I've known Heather since the *womb*, practically."

Bryan looks at Philip. "Do you remember when you first met me?"

Philip looks hard into the eyes of the man beside him. He brings the front legs of his chair back to the floor. "What's the matter, Bryan?"

"Nothing's the matter," Bryan says, conscious suddenly of the heaviness of his shoulders, the weight of his hands against his thighs. "Really. Nothing." Philip raises an eyebrow. "I'm just being *pensive*."

Underneath the table, Philip reaches out and touches Bryan's hand, his warm fingers wrapping themselves around those of the man beside him. "I wish you were having a good time," he says.

"I am."

"You have *never* been a good liar." Philip squeezes Bryan's hand. "I'm the one who's not supposed to be enjoying this, remember?"

Bryan smiles, masking, he hopes, the sudden dizzying sense of standing at the edge of the known world, staring out at territory yet undrawn.

"Hey, Hargrove," a voice behind them calls.

Philip looks over his shoulder, nods at his friend. "Coming." He turns back to Bryan. "Call of the wild."

"Go," Bryan says.

Philip squeezes Bryan's hand again and then the fingers are gone. "I'll be back," he says, scooting his chair away from the table and standing up to go. "You can't leave without me. I've got Dad's keys."

The house is quiet. Bryan listens to the steady sound of Trevor's breathing as his eyes adjust to the darkness. He had been dreaming, about what he cannot remember, when his eyes suddenly opened, as they sometimes do when a noise pierces deep sleep. He lies still, listening.

After a few minutes, he slides carefully out of the bed so as not to wake Trevor. The bedroom is blue-gray in the hazy streetlight that shines through the front window. He picks up a rumpled denim shirt from across the back of the valet and puts it on over his T-shirt and underwear. He walks down the hall to the kitchen, stopping at Philip's closed bedroom door. He puts his ear against the wood. He can hear nothing.

Slowly, like a thief caressing the lock of a huge steel safe, he turns the knob and walks silently into Philip's room. Here, too, the light is blue-gray, making everything look cold and unreal. He tiptoes to the bed and the long lump concealed beneath its covers. Philip faces the wall, the back of his head all that is visible in the room's weak light. Bryan leans over the blanket-covered form. Philip's breath is lighter than his father's, barely audible. Bryan stands there for some time, listening, until he realizes that his bare legs are growing cold, that his lower back is getting tight.

Bryan sits on the living-room couch, a blanket wrapped around his lower body. He sits in darkness, sipping from a glass of red wine, a trick he has learned to help beat his frequent bouts with sleeplessness.

And will you join with me, the reverend had said, his arms opened wide to include the entire congregation, *in support of the holy bond that Heather and Michael are making here before us today?* And the voices had called out, as one, *We do.* Bryan had felt the muscles of his throat move; had heard, as if from far away, the sound of his own voice saying the words. But what he saw, Heather and Michael and the reverend suddenly vanished, were his parents, who had no doubt envisioned a day in which *their* only son would stand before banks of flowers and rows of friends in their Sunday finery, all looking upon this spectacle as one. He saw his parents, now grown old, sitting in the morning sun on their patio, each drinking from a cup of coffee, the paper spread out between them, silently reading, the sound of waves pushing softly against the nearby beach a constant, quiet reminder of how little we can call our own.

They send Philip checks at Christmas and on his birthday, the cards written in his mother's elegant hand, signed with their Christian names: *Love, Marjorie and Clark.*

He hears his name. He feels a hand, insistent, on his shoulder. Again: "Bryan?"

He opens his eyes, sees Philip's face above him. "What?" His voice is hoarse with sleep.

"I made coffee."

"Wh' time is it?" Bryan says, pulling himself into a sitting position on the couch.

"Eight-thirty." Philip sits down beside him on the couch and holds out a coffee mug. "Want this?"

"Sure," Bryan answers, taking the coffee. "What are you doing up so early?"

"I don't know. Woke up and figured I might as well get out of bed."

"Have the Pod People taken over?" Bryan takes a careful sip from his mug. "You're not the real Philip Hargrove," he says in mock terror. "What have you done with him?"

Philip smiles. "Just drink your coffee, Mr. sleeping-on-the-couch-for-some-mysterious-reason . . . Dad kick you out of bed?"

"No. I couldn't sleep. Came out here—"

"Got sauced up." Philip nods at the wineglass sitting on the table next to the couch.

"Had *half* a glass of wine to relax me, thank you very much, and fell asleep."

"A likely story."

Bryan swats at him with one hand. "Why get up so early if you're only going to harass me, you ungrateful child?"

"You're drinking coffee made with my own two hands and *I'm* the ungrateful one?"

Bryan sets his mug on the table beside the half-filled wineglass. "Come here," he says, holding out one arm, waiting for Philip to slide in next to him. Philip rolls his eyes, sliding slowly under Bryan's arm, and leans back against the older man's chest.

"Aren't I a bit old for bedtime stories?"

"You're never too old to be hugged. Haven't you heard my mother say that a hundred times?"

"This is the last time I make you coffee if this is what I have to endure as a result of it."

"What am I going to do when you're gone?" Bryan asks, wrapping his arms around Philip's body.

"Make your own coffee, mow your own grass, run your own errands."

Bryan squeezes his arms together. Philip laughs, lets out a "hey!"

"You're so mistreated," Bryan says.

"There's a whole semester yet."

"What am I going to do, huh?"

"Miss me."

"That's right," Bryan says, lightly kissing the top of Philip's head. He waits a beat. "For about twenty minutes."

"You are such a *fart*," Philip says, wriggling out from under Bryan's arms. He scoots back to the other end of the couch, pointing his index finger: "*Fart.*"

Bryan laughs, picks up his coffee mug and drinks. "So where are you going to go on this European adventure your mother wants to send you on?"

"Who says I'm going?"

"Don't you want to?"

"Maybe I could just take the money instead."

"Whatever you want to do." Bryan takes another sip of coffee. "I'm sure your mother would understand."

"What would you do?"

Bryan looks at Philip over the top of his coffee mug. "What would *I* do?" he says.

"Uh, that *was* the question, I think."

Bryan looks at his son, at the bright eyes and delicate planes of his face. He looks into the eyes he knows so well, the eyes now searching his own for an answer. There is so much, he thinks, so much unknown until felt.

"I'd go," he says.

"You would?"

"Yes," he says, the map of his heart unfolding. "Start in Florence." He can see the world stretched out before him, its faded colors marking off the boundaries of what we know as ours. "Work your way north from there. Vienna. Prague. Berlin. Do you want to do Scandinavia?"

"I don't know. Should I?"

"Why not? There's so much," Bryan says, the past's territories taking shape with each word, rivers and plains and forests pulsing into color all around him. "So much, Philip. Like nothing you've ever seen."

Case Study　　# Three Women

ONA BREGMAN

The composite cases being presented here are not meant to represent all women, nor do they represent all approaches to working with women. This collage of cases was chosen to demonstrate a particular relationship theme. The approach comes out of this commentator's use of Bowen theory as the theoretical framework that guides her thinking and understanding of human emotional process and behavior. Some assumptions that frame this presentation follow. The emotional process in the relationship systems to which a person belongs are a major contributing factor to behavior, with the intergenerational family of origin being particularly significant. One major variable in human functioning is the degree and intensity of chronic anxiety. Anxiety is present in all living systems. It is the intensity of the anxiety and one's ability to manage oneself in the face of it that contribute to the variation in human functioning. Emotional process is common to all individuals and systems, although the content, context, biases and other societal and cultural factors will vary. If one can learn to use feelings as radar to tune into emotional process and learn to think about that process, then one is more able to be a self in relationship. These assumptions by the author grow out of her understanding of Bowen Theory.

Bowen developed his theory as a beginning attempt to move the understanding of human behavior toward a more scientific base. Bowen did not view his theory as complete. In addition, those (including this case presenter) who are using the theory as a base for clinical coaching are limited by their own degree of maturity. After many years of studying and attempting to live this theory, I continue to find new understanding of both the theory and myself. Bowen theory helps me to hold on to the big picture. Bowen theory does not provide techniques, however, so what I do in practice is a reflection of who I am in relationship with the other person(s). It is a collaborative effort in which the context of all the systems the person is a part of are examined as the person moves toward more maturity. As a Bowen coach, I do not practice therapy in the traditional sense. It is not my responsibility as the clinician to "fix" the client or the client system.

"A Bowen clinician would assume individual responses emerge from reactivity in the relationship system. Coaching would guide the client toward holding one's position in a responsible and connected manner. Taking responsibility for self moves people toward more mature and intimate relationships. The clinician would be guided by principles and assumptions but would not have any other agenda" (Bregman and De Stefano 1998, p. 6). The practitioner observes the family system and, with as much neutrality as possible, coaches the individual, couple or family toward taking responsibility for change.

"Bowen theory was never meant to be sensitive to the content of any socio-logical variable, whether it is gender, race, culture, sexual preference, or religion. It was put forth as part of a broader effort to move the study of human behavior to-ward the life sciences" (Horne 2002, p. 111). Bowen theory has been criticized by many who use a different lens. The feminist critique is particularly relevant for this section (Ault-Riche 1986, Hare-Mustin 1978, Knudson-Martin 1994, Luepnitz 1988), and the quote above provides an example of some of the content of this criticism. The feminist critique frequently comes out of a social and political posi-tion that goes on to suggest that Bowen theory is gender biased and pathology ori-ented. Without in any way minimizing the importance of the social and political realm, Bowen theory is distinct in its attempt to understand behavior through evo-lution and systems thinking. A political dimension is not part of the clinical work, though it would appear to me that the more a person is able to develop in his or her emotional maturity, the more opportunity that person will have to lead in the areas of social and political issues. Bowen theorists are concerned with mature leadership. This would include recognizing the emotional process that is an inte-gral part of oppression.

Bowen theory is frequently misunderstood as incorporating a pathologizing of clients. Psychopathology is a linear concept that doesn't fit a systems view. It is not part of any writings on the theory or any index that this contributor has seen (Bowen 1978, Kerr & Bowen 1988, Papero 1990 or Gilbert 1992, to cite a few). "All functioning is on the same continuum. Persons struggle with the same emo-tional processes and are more or less able to regulate self. One's ability to manage self and remain connected contributes to functioning; increased functioning tends to manifest fewer symptoms" (Bregman & De Stefano 1998, p.5).

Not having studied feminist theory and critique as extensively as I have Bowen theory, I can only respect the different lens and assume it makes sense to and is a fit for those who use it clinically. Since a Bowen lens makes sense to me, the presentation of this composite case comes from the perspective of Bowen the-ory. This means that coaching in a session is used by a family member outside of the session to work on self in relationships. Client and coach work collaboratively. The coach, who has also participated in such a coaching relationship in order to work on self in relationships, works with him/her to understand the emotional process in the relationship systems to which the client belongs, particularly the in-tergenerational family system. A key part of this process is the person's beginning to take responsibility for managing self. This can be a difficult process; that is, to develop one's ability to think about feelings, make choices, and take responsibil-ity for the outcome of those choices, recognizing the limitations that reality pre-sents. The issues may be clothed differently not only for different genders but also for different people of the same gender, but basically emotional process is the same. Focusing on others and pointing fingers does not change anything. Taking charge of one's own life can make a difference.

This is a composite story of three women. Each woman described is a partially fictionalized composite of several women, in order to protect the identity of each. Sharon, Patty, and Kelly were all recently separated from lovers. Sharon was a traditional woman, Patty a professional woman, and Kelly a graduate student. Although their stories differed, they had one thing in common. Once caught up in the passion and sexual activity of a romantic affair, they loaned much of whatever sense of self they had to their lovers. The lovers eagerly accepted this gift in an apparent attempt to feel more of a self themselves. This contract would work for a while. It would function until the one who loaned self would try to reclaim some piece of self in order to survive. At this point the one who borrowed self would go find another source. One broken heart followed another for each of the women. The stories are abbreviated with much detail omitted.

SHARON

Sharon had married her first love, a charming and handsome young man who was a football star. They married immediately after high school. Although he drank "a bit too much" according to Sharon and didn't take a lot of responsibility, he was so much fun and so sexy that it made up for those shortcomings. She said they loved one another passionately. Sharon grew up in a blue-collar family. She was the daughter of a sickly mother and an alcoholic father who had sexually abused her for a brief period of time when she was very young. Sharon's mother was withdrawn, depressed, and bitter. She had left her husband emotionally years before but stayed with him for her children and because her religion was against divorce. In later years she lived separately. Sharon's older brother was chronically psychotic. Sharon had felt very loved and taken care of by her husband for whom she reciprocated by fulfilling his every wish and desire. She gave up her friends and outside interests, saw her family infrequently and was always there for him. When he served in the armed forces during a conflict, she wrote him daily, listened to their songs, and waited for him to return. When he returned from the army, however, he was addicted to drugs and unable to resume his earlier role. This made it difficult for Sharon to stay connected to him. After his discharge he went into a chronic depression, stopped working, being charming, and functioning in general. She no longer felt loved and left him.

   As Sharon met new men, there would be a passionate sexual attraction and she quickly became sexually involved, leading to the belief that the relationship was committed. Generally the men involved had a different version of the relationship. One heartbreak followed another. She entered therapy after a series of such relationships, presenting with the expressed desire to stop letting her life be run by her desire to be loved by a man. Sharon finally said, "I have to learn to stop thinking with my vagina."

   At the time, Sharon's father was terminally ill. She reconnected with him and forgave him, but at the same time informed him that she would no longer keep her promise of secrecy. Not that she particularly wanted to "out" him since he was no longer a danger to children in the family, but she had even been afraid to discuss the impact of the abuse in therapy or with close friends, still fearing the threats he had made. It was those threats she wanted to be free of.

Sharon began to redefine who she was in her original family. She also changed jobs and went from being a department store clerk to becoming a very successful sales rep for a big company.

Sharon worked on self, on taking and holding a position, and on not becoming intimate physically until she had more clarity about herself. As her work progressed she was more able to take a position with men that she dated. She no longer engaged in sexual activity prematurely but worked at establishing a relationship first. She also began to make clear statements to whomever she dated about what she expected in a relationship. Some men were quick to flee. Then she began dating George, who respected her positions, didn't declare love or try to sweep her off her feet, and overall appeared to be developing a friendship with her. At the same time each of them was moving toward a more romantic relationship. Eventually they became engaged to marry.

Around this time, George was downsized and moved into Sharon's apartment. It appeared he was taking less and less responsibility for himself, and not contributing financially or physically to the household.

Each was eager to start a family, as they were in their mid-thirties. George was from a wealthy family. His parents divorced when George became an adult. His father was a successful business man and a leader in his community. His mother was a traditional woman who focused on creating the home and raising her son. The parents' relationship had been dominated by his father's desires, and his mother apparently followed a long-term plan to leave as soon as her son was no longer dependent on her. His mother had been the buffer between George and his father. George's relationship with his father had been bumpy since then, as his choices of job and lifestyle (not enough money and too much leisure activity) disappointed his father.

Sharon chose not to factor this information into her decision to marry George. She desperately wanted to be married and have a child. She was welcomed into the family by both of George's parents, who were eager to be grandparents. She and George had a son eleven months after the wedding and a daughter fourteen months later. George's mother died shortly afterwards of chronic heart disease. George decided to join his father's business at this time. The couple moved to the father's town. Initially things seemed to be going very well. Predictably, however, George's productivity did not satisfy his father and his income was cut. The couple moved into the father's home, at the father's insistence. Sharon called me the following year and asked for an appointment to see me when she came back to visit her mother.

Sharon's first statement on that occasion was, "I guess I didn't really change much at all. I can't believe what I'm into. My father-in-law runs my life, my husband ignores me and gets involved with other women, and I feel like I'm a prisoner in that house." She went on to describe a situation where she had given up her work to move and then stayed at home at the insistence of her father-in-law and then of her husband. They promised they would take care of her in style and insisted that the children needed their mother to raise them. Although she did live "in high style," it was difficult for her to get out of the house, she had no money of her own, she was literally housekeeper for her father-in-law, etc. Yet she felt she couldn't leave because her father-in-law was well-connected and with his wealth had assured her that if she left, he would gain custody of the children. George meanwhile took no responsibility for himself and basically marched to his father's drum.

Sharon asked that I not raise questions or suggest she think about her options. She had basically wanted to see me to unload but was convinced that she would lose her children if she changed anything. Basically, she would stay until her children were grown, as did her mother and mother-in-law. She was unable or unwilling to look at the relationship patterns that were repeating from previous generations.

PATTY

Patty was a professional woman in her mid-forties with one sister five years younger. She grew up in a middle-class family. Her father was a professional man and her mother was a college educated, traditional homemaker. Patty viewed her mother as having given up her life to take care of her father and resolved never to do that. Her relationship with her mother had been distant and non-conflictual. She was patronizing of her mother's life choice and her mother was at times uncomfortable with her choice, believing she had betrayed her feminist principles on some level. In fact, Patty's mother was a very independent and functional woman who had chosen to stay at home and raise her children despite her ambivalence. Patty's relationship with her father was also distant. She held him in part responsible for her mother's role. He was very career oriented and not particularly involved with the children. The relationship between her parents appeared to be loving and stable. After the children were grown, her mother completed graduate work and entered a new career. Her parents are still married as is her sister. Patty didn't have many women friends because she "didn't like women much as they weren't serious enough about achieving success and conversations with them were too frivolous." In fact, Patty didn't have much fun.

She had a series of time-limited relationships with men before meeting Dan. She usually had an income either equal to or higher than her lovers. She took pride in considering herself very independent and a match for any man professionally. Each relationship she had was exciting and passionate but would end quickly, as Patty would discover she had difficulty holding on to her sense of self as soon as her lover would ask more of her than she was willing to give. Almost all of the men asked her to leave her successful career to follow them to their own job opportunities. She viewed this as being asked to give up her own life. She was never able to think about exploring job opportunities in the new area. Nor was she able to take a position about remaining in her current position while negotiating a way to maintain the relationship. She reacted so strongly to suggestions that she move that she was unable to think about options. She would become so frightened that she would "become just like my mother" that she would leave the relationship, reluctantly and with much sadness. When she met Dan, he seemed different. After a brief and passionate courtship they moved in together. Until that time, Dan had spoken of his commitment to egalitarian relationships and expressed pride in her career accomplishments. After moving in together, however, he shifted his position. Although he wanted to show off his accomplished partner to his friends on the one hand, he resented her commitment to her job and her friendly relationships with her colleagues, who were mostly male. He wanted her to be home when he got there. He wanted her to be available to accompany him to his business functions on short notice. He said it was because he loved her so much and wanted to show her off. She said she loved him too, and by this time had decided she wanted to marry and have children. So she acquiesced to his many demands, counting on this leading to marriage. As he borrowed more and more of her to boost his own image of himself, she grew needier and needier. This was another version of the loaning and borrowing of self. Her demands increased and Dan finally left her. She crashed and wondered where her independence had gone.

As Patty met new men, when there was a passionate sexual attraction, she quickly became sexually involved and believed the relationship had potential. These relationships often paralleled her relationship with Dan, though they were shorter term. She entered therapy after a series of such relationships, presenting with the expressed desire of finding a solid relationship, so that she could marry and have children. She wanted to be able to do this without losing what she referred to as her independence.

It took a long while for Patty to recognize that her "independence" was more pseudo than real. It was a stance she had wanted to be able to take but in reality was unable to unless she was not connected to a man. It was agreed that Patty would abstain from men for a period of time while she worked to understand the intergenerational relationship patterns in her family of origin and unresolved emotional issues in these relationships. She worked on person-to-person relationships with each of her parents and others in her extended family, and began to establish for herself a clear position in those relationships.

As she clarified her own issues about independence that grew out of the family emotional system, her relationships with members of her family became more mature. She began to function more efficiently in her career and allow more time for relationships with friends.

When she met Bill, she wanted to have him meet her family and have them meet him. She had rarely introduced the men in her life to her family before. Bill and she had a ten month courtship and then announced their engagement to be married a few months later. She was surprised to realize that she wanted a traditional wedding in the family church. One month before the wedding, Bill was offered a lateral move in his job that might lead to a promotion. He would have to move to another city. Patty was able to explore the possibility of changing jobs while Bill evaluated what the value of this move would be to his career. They were able to evaluate this together and decided to stay put. The possibility was left open, however, for a move in the future.

The marriage was going well when it became apparent that they were having trouble conceiving. Patty began to fall into old patterns but returned to coaching which her husband also took part in. Following failed fertility treatments they adopted two children. They are part of an open adoption and have working relationships with the birth parents and grandparents. Still married, they and their two children are living in another city. Both are successful in their careers and their children appear to be functioning well.

KELLY

Kelly was a graduate student in her late twenties. Kelly came from a well-educated family where both parents held prestigious jobs. Her father was minister at a large church that was central to many social justice activities in her community. Her mother had a job in politics. Kelly's observation of family life growing up was mixed. The family was loving and well-connected. Although father pitched in quite a bit "for a man," she observed her mother being burdened by the combination of home and work responsibility. Her father had an affair that was never disclosed publicly, but which Kelly had learned about from the daughter of the woman involved in the affair.

From an early age, Kelly had been aware that there was something different about herself. During adolescence she acknowledged her sexual orientation and came out to her parents. They were accepting after the initial surprise.

Despite some of the struggles she experienced as a result of being a lesbian, she always thought it a gift. This would mean she could partner with a woman and have a "really egalitarian" household. Kelly had been in several short term lesbian relationships before entering a relationship with Jackie. In short term relationships Kelly was less sexually adventuresome than her lovers, who quickly moved on. She had been living with Jackie for five years. Jackie had a supervisory job in a local insurance company. She adored Kelly and had invited her to live in her home and agreed to help support her financially during the completion of graduate work. Jackie thought it only reasonable, since she was working full time and helping to get Kelly through school, that Kelly do most of the housekeeping chores. She also expected much from Kelly sexually, including having an intact hymen broken by a gynecologist in order to facilitate sexual activity. Although Kelly was shy sexually, she didn't want to lose Jackie as she had previous lovers, so she complied. She also gave up her friends in order to be there more for Jackie. As time went on, Jackie had increasing demands, and Kelly felt herself slipping away. When Kelly took a position that attempted to hold on to a bit of self, Jackie began a secret affair with someone else.

Eventually Kelly found out about the affair. Jackie wanted Kelly to stay but also wanted to continue the affair. Kelly refused to agree to this, so Jackie asked her to leave, inviting her new lover into the home. Kelly had entered therapy saying she found herself in a similar role to her mother's even though she was in a relationship with another woman. Her expressed goal was to be able to hold onto herself in her next relationship, and she worked hard to get there. She stayed out of relationships for several years. She connected to the women in her family and investigated how each of them had been in relationship. She did the same with the significant men. Kelly learned that her parents had survived the crisis of the affair by each working to take more responsibility for self in the relationship. Kelly also learned that her parents' relationship had become more intimate and satisfying after this crisis. During this period of time, Kelly completed graduate work and became successful in her field. She has now been involved in a relationship for ten years. The couple bought a house together eight years ago. Kelly had periodic sessions to continue her work and stay on track. The couple adopted a child five years ago, who at four years of age appears to be developing well. The couple relationship appears to be functional and stable. Both women have working and loving relationships with their families.

DISCUSSION

All three of these women entered into love affairs immediately after meeting a person they were attracted to following the loss of another. None really knew themselves or the partners involved. Nor did they have any understanding of the influence that emotional process in their original families could have. Biology and emotional need drove the relationships. Little if any thoughtfulness entered the scene.

Although there were no doubt many other contributing factors, each woman had been part of an emotional process in their family of origin that contributed to how they defined themselves. Each found herself not in charge of her own life and hostage to the need for a loving relationship with a partner. Each hit bottom and decided to attempt to better take charge of her life. It was at this point that each entered therapy.

The common theme in all three situations is the way in which *some* women who become involved sexually with another person sell out on self in order to hold on to the relationship. The situations may differ but the emotional process is the same. Their partner becomes the buyer and uses the purchased self in order to make himself feel complete. The partner then takes pseudo responsibility for the pair's functioning. Neither party is able to take responsibility for self in a relationship; instead each thinks in terms of a "we." Each partner plays a reciprocal role in this borrowing and lending of self. The emotional process that is occurring is rooted in the emotional process of the family relationship system. This is very powerful.

It is particularly interesting that this same pattern emerged in both the heterosexual and homosexual relationships. It is also interesting that the other person of these couples had obvious relationship issues of their own. An assumption here is that although presenting differently, each member of a couple approximates a similar level of maturity.

People have strengths and resources available to them that they may not be aware of, and all three of these women appeared to move on from the place where they were stuck. Although it appears that Patty and Kelly were able to take some significant strides, Sharon appears to have moved to a lesser degree.

It is important to remember though, that she did think it through and make a choice. She chose to pay the price she did in order to have children before the clock ran out for her. It is not possible to assess actual development of emotional maturity in the short term for any of these women. For the purpose of assessment, the indications of degree of emotional maturity realized may not be apparent until another generation or two reaches adulthood.

REFERENCES

Ault-Riche, M. ed. (1986). *Women and Family Therapy*. Rockville, MD: Aspen.

Bowen, M. (1978). *Family Therapy in Clinical Practice*. New York: Jason Aronson.

Bregman, O. C. and DeStefano, S. (1996). The Stone Center and Bowen Theory. Unpublished paper.

Gilbert, R. M. (1992). *Extraordinary Relationships: A New Way of Thinking About Human Interactions*. Minneapolis, MN: Chronimed.

Hare-Mustin, R. T. (1978). A Feminist Approach to Family Therapy. *Family Process* 17: 181–194.

Horne, K. B. (2002). All in the Family: A Belated Response to Knudson-Martin's Feminist Revision of Bowen Theory. *Journal of Marital and Family Therapy* 28: 103–113.

Kerr, M. E. and Bowen, M. (1988) *Family Evaluation*. New York: W. W. Norton.

Knudson-Martin, C. (1994). The Female Voice: Applications to Bowen's Family Systems Theory. *Journal of Marital and Family Therapy* 20: 35–46.

Luepnitz, D. A. (1988). *The Family Interpreted: Feminist Theory in Clinical Practice*. New York: Basic Books.

Papero, D. (1990). *Bowen Family Systems Theory*. Needham Heights, Mass.: Allyn and Bacon.

Watzlawick, P., Weakland, J. H. and Fisch, R. (1974). *Change: Principles of Problem Formation and Problem Resolution*. New York: W. W. Norton.

Questions for Further Study

1. Gloria Anzaldua, in this excerpt from a chapter in her book *Borderlands/La Frontera: The New Mestiza*, proclaims, in effect, that she occupies the ground on which the cultural expectations she grew up with, its gender roles, and her sexual orientation, meet. She attributes much of her desire to rebel to her "shadow beast," while at the same time recognizing that this emergence of her true self could not have taken place without leaving her community and home. What are the personal strengths, as well as the external social supports, that enabled Anzaldua to so strongly assert her identity as a minority within a minority? What lessons are inherent in this knowledge for social workers?

2. Shanlon Wu writes of the dearth of role models for Asian men in the United States and the difficulties he encountered growing up when his own talents and skills did not fit into the traditional image of Asian manhood. In fact, Wu's sense of displacement is not uncommon in those whose families may have emigrated years ago, but who themselves are American-born (the comedian Margaret Cho has built a career as an entertainer on the disconnection between the perceptions of "ideal" Asian womanhood and her own identity as an Asian-American female). How might a social worker have enabled Wu to more freely and happily pursue his own areas of strength rather than his perceptions of what he "ought" to be?

3. Shani Mootoo's "Out on Main Street" is the simple story of a walk on Main Street, during which the two women protagonists encounter threats that are both real and metaphoric, including potential threats to their physical being, to their relationship, to their gender and sexual identities, and to their identities as Indians. What are these threats? Should any of them fall within the purview of the social worker? Why? What can the social worker do about them?

4. Why do you think Karl Woelz titled the story that appears here "Cartography"? With an answer to this question in mind, consider what a helping professional might take away from the story that could be used to help individuals who find themselves in the position of the non-biological parent? In other words, what might you do to help such a person increase the fit between himself and his environment, either at a micro or macro level?

219

5. Consider the "Three Women" described in the case study by Ona Bregman. How would you, as a social worker, proceed with these women so that they might not, in the words of the author, loan their sense of self to another? In other words, what might be a reasonable plan of action (assuming their collaboration in its design, of course!).

Invited Commentary

COLLEEN REED

Consumers and social workers develop a plan of action based on the consumer's specific aims for the collaborative social work process. Still, consumers' stories are often drowned out by static from social workers' fears about enacting the work of the helping relationship, from their own personal values and biases, and from the pull of privilege to engage in social control. The stories of the protagonists in these readings are unified in their depiction of disenfranchisement. The readings give social workers the opportunity to explore the main characters' hopes, dreams, resources, successes, and challenges, while attending to their own "static" as readers.

Developing a plan of action involves understanding the consumer's goals and examining the influences of privilege and oppression on the life of the consumer. The plan of action sets the scope of the collaborative work and determines manageable steps toward the goals. These steps of action consist of mobilizing strengths and resources to reduce obstacles to enrichment and to increase personal successes. The plan for action situates the consumer as the expert of story, the goals, and the best processes by which to reach the goals. Specific ways for the social worker to support the consumer's process are illuminated in the plan of action.

In this volume, the characters' narratives are vivid yet not "live." This response, then, does not fully apply the process of developing a plan for action to the readings, as the characters-cum-consumers cannot participate fully in the process. The readings address characters' unique experiences of identity and authenticity. While each main character's personal context is distinct, all the stories are set against a backdrop of privilege and oppression. The main characters experience incongruity between sense of self and expectations about gender and sexual orientation. The readings allow readers to consider the implications of their understandings of the stories for the development of consumer-driven plans of action.

ENGAGING WITH THE STORY: ACTIVE READING / LISTENING

Active reading of these stories parallels active engagement with consumers. Social workers elicit ongoing clarifications and rich detail about a consumer's story to increase understanding not only of the consumer's goals, but also of her particular strengths and challenges. Hallmarks of active engagement with consumers include genuine interest, curiosity about consumer's creative approaches, and hope for and belief in the possibility of change.

Active engagement with the story similarly involves cultivated attention to nuances of meanings. Rich literary detail including the use of dialogue, word choice, time sequences, and glimpses into the character's internal thoughts and feelings provides clues to the character's stories. For example, Anzaldua's interlingual essay emphasizes her connection to two languages and ethnic cultures. Mootoo's main character speaks in her dialect. Her speech plainly identifies her cultural affiliation and national origin—groups to which she belongs—and groups that question her belonging.

- *Are the central struggles of the main characters resolved in similar ways across the story? How is this managed in other works by the same author?*
- *Bryan's thoughts and feelings are revealed to the reader in two ways—what might this tell the reader?*
- *What clues can a reader identify from the author's choice to organize the case study materials in this particular way?*

USING AN ADJUSTABLE ZOOM LENS: PERSONAL STRUGGLE AND SOCIETAL OPPRESSION

Developing a plan for action requires agreeing on the central purposes and aims of the collaborative process. Plans of action must account for the consumer's goals, her preferred methods for making change, and her unique set of strengths and resources, and must include clear understanding of the forthcoming contributions of the social worker.

The understanding between consumers and social workers sets the scope of the collaboration and determines the type of action to follow. Vulnerable people experience personal struggles that are inextricably connected to their experiences of institutionalized oppression. In setting the scope of work, great attention must be paid to privilege and oppression to avoid setting the spotlight on helping the individual fit an unjust environment rather than working toward justice at an environmental level.

The main characters in these readings encounter disenfranchisement from themselves, their families, their identity groups, and dominant society. Obstacles to the characters' having a sense of congruence with their environments stem from the dominant culture's heterosexism, sexism, racism, and ethnocentrism. Internalization of these institutionalized forms of oppression amplifies the characters' struggle toward a sense of wholeness.

This incongruence is exemplified both by challenges to the character's sense of identity and authenticity. Each character lives in this dissonance in a unique way. The women in the case studies engage in helping relationships based on their incongruent experiences of self and identity with their perceptions of dominant society role expectations for women. Bryan, in Woelz' essay, wrestles not only with the expectations dominant society has of men and fathers but also with his expectations for himself. He questions the very role his behavior exemplifies in the essay.

Wu recounts his painful urgent search for self amidst expectations for an Asian male. He wrestles with first developing then meeting his own gender and culture expectations as well as the cultural expectations of his family and dominant society. Anzaldua and Mootoo's protagonists similarly describe their failure to meet culture group expectations. In their stories, the mismatch results in costly disenfranchisement based on sexism and heterosexism.

Indian merchants taunt Mootoo's protagonist for her inadequate experience of culture, and this is exacerbated by her differences from gender and orientation norms. Rather than releasing her from cultural expectations in light of her different national origin, or simply broadening their expectations of cultural group members' experiences, they shame her for her imprecise vocabulary about food. "Pud," as her lover calls her, says she feels like a cultural "traitor." She pronounces herself and her lover "cultural bastards," separated from multiple identity families by the very characteristics that give them membership in others, and by differences in national origin, gender, sexual orientation, and ethnicity.

In addition to the characters' struggles about identity, the protagonists also negotiate questions of authenticity. In each of the stories, the character's cultural orientations are tested against standards employed both by the character's identity group and dominant society. Group members check one another for sufficient evidence of in-group characteristics such as gender role hallmarks, language, spiritual practices, personal choices, and values. Dominant society denies Bryan's role as authentic father and partner, in Woelz' essay. Bryan is asked about his "membership card" to his orientation identity group when he eschews a stereotypical preference. However, he also questions his authenticity in these roles. Similarly, Wu writes that he was pleased with the approval from dominant group members—business peers—that his "Chinese isn't good enough" because it meant that he was closer to having a sense of belonging, even though the belonging would have been artificial.

Anzaldua describes a perilous paradox. Her identity groups deny the legitimacy of her authentic self, based on her memberships in other identity groups. Anzaldua's authentic identities of feminist, lesbian, and woman, are the very elements of her identity that deny her access to Mexicana culture. Anzaldua highlights that each Mexicana/o faces the identity challenge when determining how to claim identity from both the colonizer and the colonized—to be mestiza/o.

- *What are the implications of the ways the following words are commonly defined: gender, sexual orientation, and ethnicity? Do common definitions reflect false dichotomous thinking?*
- *Is it feasible that a group would want to ensure the legitimacy of someone's membership for a good reason? If so, then under what circumstances? What are the implications of your responses?*
- *What are the consequences of setting the scope of work too narrowly? too broadly? How is the plan of action changed when consumers are mandated to service?*

SUMMARIZING THE MAIN POINTS OF THE STORY: POWER DYNAMICS

Social workers consider the influences of power and aspects of social control in the helping process. When developing a plan of action, then, consumers' voices must be continually and actively elevated as expert. To facilitate consumer self-determination in the helping process social workers must make the terms of the work explicit, detailing the types of services that are available, and the specific ways in which the social worker will offer help.

Social workers' strengths, sense of identity, and skills, as well as biases, ignorance, and unearned social advantages, influence understanding of consumers' stories. The personal lens of the social worker is so powerful; it exerts influence on each element of the plan for action, from determining manageable action steps and identifying strengths to evaluating the goals at the end of the process. The "default" starting place is that of one's own personal experience. Shifting this lens, widening it, involves disciplined self-awareness and reflection. To better collaborate with consumers who experience heterosexism and sexism, social workers adopt a critical perspective that examines situations through a counter-oppressive stance.

Social workers increase their knowledge through relationships with members of vulnerable groups, education, and the arts. Social workers engage in exercises to increase their understanding of bias and oppression such as wearing a sweatshirt emblazoned with "Gay and Proud" for a week without ever offering explanation to the people they meet, to gain small clues about the daily coming out experiences of gay and lesbian people. Using privilege to collaborate with vulnerable people in action for social justice perhaps best increases understanding.

The readings present different ways in which the protagonists negotiate oppressive society and choose their own manageable steps toward better understanding of their own identities. Wu sets the stage for his essay by describing his impression of Asian icons in popular culture. Despite the fact that he views the icons as inappropriate caricatures he persists in his interest by calling for a better figure to hold up as an Asian hero. Wu gets little support for his ensuing search for this hero, making his struggle more difficult. Not dissuaded from his search, Wu ultimately follows his passion to an important self-discovery.

Early in Woelz' essay, a wedding invitation arrives. This piece of mail does more than invite the family to a wedding; it invites Bryan to examine his feelings about family, and about his role within his family. Bryan does not automatically point to the dominant culture as the sole source of his disenfranchisement. He allows himself to let his own feelings bubble up and then he examines them in light of his actual experiences. In essence he checks his experiences against a series of expectations. Later in the story, Bryan simultaneously acknowledges what may be exceedingly clear to the reader—yet is not to Bryan until this point—that he is absolutely Philip's father and that he must address his sadness about his son Philip's coming of age in light of his role as father.

- *Are there ways the case studies are illustrative of bias in regards to social norms about dating and gendered critiques of sexual relationships and sexual activity?*
- *What are the role expectations that the women do not meet? Whose expectations are they? What can we glean about the women's strengths?*

- *What are the implications for the plan of action of the framework "loaning sense of self" when contrasted with the statement ". . . each found herself not in charge of her own life and hostage to the need for a loving relationship . . ."*
- *How do we view a "stall" in the work? Is the consumer ambivalent about change? What is the social worker's responsibility in the "stall"?*
- *Examine Bowen Family Systems Theory. In what ways does it counter or perpetuate gender bias & heterosexism?*

DENOUEMENT—UNTYING THE PLOT KNOT: STRENGTHS AND RESOLUTION

Cultivated curiosity about resilience fuels social workers' abilities to hear and illuminate strengths already in force in consumers' lives. Turning the attention of the collaborative process to celebration of these strengths opens up possibilities to elicit beneficial practices including mobilization of resources, reliance on well-stocked sources of inspiration and support, and the identification of successful strategies to eliminate barriers. Invigoration of inherent strengths and use of external resources bring the work of the collaborative team toward the aims identified by the consumer.

Approaching the work in manageable stages and harnessing the power of consumers' strengths means that the social worker is likely to bear witness to experiences of success and resolution. When constructing the plan of action, the collaborative team imagines these experiences in detail. This process helps to both solidify consumer's goals and determine markers of success for the collaboration. In essence consumer's stories shift with their experiences of their own strengths in light of challenges.

Strengths are mobilized toward resolution of the incongruence in identity and authenticity for the protagonists in the readings. Bryan negotiates his feelings about family while integrally connected to a loving partner and son. Wu claims the need for a model on which to hang his developmental aspirations and persists in his struggle for identity. Anzaldua aptly describes her own strengths. She separates from her ethnic cultural group enough to avoid constant injury. She balances this separation by fiercely taking her culture with her. Mootoo's protagonist honors her inner voice above the din of role expectations. She warmly describes her lover's feminine appearance yet plainly states that ". . . if I ain't walking like a strong-man monkey I doh exactly feel right and I always revert back to mih true colours."

For the character's, or perhaps the authors (and for us all), simply the telling of one's story has its own benefits. Wu says, ". . . writing gives [him] coherence," that it "reconciles for [him] the different forces [he] always feels pulling at [him]." Ultimately Wu finds himself at the center of his own story, his search for a model of Asian manhood. He reflects on his story of tenacity with compassion, acknowledging that he is his own hero. In a similar way, Anzaldua re-stories her own experience. She stakes a claim on legitimizing her own authenticity rather than focusing on disenfranchisement by oppressive norms and values. She writes, "if going home is denied me then I will have to stand and claim my space, making a new culture—*una cultura mestiza*—with my own bricks and mortar and my own feminist architecture."

- *In what ways do our perceptions of self as "helper" influence our views about consumers' successes?*
- *What implications are there for collaborations in which the "end" is determined by factors other than attainment of the consumer's goals? How might any negative implications be mitigated by the social worker?*
- *How does the framework "role dislocation" set parameters on the strengths to be used and the desired outcomes?*
- *How do social workers address behaviors and processes that act as strengths but are not valued by dominant society?*

EPILOGUE

The ways that I identify myself inform my reading and understanding of the works presented here. Some of my identity groups have voices in these stories. I read through the lens of my understandings—of constricting and liberating labels, gender bias, gender norms, heterosexual assumption, heterosexism and policies that limit the possibilities of vulnerable people to experience the advantages of people in privileged identity groups. My own experiences of vulnerability provide me an insider's perspective on oppression yet they in no way diminish my simultaneous experiences of unearned privilege. I must address, like the characters in these readings, the dynamic tension between authentic self and lack of societal legitimacy. As a social worker, my story resolves with the commitment to operationalize my privilege in action toward social justice.

Unit 5 ACCESSING RESOURCES FOR PERSONS AFFECTED BY RELOCATION AND DISLOCATION

Editors' Introduction

We, the editors, are Midwesterners by birth, transplanted to the Plains as a result of our employment. We are aware of how the archetypal story of the Wizard of Oz has powerfully shaped the perception that others have of our adopted home, Kansas. In the famous film, Kansas consists of colorless flatlands and downtrodden farmers.[1] We want to propose a more accurate view of Kansas and a new interpretation of *The Wizard of Oz*, relevant for social workers in Kansas and beyond. Although 86 percent of the 2.7 million residents of the state of Kansas identified themselves as white in the 2000 Census, the numbers of Asian and Pacific

Islanders, Hispanics, and American Indian or Alaskan Natives have increased significantly within the last twenty years. Social workers in Kansas, like those in areas more typically associated with large immigrant populations, are actively engaged in the effort of helping persons affected by relocation and dislocation to acquire necessary resources.

A superficial interpretation of *The Wizard of Oz* is that people have within them qualities—inner resources—that will move them forward to greater equanimity, better mental health, or a more prosperous life. In L. Frank Baum's classic tale, Dorothy always had the means to return home to Kansas, just as the Scarecrow, Lion, and Tin Man had the brains, courage, and heart that each sought outside of themselves. A deeper reading, however, requires us to look at the circumstances of their plights. Dorothy is brought to Oz by a cataclysmic event. She finds Oz disorienting and longs for home. As she embarks on her journey to find the all-powerful Wizard who will grant her wish, she comes upon three figures who are isolated and helpless until she brings them together in a common quest. The resources that each brings to this effort (resources that they, in fact, had all along) are what, in the end, enable Dorothy and her companions to achieve their goals and, metaphorically, return home. Thus, the other lessons contained within the story are that 1) problem solving in isolation is difficult, if not impossible; and 2) the journey, not the destination, may be the most important part of the process.

The ability to access resources—or to enable clients to access their own inner resources—is one of the most crucial skills in social work. As *The Social Work Dictionary* (1991) notes, resources are "any existing service or commodity that can be called upon to help take care of a need" (p. 201). These may include other social agencies, self-help groups, and government programs, but also individuals in the community who possess special characteristics that may be particularly helpful to the client. The importance of appropriately matching needs to resources for clients simply cannot be overstated. We hope to highlight this idea as we discuss the readings for this section.

A common thread clearly runs through all the readings we showcase in this unit: the theme of home—finding it, making it, leaving it—is extraordinarily significant to our lives, and strongly influences our sense of safety, security, and place. Thus, the ability to access resources in the service of helping others find "home," either in a real or metaphoric sense, is indeed important.

Carter Revard's "History, Myth, and Identity among Osages and Other Peoples," from *Family Matters, Tribal Affairs* certainly drives this message home, through his careful explication of home as a creation of *Usen* (God). With reference to several autobiographies, Revard demonstrates how indigenous peoples think of their place in the world far differently than do their European counterparts. Most important are their relationships: to the cosmos, to their land, to the stories passed down, and to their tribal ancestors. The individual is important only insofar as he or she represents a link in the continuing chain of stories and tradition that constitute their people's most vital resource. The essay suggests that, for the descendents of Geronimo, as well as the Pawnee, Osage, and other tribes, the acquisition of resources is likely to be viewed as helpful only insofar as such resources renew and benefit the entire community. This, of course, runs counter to prevailing Euro-American notions of individualism and the desirability of personal wealth.

Stevan M. Weine's "Doing Testimony Psychotherapy with Survivors of Ethnic Cleansing," from *When History is a Nightmare*, also focuses on the traumatic loss of home and its aftermath, working specifically with the refugees of Bosnia-Herzegovina. Weine asserts that one of the most important resources for Bosnian expatriates now living in the United States is a person able to listen to their often-horrifying testimonies. This resource of a listening ear, often taken for granted as a generic skill in social work practice texts, is not as simple to practice as it might seem. For example, Weine notes that a person listening to traumatic testimony must have a clear purpose in mind and that the purpose (and thus the skill itself) must be tailored to the political circumstances of the trauma, the time and place in which it occurred, and the reasons for which the victims were targeted for destruction (e.g. racial, religious, class-based, social). The listener must know when and how to terminate the act of bearing witness to a testimony. In order to be positioned effectively as a receiver of such testimony, the professional must go through a process of moral and psychological preparation as well as professional/technical training. Weine's extended treatise on testimony for traumatized clients effectively drives home the point that the competent professional social worker must understand that the appropriate use of self as a listener is a vitally important resource. Furthermore, Weine speculates on the uses of testimony to create community awareness and dialogue in the wake of trauma as resources for collective recovery.

Michael Yellow Bird, in "The Continuing Effects of American Colonialism on First Nations Peoples," a piece written especially for this volume, applies his professional social work skills to assessing and framing the problems that many First Nations peoples endure as the result of the ongoing effects of colonialism. Yellow Bird believes that the social worker is likely to be most effective when he or she understands the history of colonialism, the political dynamics that maintain its conditions, and the sheer magnitude of its injustice. He also offers means by which social workers can participate in the remedy, through study and research and through the action of linking First Nations Peoples to resources, such as organizations dedicated to fighting for an end to colonialism.

Sheida Bates' "The End of the Muddy Garden" carries within it themes of home and the importance of resource acquisition, albeit from a perspective that is very different from the other selections in this unit. This fictional account centers on a family's discussion of the death of Firuzeh, a relative. Through the device of what appears to be idle conversation about the circumstances surrounding Firuzeh's demise, the reader is drawn into a reflection on Iranian cultural values and attitudes. At the end of this conversation, the narrator realizes that, as a consequence of her family's emigration to this country, which appears to have been occasioned by the political upheaval in Iran in the '70s, she has lost her cultural moorings. The resources that the protagonist has acquired—her MBA, a job, and an independent life—are juxtaposed against her growing realization of all that was lost in the family's move from the old country.

The case study, "Nalani Ethel C.: Social Work with a Hawaiian Woman and Her Family," by Noreen Mokuau and Barbara Pua Iuli, invites us to look at how the social worker, through a conscious use of self and an expert ability in resource acquisition, enabled her client to find and utilize the resources necessary for keeping her children. Helping Nalani find the resources necessary to learn her native language was central to the accomplishment of all other goals. By helping her reconnect with her heritage, the social worker built a foundation for helping Nalani consider and adopt child-rearing practices appropriate to Hawaiian culture. Other goals, developed and met through the acquisition of culturally appropriate resources, allowed this worker to be of significant service to this family.

Finally, Uma Segal, in her guest commentary, notes a critical-but-overlooked problem for clients displaced from their own countries of origin: many are unaware of the resources to which they are entitled. Furthermore, the mere suggestion in the media that certain resources ought to be off-limits to emigrant populations results in a drop-off in application for those resources. Thus, a knowledgeable social worker, who can both find those persons who will not come forward and then link them to the resources they may rightfully claim, is a critical link to those clients' well-being.

More importantly, Segal reminds us that cultural sensitivity and cultural competence are two different qualities. For social workers, cultural sensitivity is necessary but not sufficient for the work we do with persons, much like those in these readings, who have been either dislocated within their own countries or displaced from their countries of origin altogether. Cultural competence, the result of an ongoing learning process, must animate our work with such clients. It is competence that lies at the core of meaningful professional relationships and determines our ability to help such clients acquire the appropriate resources.

These works, taken together, illuminate the importance of understanding who our clients are, especially from the point of view of the relationship between where they find themselves now and their home. This understanding lies at the core of meaningful professional relationships and determines our ability to help clients acquire the appropriate resources. When we do our best work, we can help them find their way home.

REFERENCES

Barker, R. (1999). *The Social Work Dictionary* (2d ed.). Washington, D.C. National Association of Social Workers: 1991.

Policy Research Institute, University of Kansas. www.ku.edu/cwis/units/pri/ksdata/census/2000/race/tables/T20.shtml

NOTE

[1]A new biography of the author of "The Wonderful Wizard of Oz," L. Frank Baum, reveals that he never even visited Kansas. The true inspiration for Dorothy Gale's Kansas home was the Dakota Territory. Baum moved to the town of Aberdeen in 1888, and the book was published in 1900. For more information about the background of this story, see: Rogers, K. (2002) *L. Frank Baum: The Man Behind the Curtain*. New York: St. Martin's Press.

History, Myth, and Identity among Osages and Other Peoples

CARTER REVARD

Something strange appears when we look at certain autobiographies of Indian people: the notion of identity, of how the individual is related to world, people, self, differs from what we see in "Euroamerican" autobiography. In "Western Civilization," an *identity* is something shaped between birth and death, largely by tiny molecules called genes, somewhat also by what the child's nervous system undergoes between birth and the first few years thereafter—and with every year past the first one, events become less and less important in shaping that identity.[1] That is not how Geronimo sees his identity in the autobiography he dictated to S. M. Barrett.[2] Nor does Geronimo begin by focusing on what a Euroamerican audience would likely consider the key to his identity: the clash with American soldiers and invaders of the Apache lands.[3] Geronimo does not even get around to mentioning his own birth until the book's third chapter. Instead, he begins the story of his life in this way: "In the beginning the world was covered with darkness. There was no sun, no day. The perpetual night had no moon or stars. There were, however, all manner of beasts and birds. . . . All creatures had power of speech and were gifted with reason. There were two tribes of creatures, the birds and . . . the beasts."[4] Geronimo then tells how the birds wanted light brought into the world, but the beasts would not have it, and there was war. The birds won, admitting light and so allowing humans to live and thrive. But the Dragon continually came down and devoured human children, until one year a son of the Rainstorm was born to the woman, and she hid her son away until he grew up to fight and kill the Dragon.[5] This boy's name was *Apache*, which (Barrett's book says) literally means *Enemy*, and he was the first chief of the people, first to wear the eagle's feathers in sign of justice, wisdom, and power such as the birds had shown in fighting for light. For Apache and his people, *Usen* created a homeland, placing within it, as in each homeland created for a people, all that was best for them: grain, fruits, game, herbs of healing, a pleasant climate, all that they could use for clothing and shelter. Geronimo concludes this opening part of his autobiography by saying, "Thus it was in the beginning: the Apaches and their homes each created for the other by Usen himself. When they are taken from these homes they sicken and die. How long until it is said, there are no Apaches?"[6] It is only after this Genesis-like history of his world's creation, his people's creation and deliverance, of their land's creation, of why they are called *Apaches*, of what it means to be taken from the land created particularly for his people, that Geronimo speaks of himself—of his individual birth into the world: "I was born in No-doyohn Canyon, Arizona, June, 1829."[7]

Whatever the order of importance among such facts might be for a Euroamerican autobiography, Geronimo ranked them from cosmic through geologic to tribal, subtribal, family and then only, last and in full context, the "individual" self that was Geronimo. And every *name* in his narrative, whenever he speaks it, has its symbolic meaning that resonates in this deeper context, can be rightly understood only in light of that part of the people's history which he is then telling. *Apache* does not "mean" only what (in Barrett's version) it "literally says," *Enemy*, but refers to The Enemy of that Dragon who threatens human children, and it is the name of the first great "Culture Hero" (as Euroamericans would call him: that Son of the Rainstorm who killed the Great Destroyer of Humankind).

I doubt that for most Euroamericans our national terms—*English, American, German, European*—resonate thus, because we lack a system of national and personal names that is openly and plainly linked to our mythic history or religious creeds.[8] There is of course the Catholic custom of naming after saints and biblical figures, and the Jewish naming arrangements that preserve religious and ethnic and family histories, and there are certainly subterranean passages between mainstream American personal names and the older familial and ethnic and national histories hidden within them. Yet particularly among Protestants, it seems, Americans have untied their names and individual histories from place and nation to an astonishing extent in the last five hundred years—precisely since the terms *individualism, self, identity* and *civilize* came into the English language in their current meanings.[9]

Now, when Geronimo told his life story, he had been a prisoner of war for twenty years, and a great deal had been done to *civilize* him.[10] As a recent editor of his autobiography puts it, "He took on all the trappings of the white man's civilization, becoming a farmer, a member of the Dutch Reformed Church, a Sunday School teacher, and a tireless promoter of himself, hawking photographs, bows and arrows at various fairs and expositions."[11] Civilized or not, Geronimo at seventy-six years of age (when dictating his life story to Barrett) still had his culture, his hierarchy of values. He knew who he was and where he came from, and he was sure that removal of the Apaches from their *homeland* meant, for him and for all of them, the loss not just of a "way of life" or a "home," but a change in, perhaps a loss of, their *beings*—or, as we might say, their *identities*. In his story, the notions of cosmos, country, self, and home are inseparable.

The result of losing that *homeland* can be seen in another Apache autobiography, though at first it seems to offer counter-evidence on the relation of being to land. This is a book narrated by one of the young Apache men who went with Geronimo on one of the last breakaways into the free Sierra Madre of

Mexico—a man named Jason Betzinez, born in 1860 and producing his autobiography in 1958 (he died in 1960, aged 100, from a car crash).[12] Betzinez tells us that in 1902, when the Apache heads of families met with military authorities at Fort Sill, Oklahoma (where they were still prisoners of war), to request once more that they be repatriated to their old homeland in New Mexico, as they had been promised when they surrendered in Mexico, Betzinez himself stood up courageously and said that he wanted to stay in Oklahoma:

> I was born and raised among these Indians. I lived just like they did—a hard life, *homeless* and *hopeless*. But through a Government school I had a chance to *better myself*. . . . I learned to be a blacksmith. I worked in a steel mill. I learned farming. Now I am being forced to choose between this new, good life and that old, primitive life out west. If I go west to live in a camp as a reservation Indian, all that I have gained, all that I have learned, will be lost. . . . My wish this day is that the Government should give me a house and land and permit me to remain. (p. 190)

Betzinez was clearly a fine person, and I would bet my life he was a good neighbor and friend—but the quoted words make him seem a perfect instance of a "wild" Indian who was "tamed" by the Euroamerican schools. Indeed, rebutting an Arizona senator, Betzinez says this himself: "At the time the removal of the Apaches from Fort Sill was . . . under consideration in Washington. One of the Senators from Arizona said, 'You can no more tame an Apache than you can a rattlesnake.' I think . . . the recent history of our people flings those words back in the worthy gentleman's teeth" (p. 199). At the age of twenty-seven, Jason Betzinez had been put into Carlisle Indian School, taught to speak and write English, converted to Christianity, and brought to be ashamed of and hostile to Apache dances and ceremonies, and now he considered his Apache life as "the old pitiful existence to which I was born" (p. 153).

Consider how different Betzinez's "old" life had been from Geronimo's. Geronimo had been born in 1829 and could grow up both "wild" and "free"; Betzinez, born in 1860 after the U. S. annexed his homeland, was from his teens onward under deadly and constant harassment. As he tells it, "As far back as I remember we had never had a permanent home or a place we could call our own. Some of us were beginning to prefer quiet and security to the ever present worry and fear of being hounded. . . . I think we realized dimly, as we jolted along in these wagons, that even as prisoners our worst troubles might be coming to an end" (p. 141). The episode he refers to here is when the Apaches, having been rounded up in Mexico and Arizona, were being railroaded off to Florida as prisoners of war, in direct violation of the agreement made when they surrendered. What Betzinez says, in effect, is that the prisoners have decided they are only safe in prison. It is meant, of course, as compliment to the jailers.

It is a hard question whether Geronimo or one of the older Apaches, if asked to describe Jason Betzinez when he returned from Carlisle to live at Fort Sill in 1900, would have described him as "Apache." His *identity* was not merely changed from "wild" to tame," from hunter/warrior to blacksmith/farmer. Consider: it was thenceforward impossible for Betzinez to begin his life story with the Apache account of the Creation, for he was now a sincere Christian. It was no longer relevant to his life to name the subtribes of Apaches as

Geronimo's autobiography does, for readers of Betzinez's story would be interested only in his being "an Apache." After going to Carlisle, Jason Betzinez had no homeland unless the United States government assigned him one. He had no religion shared with his people, no ceremonies that tied his youth to his age or self to tribe. In short, he had no IDENTITY unless he could reinvent himself in Euroamerican terms.

After 1900, that is, he was cut off completely from his first twenty-six years of life—from cosmos, tribe, homeland, and "values." From that time on, *all that made him Indian was his race*—and the chief test of that, by Euroamerican values, would be whether he could raise his status to be like a "white" man, for that alone would show whether he was racially inferior or could "make it." His sense of worth now depended on how NON-Apache he could act. Yet, of course, skin color and features would "identify" him as "Indian," no matter what his lifestyle became.

Betzinez had kept some attitudes, and he saw clearly how false was some of what Euroamericans wanted him to believe about his people's history. He could see it because he still had, in oral history, Apache truths that were omitted or distorted by printed Euroamerican accounts; he makes this clear at the very beginning of his autobiography (pp. 1–2). He quickly reveals that even though he had come to praise the non-Apache life to which Carlisle had turned him, even though he deplored the wish of "wild" Apaches to return to an existence and home country which, he insisted, was wretched and harassed, yet his feelings and memories of that homeland and existence were not negative. On the contrary, as he says: "We loved this beautiful land. . . . Between . . . 1858, when the Government granted us this reservation 'forever,' and 1876, when that same Government took it away from us forever so that white men seeking gold might have it, we lived there in peace and contentment. We hunted, gathered and traded. . . . For a short time life was . . . a happy one" (p. 25). But the official views expressed as Betzinez concludes his autobiography are very different from those at his beginning. From his Carlisle days, Betzinez had "thrown away" his Apache identity and accepted the Euroamerican self patterned for him by the soldiers at Carlisle whom he came to admire and trust. It is a remarkable and attractive self, clearly that of an unusually strong, courageous and decent man, whose life is told in this book. But it is clearly a Euroamerican self. We may account for its shaping, perhaps, by the imprisonment, penances, and education at Carlisle. If this were a U.S. citizen in 1994 we would presumably call the process brainwashing.

How, then, do we account for the different sense of self or identity in Geronimo's book? Here we have no clear description from Geronimo: he shows us an Apache self, but does not show how it was shaped. We can look into particular books for some idea of the ways Apache education shaped people—for instance, Morris Opler's *Apache Odyssey, Journey Between Two Worlds* tells how a Mescalero Apache "grew to maturity when his people . . . were experiencing defeat, confinement, and profound cultural readjustment."[13] But something more than one tribe's self-shaping is involved here, or so it appears to me from some years of having taught a course in which we read autobiographies of Indians from very different tribal cultures. Not only how Apache but how Indian beings are shaped is what I want to look into, if only a little way, in this chapter. One trail into this great Sierra is the way of naming and using language.

The autobiography that has helped me see how naming and language reflect and shape a sense of identity within the world, both outside and part of an Indian self, is Charles Eastman's *Indian Boyhood*.[14] Eastman was a Santee Sioux born about 1858 and raised, like Geronimo, "wild," but Eastman was then "brought in to the mainstream" as Betzinez was, through education, rather than through capture and imprisonment as Geronimo was. Eastman was just four years old in 1862 when the Santee took part in the great Sioux uprising and massacre in what is now called Minnesota. Eastman's father was captured and sentenced to death, but Eastman's mother and others in the family fled into Canada where Eastman was raised to age sixteen in the old ways, expecting some day to return to the United States to take revenge for the father who, he thought, had been hanged. But his father's sentence had been commuted to life in prison, where he was converted to Christianity, decided to take the white man's road, learned farming, won release on parole, and finally went to Canada looking for his son. One day, wearing white man's clothes, he walked into the Santee village where his nearly grown son was living, and presently walked out again, taking his son back to the United States. The son, given the name Charles Eastman, was put into mission school, then Beloit College, Knox College, and Dartmouth. Graduating with honors in 1887, he went to medical school at Boston University, where he got his M.D. just in time to be sent out to the Pine Ridge Sioux Agency shortly before the 1890 massacre of Sioux by the Seventh Cavalry at Wounded Knee. Eastman writes of trying to save some of the Indian children wounded there by the Hotchkiss machine guns, or the more prosaic carbines used by the troopers as they followed and shot down the women and children trying to flee the slaughter.

Such are the facts. I want to look, however, not at the Cavalry versus Redskins scenario so familiar from movies, but at one aspect of Eastman's *education as a "wild" Indian*, before being *civilized*. That aspect, briefly examined in the previous chapter, is his learning the Santee system of names for animals and plants, and how this system tied his sense of personal identity to his sense of tribal identity and relationship to the world of other-than-human "natural" beings. In his chapter on "An Indian Boy's Training" (pp. 49–56), Eastman points out that the education of Indian children was highly systematic and its customs "scrupulously adhered to and transmitted from one generation to another." While a male child was being carried in its mother's womb, she would keep in mind for him some celebrated figure from the tribe's history and "would gather from tradition all his noted deeds and daring exploits, rehearsing them to herself when alone." After he was born, her lullabies would "speak of wonderful exploits in hunting and in war," and he would be called "the future defender of his people." As he grew older, he would be hearing the hunting songs, and in these, "the leading animals are introduced, they come to the boy to offer their bodies for the sustenance of his tribe. The animals are regarded as his friends and spoken of almost as tribes of people or as his cousins, grandfathers, and grandmothers." What Eastman's account here barely hints when the animals are said to "offer their bodies"[15] may well be what is made explicit in the ceremonies of a related tribe, the Osage, particularly in the *Origin Wi-gi-e of the Buffalo Bull Clan* that might be recited as part of the feast of corn given a year after a child was named.[16] In this recitation, a member of the *Tho-xe* (Buffalo Bull) clan tells of how the Osages came from the mid-heavens, the stars, to become a people on this earth. In this journey they were directed by various powers through three "divisions" of the heavens, where they found no place to become a people, but in the fourth "division" they met "the Man of Mystery, the god of the clouds" (understood to be "Thunder," though all these terms are much more than "literal").[17] He said to them: "I am a person of whom your little ones may make their bodies. *When they make of me their bodies*, they shall cause themselves to become deathless" [emphasis added]. They then went to the Buffalo Bull, who also said they could make their bodies of him, and proceeded to throw himself upon the ground so that there sprang up for their use as medicine and food certain plants—including four kinds of corn.

What the Osage chants show is that when the "clan" animals came to offer their bodies it was not only (as Eastman's printed account seems to say) as willing sacrifices for food and clothing and ceremonial regalia—it was as part of the sacred agreement made at Origin Time between human and non-human beings of this world, between Osage beings on the one hand, and on the other hand beings from Thunder through Mountain Lion and Red Bird "down" (or "up") to the stones of the earth. I believe Eastman's account should be taken as implying that among the Santee the same was true, that when Eastman heard the "hunting songs" he would hear them as part of the Creation Stories and the Origin Stories and the Naming Stories.

Eastman's account does describe what I take to be the telling of Santee creation stories—the "legends of his ancestors and his race" were told and repeated "almost every evening," and whatever story a boy heard one night from parents or grandparents, he himself was "usually required to repeat" the next evening. In this way "his household became the audience by which he was alternately criticized and applauded." It was a schooling without having home and school separated, without creating a clerical class within the tribe.

But what interests me here is the naming system. Let's consider once more Eastman's description of how his uncle "catechized" him on his observation of animals: "It was his custom to let me name all the new birds that I had seen during the day. I would name them according to the color or the shape of the bill or their song or the appearance and locality of the nest—in fact, anything about the bird that impressed me as characteristic. . . . He then usually informed me of the correct name. Occasionally I made a hit and this he would warmly commend." Part of Eastman's Santee identity-sense came from realizing that his own close observation of the birds, and his naming them based on this, might well be at one with his community's choice of names for them. He was adjusting his own verbal creativity to his tribesmen's traditions in a very direct way. The sense of linguistic "authority" in his "oral" society seems just as strong as it is in our "literate" society, but the whole relation of individual to authority must have had a different "feel" in the oral society, where spoken language came from authorities present and known. English speakers have two sets of names for creatures—"common" and "scientific," and in neither set is it apparent to an ordinary speaker *why* a given name is used for a given creature. Our word-roots are buried far out of mind in unknown history.[18] But for Eastman, his language was "transparent," not "opaque" as English is to most of us. English is a melting-pot language, with a priestly language of Latinate terms, and a commoners' language of shorter words, but all of them are opaque so far as animals are concerned.[19] Our words no longer put us in touch with the LAND we live on and from, or the ANIMALS we live among and upon.

So far, we have focused on three autobiographies only—those of Geronimo, Betzinez, and Eastman. We have posited a "wild" sense of identity with its hierarchy from cosmic to personal firmly set, and a "tame" sense dependent on white beneficence and cultural power; and we have touched briefly on how the "wild" sense (as in Eastman) may have been shaped by the language as used by its speakers. Let's look now at two other tribes, Pawnee and Osage, to observe in more detail how the *land-orientation* of a family and individual created an Indian identity among Pawnees, and how the *naming ceremony* (for persons) helped create Indian identity among Osages. We turn to these two distinctly different tribes because they show it is *Indian* and not just an *Apache* or *Santee* "identity" we are looking at. The sample, admittedly, is limited, but it seems to me cautious inferences can be drawn from it.

For the Pawnees we draw mostly upon Gene Weltfish's beautiful book, *The Lost Universe*.[20] Our point is how powerful a force the Pawnee ceremonies were in shaping each Pawnee's sense of identity. Weltfish says: "The thing that made life most worthwhile to the Pawnees was their elaborate round of ceremonies . . . based on a complex philosophy of the creation of the universe and of man and of their ongoing nature. The ceremonies were considered as the means for keeping the cosmic order in its course and the continuance of the earth and its life processes. . . . The ceremonies were more than religious observances. They were the whole focus of Pawnee aesthetic life" (p. 8). Nor were these "ceremonial ways" only dances and songs and recitations. The shape of a Pawnee house, and the place in this house of each inhabitant, were part of an ordered patterning that placed this person in a certain clear relation to kinfolk, to household tasks, to the working areas and the sacred areas—*and to the cosmos*. That is, the circular Pawnee lodge was oriented not just within the village, but within the universe, by the sun and stars:

> Everyone in the house knew his appointed place and where he could go and . . . not go. In the sacred area at the west was an earthen platform. . . . Between the fireplace and the buffalo altar, there was a sacred spot that was invisible—the *wi-haru*, "the place where the wise words of those who have gone before us are resting." Rather than step over this place in order to pass from one side of the house to the other, everyone walked around the entire house by the way of the east. When the heads of the household sat down . . . it was to the west . . . and no one would want to pass in front of them. The house was a microcosm of the universe and as one was at home inside, one was also at home in the outside world. For the dome of the sky was the

. . . roof of the universe and the horizon . . . was the circular wall of the cosmic house. Through the roof . . . the star gods poured down their strength from their appropriate directions in a constant stream. In the west was the Evening Star, . . . and in her garden the corn and buffalo were constantly being renewed . . . and in the western part of the house the sacred buffalo skull and the bundle with its ears of corn symbolized this power. In the eastern sky was the Morning Star—god of light, of fire, and of war. As he rose every morning he sent his beam into the long entryway of the house and lit the fire in an act of cosmic procreation, symbolizing his first union with the Evening Star in the times of the great creation [when they begot] the girl that was the first human being. . . . The house was also the womb of a woman, and the household activities represented her reproductive powers. The beds of the women along the circular walls were . . . ranged by age to represent the main stages in a woman's life—the youngest woman near the west where the garden of the Evening Star was located, the mature woman in the middle . . . and the old women near the exit to the east, for at their age they were "on the way out." Being at home was spoken of as being "inside"; *ti-ka*, "he-is-inside"; the house, *a-ka-ru*, "the-inside-place"; the universe, *ka-huraru*, "the-inside-land." . . . Everyone in the house had a clear consciousness of these things as they moved about within it. Now secure in his bed, the boy was also secure in the world. (pp 63–64)

Naturally, to be oriented to heaven and the stars meant one was oriented in time as well as space, among the seasons and the ceremonies that "marked" the seasons: except that for a Pawnee, a ceremony did not merely mark, it helped in the moving of time.[21] There was, for instance, the "spring awakening": "The first ceremonial act of the year was to awaken the whole earth from its winter sleep. . . . The year began about the time of the spring equinox with the ritual recitation of the creation by the five priests. The position of the stars was an important guide to the time. . . . The earth lodge served as an astronomical observatory and as the priests sat inside at the west, they could observe the stars in certain positions through the smoke-hole and through the long east-oriented entranceway" (p. 12). Each Pawnee therefore knew from the repeated ceremonies how the Creation began, and saw the ordering of that creation symbolized in the shape and orientation of the house and its inhabitants, saw the seasonal occupations and activities closely tied to the stars, observed that the singing and dancing ceremonies were part of the link between self and tribe and universe, part of a Pawnee being.

From these facts I would argue that the "wild" Indian held quite different opinions from "civilized" Americans around 1880, concerning a person's relation to land, sky, and the creatures therewithin. They differed not only in their notions about property and ownership, or in their political views on voting, taxation, churchgoing, salvation and damnation. Geronimo, in being Apache, was like a Pawnee, or a Santee, or an Omaha, or an Osage: all were *Indian*, not *Euroamerican*. I suggest that for all the anthropologists can say about differences of high importance between cultures of Plains, Pueblo, Woodlands, Coastal and other tribes, groups, nations, there WAS such a thing as an "Indian" way beneath the differences. Succinctly put, that way's ceremonies *embodied a unified way of life*: what was Indian was the seamlessness of human life, in which it would not make sense to speak of religion on the one hand, and warfare on the other, of hunting here and naming a new chief there, of the Creation of the Universe on this side and the Naming of a Child on that. "History" and "village arrangement," "Cosmos" and "lodge architecture," were intimately related through ceremonies as well as stories and art work, the inside of a lodge, as well as placement of houses in the camp, carried historic and cosmic meanings.

The best way to demonstrate this might be a detailed discussion of ways in which, for instance, the Osage ceremonies for naming a child reflect, are linked with, those for naming a new chief, and both ceremonial cycles embody the tribe's history as well as its Genesis-Exodus version. Having discussed the Osage Naming Ceremony at length elsewhere, I will focus here on a few points from Francis La Flesche's account. Himself Omaha and speaking Osage well, La Flesche was the right person at the right time to preserve in print Osage ceremonies that would shortly afterwards be "thrown away." In the Osage *Rite of the Chiefs,* as he notes, are not only the ceremonies for naming a new chief, but (in what we may call allegorical narrative form) the history of the Osage people's becoming a nation. We are told in this rite how they came from the stars and chose bodily forms, how they took the tribal organization that simultaneously represented their history and the form of the universe. In the ceremony one finds, also, explanation of the choosing of certain animals as patrons for their clans, certain foods as the right ones, certain names for individuals as appropriate (and as tied to their mythic and in-time history). In this *Rite of the Chiefs,* therefore, what Europeans would subdivide into "history, religion, social structure, farming, hunting and ethology" are all subsumed. This rite was supplemented by another which La Flesche titles *Hearing of the Sayings of the Ancient Men,* in which we also see expressed "in mythical form, the origin of the people," here envisioned as a begetting of life between "two great fructifying forces—namely the sky and the earth," with life continuing forever to proceed from this begetting. And this notion of a continuous procreating of the universe is embodied in the tribal organization, divided into moieties of Sky and Earth divisions, with men from one of these required to marry women from the other, so that for each Osage marriage arrangement and ceremony there was a reenactment of the tribe's origins and of the cosmic reasons and theory behind this.[22] Further, the version of this origin-story recited by a given clan was modified so as to "conform to that part of nature which the [clan] represented in the tribal and the gentile organizations, for the tribe in its entirety symbolized the visible universe in all its known aspects." Specifically, the Black Bear or Thunder clan would each have its own version, with its particular patron-being giving its special name, powers, and blessing to the clan and the tribe.

Such, then, were the *Rite of the Chiefs* and the *Hearing of the Sayings of the Ancient Men.* When we now look at the Osage rite for naming a child—which as La Flesche puts it "installs the child in his proper place in the tribal organization and entitles him to recognition as a person"—we do not see an isolated and unrelated set of stories and histories. We find instead that the names bestowed in the bringing of a child into a clan reflect the tribal and gentile histories. The name *Nom-peh-wah-the,* for instance, may be literally translated as "Fear-Inspiring," but that is only the surface part of its meaning. Literally, *nom-peh* means "to be afraid," and *wah-the* means "cause or make to be." But the fear referred to in this name, it is understood, is that caused by Thunder: the sacred Thunder of the time before the Osages came to earth, when they sent ahead a messenger to discover how they might become a people, and what they could make their bodies from and what names they might take. The name *Nom-peh-wah-the* therefore embodies and recalls this part of the people's sacred history, as well as that part of its chronicle-history when certain famous men bore this name in the memory of the elders.[23]

Clearly, then, giving a clan-name involved a ceremony that itself was an epicycle on the great cycle of clan-origin, which was part of the universe's wheel that had turned to bring the entire tribe and its world into being. The Osages, we may stress, believed that the universe did move in an order given it by a "silent, invisible creative power . . . named *Wa-kon-dah*, Mysterious Power."[24] Therefore, when the first ceremony in the child-naming ritual was called *Wa-zho-i-ga-the*, "the Taking of Bodies," it was not merely that some incorporeal star-beings decided to come down and incarnate themselves, but that they were moving as part of the universe under Wa-kon-dah's guidance. When they adopted their life-symbols through which they became a people and could live on earth, they addressed these as "grandfather" and "grandmother": Sun, Moon, Morning Star, Evening Star, Dipper, Pleiades, Elk, Bear, Puma, Red Cedar, Buffalo Bull. When (at a later stage of the child-naming) the naming *wi-gi-e* of a clan was recited, the recital was called the *Zha-zhe Ki-ton*, "Taking of Names." The names were given according to a set sequence of possibilities determined in part by the order of birth within a family: first male, second male, third male; first, second, third female— each had its possible set of names.[25]

At the ceremony's end, there would be a special set of instructions for the child's mother. At the later feast (including corn ceremonially planted by the mother) for the *Xo-ka* who had presided over the naming, there might be the recitation by a member of the Buffalo Bull clan of that clan's *wi-gi-e*, telling how the Osages descended from the heavens and—most pertinently—how the Buffalo Bull had brought corn to the Osages. And to recur to the name just mentioned, *Nom-peh-wah-the*, this *wi-gi-e* tells how, when the Osages were trying to come down from stars to earth, their messenger was sent ahead to find a place where they might become a people. Having passed through three divisions of the heavens, the messenger had found no habitation for them, but in the Fourth Division he saw the "Man of Mystery, the god of the clouds"—and turning to his brothers, he said: "Here stands a *fear-inspiring man*! His name, I verily believe, is *Nom-peh-wah-the* ('fear-inspiring')!" Thereupon this mysterious and terrible man addresses the messenger and other Osages: "I am a person of whom your little ones may make their bodies. When they make of me their bodies, they shall cause themselves to be deathless."[26] He then gives them other personal names that they can use.

The name *Nom-peh-wah-the*, then, would be given in a context which would bring its new bearer into the tribe in a very complete fashion, at least as complete as a Christian or Jewish naming ceremony—and on its religious and cosmic side it would be comparable to such rites. It also referenced the tribal, family, and clan history into which the newly named child would be precisely placed. An Osage child in those "wild" times would thus have had all these placements brought to his awareness not only at the particular time he was given the name, but each time he attended another name-giving, and also when he attended the *Rites of the Chiefs* and other ceremonies.

In short, like Geronimo, or Eastman, or La Flesche, or a Pawnee child, an Osage would have had his personal identity carefully, explicitly, unmistakably linked with that of his people, with the symbolic arrangement of his village, with the marriage arrangements and hunting encampments and choosing of chiefs and war and peace ceremonies, with the animals whom he could hunt or whose feathers he could wear, the plants he would eat, the earth and sky he dwelt within. If we wanted to ask about a "wild" Indian's sense of identity, therefore, we ought to ask also about these "other" matters. The "wild" Indian was tied to land, people, origins and way of life, by every kind of human order we can imagine. "History" and "Myth" and "Identity" are not three separate matters, here, but three aspects of one human being.

NOTES

1. Erik Erikson has argued for the importance of much later periods in an individual's life as crucial to shaping and reshaping identity; the long obituary notice in the *New York Times* (Friday, May 13, 1994) gives a very useful and interesting account of his work. It mentions, for instance, that his *Childhood and Society* (1950) was published after he had studied early childhood training of Sioux people and differentiated their children's identity-sense from that of the Yurok Indians whom he also studied. He proposed that humans undergo successive "identity crises" during their lives, and applied this notion to "psychobiographic" studies of Martin Luther and Mahatma Gandhi (1958, 1969). Erikson's having himself been an "in-betweener"—illegitimate child suspended between religions (Lutheran, Jewish), taunted by Nazis as a Jew, rejected at the synagogue as of Nordic appearance—and his studies of non-European identity-formation surely made him sensitive to issues with which one is faced in looking at the "autobiographies" of American Indians with which the present essay is concerned.
2. *Geronimo: His Own Story*, ed. S. M. Barrett, newly ed. by Frederick W. Turner, III (New York: E. P. Dutton, 1970). All kinds of problems are presented to us by this work: to what extent is it an accurate transcription or paraphrase of Geronimo's account, how far does its organization and sequencing reflect Barrett's rearranging of bits and pieces, how much was added or subtracted or altered by the intermediary Apache translators used by Barrett. I cut this Gordian knot by assuming the book as printed is authentic and accurate enough for the purposes of this discussion, expressing reservations only here and there.
3. The 1993 movie called *Geronimo*, for instance, though "sympathizing" with Geronimo, presents him primarily as a larger-than-life Indian warrior

fighting American soldiers; and the soldiers are presented as, of course, highly respectful of his courage, of the relatively just causes for which he was fighting, and so on. In the end, that movie asks us to understand Geronimo as "Apache" in only two dimensions: the fierce indomitable warrior, and the man unjustly treated by mean and crooked Mexicans and Americans. There is nothing whatever of Apache cosmology, theology, ideology, customs or ways except in relation to the "war with whites," which is pictured as about a homeland but not about a way of life or world-views.

4. *Geronimo*, p. 61. Barrett's version of Apache "creation time" is probably much distorted, but my point is that Geronimo began by telling some version of the Apache Creation Story as his introduction to the story of Geronimo. One may argue that the Christian Gospel of John distorts the Judaic account of the beginning of things, since it is a late Hellenized version adapted to provide a biography of a man taken by its author to be the Messiah. The Hellenizer, nevertheless, has reasons for providing that reference to the *Genesis* story.

5. "Dragon" of course carries all kinds of European baggage, but so does "Monster," a term more usual for translators of Apache, Navajo, or Pueblo Creation Stories, in which such episodes of "Monster-slaying" set parameters for the world as humans now know it. See, for instance, Paul Zolbrod's edition of the Navajo Creation Story, *Diné Bahanè* (Albuquerque: University of New Mexico Press, 1984).

6. *Geronimo*, p. 69. I wonder about the "literal meaning" that in Barrett's account is assigned to *Apache*, and suspect some confusion on Barrett's part.

7. *Geronimo*, p. 70. Could *No-doyohn* be a mistake for *Mogollon?*

8. See the earlier essay in Revard's *Family Matters, Tribal Affairs* (Tucson: University of Arizona Press, 1998), "Making a Name," for qualifications of this.

9. Though the history of these words sheds light on the attitudes of Europeans toward "Indians" whom they civilized with such genocidal efficiency, there is not space to summarize that history here. A sketch is given in my "Why Shakespeare, Though Not Unselfish, Never Had Any Fun," in E. Cooley, Mervin R. Barnes, and John A. Dunn, eds., Papers of the Mid-America Linguistics Conference for 1978 (Norman: University of Oklahoma Press, 1979), pp. 478-487.

10. See the entry for *civilise* in the *Oxford English Dictionary*. The word was Anglicized in the early 17th century precisely to justify man's ways to man as the British began to turn the globe a shocking Imperial pink: as Captain John Smith wrote of his experiences in Virginia, it was easier to civilize "them" by the sword than by fair means (to paraphrase the *OED* citation from his 1624 *History of Virginia*).

11. *Geronimo*, p. 49. One of the "fairs and expositions" was the St. Louis World's Fair of 1904, where he was exhibited as prisoner of war. He must have been in its headquarters, the newly built Brookings Hall of Washington University. I teach and have an office across the quadrangle from Brookings. Geronimo perhaps walked round the new-built quadrangle, where Commencement ceremonies now are held.

12. Jason Betzinez, *I Fought With Geronimo*, with W. S. Nye (Harrisburg, Penn.: The Stackpole Company, 1959). (Page references to this book are given parenthetically in the text.)

13. Morris E. Opler, *Apache Odyssey: A Journey between Two Worlds* (New York: Holt, Rinehart and Winston, 1969), p. x.

14. Eastman, *Indian Boyhood,* hereafter in this chapter cited by page number alone. As with Geronimo's autobiography, I leave aside the difficult question of how non-Indian input—in this case, from Eastman's white wife, herself a teacher whom he met while at Pine Ridge where she was teaching Sioux children—may have shaped and colored Eastman's account of his life as it stands in his printed work. I ignore also (for now) the neo-historicist aspects of the case: the shifting vogues and forms of Indian autobiography; the particular and general social tasks assigned by whites to this genre during the period 1890–1940 as part of dealing with post-Wounded Knee Indian tribal entities and the "Indian question" as a whole; and the ways Eastman himself fitted his autobiographical writing and speaking into such tasks and his own personal and ethnic agenda. The very useful discussions and bibliographic account of Indian autobiographies by scholars, especially Peter Beidler, Kathleen Sands, H. David Brumble and Arnold Krupat, are essential to the full discussion such questions deserve.

15. The account as here cited from *Indian Boyhood* misses the sacred dimension of such songs, which tie intricately into the Creation Stories—though certainly Eastman would have known that dimension well, so it is likely the inadequate understanding of Santee ways by his wife Elaine Goodale Eastman that caused this lacuna in Eastman's account. We can clearly see this sacred dimension in traditional Osage naming ceremonies, as printed in 1928 (with transcription, translation, introduction and detailed commentary) by Francis La Flesche in *The Osage Tribe: Two Versions of the Child-Naming Rite,* Smithsonian Institution, Bureau of American Ethnology Annual Report, no. 43, 1924–1925 (Washington, D.C.: 1928), pp. 23–264. Other Osage ceremonies, which illustrate how members of this Siouan-language tribe were being educated at the time Eastman was growing up, are transcribed and translated by La Flesche as BAE Annual Reports numbers 36, pp. 35–597 (*Rites of the Chiefs, Sayings of the Ancient Men*); 39, pp. 31–630 (*Rite of Vigil*); 45, pp. 529–833 (*Rite of the Wa-xo-be*); and in the 1939 *BAE Bulletin* (*War Ceremony and Peace Ceremony of the Osage Indians*), *passim.* Some translations of songs and recital-chants from these ceremonies, and many useful glosses and definitions, are found in La Flesche's 1932 *Dictionary of the Osage Language.* And see, now, Garrick Bailey's account, *The Osage and the Invisible World* (Norman: University of Oklahoma Press, 1995).

16. La Flesche, *Osage Tribe,* pp. 56–58.

17. Ibid., p. 57. In Euroamerican culture, words like *electricity* and *gravity* have "literal," "figurative," and "scientific" sense-clusters. Alert and sensible readers negotiate among these flavors and quarky senses with no particular difficulty, and the same ability to negotiate among ceremonial and everyday, metaphysical and physical word-senses should be recognized

among Osages and other Indian peoples. There are actual instances within some of the ceremonial recitations or narratives where the reciter will say things, in referring to the "journey from the stars to this earth," such as "They came to a valley: verily, it was not a valley"—warning the listeners, I believe, that the language being used is special, figurative, mysterious, not everyday.

18. I happened lately to look at the words *chameleon* and *chamomile* in the *American Heritage Dictionary* and was surprised to find the same Greek word is behind the first half of each. A *chameleon* is a "ground-lion," and the herb *chamomile* is a "ground-apple." The *AHD* editors say that behind the Greek *chameleon* is a Babylonian word which itself means "ground-lion," so the Greeks must have thought the Babylonians had a good name for that little reptile, and just translated the name into their own language. As for *chamomile*, it of course is not actually a ground-apple; rather, as the *AHD* editors say, some varieties *smell* like apples. I have my doubts about this, particularly since *melon* is the Greek word behind the *-mile* part of *chamomile*, and *melon* might refer to some fruit other than what we would call an "apple." Ah well—Sprachgeschmellers differ.

19. Of course, as discussed in "Making a Name," our English is far more transparent where machines and technology are concerned and our speakers are still coining names in spoken as well as literary English: we understand *hatchback* or *Fuzzbuster* or *beeper* to be "tribal" words that are figurative, describing what they refer to.

20. Gene Weltfish, *The Lost Universe: Pawnee Life and Culture* (Lincoln: University of Nebraska Press, 1977); page references are cited in the text. A primary source, given by the Pawnee elder Tahirussawichi through the bilingual Pawnee scholar James Murie, transcribed and translated by Murie and Alice Fletcher, is printed as *The Hako: A Pawnee Ceremony*, Smithsonian Institution, Bureau of American Ethnology Annual Report, no. 22 (Washington, D.C., 1904). Fletcher for years had found no Omaha informants to recite for her the texts and songs of this intertribal ceremony, but at last located a Pawnee elder who knew and would recite it. I assume that since the Hako Ceremony was intertribal, each tribe performed it in its own language and particular format. The ceremony is an "adoption" rite in which two groups become "brothers." That it involves the sacred pipe suggests it may be one of the most important "peace" ceremonies of the pre-Columbian Great Plains tribes. Anglo accounts of Plains Indians seem always to stress their warfare, their hostilities and rivalries—making them sound very like the Europe known to history as a collection of rabidly hostile and murderous peoples always trying to slaughter or conquer or dominate each other. How the Indian nations succeeded in getting along, rather than how they conducted their warring or raiding relationships, is emphasized by Howard Meredith in *Dancing on Common Ground: Tribal Cultures and Alliances on the Southern Plains* (Lawrence: University of Kansas Press, 1995), discussing Southern Plains nations including Wichita, Pawnee, Caddo, Plains Apache,

Cheyenne and Arapaho, and Comanche (see, for the annual Pawnee-Wichita Visitation, pp. 20–21, 58–59).

21. The Pawnee images of microcosm/macrocosm ought to be compared to those of the Europeans in about the same time-frame, say 1400–1600 A.D.— there are startling resemblances as well as the expected differences. Work by Chaucer, Spenser, and Shakespeare could be set beside Pawnee texts— though it would outrage Mono-culturists to anthologize *The Faerie Queene* along with *The Hako Ceremony.*
22. La Flesche, B.A.E. *Annual Report No. 36* (1921), p. 48.
23. See La Flesche, *Osage Tribe,* especially pp. 159, 162.
24. Ibid., p. 30.
25. Ibid., p. 31.
26. Ibid., pp. 56–57.

Reading

Doing Testimony Psychotherapy with Survivors of Ethnic Cleansing

STEVAN M. WEINE

ENDING H.'S TESTIMONY

I bump into H. at the Bosnian Refugee Center in Chicago about a week after our third testimony session with him. For the first time since leaving Omarska he has not seen the man in his dreams. A few days later we meet for our fourth session.

The last three nights I didn't have any dreams. . . . When I come here, however, I am reminded and I feel very bad that day. But after that I feel better. Better and better every day. Since I have been telling you my story I am much more social. Before I avoided people, but now I like to be with people and to talk with them. I had a terrible fear of people because I did not trust them. But now I like to speak with people and I don't withdraw anymore.[1]

"Can you say more about what happened to the man in your dream?"

When I saw his face and I recognized him, I stopped dreaming of him. He doesn't come anymore. I am not avoiding talking about him. But I have nothing more to say. Before I was able to recognize his face I heard terrible voices and had hallucinations. After I saw him I lost that voice—his voice.

I still have a lot of voices from different people. I know many of them who appear in my dreams. Many are prisoners. But when I awake, I forget them all. I know who they are, but when I wake up I forget them. I can give you lots of names of victims if you want. Just tell me and I will give you many, many names.

"Yes, we must take down the names for the record [and later we did], but what seems most compelling at this moment is to talk about those whose voices you still hear, so that we may come to know them like we did that man whose face you could not see."

One voice which I hear every day and I can't forget is the voice of the young boy whom they castrated. He is with me every night, and I think all my life I will remember that voice.

He speaks in detail about that poor boy and then turns to the other voices.

During the day I hear other voices, especially when I am alone. Sometimes I have the feeling that somebody is calling me. Very often, I open the door expecting to see somebody. I avoid being alone. I go out. I like to speak with people. Because when I am alone I always hear those voices.

"What do the voices say?"

They call me. They pronounce my name. I think that's because we were always afraid of the list. When they came with the list and read off your name, you knew that was the end. They would take you and kill you. Nowadays, very often I respond to that voice, answering like I would answer that voice in the camp. I hear them speak my last name. Sometimes if my family is with me in the same room they ask me, "Are you crazy? Whom are you answering?"

We tell H. how he can talk with his family about the voices in a way that describes it not as being crazy but as having strong memories.

Today I feel 70 percent better than the first day I came to speak with you. I was so afraid. I never visited my neighbors. Now I feel relaxed. I can communicate. I can talk with people. I can visit people.

But one thing bothers me. I am afraid of big working rooms, of warehouses, because they remind me of the torture rooms. I think right now that is the only problem—and I hope I will be liberated from that fear.

His voice trails off. We ask him if he wants to talk more. He shrugs his shoulders as if to say, I don't know. It can be immensely difficult to know how or even when to end a testimony. There is the recognition that the telling of the trauma story can be an endless venture. With H., there is so much more that can be shared. We can keep going and going. What happened in the warehouse? Tell us about the other voices. In those four sessions, there is no doubt that H. has only spoken a small part of all that he has endured in the camp. But still, we choose to stop there.

Testimony cannot be about telling it all. It would be unbearable. In testimony, you must enter into the world of the traumas, but you must also leave. Both the teller and the listener must survive. The story that has been told and received creates other obligations that then must be worked on.

A difficulty arises for the listener when the survivor is simultaneously leading you in and leading you out. Which path do you then take? We have the feeling that after four intensive sessions, H. has spoken a great deal and given reasonably convincing evidence that it has helped him. The nightmare is gone. So we surmise that he is primarily leading us out, and we follow. We talk about the possibility that someday he may wish to reenter that world, and we can go together. We meet the next week to read his testimony back to him. As we do, H. listens intently. On occasion, he speaks up to add or correct something. At the end of the reading, we make the changes and he takes home a copy, thirty pages long. We arrange to meet again in one month to see how he is doing. We also give him some ideas as to what he can do with his testimony, and tell him we will keep him in mind and look for ways that his testimony might be publicly shared. That is all fine with him. He thanks us, shakes hands, and leaves.

This approach, the testimony method of psychotherapy, is one way mental health professionals have of working with survivors of state-sponsored violence. It is in part a straightforward proposition. Survivors tell the story of what happened when traumas shattered their life and the psychiatrist or psychotherapist is the listener who records it. Together they make a document of the trauma story, and then find ways to make that story knowable to others.

Yet testimony is not straightforward. Survivors do not speak only of their trauma story but also of their participation in the way of life that was, and what kind of future they foresee. The testimony yields a story that is shaped by both the survivors' and the witness's imperative to construct a narrative that is true to the events it seeks to represent, and true to itself. Remembering is itself a highly dynamic process, subject to interpersonal experience, social context, language, mental schemas, and brain functioning. Testimony has been used to reduce individual suffering, bear witness to human rights violations, collect legal evidence, and create art, and as a means of writing historical narratives. Assuming many different forms, testimony would appear to occupy a central position in late-twentieth-century Western culture.[2]

The benefits of testimony for the survivor are sometimes as plain to see as the departure of H.'s nightmares of a screaming man with no face. However, there is still much to be discovered about testimony as a means of working with survivors' remembrances of genocide or other social traumas.

HOLOCAUST, TORTURE, AND ETHNIC CLEANSING

I first learned about testimony from Dori Laub, the psychiatrist, psychoanalyst, and child survivor of the Holocaust who had cofounded the Fortunoff Holocaust Video Testimony Archives at Yale University. What Dori taught about Holocaust testimony helped to prepare my colleagues and me to respond to the call from refugee resettlement agencies when Bosnian refugees first came to Connecticut in January 1993. Our group at the trauma clinic first adopted a Holocaust testimony approach, although we knew very well that these historical events were not equivalent, and that consequently neither would be the survivors' psychological struggles. As we learned from working with the Bosnian survivors of ethnic cleansing, we kept reevaluating how Holocaust testimony could address, but was also changed by, this more recent human calamity.

The testimony approach to working with survivors of the Holocaust emphasizes remembering and knowing traumatic experiences from the distant past as a means of transforming identity, for self and community. "No one can become what he cannot find in his memories," wrote the Holocaust survivor Jean Amery.[3] And yet it is essential to note that most of the testimony work with Holocaust survivors was done forty to fifty years after the actual genocide. Consequently, what one finds in testimony is influenced by the many particulars of who one is at that time, individually and collectively.

Indeed, the scholarly work on Holocaust remembrances illustrates that the manner in which the genocide is remembered can be shaped by current sociohistorical context. There is James E. Young's study of Holocaust memorials, demonstrating a sharp contrast between how the Holocaust is remembered in Israel and in Poland. In Israel, where a Jewish nation was successfully established, the destruction and victimization of the Holocaust is collectively remembered in a way that feeds into an image of the heroic nation builder of the state of Israel.[4] In Poland, where the Jewish population of 3.5 million was annihilated, memorialization has taken the form of "broken tablets" made out of granite, railroad ties, or the shattered tombstones from destroyed Jewish cemeteries, in which "the fragments are not recuperated so much as reorganized around the theme of their own destruction" (Young, *Texture*, 185). I started wondering: which of these diametrically opposed archetypes—courageous "fighters" (pp. 209–281) or "broken tablets" (p. 185)—better captures the truth of survival in Bosnia and its Diaspora? Or is it something else still yet to be realized?

The testimony work with survivors of the Holocaust appears to be organized more around the psychology of "broken tablets." Dori Laub has characterized the experience of the Holocaust, as well as other forms of massive psychic trauma, as "an event without a witness" (p. 75). Echoing Martin Buber, he writes, "There was no longer an other to which one could say 'Thou' in the hope of being heard, of being recognized as a subject, of being answered . . . (and) when one cannot turn to a 'you' one cannot say 'thou' even to oneself" (p. 82). This yields "the loss of the capacity to be a witness to oneself" (p. 82). These traumatic experiences may not even be knowable to survivors, though their lives often bear unmistakable traces left by extremity.

Decades into their survivor experience, some kind of restoration becomes possible through testimony, when "this narrative that could not be articulated" can finally be "told," "transmitted," and "heard," and when the survivor "reclaims his position as a witness: reconstitutes the internal 'thou' and thus the possibility of a witness or a listener inside himself" (p. 85). However, Holocaust testimony is more accurately viewed as "dialogical process," "discursive practice," and "speech act," more so than the complete construction of a definitive statement, or the complete reconstruction of the "broken tablets," of one's own identity.[5] This theme is also stressed in the writings of Lawrence Langer, a scholar of Holocaust testimonies and literature, who has argued sharply against any attempts to over-evoke the heroism of Holocaust survivors. Langer uses the concept "unheroic memory," evoking far more anguish than hope.

An entirely different sense of the testimony emerges from the experiences of mental health professionals who were living and working in Chile during the time of political oppression under Augusto Pinochet. In comparison with Holocaust testimony, Chilean testimony was more explicitly a part of a political project—the active resistance of a military dictatorship. The Chilean professionals sought to deploy themselves to help recent torture victims suffering from psychological difficulties as well as to oppose the human rights abuses and political repression. The victims themselves were mostly political activists and dissidents. The Chilean professionals had the survivors tell their stories into tape recorders; these accounts were then transcribed, edited, and reworked into narratives of their torture experiences.[6]

The Chileans' understanding of their testimony work focused on its ability to mend the rupture in the self's relationship with the collective: "The therapeutic process of testimony helps patients to integrate the traumatic experience into their lives by identifying its significance in the context of political and social events as well as the context of their personal history."[7] This healing process was facilitated by the torture victim having been politicized even before the oppression, which again was not the case for Holocaust survivors. The authors report that the testimony works via a process of "catharsis," which leads to "symptomatic relief." However, testimony "does not simply express the emotional trauma, but facilitates its personal and social elaboration." This testimony "can have a wide distribution," through human rights and mental health networks, both in Chile and internationally.

These authors seem to be making three very different (though not necessarily contradictory) claims about how testimony works: through integration, a reconnection; through catharsis, a letting go; and through acknowledgment, a making known. Overall, the Chileans convey a greater sense that individual healing and social change is possible through testimony than is evident in the Holocaust testimonies of broken tablets. They make the claim that their testimony works effectively on several different levels. Survivors experience improvement in their traumatic stress symptoms; human rights abuses are documented; and the professional community becomes informed about this innovative method of treatment.

The Danish psychologist Inger Agger and psychiatrist Soren Jensen have also used the testimony method of psychotherapy in their work with refugee women survivors of sexual torture (from the Middle East and Central and South America) living in Denmark.[8] They too address the psychological complexities of how testimony works. Like the Chileans, Agger and Jensen focus on the survivor's isolation from the collective that was destroyed, her powerlessness in relation to the totalitarian regime, and her guilt over her own predicament in exile. For them, "testimony can be an offensive instrument for overcoming this guilt" and, as with the Chileans' emphasis on the political, in "strengthening the ideological commitment of the refugee."[9] Agger and Jensen also note testimony's dualism. Their testimony has a "double connotation"— that is, both "objective, judicial, public, or political" and "subjective, spiritual, cathartic, or private." Agger's *The Blue Room* provides an engaging exploration of what happens on the boundary between public and private life for these refugees.[10] Political violence is represented as an evil and brutish way of shattering a woman's capacity to achieve a more egalitarian place in society, forcing a retreat into a broken and humiliated private life. The testimony work took place in a blue room in Agger's apartment, and the figure of this room came to serve as a metaphor for the special healing space testimony offers the survivor, if not societies. How could testimony function in the very different spaces of Bosnia and its Diaspora?

Bosnians are also survivors of political violence, but under circumstances very different from these other three groups. Unlike many survivors of torture described in the literature, most Bosnians were not targeted because they were political activists. Rather, like Holocaust survivors they became subject to ethnic cleansing by the simple reason of their membership in the collective project that had been targeted for destruction. But unlike the Holocaust survivors, who gave their testimonies many decades later, the Bosnians were talking about ethnic cleansing proximate to (if not contemporaneous with) the genocide itself, and to their own desperate struggles to rebuild their lives and Bosnia, in the Diaspora and in Bosnia-Herzegovina.

Another important dimension is that for Bosnians, the genocide they survived came after over forty years of living together in a community of Muslims, Serbs, and Croats. And it bears restating that theirs was a communist society that had imposed substantial restrictions upon social, cultural, and political life, thus demarcating a rigid boundary between the realms of public and private existence. The giving of testimonies, and how they were received, communicated and interpreted, must be located within the larger process of the "construction of social memory"[11] that has been preoccupying a Bosnian communality striving to redefine itself. All of these differences, which make surviving ethnic cleansing in Bosnia unique, also made the survivors' dilemmas of memory unique, and consequently the testimony work itself.

A TESTIMONY PROJECT

Our group started receiving testimonies in January 1993, when the first refugees from Bosnia came to Connecticut. This work continued in Connecticut through 1994, then moved to Chicago, when we established a small oral history archive for Bosnian testimonies as a part of our Project on Genocide, Psychiatry, and Witnessing at the University of Illinois at Chicago. Some seventy testimonies have been collected as of this writing.

It would not be accurate to convey that the testimony work proceeded with ease and that I and the other people involved were not often beset by struggle, confusion, and doubt. At first, we started videotaping testimonies, as in the Holocaust video archives. But survivors found that videotaping was too reminiscent of television interviews, which they experienced as intrusive and exploitative. It did not set the right interpersonal milieu for the giving of a more confessional and thoughtful testimony. So we stopped the videotaping. Compiling detailed, lengthy written narratives was more acceptable to these survivors, and indeed this form seemed better able to contain the narrative, sociohistorical, and cultural complexities of the testimony that were of greatest interest to us.

We also found that often enough the concept of testimony itself was not readily grasped by Bosnians. When Bosnians use the word "svjedocenje" for testimony, it is primarily associated with a legalistic meaning that denotes making a sworn statement before a judge.[12] One survivor said, *It is something official with legal consequences.*[13] We did not want the idea of the testimony to be constrained by this legal connotation, which could encourage the refugees to speak only in the kind of public voice that they would have been expected to use in Tito's Yugoslavia. Nor did we want the testimonies to be too closely associated with the United Nations War Crimes Tribunal, then so disparaged by Bosnians who associated it with the much-despised United Nations Protectorate Forces.

A number of survivors suggested that we use a phrase like "pricanje," or *telling your story,* as an alternative to the more legalistic "testimony."[14] Others dissented, feeling that this phrase put too much emphasis on the personal and did not draw enough attention to the social and political realities of this genocide. The effort to find a voice that could speak to both public and private dimensions of the Bosnian experience of ethnic cleansing involved continual struggle.

In one of our group discussions, a survivor defiantly counters those who are backing away from the testimony concept: *I will be glad to be a witness—to tell the truth.* Indeed, many survivors feel that they are in possession of a valuable and terrible historical truth to which they must publicly bear witness. Then there are others who back away from the nightmare of history, setting their sights elsewhere. One survivor speaking in a group meeting sums up the feelings of many who have given up on history, and who want primarily to rebuild a private life for their families, when she says, *It doesn't matter what we say. The winner makes history.*

This comment really depresses me. It is a negation of the survivors' bearing witness, of the power inherent in their remembering and telling, of the very proposition of listening to and documenting their stories. As we sit around the big table in the Bosnian Refugee Center drinking warm soda in the awkward silence that follows, Robert Lifton's teachings on the special knowledge of survivors come to mind. He wrote that what the survivor knows of genocide from personal experience can be a knowledge base for the work of making peace and preventing genocide. So I tell the group, "Survivors can write history too," and speak of the significance of remembrances of survivors of Hiroshima, the Holocaust, Armenian genocide, and the Vietnam war.

But what about the children? a survivor asks. *Must our children know of these terrible memories?* A survivor replies that she does not want her children to know because she does not want them to grow up learning to hate and feeling the desire to murder. More than a few survivors take the position that if we immerse ourselves in memories of ethnic cleansing, then it will inevitably lead to passing on hatreds and the desire for vengeance. Some other survivors speak in opposition. They say that if we had only had access to our past memories of ethnic killings from World War II, then our generation would have been better prepared for ethnic cleansing.

This dialogue starts sounding familiar. Next I expect the survivors to say that if we had only kept the memories of World War II alive, then we would have known that Serbs were murderers, and that we couldn't live together. But I am surprised; these survivors are really trying to say something different. They are not telling stories of atrocities just to demonize the Serbian people. Actually, they have not made up their minds that different peoples can't live together. They do not really know what the Bosnian future will be, but they are nonetheless able to struggle with some of the more difficult questions on the boundary between the self and history: Could we have done something different with our memories of ethnic nationalist aggression in World War II? And even more pressing, what are we now to do with our memories of ethnic cleansing? Comments like these inspire us to try to use the testimonies as a means of helping Bosnians and Bosnia come to new understandings of the dilemmas of memory that come of the personal and historical nightmares of ethnic cleansing.

NARRATIVES OF THE SELF'S HISTORICAL NIGHTMARE

Testimony work with survivors of state-sponsored violence, including both torture and genocide, has always been concerned with the relationship between the self and history. But in the case of ethnic cleansing in Bosnia, our experience using testimony finds self and history intertwined in new ways that deserve further exploration.

Survivors often begin their testimony by introducing their self as directly rooted in the context of history and its past nightmares. A. begins his testimony by saying: *I was born in Gacko in the war year of 1943. My father was killed when I was three months old. He fell victim of the same goal that is killing people today. My grandfather was also a victim of the same goal but at a different time.*[15]

Survivors like A. who were old enough to have lived through World War II will often relate their direct, personal experiences of this history. Younger survivors (such as B., quoted in the Prologue of *When History Is a Nightmare*), speaking what they know about Bosnian history in stories of their parents' or grandparents' lives, also portray a strong sense of the self in history.

A certain kind of historical awareness of the nightmare of World War II has been understandably heightened as a result of surviving ethnic cleansing. However, these historical memories of atrocity are deployed here not merely to justify today's desire for vengeance toward the other side (although that is an issue for some), but often enough to face the terrible price Bosnians have paid as a result of their wars. In their testimonies, survivors find themselves sharing thoughts about how World War II damaged their lives or their families' lives in ways they were unlikely to have discussed with anyone previously. Sometimes it can seem as if chronological time has collapsed and the struggle to live with the nightmares of World War II, though actually some fifty years old, dominates the realities of here and now. Ironically, it took the recent genocide and war to give Bosnians the unwelcome but invaluable chance to grasp from those old nightmarish memories some truths that could not be grasped before, given that communism had encouraged them to push those memories aside.

Survivors give testimony in which they share vignettes about unforgettable moments in their lives in Tito's Yugoslavia, emphasizing how, contrary to the ideology of Brotherhood and Unity, the links between personal and ethnic identities were made incredibly, and often painfully, clear to them. A. describes his years in the Yugoslav National Army.

My immediate squad commander . . . asked me after a whole year of service how it was possible that I was such a nice guy when the letters in my file were indicating the opposite. Then I realized what had been written about me in their files was really dark and awful. I was sort of "an enemy of the people." They believed that I came from an Ustasha family, because my father was killed in 1943 and he was not a Partisan. The Serbs were the ones who were creating the files, writing the characterizations. And if both my father and grandfather were killed by Serbs, I had to be a bad guy too. That has really hit me hard. It was in my head for years. . . .

In his head, but not in any kind of meaningful public discourse on the dangers of ethnic nationalism. No such dialogue existed in Tito's Yugoslavia.

Now in testimony, the survivors will often struggle over their memories of Tito. Their thoughts and feelings concerning Tito, who after all was primarily responsible for managing the struggles of national identity in Yugoslavia, are understandably intense and conflicted. A. wonders:

I don't know if it was good that he existed or not. Maybe it would have been better for us if he had never existed. I think about his responsibility in solving our problem: whether he was intentionally postponing the solving of our national problem or not; whether he had the power to change anything. For me, that is the most important question. I know how successful, or unsuccessful, he was in leading the country's economy. But for us Muslims, the solving of the problem of Muslim nationality and national identity was a very important one. And I don't know whether he had the power to solve it. And for us that was crucial.

In testimony, survivors are given permission to tell these stories of the memories and dreams that one kept in one's head, or maybe told only within one's family, during Tito's Yugoslavia. The testimony becomes a place for survivors to open up other difficult aspects of the complicated relationship between self and history. They struggle over how, probably without acknowledging it, they wagered their lives on the integrity of Tito's Brotherhood and Unity and lost. A. thinks back over the years of living together.

We lived in one system, and that was Tito's Yugoslavia, and that has reflected upon our lives everywhere, in schools, factories, offices, in our homes. He was speaking about this brotherhood and unity, pushing that idea, and we believed in it. I don't know why, but we believed in it. . . . But still, we believed. And we've been cheated. We've been cheated by the brotherhood and unity concept, that apparently only we believed in. We have been used by everybody. And we've been living fine and enjoying ourselves, hoping that the bad things would never happen again.

Sometimes survivors reach a point in their testimony beyond which they cannot pass. As with A., it can be the position that says we were cheated by "them"—politicians, communists, religious leaders, other ethnic groups. Far less often will the survivor implicate himself or herself—as an individual, family, culture, or way of life—for having held to a naïve view of history.

Sometimes survivors themselves can glimpse it, but even when they do not, the testimonies provide evidence of just how problematic is the place of memories of collective traumatization in relation to the imagined community of Bosnian life. Survivors' testimonies reveal that although survivors carried memories of aggression from World War II, and often the sense of the aggressor as an enemy, this was essentially not a part of a political understanding. The testimonies do not convey the sense that those memories of aggression have been linked with the idea that ethnic nationalism is a public enemy. Some survivors will note that some war criminals were punished by the state, and others went into exile, but the testimonies do not convey the sense of participating in a political culture that had a basic political understanding of what kept living together going, and what threatened its existence. Rather, in the testimonies they tend to idealize the experience of living together as a kind of dream, and reminisce nostalgically about the good old days. The more I listen to these testimonies, the more I feel that in order to consider what made ethnic cleansing in Bosnia possible, we have to listen not only for accounts of what the aggressors did, but also for the ways in which the survivors have been constructing and relating to memories of aggression in their narratives of historical nightmares.

The close relationship between self and history takes on an added dimension in our testimony work, given that the history of ethnic cleansing was far from finished when we were receiving testimonies in 1993, 1994, and 1995. We were giving survivors a chance to tell their version of this latest chapter in Balkan history before that history had been written, let alone finished. Survivors were telling stories that bore evidence of the historical events they had just lived through. Even if they had achieved a safe haven, their families and communities were still in the grip of the historical nightmare of which they spoke. What would happen with their own lives, let alone with history, was unknowable at the time they were giving their testimonies. It is only fitting that we have not been asking survivors to predict the future, or to analyze what has happened. What then do we want?

For mental health professionals like myself, as well as journalists, human rights activists, artists, and others who were committed to receiving survivors' stories, our desire to listen during the ethnic cleansing was in part motivated by an urgency to make the historical truth of genocide more widely known.[16] Many in the mass media and governments in the West had been complicit in spreading the perpetrators' message that spoke of ancient ethnic hatreds, civil wars, and Muslim fundamentalism. We operated under the belief that if more people were exposed to the truth contained in survivors' stories, it would be harder for people to be misled by leaders seeking to avoid taking responsibility or action. We endeavored to receive survivors' stories and to get those stories out, and we hoped they would mobilize others' concern and action on behalf of the Bosnian people and in opposition to genocide. We were trying to influence people's inaccurate historical perceptions in the hope that it would help to change the course of history and to save Bosnia.

Then in September 1995, President Clinton did what we had wanted done years earlier, and the military aggression against Bosnia-Herzegovina stopped. We were then forced to shift our approach in response to the demands of the post-Dayton era, with its imperatives of stopping the war and forging a lasting peace and democratic society in Bosnia. This immediately changed the whole context for testimony.

Testimony now has to serve the processes of recovery and of peacemaking in the post-Dayton milieu, with all its burdens of too much history. Our testimony work becomes an attempt to confront the dilemmas of memory of the post-war, post-ethnic cleansing, post-living together, post-communist era. Our aim now is to work with survivors to produce narratives that might lead to new understandings of the historical nightmares in Bosnian life, and importantly, a new public ethics regarding ethnic diversity. Our belief is that the transition to democracy requires new understandings of the experience of living together in Tito's Yugoslavia; these understandings must include reassessing the attitude that has been called merhamet.[17]

REASSESSING MERHAMET THROUGH TESTIMONY

Because it has been at the center of the "Bosnian spirit" that inspired living together, one might think that merhamet would be a primary force in the evolutionary process of making peace and building solidarity in post-Dayton Bosnia-Herzegovina. However, as a woman in Grbavica said in her testimony, *The worst part is I used to be so open, now we all are so closed.*[18] This closedness, also associated with fear, mistrust, hatred, and extremism, is a truthful confession of what it is actually like to live in the aftermath of ethnic cleansing and its trauma to merhamet. The testimony offers a space where one can begin to reflect on what is left of the years of living together and merhamet after surviving the nightmare of ethnic cleansing. Listening to these testimonies, one gets the impression that merhamet is in real trouble.

As difficult as it is to speak of the nightmare of genocide, it can be even more painful for survivors to speak of this dream that once animated their lives. My belated discovery of merhamet in testimony with E. teaches me how important it is to assist survivors in putting the experience of living together into words. Sometimes, they are so understandably preoccupied by the memories of ethnic cleansing and the new mentalities it provokes that they may not spontaneously mention merhamet, or try to give any words at all to the multi-ethnic experience. Yet often enough, Bosnians show a strong desire to use testimony not only to name the traumas that have disrupted their lives but also to name what the years of living together mean to them.

A. spontaneously broaches the topic: *We Bosnians, we are different. We forget easier. That is Bosnian merhamet. It is deeply rooted in our culture.* And so you find that some who shared in the values of merhamet are still trying to evoke that mentality as a way of dealing with memories of ethnic cleansing. They say that they are ready to forgive the aggressors, to forget what they did, and to move on with life.

When faced with the awesome challenges of the Dayton peace accords— to develop common institutions; to hold democratic multiparty federal and municipal elections; to reconcile with former aggressors; to re-accept displaced persons—nationalist, nondemocratic, non-open mentalities are often provoked. In this context, merhamet is at risk of being abandoned, or of being submerged by the momentum toward an exclusive Muslim identity for Bosnians and their society. For some, merhamet is seen as a big part of the problem, not at all as a part of the solution.

For survivors occupying either of these positions, testimony is a chance to begin to reassess merhamet and to redefine its place in the new landscape of Bosnia-Herzegovina. What will the Bosnians now do with this element of their culture, these survivors are asked to wonder. Will merhamet overcome even what genocide has done? Will it survive? Or has merhamet become the geno-cide's greatest object of destruction? Was it actually responsible in part for the genocide?

In testimony, we ask survivors to share more than just their memories of aggression. We also want to know if they identify the aggressor as an enemy, and if so, in what sense. We are curious about what the survivors did or desired to do in response to the aggressors. Then we ask about their sense of merhamet toward the aggressor, be it benevolence, forgiveness, charity, mercy, or something else.

We would like to believe that the very act of speaking of merhamet in relation to memories of aggression can redeem it. That testimony stories regarding merhamet can provide narrative evidence of its centrality in the Bosnian experience. Through testimony those who say that merhamet is still alive and as strong as ever in their hearts and lives can be encouraged to talk about what they will do to make it work in the new Bosnia. But we know that that alone is not enough.

We ask them if there are contingencies associated with their sense of merhamet. Some, like A., say that we can have merhamet if a court of law prosecutes the real war criminals. Some say that we can have it if the Bosnian Serb leaders in Pale would admit their guilt in the genocide and commit to multi-ethnic living. Some say that we can have merhamet only if there is a strong enough army and police to protect us from ethnic nationalists. Thinking about contingencies is important because it serves to move merhamet in the direction of a more political approach to reality, something it has historically lacked.

Yet we find some survivors saying that after ethnic cleansing there is no contingency that is adequate to make merhamet work. Yet not even its strongest detractors would argue that merhamet has completely disappeared. We think that it can be valuable for Bosnians to know about the many ways merhamet will continue to influence their way of thinking about themselves and their world. We also believe that it is just as important that testimony be used to learn more about merhamet's problematics, revisiting the political culture of Tito's Yugoslavia and the place of memories of aggression from World War II.

After World War II, the moral community elevated the Partisans' defeat of fascism above all else. Though there was living together, the moral imperative of the day was not to look at how to reconcile the experiences of living together and memories of aggression from World War II. In that sense, we can say that merhamet was not really tested. Citizens of the Second Yugoslavia were never given the option to consider acting on behalf of their ethnic group and to reconcile the advantages of taking a pro-ethnic stance against the costs of mass violence and destruction. Because it was never tested, then, merhamet is something less than a moral attitude. Perhaps it is more a humanistic sentiment. That would account for the relatively plastic way many survivors react to a question about merhamet. *I don't have merhamet now, but maybe in two years, I will,* says one survivor.

But now, after ethnic cleansing, merhamet is being seriously tested. It cannot simply go dormant, then reappear unchanged. For one thing, too many survivors have said that merhamet let the Bosnian Muslims down, that it did not prevent nationalism and genocide in Bosnia. With such dramatic changes in the Bosnian landscape of memory, it is no exaggeration to say that ethnic cleansing has provoked a moral crisis concerning merhamet. How is it possible to face this moral crisis in the highly politicized atmosphere of Bosnia after Dayton? Now, merhamet is being subjected to far greater political pressure than it ever was in Tito's Yugoslavia.

We should not expect that testimony would simply purge survivors of nationalistic attitudes and strengthen merhamet, any more than it would magically purge them of their traumatic memories. But could it help them to contextualize their hatreds and vengeance, and to assist them in negotiating those attitudes—reconciling them with their opposites as a part of a moral struggle?

Testimony, with its insistence on honest personal accounts, is especially open to engaging the moral crisis, deepening and advancing the moral struggle. Testimony looks at the self's narrative constructions of these radically contradictory historical realities without totally subjecting them to the political order of the day and without overly privatizing or pathologizing them. It is not only that testimony takes place on the boundaries between the self and history; it is also that it encompasses four, if not more, distinct historical epochs: living together in Tito's Yugoslavia, the recent ethnic cleansing, the ethnic atrocities of World War II, and the post-Dayton period.

Listening to these testimony accounts of the mentality of multi-ethnic living suggests that merhamet was entirely apolitical in the sense discussed by the political theorist Carl Schmitt.[19] Schmitt wrote that the nature of the political centers on the distinctions a state and its people make between public "friends and enemies" (Schmitt, *The Political,* 26). The survival of a democracy depends in part upon its capacity to know its enemies and to combat them, forcefully if necessary. Liberalism is denounced as a "negation of the political" (p. 70) that throws a "smoke screen" (p. 84) over the realities of public friends and enemies, thereby endangering democracy. Although Yugoslavia was no liberal society, the ideology of Brotherhood and Unity created the illusion of liberalism amidst the totalitarian control of a political state and its culture. To Schmitt, there is nothing more dangerous than believing that you have no public enemies. Testimonies reveal that survivors really believed in Brotherhood and Unity and its sense of merhamet, which promised to deliver their historical dreams unto them. Schmitt implies that it was a shroud that kept them from seeing or attending to the very significant ethnic tensions and threats in Yugoslavian society. It also prevented them from attending to the haunting memories of ethnic nationalist violence, which would then eventually return with a vengeance, creating enemies anew.

Testimony seeks out two kinds of courage from survivors. The first is the courage that comes of surviving a genocide and enduring horrific physical and emotional hardship. The second is the courage that comes of the self facing the collision of two or more conflicting historical realities and figuring out who one is and what path one chooses. Testimony asks the self to struggle with that which cannot be reconciled, and to face the moral problems that come from that struggle. If merhamet is to be an element in the moral order of the new Bosnia, then it will surely have to survive this trial.

TOWARD A CIVIC DIALOGUE ON SURVIVORS' REMEMBRANCES

A. concludes his testimony:

> I think the stories should be collected. This time we have to know our history, because otherwise, others will be falsifying the history, as they did before. All we have to do is to record the truth. We need to have our stories, our figures, and our statistics. That is why I am happy that my story has been documented.

The psychiatrist and scholar Jonathan Shay, who explored combat soldiers returning to civilian life in a fascinating reading of Vietnam against ancient Greece, cites the need for "new models of healing which emphasize communalization of the trauma."[20] Chilean testimony addressed this through collaborations between survivors, survivor groups, mental health professionals, human rights activists and organizations, and eventually, a government truth commission.[21] Conceptually, the Chilean mental health professionals thought of this as "to de-privatize their pain" (Agger and Jensen, *Trauma and Recovery*, 146), which they considered a necessary departure from the mainstream psychiatric approach toward psychotherapeutic work. Holocaust scholars have organized testimony projects in order to build a collective, historical memory out of the many particular experiences of survival.[22] Agger and Jensen report that a major goal of testimony work is to facilitate the "construction of social memory" (p. 228), a process that must accompany reconciliation.

In Bosnia-Herzegovina, this social processing of memory has suffered greatly not only from five years of genocide and war, but also as a consequence of communism and the failed transition to democracy. Bosnia in the post-Dayton era lacks the individual habits, the professional skills or ethics, the institutions, or the cultural understandings to adequately support this kind of memory work. Therefore, the successful transition to democracy and the forging of a lasting peace in Bosnia-Herzegovina will require new understandings and new initiatives concerning memory. Memories of aggression must be openly communicated and fundamentally linked to a moral understanding of the values of liberal democracy and to the identification of ethnic nationalism as its enemy. Further, the transition requires nurturance of a social dialogue where the democratic system of values and the peoples' memories of experiences have a chance to interconnect. This in turn requires that cultural elites and institutions prioritize working with remembrances, and integrate this work with democratization and with their other aims and tasks. At this moment in time, I see this work taking shape in three approaches in Bosnia-Herzegovina and its Diaspora: (1) establishing oral history projects in civic institutions; (2) facilitating interdisciplinary approaches to the study of traumatic memory in the university; and (3) developing curriculum on memories and reconciliation in elementary and secondary schools.

Oral history projects are needed in order to collect survivors' testimonies, both in Bosnia-Herzegovina and the Diaspora. In Chicago, we found that establishing testimony archives set a large group context that helped support the testimony work with individual survivors. All too often the survivor is silent, or speaks as a lone wolf. Testimony can give the individual survivor a voice that is empowering in and of itself. Many survivors would probably not tell their story if it was only "one to one" with a therapist, but because they know that their voice will be joined with many others, they suffer less fear and aloneness. Our work attempting to gather testimonies in Sarajevo and in Germany indicates that this will be equally true in Bosnia-Herzegovina.

What should these testimonies contain? First and foremost, they are to be the survivors' accounts of ethnic cleansing. Second, they are to be remembrances of living together. Third, there are the long-suppressed stories of World War II, as well as other prior episodes of historical violence that have lived on in memory, perhaps through the family and its elders. Fourth, they are to deal with the oppressive effects of the communist system, even though it was not the harshest of those seen in Europe. These testimonies must primarily focus on the dangers of ethnic nationalism and the values of multi-ethnic tolerance and understanding.

So far we have found that after telling their stories, survivors were very well aware that the testimonies they gave were something other than a deposition for legal proceedings, as necessary as that might be. They knew that their stories deserved a special reception that would somehow acknowledge and deal with them as rich and complicated historical narratives. At our Project in Chicago, we established a small archive where survivors' stories could be held. As with the Holocaust testimony projects, we sought to locate them in proximity to the Bosnian community and to the academic and professional communities. Our belief was that by better grounding the testimonies in these worlds, we could work against marginalization, and toward developing new understandings and new approaches.

When professionals and scholars, artists and writers, community leaders and educators, groups and institutions get involved in the process of giving, receiving, and working with survivors' testimonies, there is the possibility of opening the way for societies to develop a civic dialogue on survivors' memories. A testimony project brings a critical mass of survivors' stories into a special social context. The psychologist Daniel Schaecter points out that this kind of large-scale yet individualized approach offers some increased protection against the distortion and manipulation of testimony that comes when a very small number of stories, with all their potential for being nonrepresentative, are involved.[23] It allows for the development of an open, group dialogue on the critical issues of reconciling the memories of living together with those of ethnic atrocities. It creates a safe social space in which a community can struggle toward developing a collective narrative of historical memory, and can invite others into that dialogue.

However, there are many obstacles to the gathering of testimonies. The first set of obstacles are practical: those having to do with the daily hardships that make individual, family, and institutional life so difficult for most Bosnians. The second set has to do with the legacy of communism itself, which encourages people to silence memories of ethnic atrocities in order to promote living together; to disavow any collective memory because of the taint of mistrust associated with the collective forgetting of Brotherhood and Unity; to escape from history into private life and private memories. But fear is probably the biggest obstacle to testimony. It is all too obvious, with the provisions of Dayton, that this history is not over with. The perpetrators and criminals are still on the loose. Nobody really knows who or what entity will be in power in the years to come. There is also the all too real fear of exploitation of these testimonies by anyone who wants to seize on a memory and misuse it. The shattering of trust, so common in traumatized individuals, families, and communities, is pervasive in Bosnians.[24]

The establishment of testimony projects in Bosnia-Herzegovina and the Diaspora would be a necessary step in developing a civic dialogue on survivors' memories there. That is why I have been calling for the establishment of testimony projects in Sarajevo, to start. To best reflect the multi-ethnic communality of Bosnia, these projects should include survivors of ethnic cleansing and war not only from the three major ethnic communities in Bosnia—Muslims, Orthodox, and Catholics—but also from the so-called "mixed" persons. Listening to the stories of Bosnian Orthodox and Catholics, which will undoubtedly contain some stories of persecution by Muslims, will be hard for some. But there is much more to be lost by not including their voices. It would send a clear signal that the new Bosnia has overtly nonpluralistic and nondemocratic designs.

The testimony projects in Bosnia-Herzegovina should be located in relation to institutions of higher education. This would keep the body of testimonies in contact with an interdisciplinary intellectual community of students and scholars, increasing the likelihood that the testimonies would become connected with their ongoing studies. I picture students in history, sociology, religion, literature, and psychology going to the testimony archives, using them in their papers and presentations, and growing up intellectually, morally, and politically in relation to them.

The testimonies are by no means primarily psychotherapy, and the phenomenon they bear is not exclusively psychiatric. An interdisciplinary approach will be needed to address the testimonies adequately, and especially the dilemmas of memory they contain. Psychiatrists must join with historians, anthropologists, sociologists, journalists, politicians, human rights activists, and artists. Interdisciplinary methodologies for receiving, collecting, studying, and transmitting survivors' testimonies must be developed. Yet such disciplinary boundaries are often not easy to breach. In Bosnia-Herzegovina, there is the added problem that the educational institutions are poor and depleted, and in the face of the shattering of their way of life, scholars and teachers may cling ever more tightly to that which they knew, and resist the new.

When Tvrtko Kulenovic and I presented a three-day seminar in Sarajevo in October 1997, we hoped it would serve as a step in the interdisciplinary direction. We called it "Dilemmas of Collective Memory and History: A Workshop for Interdisciplinary Inquiry in Sarajevo."[25] The very title we chose caused some sparks to fly. *We are victims of collective memory,* said one physician, to which many heads nodded in agreement. He meant the collective memory of Serbian suffering, which had been associated with virulent ethnic nationalism and which stood behind ethnic cleansing. There was also the matter of the collective forgetting of communism's Brotherhood and Unity, by which they all felt duped. I don't want to be a part of any of these collectives, they seemed to be saying. Collective had left too bad a taste in their mouths. Fortunately, we were able to examine it together and not get stuck there.

The participants were researchers, scholars, professionals, writers, or artists, actively engaged in work that addressed survivors' remembrances. We chose not to present a highly structured research plan. Rather, we presented the totality of possibilities of interdisciplinary inquiry into memory with the explicit intent of impressing people with its difference from the accustomed ways of thinking about these things in contemporary Sarajevo. We taught current methodologies, approaches, and techniques concerning the interdisciplinary study of collective memory (with an emphasis on literary and psychological approaches). We shared the language, attitude, and approaches to understanding issues and problems of collective memory. We were aiming to develop an interdisciplinary community and dialogue interested in nonpartisan approaches to survivors' remembrances. I am not proclaiming that it was a success, because to know that I would have to see it translated into actual work, which it of course has not been as yet and probably won't be for some time. On the other hand, we think that this kind of international, interdisciplinary dialogue and collaboration is just what will be needed to develop new ways of thinking and working with memories.

Just saying these words, which look forward to successful ways of working, brings to mind their opposite. One clinician who attended the workshop professed total enthusiasm for what was discussed, then before parting, let slip, *I will soon have more opportunity for creative endeavors.* In other words, he had just lost his salary. It is awfully hard to think about history when day-to-day living is so impossibly hard.

Communalization of survivors' memories will certainly require more than scholarship and intellectual dialogue. Creative artworks are necessary to confront the experience of atrocity and to help facilitate the transmission of knowledge of genocide. The imaginative force that they bear can engage traumatic memories without letting fear, hatreds, and mistrust dominate. Art can show the possibility of creating narratives and images that do not intentionally or inadvertently succumb to the violence and nationalism that has shattered the way things were. Art can bridge the personal and the historical in the most believable ways. Jonathan Shay points out that in ancient Greece, theaters were actually located in healing centers.[26] With its rich cultural history, Bosnia could yet develop new kinds of working alliances between mental health professionals and creative artists.

The issue provoked by testimonies is not only the transmission of traumatic memories, understandably of interest to trauma clinicians, but also the transmission of the totality of value systems upon which a people's survival depends. How does a society treat its younger generation and transmit to them its collective memories and values?[27] The International Commission on the Balkans recommended the establishment of joint historical commissions to make new guidelines for writing textbooks that do not abuse history "for nationalist purposes."[28] What better way to approach the telling of history than through testimonies, which provide the best possible evidence of how history has been misunderstood and misused, but which also inspired and strengthened an open, democratic view. Survivors' testimonies should be at the center of innovative curricular approaches to teaching youths about Bosnian history. Such approaches have been developed in the West concerning the Holocaust, civil rights, human rights, and international identity.[29]

As A. says, we cannot afford to end the testimony, because the survivor's story has far to go on its journey into history.

Well, this story could last for years. I have no illusions that I told you everything because each and every day of that time is a whole story. Sometimes, one hour of a day was a story. But I am pleased at being able to tell you this whole story. And I will be happy if my story can help anyone. If it is recorded for history.

As for the survivor H., in a follow-up meeting we ask if we can read from his testimony at some presentations to professional groups. He says that he would be deeply honored. After each presentation, we'd call him up to let him know how people responded, and what they said. Most memorable was the time we invited him to present his story in person with us to a group of clergy, ethicists, and mental health professionals in Chicago. His story, more so than any published book or newspaper article, really communicates the truths of surviving ethnic cleansing. When he saw for himself that his voice was being heard and that something was being understood about Bosnia, the look on his face showed he felt something strong and good.

FINDING NEW WAYS OF BEING PROFESSIONAL

From the testimonies of several academic psychiatrists, I learn that in Tito's Yugoslavia psychiatrists by and large avoided addressing the post-traumatic psychological sequelae in civilian and military survivors of World War II. They report that some professionals heard survivors' stories, but these stories were not systematically collected, reflected upon, discussed, or analyzed. (Jovan Raskovic in Croatia is a notorious exception.) Only rarely did individual psychiatrists do trauma-oriented work with survivors. This kind of work was not taught, studied, or practiced. As late as the 1980s, the leading psychiatric textbooks in Yugoslavia did not even mention post-traumatic conditions related to war or genocide.[30]

Ethnic cleansing and war made abundantly clear the immense disadvantages of Bosnian psychiatrists' not having acquired the clinical skills to address war-trauma-related conditions. It also showed that Bosnian psychiatrists had no particular expertise regarding survivors' memories, no psychological or historical view that prioritized survivors' stories, and no more investment in a civic dialogue on survivors' memories than anyone else in Bosnia.

During the ethnic cleansing and siege, mental health professionals were drowning in survivors' stories, and they did what they could. There were scores of individual efforts to hear the stories, to relieve suffering, and more than a few efforts to gather testimonial evidence for the war crimes tribunal. But neither governmental nor nongovernmental mental health organizations developed anything resembling Holocaust or Chilean testimony. This was largely a consequence of the very real problems of enduring genocide, siege, and war. After all, they did not have the tape recorders, computers, money, time, institutional support, or safe space we did in the rich world. All they really wanted to do was survive. But it was probably also a consequence of the larger tendency to push aside memories of aggression, which was the norm in Yugoslav Bosnian society.

It would be wrong, though, to imply that international mental health professionals who trained the Bosnians in trauma work during the aggression, and the whole tradition of trauma mental health work, were not in some ways also implicated by this unpreparedness. During the ethnic cleansing and war, international mental health experts poured into Bosnia-Herzegovina and Croatia in order to teach them trauma mental health work and to organize programs to help survivors. In sharing their expertise on trauma with Bosnian professionals, who had a lot to learn about trauma work, the internationals did much good. During the siege of Sarajevo and the ethnic cleansing of Bosnia, the priority was on providing humanitarian assistance. International mental health professionals were caught up in the same bind as all humanitarian projects—you may help the sufferer, but not confront the aggressors. This severing of the humanitarian from the political may have discouraged international mental health professionals from adequately attending to survivors' memories and the ethical dilemmas they present.

But now, with the transition to a postcommunist, post-genocidal, postwar psychiatry and mental health system underway, professionals redefining their work with survivors and their memories cannot afford to ignore these issues. What is required is nothing short of a radical redefinition of the professional identity of the psychiatrist in Bosnia-Herzegovina, as well as the development of new understandings by the international psychiatrists who work with them.

For the internationals and Bosnians, this will require more than attention to treating PTSD, which presents a risk of overly privatizing and pathologizing the experience. It will require that the approach to trauma survivors be accompanied by a serious consideration of the ethics of professionals' relationship to genocide and to survivors' memories in Bosnia-Herzegovina. That will require a greater depth of understanding of the Bosnian landscape of memory than most internationals, not to mention most Bosnian mental health professionals, have thus far acquired.[31]

The new understandings that need to be reached are consistent with the point of view that the medical professional participates not only in a narrow biomedical role, but actually in a broader social, political, and cultural project, especially when it comes to social traumas.[32] The basic proposition that psychiatrists and other health care workers explicitly see their work with survivors in relationship with social and political processes is familiar to the evolving movement of mental health and human rights.[33]

The Chilean professionals spoke of the position of "ethical non-neutrality" and the "bond of commitment," which reflects an ideology according to which professionals are to make links between their patients' symptoms and sociopolitical processes, and to take positions (in therapy and in public) on the etiologically significant human rights violations.[34] Dori Laub spoke of the role of the physician as a "witness" to the trauma survivor in the sense that the physician must fill the void and be there to document the historical truth of social traumas.[35] Robert Jay Lifton has described the role of the "witnessing professional," deploying professional expertise within a carefully drawn ethical and historical framework to address both the individual survivors of traumatic situations and the communal and historical dislocations within which the traumas took place.[36] Supported by these ideological structures, mental health professionals receiving survivors' stories have been able to participate in larger processes of social and political change, in a number of different sociohistorical contexts.

Yet insights such as these into the relationship between the personal and the collective, the psychological and the sociopolitical, have never come easy. Even in the relatively privileged conditions of the West, the development of a human rights and mental health movement has taken a long, long time. We should also note that it was not until three or four decades after World War II that psychiatry started to pay more systematic attention to the struggles and stories of survivors of the Holocaust and that there have been similar time gaps concerning other instances of genocide, such as the Armenians and the Cambodians. To this day, there is still a tendency to see social and political traumas through privatizing or pathologizing approaches. The paradigm of PTSD, which frames the psychiatric approach to surviving trauma, dominates the mental health professionals' approach.[37] Is there another way?

Agger and Jensen identify the "wounded healer" as one who may be able to transcend such limitations, in spite but also because of the problems their condition also presents to them (*Trauma and Recovery*, 87–88). They quote Jung: "only the wounded physician heals." They believe that the personal suffering of a healer who has also been traumatized can enable that healer to develop greater empathy and understanding of trauma survivors. What's more, the healer's involvement in human rights work and engagement in a political project can in turn be spread to other survivors through prevention and clinical work, as well as interdisciplinary collaborations with other domains of human rights work.

Dori Laub makes the claim that psychiatrists can be witnesses, not because they themselves are necessarily survivors (which in his case was true), but because they are fundamentally engaged in transmitting survivors' stories in a way that may stimulate the survivor to tell the story in the first place.[38] Now in Bosnia, most if not all professionals have their own trauma experiences and memories to draw from. If Bosnian mental health professionals are to redefine themselves, then they may very well have to begin with the understandings and approaches they derive from their relationship with their own traumatic experiences, memories, and nightmares.

This is not to say that mental health professionals are the only people who can be witnesses. But their work as psychological trauma healers puts them in a likely position to receive survivors' stories, and gives them the means to interpret and transmit those stories. They have the skills of nuanced interviewing and listening that can help to establish the interpersonal conditions that make testimony possible. Their expertise with narrative approaches embraces a special commitment to eliciting, receiving, documenting, understanding, and communicating survivors' stories. Psychiatrists and other mental health professionals who work with survivors are in a privileged position for developing a civic dialogue on survivors' memories. It can be done with activities that are a part of many professionals' lives: teaching other professionals, educating the public, building and strengthening social networks, changing organizations and institutions.

Testimony work requires not only certain technical skills, but also an ethical knowing of survivors' memories and one's own relationship with them. Before doing testimony work, the professional must undergo a process of moral and psychological preparation in order to be positioned as a receiver of testimony. Little is known about the nature of this process or how to nurture it. We stand to learn a great deal from those Bosnian professionals who will chronicle their own journeys to redefine themselves as professionals in this time of great historical change.

Another important aspect of the possible transformation in professional work stems from how the testimonies open up new approaches to conducting research. As in the testimony itself, the primary commitment in the intellectual inquiry into testimonies is to survivors and their stories. The testimony researcher endeavors to avoid becoming merely an appendix to a diagnosis, a scale, or a theory. The researcher is as committed to questioning his or her own beliefs as to questioning the survivors in testimony. This may render the work nonobjective, in the sense that it does not follow a scientific methodology. However, that does not mean that it is without discipline. Nor is it without precedent: the emphasis upon intensive biographical interviewing, survivors' narratives, ethical commitment, and moral reading has also been evident in the "advocacy research" of Robert Jay Lifton, the "normative ethics" of Philip Hallie, and the testimony writings of Inger Agger and Soren Jensen, Dori Laub and Shoshana Felman, to name a few.[39]

The testimony sets up a comparatively egalitarian relationship between the survivor and the researcher.[40] The latter is there to listen and learn from the survivors. The survivor is encouraged to raise questions about the researcher and all that role represents to the survivor. This unique relationship then becomes a part of the researcher's intellectual inquiry in the form of a double confession. The survivor has given testimony to the researcher, who in turn gives testimony to the reader, with the same commitment to detailed, close, honest reflection. In doing so, the researcher, like the survivor, cannot stay removed from the stories. The professional must necessarily take sides.

Testimony translates into a kind of scholarship that is not necessarily about constructing a theory or testing a hypothesis. Testimony research yields a narrative that can be of use for survivors, educators, professionals, intellectuals, artists, and others. This narrative does not invite within only a narrow group of readers who share a common professional language or preoccupations. Like the testimonies themselves, this narrative of intellectual inquiry focuses us on major social issues, but also on the question of how we define ourselves.

The researcher seeks not so much to avoid the problems of nonobjectivity as to exploit its possible benefits. The inquiry seeks out encounters, collisions, conflicts, and confrontations between the different voices, different sides, including that which is known and that which is not. For survivors, professionals, and readers, the aims of entering into this narrative can be to become more aware of: how we listen and know; how we live with suffering in our midst; how we live with oppression and traumas in our midst; how we can make meaningful changes in the self that support taking action in the social and political realms.

And yet the inescapable fact of Bosnia-Herzegovina today is that there are far more suicides than testimonies. Isn't there a way in which each suicide says that taking one's life is a sensible response to the weight of living with too much history? The futility of their struggle was also anticipated by Joseph Roth. "The old revolver that Herr von Trotta had taken along pressed in his back pocket. What good was a revolver? They saw no bears and no wolves in the borderland. All they saw was the collapse of the world!"[41]

No countervailing narrative proposition exists in Bosnia-Herzegovina that can overcome all the loss, destruction, and misery. The search for memory cannot be readily resolved, despite the yearnings. Not tens of thousands of Schindler-inspired testimonies would be enough to contain much too much history to bear. Testimony work is based on the human desire to tell and to listen to stories no matter how difficult things are in reality. It could be said to "work" to the extent that it brings the survivor, the researcher, and the listeners into contact with the dilemmas of memory that are at the center of the struggles for individual and societal recovery. By no means should we ever consider the proposition of testimony to be some kind of solution to Bosnia's current and future dilemmas. It cannot guarantee healing or justice, at an individual or a collective level; but perhaps it can assist in the development of a better knowing, where many have their say, and the history that is learned is also more knowledgeable about memory processes and the significance of remembrances. Now, in the post-Dayton era, as Bosnians wake up from their nightmare, the time is right to begin.

NOTES

1. H. [pseud.], interview with author, tape recording, March 1995, Bosnian Survivors Oral History Archives, Project on Genocide, Psychiatry and Witnessing, University of Illinois at Chicago.
2. Shoshana Felman and Dori Laub, *Testimony: Crises of Witnessing in Literature, Psychoanalysis and History* (New York and London: Routledge, 1992); Geoffrey Hartman, *The Longest Shadow: In the Aftermath of the Holocaust* (Bloomington: Indiana University Press, 1996); Lawrence Langer, *Holocaust Testimonies: The Ruins of Memory* (New Haven and London: Yale University Press, 1991); Terrence DePres, *The Survivor: An Anatomy of Life in the Death Camps* (Oxford: Oxford University Press, 1976).
3. Jean Amery, *At the Mind's Limits: Contemplations by a Survivor at Auschwitz and Its Realities* (Bloomington: Indiana University Press, 1980), as quoted in James E. Young, *The Texture of Memory: Holocaust Memorials and Meaning* (New Haven and London: Yale University Press, 1993), 1.
4. Young, *Texture*, as well as his *Writing and Rewriting the Holocaust* (Bloomington: Indiana University Press, 1988).
5. See Felman and Laub, *Testimony*; Langer, *Holocaust Testimonies*; and Hartman, *The Longest Shadow*.
6. Inger Agger and Soren Jensen, *Trauma and Recovery under State Terrorism* (London: Zed Books, 1996).
7. See A. J. Cienfuegos and C. Monelli, "The Testimony of Political Repression as a Therapeutic Instrument," *American Journal of Orthopsychiatry* 53, no. 1 (1983), 43–51.
8. Agger and Jensen, *Trauma and Recovery*.
9. Inger Agger and Soren Jensen, "Testimony as Ritual and Evidence in Psychotherapy for Political Refugees," *Journal of Traumatic Stress* 3 (1990), 115–130.
10. Inger Agger, *The Blue Room: Trauma and Testimony among Refugee Women: A Psychosocial Exploration* (London: Zed Books, 1992).
11. Agger and Jensen, *Trauma and Recovery*, 228.
12. Alija Isakovic, *Rjecnik bosnakskog jezika (Karakteristicna leksika)* (Sarajevo: Bosanska knjiga, 1995), 304.
13. Bosnian survivor, personal communication.

14. "pricanje" means to tell a story. See Isakovic, *Rjecnik bosnakskog*, 250.
15. A. [pseud.], interview with Alma Dzubur, tape recording, 1995, Bosnian Survivors Oral History Archives, Project on Genocide, Psychiatry and Witnessing, University of Illinois at Chicago.
16. Some leading activists in the United States were Steven Walker, Roy Gutman, Susan Sontag, and Catherine Mackinnon. See Susan Sontag, "Godot Comes to Sarajevo," *New York Review of Books*, 21 October 1993, 52–59; Stephen W. Walker, "Genocide: We are Responsible," *Tikkun* (November/December 1993), 19–22; and Steven A. Holmes, "State Department Balkan Aides Explain Why They Quit," *New York Times*, 26 August 1993, A12.
17. I strongly believe that these experiences also have to be documented as historical and legal evidence of war crimes for possible use in a truth commission or war crimes tribunal. See Theodore Meron, "The Case for War Crimes Tribunal in Yugoslavia," *Foreign Affairs* 72, no. 3 (summer 1993), 122–135.
18. I. [pseud.], interview with author, tape recording, 1997, Bosnian Survivors Oral History Archives, Project on Genocide, Psychiatry and Witnessing, University of Illinois at Chicago.
19. Carl Schmitt, *The Concept of the Political* (Chicago and London: University of Chicago Press, 1996).
20. Jonathan Shay, *Achilles in Vietnam: Combat Trauma and the Undoing of Character* (New York: Atheneum, 1994), 229 n. 13.
21. See Agger and Jensen, *Trauma and Recovery.*
22. See Felman and Laub, *Testimony;* Geoffrey Hartman, *The Longest Shadow;* and Langer, *Holocaust Testimonies.*
23. Daniel Schaecter, *Searching for Memory: The Brain, the Mind, and the Past* (New York: Basic Books, 1996).
24. For a discussion of the shattering of trust after trauma, see Judith Herman, *Trauma and Recovery* (New York: Basic Books, 1992); Jennifer J. Freyd, *Betrayal Trauma: The Logic of Forgetting Childhood Abuse* (Cambridge and London: Harvard University Press, 1996); and Ronnie Janoff-Bulman, *Shattered Assumptions: Towards a New Psychology of Trauma* (New York: The Free Press, 1992).
25. Interviews and discussion at Sarajevo Seminar, October 1997, Bosnian Survivors Oral History Archives, Project on Genocide, Psychiatry and Witnessing, University of Illinois at Chicago.
26. Jonathan Shay, A*chilles in Vietnam: Combat Trauma and the Undoing of Character* (New York: Atheneum, 1994), 194.
27. See Claude Lévi-Strauss and Didier Eribon, *Conversations with Claude Lévi-Strauss* (Chicago and London: University of Chicago Press, 1991); and Leszek Kolakowski, *The Presence of Myth* (Chicago and London: University of Chicago Press, 1989).
28. *Unfinished Peace: Report of the International Commission on the Balkans* (Washington, D.C.: Carnegie Endowment for International Peace, 1996), 152.

29. Herbert Hirsch, *Genocide and the Politics of Memory: Studying Death to Preserve Life* (Chapel Hill and London: University of North Carolina Press, 1995), 178–180.

30. Dusan Kecmanovic, ed., *Psihijatrija* (Beograd i Zagreb: Medicinska kniga, 1989).

31. For the army of international mental health consultants, it will also require a different mentality than is commonly expressed by trauma mental health professionals whose investment in the sense of their being a movement goes along with a belief that we possess a terrific body of knowledge that must be shared the world over,

32. See Arthur Kleinman and Joan Kleinman, eds., "Social Suffering," *Daedalus: Journal of the American Academy of Arts and Sciences* 125, no. 1 (winter 1996), special issue.

33. See Inger Agger and Soren Jensen, "Introduction: Mental Health and Human Rights," in Inger Agger, *Mixed Marriages: Voices from a Psycho-Social Workshop held in Zagreb, Croatia* (Brussels: European Community Humanitarian Office, 1996), 12–14.

34. Agger and Jensen, "Introduction."

35. Felman and Laub, *Testimony*, 74–75.

36. Robert Jay Lifton, lecture delivered at the 9th Annual Meeting of the International Society for Traumatic Stress Studies, 1993.

37. See Anthony Marsella, Matthew Friedman, Ellen Gerrity, and R. Scurfield, eds., *Ethnocultural Aspects of Posttraumatic Stress Disorder* (Washington, D.C.: American Psychological Association, 1996).

38. See Felman and Laub, *Testimony*, 75–76.

39. See Robert Jay Lifton, *Death in Life: Survivors of Hiroshima* (New York: Random House, 1967), 3–12; Felman and Laub, *Testimony*; also Phillip Hallie, "Skepticism, Narrative, and Holocaust Ethics," *Philosophical Forum* 16, nos. 1–2 (fall/winter 1984/5), 33–49.

40. See Alessandro Portelli, *The Death of Luigi Trastulli and Other Stories* (Albany: State University of New York Press, 1991), 29–58.

41. Joseph Roth, *The Radetzky March* (Woodstock, N.Y.: Overlook Press, 1932) and *The Emperor's Tomb* (Woodstock: Overlook Press, 1950), 164.

The Continuing Effects of American Colonialism upon First Nations Peoples[1]

MICHAEL YELLOW BIRD

> It is comfortable for us to believe that colonialism is something which happened two hundred or more years ago, and which involved injustices which never could happen today. Yet, colonialism is a continuing process.
>
> Carmel Tapping, *Other Wisdoms, Other Worlds*, 1993

I am happy that my colleagues Alice Lieberman and Cheryl Lester have given me the opportunity to write this essay for their book. It is rare that we First Nations Peoples are invited to give our opinion, share what we know, or tell our stories. Almost without exception, our voices, concerns, and experiences are ignored as if we no longer exist or as if what we have to say is not important. This is upsetting and insulting because we are not immigrants, visitors, or refugees to this country. We are the aboriginal peoples; these are our aboriginal homelands. It is disrespectful to overlook us in our own country. Such treatment reinforces our invisibility and reduces us to strangers in our own home.

Many who now occupy and control our lands do not know, or in some cases refuse to acknowledge, that they are the descendants of uninvited, ungracious visitors who not only caused the destruction of our peoples and cultures, but also falsely advanced the belief that this nation was founded on the principles of freedom, democracy, and justice for all. Today, as in the past, few ever talk about how, in order to achieve these principles, this nation murdered millions and millions of our peoples, stole billions of acres of our lands, intentionally eliminated most of our tribal languages, beliefs, and values, and reduced us to second class citizens in our own homelands. In effect, we are America's dirty little family secret, kept hidden from view.

It is convenient for the United States of America to forget about us as if we don't exist, except when we are used as romantic archival relics or props in colonial films and stories to advance the one-sided, distorted myths declaring

Source: A partial and earlier version of this paper was presented at the Task Force Meeting of Cultural Competence in Child Welfare Practice: A Collaboration between Practitioners and Academicians, University of Texas at Austin, February 9–10, 2001.

the "greatness" of this nation. Rarely has responsibility been taken, or have apologies been made, for what happened and continues to happen to our peoples. We are, without question, the most impoverished, disenfranchised, dispossessed, invisible, least heard, and least supported racial/ethnic group in this country and few seem to care or have knowledge of our situation. From where I am situated, as an Indigenous person and social work scholar, it appears that the United States suffers from two phobias with respect to Indigenous Peoples: *"dikephobia,"* (the fear of justice) and *"hypegiaphobia"* (the fear of responsibility). More than ever there is a need for social workers to understand and remedy this nation's past and present mistreatment, control, and oppression of Indigenous Peoples. At the end of this essay, I suggest several things that can be done.

Today, more than ever, I am convinced that many of the problems, and much of the suffering, experienced within First Nations communities is the result of the past and present effects of American colonialism. First Nations Peoples are the survivors of a massive and prolonged campaign of racial and cultural terrorism, which was perpetuated by the United States of America as it colonized our lands and lives. Colonialism is the invasion and subjugation of one people by another from a different race and culture and is often a brutal, humiliating, and alienating experience and process for the colonized. Under colonial rule, the colonizer appropriates, often through force or deception, the lands, resources, and wealth of Indigenous Peoples while deliberately and systematically destroying their lives, numbers, spirit, and cultural integrity.

The past and present experience of colonialism has caused many Indigenous Peoples to become either silent, passive, and accommodating or resentful, mistrusting, angry, and defiant toward the colonizer. Since, in many cases, they have limited abilities, resources, or systems, which allow them to effectively resist or strike back at their colonial oppressors, many Indigenous Peoples capitulate to this situation and often engage in destructive behavior toward themselves or one another. In fact, Jean-Paul Sartre (1963, p. 18) says that if the suppressed fury of the colonized fails to find an outlet, "it turns in a vacuum and devastates the oppressed . . . the different tribes fight between themselves since they cannot fight the real enemy—and you can count on the colonial policy to keep up the rivalries."

The above discussion and definitions cannot begin to describe the human suffering, loss, and oppression that are experienced over and over again by Indigenous Peoples under colonial rule. Much of the suffering happens in silence, in secret, away from the eyes, hearts, and minds of the oppressor and can never be known unless our voices are heard and stories are told. For those of you who do not know the pain of losing your lands, children, culture, language, identity, and hope at the hands of invading peoples, it will be difficult to understand what our peoples have gone through to survive American colonialism. In fact, Julian Burger (1990) speaking generally about colonialism says it is such a vicious event for the colonized that it can be regarded as one of the most destructive processes in human history. And as Carmel Tapping (1993) cautions in the opening quote, colonialism does not just simply end.

To help describe the effects that colonialism has had on Indigenous Peoples, I share, in the following section, what happened to people from my tribal community.

MANUFACTURING MISERY AND INSTABILITY: THE LEGACY OF COLONIALISM AMONG THE SAHNISH

> Through the politics of colonization, we were made to believe that we were inferior, stupid, lazy, and worthless. Self-hatred naturally followed. I soon began to hate myself for how I looked, behaved and spoke. The indoctrination is as powerful and pervasive as the catechism of any religion. In school we were taught that we were retarded. I believed I was dumb compared to white students and that I was low class, crude, and dirty.
>
> Howard Adams, *Tortured People: The Politics of Colonization*, 1999

I am Sahnish and Hidatsa First Nations, a child of hereditary chiefs of the Awahu village of the Sahnish, and I am convinced that many of the problems and much of the misery in my reservation community is a direct result of our people's subjugation under American colonialism. I know that my people did not suddenly wake up one day and decide to abuse their children and spouses, kill one another, commit suicide, drink ourselves to death, act like fools, become addicts, go to prison, and lose our language, beliefs and values. Rather, the disintegration of our society, and the struggles we have faced and continue to face, are a result of the oppressive policies and behavior of our colonizer: The United States of America.

I grew up in a small tribal community where many of our members used alcohol and violence to numb the pain and humiliation of colonialism. For years, I didn't know why our people engaged in so much destructive behavior and had so many tragic problems. Not knowing that American colonialism was at the root of our misery and instability, I often harbored a deep, penetrating, and persistent shame about being an Indigenous person and, in silence, blamed our dire circumstances on ourselves: we weren't good enough, smart enough, rich enough, or white enough. As Howard Adams states above, my colonizers had led me to believe that we were inferior, stupid, lazy, and worthless people who were solely responsible for causing our own pain and confusion. Although, there were (and remain) many strengths in our community, our repeated exposures to trauma, shame, and domination often seemed to cancel out the good.

From my earliest years, I still cannot forget the cultural, spiritual, and physical carnage spawned by the use of alcohol and violence in our small community. Shootings, stabbings, drownings, car accidents, hangings, beatings, and freezing to death were the more common ways that people died under the influence. For those who did not suddenly perish in these ways, alcohol poisoning, mostly in the form of cirrhosis, waited impatiently for them. The latter fatalities were, perhaps, the most debilitating for our community because we would experience, on a daily and nightly basis, the slow and drawn out death of our relatives. I remember a period of time when I became so accustomed and desensitized to the pervasive death of people from my community that, long after I had left the reservation, one of the first things I would ask my mother whenever I called home was "who died?" It would be years later when I finally realized that my "don't feel" response was one way that I, and many people from my community, coped with all the loss we experienced.

Death was not the only form of misery that we endured due to substance abuse. I recall that we also experienced high rates of family breakups, accidents, injuries, arrests, jail terms, fires, sexual abuse, child abuse and neglect, poor health, child apprehension by white social workers, unemployment, and welfare dependency (Maracle 1993). On the rez (reservation), keeping track of family members who were actively using substances was an ongoing struggle for many families. When those members of a family who had been drinking didn't come home when they were expected, other family members would often go looking for them. Sometimes they would find their relatives passed out, quivering in their urine-soaked nightmares, exuding the heavy smell of death in a house where people regularly "partied." At other times, they would see their family member's wasted, intoxicated frame walking slowly down the road attempting to hitch a ride to the nearest rez bar to get a drink to quiet the demons and tremors that had made a home in his or her soul. Still other times, they would embarrassingly encounter their relatives on the streets of some off-rez white border town begging white people for change for their next drink.

There were many times when the trauma of violence and substance abuse was personalized and embedded deep within the psychological structure of our people. I recall when it happened to me. When I was a little boy, one of my earliest and most vivid memories was not of getting a beautiful pony for my birthday, or my mother reading me my favorite bedtime story. It was about being picked up and held by an intoxicated uncle whose face was beaten badly and bloodied by his drinking "buddies," and whose pores, clothes, and breath radiated with the sickening smell of many days of drinking cheap wine. It was late one night when he came pounding and crying at the door of my parents' house. When my mother opened the door and saw him, she cried out, and her face and body fell into a brief, but profound, state of shock. My father, having much more experience with such things, reacted with silence and an odd smile. I remember all the blood, and that the grotesque, lumpy shape of his face reminded me of a monster. Yet, this monster was sobbing like a child who had lost his mother, so many of the sounds he made were soft and pitiful. I was terrified by how he looked and the noises he made. When I cried out in fear to my mother, my uncle stopped weeping and looked and smiled at me through all the blood. He walked over, picked me up, and gently hugged me and patted my back to comfort me. However, I frantically screamed and cried as I made contact with the blood on his face and shirt. Even though I shrieked and pushed to get away from him, he didn't let me go until one of the drunken ladies he was with scolded him and took me and set me back on the couch where I had been sleeping. As I trembled with uncontrollable shock and tried to suck back my deep sobs of fear and confusion, my mother made my uncle and the other late night visitors sit down at our kitchen table. As she prepared a meal for them, she quietly reminded them they shouldn't be drinking. This uncle died about ten years later from having his head run over by the rear wheel of a white man's car he had passed out under. Some witnesses said the white man knew he was there and that it was a deliberate act, yet he was never even questioned about what happened.

Although these kinds of events occurred over and over again in our community, our people were not always this way. I recall many times when my mother and aunties have emphatically stated that alcoholism, welfare, unemployment, and family violence were almost non-existent in our villages when they were growing up. I remember them saying, "You could count the number of families on one hand who had these kinds of problems." The time they spoke of was before the 1950s when the federal government forced us out of our villages, off of our aboriginal homelands which were located alongside the "Mysterious River" (what whites call the Missouri River). It seems that even in the face of the oppressive and destructive colonialism that had preceded my mother's childhood experience, our people had found ways to work closely together and care for one another in order to counter the damaging effects of their colonial experience. My mother says that even as our people were forced to send their children to boarding schools and assimilate into white religions, many of our people continued, usually in secret, to perform our most sacred ceremonies to renew our lives, commune with our Creator, and help our children through various rites of passage to become responsible members of our society.

Before the United States of America drove us out of our home, caring for our children was a responsibility shared by the entire village. Among the Sahnish, "protecting, nurturing, and teaching children were shared between parents and clan membership" (Yellow Bird 1999b, p. 231). Our elders say that to be lazy, intoxicated, or abusive was taboo and strongly discouraged. Our very survival depended upon our people being industrious, generous, kind, compassionate, courageous, intelligent, and lucid. However, after the illegal seizure and flooding of our lands and destruction of our villages, our existence changed for the worse. As our people's way of life was increasingly condemned and controlled by Christian missionaries and the federal and state government, we were forced to begin abandoning more and more of our cultural beliefs and values.

Under colonial rule, our people were confined to reservations and, in many ways, were no longer able to provide or produce their own food. Thus, they became dependent upon the food rations, often of inferior quality, handed out by the colonizers. Having this advantage, white missionaries and bureaucrats routinely threatened our Chiefs that the village would lose its rations if they asserted leadership that was in conflict with the rules and goals of white society. Our warriors, who once protected our villages against colonial invasion, were co-opted and conscripted to fight for the colonizer against old enemies, which further heightened animosities and derailed any hopes for peace. Our spiritual leaders, who many times represented our first and last defense against evil, oppression, and hopelessness, were jailed for conducting traditional religious and spiritual practices and were only released when they denounced what they were doing and joined a Christian religion.

To drive a stake deep into the heart of our culture, the socialization and teaching of our children was stripped from our peoples and taken over by white ministers, priests, teachers, and bureaucrats who believed we were primitive, dirty, savage, ignorant heathens whose beliefs, values, and knowledge had little or no redeeming qualities (Yellow Bird 1999c). To ensure the success of their "Indian" education programs, colonizers took many of our best and brightest children from our villages and sent them to boarding schools, where they were taught to ignore and/or despise themselves and our culture. When they returned home with their new colonial education, some were able to return to practicing our traditions, but mostly in secret because they feared reprisals or ridicule by white colonizers who now resided among them and continued to control their thinking and actions. Others who responded positively to white imperialism were rewarded with positions of authority in the colonial bureaucracy, which encouraged our people to further abandon our ways in order to assimilate into white society. Students who did not attend off reservation boarding schools were required to attend day schools on the reservation which were no better at respecting the children or our culture.

Today, American colonialism continues to pervade my tribal community and those of most First Nations Peoples. I am not alone in my thinking that this destructive system has taken a great toll upon our peoples. Many Indigenous grassroots activists, intellectuals, elders, and political leaders agree that the colonial polices of the federal and state governments have been directly responsible for a significant amount of our high rates of mortality, morbidity, poverty, substance abuse, family and community disintegration, depression, trauma, unemployment, and cultural disorganization.

The instability, self-destructive tendencies, infighting, and hopelessness of many people within our tribal communities continues at unprecedented levels, and I am disturbed by these realities. I am haunted by the historical and ongoing pain, destruction, and death of our peoples. Many times I can still see the grotesque face of my dead uncle smiling at me through all the blood. And there are times when I can still hear his cries and smell the cheap wine he drank and the dirty clothes he wore. However, I no longer cry out and try to push myself away from him as I did when I was a child. Instead, I gently hug him and silently promise him that I will not forget him or any of our relatives who have died under American colonial rule. I promise him that I will tell the truth of what has happened to us as I write these stories.

Recently, I called my mother, and as always asked her "who died." This time she didn't answer me as she usually does. Instead, I could feel her heart ache, her hand squeeze the phone more desperately, and her lips tighten as she said "Oh Michael, don't ask me who died. There are just too many of us dying these days."

WHAT SOCIAL WORKERS CAN DO

On a structural level there are several things that social workers can do to challenge the ongoing effects of American colonialism upon First Nations Peoples.

To begin with, it is critical to acknowledge the existence of this oppressive structure and its destructive effects. Colonialism is a system of oppression and racism which produces a humiliating and alienating experience for the colonized. It is antithetical to the professional values of social work practice and must be courageously and intelligently challenged on micro and macro levels.

Second, social workers must undertake formal, focused studies of colonialism, paying special attention to how it subjugates the social, political, and economic lives of First Nations Peoples in the United States. To help broaden an understanding of this unjust system, social workers should examine American colonialism as a global phenomenon and the effects it has on other Indigenous peoples throughout the world. In tandem with this, it is also important to become informed of the opinions that other nations have regarding America's foreign policies and presence in the world community. There are numerous alternative websites, magazines, books, news programs, and videos which offer clear and compelling analyses of American colonialism that can be used by social workers in their search to understand this phenomenon.[2]

Third, social work students must demand that the professional curriculum of their schools include significantly more courses which focus on social justice within the context of local, national, and international affairs. They must also demand that they be trained in the tactics necessary for combating social injustices such as colonialism and institutional racism. For instance, activist skills such as mobilizing, organizing, advocacy, and consciousness-raising are critical for creating structural changes in society and must be emphasized in professional education if social workers are to be effective change agents.

Indigenous Peoples in the United States are invisible peoples whose voices, concerns, and experiences receive little serious attention or exposure. Social workers have many micro skills that can help correct this disparity. Using their skills of listening and recording social histories, they can encourage and collect stories from Indigenous Peoples about how colonialism, racism, and other injustices have affected their lives. With permission from the storytellers, these narratives can be shared with the general public, policy makers, service providers, and political representatives to create understanding of the past and present injustices. These stories can also be used to improve and create needed services, outreach, and resources to Indigenous communities. For instance, if language loss is a major concern for a community, social workers can bring this to the attention of others and proactively use their organizing and fund-raising skills to help Indigenous Peoples start language programs (Yellow Bird 2001).

Fourth, social workers can use their networking skills to strategically connect Indigenous Peoples to various organizations that focus on addressing issues of injustice and inequality. Such links will enable First Nations to bring their issues into larger forums of public debate to create a greater knowledge of their circumstances and viewpoints. In addition, these partnerships will help develop greater support networks for Indigenous Peoples' causes. Finally, since Indigenous communities have limited abilities, resources, and systems to effectively deal with the oppressive aspects of American colonialism, social workers can be helpful in at least three ways. First, they can work to make sure that the

United States lives up to the past and present agreements it made with First Nations Peoples. This nation has a legal and moral obligation to provide for the well-being of Indigenous Peoples because of the past treaties it made with these groups. In most of the treaties, native people gave up land in exchange for promises that the United States "would protect the safety and well-being of tribal members. The Supreme Court has held that such promises create a trust relationship" (Pevar 1992, p. 26). However, the United States has rarely lived up to its agreements, and the well-being of most tribes hangs in the balance; most desperately need financial resources for health and human services, education, employment, and other important services. Because of agreements struck in past treaties, social workers are in a strong moral and legal position to demand that the U.S. government live up to its promises with Indigenous Peoples.

Second, social workers can work to ensure that the United States corrects its unjust, oppressive policies and behavior toward First Nations. Since Indigenous Peoples are diverse groups with different experiences and resources, the policies of the United States affect them in different ways. To determine which policies are damaging to these groups and how they might be changed or disposed of, social workers must meet with tribal governments, organizations, scholars, and grassroots people. Finally, the sovereignty of tribal peoples and their governments must be acknowledged and morally and legally supported by the U.S. government. Indigenous Peoples must have the freedom to determine their own futures, and they must have the opportunity to remove themselves from the control and domination of this nation if they so desire. They must be treated with respect and regarded as legitimate governments with all the powers necessary for nationhood.

American colonialism has, and continues to have, numerous damaging effects and is responsible for many of the past and present problems in Indigenous communities. While there are many ways that social workers can assist Indigenous Peoples, perhaps the most effective is to courageously and intelligently confront the continuing effects of American colonialism. Perhaps such efforts will not only help First Nations, but also assist the United States to overcome its two greatest phobias: *dikephobia* (the fear of justice) and *hypegiaphobia* (the fear of responsibility).

REFERENCES

Adams, H. (1999). *Tortured People: The Politics of Colonization.* Penticton, BC: Theytus Press LTD.

Burger, J. (1990). *The Gaia Atlas of First Peoples.* New York, NY: Anchor Books.

Crawford, J. (1994). Endangered Native American Languages: What Is to Be Done, and Why? Available: www.nceb.gwu.edu/miscpub/crawford [1999, August].

Maracle, B. (1993). *Crazywater: Native Voices on Addiction and Recovery.* Toronto, ON: Penguin Books Canada.

Pevar, S. (1992). *The Rights of Indians and Tribes: The Basic ACLU Guide to Indian and Tribal Rights.* Second Edition. Carbondale and Edwardsville, Ill.: Southern Illinois University Press.

Sartre, J. P. (1963). Preface. *The Wretched of the Earth*, Frantz Fanon. New York, NY: Grove Press, Inc.

Tapping, C. (1993). Colonialism—Then and Now. In Carmel Tapping (ed.), *Other Wisdoms, Other Worlds: Colonisation and Family Therapy.* Dulwich Centre Newsletter, 1.

Yellow Bird, M. (1999a). Indian, American Indian, and Native Americans: Counterfeit Identities. Winds of Change: A Magazine for American Indian Education and Opportunity (14), 1.

Yellow Bird, M. (1999b). Indigenous Peoples Parenting. In Charles A. Smith (ed.), *Encyclopedia of Parenting* (pp. 231–233). Greenwood Press Publishers.

Yellow Bird, M., and Chenault, V. (1999c). The Role of Social Work in Advancing the Practice of Indigenous Education: Obstacles and Promises of Empowerment-Oriented Social Work Practice. In Karen Gayton Swisher and John Tippeconnic III (eds.), *Next Steps: Research and Practice to Advance Indian Education* (pp. 201–236). Charleston, WV: ERIC Clearinghouse on Rural Education and Small Schools.

Yellow Bird, M. (2001). Critical Values and First Nations Peoples (pp. 61–74). In Rowena Fong and Sharlene Furuto (eds.), *Culturally Competent Social Work Practice: Practice Skills, Interventions, and Evaluation.* Longman Press.

NOTES

[1]In this paper, the terms First Nations and Indigenous Peoples are used rather than Indians, American Indians, and Native Americans. These latter terms are used only when directly quoting another source. The substitution of labels is necessary because the labels Indians, American Indians, and Native Americans are "counterfeit identities" resulting from the hegemony of European-American colonialism and linguistic imperialism (Yellow Bird 1999a, p. 86). Indigenous Peoples are "*not* Indians or American Indians because they are not from India. They are *not* Native Americans because Indigenous Peoples did not refer to these lands as America until Europeans arrived and imposed this name" (Yellow Bird 2001, p. 61). The change in terminology is a matter of social justice because Indigenous Peoples have struggled and continue to struggle against the oppressive paradigms of American linguistic colonialism that ignores individual tribal identities and falsely names Indigenous Peoples to serve the needs and history of the colonizer. Counterfeit labels are dangerous because "they are historically entangled in American racist discourses that claim Europeans discovered a new world that needed to be settled, claimed, and civilized. This myth-making has promoted the notion that the original inhabitants were unable to settle, claim, and civilize these lands because they were nomadic, unsettled, savage peoples" (Yellow Bird 1999a, p. 86).

[2]Some alternative sources for gaining a perspective on American colonialism include the following:

Websites: Center for World Indigenous Studies, Fourth World Documentation Project (www.cwis.org), Third World Traveler, Progressive Media Links, Speaking Truth to Power (www.thirdworldtraveler.com/General/Prog_Media_Links.html)

Radio News Programs: AIROS/Native America Calling (www.nativetelecom.org/); Native America Public Telecommunication (www.nativecalling.org); Democracy Now (www.democracynow.org)

Magazines: Z Magazine, Dissent Magazine, The Progressive, Cultural Survival Quarterly

Books: *The Gaia Atlas of First Peoples: A Future for the Indigenous World,* by Julian Burger with campaigning groups and native peoples worldwide, Anchor Books: New

York, 1990; *The State of Native America: Genocide, Colonization, and Resistance,* edited by M. Annette Jaimes, South End Press: Boston, 1992; *Indians are Us? Culture and Genocide in Native North America,* by Ward Churchill, Monroe, ME: Common Courage Press, 1994.

Newspapers: *Indian Country Today, News From Indian Country: The Independent Native Journal*

Videos: *"Teaching Indians to be White"* (1993), Available from: Films for Humanities and Sciences, P.O. Box 2053, Princeton, NJ, 08543 (800) 257-57-26, Cataloging: 306.08'97, Indians of North America—Government relations, Print Entry #: 4:1221; *"Healing the Hurts"* (1989), Distributed by Phil Lucas Productions, P.O. Box 1274, Issaquah, WA, 98027 (206) 979-9819

The author gives special thanks to Magdalene Yellow Bird and Jana Haimsohn for comments, insights, and feedback.

Reading

The End of the Muddy Garden

SHEIDA BATES

Her name, Firuzeh, is old and Persian and strong. I knew it meant Turquoise in Farsi and while we discussed her death I wondered whether it did not have the same root as "Piruz," a winner, a conqueror, and I found the analogy ironic. I tried to read symbolism in it but could not so I kept my dwindling knowledge of Farsi to myself.

Nordstrom was having a sale the day we talked about Firuzeh's death. It was a hot Saturday in Calabasas, and at three in the afternoon, my father called to say there was a problem with a client's payroll and he would be working for another two hours. He owns an accounting firm in Glendale.

"Should we wait, then?" My mother asked.

Our vacationing relatives, my uncle and his wife, Nushin, answered in the affirmative but I thought the delay unnecessary. The plan was to drop off my uncle at my father's firm and go shopping at the Galleria. It would make more sense if my uncle took my mother's car and we went shopping in mine but of course that was not what we did.

I put the kettle on and warmed up the leftover pecan pie. I brought it to the table, along with a bowl of oranges. I like my parents' dining room. Its large windows make the room airy, and I also like the intimacy of the dining table.

My mother and Nushin joined us after they made their selection from the Persian CDs. In a minute, Parisa's clear voice filled the room. She is a traditional singer, talented, classically trained, with a voice that ranges far. She is well-loved among the Iranian community, and I cannot stand her.

A sitar accompanied her rendition of a Persian poem. Nushin, endowed with a beautiful voice herself, sang along about the fleeting quality of life, and I went to the kitchen to check on the progress of the tea.

Coming back, I heard the last half of my uncle's comment about someone named Goli.

"What's that?" I asked.

"We're talking ancient history," he said, "Seven or eight years ago."

"Yes?" I said.

"When Firuzeh died, Goli became the guardian."

"Who's Firuzeh? I know the name."

"Don't let your father hear you say that," my mother said, "He doted on Firuzeh."

In exile, the old generation clings to the past, and the westernization of their children does not bother them nearly as much as their children forgetting the past.

"She's a relative," my uncle said, "Her mother was cousin to our un . . . ."

I could never get those relations straight, not having the advantage of growing up among extended relatives. I grew up in Tehran. And although we went to Mazandaran every summer, I spent my time with my Aunt Mina in Sari. But I remembered having seen Firuzeh at some point.

"She used to take care of us," he continued, "when your father and I were little."

And I remembered a moment when a dark, petite woman kissed my father's face with the kind of tenderness that people of the same blood feel.

"I do remember Firuzeh," I said.

The scene was blurry with damp and rain, consisting of leafless trees, a muddy yard, and a two-bedroom house filled with children. The youngest was barely four. Firuzeh's husband must have died shortly before that because, along with the kiss, I had an impression of my mother feeling sorry for the fatherless child.

"Didn't her husband die quite a few years ago?" I continued.

Affirmations came from all three at the table.

"So she died too?"

"Yes," my mother said, "We told you."

"It was eight years ago," my uncle said, "You forgot."

"No. No one told me. I would remember a death."

"We told you," my mother said, "You don't remember. You were busy getting ready for Cabaret Tehran or some rock concert."

My mother remembers parties and rock concerts, but she cannot say that I might have been working or studying. I have an MBA from Cal State Northridge and work for Pacific Bell and my mother is proud of me. But she believes that my friends, Persian and otherwise, keep me from what she calls "being serious about life."

"Anyway," my uncle said, "Goli, Firuzeh's oldest daughter, took guardianship. You remember her: nice looking girl, tight curly hair—"

Nushin gave clicks of the tongue.

"Poor girl," my mother said, "Stuck with eight children."

"And not married," Nushin said, taking up my mother's thought.

"Well," my mother said, a passionate edge in her voice directed at me, "She had a lot of suitors."

"She should have married when she was young," Nushin said meaningfully.

I was used to this pressure, being thirty and unmarried.

"Maybe she liked her life the way it was," I said, winking at my uncle.

"A woman," my mother said, "should marry when she is young and beautiful."

"Those are assets," Nushin said, "that we lose as we age."

"Then college has been a waste," I said, "So has my career, my independence."

"Your independence is fine," my mother said. "I want to have grandchildren before it's too late."

"We want to see you settled," Nushin said, "We want your happiness."

"And I want my tea," my uncle said, releasing me.

I went into the kitchen. The water had come to a boil. I poured it over the tea-leaves and inhaled the scent of the cardamom seeds.

The last time we went to Mazandaran I was fifteen. My memories of the North, as Mazandaran is often called, are sun-drenched and green, imbued with the salty scent of the Caspian and the flowers in my Aunt Mina's garden. We stayed with her every summer and I watered her flowers every other day at sunset when the brick walls of her yard would glow violently orange and I would float on the warm scent of petunias. Some days, Haji's wife, my aunt's nosy neighbor, would talk to me from her second story window.

The water turned amber and I got the tea glasses ready. My mind went back to that scene in Firuzeh's house and I remembered they lived in the outskirts of Shahi (now called Ghaem-Shahr). Shahi was fifteen miles from Sari. It was an industrial town which even the sunny days of Mazandaran could not rescue from being ugly.

Gradually Goli took shape in that scene. Yes, Goli—attractive in a strong, big-boned way in her early twenties—wearing a red sleeveless shirt. It was not until then that I remembered Bijan, her older brother, Firuzeh's eldest son.

I fell in love with Bijan twice—that is, every time I saw him.

The first time was during the first months of the revolution and I was fourteen. Schools were closed and we went to Mazandaran to wait for the end of the strikes. My parents insisted that I continue studying on my own. One day Bijan came to visit and my father suggested that he help me with calculus.

During the two hours of our math session I couldn't take my eyes off him. Unfortunately for me, he was twenty-six years old. A moment came when our eyes locked for a few seconds more than was appropriate, and to my dismay he turned a patronizing smile on me, the way an older man smiles at a child, but I fell in love with him anyway.

Back in Tehran, my mind wandered to other boys. Sina, for instance, the neighbor's boy, who gave me my first kiss.

A year later, we went to Mazandaran for the last time. I saw Bijan a few times—each time briefly and at large, family gatherings in Sari. I wondered now if this was the reason I hadn't associated him with their depressing house in Shahi, and thus, with Firuzeh. The last time I saw him he introduced us to his fiancé, a beautiful girl from Azerbaijan. She was so sweet to me I couldn't stay jealous long.

"I remember Bijan and Goli," I said, bringing the tea.

The three of them nodded in approval and affirmation.

"That's right," my mother said, "You should remember Bijan."

"It's funny, though. I didn't associate him with Firuzeh."

"Well, you've seen him more often."

"I must have been fourteen," I said, recalling the math tutorial.

"Fourteen?" my mother said, "He came to see you all the time when you were a baby. He loved playing with you. He had started college and you were four or five . . . ."

"Seven," I said with conviction, "I must have been seven because he was twelve years older than me."

I was thinking of puberty when my mother brought up my childhood—a time I could not possibly remember, but doubtless, the only time when I obeyed her unquestioningly.

"Whatever it was," she said, ignoring my excitement. "He came to our house once a week for dinner. Well, he was a bachelor," she said, more as a matter of reminiscence than to impart information. "He didn't know anyone in Tehran, and he *was* a relative. We were living in a one bedroom, but we had him come over so he wouldn't be lonely."

I smiled at the thought. I could imagine my mother fussing over the young man, preparing a meal—a habit that was a source of pride and honor to her. And I could see my father too, dispensing advice even at his young age. And yes, Bijan, I could see him impressed and grateful, perhaps having his own life with his friends in the big city but being pulled to my parents' hospitality.

Then my mother turned towards me. "You used to say you'd marry him when you grew up. And he'd tease you every time, saying he was holding you to it."

I laughed.

"I must've had good taste," I said, "Bijan was handsome."

"Yes," my uncle said, "He was striking."

"And he married that girl," I said, "I met her once."

Nushin, playing with the rim of her tea glass, raised her eyebrows. A "Hum" was all that came from my mother. I looked at my uncle, who looked up and acknowledged the strangeness of their reaction.

"Did something happen?" I asked, "Did they divorce?"

"Oh, no," everyone said simultaneously.

"What, then?"

"Some things we've heard," Nushin said.

"Rumors," my mother said, "Unfounded, stupid talk."

I turned to my uncle for an explanation.

"Firuzeh died under suspicious circumstances," he chose his words. "She did not die of old age."

"Foul play?" I asked, laughing. "What? A murder mystery in Iran?"

"No," Nushin said, "Not exactly."

"Firuzeh committed suicide."

I wanted to tell my mother, "I would definitely remember a suicide in the family." But my point seemed insignificant.

My uncle reached for an orange, observing and appreciating it before he cut into it. Mazandaranis examine and savor citrus fruit the way wine connoisseurs cherish a glass of good wine.

"How did she?" I asked.

"She set herself on fire."

"How theatrical."

"She was unfortunate," my mother said, her tone suggesting that I should be more compassionate of people's misfortunes.

"Such a hard life," Nushin added.

"Yes, well," I said, "And I suppose setting herself on fire made it easier."

"Don't mock the dead," my mother said.

"I'm thinking about the living. Her children. They're the ones who got hurt. How can they handle the fact that their mother committed suicide?"

"You didn't know her well," my mother said, "You shouldn't judge."

I felt my head overloading on the whining of Parisa.

"Can I turn the music off?" I asked.

A loud, firm "no" came from Nushin and my mother.

I picked up an orange and started peeling it.

"So," I said, maneuvering my knife under the orange skin, "What sent Firuzeh over the edge?"

Nushin shook her head.

"Money problems," my uncle said, "Bijan was not doing well. So he asked for his portion of the inheritance. Firuzeh didn't want to give it to him. She said her children were small, and she had no other means of support."

I looked up from my peeled orange when my uncle became silent.

"That's it? That's why she killed herself? Because Bijan wanted what was rightfully his?"

"Bijan had a job," Nushin said, "He was supporting himself and his wife."

"He might have needed it for an investment," I said, and I turned to my uncle who was nodding in agreement.

"You are right. He was thinking of opening his own business. There is no crime in that. But think of Firuzeh's position. Who else was going to secure the future for her children?"

"Bijan," I said firmly, "Her oldest son. If she gave him the chance, that is."

"And what if he bungled it?" my mother said and pushed her glass towards me.

I got to my feet and asked everyone if they wanted more tea, and I went into the kitchen with all four glasses.

I felt sorry for the younger generation who had to survive under desperate economic conditions in Iran. And I was sorry Firuzeh was dead, but I could not empathize with her. There was no sense in her suicide, no nobility, and therefore, no value.

I thought of the song "Kevin Carter" on my new Manic Street Preachers CD. Kevin Carter took a picture of a vulture stalking a starving African child, won the Pulitzer Prize for it and shot himself four months later. At least, there was a moral dilemma, even if I could not excuse the act. I tried humming the song but Parisa was loud and I could not concentrate.

And I thought of a suicide bombing shortly after the revolution. One day, a young man, whose brother (a communist, I believe) had been executed by the government, taped a bomb to himself and walked to the center of a religious gathering. He found the Muslim cleric who had ordered the execution of his brother, pretended to be an admirer, and held the cleric in his arms. We watched the whole thing on television, as it was being broadcast live.

I inhaled the lovely scent of cardamom tea, and I thought of the desperate anger of a young man whose face I never saw, who I only knew as the back of a white shirt in a crowd of thousands, and that fierce, immovable embrace.

"If anything," Nushin said when I walked in, "the wife should have had more sense, and talked Bijan out of it, instead of instigating the whole thing."

"Don't tell me," I said mockingly, "back home, people blame Bijan's wife."

"There *was* a police inquiry," Nushin blurted out.

"You're joking. Inquiry into what?"

"Wait," my uncle said to Nushin. Turning to me he continued, "The police inquiry was routine. See, they found her body at the end of the garden."

"Whose garden?" I asked.

"Theirs. It was behind the house. Don't you remember?"

I wondered if the leafless trees in my memory were in the garden.

"She had wrapped a blanket around herself," he continued, "and soaked the blanket with gasoline. Around two or three in the morning."

And I saw Firuzeh, dragging a blanket in the dark hours of the morning to the end of a wet, rainy, leafless garden. Perhaps she sat on the roots of a tree at the wooden border—the entwined branches that are used as fences in the villages of Mazandaran—and contemplated her life and death. There, she took the gasoline, poured it on herself and on the blanket. When she lit the match she was no longer conscious that the ground was wet, the air, damp and cool, that mud had accumulated on her galoshes.

"The problem is," my uncle continued, "no one saw it happen."

"Which means . . . ." Nushin said.

"Which means," I said, "that someone else could have wrapped the blanket on her and set her on fire—namely, Bijan and his wife."

My uncle leaned back and turned up the palms of his hands to indicate confirmation.

"For God's sake," I said.

"People do strange things where money is concerned," Nushin said.

"It had to be taken into consideration," my mother said.

"C'mmon," I said, "We all know Bijan. He is no more capable of killing any-one, let alone his own mother, than I am."

"Of course he isn't," my mother said.

"No, of course not," Nushin agreed.

"It's the way things are over there," my mother said, "Rumors and gossip, you know. So the police had to make sure. That's all we're saying."

"And as for his wife," I said, encouraged and relieved by Bijan's exoneration, "if she wanted to do away with the mother-in-law, I'm sure she'd find a more convenient way. Why not stick a knife in her? Why not feed her rat poison?"

My uncle played with the shredded orange peels on his plate. His lower lip was twisted, as if he were contemplating the truth of the matter.

"No," I continued, "Firuzeh had to make a dramatic exit."

"Well," my mother said, "the poor woman had more problems than most people. Her mother died when she was a baby. A stepmother raised her."

"And the stepmother was vicious," my uncle said, "I remember her."

"Which is not to say," my mother continued, "that Firuzeh would have been better off with her own mother."

Nushin nodded and I waited.

"Firuzeh's mother was crazy," my mother said, "It was fortunate that she died young. She was released from a life of misery."

"Mental illness?"

"They used to call her Nut-case Naaheed," my uncle said.

"What about Firuzeh? She could have inherited the genes. Some mild form of—I don't know—paranoia or something?"

"It's possible," my uncle murmured.

Parisa's CD had come to an end a while back, and the tea glasses were empty.

"Would anyone like more tea?"

My mother motioned with her head towards the living room and I gathered the glasses. I put on another CD by Parisa and I took the glasses away.

The three had started another conversation, something mundane, some-thing lighter than suicide by fire. We were all older now, sixteen years older than the last time we were in Iran. Bijan was forty-two, Goli, who ended up tak-ing care of her siblings, a couple of years younger than that. And the fatherless boy was a grown man.

I tried to recall Bijan's face, but the details had faded from my memory. Only a strong impression of dark and masculine beauty remained. It was a shame because he was beautiful, but there, I could not get to the details. A shame also because I wanted to remember him clearly.

I remembered the face of a vendor in Tehran who sold ice cream and deli sandwiches out of a tent. He had a distinguished forehead, aquiline nose and soft sleepy eyes. I could also remember his partner who gave me free straw-berry ice cream once. He wore round spectacles and he looked like the British actor, Colin Firth. All useless details, but they were etched in my brain.

The garage had the quiet air of a wine cellar, where noise is subdued and transient. I took the car out, and turned the air-conditioner on, leaving the windows down so I could breathe. So that was the end of Firuzeh, I thought, as I searched through my CDs for something that would get Parisa's whining out of my head. One afternoon, on the other side of the ocean, over tea and pie, Firuzeh became the subject of our conversation. She lingered among the talk of death and paranoia and the thought of sun and blown-up white shirts, spectacles and mud, oranges and lust.

I felt exhausted with remembering. The memories were there, but so was the pain and all that was lost.

And I found the perfect song by Manic Street Preachers. It was the title song, "Everything Must Go," and my cousin, who sent me the CD from England, had explained the story behind it in an e-mail. I had dismissed it at first, not being able to relate to the content.

Richey Edwards, my cousin's favorite band member, disappeared a while back and the search had turned up nothing. The song was a farewell to him, a declaration that the band had decided to move on. I lit a cigarette while the first foreboding, drum-dominated notes played.

Freed from the memory
Escape from our history, history

I enjoyed the young, raspy voice of the lead singer. I found it unpretentious and honest. And I liked the force of his passion, his interpretation of the lyrics. While I could hear the release in "escape from our history," I was taken aback by the frustrated anger—which came from regret—in the final "history." This was the process of letting go, I thought. And then came the chorus.

Case Study   # Nalani Ethel C.: Social Work with a Hawaiian Woman and Her Family

NOREEN MOKUAU

BARBARA PUA IULI

INTRODUCTION: THE PROFESSIONAL SOCIAL WORK CONTEXT

Malia, a social worker for the Horizons project, provided services to families with children under 3 years old. The majority of the families she worked with were considered to be "environmentally at risk" and resided in various low-income housing projects. Many of Malia's clients were of Pacific Islander descent, particularly of Hawaiian and Samoan ancestries. Malia received referrals from pediatricians, family physicians, public health nurses, and other health care professionals.

While the "target child" was often the foremost reason for the referrals, the entire family was involved in intervention and were frequently assisted through provision of resources, networking, advocacy, counseling, and other services. The main objective of the Horizons project is to provide care coordination services to families with very young children who are at risk. As a care coordinator, Malia's primary responsibilities were to initiate contact with the families, help them identify their needs, and link them with appropriate resources for support. In addition, she monitored and evaluated the effects of these services on her clients.

In the early stages of intervention, Malia often worked with the mothers of the children referred to her. Since mothers were frequently the primary caretakers, once their situations were stabilized they were in a better position to care for their children. Work with the children was carried out after assisting the caretaker and the family.

ENGAGEMENT: DEVELOPMENT OF THE RELATIONSHIP

A public health nurse at the state's Department of Health referred Nalani Ethel C. to Malia at the Horizons project. Nalani fit the criteria for referral because of her high-risk status as a parent with very young children. As a condition of the referral, Nalani insisted that she work only with a Hawaiian social worker.

Thus, Malia, a Hawaiian social worker who specialized in practice with Pacific Islander families, seemed a compatible choice.

Malia noted in the referral that Nalani (24 years old) was married to Pohaku (24 years old), and they had a daughter, Kahea (4 years), and twin sons, William and David (16 months old). At the time of the referral, Nalani was six months pregnant. Her high-risk status was reflected in several ways, including:

- previous experiences of homelessness;
- permanent removal of her oldest child based on findings of neglect by the court and by the state's Department of Human Services;
- low socioeconomic status, with a gross family income of $10,000; and
- low educational attainment.

Nalani and her family resided in a high-rise, low-income apartment complex. Having worked with several Samoan and Hawaiian families from this neighborhood, Malia was very familiar with the surroundings and the people who resided there. However, her earliest home visits to Nalani were awkward. The first home visit was conducted in an open corridor of the building, because Nalani said that her apartment was too untidy for visitors. The second home visit was conducted in a neighbor's apartment because Nalani again expressed embarrassment over the cleanliness of her own home. Nalani's hesitance to invite Malia into her home appeared to indicate both embarrassment about the condition of her home as well as, perhaps, a lack of trust in her new social worker.

Malia wondered about the best ways to establish trust with Nalani. She thought that there must be a way to help Nalani feel more comfortable with her, but she also recognized the need to make an actual home visit to Nalani's home, meet her husband and children, and assess her home situation.

The two earliest "home visits" illustrated the importance of trust in the evolving relationship between Malia and Nalani. The discussions focused on two issues: Nalani's challenge of the legitimacy of the "Hawaiian-ness" of Malia, and Nalani's interest in her Hawaiian heritage. In the first home visit, Nalani expressed surprise at meeting a Hawaiian social worker with blond hair, fair skin, and blue eyes. Her expectation was that Malia would have dark hair, tanned skin, and brown eyes. Nalani's challenges to Malia's Hawaiian-ness appeared in a series of questions pertaining to Hawaiian culture:

Nalani: Where is your family from?

Malia: I was born and raised in Wai'anae (O'ahu), moved to the mainland for several years, returned to the islands, and now live in Wahiawa (O'ahu) with my husband and two children.

Nalani: How old are your children?

Malia: Kimo is 7 years old and Haunani is 5.

Nalani: So you have some young ones too! I guess you know about children.

Malia: I have been learning as I go along. Even my social work training hasn't prepared me much for some of the things I have to deal with as a parent.

Malia's ability to respond to such questions and to disclose in a culturally appropriate way assisted her in gaining Nalani's beginning trust. Malia recalled other events that assisted her in the engagement process, including the fact that she knew several people in Nalani's building and greeted them in culturally acceptable ways by physically embracing them and sharing information about each other's families. In the earliest meetings with Nalani, Malia used Hawaiian words interspersed throughout the interview, and her ability to speak the Hawaiian language was a definite asset. Finally, Malia shared other personal information about herself, including information about her family and background. This self-disclosure was then used to focus on identifying places, persons, and experiences she and Nalani might have in common. Establishing connections or "binders" with people is vital to trust-building among Hawaiians and reflects their cultural norms of openness and sharing.

DATA COLLECTION AND ASSESSMENT: USING CULTURAL INFORMATION

As Malia was able to establish a beginning relationship with Nalani, she collected additional information about her situation The assessment phase focused on three areas, with the greatest attention being paid, in the beginning, to Nalani's self-development and identification as a Hawaiian. This initial focus was identified by Nalani as her most difficult problem, although Malia realized that Nalani's parenting skills and her relationship with her husband were also problematic. Typically, social workers from the Horizons project conduct assessments of the entire family. However, Malia recognized that Nalani's personal needs seemed to overwhelm her, so the nature of assessment tended to focus on her.

Self-Development

Nalani was very proud to be Hawaiian but was not quite sure what it meant to be Hawaiian. She was aware that genealogy played an important part in any Hawaiian family's self-concept because it is critical to identification and a sense of rootedness. However, there were gaps in Nalani' s knowledge about her own family tree, and she could not fully remember the names of several ancestors. As Malia helped to explore Nalani's genealogy, it became evident that they shared some genealogical connections and were related. This connection served as another "binder" for the two women and further enhanced their relationship.

The exploration of genealogy became important for another reason. Proof of genealogy was a means to secure federally sanctioned homestead land. To qualify for Hawaiian homestead lands, it was necessary to provide evidence of "Hawaiian blood quantum." This meant that an individual's genealogy must include at least one native born Hawaiian parent. The idea of applying for homestead land represented a beacon of light for Nalani, who recalled the anguish of being homeless and who currently resided in a less than ideal living situation.

Another critical issue for Nalani was not being able to understand and speak Hawaiian, the native language of her heritage. Malia recognized that in translating Hawaiian to English much of the meaning can be changed and sometimes distorted. Thus, for many Hawaiians who are seeking to establish their Hawaiian identities, learning the language becomes extremely important. While many young Hawaiians are not fluent in their native tongue, more were making the effort to learn the language in the 1990s. Nalani appeared "hungry" for lessons on language, as Malia would often use Hawaiian words interspersed in their discussions and Nalani seemed interested in learning these words.

Nalani's strong desire to understand her Hawaiian heritage provided Malia with opportunities to work on other issues. Malia noted, for example, that Nalani mistakenly believed that child abuse was common among Hawaiians, stemming from cultural origins. It became apparent that focusing on Nalani's identification and development as a Hawaiian woman meant educating her on the accuracies of history, language, values, and behaviors of the Hawaiian culture. This would include "unlearning" other values and behaviors she had mistaken as cultural. For example, Malia observed that Nalani lacked good parenting skills, was often abrupt with her sons, and would make reference to the need for physical discipline.

Child Care and Parenting Skills

Prior to the birth of the twins, the Hawaii Department of Human Services permanently removed the oldest child from Nalani and Pohaku because they could not provide a safe environment. There had been reports of child neglect, and the family had been homeless and living in a tent for a year. Malia felt that Nalani was still dealing with her grief over the loss of her daughter. She stated to Malia that she really wants to learn to be a good mother to the other children, but it was apparent that her parenting skills needed improvement. Malia learned that she was not seeing her obstetrician on a regular basis for prenatal care, even though she was six months pregnant.

Marital Relationship

Nalani did not express any marital difficulties, suggesting that her relationship with Pohaku was fine. However, she indicated that she wished Pohaku could become more involved in parenting the twins. She said that Pohaku was ashamed of being a high school dropout and was afraid that he would fail a written examination for a refuse truck driving position. His present employment as a part-time maintenance person was not satisfying, and he hoped for full-time employment with the refuse department of the city and county.

GOAL PLANNING: WORKING TOGETHER

Based on the problems and issues identified in Malia's work with Nalani, several goals were collaboratively established. Malia was careful to make sure the goals reflected the pertinent information obtained during the data collection and assessment phase and that they were acceptable to Nalani.

Self-Development

Nalani's struggle for personal development and growth was similar to struggles experienced by many Hawaiians in the 1990s. There was an increased awareness among Hawaiians regarding the historical devastation of their culture and traditions and a concurrent commitment to recapture the strengths of their cultural past. However, while many had an awareness of cultural loss, they were not fully cognizant of their traditional cultural values and norms. As was the case with Nalani, many did not know their cultural history, speak their native language, or practice cultural norms and behaviors. The search for one's Hawaiian-ness can be an intense experience, initiated by learning about Hawaiian values and norms and thereby strengthening an individual's own identity as well as the collective identity. Nalani's goals for self-development were:

- to learn about her genealogy and simultaneously apply for Hawaiian homestead land (a federal provision designating land entitlement for eligible Hawaiians),
- to learn to speak the Hawaiian language,
- to learn anger management skills and to specifically understand the perspective that Hawaiians adopted in disciplining their children, and
- to complete her graduate equivalency diploma (GED).

Child Care and Parenting Skills

The welfare of the children was central to the mission of the Horizons project, and goals related to child care and parenting skills were an important part of the overall intervention with Nalani. Specifically, the goals for Nalani were: (1) to deal with the grief resulting from her daughter's removal from her home, and (2) to develop and follow a prenatal care plan to assure a healthy pregnancy and birth.

Marital Relationship

Goals related to strengthening the marital relationship and supporting Pohaku's role as husband and father were also identified. These joint goals for Nalani and Pohaku included: (1) learning about their joint responsibilities as parents, and (2) securing employment as a truck driver (Pohaku).

INTERVENTION: COORDINATING CARE

As a care coordinator, Malia's primary responsibility was to link Nalani with appropriate community resources that would support her in getting her needs met. Secondary responsibilities included role modeling, counseling, and information sharing.

Malia promoted Nalani's search for her Hawaiian-ness in several ways. She helped connect Nalani to the state agencies where historical and archival information was available. At the same time, she encouraged Nalani to "discover" her family tree. She also continued to provide counseling on the cultural importance of family lineage and shared personal information on the value of knowing her own ancestors. Finally, Malia supported Nalani's application for Hawaiian homestead lands by picking up the forms and assisting her in filling them out. There were areas on the application that could be filled out only after Nalani went to the appropriate state offices and learned more about her ancestors. Nalani was able to negotiate this by herself.

In terms of language familiarity, Malia connected Nalani to an older Hawaiian woman (a Kupuna) who was a fluent native speaker and who lived in the same building complex as Nalani. The first meeting, spontaneous and casual, occurred as Nalani and the Kupuna collected their mail at the building complex mailboxes.

Malia: Aunty Kuuipo, this is the Hawaiian girl I was telling you about who wants to learn Hawaiian from you. This is Nalani Ethel C.

Aunty: Aloha Nalani, pehea'oe? This is my mo'opuna nui (as aunty makes this statement, she simultaneously taps Nalani's stomach). Do you know what I said?

Nalani: No aunty, I don't understand.

Aunty: I said, hello, how are you. I also said that this is my great grandchild— my mo'opuna nui.

Malia: Aunty, Nalani wants to learn how to speak Hawaiian. Would you be able to help her?

Aunty: (to Nalani) I live in the same building as you, come see me anytime.

Two important things occurred in this brief but positive interaction. First, Malia's use of the title "aunty" was deliberate and conveyed a sense of respect for "family." Second, Aunty Kuuipo acknowledged Nalani's unborn child to be her own grandchild even though the two women were biologically unrelated. This acknowledgment was made so that Nalani understood that Aunty Kuuipo would regard her with the same esteem she would a member of her family. This traditional idea suggested an important cultural value of family loyalty, thereby facilitating the relationship between aunty and Nalani.

Malia had prepared both women for meeting each other but took the opportunity of introducing them to each other as the opportunity presented itself. The spontaneous interaction at the mailboxes was a positive one. Another meeting was set up, and an informal schedule was established to assist Nalani in learning the language.

Malia also provided Nalani with several learning resources, including a Hawaiian dictionary, pictures, and information on Hawaiian phrases. Finally, Malia continued to familiarize Nalani with the language by using words and phrases in their meetings together. For example, they would practice simple phrases such as good morning (aloha kakahiaka) and how are you (pehea'oe).

In providing information to Nalani, Malia emphasized the cherished role of children in Hawaiian culture. Malia recognized the need to correct Nalani's misperception that physical discipline was a common practice in traditional Hawaiian culture. Malia also felt it important that Nalani and Pohaku learn alternative ways of caring for their children. For example, during one home visit, Malia was able to provide information on child-rearing in Hawaiian culture. At one point during the visit, the twins were unintentionally disturbing their mother by racing back and forth down the hallway and laughing loudly.

Nalani: If my kids don't listen, I lick 'um (hit them). (She called to the twins and as they approached her, she hit them with her slippers.)

Malia: You know, there is a myth that Hawaiians show love by beating their wives and children. Hawaiians love children. For many Hawaiians, the lei (flower garland) is a symbol of a child's arms wrapped around a parent's or grandparent's neck.

Nalani: I was abused when I was a kid because my father used to beat me all the time. Because of him, they took me away and put me in foster care. (pause) I don't want that to happen to my kids.

Malia: With what happened to you, and to Kahea, you don't want to place yourself in that position where the state may come in and take your twins.

Nalani: Oh yeah, I don't want to lose my two kids. I lost Kahea, I don't want to lose my two kids.

Shortly after this home visit, Malia referred Nalani to a parenting skills class called Malama Na Keiki (Taking Care of the Children), which teaches skills in anger management and positive child-rearing techniques. The timing was good, as Nalani was intent on learning alternative ways to manage the children. This was, in part, motivated by her wanting to keep her family together and avoid removal of the children by Child Protective Services.

The achievement of goals established for child care and the marital relationship continued. Malia counseled Nalani on the loss of her oldest child and reinforced her resolve to "be a good mother" to the other children. Malia also counseled Nalani on the importance of prenatal care as a form of "good mothering," and Nalani obtained adequate prenatal care. Efforts were also made to secure a tutor for both Nalani and Pohaku to assist them in working toward a graduate equivalency diploma.

EVALUATION: A CULTURE-SENSITIVE APPROACH

Throughout the social work process, from engagement to evaluation, Malia tried to be sensitive to the influence of culture on Nalani as well as considering the entire case situation. For example, Malia utilized a cultural style of discussion called "talk story," in which personal themes were shared in an informal and relaxed way. Talk story emphasizes the mutual exchange of information between participants and minimizes the question-answer format sometimes adopted by social workers. Cultural activities, such as genealogy explorations, language lessons, and teaching Hawaiian values and mores related to child-rearing, were the predominant points of intervention for Malia. It is believed that the infusion of cultural sensitivity into work with Nalani contributed to the ongoing positive nature of the relationship and the outcome of this case.

Accomplishment of the identified goals proceeded in stages, indicative of the ongoing nature of the relationship. Achievement of some goals may lead to termination of the relationship or to establishment of other goals and issues. Clients of the Horizons project are voluntary, and Nalani's choice was to maintain contact with Malia. Outcomes include:

- Nalani's ability to understand and speak Hawaiian words and phrases,
- an understanding of Nalani's familial lineage and completion of a Hawaiian homestead lands application,
- weekly participation in a parenting class and learning anger management skills,
- increased acceptance of the loss of her daughter and increased motivation to "be a good mother" to the other children,
- regular visitations to her obstetrician for prenatal care,
- participation by Nalani and Pohaku in counseling sessions with Malia on parenting responsibilities, and
- locating a tutor for Nalani and Pohaku.

Achievement of several outcomes indicates some measure of success, yet issues in life are continuous. Nalani expressed a desire to continue to work with Malia on several issues, old and new. For example, Nalani wanted to learn more about budgeting and financial planning, and Malia planned this as another area for exploration. The work between Malia and Nalani continued.

READINGS

Ishisaka, H. A., & Takagi, C. Y. (1982). Social Work with Asian- and Pacific-Americans. In J. W. Green (Ed.), *Cultural Awareness in the Human Services* (pp. 122–156). Englewood Cliffs, NJ: Prentice-Hall.

Kumabe, K., Nishida, C., & Hepworth, D. (1985). *Bridging Ethnocultural Diversity in Social Work and Health.* Honolulu: University of Hawaii Press.

Omizo, M. M., & Omizo, S. A. (1989). Counseling Hawaiian children. *Elementary School Guidance and Counseling, 23,* 282–288.

Questions for Further Study

1. Carter Revard, in "History, Myth, and Identity among Osages and Other Peoples," from *Family Matters, Tribal Affairs* demonstrates that the history and worldview of the Osage Indians differs vastly from the worldview that predominates in the United States. What can we take from his essay that would help us as social workers in our efforts to assist persons whose backgrounds, values, and interests differ from our own?

2. Consider the reading "Doing Testimony Psychotherapy with Survivors of Ethnic Cleansing," from *When History Becomes a Nightmare*, by Stevan Weine. For those individuals relocating from war-torn countries like Bosnia-Herzegovina, the task of acquiring resources would be affected by the specific circumstances of their relocation and degree of cultural displacement. How would these two variables impact the resources needed? What might be the first thing you would do if, as a social worker, you were assigned the responsibility of helping such a person transition comfortably into U.S. society?

3. "The Continuing Effects of American Colonialism upon First Nations Peoples," by Michael Yellow Bird, uses both academic scholarship and personal experience to illuminate the continuing legacy of colonialism on his reservation in particular and on First Nations peoples in general. Specifically, Yellow Bird views the high rates of alcoholism, violence, and unemployment among his people as rooted in the theft and destruction of his peoples' lands and culture by the U.S. government. Given this, how should social workers alter their practice with First Nations Peoples in these areas? What must be done to build a relationship between non-First Nations social workers and First Nations clients?

4. Sheida Bates, in "The End of the Muddy Garden," offers a view inside Iranian culture. Is there any evidence, in this story, that the stresses of growing up in fear and repression, and eventually living in exile, have made her or her family different from those who have spent their lives calmly and in one place?

5. Consider the case, "Nalani Ethel C: Social Work with a Hawaiian Woman and Her Family," by Noreen Mokuau and Barbara Iuli. How does the social worker use the strong identification of the Hawaiian mother with their common heritage as a resource in bringing about change? When is a common heritage between worker and client likely to be most useful? When is it likely to have little or no bearing?

Invited Commentary

UMA A. SEGAL

FROM CULTURAL SENSITIVITY TO CULTURAL COMPETENCE

The call has long been out for cultural sensitivity. The more recent call is for cultural competence. It is infinitely easier to be culturally sensitive in this multiethnic, multicultural society than it is to be culturally competent. Yet it is virtually impossible to be culturally competent without being culturally sensitive. Where does the social work practitioner begin? How does the practitioner become culturally sensitive? What *is* cultural sensitivity? And to what culture is one supposed to be sensitive? The American society is a mosaic of cultures. The Euro-American one is clearly the dominant, mainstream one, yet, what is it? Is it Anglo-American? French-American? German-American? No longer are all descendants of European immigrants content with being a part of the "melting pot" in this twenty-first century. Many proudly speak of their origins from nations other than the United States, learn the language of their forefathers, and seek to maintain or develop ties with distant relatives. However, Euro-Americans have a choice that people of color do not: they can become "unhyphenated" Americans. The social worker must first be sensitive to the reality that ethnic minorities in the United States are first defined by their color and, hence, regardless of their preferences, are inexorably tied to their non-Euro-American origins. They are bound by their personal history and experiences, but they are also tethered by how they are perceived and categorized by others. Thus, once social workers are sensitive to this reality, they may move toward cultural competence in providing services to ethnic minorities.

For competent social workers, cultural pluralism and the realization that many different values, behaviors, and views of the world can exist side-by-side is not sufficient. It is essential that they ensure that their knowledge and skills are tempered with beliefs in at least the following fundamental values of social work: (1) social justice, (2) the intrinsic worth and dignity of the individual, (3) the uniqueness of the individual, (4) that society must provide opportunities, and (5) that society must help eliminate specific problems. In a nation that is composed of so many ethnic minorities, most of whom have been oppressed in some manner and at some time, a single social worker can never be "competent" in working with *all* groups, and may not even be thoroughly competent with one particular group, as all individuals and their life experiences vary. It is necessary, however, that social workers' sensitivity lie in a realization that minority individuals (and the minority group) must be viewed within a holistic

framework, and interventive competence can develop through the joint endeavors of the worker and the client. A fundamental truth in the quest for sensitivity and competence is often overlooked—*the human condition is universal*. All
human beings have the same basic needs, feelings, hopes, and dreams, and all,
at some level, respond to their environment and to others from this fundamental truth. Bearing in mind the universality of the human condition and adhering
to social work values will move the practitioner rapidly in the direction of cultural competence.

The preceding collection of four articles provides a collage of peoples who
have been displaced,[1] who are refugees,[2] and who are immigrants.[3] Carter Revard and Michael Yellow Bird write of Native Americans (Yellow Bird prefers
the term *Indigenous Peoples*), Stevan Weine's focus is on the Bosnians, and Sheida
Bates concentrates on one Iranian family. A non-Western European-North
American picture emerges that emphasizes the importance of temporal conti-
nuity as history defines the present and unites with it to mold the future. Societal and personal histories are intertwined with present identity and have
implications for future trends. In some societies, the individual and the nuclear
family are of most importance. However, in many other cultures, the individual
is an extension of the family or the community, and in yet others, as discussed
by Revard, the individual is defined within the context of ancient history and
culture. What, then, does it mean to work with minorities in the U.S. who, either
involuntarily or by choice, are distant from their cultures of origin and from that
which is familiar?

While living within one's culture and sharing a history with the majority
society, one takes both culture and history for granted. History and culture
shape and provide the boundaries and context of one's identity, and it is only
when one is removed from the familiarity of these boundaries, and when one's
culture is challenged, that one consciously attempts to adhere to the once familiar or begins to critically examine it. Furthermore, as groups are displaced or
migrate, they find they are required to readjust their perceptions and behaviors.
While immigrants who move by choice may find it easier to make many adjustments because changes were expected and may even have been eagerly anticipated, involuntary displacement or migration (as with Native Americans and
with refugees), brings unwanted and unanticipated changes.

Before involuntarily moved groups are uprooted, they generally experience
intense trauma, violence, and violation of a magnitude that most others cannot
begin to comprehend. Revard suggests that, in addition, they must not only
survive in the face of the aggressors' behavior but also try to process and understand that behavior. Most are neither able to understand it nor to live with it,
hence the high rate of post-traumatic stress disorder (PTSD) among refugees
and recently displaced persons. With movement from the familiar to the unfamiliar, they are presented with a mainstream America that wishes that they assimilate and become a part of the "melting pot," which, in reality, does not exist
for people of color. Thus, unable (and/or unwilling) to assimilate, many continue to be exposed, if not to physical violence, to emotional violence and xenophobia. Their origins are neither understood nor appreciated, and they are

expected to sever ties to their culture, ancestry, and history, but as people of color, they do not have the opportunity to truly assimilate into the new society to which they have moved.

Historical and current evidence in the U.S., as in many other nations, speaks not only of xenophobia but also of oppression and institutional discrimination. Paradoxically, this nation of opportunity and largesse is also a nation of prejudice and inequality. Immigration laws have evidenced it since the 1880s, and, unfortunately, the openness of immigration policies and refugee programs of the latter third of the twentieth century have been drastically affected by the horrors of the September 11, 2001 terrorist attacks on New York's World Trade Center and the Pentagon in Washington, D.C. Institutional discrimination and oppression ebb and flow, based on the nation's and the world's political and social climates. While working with displaced persons, refugees, and immigrants, practitioners may also address social injustice and aim to change mainstream attitudes and policies, but working specifically with these populations requires a movement from cultural sensitivity to cultural competence. Underlying commonalities in major barriers to intervention must be addressed, and many are couched in the interplay among history, culture, and life experience.

Clearly the experience of displaced persons and refugees is substantially different from that of the immigrant, whether legal or undocumented. In addition, their experience is more complex, causes greater trauma and dysfunction, and more strongly challenges abilities, values, and self-esteem. The discussion below simplifies, and perhaps does an injustice to, some of the difficulties confronting these groups, but is an attempt to isolate the more distressing and shared conflicts facing these groups.

At least four sets of issues confront displaced persons, particularly Native Americans in the United States: (1) evaluation and understanding of historical/current aggressor behavior, (2) personal minimization of culture and identity in the process of enforced assimilation, (3) loss of status and position held in the indigenous culture and society, and (4) as suggested by Yellow Bird, early development from childhood of a form of "self-loathing" because of destructive forms of indoctrination by the majority society and observations of community dysfunction emanating from oppression and debasement. Overlapping issues affect refugees to the United States who must (1) evaluate and process aggressor behavior, (2) recognize that people in authority in the United States are not going to violate them, (3) cope with the causes and symptoms of PTSD, (4) adjust to loss of status and earning capacity in the face of non-transferable skills, and (5) handle changes in intrafamilial role relationships and social norms. Immigrants may not have to manage such significant issues; however, they do have to face changes in social and cultural norms and values and subsequent role relationships. Movement to a minority status, furthermore, affects their perception and definition of self.

Other issues, many of which are discussed in depth in extant literature, are (1) cultural conflicts, as indicated above, experienced by both the immigrant/refugee/displaced generation and its progeny in values, perceptions, behaviors, and relationships, (2) as suggested by Weine, how much of its experience the first generation should convey to the second, for both sharing and preventing feelings of anger and hatred are necessary, and (3) what is to become of their dreams and hopes that existed prior to their movement, and what is to be the direction of their futures (for displaced persons and refugees).

To be truly sensitive to the needs of people removed from their origins, social workers must seek a holistic picture of those individuals, beginning with the impetus that moved them out of their original homes. In doing so, they must aim to understand the political, social, economic, and cultural factors and the individuals' positions and resources in their societies of origin, and this will serve to provide a framework for understanding why they left. Refugees and displaced persons leave their origins because they are driven out, while immigrants frequently move for improved opportunities. This should immediately alert practitioners to the realization that the transitions of the former two groups are usually substantially more traumatic and stressful than are those of the latter.

Once in the new environment, acclimatization and adjustment are the outcome of two major factors: (1) The individual's resources for adjustment in the United States and (2) mainstream American readiness to accept the individual. Immigration literature can be extrapolated to include displaced persons in exploring both these factors. The former—the individual's personal resources—include (a) psychological strengths, (b) language competence, (c) social supports, (d) vocational/professional skills, (e) economic resources, and (f) color of skin. For Bosnian refugees, for example, color of skin is not a barrier, however, it is for Vietnamese or Ethiopians, who are less readily accepted into the workforce despite similarly low levels of English language competence as the Bosnians. The latter factor—the readiness of the United States to accept the individual—is reflected in its (a) immigration and refugee policies, (b) the opportunities and obstacles presented to these newcomers, (c) programs and services available to meet needs, and (d) acceptance of non-white populations. The variables identified in the "readiness" factor may apply more to refugees/immigrants than to displaced persons who are U.S. citizens and entitled to programs and services available to others. However, although they are not affected by immigration and refugee policies, displaced U.S. citizens are influenced by the opportunities and obstacles mainstream America presents, as well as by its level of social and political acceptance. An assessment of this combination of variables will allow service providers a broader and deeper perspective of the experience of displaced persons/refugees/immigrants and allow greater cultural sensitivity, establishing a foundation from which they can move toward cultural competence.

Intrinsic to this cultural sensitivity is the awareness of obstacles (both those raised by the majority society as well as those erected by the minority group itself) to accessing resources and services. Most importantly, social workers must recognize that all U.S. resources should, by right, be available to those who are eligible, and be based on need and *eligibility* criteria, not on ethnicity. Indigenous peoples may justifiably argue, as do both Revard and Yellow Bird in their compelling arguments, that they were forcibly deprived of the very resources (specifically land and a means of subsistence) that are so frugally and grudgingly now meted out to them. The majority of displaced persons, refugees, and immigrants neither know nor understand their rights, the resources available to them, or the means to access them. It is the responsibility of social workers to identify and make opportunities accessible to these groups—which may mean advocating for the populations they represent or working with minority group norms (such as pride and "face-saving") in allowing them to utilize that to which they are entitled.

Cultural and social sensitivity based on issues discussed above will allow practitioners to provide these groups the specific services they require. It should also enhance their awareness of the need to tailor their skills to work with clients who differ from themselves, particularly if they bear in mind social work values of the intrinsic worth and dignity of the individual, and that society should provide opportunities and acknowledge that all peoples have the same fundamental needs. Some basic guidelines are consistent with working with all clients, and practitioners who are client-centered, especially in the early stages of the relationship, are more likely to establish the rapport and trust so essential in any interventive relationship.

Among people who have been traumatized and violated, as most displaced persons and refugees have been, establishing a trusting relationship is often time consuming and requires patience and compassion. It is during this period that many of the barriers to intervention can occur. Authority figures, often those who are placed in positions to protect citizens, are the perpetrators of violence against displaced persons and refugees in their homelands. That causes these groups to distrust people in authority, and social work practitioners are perceived as being people with power and influence because they are able to deliver the services that most refugees and displaced persons seek: financial assistance, employment and housing, referrals to language assistance programs, and health care. Most do not come to the attention of the social services for psycho-social difficulties. However, experience has generated a dissonance, since in their lands of origin those who were in positions to help them often harmed them instead. Therefore, there is great reticence to use social services, and there is fear and suspicion toward those who offer them.

In addition to dealing with suspicion and distrust while establishing the relationship, workers may be confronted by values and norms that prevent the "airing of dirty laundry" outside the boundaries of the family or that engender shame at having to seek non-familial assistance. Both these behaviors are considered unacceptable in many cultures, and having to discuss problems with strangers or receive assistance from "outsiders" is demeaning. Therefore, even while presenting themselves at social service agencies, these clients may not share their real concerns for a long time, and perhaps never. In many societies, furthermore, it is more acceptable to have physical rather than mental health problems, and many displaced persons and refugees may somatize their difficulties, seeking medical care, which provides them with some much needed attention, but which is more acceptable than any form of mental health intervention. However, it is not until the mental health needs are addressed that the somatic ailments abate.

Some interventive skills considered appropriate, furthermore, with the Euro-American population, may be less than useful with people from other cultures. For instance, social workers in the United States are taught to be non-directive and to engage in appropriate self disclosure to establish rapport; with some groups, these skills may be counterproductive. In many cultures, people do not seek assistance unless they plan on taking the advice offered by the expert. As such, when they have appointments with social workers, they expect to be told what to do. Even when all options with the resulting consequences are explored with them, they expect to be guided toward that option that the social worker believes is the most beneficial. After all, if they knew what to do, they would not need the social worker! In addition, self-disclosure that so often is used as a tool to establish empathy with the mainstream population must be used with extreme caution, and used primarily to establish credibility, expertise, roles, and authority—all important ingredients in working with displaced/refugee/immigrant populations. The disclosure of problems or experiences similar to those of the refugees and/or displaced persons may be unsuccessful in establishing rapport; these groups would prefer working with someone who is not mired in the same issues in which they find themselves.

Practice in the human services is, intrinsically, fraught with a variety of difficulties. As clients in the United States become increasingly ethnically and culturally diverse, it becomes important to recognize that a range of additional factors can complicate service provision. While focus on providing social work services to ethnic minorities is increasing, efforts toward displaced persons and refugees continues to be relatively limited, and extant knowledge about them is scattered. Several practice issues confound effective service provision and intervention related to the client system. Resistance, communication barriers, personal and family background, and ethnic community identity are exacerbated by the experience of many displaced persons and refugees, who closely guard information because of fears (perhaps unfounded) of exposure, past experience with oppression, and mistrust of authority. A number of refugees arrive from nations in which they do not have the freedom of speech or of choice. The fears surrounding authority, including the possibility of deportation from the United States can often erect formidable barriers as service providers probe into the lives, experiences, and feelings of refugees.

Ultimately, service providers must become aware of these conditions that can hinder the development of an adequate working relationship with displaced persons, refugees, and immigrants. In order to develop rapport based on understanding and trust, it is essential that service providers educate themselves about both general and specific minority group experiences, adjustment in mainstream America, and the community culture. Interventions, services, and resources must be applied with an awareness of their implications for the cultures involved. To the extent possible that they can be explained in understandable terms, within the context of the particular client group's norms, it behooves the practitioners to so do. Only when service provider credibility, rapport, and sensitivity are established will a large segment of the displaced person/refugee/immigrant population provide sufficient information or be compliant with the guidelines of intervention.

Self-disclosure must be used to increase credibility and authority, while *understanding* must be used to develop the relationship. Although many displaced persons and refugees may fear authority and seek to avoid it, individuals from among the Native Americans and many of the cultures represented by refugees that are currently in the United States are socialized to respect (and obey) it. Hence, directiveness, a skill that is suggested only minimally with the majority U.S. population, is one that can be most effective with these groups. Despite American emphasis on allowing people to make their own decisions, in these minority cultures, once rapport and trust have been established between practitioners and clients, a clear directive is most effective in helping in the resolution of problems.

Thus, cultural sensitivity is the learning of a culture. But learning about a culture means going beyond exploring the norms, values, and behaviors of a particular group. It requires that one appreciate the context of this group, both in its original home and in its new one, in the case of refugees, displaced persons, and immigrants, and comprehend the entire process and effects of their move, while bearing in mind that each individual is unique. Through this process, the social worker must bear in mind not only the experience of the individual, but the historical experience of the group, its experience of oppression, and the continuing obstacles to equal access to opportunities and resources because of xenophobia and ignorance. Cultural competence necessitates working with the idiosyncratic differences between cultures but also requires the essential skills of advocacy and negotiation so that groups that have been oppressed and stripped of their self-confidence struggle through the complexities of the majority society.

Thus, cultural competence requires a realization of the barriers that will be erected because of the culture and because of experience, recognizing that since the source is different, the intervention skills employed may have to differ. Nevertheless, the human condition and its similarities bind peoples together to a much greater extent than one tends to expect. Regardless of social norms, culture, religion, or language, all people, at the very least, have the same desires for health and the ability to provide for their families. All people experience joy, fear, pain, hope, despair, and the entire range of emotions. All are vulnerable, need other human beings, and are influenced by environmental factors. If practitioners bear this in mind, begin "where the client is," maintain social work values, are knowledgeable about appropriate resources, explore the client culture and experience, and non-judgmentally seek to comprehend their implications and adapt practice intervention skills, cultural competence will ensue.

NOTES

[1]Displaced persons are those who are forced to move from one place to another within their own country.

[2]Refugees are those who, because of a fear of persecution, flee their countries.

[3]Immigrants are individuals who move voluntarily, generally for improved opportunities.

Unit 6   NEGOTIATING MULTIPLE SYSTEMS ON BEHALF OF CHILDREN AND FAMILIES

Editors' Introduction

The stories and case study in this unit all concern children and families: biological, step-, foster, and possibly adoptive. Each demonstrates, to very different effect, the impact of "helping" systems upon those families, particularly the children, and the potential for multiple systems, wrapped around a client system, to make dramatic differences, for better yet sometimes for worse.

The Social Work Dictionary (Barker 1991) defines negotiation as a process of bringing together opposing parties for the purpose of coming to mutually acceptable agreements (p.154). In our view, negotiating multiple systems on behalf of clients involves the complex management of interactions and relationships that occur both inside and outside the family, particularly when an effort is made to provide a family with professional services intended to help them. Ideally, social workers guide clients to smooth, cooperative, non-violent interactions when they link them with an array of services aimed at increasing the stability and effective functioning of the family. However, as the readings we offer suggest, this is not always the case; cultural insensitivity and incompetence can sometimes exacerbate rather than improve the experience of children and families as they come into contact with a broadening network of interacting individuals and systems.

Told from the point of view of a floundering father, Bharati Mukherjee's "Fathering," concerns a family on the brink of disintegration. At the age of ten, Eng has come to the United States to meet and live with her biological father Jason and his partner Sharon. Although Sharon initially encouraged Jason to find out what happened to his child and permitted him to bring her into their home, it becomes clear that the needs of this traumatized child quickly outstrip their capacity to meet them. Although a fourth character, Dr. Kearns, offers support to this struggling family unit, the divorced Vietnam War veteran and his ambivalent partner need more support systems to effectively care for the child they recently discovered and recovered from Vietnam. A social worker might help identify and connect this couple with support systems of various types to address their own needs as well as to maximize their ability to help Eng and to parent her effectively. The difficulty this family has coordinating their connection with their sole source of support, Dr. Kearns, illustrates the complexity of negotiating support systems and suggests the skill needed to develop and maintain effective interactions with appropriate support.

Louise Erdrich's "American Horse," in some ways, serves as a counterpoint to "Fathering": once again, we are witnessing the dismantling of a family, but under very different circumstances. "American Horse" portrays a First Nations family, living in poverty and deprivation. As the story opens, there are ominous portents; in short order, we see this family's misfortune arrive in the form of two officers and a social worker, who have come to remove Woodrow (Buddy) American Horse, a little boy, from the care of his mother Albertine and his Uncle Lawrence, and to place him in foster care. The little the narrator of the story tells us about this family's past makes us painfully aware of the need for a thorough assessment in child welfare practice. The comic caricature of the insensitive and self-righteous social worker asserts the need for culturally sensitive social workers who can approach families with an understanding of the people with whom they are dealing and who have adequate knowledge of the laws whose violations they are investigating. For all the poverty of Buddy's circumstances, it is clear that he feels attached to his mother and uncle and that they are opposed to his removal. Moreover, the circumstances of his removal are disturbingly abrupt and violent, and they disorient and traumatize the child whose welfare is presumably at issue. Erdrich's story underscores the importance for social workers of using all their skills to put supports in place that will obviate the need for the last-resort action of removal of a child from his home.

Vicki Sear's "Grace" tells the heartbreaking story of Jodi and her brother Billie Jim and their developing relationship with foster parents Paul and Grace. Told from the watchful point of view of Jodi, "Grace" offers the reader a sense of the horrors of the orphanage and foster homes in which these siblings have grown up prior to becoming the wards of Paul and Grace. Under the care of these two people, old enough to be their grandparents, Jodi and Billie Jim have an opportunity to be children again, and to respond to kindness and generosity. They also benefit from the guidance of Indigenous people, who approach their common heritage with knowledge and respect and offer a critical alternative to the negative view of themselves that was fostered in the orphanage. The understanding and patience demonstrated by these foster parents as they connect these orphaned and abused children with the knowledge of their history and traditions offers an example of the type of resources that a social worker ought to provide for children who have lost connection with their family and culture. When such supports for children are lost or diminished, the most important thing that social workers can do is to find substitutes or reestablish those supports in order to maintain their link to the family or cultural system.

"Ruth's Song (Because She Could Not Sing It)," by Gloria Steinem, is both a biographical and autobiographical exploration of the author's life with an emotionally unstable mother. Following her parents' divorce, Steinem is left, without her father or elder sister, to care for her mother on her own. Looking back on those years, when she developed from the age of ten to seventeen, Steinem seeks to understand and explain how they became so isolated and bereft of the supports that might have offered them stability. She finds patterns of emotional instability in other members of her mother's family, but more pertinent, she believes, is the fact that her mother was excluded from the multiple systems that would have made her life meaningful and lent her social and emotional support. Steinem's personal essay suggests that maintaining contact with and successfully negotiating multiple systems is the primary way that individuals maintain system balance.

We conclude our readings with a case study with a hopeful ending, perhaps an antidote to some of the stories told here. The case of Tanya, by Elizabeth Kenny and Kathleen Belanger, presents an assessment, intervention, and evaluation of a young girl who finds help for herself, her child, and her brothers by turning to social workers, church, and schools. Most important were the close, supportive, and enduring relationships between the foster parents and children. This case study demonstrates that, in spite of the difficulties of working in a community with few formal supports, social workers can make a difference when they work successfully with even the few effective systems that are in place. When family social work arrays an appropriate network of social, financial, and structural supports around a family system in an appropriate manner, it is much more likely to bring about the result of an empowered, appropriately interdependent family. However, as these readings suggest and as Vanessa Hodges notes in her Invited Commentary, children and families often suffer from the paucity of "empowering, culturally relevant, evidence-based, and effective [services,]...offered with a profound understanding of a family's culture, history, and strengths." It is our hope that a reflection on the successes and failures represented in these readings will inspire more social workers to provide children and family with such services, knowledge, and understanding.

Fathering

BHARATI MUKHERJEE

Eng stands just inside our bedroom door, her fidgety fist on the doorknob which Sharon, in a sulk, polished to a gleam yesterday afternoon.

"I'm starved," she says.

I know a sick little girl when I see one. I brought the twins up without much help ten years ago. Eng's got a high fever. Brownish stains stiffen the nap of her terry robe. Sour smells fill the bedroom.

"For God's sake leave us alone," Sharon mutters under the quilt. She turns away from me. We bought the quilt at a garage sale in Rock Springs the Sunday two years ago when she moved in. "Talk to her."

Sharon works on this near-marriage of ours. I'll hand it to her, she really does. I knead her shoulders, and I say, "Easy, easy," though I really hate it when she treats Eng like a deafmute. "My girl speaks English, remember?"

Eng can outcuss any freckle-faced kid on the block. Someone in the killing fields must have taught her. Maybe her mama, the honeyest-skinned bar girl with the tiniest feet in Saigon. I was an errand boy with the Combined Military Intelligence. I did the whole war on Dexedrine. Vietnam didn't happen, and I'd put it behind me in marriage and fatherhood and teaching high school. Ten years later came the screw-ups with the marriage, the job, women, the works. Until Eng popped up in my life, I really believed it didn't happen.

"Come here, sweetheart," I beg my daughter. I sidle closer to Sharon, so there'll be room under the quilt for Eng.

"I'm starved," she complains from the doorway. She doesn't budge. The robe and hair are smelling something fierce. She doesn't show any desire to cuddle. She must be sick. She must have thrown up all night. Sharon throws the quilt back. "Then go raid the refrigerator like a normal kid," she snaps.

Once upon a time Sharon used to be a cheerful, accommodating woman. It isn't as if Eng was dumped on us out of the blue. She knew I was tracking my kid. Coming to terms with the past was Sharon's idea. I don't know what happened to *that* Sharon. "For all you know, Jason," she'd said, "the baby died of malaria or something." She said, "Go on, find out and deal with it." She said she could handle being a stepmother—better a fresh chance with some orphan off the streets of Saigon than with my twins from Rochester. My twins are being raised in some organic-farming lesbo commune. Their mother breeds Nubian goats for a living. "Come get in bed with us, baby. Let Dad feel your forehead. You burning up with fever?"

"She isn't hungry, I think she's sick," I tell Sharon, but she's already tugging her sleeping mask back on. "I think she's just letting us know she hurts."

I hold my arms out wide for Eng to run into. If I could, I'd suck the virus right out of her. In the jungle, VC mamas used to do that. Some nights we'd steal right up to a hootch—just a few of us intense sons of bitches on some special mission—and the women would be at their mumbo jumbo. They'd be sticking coins and amulets into napalm burns.

"I'm hungry, Dad" It comes out as a moan. Okay, she doesn't run into my arms, but at least she's come as far in as the foot of our bed. "Dad, let's go down to the kitchen. Just you and me."

I am about to let that pass, though I can feel Sharon's body go into weird little jerks and twitches when my baby adds with emphatic viciousness, "Not her, Dad. We don't want her with us in the kitchen."

"She loves you," I protest. Love—not spite—makes Eng so territorial; that's what I want to explain to Sharon. She's a sick, frightened, foreign kid, for Chrissake. "Don't you, Sharon? Sharon's concerned about you."

But Sharon turns over on her stomach. "You know what's wrong with you, Jase? You can't admit you're being manipulated. You can't cut through the 'frightened-foreign-kid' shit."

Eng moves closer. She comes up to the side of my bed, but does touch the hand I'm holding out. She's a fighter.

"I feel fire-hot, Dad. My bones feel pain."

"Sharon?" I want to deserve this woman. "Sharon, I'm so sorry." It isn't anybody's fault. You need uppers to get through peace times, too.

"Dad. Let's go. Chop-chop."

"You're too sick to keep food down, baby. Curl up in here. Just for a bit."

"I'd throw up, Dad."

"I'll carry you back to your room. I'll read you a story, okay?"

Eng watches me real close as I pull the quilt off. "You got any scars you haven't shown me yet? My mom had a big scar on one leg. Shrapnel. Boom boom. I got scars. See? I got lots of bruises."

I scoop up my poor girl and rush her, terry robe flapping, to her room which Sharon fixed up with white girlish furniture in less complicated days. Waiting for Eng was good. Sharon herself said it was good for our relationship. "Could you bring us some juice and aspirin?" I shout from the hallway.

"Aspirin isn't going to cure Eng," I hear Sharon yell. "I'm going to call Dr. Kearns."

Downstairs I hear Sharon on the phone. She isn't talking flu viruses. She's talking social workers and shrinks. My girl isn't crazy; she's picked up a bug in school as might anyone else.

"The child's arms are covered with bruises," Sharon is saying. "Nothing major. They look like . . . well, they're sort of tiny circles and welts." There's nothing for a while. Then she says, "Christ! no, Jason can't do enough for her! That's not what I'm saying! What's happening to this country? You think we're perverts? What I'm saying is the girl's doing it to herself."

"Who are you talking to?" I ask from the top of the stairs. "What happened to the aspirin?"

I lean as far forward over the railing as I dare so I can see what Sharon's up to. She's getting her coat and boots. She's having trouble with buttons and snaps. In the bluish light of the foyer's broken chandelier, she looks old, harrowed, depressed. What have I done to her?

"What's going on?" I plead. "You deserting me?"

"Don't be so fucking melodramatic. I'm going to the mall to buy some aspirin."

"How come we don't have any in the house?"

"Why are you always picking on me?"

"Who was that on the phone?"

"So now you want me to account for every call and every trip?" She ties an angry knot into her scarf. But she tells me. "I was talking to Meg Kearns. She says Dr. Kearns has gone hunting for the day."

"Great!"

"She says he has his beeper on him."

I hear the back door stick and Sharon swear. She's having trouble with the latch. "Jiggle it gently," I shout, taking the stairs two at a time. But before I can come down, her Nissan backs out of the parking apron.

Back upstairs I catch Eng in the middle of a dream or delirium. "They got Grandma!" she screams. She goes very rigid in bed. It's a four-poster with canopy and ruffles and stuff that Sharon put on her MasterCard. The twins slept on bunk beds. With the twins it was different, totally different. Dr. Spock can't be point man for Eng, for us.

"She bring me food," Eng's screaming. "She bring me food from the forest. They shoot Grandma! Bastards!"

"Eng?" I don't dare touch her. I don't know how.

"You shoot my grandmother?" She whacks the air with her bony arms. Now I see the bruises, the small welts all along the insides of her arms. Some have to be weeks old, they're that yellow. The twins' scrapes and cuts never turned that ochre. I can't help wondering if maybe Asian skin bruises differently from ours, even though I want to say skin is skin; especially hers is skin like mine.

"I want to be with Grandma. Grandma loves me. I want to be ghost. I don't want to get better."

I read to her. I read to her because good parents are supposed to read to their kids laid up sick in bed. I want to do it right. I want to be a good father. I read from a sci-fi novel that Sharon must have picked up. She works in a camera store in the mall, right next to a B. Dalton. I read three pages out loud, then I read four chapters to myself because Eng's stopped up her ears. Aliens have taken over small towns all over the country. Idaho, Nebraska: no state is safe from aliens.

Some time after two, the phone rings. Since Sharon doesn't answer it on the second ring, I know she isn't back. She carries a cordless phone everywhere around the house. In the movies, when cops have bad news to deliver, they lean on your doorbell; they don't call. Sharon will come back when she's ready. We'll make up. Things will get back to normal.

"Jason?"

I know Dr. Kearns's voice. He saw the twins through the usual immunizations.

"I have Sharon here. She'll need a ride home. Can you drive over?"

"God! What's happened?"

"Nothing to panic about. Nothing physical. She came for a consultation"

"Give me a half-hour. I have to wrap Eng real warm so I can drag her out in this miserable weather."

"Take your time. This way I can take a look at Eng, too."

"What's wrong with Sharon?"

"She's a little exercised about a situation. I gave her a sedative. See you in a half-hour."

I ease delirious Eng out of the overdecorated four-poster, prop her against my body while I wrap a blanket around her. She's a tiny thing, but she feels stiff and heavy, a sleepwalking mummy. Her eyes are dry-bright, strange.

It's a sunny winter day, and the evergreens in the front yard are glossy with frost. I press Eng against my chest as I negotiate the front steps. Where the gutter leaks, the steps feel spongy. The shrubs and bushes my ex-wife planted clog the front path. I've put twenty years into this house. The steps, the path, the house all have a right to fall apart.

I'm thirty-eight. I've let a lot of people down already.

The inside of the van is deadly cold. Mid-January ice mottles the windshield. I lay the bundled-up child on the long seat behind me and wait for the engine to warm up. It feels good with the radio going and heat coming on. I don't want the ice on the windshield to melt. Eng and I are safest in the van.

In the rear-view mirror, Eng's wrinkled lips begin to move. "Dad, can I have a quarter?"

"May I, kiddo," I joke.

There's all sorts of junk in the pockets of my parka. Buckshot, dimes and quarters for the vending machine, a Blistex.

"What do you need it for, sweetheart?"

Eng's quick. Like the street kids in Saigon who dove for cigarettes and sticks of gum. She's loosened the blanket folds around her. I watch her tuck the quarter inside her wool mitt. She grins. "Thanks, soldier."

At Dr. Kearns's, Sharon is lying unnaturally slack-bodied on the lone vinyl sofa. Her coat's neatly balled up under her neck, like a bolster. Right now she looks amiable, docile. I don't think she exactly recognizes me, although later she'll say she did. All that stuff about Kearns going hunting must have been a lie. Even the stuff about having to buy aspirins in the mall. She was planning all along to get here.

"What's wrong?"

"It's none of my business, Jason, but you and Sharon might try an honest-to-goodness heart-to-heart." Then he makes a sign to me to lay Eng on the examining table. "We don't look so bad," he says to my daughter. Then he excuses himself and goes into a glass-walled cubicle.

Sharon heaves herself into a sitting position of sorts on the sofa. "Everything was fine until she got here. Send her back, Jase. If you love me, send her back." She's slouched so far forward, her pointed, sweatered breasts nearly touch her corduroy pants. She looks helpless, pathetic. I've brought her to this state. Guilt, not love, is what I feel.

I want to comfort Sharon, but my daughter with the wild, grieving pygmy face won't let go of my hand. "She's bad, Dad. Send *her* back."

Dr. Kearns comes out of the cubicle balancing a sample bottle of pills or caplets on a flattened palm. He has a boxer's tough, squarish hands. "Miraculous stuff, this," he laughs. "But first we'll stick our tongue out and say *ahh*. Come on, open wide."

Eng opens her mouth real wide, then brings her teeth together, hard, on Dr. Kearns's hand. She leaps erect on the examining table, tearing the disposable paper sheet with her toes. Her tiny, funny toes are doing a frantic dance. "Don't let him touch me, Grandma!"

"He's going to make you all better, baby." I can't pull my alien child down, I can't comfort her. The twins had diseases with easy names, diseases we knew what to do with. The thing is, I never felt for them what I feel for her.

"Don't let him touch me, Grandma!" Eng's screaming now. She's hopping on the table and screaming. "Kill him, Grandma! Get me out of here, Grandma!"

"Baby, it's all right."

But she looks through me and the country doctor as though we aren't here, as though we aren't pulling at her to make her lie down.

"Lie back like a good girl," Dr. Kearns commands.

But Eng is listening to other voices. She pulls her mitts off with her teeth, chucks the blanket, the robe, the pajamas to the floor; then, naked, hysterical, she presses the quarter I gave her deep into the soft flesh of her arm. She presses and presses that coin, turning it in nasty half-circles until blood starts to pool under the skin.

"Jason, grab her at the knees. Get her back down on the table."

From the sofa, Sharon moans. "See, I told you the child was crazy. She hates me. She's possessive about Jason."

The doctor comes at us with his syringe. He's sedated Sharon; now he wants to knock out my kid with his cures.

"Get the hell out, you bastard!" Eng yells. "*Vamos!* Bang bang!" She's pointing her arm like a semiautomatic, taking out Sharon, then the doctor. My Rambo. "Old way is good way. Money cure is good cure. When they shoot my grandma, you think pills do her any good? You Yankees, please go home." She looks straight at me. "Scram, Yankee bastard!"

Dr. Kearns has Eng by the wrist now. He has flung the quarter I gave her on the floor. Something incurable is happening to my women.

Then, as in fairy tales, I know what has to be done. "Coming, pardner!" I whisper. "I got no end of coins." I jiggle the change in my pocket. I jerk her away from our enemies. My Saigon kid and me: we're a team. In five minutes we'll be safely away in the cold chariot of our van.

Reading   # American Horse

LOUISE ERDRICH

The woman sleeping on the cot in the woodshed was Albertine American Horse. The name was left over from her mother's short marriage. The boy was the son of the man she had loved and let go. Buddy was on the cot too, sitting on the edge because he'd been awake three hours watching out for his mother and besides, she took up the whole cot. Her feet hung over the edge, limp and brown as two trout. Her long arms reached out and slapped at things she saw in her dreams.

Buddy had been knocked awake out of hiding in a washing machine while herds of policemen with dogs searched through a large building with many tiny rooms. When the arm came down, Buddy screamed because it had a blue cuff and sharp silver buttons. "Tss," his mother mumbled, half awake, "wasn't nothing." But Buddy sat up after her breathing went deep again, and he watched.

There was something coming and he knew it.

It was coming from very far off but he had a picture of it in his mind. It was a large thing made of metal with many barbed hooks, points, and drag chains on it, something like a giant potato peeler that rolled out of the sky, scraping clouds down with it and jabbing or crushing everything that lay in its path on the ground.

Buddy watched his mother. If he woke her up, she would know what to do about the thing, but he thought he'd wait until he saw it for sure before he shook her. She was pretty, sleeping, and he liked knowing he could look at her as long and close up as he wanted. He took a strand of her hair and held it in his hands as if it was the rein to a delicate beast. She was strong enough and could pull him along like the horse their name was.

Buddy had his mother's and his grandmother's name because his father had been a big mistake.

"They're all mistakes, even your father. But *you* are the best thing that ever happened to me."

That was what she said when he asked.

Even Kadie, the boyfriend crippled from being in a car wreck, was not as good a thing that had happened to his mother as Buddy was. "He was a medium-sized mistake," she said. "He's hurt and I shouldn't even say that, but it's the truth." At the moment, Buddy knew that being the best thing in his mother's life, he was also the reason they were hiding from the cops.

He wanted to touch the satin roses sewed on her pink tee shirt, but he knew he shouldn't do that even in her sleep. If she woke up and found him touching the roses, she would say, "Quit that, Buddy." Sometimes she told him to stop hugging her like a gorilla. She never said that in the mean voice she used when he oppressed her, but when she said that he loosened up anyway.

There were times he felt like hugging her so hard and in such a special way that she would say to him, "Let's get married." There were also times he closed his eyes and wished that she would die, only a few times, but still it haunted him that his wish might come true. He and Uncle Lawrence would be left alone. Buddy wasn't worried, though, about his mother getting married to somebody else. She had said to her friend, Madonna, "All men suck," when she thought Buddy wasn't listening. He had made an uncertain sound, and when they heard him they took him in their arms.

"Except for you, Buddy," his mother said. "All except for you and maybe Uncle Lawrence, although he's pushing it."

"The cops suck the worst, though," Buddy whispered to his mother's sleeping face, "because they're after us." He felt tired again, slumped down, and put his legs beneath the blanket. He closed his eyes and got the feeling that the cot was lifting up beneath him, that it was arching its canvas back and then traveling, traveling very fast and in the wrong direction for when he looked up he saw the three of them were advancing to meet the great metal thing with hooks and barbs and all sorts of sharp equipment to catch their bodies and draw their blood. He heard its insides as it rushed toward them, purring softly like a powerful motor and then they were right in its shadow. He pulled the reins as hard as he could and the beast reared, lifting him. His mother clapped her hand across his mouth.

"Okay," she said. "Lay low. They're outside and they're gonna hunt."

She touched his shoulder and Buddy leaned over with her to look through a crack in the boards.

They were out there all right, Albertine saw them. Two officers and that social worker woman. Vicki Koob. There had been no whistle, no dream, no voice to warn her that they were coming. There was only the crunching sound of cinders in the yard, the engine purring, the dust sifting off their car in a fine light brownish cloud and settling around them.

The three people came to a halt in their husk of metal—the car emblazoned with the North Dakota State Highway Patrol emblem which is the glowing profile of the Sioux policeman, Red Tomahawk, the one who killed Sitting Bull. Albertine gave Buddy the blanket and told him that he might have to wrap it around him and hide underneath the cot.

"We're gonna wait and see what they do." She took him in her lap and hunched her arms around him. "Don't you worry," she whispered against his ear. "Lawrence knows how to fool them."

Buddy didn't want to look at the car and the people. He felt his mother's heart beating beneath his ear so fast it seemed to push the satin roses in and out.

He put his face to them carefully and breathed the deep, soft powdery woman smell of her. That smell was also in her little face cream bottles, in her brushes, and around the washbowl after she used it. The satin felt so unbearably smooth against his cheek that he had to press closer. She didn't push him away, like he expected, but hugged him still tighter until he felt as close as he had ever been to back inside her again where she said he came from. Within the smells of her things, her soft skin, and the satin of her roses, he closed his eyes then, and took his breaths softly and quickly with her heart.

They were out there, but they didn't dare get out of the car yet because of Lawrence's big, ragged dogs. Three of these dogs had loped up the dirt driveway with the car. They were rangy, alert, and bounced up and down on their cushioned paws like wolves. They didn't waste their energy barking, but positioned themselves quietly, one at either car door and the third in front of the bellied-out screen door to Uncle Lawrence's house. It was six in the morning but the wind was up already, blowing dust, ruffling their short moth-eaten coats. The big brown one on Vicki Koob's side had unusual black and white markings, stripes almost, like a hyena and he grinned at her, tongue out and teeth showing.

"Shoo!" Miss Koob opened her door with a quick jerk.

The brown dog sidestepped the door and jumped before her, tiptoeing. Its dirty white muzzle curled and its eyes crossed suddenly as if it was zeroing its cross-hair sights in on the exact place it would bite her. She ducked back and slammed the door.

"It's mean," she told Officer Brackett. He was printing out some type of form. The other officer, Harmony, a slow man, had not yet reacted to the car's halt. He had been sitting quietly in the back seat, but now he rolled down his window and with no change in expression unsnapped his holster and drew his pistol out and pointed it at the dog on his side. The dog smacked down on its belly, wiggled under the car and was out and around the back of the house before Harmony drew his gun back. The other dogs vanished with him. From wherever they had disappeared to they began to yap and howl, and the door to the low shoebox-style house fell open.

"Heya, what's going on?"

Uncle Lawrence put his head out the door and opened wide the one eye he had in working order. The eye bulged impossibly wider in outrage when he saw the police car. But the eyes of the two officers and Miss Vicki Koob were wide open too because they had never seen Uncle Lawrence in his sleeping get up or, indeed, witnessed anything like it. For his ribs, which were cracked from a bad fall and still mending, Uncle Lawrence wore a thick white corset laced up the front with a striped sneakers' lace. His glass eye and his set of dentures were still out for the night so his face puckered here and there, around its absences and scars, like a damaged but fierce little cake. Although he had a few gray streaks now, Uncle Lawrence's hair was still thick, and because he wore a special contraption of elastic straps around his head every night, two oiled waves always crested on either side of his middle part. All of this would have been sufficient to astonish, even without the most striking part of his outfit—the smoking jacket. It was made of black satin and hung open around his corset, dragging a tasseled belt. Gold thread dragons struggled up the lapels and blasted their furry red breath around his neck. As Lawrence walked down the steps, he put his arms up in surrender and the gold tassels in the inner seams of his sleeves dropped into view.

"My heavens, what a sight." Vicki Koob was impressed.

"A character," apologized Officer Harmony.

As a tribal police officer who could be counted on to help out the State Patrol, Harmony thought he always had to explain about Indians or get twice as tough to show he did not favor them. He was slow-moving and shy but two jumps ahead of other people all the same, and now, as he watched Uncle Lawrence's splendid approach, he gazed speculatively at the torn and bulging pocket of the smoking jacket. Harmony had been inside Uncle Lawrence's house before and knew that above his draped orange-crate shelf of war medals a blue-black German luger was hung carefully in a net of flat-headed nails and fishing line. Thinking of this deadly exhibition, he got out of the car and shambled toward Lawrence with a dreamy little smile of welcome on his face. But when he searched Lawrence, he found that the bulging pocket held only the lonesome-looking dentures from Lawrence's empty jaw. They were still dripping denture polish.

"I had been cleaning them when you arrived," Uncle Lawrence explained with acid dignity.

He took the toothbrush from his other pocket and aimed it like a rifle.

"Quit that, you old idiot." Harmony tossed the toothbrush away. "For once you ain't done nothing. We came for your nephew."

Lawrence looked at Harmony with a faint air of puzzlement.

"Ma Frere, listen," threatened Harmony amiably, "those two white people in the car came to get him for the welfare. They got papers on your nephew that give them the right to take him."

"Papers?" Uncle Lawrence puffed out his deeply pitted cheeks. "Let me see them papers."

The two of them walked over to Vicki's side of the car and she pulled a copy of the court order from her purse. Lawrence put his teeth back in and adjusted them with busy workings of his jaw.

"Just a minute," he reached into his breast pocket as he bent close to Miss Vicki Koob. "I can't read these without I have in my eye."

He took the eye from his breast pocket delicately, and as he popped it into his face the social worker's mouth fell open in a consternated O.

"What is this," she cried in a little voice.

Uncle Lawrence looked at her mildly. The white glass of the eye was cold as lard. The black iris was strangely charged and menacing.

"He's nuts," Brackett huffed along the side of Vicki's neck. "Never mind him."

Vicki's hair had sweated down her nape in tiny corkscrews and some of the hairs were so long and dangly now that they disappeared into the zippered back of her dress. Brackett noticed this as he spoke into her ear. His face grew red and the backs of his hands prickled. He slid under the steering wheel and got out of the car. He walked around the hood to stand with Leo Harmony.

"We could take you in too," said Brackett roughly. Lawrence eyed the officers in what was taken as defiance. "If you don't cooperate, we'll get out the handcuffs," they warned.

One of Lawrence's arms was stiff and would not move until he'd rubbed it with witch hazel in the morning. His other arm worked fine though, and he stuck it out in front of Brackett.

"Get them handcuffs," he urged them. "Put me in a welfare home."

Bracket snapped one side of the handcuffs on Lawrence's good arm and the other to the handle of the police car.

"That's to hold you," he said. "We're wasting our time. Harmony, you search that little shed over by the tall grass and Miss Koob and myself will search the house."

"My rights is violated!" Lawrence shrieked suddenly. They ignored him. He tugged at the handcuff and thought of the good heavy file he kept in his tool box and the German luger oiled and ready but never loaded, because of Buddy, over his shelf. He should have used it on these bad ones, even Harmony in his big-time white man job. He wouldn't last long in that job anyway before somebody gave him what for.

"It's a damn scheme," said Uncle Lawrence, rattling his chains against the car. He looked over at the shed and thought maybe Albertine and Buddy had sneaked away before the car pulled into the yard. But he sagged, seeing Albertine move, like a shadow within the boards. "Oh, it's all a damn scheme," he muttered again.

"I want to find that boy and salvage him," Vicki Koob explained to Officer Brackett as they walked into the house. "Look at his family life—the old man crazy as a bedbug, the mother intoxicated somewhere."

Brackett nodded, energetic, eager. He was a short hopeful red-head who failed consistently to win the hearts of women. Vicki Koob intrigued him. Now, as he watched, she pulled a tiny pen out of an ornamental clip on her blouse. It was attached to a retractable line that would suck the pen back, like a child eating one strand of spaghetti. Something about the pen on its line excited Brackett to the point of discomfort. His hand shook as he opened the screen-door and stepped in, beckoning Miss Koob to follow.

They could see the house was empty at first glance. It was only one rectangular room with whitewashed walls and a little gas stove in the middle. They had already come through the cooking lean-to with the other stove and wash-stand and rusty old refrigerator. That refrigerator had nothing in it but some wrinkled potatoes and a package of turkey necks. Vicki Koob noted in her perfect-bound notebook. The beds along the walls of the big room were covered with quilts that Albertine's mother, Sophie, had made from bits of old wool coats and pants that the Sisters sold in bundles at the mission. There was no one hiding beneath the beds. No one was under the little aluminum dinette table covered with a green oilcloth, or the soft brown wood chairs tucked up to it. One wall of the big room was filled with neatly stacked crates of things—old tools and springs and small half-dismantled appliances. Five or six television sets were stacked against the wall. Their control panels spewed colored wires and at least one was cracked all the way across. Only the topmost set, with coathanger antenna angled sensitively to catch the bounding signals around Little Shell, looked like it could possibly work.

Not one thing escaped Vicki Koob's trained and cataloguing gaze. She made note of the cupboard that held only commodity flour and coffee. The unsanitary tin oil drum beneath the kitchen window, full of empty surplus pork cans and beer bottles, caught her eye as did Uncle Lawrence's physical and mental deteriorations. She quickly described these "benchmarks of alcoholic dependency within the extended family of Woodrow (Buddy) American Horse" as she walked around the room with the little notebook open, pushed against her belly to steady it. Although Vicki had been there before, Albertine's presence had always made it difficult for her to take notes.

"Twice the maximum allowable space between door and threshold," she wrote now. "Probably no insulation. Two three-inch cracks in walls inadequately sealed with white-washed mud." She made a mental note but could see no point in describing Lawrence's stuffed reclining chair that only reclined, the shadeless lamp with its plastic orchid in the bubble glass base, or the three-dimensional picture of Jesus that Lawrence had once demonstrated to her. When plugged in, lights rolled behind the water the Lord stood on so that he seemed to be strolling although he never actually went forward, of course, but only pushed the glowing waves behind him forever like a poor tame rat in a treadmill.

Brackett cleared his throat with a nervous rasp and touched Vicki's shoulder.

"What are you writing?"

She moved away and continued to scribble as if thoroughly absorbed in her work. "Officer Brackett displays an undue amount of interest in my person," she wrote. "Perhaps?"

He snatched playfully at the book, but she hugged it to her chest and moved off smiling. More curls had fallen, wetted to the base of her neck. Looking out the window, she sighed long and loud.

"All night on brush rollers for this. What a joke."

Brackett shoved his hands in his pockets. His mouth opened slightly, then shut with a small throttled cluck.

When Albertine saw Harmony ambling across the yard with his big brown thumbs in his belt, his placid smile, and his tiny black eyes moving back and forth, she put Buddy under the cot. Harmony stopped at the shed and stood quietly. He spread his arms to show her he hadn't drawn his big police gun.

320   Reading   American Horse

"Ma Cousin," he said in the Michif dialect that people used if they were relatives or sometimes if they needed gas or a couple of dollars, "why don't you come out here and stop this foolishness?"

"I ain't your cousin," Albertine said. Anger boiled up in her suddenly. "I ain't related to no pigs."

She bit her lip and watched him through the cracks, circling, a big tan punching dummy with his boots full of sand so he never stayed down once he fell. He was empty inside, all stale air. But he knew how to get to her so much better than a white cop could. And now he was circling because he wasn't sure she didn't have a weapon, maybe a knife or the German luger that was the only thing that her father, Albert American Horse, had left his wife and daughter besides his name. Harmony knew that Albertine was a tall strong woman who took two big men to subdue when she didn't want to go in the drunk tank. She had hard hips, broad shoulders, and stood tall like her Sioux father, the American Horse who was killed threshing in Belle Prairie.

"I feel bad to have to do this," Harmony said to Albertine. "But for godsakes, let's nobody get hurt. Come on out with the boy, why don't you? I know you got him in there."

Albertine did not give herself away this time. She let him wonder. Slowly and quietly she pulled her belt through its loops and wrapped it around and around her hand until only the big oval buckle with turquoise chunks shaped into a butterfly stuck out over her knuckles. Harmony was talking but she wasn't listening to what he said. She was listening to the pitch of his voice, the tone of it that would tighten or tremble at a certain moment when he decided to rush the shed. He kept talking slowly and reasonably, flexing the dialect from time to time, even mentioning her father.

"He was a damn good man. I don't care what they say, Albertine, I knew him."

Albertine looked at the stone butterfly that spread its wings across her fist. The wings looked light and cool, not heavy. It almost looked like it was ready to fly. Harmony wanted to get to Albertine through her father but she would not think about American Horse. She concentrated on the sky blue stone.

Yet the shape of the stone, the color, betrayed her.

She saw her father suddenly, bending at the grille of their old gray car. She was small then. The memory came from so long ago it seemed like a dream—narrowly focused, snapshot-clear. He was bending by the grille in the sun. It was hot summer. Wings of sweat, dark blue, spread across the back of his work shirt. He always wore soft blue shirts, the color of shade cloudier than this stone. His stiff hair had grown out of its short haircut and flopped over his forehead. When he stood up and turned away from the car, Albertine saw that he had a butterfly.

"It's dead," he told her. "Broke its wings and died on the grille."

She must have been five, maybe six, wearing one of the boy's tee shirts Mama bleached in Hilex-water. American Horse took the butterfly, a black and yellow one, and rubbed it on Albertine's collarbone and chest and arms until the color and the powder of it were blended into her skin.

"For grace," he said.

And Albertine had felt a strange lightening in her arms, in her chest, when he did this and said, "For grace." The way he said it, grace meant everything the butterfly was. The sharp delicate wings. The way it floated over grass. The way its wings seemed to breathe fanning in the sun. The wisdom of the way it blended into flowers or changed into a leaf. In herself she felt the same kind of possibilities and closed her eyes almost in shock or pain, she felt so light and powerful at that moment.

Then her father had caught her and thrown her high into the air. She could not remember landing in his arms or landing at all. She only remembered the sun filling her eyes and the world tipping crazily behind her, out of sight.

"He was a damn good man," Harmony said again.

Albertine heard his starched uniform gathering before his boots hit the ground. Once, twice, three times. It took him four solid jumps to get right where she wanted him. She kicked the plank door open when he reached for the handle and the corner caught him on the jaw. He faltered, and Albertine hit him flat on the chin with the butterfly. She hit him so hard the shock of it went up her arm like a string pulled taut. Her fist opened, numb, and she let the belt unloop before she closed her hand on the tip end of it and sent the stone butterfly swooping out in a wide circle around her as if it was on the end of a leash. Harmony reeled backward as she walked toward him swinging the belt. She expected him to fall but he just stumbled. And then he took the gun from his hip.

Albertine let the belt go limp. She and Harmony stood within feet of each other, breathing. Each heard the human sound of air going in and out of the other person's lungs. Each read the face of the other as if deciphering letters carved into softly eroding veins of stone. Albertine saw the pattern of tiny arteries that age, drink, and hard living had blown to the surface of the man's face. She saw the spoked wheels of his iris and the arteries like tangled threads that sewed him up. She saw the living net of springs and tissue that held him together, and trapped him. She saw the random, intimate plan of his person.

She took a quick shallow breath and her face went strange and tight. She saw the black veins in the wings of the butterfly, roads burnt into a map, and then she was located somewhere in the net of veins and sinew that was the tragic complexity of the world so she did not see Officer Brackett and Vicki Koob rushing toward her, but felt them instead like flies caught in the same web, rocking it.

"Albertine!" Vicki Koob had stopped in the grass. Her voice was shrill and tight. "It's better this way, Albertine. We're going to help you."

Albertine straightened, threw her shoulders back. Her father's hand was on her chest and shoulders lightening her wonderfully. Then on wings of her father's hands, on dead butterfly wings, Albertine lifted into the air and flew toward the others. The light powerful feeling swept her up the way she had floated higher, seeing the grass below. It was her father throwing her up into the air and out of danger. Her arms opened for bullets but no bullets came.

Harmony did not shoot. Instead, he raised his fist and brought it down hard on her head.

Albertine did not fall immediately, but stood in his arms a moment. Perhaps she gazed still farther back behind the covering of his face. Perhaps she was completely stunned and did not think as she sagged and fell. Her face rolled forward and hair covered her features, so it was impossible for Harmony to see with just what particular expression she gazed into the head-splitting wheel of light, or blackness, that overcame her.

Harmony turned the vehicle onto the gravel road that led back to town. He had convinced the other two that Albertine was more trouble than she was worth, and so they left her behind, and Lawrence too. He stood swearing in his cinder driveway as the car rolled out of sight. Buddy sat between the social worker and Officer Brackett. Vicki tried to hold Buddy fast and keep her arm down at the same time, for the words she'd screamed at Albertine had broken the seal of antiperspirant beneath her arms. She was sweating now as though she'd stored an ocean up inside of her. Sweat rolled down her back in a shallow river and pooled at her waist and between her breasts. A thin sheen of water came out on her forearms, her face. Vicki gave an irritated moan but Brackett seemed not to take notice, or take offense at least. Air-conditioned breezes were sweeping over the seat anyway, and very soon they would be comfortable. She smiled at Brackett over Buddy's head. The man grinned back. Buddy stirred. Vicki remembered the emergency chocolate bar she kept in her purse, fished it out, and offered it to Buddy. He did not react, so she closed his fingers over the package and peeled the paper off one end.

The car accelerated. Buddy felt the road and wheels pummeling each other and the rush of the heavy motor purring in high gear. Buddy knew that what he'd seen in his mind that morning, the thing coming out of the sky with barbs and chains, had hooked him. Somehow he was caught and held in the sour tin smell of the pale woman's armpit. Somehow he was pinned between their pounds of breathless flesh. He looked at the chocolate in his hand. He was squeezing the bar so hard that a thin brown trickle had melted down his arm. Automatically he put the bar in his mouth.

As he bit down he saw his mother very clearly, just as she had been when she carried him from the shed. She was stretched flat on the ground, on her stomach, and her arms were curled around her head as if in sleep. One leg was drawn up and it looked for all the world like she was running full tilt into the ground, as though she had been trying to pass into the earth, to bury herself, but at the last moment something had stopped her.

There was no blood on Albertine, but Buddy tasted blood now at the sight of her, for he bit down hard and cut his own lip. He ate the chocolate, every bit of it, tasting his mother's blood. And when he had the chocolate down inside him and all licked off his hands, he opened his mouth to say thank you to the woman, as his mother had taught him. But instead of a thank you coming out he was astonished to hear a great rattling scream, and then another, rip out of him like pieces of his own body and whirl onto the sharp things all around him.

Grace

VICKIE SEARS

I thought we were going to another farm because it was time for spring plant-ing. But the lady, she said, we were going to be her children. You know how it is grownups talk. You can't trust them for nothing. I just kept telling my brother that we best keep thinking of ourselves as orphans. Our parents got a divorce and we don't know where they are, so we need to keep our thinking straight and not get fooled by this lady. I don't care if her skin is brown just like us. That don't mean nothing.

I hear my brother dozing off and I want to shake him to wake up, but these people are driving this truck and they can hear everything I say anyhow, so I just let him sleep.

This is the second time we've been riding in this old beat-up green pickup. The first time they came and got us from the children's home, they took us down to Pioneer Square. I could see right away they was farm people by the truck having straw in the back and them not having real good clothes like they wear in the city. City people talk more, too. These people were real quiet right off. They answered the questions the orphanage people asked them but they didn't tell them much of anything. I guess I liked that some, but I wasn't going to tell them nothing about me. Who knew what they'd do? We never went nowheres before with brown people.

The man, he had on blue jeans and a flannel shirt and a jeans jacket. His hat was all sweaty and beat up like his long skinny face. His boots was old, too. I guessed they didn't have much money and were needing to get some kids to help them with their work. Probably we'd stay with them until harvest time and then go back to the orphanage. That happened before, so it didn't matter much anyhow.

The woman was old and skinny. She had hands that was all chewed up and fat at the knuckles and she kept rubbing them all the time. She had white hair with little bits of black ones popping out like they was sorry to be in there by themselves. She had a big nose like our daddy has, if he still is alive, that is. She and the man was brown and talked kind of like my daddy's mother, slow and not so much in English. These people, though, they talked English. They just didn't talk much.

When they said they was going to take us downtown, I thought they was going to take us to a tavern. That's where Mrs. Dopler, one of the orphanage housemothers, took me real late one night to show me where all the Indian women was and what kind of people they are, always being drunk and laying up with men. The woman said that that is all us Indian girls like to do, and I will be just like that, too, so I thought that's where these people would take us. But they didn't. They took us to dinner at this real nice place and let us have soda pop and even bought us a dessert. Me and brother both got us apple pie, with ice cream, all to ourselves.

I started thinking maybe these people was O.K., but a part inside me told me I best not get myself fooled. So I told them they wouldn't want us to live with them because my brother is a sissy and I'm a tomboy. The lady said, "We like tomboys, and Billie Jim looks like he is a strong boy. You both look just fine to us." Then, they took us to walk in the Square and we stopped by this totem pole. Mrs. Dopler told me that pole was a pretend God and that was wrong because God was up in heaven and Indian people was bad, especially the ones who made the pole. This lady, though, she said that the totem pole was to make a song about the dead people and animals, and that it was a good and beautiful thing. She had brother and me feel the inside of the pole. Like listening to its belly singing. I don't know what she meant by that, but the wood was nice. I liked better what she said about the pole.

We walked around for a while and then they took us back to the orphanage. The lady said they would come back, when all the paperwork was done, to get brother and me. I thought she was just talking big, so I said, "Sure," and me and brother went inside. We watched them drive away. I didn't think they would come back, but I thought about them being brown just like my daddy and aunts and uncles and brother and me. They were more brown than us, but I wondered if they were Indian. They didn't drink though, so maybe not.

We didn't see those people for a long time. Brother and me went to a big house to help clean for spring coming. I don't see why you clean a house so good just because the seasons change, but we done that anyway and then went back to the orphanage. I kept thinking on how nice those farmers were and how they might be Indians, but I didn't want to ask anybody about them. Maybe, if it was for real that they were going to come back for us, it would spoil it to ask about them. Seems like you don't ever get things just because you want them, so it's better not to ask.

Then, one day, one of the matrons tells me to find Billie Jim because there are some people come to visit.

My brother was up in a tree hiding from a couple of the big boys. First, I had to beat up Joey so's he would let Billie Jim come out the tree. We rolled in the dirt fighting, and I knew I was going to be in trouble because I was all dirty and there was blood on my face. I thought I would get whomped, too, for getting in a fight. I spit on my hand to try to clean up my face, but I could see by the matron's scowl that I didn't look so good. I pushed my brother in front of me because he was clean and maybe the people wouldn't see me so much. We went into the visiting room, and I saw it was those farmers whose names I didn't remember. They asked the director of the home if they could take us now. He said, "Yes. It's so nice to place these *special* children. I hope they'll be everything you want."

Then he reached out his hand, and the farmer brought his long arm out of his sleeve. The orphanage man pumped his arm up and down, but the farmer hold his still. It was funny to see. The woman, she barely touched the hand of the man. She was not smiling. I thought something was wrong, but I knew we were going with these people anyhow. I never cared much about where I went, long as the people didn't beat on us with sticks and big belts.

We didn't have to do nothing to get ready because we found our suitcases in the hall by the bottom of the stairs. The director, he gave brother and me our coats and said, "You be good children and perhaps we won't have to see you here again."

I wanted to tell him I didn't like him, but I just took brother's hand and we walked out the door.

The people stopped at lots of stores downtown, and then we went to lunch again.

"I asked them, "Do you use a stick or strap for spanking?"

The man said, "We don't believe in spanking."

Before I could say anything, Billie Jim pinched me under the table and I knew he had to go to the bathroom. So I said, "Excuse us," and we got up to leave. The lady, she asked Billie Jim, "Do you have to go to the bathroom?"

Brother just shook his head, and the woman said, "Paul, you take him."

They left, and I worried about Paul messing with Billie Jim. My stomach felt all like throw-up. When they came back I asked Billie Jim, in our secret way, if something happened. He whispered, "No."

I wondered if these people were going to be all right, but I kept on guard because grown-ups do weird things, all the time, when you never know they're going to.

After we ate, we walked and stopped at this drinking fountain what is a statue of Chief Sealth. Paul, he told us what a great man Sealth was, and Billie Jim asked, "You know him?"

Both Paul and the woman laughed, and Paul said, "No. He lived a long time ago. He's a stranger with a good heart."

Then the woman reached down to take my hand, but I didn't want her to get me, so I told her I had to take care on my brother and took Billie Jim's hand.

Then we were riding in this truck going to someplace I never heard of called Walla Walla. Grace, that's the lady's name, said they lived on a farm with chickens, pigs, a horse, and lots of things growing. She said we can have a place all our very own to grow things. When I sat down next to her, she let me ride by the window. I seen how my legs didn't touch the floor and how long hers were. She wasn't as long as her husband, but way bigger than me. She put my brother in her lap, where he went to sleep with his chubby fingers in her hand, but I stood guard just in case things got weird.

Paul said I should help him drive home by looking at the map so he'd know the roads he was going on. I thought that was dumb because I knew he came to the city lots and must know how to get hisself home. I went along with him, though. He seemed to be nice, and besides, it was easy for me. I can read real good cause I'm nine years old. I told him that and saw Grace is smiling. She's got wrinkles that come out the corners of her eyes and more that go down her cheeks. She has on a smelly powder that reminds me of cookies. She says there are lots of other children on neighbors' farms, and that they have grandchildren who always visit them. I guessed I would have to do a mess of babysitting.

It's a long, long ways to where they live, and I couldn't stay awake the whole time. I woke up when Grace said, "Come on, sleepyheads. It's time to go to bed."

She gave my brother to Paul to carry, but I walked by myself; up one step into the house. We went through the kitchen and climbed some stairs to the second floor. She asked me if I had to go to the bathroom and I said, "Yes." She showed me it and then closed the door. That was funny because she didn't stay. After awhile she came to knock and say, "There's a nightgown on your bed. I'll show you where you'll sleep."

She took me to a room with only one bed with nobody else in it. I asked her, "Where's brother going to sleep?"

Grace tried to take my hand to go with her, but I put it behind my back and followed her. She led me down the hall to a room where Billie Jim was already in a bed, all by hisself, sound to sleep. Then we went to a room Grace said was for her and Paul, and she said I could come there if I was scared or having a bad dream.

I told her, "I don't never have bad dreams and can take care on myself."

She asked me, "May I help you with your nightgown?"

Then I knew she was going to do bad things like the orphanage woman and I wanted to grab Billie Jim and run, but I didn't know where I was. I started to back down to where she said to sleep and she said, "It's all right if you don't want any help. Have a good sleep."

She went into her room, and I watched until she closed the door. There was a lamp beside the bed. I slept with it on.

The first thing I did the next morning was check on Billie Jim. I asked him if they messed with him, and he told me no again. Nobody came into the room I was in either. We got dressed together and then went downstairs. Paul and Grace were already up and at the breakfast table.

Grace asked, "What would you like for breakfast? Pancakes or bacon and eggs?"

Billie Jim said, "We can pick?"

"Sure," Grace said. "All you have to do is to wash your face and hands before coming to table. Can't have you start the day with a dirty face."

We looked on each other and saw we was dirty.

Grace said, "There's a pump here, if you want, or you can go upstairs to the bathroom."

We wanted to use that red pump with the very high handle. I tried to make it give water, but Grace thought she had to help push it down. She put her hand over mine, but I moved mine. She smiled, so I let her pump the water into a tin basin and give me a big brown bar of soap. She said she made it out of pig fat. It smelled icky but made lots of bubbles.

After we ate, Paul said, "Come on, kids. I'll introduce you to our animal friends."

He put on his hat and opened the green screen door. There wasn't no grass nowhere. Just dirt, except where there was tall stuff growing. Paul told us it was alfalfa and wheat and that it got really high before you cut it. He took us into the barn to show us Henry, who was this old horse that lived there forever.

Out back of the barn was a pen with big fat pigs and a mommy one with some babies. I didn't like them much, but Billie Jim asked if he could touch them and Paul said, "Sure." Billie Jim went into the pen, and one of them pigs ran after him. Then Billie Jim screamed, the pig pushed him up against the barn wall, and Paul had to chase the pig away. Billie Jim done good, though, and didn't even cry.

Paul walked us to the chicken house and showed us Rhode Island Reds and Bantams. He taught us how to fill a basket with eggs by taking them out from under the chickens. I thought the chickens was mean because they tried to bite us. Paul laughed and said as how it would get easier to do. Then we met the cows. Paul tried to teach us to milk them. I couldn't make nothing come out, though Billie Jim got a little. The warm milk tasted icky. We walked all over the place that morning and then we got to ride on a tractor with Paul for a long time.

I was sleepy, but Billie Jim, he wanted to do more things, so we went down to this wooden bridge that went over this river that Paul showed to us. He said we should be very careful not to fall into the river because it was very fast and we would be drowned.

Down to the bridge I laid on my belly, and Billie Jim was on his, and we poked at knotholes in the wood. The water was so fast it went around and around while it was going all wavery at the same time. When we put sticks through the knotholes, the water would just pull them right away like it was never going to get fed another stick. We did that a long time until we heard Grace calling us to lunch.

At the lunch table I asked, "When will we start doing the work we came to do?"

Paul and Grace looked on each other as though I had asked something stupid, and then they smiled.

Paul said, "You came to live with us to be just like one of our own children. You will have lots of time to play and go to school. You'll have some chores because everybody on a farm has to work. One of you will help feed the chickens. One of you can care for the pigs. You can both help with Henry, and there'll be times when you can ride Henry, all by yourselves, into the woods or across the fields, after you learn to ride. Other times we'll all go to town or picnics or powwows or rodeos. Everybody has to have time to play. That's the way it is."

Then Grace said, "I'll teach you how to sew and can and cook, Jodi Ann. You and I will go on special walks and plant a garden together. You, too, Billie Jim, if you want. I want us to be friends and happy together."

I heard everything they had to say, but I was waiting, anyway, for the strange things I was sure they would do. I meant to keep my ears and eyes open just in case we needed to run somewheres.

About three days after going to their house, Grace tells us, at the breakfast table, "Today is a good day to plant the garden. What would you like to grow, Billie Jim?"

"Potatoes and rhubarb!" he says, all excited.

Then she asks me and I said, "Carrots and string beans, ma'am, because they're orange and green. It'd be pretty."

She patted my shoulder and said, "Yes, it would be lovely. It's nice you can see that, Jodi."

I put my head down so she wouldn't see me smile.

Grace got this basket with lots of little envelopes and told us, "Come on."

We went outside, round to the side of the house. Paul was waiting, sitting on his tractor. He said, "It's all turned over for you."

Grace said, "Thank you, Paul," to him, and to us she said, "Here's two places for each of you. I'll walk to the other end."

She moved to her place, going down to the ground on her knees and hands. Billie Jim and me just stood there because we never planted nothing before. She gave us some envelopes that shook with stuff, but they didn't mean nothing to us. Grace saw us standing and asked, "Have you kids ever planted things?"

We shook no, so she came over and give us little shovels, like spoons, and took hers and made a hole and put in a seed and covered over dirt. Then she put water on the place. She said, "You just do it like that, all in rows. Then you put the envelope on a stick here at the back of where you're planting. Then we wait for the rain and sunshine to help them grow."

She patted brother on the hand and went back to where she was working.

We spent a long lime doing gardening. The dirt felt good, like stored-up rain smells. We ate lunch by the garden, and Grace said, "I think we deserve a walk. Let's go down by the river, kids."

Down to the river, Grace showed us different plants and birds. She knew a lot about birds. She told us the songs by making whistles through her teeth. She tried to show us to do whistles with grass between her thumbs, but I think my teeth weren't big enough. Billie Jim didn't have a tooth in the front, so he couldn't do it either. She showed us these grasses, too, that she said made baskets, and we picked some. When we got back to the house, she put them in a big round pan, like for taking baths, and filled it up with water. That night she bit some grass apart with her teeth and showed me how to weave them in a basket. She thought I didn't know how to do this, but my grandmother already showed me before. I forgot some, though, and my basket wasn't so good. She said, "You'll get better."

Grace read a story to us, then Billie Jim and me went to bed. When I was going to sleep, I thought on her telling about the birds.

One morning time I woke up extra early. The house was all quiet, and I thought to go see some birds. I got dressed and went, real soft, down the stairs. I stopped on hearing noises in the kitchen. I crept up to the door and saw Grace putting water in the coffee pot, then poking embers in the stove. She went back to the sink and stood in the new sun coming in the window. She took one hand in the other and rubbed her swollen-up knuckles and all slow up and down her fingers. She put some stuff, what smelled like Vicks, on her hands and slow-rubbed her knuckles. Then she opened and closed her hands over and over and rubbed more. Grace looked out the window the whole time, making a little smile while she was rubbing on her fingers. It seemed like she done that lots of times before, so I stood still. I didn't want her to see me because the sun was nice on her skin and shining in her hair, kind of like baby rainbows. I just wanted to watch. I did that for a while, then made sounds like I was first coming down the stairs.

Grace said, "You're up very early, Jodi."

I said, "I wanted to go see birds and stuff."

She said, "If you want to come with me, I'll show you something magic."

She reached out her hand, but I put both arms behind my back and took hold of my own hands. She smiled and opened the door.

"We'll take a walk over to the alfalfa. I want to show you some colors."

We walked between the wheat and alfalfa, the air swollen up with their sweetness. Grace pulled down a piece of alfalfa and said, "Smell."

It was all sharp and tickled inside my nose, kinda like medicine. It had dew on it, and the wetness landed on my cheek. Grace got some on her nose. I wanted to touch it but didn't.

Grace said, "See the different colors?"

She ran a finger down the alfalfa, and I saw there was places where it was real dark, then lighter, then sorta like limes are colored. I always thought it was all one color but I was fooled. Grace did the same thing with the wheat and said, "And here's something else that's wonderful. Look what happens when the sun comes to the plants."

Grace moved them around and I saw that the light changed the colors too. It's almost like you can look right through them.

She said, "If we come back at lunch and suppertime, when the sun has gone, they'll be different again. Do you want to?"

"Yeah!" I answered.

"O.K.," she said. "It's just for you and me though, Jodi."

Grace told me about the red-winged blackbird, what I never saw before, while we went back to the house.

Later, Grace called me, and we went to see the colors again. They were changed. This time I saw, too, the little hairs each one had, what makes a wheat kernel, all full of lines and different parts just like people.

Then Grace said we had to get a chicken for dinner. In the chicken yard there was chickens scratching at the ground and picking in it for bugs. Their heads bobbed up and down and jerked from side to side. It was funny to watch them. All of a sudden, they ran to the coop. I didn't see no reason for it, but Grace pointed up in the sky and told me, "They see the shadow of the hawk. They're afraid and hide because they know hawks like to eat chickens."

The hawk circled awhile but finally went away, and the chickens came back into the yard, scratching and clucking like nothing ever happened. Grace walked around looking at all the birds and finally spied one she liked. She chased it until she caught both the wings flat, with the chicken squawking the whole time we was walking to the clearing between the barn and house, to a stump where I had seen Paul split the kindling. Grace said, "You hold the chicken by the feet and give it a quick, clean cut with the ax. Do you want to try it?"

I didn't never think on killing nothing to eat and didn't want to do it. I remembered the wild kitten I made friends with out in the tall grass back at the orphanage. I thought about how one of the orphanage matrons killed the kitten and hung it round my neck and told everybody I killed it. All day I had to wear the kitty, but I didn't cry. I just pretended like the kitty never was important. Now Grace wanted me to kill the chicken, and I didn't want to. I tried to back away, only she said, "I know you are strong enough to do this, Jodi."

She stuck out the handle to the hatchet, but I couldn't take it. I shook my head no and said, real quiet, "I don't want to, ma'am."

I backed up more and she said, "Well, we need supper. You watch and perhaps you'll be able to do it the next time."

Grace took that chicken and held it on the chopping block and chopped off the head so quick I almost didn't see her do it. I jumped back when the blood went flying everywhere, all hot-smelling in the sun and making dark plops in the pale dust. She let the chicken go. There wasn't no noise except chicken toenails scratching in the dry, hard dirt and wings trying to fly when the chicken ran around and around. I didn't want to see it do that, but it was hard to stop looking. It ran circles whole bunches of times and then fell down, sort of jerking, till it stopped. That's when I looked at the head. Its eyes were like kitty's and my stomach felt like throw-up. I wanted to run. Grace pulled out a big piece of string from her apron pocket, and I knew it was going to be just like before with Mrs. Dopler. Grace said, "Jodi, come on over. We'll tie the chicken upside down and take off the feathers."

But I couldn't go near her. I yelled, "No!" and ran into the barn. I climbed the ladder and went behind some hay and pulled it all over me till nobody could see me and stayed real quiet. I sucked in air and didn't give it back. Grace came and called out, "Jodi, I'm sorry if I scared you. It's all right if you don't want to help. Jodi? You don't have to hide. It's all right."

But I was thinking on how I told a grownup no and didn't do what she said. I knew I was going to get whipped. Paul and Grace would send me and brother back because I was bad. Billie Jim was going to be all mad with me because we had to leave. Didn't nobody want to keep us if I'm bad. Brother and me most always went to places together.

I stayed in the hayloft a long time. Then I heard Paul and brother calling me. They was yelling it was suppertime like nothing was wrong. I peeked through the slats of the door to the hayloft and saw Grace standing in the kitchen doorway. She didn't look mad. Paul and Billie Jim were holding hands, walking toward the fields, calling my name. Grace looked up to the barn like she knew I was there and started out to the barn.

I heard her shoes scrape on the rocks in the barn doorway when she stopped walking. She said, "Hello, old Henry. You need some water, friend?"

The bucket handle squeaked and there was walking. The yard pump handle went crank-crank-crank, and then water gushed into the bucket. Footsteps came back, and there was a horse tongue slurping, like Henry was real thirsty.

Grace said, "You know, Henry, when I was little, I used to do some of my best thinking sitting in the grass up on a hill behind my house. I guess the best place now would be up in the hayloft. It's the most like a grassy hill right around here."

Then I heard the dry snaps of weighted wood as Grace bent the ladder steps coming up. She was puffing a little when she reached the loft ledge and climbed over. I peeked out the hay and saw her dangling her legs and making a hum.

"Yes sir, Henry, old friend," says Grace, "this feels almost like my hill. If I were little and scared, this might be the right place to come think. I guess I'd know I was in just about the safest place in the world. Everything would be all right up here. After I had things all sorted out, I could come down and run on home to momma and know she loved me, no matter what."

That was the most I ever heard Grace say at one mouthful of talking. I still didn't make noise, though. She was talking true talk but she was still a grownup. She sat there awhile, swinging her legs and humming. Then she said, "Well, Henry, guess I'll go into the house. I'm getting cold and hungry."

Grace climbed down, and I saw her go to the screen door. She stopped and called out in a loud voice, "Jo-o-o-d-d-i-i!" She waited a little bit, then went in the house.

I wanted to think nothing was going to happen, but I knew I was going to get whomped. I had been spending most of the day in the barn but couldn't think on nothing to do, except face the punishment. I went down the ladder and out the barn. I peeked around the corner of the parlor window. Billie Jim was listening to Charlie McCarthy on the radio. He was sitting in Paul's lap while Paul read the paper. Grace was rocking in her chair, knitting. She looked like my grandmother, except my grandmother is short. I missed my grandmother. Only thinking on her won't do no good, so I went around to the back door and slammed it real loud when I came into the house, and marched right to the living room. Billie Jim jumped up and ran to me and said, "You made us real worried. Where was you?"

He grabbed my arm, but I pulled away and said, "I don't know why you was worried. I was only up to the top of this grassy hill what I found, thinking about things."

Grace put down her knitting and looked at me. I felt my heart running fast when she looked at Paul. He looked back on her for a little, then said, "Was it a nice hill, Jodi?"

I knew I couldn't say no more lies without making spit in my mouth because my throat was all dried up and my tongue would stick and not make words, so I just shrug a shoulder. Grace stood up and started coming toward me. I figured to stay where I was to take the hit. I was getting ready. Instead, she said, "I'm glad you're home. Now we can eat supper. I hope you had a nice adventure."

She reached me, and my body was stiff with waiting, but her arms was out like she was going to hug me. I didn't back down, and she closed her arms around me and hugged. I just stood there, still stiff. Then she bent down to whisper in my ear, "You've got straw in your hair, Jodi." She patted me on the shoulder, and we went to the kitchen.

While she was putting food on the platters, Grace said, "Jodi told me she doesn't like fried chicken much, so she doesn't have to eat any if she doesn't want. We even have two nice pork chops here, with mint jelly, in case Jodi would rather not eat the chicken."

She turned around with a platter filled up with chicken, and on the end was the pork chops. They tasted good with jelly. We never got that in the orphanage.

I watched Grace real good the rest of the time before bed, but she never said nothing about the chicken or me not being good. She never said nothing about it ever again.

The April we came in turned into July, with everybody just doing their work and playing, too.

We met Jim and Sara and Crystal, Paul and Grace's kids. Between them three they had twelve kids. Sometimes, everybody came over at once—cousins and other people, too. Lots of times we cooked outside, and sometimes we ate things that we growed in the garden. It was just like at our daddy's house a long time before, except there weren't no grandparents because Grace and Paul were the grandmother and grandfather. Their parents was dead.

We did lots of things together. Paul taught brother to fish and both of us to swim. When brother and him went away for fishing, Grace and me did beading. She showed me how to do beads in a circle. We made lots of things to take to powwows. I sold one I made, but Grace sold lots. I made two baskets I liked but I kept them. We went to a powwow over to the reservation and one at White Swan and down to Oregon. Everybody in the family went, in all the trucks, lined up on the highways, and we all stopped together to eat.

One day, Paul said to Grace, "Their hair is long enough now. I guess it's time."

Billie Jim looked at me across the table and motioned at me to come with him. He took his short legs up the stairs to the bathroom as fast as he could, and said, "Hurry up, Jodi."

He left the door barely open enough for me to squeeze in after him, then slammed and locked it.

He whisper-yells, "They're gonna cut our hair, Jodi! Don't let 'em do it. Please make 'em not do it, Jodi!"

I asked him, "How come you think they're going to do that, Billie Jim? This ain't the orphanage. They won't cut it off like there. Grace and Paul and everybody, almost, gots long hair."

"But Jodi Ann, didn't you listen when Paul said it was long enough. It means a cutting."

I started to say more, but Paul called to us. "Come on downstairs, kids, and meet us outside."

We went downstairs and out the door and walked slow to where Grace was standing. She had her hands behind her back. Paul was rolling a big log from the woodpile toward where the chopping block was. Paul set the log up like the block and said, "O.K., kids, we have a surprise for you. Take your seats and face each other."

My stomach was sick, and I started to think Billie Jim might be right. After we sat down I looked on Billie Jim and knew how much of a little kid he was and how I was supposed to take care on him, but it felt like the best thing was to run away.

Grace stood by me, and Paul was by Billie Jim. Paul said, "O.K., Grace, count with me. Ready? One, two, three, now. Surprise!"

When they yelled surprise, all their arms go up, and I jumped and grabbed Billie Jim, pulling him off the log, and we ran backward.

Grace said, "Wait, Jodi! Look."

In each of their hands were ribbons, streaming out in the breeze.

Paul said, "It's time to teach you how to braid your hair. Come on over."

We walked over, still holding hands, and all that got said was when Paul said, "O.K., now Jodi, you watch me while I do Billie Jim. Then, Billie Jim can watch Grace and you."

They slowly weaved the ribbons in the shiny black of our hair. In and out go hair and ribbon until the end, when there was just enough to tie the braid tight. We did it to each other until we were real good at it, and sometimes Paul and Grace let us braid their hair. We all went to the next family picnic with ribbon braids.

Paul showed us how to ride and take care of Henry, too. We went lots of places all by ourselves on Henry. He never went too fast, but sometimes he tried to scrape us off on trees. He also liked to go through the barn door with the top part closed. Once he knocked me off and I didn't want to ride no more, but Grace said I got to because Henry would think he won something and wouldn't let me ever ride him again. We brought the box for me to stand on, and I got back up.

I got to spend lots of time with Grace. Many mornings I watched her doing her finger rubs while seeing the morning coming as I peeked around the doorway. We went on walks together, and she taught me about flowers and birds. Usually, most times just her and me went, but sometimes we let brother come. I even let her hold my hand sometimes because it seemed like the bumps in her fingers felt better when I did. Least she always smiled. She didn't squeeze my hand or put it in her tee-tee. She didn't never put her fingers in my tee-tee either, or play with Billie Jim's pee-pee. Neither did Paul. Brother and me both liked that.

One day, Billie Jim and me was brushing Henry when Grace yelled, "Oh, Jodi and Billie Jim. Come see what Pickles is doing."

We ran to the other side of the barn by the door where hay was stacked. There was a big pile not in a bale, so Billie Jim and me could feed the cows and Henry, and there, in the middle of the pile, was Pickles, the cat. She was laying on Paul's bathrobe, sort of all crookedly on her side, making strange noises. Rufus the dog was sitting by her, and sometimes Pickles hissed at him when he stuck his nose near her. That was funny to see cause they were friends.

I asked Grace, "What's the matter with Pickles?"

Billie Jim said, "She's sick, you dummy."

I wanted to pinch him, but Grace took our hands, pulling us into the straw. She said, "You watch. Something amazing is going to happen. Pickles is having babies."

We sat forever, but nothing happened except Grace talked real slow and stroked Pickles. Pickles made funny noises and her stomach swelled up and down and moved and she licked her bottom, but that's all. The screen door banged, and Billie Jim jumped up, yelling, "I'm gonna get Paul!"

When he was gone, Grace asked, "What are you thinking, Jodi?"

I said, "I don't see how Pickles can make babies, and besides, it's boring."

Grace pulled me up to her lap and told me about how the babies got inside and growed, and I thought it was icky. She said, "It takes a long time and lots of hard work to make something as special as a baby. Someday you might want to do it. Here, you pet Pickles, too."

It felt good in Grace's lap, and we stuck our arms out at the same time to pet Pickles.

Just about then we heard a squishy noise with a grunt from Pickles. This icky stuff came squirting out and Pickles acted like she couldn't get no air. She was panting, and then this kitten popped out in a white sack and Pickles bit it open and ate it up and licked the sticky stuff off the kitten. I heard what Grace said but was thinking on not having no babies if I have to do that.

Billie Jim came back with Paul, and Paul said, "Aa-a-y, that's where my bathrobe went. I couldn't find it this morning. You're doing a nice job, Pickles." He pats her head, and she meows to him.

Grace said, "Paul, you take Billie Jim for a walk and tell him some things."

Paul said, "We did that before we came out, Grace."

He put his arm on Billie Jim's shoulder, and my brother was smiling like he was all full up with something nobody ever knew before.

Paul said, "Let's all sit down together here."

All of us watched Pickles have two more kittens and then Grace said, "Well, it's time to give our new momma a rest. Billie Jim, you bring her some water. Jodi, you run get an egg and put it into a bowl. Rufus, you come inside with me before you get your nose scratched."

Billie Jim and me came and went lots of times to see Pickles that night. The kittens were crawling on Pickles' tummy and pushing for milk and making soft cries while Pickles was licking their fur all soft and clean. Grace was right that they were beautiful.

In August, everybody in the family came around everyday for the harvest. It was real hard work. Brother and me helped too, but mostly the grownups did it. Grace and Sara and me cooked lots. Outside the air was pale green and sort of fuzzy with little pieces of the cutted stuff filling the wind. It smelled clean and wet even though days were hot. I liked it except it made me sneeze. Grace said, "It's best if you stay inside, Jodi, and help with cooking. You can make your biscuits."

I made good biscuits. We all worked really hard.

One harvest day, it was after a big rain in the night, Billie Jim and me were playing Huckleberry Finn on these boards we made into a raft in a pond at the bend of the road. All of a sudden there was this high, screaming sound and a long white ambulance coming down our road. It went by us fast, making mud fly all over. We ran after it, up to the house. Jim said, "Stay back, kids. Give them room."

Some men went into the house and came back with Paul sleeping in this bed they carried. Paul had a thing on his face with a bag going in and out like wind. Grace came behind him, and she looked like she was going to throw up. They speeded away. Everybody else got in the green truck, and we went to the hospital where we sat in a hall. Then came a medicine man who sang songs with his rattle, but the nurse people made him sit in the hall, too. He didn't care, though. He still sang real soft, and whenever there wasn't no nurse around, he went back in the room. After a long time, a doctor came to say, "Each of you can go in, two at a time." Then he went away.

Sara took me in, and I see Grace was looking really sad. I look on Paul and knew he was dead. His skin felt all cold and he didn't have no smile. I couldn't think on what it meant. I wanted Grace to make it not be, but she just patted my hand. I wanted to hold hers, but she didn't do nothing but pat me.

A long time later, we went back to the house with Sara. Grace didn't come home for three days. When she saw brother and me, she said, "Come into the living room, children. I need to talk with you."

Me and Billie Jim went in, and Sara and Jim and Crystal were there too. Everybody was all quiet.

Grace said, "In a little while the county car will be here to pick you up because you are going back to the orphanage. They say I'm too old to keep you children by myself. I told them we would be fine together, but they tell me a woman alone isn't enough. So you have to go."

Billie Jim asked, "Didn't we do enough work?"

I pinched him and he yelped. Grace took my hand and Billie Jim's too. Then she said, "You're wonderful children, but they won't let you stay. You be strong, and make us all proud of you."

I wanted to run, but I didn't know how come.

Then Grace said, "Let Sara and Crystal help you while I rest here."

Nobody said nothing while we packed up. I saw a car coming what had writing on it. It was the kind that most always takes and gets us from foster homes. It stopped, and the driver started honking. Billie Jim and me didn't walk too fast going downstairs, but didn't no one say we were bad because we were slow. Everybody walked by us to say a good-bye except Grace. She took our hands to go out the back door.

"You be good children," she said to us. "Listen to the Creator like Paul told you and you'll stay strong."

Grace took Billie Jim in a hug and kissed him. He squeezed her neck, and I saw he was crying, but he didn't make no noise. Then she took both my hands. I looked on her big brown knuckles and didn't want to leave watching her in the sun. She hugged me real hard, and I hugged her, too. We didn't say nothing.

The county man put us in the back seat and started to drive, right away. We both got up on our knees to see out the back window, but the man yelled to us, "Sit down," so we did and we couldn't see nobody until we went over the bridge and turned onto the highway. Then we saw Grace, still standing by the door, waving. Billie Jim and me held hands to wave back.

Reading

Ruth's Song

(Because She Could Not Sing It)

GLORIA STEINEM

Happy or unhappy, families are all mysterious. We have only to imagine how differently we would be described—and will be, after our deaths—by each of the family members who believe they know us. The only question is, Why are some mysteries more important than others?

The fate of my Uncle Ed was a mystery of importance in our family. We lavished years of speculation on his transformation from a brilliant young electrical engineer to the town handyman. What could have changed this elegant, Lincolnesque student voted "Best Dressed" by his classmates to the gaunt, unshaven man I remember? Why did he leave a young son and a first wife of the "proper" class and religion, marry a much less educated woman of the "wrong" religion, and raise a second family in a house near an abandoned airstrip; a house whose walls were patched with metal signs to stop the wind? Why did he never talk about his transformation?

For years, I assumed that some secret and dramatic events of a year he spent in Alaska had made the difference. Then I discovered that the trip had come after his change and probably had been made because of it. Strangers he worked for as a much-loved handyman talked about him as one more tragedy of the Depression, and it was true that Uncle Ed's father, my paternal grandfather, had lost his money in the stockmarket Crash and died of (depending on who was telling the story) pneumonia or a broken heart. But the Crash of 1929 also had come long after Uncle Ed's transformation. Another theory was that he was afflicted with a mental problem that lasted most of his life, yet he was supremely competent at his work, led an independent life, and asked for help from no one.

Perhaps he had fallen under the spell of a radical professor in the early days of the century, the height of this country's romance with socialism and anarchism. That was the theory of an uncle on my mother's side. I do remember that no matter how much Uncle Ed needed money, he would charge no more for his work than materials plus 10 percent, and I never saw him in anything other than ancient boots and overalls held up with strategic safety pins. Was he really trying to replace socialism-in-one-country with socialism-in-one-man? If so, why did my grandmother, a woman who herself had run for the school board in coalition with anarchists and socialists, mistrust his judgment so much that she left his share of her estate in trust, even though he was over fifty when she died? And why did Uncle Ed seem uninterested in all other political words and acts? Was it true instead that, as another relative insisted, Uncle Ed had chosen poverty to disprove the myths of Jews and money?

Years after my uncle's death, I asked a son in his second family if he had the key to this family mystery. No, he said. He had never known his father any other way. For that cousin, there had been no question. For the rest of us, there was to be no answer.

For many years I also never imagined my mother any other way than the person she had become before I was born. She was just a fact of life when I was growing up, someone to be worried about and cared for; an invalid who lay in bed with eyes closed and lips moving in occasional response to voices only she could hear; a woman to whom I brought an endless stream of toast and coffee, bologna sandwiches and dime pies, in a child's version of what meals should be. She was a loving, intelligent, terrorized woman who tried hard to clean our littered house whenever she emerged from her private world, but who could rarely be counted on to finish one task. In many ways, our roles were reversed: I was the mother and she was the child. Yet that didn't help her, for she still worried about me with all the intensity of a frightened mother, plus the special fears of her own world full of threats and hostile voices.

Even then I suppose I must have known that, years before she was thirty-five and I was born, she had been a spirited, adventurous young woman who struggled out of a working-class family and into college, who found work she loved and continued to do, even after she was married and my older sister was there to be cared for. Certainly, our immediate family and nearby relatives, of whom I was by far the youngest, must have remembered her life as a whole and functioning person. She was thirty before she gave up her own career to help my father run the Michigan summer resort that was the most practical of his many dreams, and she worked hard there as everything from bookkeeper to bar manager. The family must have watched this energetic, fun-loving, book-loving woman turn into someone who was afraid to be alone, who could not hang on to reality long enough to hold a job, and who could rarely concentrate enough to read a book.

Yet I don't remember any family speculation about the mystery of my mother's transformation. To the kind ones and those who liked her, this new Ruth was simply a sad event, perhaps a mental case, a family problem to be accepted and cared for until some natural process made her better. To the less kind, or those who had resented her earlier independence, she was a willful failure, someone who lived in a filthy house, a woman who simply would not pull herself together.

Unlike the case of my Uncle Ed, exterior events were never suggested as reason enough for her problems. Giving up her own career was never cited as her personal parallel of the Depression. (Nor was there discussion of the Depression itself, though my mother, like millions of others, had made potato soup and cut up blankets to make my sister's winter clothes.) Her fears of dependence and poverty were no match for my uncle's possible political beliefs. The real influence of newspaper editors who had praised her reporting was not taken as seriously as the possible influence of one radical professor.

Even the explanation of mental illness seemed to contain more personal fault when applied to my mother. She had suffered her first "nervous breakdown," as she and everyone else called it, before I was born and when my sister was about five. It followed years of trying to take care of a baby, be the wife of a kind but financially irresponsible man with show-business dreams, and still keep her much-loved, exhausting job at the newspaper. After many months in a sanitarium, she was pronounced recovered. That is, she was able to take care of my sister again, to move away from the city and the job she loved, and to work with my father at the isolated rural lake in Michigan he was trying to transform into a resort worthy of the big dance bands of the 1930s.

But she was never again completely without the spells of depression, anxiety, and visions into some other world that eventually were to turn her into the nonperson I remember. And she was never again without a bottle of dark, acrid-smelling liquid she called "Doc Howard's medicine": a solution of chloral hydrate that I later learned was the main ingredient in "Mickey Finns" or "knockout drops," and that probably made my mother and her doctor the pioneers of modern tranquilizers. Though friends and relatives saw this medicine as one more evidence of weakness and indulgence, to me it always seemed an embarrassing but necessary evil. It slurred her speech and slowed her coordination, making our neighbors and my school friends believe she was a drunk. But without it, she would not sleep for days, even a week at a time, and her feverish eyes began to see only that private world in which wars and hostile voices threatened the people she loved.

Because my parents had divorced and my sister was working in a faraway city, my mother and I were alone together then, living off the meager fixed income that my mother got from leasing her share of the remaining land in Michigan. I remember a long Thanksgiving weekend spent hanging on to her with one hand and holding my eighth-grade assignment of *A Tale of Two Cities* in the other hand, because the war outside our house was so real to my mother that she had plunged her hand through a window, badly cutting her arm in an effort to help us escape. Only when she finally agreed to swallow the medicine could she sleep, and only then could I end the terrible calm that comes with crisis and admit to myself how afraid I had been.

No wonder that no relative in my memory challenged the doctor who prescribed this medicine, or asked if some of her suffering and hallucinating might be due to overdose or withdrawal, or even consulted another doctor about its use. It was our relief as well as hers.

But why was she never returned even to that first sanitarium? Or to help that might come from other doctors? It's hard to say. Partly, it was her own fear of returning. Partly, it was too little money, and a family's not-unusual assumption that mental illness is an inevitable part of someone's personality. Or perhaps other family members had feared something like my experience when, one hot and desperate summer between the sixth and seventh grade, I finally persuaded her to let me take her to the only doctor from those sanitarium days whom she remembered without fear.

Yes, this brusque old man told me after talking to my abstracted, timid mother for twenty minutes: she definitely belongs in a state hospital. She should be put there right away. But even at that age, *Life* magazine and news-paper exposés had told me what horrors went on inside those hospitals. As-suming there to be no alternative, I took her home and never tried again.

In retrospect, perhaps the biggest reason my mother was cared for but not helped for twenty years was the simplest: her functioning was not that neces-sary to the world. Like women alcoholics who drink in their kitchens while costly programs are constructed for executives who drink, or like the home-makers subdued with tranquilizers while male patients get therapy and per-sonal attention instead, my mother was not an important worker. She was not even the caretaker of a very young child, as she had been when she was hospi-talized the first time. My father had patiently brought home the groceries and kept our odd household going until I was eight or so and my sister went away to college. Two years later when wartime gas rationing closed his summer re-sort and he had to travel to buy and sell in summer as well as winter, he said: How can I travel and take care of your mother? How can I make a living? He was right. It was impossible to do both. I did not blame him for leaving once I was old enough to be the bringer of meals and answerer of my mother's ques-tions. ("Has your sister been killed in a car crash?" "Are there German soldiers outside?") I replaced my father; my mother was left with one more person to maintain a sad status quo, and the world went on undisturbed.

That's why our lives, my mother's from forty-six to fifty-three, and my own from ten to seventeen, were spent alone together. There was one sane winter in a house we rented to be near my sister's college in Massachusetts, then one bad summer we spent house-sitting in suburbia while my mother hallucinated and my sister struggled to hold down a summer job in New York. But the rest of those years were lived in Toledo where both my mother and father had been born, and on whose city newspapers an earlier Ruth had worked.

First we moved into a basement apartment in a good neighborhood. In those rooms behind a furnace, I made one last stab at being a child. By pretend-ing to be much sicker with a cold than I really was, I hoped my mother would suddenly turn into a sane and cheerful woman bringing me chicken soup a la Hollywood. Of course, she could not. It only made her feel worse that she could not. I stopped pretending.

But for most of those years, we lived in the upstairs of the house my mother had grown up in and that her parents left her—a deteriorating farmhouse engulfed by the city, with poor but newer houses stacked against it and a major highway a few feet from its sagging porch. For a while, we could rent the two downstairs apartments to a newlywed factory-working couple and a local butcher's family. Later, the health department condemned our ancient furnace for the final time, sealing it so tight that even my resourceful Uncle Ed couldn't produce illegal heat.

In that house, I remember:

. . . lying in the bed my mother and I shared for warmth, listening on the early morning radio to the royal wedding of Princess Elizabeth and Prince Philip being broadcast live, while we tried to ignore and thus protect each other from the unmistakable sounds of the factory worker downstairs beating up and locking out his pregnant wife.

. . . hanging paper drapes I had bought in the dime store; stacking books and papers in the shape of two armchairs and covering them with blankets; evolving my own dishwashing system (I waited until all the dishes were dirty, then put them in the bathtub); and listening to my mother's high praise for these housekeeping efforts to bring order from chaos, though in retrospect I think they probably depressed her further.

. . . coming back from one of the Eagles' Club shows where I and other veterans of a local tap-dancing school made ten dollars a night for two shows, and finding my mother waiting with a flashlight and no coat in the dark cold of the bus stop, worried about my safety walking home.

. . . in a good period, when my mother's native adventurousness came through, answering a classified ad together for an amateur acting troupe that performed biblical dramas in churches, and doing several very corny performances of *Noah's Ark* while my proud mother shook metal sheets backstage to make thunder.

. . . on a hot summer night, being bitten by one of the rats that shared our house and its back alley. It was a terrifying night that turned into a touching one when my mother, summoning courage from some unknown reservoir of love, became a calm, comforting parent who took me to a hospital emergency room despite her terror at leaving home.

. . . coming home from a local library with the three books a week into which I regularly escaped, and discovering for once that there was no need to escape. My mother was calmly planting hollyhocks in the vacant lot next door.

But there were also times when she woke in the early winter dark, too frightened and disoriented to remember that I was at my usual after-school job, and so called the police to find me. Humiliated in front of my friends by sirens and policemen, I would yell at her—and she would bow her head in fear and say, "I'm sorry, I'm sorry, I'm sorry," just as she had done so often when my otherwise-kindhearted father had yelled at her in frustration. Perhaps the worst thing about suffering is that it finally hardens the hearts of those around it.

And there were many, many times when I badgered her until her shaking hands had written a small check to cash at the corner grocery and I could leave her alone while I escaped to the winter comfort of well-heated dime stores that smelled of fresh doughnuts, or to summer air-conditioned movies that were windows on a very different world.

But my ultimate protection was this: I was just passing through, a guest in the house; perhaps this wasn't my mother at all. Though I knew very well that I was her daughter, I sometimes imagined that I had been adopted and that my real parents would find me, a fantasy I've since discovered is common. (If children wrote more and grown-ups less, being adopted might be seen not only as a fear but also as a hope.) Certainly, I didn't mourn the wasted life of this woman who was scarcely older than I am now. I worried only about the times when she got worse.

Pity takes distance and a certainty of surviving. It was only after our house was bought for demolition by the church next door, and after my sister had performed the miracle of persuading my father to give me a carefree time before college by taking my mother with him to California for a year, that I could afford to think about the sadness of her life. Suddenly, I was far away in Washington, living with my sister and sharing a house with several of her friends. While I finished high school and discovered to my surprise that my classmates felt sorry for me because my mother *wasn't* there, I also realized that my sister, at least in her early childhood, had known a very different person who lived inside our mother, an earlier Ruth.

She was a woman I met for the first time in a mental hospital near Baltimore, a humane place with gardens and trees where I visited her each weekend of the summer after my first year away at college. Fortunately, my sister hadn't been able to work and be our mother's caretaker, too. After my father's year was up, my sister had carefully researched hospitals and found the courage to break the family chain.

At first, this Ruth was the same abstracted, frightened woman I had lived with all those years; though now all the sadder for being approached through long hospital corridors and many locked doors. But gradually she began to talk about her past life, memories that doctors there must have been awakening. I began to meet a Ruth I had never known.

A tall, spirited, auburn-haired high school girl who loved basketball and reading; who tried to drive her uncle's Stanley Steamer when it was the first car in the neighborhood; who had a gift for gardening and who sometimes, in defiance of convention, wore her father's overalls; a girl with the courage to go to dances even though her church told her that music itself was sinful, and whose sense of adventure almost made up for feeling gawky and unpretty next to her daintier, dark-haired sister.

. . . A very little girl, just learning to walk, discovering the body places where touching was pleasurable, and being punished by her mother who slapped her hard across the kitchen floor.

. . . A daughter of a handsome railroad engineer and a schoolteacher who felt she had married "beneath her"; the mother who took her daughters on Christmas trips to faraway New York on an engineer's railroad pass and showed them the restaurants and theaters they should aspire to—even though they could only stand outside them in the snow.

. . . A good student at Oberlin College, whose freethinking traditions she loved, where friends nicknamed her "Billy"; a student with a talent for both mathematics and poetry, who was not above putting an invisible film of Karo syrup on all the john seats in her dormitory the night of a big prom; a daughter who had to return to Toledo, live with her family, and go to a local university when her ambitious mother—who had scrimped and saved, ghostwritten a minister's sermons, and made her daughters' clothes in order to get them to college at all—ran out of money. At home, this Ruth became a part-time bookkeeper in a lingerie shop for the very rich, commuting to classes and listening to her mother's harsh lectures on the security of becoming a teacher; but also a young woman who was still rebellious enough to fall in love with my father, the editor of her university newspaper, a funny and charming young man who was a terrible student, had no intention of graduating, put on all the dances, and was unacceptably Jewish.

I knew from family lore that my mother had married my father twice: once secretly, after he invited her to become the literary editor of his campus newspaper, and once a year later in a public ceremony, which some members of both families refused to attend as the "mixed marriage" of its day.

And I knew that my mother had gone on to earn a teaching certificate. She had used it to scare away truant officers during the winters when, after my father closed the summer resort for the season, we lived in a house trailer and worked our way to Florida or California and back by buying and selling antiques.

But only during those increasingly ambitious weekend outings from the hospital—going shopping, to lunch, to the movies—did I realize that she had taught college calculus for a year in deference to her mother's insistence that she have teaching to "fall back on." And only then did I realize she had fallen in love with newspapers along with my father. After graduating from the university paper, she wrote a gossip column for a local tabloid, under the name "Duncan MacKenzie," since women weren't supposed to do such things, and soon had earned a job as society reporter on one of Toledo's two big dailies. By the time my sister was four or so, she had worked her way up to the unusual position of Sunday editor.

It was a strange experience to look into those brown eyes I had seen so often and realize suddenly how much they were like my own. For the first time, I realized that I might really be her daughter.

I began to think of the many pressures that might have led up to that first nervous breakdown: leaving my sister whom she loved very much with a grandmother whose values she didn't share; trying to hold on to a job she loved but was being asked to leave by her husband; wanting very much to go with a woman friend to pursue their own dreams in New York; falling in love with a co-worker at the newspaper who frightened her by being more sexually attractive, more supportive of her work than my father, and perhaps a man she should have married; and finally, nearly bleeding to death with a miscarriage because her own mother had little faith in doctors and refused to get help.

Did those months in the sanitarium brainwash her in some Freudian or very traditional way into making what were, for her, probably the wrong choices? I don't know. It almost doesn't matter. Without extraordinary support to the contrary, she was already convinced that divorce was unthinkable. A husband could not be left for another man, and certainly not for a reason as selfish as a career. A daughter could not be deprived of her father and certainly not be uprooted and taken off to an uncertain future in New York. A bride was supposed to be virginal (not "shopworn" as my euphemistic mother used to say), and if your husband turned out to be kind, but innocent of the possibility of a woman's pleasure, then just be thankful for the kindness.

Of course, other women have torn themselves away from work and love and still survived. But a story my mother told me years later has symbolized for me the formidable forces arrayed against her:

"It was early spring, nothing was open yet. There was nobody for miles around. We had stayed at the lake that winter, so I was alone a lot while your father took the car and traveled around on business. You were a baby. Your sister was in school, and there was no phone. The last straw was that the radio broke. Suddenly it seemed like forever since I'd been able to talk with anyone—or even hear the sound of another voice.

"I bundled you up, took the dog, and walked out to the Brooklyn road. I thought I'd walk the four or five miles to the grocery store, talk to some people, and find somebody to drive me back. I was walking along with Fritzie running up ahead in the empty road—when suddenly a car came out of nowhere and down the hill. It hit Fritzie on the head and threw him over to the side of the road. I yelled and screamed at the driver, but he never slowed down. He never looked at us. He never even turned his head.

"Poor Fritzie was all broken and bleeding, but he was still alive. I carried him and sat down in the middle of the road, with his head cradled in my arms. I was going to *make* the next car stop and help.

"But no car ever came. I sat there for hours, I don't know how long, with you in my lap and holding Fritzie, who was whimpering and looking up at me for help. It was dark by the time he finally died. I pulled him over to the side of the road and walked back home with you and washed the blood out of my clothes.

"I don't know what it was about that one day—it was like a breaking point. When your father came home, I said: 'From now on, I'm going with you. I won't bother you. I'll just sit in the car. But I can't bear to be alone again.'"

I think she told me that story to show she had tried to save herself, or perhaps she wanted to exorcise the painful memory by saying it out loud. But hearing it made me understand what could have turned her into the woman I remember even while my parents were married: a solitary figure sitting in the car, perspiring through the summer, bundled up in winter, waiting for my father to come out of this or that antique shop, grateful just not to be alone. I was there, too, because I was too young to be left at home, and I loved helping my father wrap and unwrap the newspaper around the china and small objects he had bought at auctions and was selling to dealers. It made me feel necessary and grown-up. But sometimes it was hours before we came back to the car again and to my mother who was always patiently, silently waiting.

At the hospital and later when Ruth told me stories of her past, I used to say, "But why didn't you leave? Why didn't you take the job? Why didn't you marry the other man?" She would always insist it didn't matter, she was lucky to have my sister and me. If I pressed her hard enough, she would add, "If I'd left, you never would have been born."

I always thought but never had the courage to say: *But you might have been born instead.*

I'd like to tell you that this story has a happy ending. The best I can do is one that is happier than its beginning.

After many months in that Baltimore hospital, my mother lived on her own in a small apartment for two years while I was in college and my sister married and lived nearby. When she felt the old terrors coming back, she returned to the hospital at her own request. She was approaching sixty by the time she emerged from there and from a Quaker farm that served as a halfway house, but she confounded her psychiatrists' predictions that she would be able to live outside for shorter and shorter periods. In fact, she never returned. She lived more than another twenty years, and for six of them, she was well enough to stay in a rooming house that provided both privacy and company. Even after my sister and her husband moved to a larger house and generously made two rooms into an apartment for her, she continued to have some independent life and many friends. She worked part-time as a "salesgirl" in a china shop; went away with me on yearly vacations and took one trip to Europe with relatives; went to women's club meetings; found a multiracial church that she loved; took meditation courses; and enjoyed many books. Still, she could not bear to see a sad movie, to stay alone with any of her six grandchildren when they were babies, to live without many tranquilizers, or to talk about those bad years in Toledo. The old terrors were still in the back of her mind, and each day was a fight to keep them down.

It was the length of her illness that had made doctors pessimistic. In fact, they could not identify any serious mental problem and diagnosed her only as having "an anxiety neurosis": low self-esteem, a fear of being dependent, a terror of being alone, a constant worry about money. She also had spells of what would now be called agoraphobia, a problem almost entirely confined to dependent women: fear of going outside the house, and incapacitating anxiety attacks in unfamiliar or public places.

Would you say, I asked one of her doctors, that her spirit had been broken? "I guess that's as good a diagnosis as any," he said. "And it's hard to mend anything that's been broken for twenty years."

But once out of the hospital for good, she continued to show flashes of the different woman inside; one with a wry kind of humor, a sense of adventure, and a love of learning. Books on math, physics, and mysticism occupied a lot of her time. ("Religion," she used to say firmly, "begins in the laboratory.") When she visited me in New York during her sixties and seventies, she always told taxi drivers that she was eighty years old ("so they will tell me how young I look") and convinced theater ticket sellers that she was deaf long before she really was ("so they'll give us seats in the front row"). She made friends easily, with the vulnerability and charm of a person who feels entirely dependent on the approval of others. After one of her visits, every shopkeeper within blocks of my apartment would say, "Oh yes, I know your mother!" At home, she complained that people her own age were too old and stodgy for her. Many of her friends were far younger than she. It was as if she were making up for her own lost years.

She was also overly appreciative of any presents given to her—and made giving them irresistible. I loved to send her clothes, jewelry, exotic soaps, and additions to her collection of tarot cards. She loved receiving them, though we both knew they would end up stored in boxes and drawers. She carried on a correspondence in German with our European relatives, and exchanges with many other friends, all written in her painfully slow, shaky handwriting. She also loved giving gifts. Even as she worried about money and figured out how to save pennies, she would buy or make carefully chosen presents for grandchildren and friends.

Part of the price she paid for this much health was forgetting. A single reminder of those bad years in Toledo was enough to plunge her into days of depression. There were times when this fact created a loneliness for me, too. Only two of us had lived most of my childhood. Now, only one of us remembered. But there were also times in later years when, no matter how much I pleaded with reporters *not* to interview our friends and neighbors in Toledo, *not* to say that my mother had been hospitalized, they published things that hurt her very much and sent her into a downhill slide.

On the other hand, she was also her mother's daughter, a person with a certain amount of social pride and pretension, and some of her objections had less to do with depression than false pride. She complained bitterly about one report that we had lived in a house trailer. She finally asked angrily: "Couldn't they at least say 'vacation mobile home'?" Divorce was still a shame to her. She might cheerfully tell friends, "I don't know *why* Gloria says her father and I were divorced—we never were." I think she justified this to herself with the idea that they had gone through two marriage ceremonies, one in secret and one in public, but had been divorced only once. In fact, they were definitely divorced, and my father briefly had been married to someone else.

She was very proud of my being a published writer, and we generally shared the same values. After her death, I found a mother-daughter morals quiz I once had written for a women's magazine. In her unmistakably shaky handwriting, she had recorded her own answers, her entirely accurate imagination of what my answers would be, and a score that concluded our differences were less than those "normal for women separated by twenty-odd years." Nonetheless, she was quite capable of putting a made-up name on her name tag when going to a conservative women's club where she feared our shared identity would bring up controversy or even just questions. When I finally got up the nerve to tell her I was signing a 1972 petition of women who publicly said we had had abortions and were demanding the repeal of laws that made them illegal and dangerous, her only reply was sharp and aimed to hurt back. "Every starlet says she's had an abortion," she said. "It's just a way of getting publicity." I knew she agreed that abortion should be a legal choice, but I also knew she would never forgive me for being honest in public.

In fact, her anger and a fairly imaginative ability to wound with words increased in her last years when she was most dependent, most focused on herself, and most likely to need the total attention of others. When my sister made a courageous decision to go to law school at the age of fifty, leaving my mother in a house that not only had many loving teenage grandchildren in it but a kindly older woman as a paid companion besides, my mother reduced my sister to frequent tears by insisting that this was a family with no love in it, no home-cooked food in the refrigerator; not a real family at all. Since arguments about home cooking wouldn't work on me, my punishment was creative and different. She was going to call up the *New York Times*, she said, and tell them that this was what feminism did: it left old sick women all alone.

Some of this bitterness brought on by failing faculties was eventually solved by a nursing home near my sister's house where my mother not only got the twenty-four-hour help her weakening body demanded, but the attention of affectionate nurses besides. She charmed them, they loved her, and she could still get out for an occasional family wedding. If I ever had any doubts about the debt we owe to nurses, those last months laid them to rest.

When my mother died just before her eighty-second birthday in a hospital room where my sister and I were alternating the hours in which her heart wound slowly down to its last sounds, we were alone together for a few hours. My mother seemed bewildered by her surroundings and the tubes that invaded her body, but her consciousness cleared long enough for her to say: "I want to go home. Please take me home." Lying to her one last time, I said I would. "Okay, honey," she said. "I trust you." Those were her last understandable words.

The nurses let my sister and me stay in the room long after there was no more breath in her body. She had asked us to do that. One of her many fears came from a story she had been told as a child about a man whose coma was mistaken for death. She had made out a living will requesting that no extraordinary measures be used to keep her alive, and that her ashes be sprinkled in the same stream as my father's.

Her memorial service was in the Episcopalian church that she loved because it fed the poor, let the homeless sleep in its pews, had members of every race, and had been sued by the Episcopalian hierarchy for having a woman priest. Most of all, she loved the affection with which its members had welcomed her, visited her at home, and driven her to services. I think she would have liked the Quaker-style informality with which people rose to tell their memories of her. I know she would have loved the presence of many friends. It was to this church that she had donated some of her remaining Michigan property in the hope that it could be used as a multiracial camp, thus getting even with those people in the tiny nearby town who had snubbed my father for being Jewish.

I think she also would have been pleased with her obituary. It emphasized her brief career as one of the early women journalists and asked for donations to Oberlin's scholarship fund so others could go to this college she loved so much but had to leave.

I know I will spend the next years figuring out what her life has left in me.

I realize that I've always been more touched by old people than by children. It's the talent and hopes locked in a failing body that gets to me; a poignant contrast that reminds me of my mother, even before she was old.

I've always been drawn to any story of a mother and daughter on their own in the world. I saw *A Taste of Honey* several times both as a play and a film, and never stopped feeling it. Even *Gypsy* I saw over and over again, sneaking in backstage for the musical and going to the movie as well. I told myself that I was learning the tap-dance routines, but actually my eyes were full of tears.

I once fell in love with a man only because we both belonged to that large and secret club of children who had "crazy mothers." We traded stories of the shameful houses to which we could never invite our friends. Before he was born, his mother had gone to jail for her pacifist convictions. Then she married the politically ambitious young lawyer who had defended her, stayed home and raised many sons. I fell out of love when he confessed that he wished I wouldn't smoke or swear, and he hoped I wouldn't go on working. His mother's plight had taught him self-pity—and nothing else.

I'm no longer obsessed, as I was for many years, with the fear that I would end up in a house like that one in Toledo. Now, I'm obsessed instead with the things I could have done for my mother while she was alive, or the things I should have said.

I still don't understand why so many, many years passed before I saw my mother as a person and before I understood that many of the forces in her life are patterns women share. Like a lot of daughters, I suppose I couldn't afford to admit that what had happened to my mother was not all personal or accidental, and therefore could happen to me.

One mystery has finally cleared. I could never understand why my mother hadn't been helped by Pauline, her mother-in-law; a woman she seemed to love more than her own mother. This paternal grandmother had died when I was five, before my mother's real problems began but long after that "nervous breakdown," and I knew Pauline was once a suffragist who addressed Congress, marched for the vote, and was the first woman elected to a school board in Ohio. She must have been a courageous and independent woman, yet I could find no evidence in my mother's reminiscences that Pauline had helped my mother toward a life of her own.

I finally realized that my grandmother never changed the politics of her own life, either. She was a feminist who kept a neat house for a husband and four antifeminist sons, a vegetarian among five male meat eaters, and a woman who felt so strongly about the dangers of alcohol that she used only paste vanilla; yet she served both meat and wine to the men of the house and made sure their lives and comforts were continued undisturbed. After the vote was won, Pauline seems to have stopped all feminist activity. My mother greatly admired the fact that her mother-in-law kept a spotless house and prepared a week's meals at a time. Whatever her own internal torments, Pauline was to my mother a woman who seemed able to "do it all." "Whither thou goest, I shall go," my mother used to say to Pauline, quoting the Ruth of the Bible. In the end, her mother-in-law may have added to my mother's burdens of guilt.

Perhaps like many later suffragists, my grandmother was a public feminist and a private isolationist. That may have been heroic in itself, the most she could be expected to do, but the vote and a legal right to work were not the only kind of help my mother needed.

The world still missed a unique person named Ruth. Though she had longed to live in New York and Europe, she became a woman who was afraid to take a bus across town. Though she drove the first Stanley Steamer, she married a man who never let her drive at all.

I can only guess what she might have become. The clues are in moments of spirit or humor.

After all the years of fear, she still went to Oberlin with me when I was giving a speech there. She remembered everything about its history as the first college to admit blacks and the first to admit women, and responded to students with the dignity of a professor, the accuracy of a journalist, and a charm that was all her own.

When she could still make trips to Washington's wealth of libraries, she became an expert genealogist, delighting especially in finding the rogues and rebels in our family tree.

Just before I was born, when she had cooked one more enormous meal for all the members of some famous dance band at my father's resort and they failed to clean their plates, she had taken a shotgun down from the kitchen wall and held it over their frightened heads until they had finished the last crumb of strawberry shortcake. Only then did she tell them the gun wasn't loaded. It was a story she told with great satisfaction.

Though sex was a subject she couldn't discuss directly, she had a great appreciation of sensuous men. When a friend I brought home tried to talk to her about cooking, she was furious. ("He came out in the kitchen and talked to me about *stew!*") But she forgave him when we went swimming. She whispered, "He has wonderful legs!"

On her seventy-fifth birthday, she played softball with her grandsons on the beach, and took pride in hitting home runs into the ocean.

Even in the last year of her life, when my sister took her to visit a neighbor's new and expensive house, she looked at the vertical stripes of a very abstract painting in the hallway, and asked, tartly, "Is that the price code?"

She worried terribly about being socially accepted herself, but she never withheld her own approval for the wrong reasons. Poverty or style or lack of education couldn't stand between her and a new friend. Though she lived in a mostly white society and worried if I went out with a man of the "wrong" race, just as she had married a man of the "wrong" religion, she always accepted each person as an individual.

"Is he *very* dark?" she once asked worriedly about a friend. But when she met this very dark person, she only said afterward, "What a kind and nice man!"

My father was the Jewish half of the family, yet it was my mother who taught me to have pride in that tradition. It was she who encouraged me to listen to a radio play about a concentration camp when I was little. "You should know that this can happen," she said. Yet she did it just enough to teach, not to frighten.

It was she who introduced me to books and a respect for them, to poetry that she knew by heart, and to the idea that you could never criticize someone unless you "walked miles in their shoes."

It was she who sold that Toledo house, the only home she had, with the determination that the money be used to start me in college. She gave both her daughters the encouragement to leave home for four years of independence that she herself had never had.

After her death, my sister and I found a journal she had kept of her one cherished and belated trip to Europe. It was a trip she had described very little when she came home: she always deplored people who talked boringly about their personal travels and showed slides. Nonetheless, she had written a descriptive essay called "Grandma Goes to Europe." She still must have thought of herself as a writer. Yet she showed this long journal to no one.

I miss her—but perhaps no more in death than I did in life. Dying seems less sad than having lived too little.

But at least we're now asking questions about all the Ruths and all our family mysteries.

If her song inspires that, I think she would be the first to say: It was worth the singing.

Tanya

ELIZABETH KENNY AND KATHLEEN BELANGER

ENGAGEMENT AND DATA COLLECTION

Presenting problem: A fourteen-year-old African American girl is pregnant and rejected by her parent.

The referral to Child Protective Services (CPS) in a rural county in Texas was made by the county health unit where Tanya had gone with a friend to get a pregnancy test. She told the nurse practitioner that she was afraid to go home, and told how she and her brothers slept in the woodshed on the rear of the house where there was no heat. She cooked for her brothers and herself on a wood stove. They did not have access to the refrigerator in the main part of the house, where her mother Katia and mother's boyfriend Charles lived. Tanya told the nurse that she would be beaten for being pregnant, and the reporter also confirmed signs of abuse as well as neglect—Tanya was poorly groomed, her clothing was not clean, she had bruises on her back, and her skin, hair, and very slender build indicated inadequate nutrition.

CPS investigation confirmed that Tanya's mother would not be supportive of her daughter during her pregnancy. She viewed her children as "bad" and shifted blame from her lack of supervision of her children to Tanya's "wildness" as a cause of the girl's pregnancy. Katia and Charles would not consider having the children back in the home after Tanya had caused an investigator to come out, and the CPS worker and her supervisor felt that there was considerable risk of further physical and emotional abuse, as well as poor nutrition and care for Tanya and her brothers.

The only relative the children were aware of was an aged grandmother, whose circumstances were physically less promising than those of Katia's home; because of the grandmother's deteriorating home and withdrawn, hostile behavior, she was referred to adult protective services as possibly in need of aid herself.

According to Katia, Tanya and her brother Tony (12) had the same father, who had been killed several years before. The children did not recall ever seeing him or his family. Since the couple had never married and Katia had never applied for any assistance for these children, they did not receive any financial support in their father's name (which might have included Social Security survivors' benefits. Their younger brother was Tommy (11) whose father, Katia said, was Charles' brother Tirrell, who had left the state. Katia had applied for and received AFDC for Tommy, although the father had not been located to pay child support. Charles and Tirrell had no siblings or living parents, according to Charles.

The children attended Country Prairie Elementary and Middle Schools, in a county school district. School authorities knew of the children's state of poor physical care, but because they felt "nothing had been done" when a neglect report had been made when Tanya was in first grade, they had not further reported to Child Protective Services. The children's teachers over the years had provided school supplies and clothing, made personal calls to Katia so the children would be certified for free meals, referred them for Christmas help, and made other efforts to improve the children's lives. The school was unaware of the physical abuse and Tanya's pregnancy. All three children were at least one year behind in grade. Tommy had been referred for testing for a learning disability, although his mother was initially unwilling to sign the necessary release—"My kid ain't crazy" was her interpretation. Testing had recently taken place. School authorities viewed the children in the following terms: "no problems with behavior, very quiet, do not talk about their lives or family, play with a few children, are teased about their appearance, but generally do not have trouble with adults or children."

Removal and placement in substitute care seemed to be the sole option to provide care for these children and to provide appropriate physical and emotional care for Tanya during her pregnancy. All three siblings could not be placed in the same home, but the optimal placement under the circumstances was placement with two separate foster families in the same community, who were related and were heavily involved with activities in the same school and church, to have as much sibling contact as possible. A change of schools was necessary, but Tanya said she was pleased to have a chance to start over.

The process of removal from parental supervision and placement in the care of Child Protective Services in Texas, as in most states, is a civil court procedure. The court considers information from the investigating caseworker and gives permission for emergency custody and placement, with an adversarial hearing to follow. At this time, the parent or parents present their reasons for the court to deny temporary conservatorship to the state agency. They may have obtained the services of an attorney, or may request a court-appointed attorney if they have insufficient finances to hire an attorney on their own. If the court grants temporary conservatorship to Child Protective Services, this does not indicate that the parents no longer have rights to their children. If termination of parental rights takes place, it occurs later, when the agency can demonstrate to the court that the parents remain unable to assure the safety and care of their children.

The purpose of removal of children, as defined in the code of family law in each state, is to ensure the immediate safety of the children and then to muster resources so that the parents may resume care of their children, or so that others (ideally, relatives or other people important to the children and family) may assume permanent conservatorship of the children.

In Katia's case, she was told of the hearing and only attended when the CPS worker furnished transportation. She remained sullen with the judge, but indicated with "Yes, Sir" that she understood that the children were being removed for their safety and that she had an obligation to cooperate with Child Protective Services to regain care of them. Good practice upholds the responsibility of the agency to foster contact between parent and child while the children are in care, and the agency set up a program of visits between Katia and the children. She said she had no reliable transportation, but Charles agreed to bring her to the CPS office for a late-afternoon weekly visit with her sons and daughter.

INTERVENTION:

Work with Parent: A search was instituted for Tommy's father, to inform him of his son's situation as well as to search for other relatives. Information given to Child Support Enforcement of the Attorney General's Office was cross-checked to obtain as much information as possible. Application was made for benefits for Tanya and Tony on their father's Social Security record, as well as for information concerning possible relatives. Katia's cooperation on these and other issues was mixed: one day conciliatory and helpful as if relieved that the children were being cared for by others, the next defensive about her inability to care appropriately for her children. The worker was concerned about the possibility of domestic violence between her and Charles, and about the possibility that that fear had led her to abandon her children in deference to him. Katia would never admit that possibility, and the worker's only recourse was to leave information and a phone number for the nearest shelter with Katia. Although it was not located in their county, there was a toll-free telephone number.

As contact continued with Katia, another concern was her mental health. Her mood swings, lack of concern for the comfort of her surroundings and her grooming alternating with improved housekeeping and grooming, and conflicted relationships with her neighbors, her mother, and authority figures, such as income assistance workers, were possible indications of some mental pathology. Psychological evaluation is usually offered to parents in order to assess their needs and match them with services. However, Katia was very resistant to the idea, as she had been for Tommy's assessment, stating that she wasn't "crazy," and ongoing efforts to explain the process and reasons for it were unsuccessful.

The caseworker for Katia soon realized that this was a multi-problem family. Besides the documented lack of supervision, physical abuse and neglect relative to the children, Katia had not held a job since she was a teenager, before Tanya was born. She had dropped out of the eighth grade, begun to work in food service, and stopped during her first pregnancy. She made use of the family planning clinic for herself (but had never discussed sexual matters with Tanya and her brothers) and had not taken her children for medical care beyond minimal check-ups and the immunizations necessary for school attendance. Since she lived several miles outside the Country Prairie community and depended upon Charles and friends for transportation to buy groceries and go to a few necessary appointments, Katia had used lack of transportation as her chief reason for not applying for benefits for the children, attending school conferences, taking her children for medical care, and seeking employment. She also said lack of transportation prevented her and her family from making other social contacts, such as church attendance, that are seen as desirable in her rural community.

Transportation is indeed a problem in rural communities. Often mental health, educational, legal, casework, and health services are located in several different small towns or solely in the county seat in rural counties. Lack of public transportation is a major barrier to accessing services in rural settings. And for people in poverty, who very often live in rural communities, the ownership of an automobile is a financial impossibility. Practitioners in mental health, elderly services, outreach health services, and school social workers, to name only a few individuals providing services to rural clients, often spend a good deal of time arranging or providing transportation to counseling, psychiatric appointments, trips to a food bank, well-child visits to a clinic, physical therapy, parenting classes, parent-teacher appointments, and many other important appointments for clients. However, Katia knew a good excuse which no one pressuring her to change her behavior could deny: she had no transportation. Rural neighbors often charged Katia five or ten dollars a trip to transport her for groceries or a food stamp appointment. Charles got irregular day jobs from a local farmer and was sometimes unavailable or unwilling to transport her. This is why her caseworker made a point of planning with her and Charles for transportation to her visits with the children. Even so, there were times when she did not come to visits, nor did she call to cancel or re-schedule. When the caseworker went to her home, she was not there. In time, she responded well to the foster parent of Tanya, who agreed to pick her up when she was transporting Tanya to the visit. Occasionally, they conducted their visit in the park or at a fast-food restaurant, in an effort to meet in a more natural setting. The children all enjoyed this, and Katia seemed relieved to focus less on her interaction with the children and more on watching other people.

At early visits, she focused on the boys and seemed to be ignoring Tanya. Her caseworker wondered if Katia had always showed a preference for her sons. When she talked to Tanya about her perceptions of visits with her mother, she realized that Tanya felt her mother was punishing her for calling attention to the siblings' condition, blaming her for having the children removed. Reassurance that "grownups made that decision" and "you deserve to be cared for in safety" seemed to help Tanya not to accept responsibility for the breakup of the family. On their third visit, however, while the caseworker was showing Tony and Tommy the pictures she had taken at their last visit, Katia started talking to Tanya in a low voice. The caseworker overheard "all your fault" and "because of you I don't get Tommy's check" and intervened. She asked Katia to step outside the visiting room with her and reminded her that, as the adult in the family, it was her, Katia's, choices that had left the children unsupervised and neglected, and that Tanya had not reported her family's situation but had sought medical care for herself. She reminded Katia that, although her right to visit the children was assured, she could not use the time to blame the children for the past but was responsible for using the time to build relationships which would last.

Work with children: Tommy and Tony adjusted fairly easily to life with their foster family. The foster parents reported that they had to teach some basic hygiene procedures, such as frequent toothbrushing, and obtain corrective dental work to counteract the previous neglect, but that the boys were both "big eaters—and not fussy!" Like many neglected children, they for a while hoarded food, hiding it in their pockets and under their beds, until repeated assurances by the foster families that there would continue to be food whenever the children wanted it gradually convinced Tony and Tommy that they did not need to hide food. Another characteristic of children who have experienced this kind of deprivation is that they find it difficult to read their body's signals—each would overeat until he was uncomfortable and even ill, and they needed help in knowing when they had eaten enough. Both boys were anxious about separation from their sister, and welcomed the daily contacts with her at school, on the bus, and in shared activities of the foster families. The new school system, Red Rock Independent School District, which all three children entered, was at first unwilling to access special education services for Tommy without repeating the testing already completed; the foster parents and caseworker talked with them and persuaded them to make his initial placement on the basis of the records obtained from Country Prairie ISD.

Tanya had other problems in her placement. Counseling was begun immediately because of her pregnancy, her reluctance to discuss the father of her child, her feelings of guilt for causing the break-up of the family because of her pregnancy (which is what Katia told her), and some indications of real denial. Instead of hoarding food like her brothers, she began to overeat, another common reaction of neglected children, but with the half-expressed statement that "I'm not pregnant, I'm fat." It was not clear from talk with Tanya if she had become pregnant through sexual activity with a "boy friend" or if an adult had sexually exploited her, since a number of men friends of Charles frequented the home. Tanya's caseworker began to explore with her immediately the implications of her pregnancy, informing her of the options available to her. One need, as for other youth who have been sexually active, was complete information on sexuality, which Tanya had never received. This helped Tanya understand how the pregnancy had occurred and realize the need for good care. Because a safe abortion could only be done within a limited time frame, Tanya had to be able to consider this choice, among others. She also was informed about her option to keep and raise her child, with information about the assistance available to her, and also about adoption as a plan for her and the child. Her counselor had a group for teen parents, as well as one for pregnant teens, and Tanya chose to enter both groups. She began to acknowledge the reality of her pregnancy, and it became clear that an adult visiting the home had probably been responsible for her pregnancy, although she said she feared her mother's anger if she told who.

Tanya asked her therapist about adoption, and an interview was arranged with the outreach worker from a private adoption agency who handled adoptions in the rural counties in that part of the state. In the meantime, Red Rock

High School was unwilling to make arrangements for her continued education after the baby's birth—most teenaged mothers in the district dropped out of school. Tanya wished to attend until close to the birth, take her midyear exams early, and return to school a week later than the other students to resume the second semester. Even with the support of her doctor, her therapist, and her caseworker, Tanya was discouraged by the lack of cooperation of her school, until her foster mother, who had worked with the school district for many years, in an assertive interview with the superintendent, pointed out the obligation of the school district to provide an education for Tanya and suggested that, rather than a home teacher, she would best be educated in the regular classroom. Accommodations were made for completion of her semester, time off for birth and recovery, and return to school, according to Tanya's original plan and with the backing of medical personnel. Although the school system had not previously made much accommodation for pregnant students, Tanya did not experience any social problems with other students or faculty, and was able to make friends and gain the support of her teachers.

The effort to locate Tommy's absent parent and/or any appropriate relatives who might take responsibility for these young people was fruitless. A few identified cousins in Charles' and Tirrell's family were unwilling to develop a relationship with them, and also seemed poor possible guardians due to risky life styles.

EVALUATION AND TERMINATION

Long term outcomes: Tanya's son was born healthy and on time. She chose to spend time with him in the hospital, but Tanya had opted for open adoption through a church agency, and he went to his adoptive family at two days of age. Tanya did not choose to meet them in person, although she had received letters from them and spoken with them on the telephone before the baby was born. From time to time she received pictures of her son in his adoptive home. The adoption agency worked with her caseworker and therapist to ensure that counseling continued for Tanya, concerning issues of loss and grieving.

She and her brothers remained in care until each graduated from high school. Theirs was an unusual history for older children and adolescents who come into substitute care, for they remained in the same foster homes and thus were able to find stability and continued contact with one another. This is in part a tribute to the experience and commitment of their foster parents, who were able to tolerate the normal turbulence of adolescence, which is often even more turbulent for youth-in-care because of issues of loss, anger, loyalty, and long-term dysfunction in communication and behavior patterns. Many youth who experience behavior problems in their teens are moved to more restrictive settings, where more therapeutic intervention is possible. Often, adolescents are impatient within a foster family and are better able to adapt to a group or residential setting, where they can connect emotionally with others without having to accept caretakers as parents. These choices usually mean decreased contact with the biological family and with siblings. However, in the case of Tommy, Tony, and Tanya, their placement in families met their emotional needs, as well as their need for connection with one another and their mother. In their adolescent years, they were able to gain not only an education, but also a network of family, friends, church and community contacts. These are substantial resources for young people as they emancipate, and such resources are particularly important in rural settings. Although Tommy continued in special education while in high school, he was able to learn the skills to maintain himself and hold a job as a greenhouse worker, which he began in high school in work/study and continued after graduation. His former foster parents remained a resource for him, supporting him in maintaining a job, paying taxes, and meeting other responsibilities. Tanya got a job and was able to rent a small apartment near her foster parents, who were a resource for her when she graduated from high school (foster children are able to remain in substitute care after their eighteenth birthday until completing high school). The support system for youth leaving foster care helped her learn how to be on her own and to purchase some equipment for her apartment, financed health insurance for six months, and provided her with information and referrals to a local clinic and other services which she might need. Her foster parents invited her for dinner at least once a week, encouraged her to do laundry at their home, and took her to church and to family occasions. This help is the kind of support young people receive from their biological families when they are on their own and is not often available to youth leaving foster care.

When Tony finished high school, he moved in with his sister. He had a more difficult time than she in getting and keeping a job but finally obtained regular work in a filling station, where his hard work over six months caused his supervisor to give him some special notice and training. Tanya's apartment was within walking distance of both her and Tony's jobs, but Tony felt that as a young adult he was truly deprived in not having his own vehicle. His boss advised him and then helped him find a working car. His foster parents helped him with insurance, and Tanya paid part of the monthly insurance premium in return for Tony's helping with errands, grocery shopping, and so forth. Tony became interested in further education in auto mechanics, which was offered by a coalition of county businesses and the educational system of their county.

As mentioned earlier, Tommy began working in a greenhouse during high school. Special education services emphasized vocational planning for students who would be able to assume some independence, and this job suited his interest in plants and growing things. His employers were pleased with his attitude and work and offered him a job on completing high school. By this time, Tanya and Tony had a larger apartment, where there was room for Tommy to join them. The siblings had a close interest in one another, a real strength, and they always assumed they would live together and take care of one another. Former foster parents continued to be advisors when asked, but the older siblings had made relationships of their own at work and in the church, and were able to include Tommy in their lives. They visited with their mother once or twice a month and kept this relationship alive, although each had to deal with the fact that they felt she had neglected and then abandoned them.

The rural setting presented special problems for this family: transportation and housing problems have been mentioned. Access to many recreational, mental health, and remedial educational services customarily found in urban areas were unavailable to help these young people (for example, Tony and Tanya never were able to catch up with their age groups in school). Special independence services for youth leaving foster care, such as subsidized apartment living with help in finances, job search, etc., are unavailable to foster children in rural areas. Distances can be great for attending therapy, visiting family, visiting siblings in other placements, finding jobs, and so forth. There is often less funding for special programs in rural child welfare, since urban settings present more horrifying statistics.

The strengths in rural settings lie in the feelings of community which many times are found in small and isolated communities. Recall how the teachers of Country Prairie Independent School District made many efforts, both as educators and as community members, to provide for these children whom they had identified as neglected. The African-American community, especially in stable rural settings, may have particular strengths in family, community, and church connections such as Tanya and her brothers benefited from. Their strong foster parents were interested in fostering the children in their care over time, were willing to advocate for them in the school system, and felt the need to be role models for an extended period of time as part of their responsibility to the community as a whole as well as to these individual children.

Why did these children remain in substitute care? As has been described, there were few resources for them to turn to in their biological family, which would be the optimal solution for child placement. Quite severe neglect, both physical and medical, physical abuse, and lack of supervision leading to Tanya's pregnancy, had all occurred to the children. There was no sense that they would be cared for or protected if returned to their mother's care. Her refusal to take part in any evaluative or counseling services was the ongoing factor that ultimately was presented to the court along with the conditions that had brought the children into substitute care to request termination of parental rights. These children, like many older children, did not wish to be adopted; they had close relationships with one another and with their foster families, and for them the permanency plan of remaining in foster care until emancipation was appropriate.

One of the main factors influencing good outcomes in this case, as well as others when children come into substitute care, is the dedication of the two sets of foster parents. These were experienced parents, solidly a part of their community and firmly committed to values of self-sufficiency for their young people. These foster parents were committed to the value of church and family, which they instilled in Tanya and her brothers, skilled in advocacy for their young people—obtaining appropriate school services, for example, for Tommy and Tanya while they were in foster care—and willing to remain a presence in the lives of their foster children after the period of foster care.

*This case was opened prior to the signing of welfare reform in 1996. Thus, some terms used here may no longer be applicable. However, the intervention on behalf of the children represents contemporary practice.

Questions for Further Study

1. "Fathering," by Bharati Mukherjee, tells the story of the dissolution of a family, from the point of view of the father. From the reader's perspective, it appears that a *triangulated* relationship exists between the members of this household. That is to say, Eng's overwhelming needs have distracted her father and his partner from focusing on their own problems and needs. It also seems clear that Eng is suffering from post-traumatic stress and is in need of an intensive intervention. How might a social worker go about the task of assisting this family? What information (both included and not included in this story) is essential to figuring out how this family might best be helped? Has the father changed any aspect of his thinking about the family from the beginning to the end of the story? If so, how?

2. In Louise Erdrich's "American Horse," we follow the efforts of three people—two policemen and a social worker—as they attempt to remove a child from his mother's care. It seems to us that, under the current Indian Child Welfare Act, the removal of this child might have been very different—if, in fact, the removal had to occur at all. If you could rewrite this story to portray a more culturally sensitive or effective social worker, how would you have her approach this family? What might she do to help this mother avert removal of the child from their home?

3. Vicki L. Sears' story "Grace" is told from the point of view of Jodi. How does Jodi change emotionally from the beginning of the story to the end? What are the implications of those changes for any social worker whose job it is to develop foster care placements?

4. In her essay "Ruth's Song: Because She Could Not Sing It," Gloria Steinem becomes what family theorists call a "parentified child." In other words, she is compelled to perform the role of the parent at the expense of her own social and developmental needs. How do you think her experience as a parentified child shaped her relationship with her mother later in their lives? How do you think her experience growing up shaped the feminist identity for which she is now famous?

5. Elizabeth Kenny and Kathleen Belanger's study of Tanya illustrates the importance of social (and social work) support for multi-problem families. What are the social supports that bolster these children's chances for a better life than the one they experienced with their mother? What strengths does Tanya possess that make her ultimate success more likely?

Invited Commentary

Negotiating Multiple Systems

VANESSA HODGES

Social work practice with families and children is a rewarding yet challenging and complex undertaking. Social problems continue to grow and worsen while providers are faced with insufficient staff that often lacks social work education and training, as well as a paucity of supports and resources to adequately address family and community needs. In the communities depicted in these readings, these problems and others are abundantly evident.

The increasing numbers of diverse families in need of services present new challenges to already burdened systems of care. In my experience as a clinician and educator, I find that adopting a strong set of values and beliefs about families and communities can guide one's practice and ensure that services are empowering, culturally relevant, evidence-based and effective. Indeed, I believe that one of the points the authors were trying to make in their stories was that a paucity of such services, offered with a profound understanding of a family's culture, history, and strengths, is likely to produce some of the sad results we see here. This commentary will identify guiding principles and beliefs of family social work practice (Collins, Jordan, Coleman 1999) illustrating the benefits and risks of these concepts as they relate to our compilation of readings.

VALUES AND BELIEFS ABOUT FAMILIES

All people need a family and all family members need nurturing and deserve respect from each other.

All people need to belong, to teach and learn from others, to be responsible to and responsible for others and to engage in relationships with others. Family is the typical unit to provide such functions. Family is defined broadly to include two or more individuals that are committed to each other and who share the responsibility of meeting each other's needs and fostering growth. This commitment could be by blood as in offsprings, siblings, parents, grandparents, legally—marriage, adoption, fostering, or choice—cohabitation. The need for family, particularly a nurturing and respectful family, was aptly illustrated in the story *Grace*. Jodi and Billie Jim were Native American foster children living in an orphanage where they learned not to trust or believe adults, to expect unwanted sexual behavior, to trust and to depend only on each other. Jodi and

Billie Jim were fortunate to leave the institution to live in foster care with a Native American couple. These wise and experienced parents gently and quietly introduced them to a life of unconditional love and respect. The children were taught to value, appreciate, and live in harmony with the land. While in the care of foster parents, Jodi and Billie Jim began to remember and more closely identify with their own Native heritage, to grow and develop individual strengths and talents, and to develop a trusting and nurturing relationship with adults. This family joined together legally and significantly enhanced the quality of life for the children.

Similarly, the overwhelming love that Buddy and his mother feel for each other, evident in the vivid descriptions of Buddy's feelings for her and in the way she fought, physically, to try to prevent their separation from each other, cannot be ignored. Hopefully, there is a compelling "back-story" that explains the reason for the removal of this child from his home, but Erdrich never explains it.

Basic needs must be met before assisting families to make emotional or behavioral changes.

Basic needs of food, clothing, and shelter must be present before families are able to engage in other types of change. The nature of community-based practice accelerates the worker's awareness of basic needs of client families. Many volunteer, secular, and community agencies provide assistance for families in need, and the worker is responsible for making these connections. In the Case Study "Tanya," teachers and school counselors identified basic needs of Tanya and her siblings and referred the family for clothing, food, and other assistance. Some agencies provide a team approach and designate case managers to help family members negotiate and secure basic services, while other agencies expect the primary worker to be responsible for both basic and therapeutic needs. One could argue about the value and economy of both models, and while I prefer a single primary worker for the family, the fundamental point remains that families can't and won't move forward until these needs are addressed. It is prudent and advisable that basic needs be assessed and addressed in initial meetings. In *American Horse*, Buddy and his family appeared in need of help with basic services. Would the social worker have insisted in removing Buddy from his home if his basic needs were adequately met? As I see it, this can be the only explanation for Buddy's removal. Yet, while it may be a necessary condition for removal, it is certainly not sufficient. Trained social workers, aware of the need for basic needs to be met before other services can be utilized, must focus on such needs for this family. Alternatively, Billie Jim and Jodi's basic needs seem adequately cared for by their foster mother and father.

Families require fair and equal treatment from environmental and service systems.

Fair and equal treatment is a fundamental right of all individuals. Historically, people and families of color have been abused and mistreated, experienced personal and institutional discrimination and have been forced to extinguish long-held beliefs and traditions. Unfair treatment ranges from service providers who do not practice with knowledge and skills that are culturally relevant—for example teaching all students in a classroom to use direct eye contact and speak assertively to parents and adults—a behavior that offends many Asian and Native American cultures. Social services programs can also be unfair to diverse cultures as they tend to be designed and developed without consideration or incorporation of cultural beliefs and values. The story of *American Horse* illustrates the failure of a program to integrate cultural traditions. Buddy lived on a reservation with his mother and uncle. As noted previously, the "backstory" was not revealed to the reader; however, Buddy was apparently at risk, and a social worker and police officers were dispatched to his home to remove him. One of the first clues to unfair treatment was the social worker's statement—"I want to find that boy and salvage him." This statement assumes that Buddy is not receiving proper care from his family and that his life is in danger. Furthermore the implication is that that Ms. Koob, the social worker, understands what is best for Buddy, which includes removing him from familiar surroundings and people that know him and love and care for him. While child safety is extremely important, at no time was consideration given to deploying resources and services to the child's home to keep him safe and enable him to remain living in the home. Furthermore, it is unlikely that Buddy would be placed with another Native family, and he might experience a family or institution that ridiculed or punished him for speaking his language or practicing his traditions.

Most problems in families do not appear overnight but have developed gradually over the years.

Typically, when families present or are referred to social service agencies, they have been attempting to address problems privately or informally—by seeking support from family and friends. Families have been coping with problems for many months or even years before they reach the agency. This may be especially true for families of color who have deep distrust in formal services because of historical treatment and discrimination. Providers should recognize these attempts and reinforce families for successful coping and problem solving efforts, and consider past efforts when developing an intervention plan.

In *Ruth's Song*, Gloria Steinem describes what it is like to grow up in a family when a parent has a mental illness. Her mother lived with major depression for most of the author's childhood and adulthood. In the essay, Steinem describes two specific episodes when the family entered the formal mental health system: once when her mother was hospitalized before she was born, and again during her first year in college. *Ruth's Song*, however, vividly describes how the family cared for the mother and each other during the depressive episodes and struggled to cope in the face of such adversity. It poignantly illustrates how families struggle, adapt, and survive without formal services.

Parents need understanding and support for the challenges of maintaining relationships and raising children.

Parenting is the most significant responsibility that an adult will ever assume, yet little or no formal education, training or support is available to prepare and sustain parents through the joys and pitfalls of the job. Extended family networks have been a strength for families of color, particularly African-American families. Extended families include blood and fictive kin that form a coherent system to provide emotional and financial support to each other. Recent research is conflicting regarding the stability and growth of extended family. Industrial and technological changes coupled with families living in large urban communities have decreased the availability and support offered by extended family systems. Parents look to friends, relatives and formal networks for the understanding and support needed to parent.

Eng's father is a Vietnam Veteran who returned to the States leaving Eng behind. Eng was eyewitness to the violence and danger associated with war. She had no contact with her father for more than ten years and eventually came to the States to live with him. In her new home, Eng experienced vivid flashbacks and visions that haunted her. Not only was she in a new environment with people, foods, language, sounds, and smells, that were foreign to her, she lived in a home with conflict, resentment, and rejection from her father's partner. Eng's father was caught between parenting a child experiencing cultural adjustment and mental health problems, and nurturing a relationship with a partner unwilling to provide support and who in fact behaved in a jealous and antagonistic manner towards Eng. Formal support, such as a home-based social worker, could have assisted Eng's father and provided him with an outlet for sharing feelings and emotions and learning new skills to provide for Eng, while exploring his commitment and future in a committed relationship with his partner. A psychoeducational or support group for parenting children with mental health problems would also be an avenue to seek to provide support to other families with similar challenges.

The safety of the child is paramount and should be assessed early in one's work with families.

Protecting the rights and safety of children is one of the fundamental responsibilities of society in general but social workers in particular. Child safety is paramount and assessment and intervention plans must be designed to evaluate and maintain a safe environment. Standards for assessing indicators of child safety have been improved with the advent of risk assessments, however some areas remain subjective and especially important in cross-cultural evaluations. This point was illustrated beautifully in *"American Horse"* and *"Tanya."* Presumably, the social workers and police were sent to Buddy's home because of reports or observations of Buddy's lack of safety. As reported, the investigation was not very complete and leaves one wondering if the decision to remove was because Buddy was unsafe or because he was not living a life that Ms. Koob believed to be safe? Did Ms. Koob understand Buddy's Native American culture and misinterpret differences as deficits? In Tanya's case study, the social worker made a careful assessment of the physical and emotional safety of Tanya and her siblings and made a decision that the children could not be protected in the Mom's home and therefore placed the children in foster care.

PRACTICE PRINCIPLES OF FAMILY SOCIAL WORK

Community-based practice is an ideal service setting.

Family social workers strongly advocate for services to occur in the family's home community, that is, in the family's home, school, workplace, and neighborhood. Community-based practice affords workers an opportunity to relate to families in their natural environment where problems arise and are resolved. Community-based practice offers many advantages over agency or office-based services. For families, community-based services increase availability, convenience, and the likelihood that all family members will participate, and they decrease problems associated with unreliable or no transportation or childcare. Community-based workers can assess and intervene with families as problems occur rather than family members describing events retrospectively, as is the case in office settings. Furthermore, the worker has an opportunity to design and modify interventions based on observations made in the home or community. Finally, learning, practicing, and incorporating new skills is more likely to be accomplished in the setting in which they will be utilized rather than generalizing from office to the home. For example, Tanya's foster care worker was well aware of the limitations presented by the rural community such as transportation, recreation, and social activities for the children. The worker's knowledge of the community along with foster parenting resources enabled her to place the children in close proximity to each other in hopes of increasing contact. Knowledge and practice in the community enabled a favorable placement decision for the children (Collins, Jordan, and Coleman, 1999).

Family social work empowers families to solve their own problems.

Empowerment of families is the core of all service relationships. An empowered family is able to identify obstacles or problems, make decisions and secure resources to nurture, support, protect and develop individual family members and the family unit as a whole. The consequences of decades of inequalities based on race, class, gender, or ability have prevented some families from believing empowerment exists and is achievable.

Interventions should be individualized and based upon an assessment of the social, psychological, cultural, educational, economic, spiritual, and physical characteristics of the particular family.

During assessment, community-based practitioners explore family needs and strengths in the context of their environment. Families are unique and therefore have different experiences and expectations of the community and social system. Families typically come to the attention of an agency because one or more members is in crisis; while it is easy to focus solely on the crisis, community-based practitioners explore the entire context of family functioning as aspects of each domain (social, psychological, cultural, educational, economic, spiritual and physical) may contribute to the problem or hold the solution. Community-based practitioners have the added advantage of gathering information in the family's home and community which enables them to gather assessment data and information that might not otherwise be available. For example, workers are able to note if pictures of family members are displayed in the home, whether children have access to age-appropriate playmates and safe places to play, and the nature of relationships with neighbors and friends.

None of the families, as presented in the readings, benefited from a comprehensive assessment of family functioning though all could have been helped by such an assessment.

Collaborative helping relationship should exist between social workers and families.

Collaborative partnerships are characterized by mutual respect, a caring and non-blaming relationship, and shared service planning and decision-making (Dunst, Trivette, and Deal 1988). The ability to join in partnership with families is intentional and requires an investment and skills of both workers and family members. In addition to professional training, social workers must honor and respect cultural differences, recognize and utilize the expertise of families, and maintain open lines of communication that share and exchange information and support parental decision-making. Family members also need to fully participate as partners by teaching workers about their culture and helping them to understand how certain outcomes could be inconsistent and detrimental, and by behaving as equal partners and freely making suggestions and expressing opinions about the service. The key to a successfully collaborative partnership is how power is introduced and perceived. First and foremost, social workers must believe that collaboration is important, and establish expectations of a collaborative relationship with the family. Collaboration is likely a new concept to families and therefore they may be uncomfortable and hesitant to take the risk. It is the worker's responsibility to encourage and support families as they engage in this different type of service relationship. A family's ability to fully engage in a collaborative relationship is a good indicator that its members are feeling empowered.

A final note: these stories, and the case study, were all written before the development of the Adoption and Safe Families Act (ASFA) (PL 105-89) in 1997. Briefly, among other things, ASFA speeds up the timing of dispositions in child welfare cases. To the student: think of how ASFA might help or harm the children in the stories depicted here. Do you think these children would be better off? Worse off? Would ASFA make any difference at all? Thinking about how

ASFA might apply makes the policy-practice connection "live" and compels us to think carefully about the consequences of policy action upon our most vulnerable citizens.

REFERENCES

Collins, D., Jordan, C., and Coleman, H. (1999). *An introduction to family social work:* Itasca, IL.: F. E. Peacock.

Dunst, C., Trivette, C., and Deal, A. (1988). *Enabling and empowering families: principles and guidelines for practice.* Cambridge, MA: Brookline Books.

Unit 7 INVOKING OUR CODE OF ETHICS WITH CLIENTS IN THE CRIMINAL JUSTICE SYSTEM

Editors' Introduction

The criminal justice system consists of the programs, policies, institutions, and infrastructure designed to prevent and control crime, as well as to adjudicate, incarcerate, and rehabilitate people engaged in illegal behavior (Barker 1991). Social workers provide critical services to those in the system, much of it in the form of prevention and rehabilitation programming. Drug and alcohol treatment, case management, victim-offender mediation, and family counseling are primary among those services.

Many authors have noted the historically conflictual relationship between the social work profession and the criminal justice system (Fox 1983; Mitford 1974).

This is due, in part, to their very different missions: social workers believe that their role is to both help the person in this system reach his/her goals, as well as to protect the public (the "other" client) from the results of unlawful behavior. The criminal justice system, however, views its role as only to protect the public. Given that the profession and the system do not always share the same goal, it is not surprising that the social worker may sometimes feel that his/her work with clients falls outside the purview of the system, or that his/her work with inmates is not really "social work." This dilemma is illuminated and a resolution set forth in our guest commentary by Diane Young.

Any social worker working in a host system whose mission differs from the profession faces a difficult task. On the one hand, social workers must follow the rules, regulations, and policies governing that system. Simultaneously, they must remain true to the values and ethics of the profession they represent. Often, this results in a conundrum for the social worker. In these cases, the Code of Ethics can be an invaluable guide.

The National Association of Social Workers (NASW) Code of Ethics was first developed in 1960. From its humble beginnings as a one-page document consisting of fourteen first-person statements, to its current form of ten-plus pages that include six core values and five domains of responsibility, the Code has set forth the standards of conduct to which we all aspire, and a basis by which our conduct may be judged (Linzer 1999).[1] Although no professional code can predict, and thereby resolve, all ethical issues, the Code does provide a basis for action in work with clients that may be fraught with ethical dilemmas, as illuminated in the readings and case study that make up this unit.

We begin with a reading from *Black Eagle Child: the Facepaint Narratives,* by Ray Young Bear. Written in unconventional form, it tells a story, at once tragic and humorous, of how bilingual and bicultural misunderstanding results in a gross injustice for Claude Youthman, the protagonist. During the five years of Youthman's almost unendurable incarceration, he seizes upon the opportunities provided to learn English, to earn a degree in art history, to develop his talents and become a well-known artist, and to ultimately use his notoriety as an artist to protest prison conditions. Upon his release and return to the fictional tribal community of Black Eagle Child (BEC), he is filled with hope that he might contribute to the fight to obtain social services and resources for his people. Once there, he finds the BEC community leadership rife with corruption. He is frustrated by his inability to reform the leadership of his community or to improve its resources.

Young Bear's story illuminates many lessons for the ethical social worker: first, it requires us to think about the many indignities suffered in a prison environment, and the role of the social worker in a system that may well be impervious to change. Social workers must be prepared to behave ethically, and to forcefully advocate for changes that promote client well-being when and where they can, but to also be cognizant of their roles as representatives within this system (see: Code of Ethics: 3.09 a-g). Second, Young Bear's story is ultimately one of transformation, with unintended results. The prison experience transforms people, sometimes for good, sometimes not, but almost always the result is difficulty with re-entry into the community that the person left. Finding corruption within the leadership of his community, Claude Youthman assumes the lonely role of whistle blower.

We are asked by Ellis Cose to reflect upon the relationship of racial and ethnic minorities to the American criminal justice institution in his book *The Darden*

Dilemma. We reproduce here Cose's introduction to a collection of essays authored by a stellar assortment of scholars. Briefly, the "Darden dilemma" refers to the ethical responsibilities of the African-American professional male, working in a criminal justice system that patently discriminates against African-American males. Named after Christopher Darden, one of the attorneys who (with Marcia Clark) unsuccessfully prosecuted the criminal trial of O. J. Simpson, the dilemma involves the conflict of interests and values faced by the professional African-American male. Some argue that Darden should have executed his professional responsibilities as a prosecuting attorney impartially, which he did, without any regard for the race of the defendant. Others argue that Darden's efforts to prosecute O. J. made him a traitor to the race. From this perspective, Darden's ethical responsibility would be to lend support to members of the race whenever possible, given the context of a hostile social institution in a racist society. Darden's sentiments, according to this argument, should have been with the jury members who pronounced the innocence of their African-American brother. The Darden dilemma parallels the challenge to the ethical responsibilities of all social workers operating in the context of social institutions, like the criminal justice system, that are unjust (see: Code of Ethics 6.01).

We have also placed in this unit an excerpt of an interview from Leon Pettiway's *Workin' It: Women Living through Drugs and Crime.* Pettiway interviews Margaret, a drug addict and prostitute. The interview reveals that, although everything related to the drugs Margaret consumes—from possession to consumption to sale to the way she raises the money to support her habit—constitutes criminal activity, the person who suffers most is Margaret herself. Toward the end of the excerpt, Margaret says, "You always hope . . . that one day you might wanna stop. . . ." (p. 34). Margaret seems to be saying that she is not ready or able to stop using drugs or supporting herself through prostitution. For the social worker, the circumstances—that these are arguably victimless crimes and that the client is unwilling or unable to change—raise the issue of how, whether, and when to intervene, in a way that will be both ethical and effective. We know, from some of the "best practices" literature in addiction, that remanding a client like Margaret to a drug rehabilitation program at this point is doomed to failure (cf. Prochaska, et. al. 1992). Moreover, it might be considered unethical to recommend treatments from which a client is unlikely to benefit. Margaret's situation illuminates the dilemma social workers often face when working with persons whose crimes primarily victimize themselves.

Luis Rodriguez's description of his life as a gang member in Los Angeles offers us another view of a person trapped by negative, life-threatening chronic behaviors in which few incentives or opportunities for change are offered. As is the case of Margaret, Chin's behaviors are themselves rooted in close relationships, which makes them even more difficult to change. Even though gang member Chin was weary and wary of the house-bombings, shootings, and rapes, he was expected by close friends to participate. He, his family members, and his friends were constant prey to acts of reciprocal violence. A social worker might seize on Chin's moral resistance to gang behaviors as a point of departure for helping Chin extricate himself from the gang life. However, from an ethical perspective, the social worker must fully explore with Chin the multiple consequences that may come from an effort to change his behaviors and his relationships. Such consequences may include a loss of companionship and social support (and the attendant emotional sequelae), violence directed against him and/or his family, and the difficulty of establishing new directions, friendships, and goals.

Finally, Patricia O'Brien offers us the case study "Shirley: Navigating the Way Home from Prison." Incarcerated for fifteen months and transitioning to a halfway house, Shirley realistically details her hopes, dreams, disappointments, and determination to make it on the outside. Assisting her in this endeavor is Beth, the social worker at Grace House. At one point, Shirley bridles at the rules and restrictions that accompany life at Grace House. Beth then explains to Shirley the reasons for those rules, and Shirley accepts them. This small exchange, in which rules are made known and explained, probably departs from the customary application of rules within the prison. Difficulty complying with authority and rules is a frequent hallmark of criminal offenders. Working with such clients, social workers must be especially mindful of the ethical mandate to treat people with dignity. Responding to Shirley's discomfort, Beth treats Shirley as an adult and lets her know that she must make the choice of whether to abide by these rules or leave Grace House. Had Shirley broken the rules, she would have been held accountable for her actions and expelled from the house. This too would have been an ethical course of action: our Code is predicated upon five core values, one of which is the treatment of all clients with dignity and worth. Thus, to treat her otherwise would be to treat her as less than a full adult, with the capacity to accept the consequences of her actions.

Especially noteworthy is O'Brien's use of shifting points of view—sometimes presenting Shirley's experience from the first-person perspective but at other times speaking of Shirley in the third person—along with her use of slang and other colloquialisms in order to give more voice and visibility to Shirley herself. As Young notes in her invited commentary, such an approach to Shirley meets one of the standards for cultural competence in social work practice, namely, to empower clients and to advocate for and *with* them.

NOTE

[1]The six core values of the profession, from which flow the five domains of responsibility, are: (1) service; (2) social justice; (3) the dignity and worth of the person; (4) importance of human relationships; (5) integrity; and (6)) competence. The five domains of responsibility contained in the Code are: (1) to clients; (2) to colleagues; (3) to employers; (4) to the profession; and (5) to society as a whole.

REFERENCES

Barker, R. L. (1991). *The Social Work Dictionary.* Washington, D.C., NASW Press.

Fox, V. (1983). "Introduction." In *Social Work in Juvenile and Criminal Justice Settings,* ed. A. R. Roberts. Springfield, Il.: Charles C. Thomas.

Linzer, N. (1999). *Resolving Ethical Dilemmas in Social Work Practice.* Needham Heights, MA: Allyn and Bacon.

Mitford, J. (1974). *Kind and Usual Punishment.* New York: Knopf.

Prochaska, J., Norcross, J., and DiClemente, C. (1992). *Changing for Good.* New York: William Morrow and Co.

Black Eagle Child Quarterly

RAY YOUNG BEAR

The fall 1965 issue of the *Black Eagle Child Quarterly* contained the sad news that the state legislature had reneged on its long-held promises of twenty new houses with indoor plumbing. The prominent headline read: "Youthman Throws Cantaloupes at State Officials." The caption and text below the photograph of the splattered cantaloupes read:

"All Hope of Flushing Toilets Down the
	Drain
for Twenty BEC Households:
Claude Youthman, 35, of Cutfoot Crossing,
walked out the courtroom on August 14,
Tuesday, under the assumption he was
	acquitted
of charges of deadly assault with a 'round-
	shaped
projectile' levied against him by the state.
When the prosecuting attorney proclaimed,
'Your Honor, we submit,' in reference
to the visual evidence of the weapon,
Youthman misinterpreted 'we submit'
to mean the attorney had given up.
He was subsequently apprehended
for serious assault and terrorism
before he stepped off the courthouse
lawn.

"During Farmers Market in downtown Why
	Cheer
a month previous, Youthman contended 'a
	mean group'
of white men 'in good, clean clothes were
	listening
when theys weren't suppose ta' when his
	wife Henrietta
was accosted by a farmer with lewd
	suggestions.
'She knows little language. The white man's.
	Yours,'
he said to Judge Manez. 'When farmer say
	"put it in,"

she ran away and told me. I get mad and go
	ask farmer
why talk dirty? To get soap and wash mouth.
But they laugh, the farmer and men in the
	long
black car. I not know he (farmer) mean a sack
to put cantaloupe in.'

"Representing the state was the county
	attorney,
Tom Katz, who based the case on a series
of photographs taken at the scene.
One photograph of split cantaloupes
was enlarged to the size of a blackboard,
and another showed the open-mouths of a
	crowd
in dismay. 'This is a mockery of the good
relations we have with our Indians,'
testified the mayor, who later said
he wasn't anywhere near Farmers Market
where the event transpired. 'Whether I was
there or not is irrelevant. I came to tell
the folks at the capital we are genuinely
sorry for what happened. We vow to take
	better
care of our natives. We'll drive them home,
if necessary, when we detect telltale breath.'
When Judge Manez asked the mayor if he felt
the subject was under the influence at the
	time,
he said, 'When are they not? He probably
	was.
They are no different than children who need
strict supervision. The sad part is, they're

full-grown Adults who oughta know better
      than
to act out their frustrations in a public forum.
That's why they're overly dependent on us.
They need to be more appreciative of what
they acquired from us thus far and not be
a burden to us good, tax-paying folks.'
The jury and courtroom audience applauded
the mayor's words of wisdom . . ."

Getting arrested proved to be the most
      audacious
thing that ever happened to Claude
      Youthman.
But he had this queer, nagging feeling
a monumental change was taking place.
Where it would take him and when
and how he would unboard he did not know.
All his life he had taken precautions
to maintain a mile's distance from
the type of inhumanity represented
in the county. In his wildest fears
Youthman never anticipated becoming
an innocent passenger aboard a train
of outcasts. Being away for five years
was, therefore, an unnerving experience.
He now knew where the two railroad
      tracks
that diagonally crisscrossed the Settlement
went. He was enlightened. The trains were
capable of stealing breath from those
he knew and dearly loved, but the rails
also led to federal prisons.

Abandoned as a child—the stories of his
      origins
were purposely kept vague—he grew up
      under
the care and attention of his grandfather,
Jim Percy, a kind-hearted leader
of the Star-Medicine Society.
Never quite understanding his
purpose, Youthman became hermitlike
after dropping out from Weeping Willow
Elementary in the fifth grade. He could
not stand the prospect of one day being
questioned about his mother and father.
They were unknown; he knew of none.
This blank spot had a frightening
effect on his psyche.

If there were doings sponsored
by his grandfather, he would lock himself
in the attic with his magazines of sensational
crime and jubilant Hollywood personalities—

Audie Murphy, the war hero, and the
      exquisite
Elizabeth Taylor. Those who came up the hill
to participate in ceremonies never sought
him out of curiosity, for all were aware
the darting figure or a creaking tree branch
was indication he was nearby. If by chance
someone accidentally caught him around
a corner or in a closet, he would look
down, stumble out sideways, and not look
      up
until he maneuvered his way to the staircase.
In spite of his introvertedness, the visitors
found him pleasing in appearance. He had
      oily,
jet-black hair that graced his classic slanted
eyes and high cheekbones, and he wore
      brown
summer shirts and gray baggy denims.
What did bother people was the fact
they only saw a profile. Even though
Youthman would tense up around strangers,
he remained photogenic. The people
      glanced
at his visage and then politely looked away.
Hunching his bony back over his tightly
      folded
arms, he brought his jaw to one of the
      shoulders
and kept it there. When addressed directly
the young man would pucker his large lips
and speak in a deep voice. He was his own
ventriloquist and wooden dummy.
      Ed Sullivan.
He made speech without facial gestures
an art form. A renowned spearfisherman
      once
equated the "young hermit's" lips to the lips
of a walleye in its last throes of life
over the frozen river. "As the walleye dies
from the puncture wounds of the barbed
      tines
and the subzero weather, it stiffens
and every fiber and nerve can be seen on
its lips. This is the way I see Claude when
he talks. He grits his parched mouth so much
the only movement you see is his quivering
lip muscles. Why does he do that anyway?"
The grandfather of the recluse usually
had no explanations.

Enclosed in the subhuman surroundings
of a Kansas prison, Youthman completely
reversed his outlook and philosophy.
By scooping up triangular edges

of his facial skin with a jagged piece
of glass he sewed himself with carpet
thread and curved needle to the iron bars.
Satisfied the exterior mask would peel
cleanly at the end of a backward run,
he severed himself from the hunchbacked
figure—and was born. From the musty
compartments of his paranoia the black-
and-yellow wings broke out, extended,
and dried out in the red prairie wind.

He took advantage of the prison's exemplary
reeducation program to acquire an art history
degree with an emphasis in
    Postimpressionism.
The numbness that came with incarceration,
a condition he felt was as close to death
as anything, prompted his obsession
with school and eventual survival
in prison. More important, he pledged
to forever understand the English language,
to avoid finding himself in dire
    circumstances
again. The world would not be right without
a walleye-lipped, oily-haired hunchback
who kept a shriveled image of his aboriginal
self in a Kinney's shoebox. In the dark before
dawn, he would unravel the tanned, glossy
    face
and suspend it on a wire hanger. Growing
    tired
of holding it at arm's length, he would
    hang
the mask on the gray wall and stare at it.
By so doing he was able to train the wings
to flex from their shoulder harnesses.
At first light the butterfly's hold on
the ceiling weakened, and Claude Youthman,
who long concerned himself with aspects
of aerodynamics, flew.

By the fourth year he was writing editorials
for the *Wichita Times-Republican,* the exclusive
Sunday issues. He penned treatises on the
    redundancy
of corporal punishment of American Indians.
"It is noteworthy to keep in mind," wrote one
    editor
as part of a series introduction, "that while
    Youthman
is a convicted felon, his arguments on federal
    law
vs. state law vs. tribal sovereignty issues
    deserve
consideration. What is especially startling

is the fact he is one person who benefited
from the penal system. Without the
    ridiculous
'cantaloupe' crime for which he was unjustly
    indicted
Youthman was destined to merely live out his
    life
as a woodsman and illiterate dreamer."
(July 6, 1970)

Throughout internment Youthman balanced
social concerns with neck-deep studies
in cathedral structures and ancient marble
sculptures. In those years in Grandfather's
    attic,
listening to Perry Como and the McGuire
    Sisters,
he chipped and gouged his way with a
    sharpened
spoon and rusty penknife, producing
    thornwood
statues of "Audie" and "National Velvet."

It was then that a Father Jeff Caster heard
of his skills and gave him an art history book
and a set of expensive oils and brushes.
Of the art that Youthman could duplicate
on canvas and thumbtack to the attic wall,
it was the works of Toulouse-Lautrec and
    Seurat.
Youthman's late interest had complications.
The *A tta i ka na ni,* Sioux tipis, he did
in pointillism resembled cone-shaped
    bubblegum
vending machines. He longed for exact
    reproduction,
images you could almost touch, like Christ's
    crown
of thorns he made for Grandfather or the
    duplicates
of Elizabeth's horse, but there he remained,
right on through college, with a painting
technique he was comfortable with and stuck
    with.

Taken by postcard renditions one day of what
an incarcerated Indian sees in a glance,
he initiated the "Gray Indian Series."
The act itself was controversial.
Using large canvases made of layered
newspaper and flour paste, he depicted
365 days of the color of imprisoned light.
On each of the twelve canvases
he divided the days as geometric shapes—
octagons, diamonds, circles, rectangles,

and stripes. Into each shape was filled
an intense or subtle degree of gray.
That was all. There wasn't any kind
of humanness. Just a different shape
of gray he saw each day. The Goslin Art
Institute of Omaha, Nebraska, upon seeing
photographs that accompanied the editorials,
sponsored the first exhibition. *LIFE* magazine
followed with an interview with the
    celebrated
"American Indian Artist and Self-proclaimed
Revolutionary: From Cantaloupes to
    Cathedral
Buttresses." The Honorable Governor was
    obligated
to attend, and he sat at the reception table
with Youthman. "Then what does the 'Gray
    Series'
have to do with Postimpressionism?" opened
    Youthman
rhetorically upon his introduction, shaking
the silver chains and the wrist of a federal
marshal he was shackled to in protest.
"This is what I was asked by the warden
when the Goslin Institute first proposed
the exhibit. The warden's no dummy,
I told myself, but I'd be a darn fool
to believe he came up with the question.
He was coached, and all in an effort
to stifle my notoriety. He knows I will
speak of deplorable conditions, maggot-
infested food, and the urinal stench
of my living quarters. Simply posing
an 'art' question carries little weight.
Studying Postimpressionism was the best
    choice,
and it is a tranquil place from where
abstract visions are shaped—today."

National celebrities are made daily,
and their reigns end just as quickly.
The world is full of actors who weep
at footage of old but famous movies.
It pains them to remember the short-lived
glory. For artists and revolutionaries
    nothing
remains but laminated clippings and
    embossed
invitations with signatures of dignitaries
who later became unknown themselves.
And so it was for Claude.
The good people of Kansas wrote a total
of four replies to his editorials
from a circulation of four million.
From the publicity of *LIFE* he received

$10,000 for the paintings
and invitations to sit on several prominent
boards in the East. He also obtained
    permission
to purchase art supplies for prisoner-artists,
but a few found ways to inhale the paints,
thinners, and aerosols, killing the project.
Upon hearing this, museums and galleries
ceased communication. The public
    television
crew from WITC who had stated
    categorically
they'd be there to film his prison release
and drive him back to Iowa never showed.
It was only after he had been waiting four
    hours
that an apologetic telephone message arrived:
"Mr. Youthman: We are sorry but WITC has
    changed
priorities midstream and has opted to do
a piece on Molly Dolly, chosen this year
as the loveliest artist by People of America.
We are sending a taxi instead and will be
glad to pay for the first twenty miles
to the interstate." Claude Youthman took
the taxi ride, got off at an overpass,
and hitchhiked the rest of the way
to Black Eagle Child.

Henrietta, Mrs. Youthman, the ingenuous one
whose honor Claude was defending on that
    day
of infamy at Farmers Market, cried at the
    sight
of her husband as he limped up the hill
past the water tower. She dropped the plate
of beads and rushed out to the porch. She
    stood
and waited while the miniature souvenirs
of moccasins and canoes (what would have
    been
Claude's bus fare) dangled from her blouse.

Claude's homecoming was largely
    uneventful.
Except for the brief hugs and touches
he received from his wife and grown
    children,
nothing had changed: the front door still
had one hinge missing; the same greasy
    curtains
were there, held by a stone-smooth yarn
    string;
and the tribe was still without indoor
    plumbing.

While impermanence was not a reality they
   knew,
he became embittered. When his family made
the first physical contact with him ever,
he openly wept. Indians never needed to
   touch
each other to demonstrate love and affection.
More so if you were once a recluse like
   Claude.
You could touch or kiss someone in the
   family
all your life—or you could not. In the end,
when someone's presence was no longer,
the pain of their loss or absence
was the same. He planned to rest
before venturing back to society
to pick up where he left off—
or would he?

He had learned to fight the establishment
from behind the prison walls, to correct
injustice. He hoped he could do the same
for his home. "To make this a better place
to live" as the billboard on Highway 63 read.
At first, he was welcomed with a community
   dance,
and the BEC Business Council congratulated
   him
with pithy sentences. The tribe knew about
   his
exploits, for Henrietta had submitted his
   editorials
to the *BEC Quarterly*. The neighbors were
   amazed
how "an illiterate woodsman" was able to
   circumvent
disaster. After that, getting rides into Why
   Cheer
for groceries and typing paper was easy.
The people were glad to chat with a notable.
But they couldn't fathom his intellect.
Instead of listening and responding
to what he planned to do with health,
education, and socioeconomics, they spoke
about family spats and burned food.

Claude Youthman had taken five years off
from social or family responsibility.
The small benign things began to take
precedent. He wanted to savor lost moments
with Henrietta and their grown children.
From afar, however, he began to jot notes
   why
the tribe could not prosper economically.
Later, he read them aloud to himself,

Henrietta, and admirers who visited:

"Politics here are comparable to a birthday
   party
attended by a dozen robust children on a hot
   summer
afternoon. There is excitement, as well as
   appre-
hension. The fun and honor of it is simply
   being
invited to the affair; the reality is that only
one birthday occurs per child per year.
   Picture
this, if you will. After the party has swiftly
gone past the food, dessert, and the
   unwrapping
of presents, the children sit back, digest,
and exchange idle chitchat. Soon, even before
the parents are finished cleaning and clearing
the tables, some children demand the games
commence. The parents smile kindly before
wiping their sweaty brows. The children
giggle uncontrollably as balloons are inflated
and attached to their ankles with string.
They are then herded to the center
of the room where everyone can see them.
One concerned parent leans down and gives
last-second instructions. The object,
of course, is to bust as many balloons
as possible while keeping yours intact.
Those who cannot stand the thought
of losing 'jump the gun' by stomping
on the balloons of unsuspecting participants
before the countdown is given. The game
   stalls
and new balloons are inflated. When the
   game
finally starts there is chaos. In the same
vein, the tribe will cooperate to a certain
degree. Food and pleasantries will be shared
and exchanged. The trouble starts when a
   novel
proposal is submitted for consideration.
Someone will become outraged for not
having thought of it before. And that person
will instigate the first trampling, and others
(relatives and loyal band members) will
   follow
suit. Without evaluating if the novelty could
benefit the tribe, the balloon-busters begin
jumping up and down without really
   knowing
why. How does this tribe function then?
People are not apprised of anything that
may affect them. All is done without

their knowledge and approval by false
leaders. That means you, Lardass . . ."

As the years progressed, the rebellious
vigor he acquired in prison began to
        diminish.
Stirring changes he once shared with people
        on
rides to town were next to zero. He began
to realize why no one ever paid attention:
few possessed the voracity to follow
        through
with their own ideas.

By the time he secured a part-time position
as "tribal arts instructor" at Weeping
        Willow
Elementary in 1988—a program which had
        been
written by a former teacher, Lorna Bearcap,
(another success story)—he had a master's
in art history. He should have been content
with published articles on the "Post-Gray
Indian Series," but insights as to why
the tribe was an inept, bureaucratic
monstrosity were formulated. He concluded
the people who were running the tribe
were the real "illiterate dreamers."
The BEC Business Council allowed its
welfare, health, education, and commerce
committees to promote a greed or help thy-
self system. This is what Lorna Bearcap
had desperately tried to convey shortly
before she was dismissed from Weeping
        Willow.
As the only BEC college-educated teacher,
she had been instrumental in developing
programs whereby students were taken
        beyond
the barbed-wire fence. But her feats drew
the ire of the retarded advisory board.
After she had obtained grants in excess
of half a million dollars, she was accused
of "exploiting the school's singers and
        dancers."
The funds were then embezzled or shifted
to baseball diamond restoration (located
on a known floodplain), intertribal basketball
tournament trips (party time), or (rigged)
dance competitions. Nepotism brought about
a school principal with a degree in
        mechanical
drafting and welding. There were
        embarrassing

audits that made the lead-ins on television
        news.

Lorna Bearcap's last memo to the advisory
board chairman (who was reportedly caught
lollipopping one of the Hyena brothers) read:
"When a true genius appears in the world,
you may know [her] by this sign, that the
        dunces
are all in confederacy, against [her]—
        Jonathan Swift."
Thus ended the extraordinary efforts of a
        person
who crawled out from the brewery ditches
and made a drastic change for herself—
and for students whom she deeply cared
        about.
Like Claude, Lorna took the highway sign
seriously. Because her employers could not,
she was viewed as an obstructionist.

"The school has been relegated for years
with a monumental task of being the last
        carrier
and bastion of identity. To this end a unique
bilingual/bicultural curriculum has been
written and adopted. Unfortunately,
it is a disgrace. The school tries
in vain to convey the most rudimentary
skills, yes, but the students' retentive
abilities—to think, speak, and write
in our language and to recall precepts,
myths, and rules to live by—are far
from exemplary . . .

"We perceive the antiquated institution
as a gleaming aircraft whose defective
nuts and bolts are about to pop in flight
eight miles above. With all due respect
to our alma mater, unless the craft
can be completely 'overhauled,'
administration and direction-wise,
it faces further structural and academic
deterioration. There is something deeply
disturbing about a child who cannot begin
a conversation in our mother tongue,
and even more if a proper sentence
cannot be composed in English . . ."

The tribe patched itself back up by shinnying
up a tree, licking its wounds, and forgetting
anyone ever took the thousands of dollars.
Disguises were poor: new trucks were driven
and satellite dishes installed, but the children

of the suspects wore ragged clothes.
　　Unfortunately,
the state and federal agencies chose not to file
charges, which gave a green light for
　　repetition.
The commodity surplus cheese and flour
　　supplies
were depleted by various committees for
　　Indian
taco sales; clothing items that had been
　　donated
and trucked in by wealthy Boston people
were resold to the tribe; gas and clothing
assistance through the welfare department
were distributed among the working people
at the BEC tribal center; Social Security
checks and ADC checks were channeled,
skimmed, and reissued; monetary or land
donations were kept a secret and divided
by the Business Council. The list
of improprieties grew, and Bingo
Extravaganza was just around the corner.

Claude Youthman forgot about enlightening
the "Outside World." He set aside his paints
and brushes, and he sat down to write a letter
of complaint to a reputable Republican.
He detailed the despicable goings-on
in the *BEC Quarterly.* "Before we can
even begin to focus on the future we
must dispose of our own pretentious scum."
Before the Weeping Willow advisory board
had a chance to fire him, he resigned

under the lights of a press conference.
Lorna Bearcap was there also. Here they
　　were,
the only people who had miraculously
　　educated
themselves and remained. Now they were
　　being
ostracized for revealing ugly truths.

But the infighting was far from over. In fact,
it had just begun. The common BEC man or
　　woman
had no right to define and dictate policy.
They sought the advice of hereditary leaders
in absentia, and they grew more determined
than ever that all problems were attributable
to the lack of divine leadership.
In their opinion elections were over with.
With divine leadership, the Black Eagle Child
Nation would grow strong again.

Even though the blood which coursed
through the veins of the true Chieftains
coursed through theirs vicariously,
Claude Youthman and Lorna Bearcap sat
together at the kitchen table and penned
the first of their diatribes,
the WEEPING WILLOW MANIFESTO.
There was no other resolution.
There had to be an immediate
return to the Old Ways
beginning from the bottom
up.

Reading

The Darden Dilemma: Introduction

ELLIS COSE

Before the O. J. Simpson trial, black prosecutors were all but invisible, toiling, for the most part, in various degrees of obscurity. Christopher Darden's front-and-center role in the so-called trial of the century brought them out of the shadows, but it did much more. The endless media coverage and Darden's subsequent best-selling book created a compelling and indelible portrait of the black prosecutor as a tortured soul—as a conflicted laborer in a perfidious place where celebrity, crime, and conflicting racial perceptions collide.

Darden's very selection as a Simpson prosecutor was rich with racial connotations—so much so that Darden felt it essential to establish early on, to his satisfaction at least, that his role was not primarily symbolic. "If I thought I was being named to the case primarily because I was black, I would've rejected it. It was as simple as that. But I knew that wasn't why I had been chosen." He was chosen, instead, Darden insisted, because he was good, because he knew the case, because he was available and willing. Nonetheless, in the eyes of his critics, such facts seemed irrelevant: "I was a black prosecutor, nothing more," he complained in *In Contempt,* as he responded to the pundits' reviews of his opening statement in the O. J. Simpson trial. "None of these armchair lawyers paid attention to the content of what I had said, only the pigmentation of my skin, the breadth of my nose, the thickness of my lips. 'Yes, he's black all right. That must be why he's up there.' Everything in this case was sifted through a filter of bigoted expectations, like the pressure Jackie Robinson faced when he broke the color barrier in baseball. 'Pretty good hitter for a darkie.'"

Darden's relationship with defense counsel Johnnie Cochran was no less defined by racial preoccupations: "Beneath the court case that everyone else saw, Cochran and I fought another battle, over the expectations and responsibilities of being a black man in America. He took shots at me . . . I listened with clinched jaw. Later, I began to fire back, to show there were responsibilities as a human being that were just as important as the responsibilities of being an African American."

Darden's inner turmoil was poignantly obvious during the trial as he wrestled with painful questions about the perception of his role. "Was I going to be seen as a brother putting another brother in jail?" Such issues, Darden concluded, would not keep him from the task at hand—or from the larger mission of opening up the justice system for blacks. "Perhaps I was naive, but I convinced myself that African Americans had to be represented in all segments of the law if we were ever to believe that the system was ours too."

380

From the moment he decided to accept his appointment to the case, Darden realized he could not afford to see himself as simply a prosecutor doing his job, for too many other people defined the role otherwise—and almost always racially. In some circles (usually white) he was seen as a principled, compassionate black tribune speaking out against racism among his fellow blacks. In other circles (generally black) he was viewed as a dusky Judas, dispatched by a hostile white society to bring a strong black man down. He apparently saw himself as a man in the middle, caught between black and white racism, trying diligently to get jurors—and America—to focus on motive, opportunity, and evidence instead of race. By his own reckoning, he failed in that pursuit, largely, he believes, because of bigotry—or, as he put it, because the jury attempted to "defeat bigotry by cheating justice." The jurors, in other words (at least in Darden's estimation), rejected his view that they should play by the rules of the system to which Darden has dedicated much of his life. Darden's opinion about the jury is obviously disputable, and many of the contributors to this collection take issues with it. Still, his concern about the role of race in the justice system cannot be dismissed.

Since well before the dawn of the civil rights movement, black Americans have debated whether "the system" can be "ours too," whether America will ever fully honor its promise of freedom and justice for all. The nation's early history is not reassuring. There would have been no need, after all, for the Fourteenth and Fifteenth Amendments (intended to protect blacks against state persecution and discrimination), if authorities in many states had not been utterly hostile to the most basic notion of fairness for blacks. Though, in recent years, the concept of equality under the law has been widely accepted, the justice system in practice has not always lived up to that ideal. As Clarence Page makes clear in his essay in this collection, many blacks have sound reasons—reasons rooted in personal experience—to distrust at least some aspects of the justice system. The shooting of a black motorist by a white police officer in St. Petersburg, Florida, in October 1996 and the riots that ensued in its wake reminded Americans, yet again, of why suspicions of the police (and the justice system they represent) refuse to disappear from America's black communities.

Darden concedes that "the system" harbors racial bias but suggests that, rather than defy or reject the system, blacks should strive to make it better. It makes little sense, in his mind, for blacks to "take themselves out of the justice system because it is sometimes unfair." If blacks are ever to have "real ownership in the system," Darden argues, principled and prominent black prosecutors are essential, for only through enforcing the laws can blacks really take ownership of them.

In the essays that follow, twelve (one is tempted to say, "a jury of") black thinkers grapple with various aspects of the "Darden Dilemma." The contributors differ, sometimes sharply, in their assessments of Darden—as a man and as a prosecutor. Stanley Crouch sees him as a whiner and as one who did a horrible job with the Simpson case and who yet, in the manner of George Armstrong Custer, has somehow emerged a hero. Marcia Ann Gillespie sees him as a naive soul. "It shouldn't take a jury acquittal to make a black district attorney face the fact that . . . an admittedly racist cop is a detriment to your case if the defendant is black."

Whatever their feelings about Darden, however, all the contributors agree that, as Roger Wilkins puts it, he "had a tough job in a rough town," and a job made infinitely tougher by the mine fields of race. Darden himself equates the Darden Dilemma with the criticism black prosecutors get from other blacks for "standing up and convicting black criminals." Yet, more broadly defined, the dilemma is really about the pressures of being black in a society that has not always valued black life—and that continues to penalize black people for the color of their skin. As Elijah Anderson observes in the pages ahead, "simply being black poses a special problem of social, psychological, or even physical survival." Just to make it through the day, he argues, blacks pay a psychic tax: "Since the Rodney King beating, in particular, middle-class blacks, working-class blacks, and poor blacks often, and perhaps increasingly, agree on this point. As a young black man once told me, '. . . . When you see another black man get stopped by the police, you wonder how race figured into it. When you go into a store and the salespeople give you an extra bit of scrutiny, you wonder. When you're on the elevator in your apartment building and the elevator stops at a floor and the white woman waiting moves to another elevator, your first thought is race. Little things like that remind you as a black person that you are paying your black tax.'" And to make matters worse, America is imprisoning blacks (particularly black men) at a horrifying rate, in large measure because of drug laws that hit blacks with disproportionate force.

Former prosecutor Paul Butler is far from convinced that Darden's faith is well-placed and in his searchingly candid contribution to this collection, he explains his pessimism. The Willie Horton incident, and others like it, believes Butler, establish "that it will be impossible for African Americans to achieve justice through traditional politics, including exercising their hard-gained franchise. Perhaps 'impossible' is too strong; it is better to say that it will take too long, and African Americans can't afford to wait, considering the emergency nature of the crisis. . . . If it took the white majority more than two hundred years to understand that slavery was wrong, and approximately one hundred years to realize that segregation was wrong (and still many don't understand), how long will it take them to perceive that American criminal justice is evil?"

Even many blacks who do not see American justice as evil do believe it has been and continues to be considerably less than fair. As Roger Wilkins observes: "There is no more important concept in American criminal law than the presumption of innocence. . . . Unfortunately, it still doesn't always work. In some places, poor, alienated black males are *presumed guilty,* not because of who they are as individuals, but because of where they are from, what they look like, and what their cultural affect is. In too many big cities, criminal justice is an ugly business. It is often carried on in battered courtrooms by overburdened and harried people. . . . However we Americans may have viewed the 'refuse of [somebody else's] teeming shore,' the refuse of America's poorest streets doesn't look very attractive to these overburdened people. The task of sorting out the individuality of surly, beaten, often defiant (and often guilty) people is sometimes beyond the capacities of the workers in this strained system."

According to a much-quoted analysis by a nonprofit Washington-based organization called the Sentencing Project, roughly a third of black men in their twenties are either in prison, in jail, on probation, or on parole. And the numbers, says the Sentencing Project, are virtually certain to get worse. Given that grim statistical reality, George Curry argues, "African Americans had more than ample reason to be suspicious of the criminal justice system as O. J. Simpson went on trial for murder. It was not that O. J. loomed large as an endearing figure among blacks—the *Pittsburgh Courier* sardonically noted that even his Ford Bronco was white—it was that African Americans continue to view the criminal justice system as a criminal injustice system." Inevitably that suspicion of the justice system colors how prosecutors (particularly nonwhite prosecutors) are perceived, and black prosecutors are acutely aware of their often suspect status. During an interview, Jeffrey Craig, deputy attorney general of Pennsylvania, confided, "Sometimes I'm very apprehensive about even telling black people what I do." The reason, as I explain in a separate essay, is that the information about his job often prevents people from seeing him for who he is: "[T]hough he prosecutes primarily white-collar crimes and most of his defendants are white, he knows that people won't recognize that fact from his job title. Nor will they understand that he is a critic of a system that, at times, especially when it deals with petty criminals, ends up 'putting a bandage on an infected sore.' The general public, he realizes, has no way of knowing that he goes out of his way to be fair to black defendants, that he shares many of the experiences they have had. . . . All his critics know or think they know, said Craig, is that 'I'm a turncoat, that I'm not helping my brothers and sisters.' They see him, in short, as 'part of the assembly line of degradation and oppression of black people.'"

It is hardly surprising, in light of such sentiments, that black prosecutors sometimes feel conflicted. Nonetheless, Darden and many of his counterparts argue that they are doing the best they can with the hand that fate, circumstance, and the perpetrators' own actions have dealt them. "How could I put other brothers in jail?" Darden asked rhetorically and dramatically. "How could I not? As long as they were victimizing old people and making orphans of children, how could I not?"

Robert Grace, a young deputy district attorney in Los Angeles who was on the losing end of the 1996 murder prosecution of rapper Calvin Broadus (better known as Snoop Doggy Dogg), has made much the same argument. Grace bristled at Broadus's description of him as an "Uncle Tom." Broadus, he snorted, "had an entire table of white lawyers. And *he* talks about a sellout?"

At a meeting of fellow black prosecutors, Grace described a dinner with several black professionals at which the O. J. Simpson case was discussed. When it came to light that Grace was involved in the prosecution of Broadus, he noted, the atmosphere suddenly turned chilly. "Another brother trying to take another brother down," was one guest's description of his role. Grace was stunned. "Why," he asked himself, "are these people groaning at the fact that

I'm involved in this case as an African American prosecutor?" Didn't they realize, he found himself asking, that the victim was a person of African descent? Didn't they know that people, black people, were dying of gun violence every day and that somebody needed to stand up and say, "This is wrong"?

From Grace's perspective—and from the perspective of many of his peers—getting killers (whatever their color) off the streets is a valuable, even essential, public service. "This is where I feel I can make the most difference every day," he said. And yet, he acknowledges (as a specialist in gang violence cases) that those he prosecutes are invariably black or Latino—a fact which serves as a disturbing reminder of the centrality of race on the streets and in the courts of Los Angeles.

In one of the most famous dissents in Supreme Court history Justice John Marshall Harlan lectured his peers that the U.S. Constitution is "color-blind." "The destinies of the two races, in this country, are indissolubly linked together," asserted Harlan. In 1896, Harlan's colleagues on the Court were not prepared to accept such blasphemy, but in 1954 the Supreme Court reversed itself and granted blacks full equality under the law. Yet, in a country where blacks are roughly eight times as likely to end up in jail as whites, the very notion of color-blind justice is endangered, even if most of those blacks are guilty. Darden's dream of making the justice system "ours too" means little to defendants, or their families, who see that the only blacks present in any substantial numbers in court are those sitting in the docks. And as Andrea Ford, who covered the criminal court beat for the *Los Angeles Times*, reports, blacks in the court are not necessarily treated with respect: "I recall once almost colliding with two white police detectives at the entrance to the courthouse. After I slipped in ahead of them and walked toward the elevators, I heard someone behind me singing, "Hey, hey, she's a monkey," to the tune of the theme song of the old *Monkees* television show." When Ford turned she found the two cops smirking, causing her to wonder: "If this is the way they treated me . . . how did they treat the suspects they brought into court?"

Confronted with an overwhelmingly white structure and often with nasty attitudes as well, many blacks conclude, for obvious reasons, that there is more virtue in fighting such a system than in joining it, especially when that system seems hell-bent on putting huge segments of the black community under lock and key. As Butler puts it: "I know that one-third of my sisters and brothers are not dangerous or evil, and that any system of law that places them under its supervision is morally bankrupt and in need of immediate subversion."

In explaining the appeal of one of his fictional characters named Mouse (a stone-cold killer who "could gut a man and then sit down to a plate of spaghetti"), novelist Walter Mosley observed: "For a group of oppressed people a man like Mouse is the greatest kind of hero. He's a man who will stand up against bone-cracking odds with absolute confidence. He's a man who won't accept even the smallest insult. And for a people for whom insult is as common as air, that's a man who will bring joy." Often, added Mosley, "black men have to cross the white man's rules because we know those rules never applied to us anyway."

That sense of being excluded from and abused by the system is pervasive in certain black neighborhoods. And it is based not merely on theory but on painful personal experiences. As Clarence Page relates in these pages, a typical black response to an inquiry about the justice system would go something like: *"Sure, I know the system doesn't work because my uncle got arrested and beat up by the cops the other night and he ain't done nothin'!"*

Like Butler, Page parts company with Darden on the issue of whether such experiences—and the anger and resentments they create—interfere with the quest for justice in the courtroom. To the contrary, argues Page, those resentments, in large part racial, enhance the integrity of the judicial process by allowing real life to influence and inform the proceeding of the court. History tells us, argues Page, "that juries were created precisely to bring values of the street to the courtroom"—even if that sometimes meant ignoring evidence and setting guilty defendants free as a means of passing judgment on the justice process itself.

Page nonetheless worries that alienation from the system can sometimes be self-defeating. For it can not only lead jurors to reject evidence, but can lead people to reject a productive role in the larger society. It can lead young people, for instance, to dismiss book learning out of a mistaken notion that such a thing is "white" or to spurn mainstream jobs out of an untested belief that life in the white man's world will never be fair.

Yet, as Elijah Anderson argues, alienation among blacks—and certainly among black, inner-city youths—may be inevitable as long as America remains such a racially rancorous place. "Resigned to a society that does not include him in the American Dream," the young inner-city black man, writes Anderson, "comes of age realizing the hard truths that American society is not there for him, that a racially stratified system is in place, and that his place, fortified through acts of prejudice and discrimination, is at the bottom of it. This creates in him a profound sense of alienation and forces him to adapt, to make some adjustments. That resignation can be observed in the young men's looks, in their actions, and in their tendency to disparage white people. . . . Life has taught the young black man that he can do certain things but cannot go beyond his limited situation; dreams are simply never fulfilled." It has taught him, in short, that he is trapped on a road to nowhere, and that perhaps the only honorable thing to do is to die with dignity.

That misbegotten quest for honor too often leads to tragedy—not only for the young men abandoned by society, but for anyone who chances to get in their way. To their credit, many blacks (including some who are custodians of the criminal justice system) are searching for ways to get beyond that lose-lose situation. Betty DeRamus introduces us to several such exceptional individuals, including the memorable Willie Lipscomb, a Detroit judge who prefers turning people around to locking them up, and who has made it his mission to persuade young people to give up their guns.

As DeRamus explains, "Lipscomb began the Handgun Intervention Program . . . after nineteen-year-old, college-bound Kowan Comer, a boy he loved like a son, was shot to death at a party. Starting HIP in 1993 was Lipscomb's response to the shock of losing Comer. Under the program, bail-bond-seeking defendants who are charged with carrying concealed weapons—people who usually get probation if convicted—attend HIP's three-hour Saturday-morning class. Defendants as young as ten and as old as sixty-five have shown up for sessions, but most are in their late teens and early twenties. Usually, they come only once, but sometimes a judge orders them to return. Lipscomb made one young man who was arrested for carrying an AK47 attend thirty sessions of HIP." And the results, reveals DeRamus, have been astounding. Virtually none of the defendants who attend the program return with new charges within six months. Lipscomb's experience in losing a friend was not the only force propelling him to seek out an alternative way of life for gun-obsessed young black males: "His concern started in the late 1970s when he was a Wayne County prosecutor, specializing in murder cases. He was struck—no, shattered—by the autopsy reports. 'I saw one little young nineteen year old after another, dead with one gunshot wound in the chest,' he recalled. 'All of the autopsy protocols were the same—healthy, well-nourished young black males. . . . I started to see how guns would devastate young black men.'"

Young black men, of course, are not the only victims of pointless violence. Nor are black prosecutors the only ones conflicted over the prospect of sending felonious black men to prison. As Anita Hill makes clear, black women—particularly those who have been brutalized by the men they love—sometimes find themselves torn between the mandates of the law and loyalty to an abusive man. Hill recounts the story of Felicia and Warren Moon: a former cheerleader and a professional football player who, like Nicole and O. J. Simpson, briefly came to be seen in some circles as the public face of domestic violence. The Moon case came to light because a horrified child called 911 to exclaim, "My daddy is going to hit my mommy." Police ultimately found a bruised Felicia Moon, who allowed them to photograph the injuries she had suffered at her husband's hands and who told of fleeing the house in fear, but who refused to press charges. When prosecutors insisted on taking the case to court anyway, she testified in such a way—effectively taking all the blame for the incident herself—as to make her husband's conviction impossible. The issue in Felicia Moon's mind apparently was not just that of loyalty to a spouse, but to a spouse who she evidently felt had been unfairly targeted for racial reasons. As Hill writes: "Felicia Moon did what many women do: she stood by her man. But more than devotion to Warren Moon may have led to her choice. For Felicia Moon, a whole host of factors, some that she mentioned and others that were drawn from the circumstances, might have led her to resist filing charges and testifying. Money, fame, gender, and race all entered into the equation. Few of us dared to say what we instinctively knew was the truth: Felicia Moon could easily have been driven by a desire to save the reputation of a well-known Black man not only for himself but for the entire African American community. She ultimately decided that the loss of her reputation would be less damaging to her standing in the community than would be her disloyalty to a Black male hero."

To understand community loyalty to black men who are not good people (to men who beat their wives or prey on vulnerable people in their own communities) it is necessary to look beyond the individual miscreant and to the larger issue of racial persecution. One does not have to be an extremist to agree with Paul Butler's observation that a third of black men cannot be dangerous or evil, that there is something fatally wrong in a system (or with a society) that puts so many black people in jail. The very fact that so many black men are being consumed by the prison industry is enough to cause many people to rally, almost reflexively, around virtually anyone denounced by white authority. By the same token, distrust of black law enforcers is not an irrational sentiment lacking an antecedent. As Roger Wilkins points out: "The history of using blacks against other blacks has deep roots in slavery. There were brutal black overseers. There were also black informers. Plans for slave insurrections and escapes were often betrayed by other slaves seeking the masters' favor. In later generations, some blacks in law enforcement played out those roles, having concluded that they were accountable only to white power. Blacks working in the order-keeping system today carry the burden of that history."

Clearly, however, we are no longer in the age of slavery—or even Jim Crow. So to what extent is the history of a blatantly racist age relevant to black behavior today? Stanley Crouch argues that its relevancy has obvious limits. Similarly, suggests Crouch, arguments about the disproportionate impact of the justice system on blacks may be somewhat overblown: "Even if we accept the idea that the justice system unfairly tilts punishment toward lower-class black defendants and that the penal system imprisons a disproportionate number of convicted black men, we have to wonder what this idea actually means when we balance it against the equally disproportionate numbers of murders, rapes, robberies, and assaults that black people suffer at the hands of other black people who reside in the same communities. The yearly body counts extend far beyond what they were in even the most brutal periods of redneck Southern rule and Northern race riots." At some point, argues Crouch, rationalizations rooted in suppositions about consequences of a history of oppression must give way to some notion of free will, to some sense of individual responsibility. Moreover, the very fact of Simpson's acquittal is clear evidence of how much things have changed. As Wade Henderson points out, "Just two generations ago, a black man who was accused of Simpson's crime would have been lucky to survive the trial, much less be acquitted by a 'jury of his peers' for killing a white woman, at least in the South."

Is Clarence Page therefore right to suggest that it may be time for a reassessment? Can blacks forever think of ourselves as outsiders in our own country? Crouch believes the only sensible answer to the latter question is no. There is a certain lunacy, he contends, in the notion that we are defined solely by race, that our aspirations, our behavior, or our place in society should be dictated by race. At the center of the Simpson controversy, writes Crouch, "is the question of whether or not one's actions can yet be assessed on individual terms. . . . Was it possible for O. J. Simpson to be an individual first and a Negro either second or only incidentally? Was it possible for a predominantly black jury to be a gathering of individual experiences and perspectives instead of largely a mass of Pavlovian darkies ready to drool in unison at the opportunity to vent revenge on a legal system demonstrably mottled by racism?"

Darden clearly believes that, in many quarters, the answer is no, that despite his best efforts, his individuality (as far as much of the public was concerned) was subsumed within a racial stereotype. Yet, as Crouch points out, Darden had his own somewhat stereotypical ideas about race. When Darden writes, for instance, about "responsibilities as a human being" being "as important as the responsibilities of being an African American," does he mean to imply that those responsibilities are somehow in conflict? And, if in fact they are, what does that say not just about the justice system but about the fate of blacks in this country? Indeed, the larger issue raised by Darden, as well as many of the writers in the collection, is, "What does it mean to be a black person in America today?" To what extent is America truly our country too? To what extent will we continue to be defined—by ourselves and by the larger society—by stereotypes of criminality and intellectual defeat? How long, to put it bluntly, will black people in America continue to be "niggers"? Such questions ultimately can only be answered by African Americans, but they must be answered within the context of a society that clings to its stereotypes and that remains uncertain of what to make of its darker citizens.

However they perceive Darden, though, all the contributors agree that the Darden Dilemma is only one element in a much larger set of problems having to do with race and justice in America, and that that larger set of problems must be addressed. In an era in which more and more young black men (and boys) are coming to view a stint in jail as an inevitable rite of passage, it is not alarmist to point out that something has gone horribly wrong in America, and that as judges send more and more blacks to prison, they may also be destroying America's long-cherished dream of racial equality. At some point—and one hopes it is long before we have turned vast parts of our nation into penal colonies—Americans must face up to the fact that prison is a poor substitute for effective social policy. Without doubt, violent criminals belong off the streets, and many of them should spend their natural lives behind prison bars—or as far from human prey as the law and human ingenuity can keep them. Yet, as many of the authors of this collection suggest, street crime does not break out in a vacuum; it typically thrives in environments that are not only impoverished financially, but that lack strong social, educational, and family support networks and that offer no compelling reason to believe in a better future. Until we, as a society, become as eager to provide those things for young black men as we are to provide them with jail cells, future Christopher Dardens will continue to face a dilemma—as they wonder whether they were truly placed on this earth for the primary purpose of putting other blacks behind bars; and future black jurors will find themselves sorely tempted to weigh the option—even if they know it to be wrong—of freeing black defendants simply because of the color of their skin.

Reading

Workin' It: Women Living Through Drugs and Crime

LEON PETTIWAY

The worst fight I've ever had with a man was when I got my jaw broke. I was downtown then with the guy that was such good friends of mine. I got with him and he broke my jaw. He said I was being too nice. I never did understand that. But he was at this hotel with this girl and I went around there and all I did was ask him what time he was coming home. That was bad. To him I came 'round there to catch him doing this, but that wasn't why I came there. How was I 'posed to know he was there with her, you know? But in his mind, I came there for that purpose, to find something, you know, that he was doing wrong. Hit me with his fist and broke my jaw. He's not a big guy but he's strong. He's muscular like, you know.

I stayed in the hospital from like January to June because it kept getting infected. I mean, my face was messed up. I came out once and had to go right back because he hit me again in the same place and I had to go right back. So they just said, "Well, we gonna keep you here because we have to put a piece of metal in here." They operated on my face three times, trying to set it back so it would grow, you know, where it be normal, and it still not straight, but it's better than I ever expected to see myself 'cause my face was totally, I mean, you know, it was . . . I mean, you know, it was twisted. It was messed up.

Then I kept . . . people were still bringing me drugs at the hospital, and I didn't know long as you do drugs that you won't heal. I didn't know that. Then one day, the doctor say, "Are you still doing drugs?" And I say, "Yeah." He say, "As long as you do drugs, you're not gonna heal. We might as well send you home." I said, "Don't send me home, not with my face like this. Not with my face like this. I won't do the drugs." I stopped doing the drugs. . . . That's another time I stopped doing the drugs. Then I started healing up. They put a hole under there to drain the infection and stuff. But my face was really . . . I didn't even know myself when I looked in the mirror 'cause it was all, you know . . . all this up here was twisted around, you know. It was just all twisted.

It wasn't no way I could make money then, you know, but I tried. I went out there wired up and everything and it was real difficult for me then. I had a nice apartment and I lost that 'cause I couldn't pay the rent, you know. And I didn't want him back, right? So I didn't go home. I didn't go to my mother's 'cause I didn't go when I was well, I wasn't going then neither. But I made it . . . I made out all right. I had a few tricks that was relatives of mine and they took care of me. When you become a prostitute, your tricks is your best friends, you know.

My tricks sort of helped me through that very difficult period. That's right. They're the only ones that did. My sister came to see me one time in the hospital and that was that. My tricks helped and other drug addicts who I helped get on their feet and other guys that I helped get started, like they mighta needed a thousand dollars to buy their first package, helped me. I mighta gave them five hundred to help them out. They never forgot me and I appreciate things like that. They never forgot me when I was down and out. They came, you know.

Besides my husband I've never been in a relationship with someone who I could say I really loved. So I really don't know what love is. I wouldn't mind having a man that didn't do drugs, that worked for a living. Perhaps he's an ex-drug addict, 'cause then he would understand, you know. If he never did drugs, he would never understand a person that do do drugs. You never felt the way they feel so you can't understand it. But if you've been on drugs, then you can understand somewhat. I'm not saying that you have to go along with it, but you would understand. So I think I would like to have a man that's been on drugs before but has recovered, not only because he could understand me, but then it's something to look up to, you know.

If I wasn't a drug addict, I don't know what kind of man I would want. Probably a stiff-necked man. You know, real proper one, one that didn't do anything but go to work and buy nice things and stuff like that. Real square. If I was in recovery, . . . I don't know if it's true or not, but I've been around a whole lot of people that's been on drugs and not on it anymore, they still keep some of their dope fiend ways. There's still something about them that you can tell, if they don't do drugs, they used to do drugs. There's something, you know, it's something, and so I guess I'll always have that trait from now on. I would hope the person that I would be with would be able to understand that, like I said. Only way to understand that is to have a whole lot of knowledge about drug addicts or you've been one yourself. And not many people favor drug addicts.

I do like black, real dark-skinned guys and bow-legged guys, but I have more physical attraction to females than I do to males. And I like nice-looking girls. Girls that wear dresses and heels and things like that. I might see a guy and he's cute, black and bow-legged, but he don't do that, you know, that little thing, that little tingle. I don't get that with guys, but looking at some women, I get that.

I would consider myself bisexual 'cause I have been with a woman before. Girls make you feel different. Although this one woman, we fought a lot, too. But I feel better as a all-around person, I feel better. I do. I do better when I'm with a woman than when I'm with a man. I don't know why. I guess 'cause men don't really like me, see. They really don't. They act like they do until they get me, and then once they got me, they act like they hate me. And that's the truth. So I don't know if I bring that out in them or if that's just how they are.

Oh, I was grown, fully grown and separated and everything from my husband when I had my first relationship with a woman. In my twenties. Well, this is when I was living around there at Quincy Street. She was living around that way and I met her around there. And I felt like I wanted to be with her. She let me know how she felt and everything. And I did it. So I met her by just being in the neighborhood, speaking, saying hello to each other. Then I started going over there all the time. She was having this girl named Regina babysit for her all the time and I used to go over there with Regina to watch the kids and stuff. And she told me she was gay, and I was interested. And so we started being friends and then one day she kissed me and it went on like that. My family knew. I told my family and everything.

So give me the woman! It just feels better! Everything about it is better. Ain't nothing going up in you, making you uncomfortable. All right? It's just your body and her body and it feels better. It's softer. When she touch you, ain't nothing hurt, nothing at all hurts. There's nothing that's gonna give you any kind of discomfort, any kind of pain, any kind of "Oh, you gotta do that." If she's like sucking your tittie, you don't feel like she's biting you. She's use her mouth and not her teeth. It's just all around better.

Do I think of myself as being gay? I don't know what to consider myself. That happened once in my life, and I haven't practiced it since then. Although there have been times when I was in the street—not like I am now, before I got strung out, when I was downtown working—it's been plenty of times when men wanted to see two women, and that was no problem, you know. Even right now, if a guy spend enough money, he wants to see two women, it's no problem with me. I guess I would consider myself bisexual because I do still have relationships with men. And although it's the same way with a male or female, it's hard to find a woman that's a square, that doesn't do drugs, that would take time to be with you if you strung out on drugs, especially female. They seem to have stronger feelings about that than men do.

I don't know any homosexual men that's drug addicts. I know a few lesbians though. Drug users treat them all right, but the guys don't like them 'cause . . . 'cause they be saying she thinks she's a man, you know, and because half of they manhood is already taken away by the drugs, . . . that really intimidates them.

I only started drinking like here lately, like a year or so. I never really drank. If I went out to a bar or something, I might have ordered, like I said, a creme de cocoa and milk, but I never got high off the alcohol, you know. Then I did diet pills. Popped a few diet pills here and there. I smoked joint a little bit. But when I started doing drugs is when I started drinking and snorting that monster. So from drinking and snorting that monster, I started shooting up. I started mainlining 'cause I moved from one place to another. The next place I moved, the people didn't snort. They was banging.

First time I banged I was over this . . . it's a whole family that lives in this one house, right? It was a lotta kids and everything, but we used to go in the basement. I was still drinking it and snorting it, right? So then I was watching everybody do it. Banging. I told Stella . . . say, "Stella. Hit me." It's no problem. No questions asked. Nothing. Right away she hit me.

Then like a week later I was home and this guy came over my house and I wanted him to hit me 'cause I didn't know how to do it in the beginning, right?

. . . There's lots of kinds of syringes, but I had the ones they call these buffalo things, right? They real short but they real fat. By me not knowing a lot about this stuff, I didn't know that what you had in a little skinny, regular syringe, when you put it in the big works, it look like you ain't got nothing in there. But it can be a whole lot. It just look like a little bit 'cause it's in a fat thing. So the guy asked me for something, I told him, "Naw. Look at all that I got." I mean, it was like this, but it was still a whole lot in those fat syringes. Said, "No. This is all I got." I said, "You gonna hit me?" Boy, when he hit me with that shit, he ran it straight in. I heard bells ringing. I couldn't see, and this went on for like a hour. I got in the shower just so I could, you know, bring myself around and stuff. And he told me, "See, that's how you get kilt." That's what he told me, "That's how you get kilt. You be greedy. That's how you die." But I didn't know.

So ever since then I got me a pair of works. I went in my room. I put a stocking around my arm. I look for that vein. I found it. I went in it, and I was hitting myself ever since. That's how he taught me. You're supposed to hit your own fucking self, especially if you don't wanna give nobody nothing for doing it for you, you know. 'Cause if you don't wanna pay them, they might fuck you up.

So over the course of a week or two I learned how to mix it up, draw it up, and put it in. This is with the monster. It's pretty much the same with all drugs you do except for now, with this cocaine they selling, you got to cook all this cut off of it because the cut is what was making people sick—these different cuts they put in them—so usually I cook as much of the cut off of it as I can.

How many hits do I take like during the course of a day? A day? Oh, boy, many as I can get, but I'd say about nine, ten, and would have spent about fifty, sixty dollars, and that's just for me. There wouldn't be any time between the first shot and the second shot if I got five dollars in my pocket. If I could get it all at one time, it would be enough to satisfy me. Now with this cocaine I want a drink after I do it because I be feeling real jittery and you be nervous and anxious, you know. So you drink some wine and it'll calm you down and mellow you out, or take a drink of any kind of strong liquor. I'd rather wait till I'm not gonna shoot up no more to drink or I'll drink because I don't have any more to shoot up.

After I shoot up, it lasts about five or ten minutes, really. You know, the rush that you get from it. But there's stuff they selling nowadays, I don't know what they putting in it. It makes you bug a little bit. Like I never bug like that. Stare in one place for a long time, stare one way or just be looking down on the ground. I never did that till I started doing cocaine here lately. And then I noticed that it'll last for like fifteen or twenty minutes. You be realizing that you looking like that, but you can't stop. Yeah, you schitz longer than the high lasts. As a matter of fact, you don't schitz while you rushing, you know. While you feeling the rush, you feeling the rush, then after the rush go, you start schitzing.

I don't wake up wanting drugs 'cause I don't usually wait till I want them. Like there's a routine. I usually just go on and get it. I feel cotton-mouth though. I gets up early in the morning. I get up about eight or nine o'clock, sometimes earlier than that—I been babysitting for three weeks so now I get up six o'clock, okay?—but before that I'd get up at eight or nine o'clock 'cause I can't sleep. I have my first shot about twelve. I might eat breakfast and I won't eat no more until nighttime.

So the routine is get up, watch the morning stories—I watch "Santa Barbara"—eat, then I might watch "Wheel of Fortune." Okay? Then that other word game, you know, the "Family Feud" thing, watch that one. And by twelve o'clock, either if I didn't . . . if I don't already know where I'm gonna get five dollars from, then I go out and I find someplace to go get five dollars from. I go get high and then between that time and the time I go home, that's when I'm steady doing, getting high or getting the money to get high.

After I get my first hit I go back out and get more money and come back and get high and do that all day. And that's what I do all day long. As far as getting in? Oh, man, 'bout normally I would say . . . I guess about eleven or twelve o'clock. I could go home if I wanted to 'cause by that time I done had a drink and I'm calmed down. I always end the evening with a little wine. Every time I go home, if I don't have a drink, a bottle to take with me, I'm going to a speakeasy and they gonna give me a drink, that's all.

I never have money left from the day before. I might have two or three dollars, but it's no way people gonna let me come in the house with five dollars. Ain't no way. That five dollars is gonna stay in that house. And if I do come in the house with five dollars, the only way I'll keep it is that Shaft don't know nothing about it. And since he's always out there looking and make sure he don't miss nothing, he always know.

Now I'll go on Sixteenth Street to cop. Before that I was going to the projects. Twenty-second, Twenty-first and Ludlow, and Twenty-first and Hering, those projects. But now they're gone. They got locked up. They was on television when they ran up there and busted them boys outside. So now I go on Sixteenth Street, and if not Sixteenth Street, it's in the neighborhood where I used to hang out, where I first met Shaft. This little street called Cardinal Street. They selling drugs again. They got three dollar bags on Tuesdays and Thursdays and they be the regular nickels but they just sell them for three dollars on Tuesdays and Thursdays. So on Tuesdays and Thursdays, that's where I go. So where I could get one bag for five dollars, I can get two for six. So that gives me a break. And that's where we usually go on Tuesdays and Thursdays. But every other day we be on Sixteenth Street. If you're a dollar short, they let you go anyway. I could really make out on Tuesdays and Thursdays, if I had a lotta money. Man, yeah.

Never been in shooting galleries. I'm a drug addict, but I'm scared of a lot of drug addicts all in one place at one time. I'm scared of them because I know what a lotta ways people think, you know. And usually they think prostitutes have a lot of money, but that's not the case all the time. I know how sometimes I'd be fiending and I'd be wanting me a hit real bad, and if they think I've got the money, I know they gonna take it from me at all costs. No, I don't go to shooting galleries, and I don't go to smoke houses.

I don't mind being around other drug users as long as it ain't personal, you know. If they come to my house, I don't have nothing that they might wanna steal, but they disrespect places so bad, you know. Like when you're using . . . when you clean up the syringe, ask me for something. If I don't have it right there for you, just don't squirt the blood and stuff on my floor—just take it for granted that that's where I want you to squirt it at. 'Cause blood stinks after it sit for a while. Don't just take for granted that you could just pluck the ashes on the floor. You know what I'm saying? Just don't take these things for granted. I could see if you seen blood and cigarette butts all over the floor, then I could see you doing that. But you don't see that.

I stay pretty much by myself. Me and whoever I'm with. 'Cause things happen to you in them places. See, people think just by you being a drug addict these things can happen to you. It's not always the case. Sometimes you put yourself in that predicament where it can happen to you. If I'm home shooting up, I ain't expecting nothing to happen to me in my house. But if I'm in a shooting gallery where any and everybody can come in who gives the man two dollars and they got guns and knives, anything could happen to me, you know. I know it's not much protection but I try to put at least that much on myself.

Money determines how much drugs I'll do. Now, say on a check day . . . usually it's his check day . . . on his check day, we spend more money in a hour than we spend all day, any other day. Do you know what I mean? If we have a hundred dollars this day, it'll all be gone in an hour on check day. But if it's any other day, we might spend a hundred dollars or a little more, but it will take us all day to spend that. You following me? 'Cause you got it right there in your pocket, you spend it all right away. Now I don't agree with that 'cause I be wanting to wait sometimes 'cause I know I be wanting another hit. When it's your check day you feel bad when you gotta go out there right away and turn a trick and you just got the check.

I carry my works all the time. Yeah, if I know I'm coming out. Yeah, all the time. If not, I'll go 'round the corner and I'll get a pair for a dollar. I never know who I'm gonna see or who I'm not gonna see. When we go to his friend's houses, his friend sells works, so we usually get a set from over there.

A lot of needle sharing is going on. Maybe not as much as used to be, but it's still a lot of it going on. People aren't cleaning their works with bleach, not like they should be. Since bleach is supposed to be the only thing that kills them.

I share my works with him. We clean them, but not with bleach but with alcohol. As far as HIV, you know, you just put it in your mind that your partner doesn't have it, so it's just in my mind that he doesn't have it. Although I don't think about what he does when I'm not around. I don't think about maybe he used somebody else's works, you know. I don't think about that. I've been tested not too long ago. Negative. I got tested last Thursday again because, when you take one test, it does not . . . what they say . . . it's not proven. You can always have it and, you know, you should take another test. Well, we took that one, both of us took it. We took the second one so. . . . Yeah, because you know Kim, right? You know the one—Dude's daughter's mother? She supposed to have that and Shaft used to go with her too. When I heard she had AIDS, I got concerned then.

You know what's good on the streets 'cause that's where everybody goes. You can see the line standing there. You watch the traffic. Whichever way everybody's going, or even you see one of your friends and you say, "Where's it at?" And they'll tell you.

I haven't been given garbage that often, but a few times. You won't know till you shoot it up, and how you feel from it. It's been a couple times when some people OD'd off the same thing I done shot, you know. And I be saying, "How? We did the same thing. How could this. . . . " You know, it don't be the potency of the drug, it be your body. Sometimes your body rejects the stuff and so if it's one of them times where your body just doesn't want it, it rejects it and your brain does the same thing. You're just unlucky, but you never know when that might happen.

It's not that the drug is that good 'cause they don't sell that good of drugs on the street anymore, you know. You have to know somebody to get drugs like they be saying eighty percent pure and all this kinda mess. The drugs we shooting right now is less than probably forty percent pure. It's probably less than that, 'cause that's why you have to shoot so much of it.

So you really don't know till you put it in your body. It could be like aspirins or something, or sugar or something, and you put the water on it and you try to cook the cut out and it like thickens up and it like you cooking some kinda food, you know. It lumps up or something, you know. Then you know it's garbage. But if whatever they selling you dissolves just like cocaine when you put a little heat to it to cook the cut away and it just leaves a liquid, you won't know until you shoot it. Somebody could be giving you acid, and you won't know. But if your body is feeling . . . you can tell when you don't feel right. Okay, you might be jittery or you might feel a little light-headed. If you're light-headed, I think you should wait for a little while, you know. I've had a lot of seizures. I'm an epileptic anyway.

Since you don't know how strong it is either you inject it very slowly, very slowly. Sometimes you be wanting a hit so bad, till you just push it right on in and those would be most of the times when I have seizures. 'Cause when I want it I'm running it straight in without stopping and waiting, you know, like you go halfway, then you wait, then you feel a little rush, then you know if you can take the rest of it. But sometimes you want a hit so bad, you just rush it right on in.

I feel that one day eventually everybody that does drugs is gonna die from it. How long can your body . . . since it's something that's not supposed to be inside your body anyway. You always hope that you never die from it or hope that one day you might wanna stop because you're doing it, you know. But I believe that everybody that does drugs, especially as regularly as I do, something is gonna happen to them.

I did try smoking a pipe when I first came back to Jefferson, right? Couple years ago. When I started smoking a pipe, I didn't wanna change my clothes. I didn't wanna wash up. I didn't wanna do nothing. And still I haven't gotten back to the way that I used to be, far as doing my hair and this kinda of stuff. . . . Whereas I would-never come outside like this with toy hair like this, if it wasn't done up—I'd put a scarf on or something—now I'll come outside with it all going back, with a big forehead. And I know that's just me being slack, you know. So it do take an effect on that.

Reading

Always Running: La Vida Loca: Gang Days in L.A.

LUIS V. RODRIGUEZ

Many nights in the garage, while in the throes of sleep, I heard knocking and voices. They appeared to be woven into the dreams. But I'd wake up and realize it was no dream but Chicharrón or another homeboy or homegirl needing a place to crash, to party or just hang.

On such a night, I woke up to raps on the window. I yanked myself out of the blankets and opened the door. Santos, Daddio and Pokie, three of the Lomas crazies, were standing there.

"*Qué hubo*, homes?" I greeted.

"Chin, we need to do something tonight," Santos responded. "You with it man."

I already sensed what they meant. They wanted me to do a *jale*, a hit against Sangra. The night before Tutti from Los Diablos had gotten into a big argument with his long-term girlfriend, Cokie. In anger, Tutti drove up to Las Lomas and shot Little Man, killing him instantly. The police had already busted Tutti, but Lomas needed to exact some revenge. I knew the whole story. What I didn't know was Puppet, Ragman and the other main dudes had decided I needed to help "take care of it."

"*Orale*, let me get ready."

I put on dark clothes and my trench coat. It became a habit for me to take the trench coat whenever I did jobs like this.

We climbed over fences behind the garage and emerged onto Ramona Avenue. A car was there already. I entered, sitting in between Pokie and Little Man's brother, Beto, who had been sitting, deathly still, in the car. Santos and Daddio sat up front.

"What we got to do?" I asked.

"Look under the seats," Santos casually suggested.

I looked down with my eyes, without moving, and could see the edges of bottles and some rags. Shit, I thought, they want to firebomb a house. This meant somebody's mother, little sister or brother could be hurt or killed. But this is how things had gotten by then. Everyone was fair game in barrio wars; people's families were being hit all the time.

We cruised toward Sangra. Santos knew the police would be extra heavy the night after a shooting. But if we didn't move in a timely manner the impression would be anyone could hit us, anytime.

"Where we going?" I asked.

"We're going to Chava's *cantón*."

This was heavy. We were going after Sangra's main warrior. Who knows how they found out where his family lived, because Chava had moved in with Dina somewhere else. But the idea was to make him pay dearly, going after his mother's house, and if need be, anybody who might have the misfortune of being there.

I felt edgy, my muscles straining, my leg striking a beat against the back of the seat. I didn't want to do this. But once you're asked to do a hit, you can't refuse, can't question or even offer an excuse. Since I was easily accessible in the garage, I became a good candidate for these undertakings.

We pulled up to a quiet, suburban-looking street. Chava's family actually lived outside the barrio, in a better part of San Gabriel, pretty much like me. We parked down a ways and climbed up an embankment behind a row of houses.

Pokie brought up a bag filled with the bottles and rags. Daddio had cans of gasoline. We squatted in weeds behind a brick-fenced house with a back yard full of flowers and exotic plants, the way of many Mexican homes. A back porch had leisure chairs and gaily-painted rubber tires filled with soil and topped with purple, red and yellow petals.

It looked similar to my mother's back yard.

Santos poured gasoline into the bottles and stuffed the rags at the top, leaving a section hanging over. We each had a bottle. We were to toss them at the back porch, then run like hell to the car where Beto kept the engine running.

I didn't want to do it, but I couldn't stop. I felt trapped. I knew the only thing for me was to go through with it, and get out of there as fast as possible. I felt excitement. And an ache of grief.

A news account reported five people ran out of a house in San Gabriel after four molotov cocktails struck its back porch. Everybody got out safely, but the back of the house went up in flames and the rest of it sustained irreparable water damage from the fire hoses.

Little Man's death and the firebombing were part of a series of violent incidents between Lomas and Sangra which stretched back generations. Dudes had fathers and even grandfathers involved in the feud.

Of course, word got around about who did Chava's house. I don't know how this happened. But it soon involved my family.

By then my sister Gloria, 13 years old and a student at Garvey, looked up to me. To her, I was independent, in starched khaki pants, tattooed, with an earring in one ear before anybody did this kind of thing; always full of stories and good times. Her inexperienced mind soaked it all up.

Gloria joined a younger set of Lomas girls called United Sisters or US, and called herself Shorty. Sometimes I hung out with them, just for the kicks. I didn't see Shorty becoming a crazy Lomas girl. I saw it only as something she would get over as she matured.

One night she attended a dance at the San Gabriel Mission sponsored by Thee Prophettes, another girl's club. I didn't go, so Shorty played it smooth, hanging with her homegirls Cece and Huera from US.

Sure enough, Cokie and Dina showed up at the dance with a few Sangra girls. One of them was Spyder, who knew me from Garvey before she moved to Sangra and became one of the *locas*. When Spyder first noticed Shorty she felt a tug of recognition.

The Sangra girls gave everyone hard looks. US and Thee Prophettes kept cool, not wanting anything to undermine the benefit dance. Later that evening, though, Spyder figured out Shorty was my sister. I was "marked," meaning Sangra members were obligated to shoot Chin from Lomas. But a sister would do as well, Spyder reasoned.

Spyder relayed the information to Cokie and Dina. They had small caliber handguns. They discussed how they would corner Shorty and then let her have it, possibly in the girl's restroom.

Sometime later, my brother Joe received a phone call.

"Pick us up Joe," Shorty whispered in a frightened tone. "There's something happening here—and I'm scared."

Shorty told Joe to drive around the dance hall to a back entrance. Shorty, Cece and Huera planned to be there and get into the car. Timing was everything.

Joe didn't know what the problem might be. He got into his car and proceeded to do as Shorty asked.

He drove to the side of the dance hall where a door entrance was located, but Shorty and her friends weren't around. He waited. Suddenly the doors burst open. Shorty, Cece and Huera ran out, almost tripping as they held their heels in their hands.

"Joe, get the car going—hurry!"

"What the . . ."

But Joe couldn't get the final words out. A volley of gunfire came toward him. My sister and her friends rushed into the car, piling on top of one another. Joe pressed the accelerator, forcing the car to peel across the asphalt. Shorty didn't quite get inside but she held on as the car sped off; Cokie and Dina stood in the entranceway, and, firing from the shoulder, continued to pump .22 bullets toward the car as it vanished into the fog-drenched distance.

Sheriff's helicopters were a nightly annoyance. It could have been Vietnam, only we were the enemy. They hovered above the slopes and ravines, covering the ground with circles of lights. Deputies drove by often, pushing dudes against walls, detaining them and dispersing crowds of two or more. The homeboys shot out the few lampposts to keep the place in darkness. We hid in bushes, in basements and abandoned buildings. We were pushed underground. Codes, rules and honor became meaningless.

Rapes became a common circumstance in the Hills. They began as isolated incidents, then a way of life. Some believed this ritual started with outsiders, not from within the Hills. Others said it began with one guy who happened to be crazy, but the rest followed suit as the attacks signified a distorted sense of power. One dude was said to have raped 17 girls one summer.

Enano once pulled up in a four-door green Chevy as Chicharrón and I lolled around on Teresa Avenue. He climbed out of the car, opened the back door and invited us to "get in on this." A naked girl, passed out, lay in the back seat. A black patch of pubic hair stood out on a shock of white skin which looked as if she had been immersed in flour.

"*Chale,* homes," I responded. "I ain't with it."

Chicharrón nodded the same sentiment.

Without hesitation, Enano closed the door, entered the front seat and took off, perhaps looking for somebody else to approach.

A rainy evening greeted Yuk Yuk, Fuzzy, Ernie López and me as we left a *quinceñera* dance in the Avenues, a barrio northeast of downtown Los Angeles. We jumped into Ernie's lowrider van. Paco and two girls were inside the van. Ernie put on some music which rattled the brain cells through speakers in the front and back of the van. Fuzzy and Yuk Yuk talked with the girls as I took swigs of Silver Satin wine and snorts of heroin. Mellowed and mumbling, we drove through the wet side streets toward the Hills.

The girls were loaded; incoherent and sleepy. Makeup smeared their faces. Paco groped through the blouse of one of the girls, who faintly tried to pull him off. Fuzzy held the other girl up as he smiled at Yuk Yuk and me. I nodded off, and then woke, nodded off and then woke. Soon I noticed Paco on top of the girl he had been manhandling. Her legs were spread outward, and a torn underwear twisted around an ankle. Paco's pants were below his knees and I could see his buttocks rise up and down as he thrust into her, her weak moans more from the weight of the body than anything else.

Ernie pulled up to Toll Drive. Yuk Yuk and Fuzzy pulled the other girl out and down the slope to the field. Paco kept at it with the girl in the van. I clambered out, the cold humid air jolting me to my feet. Ernie passed me the bottle of Silver Satin as he wobbled down to where Yuk Yuk and Fuzzy were already situated. I looked back. I could hear Paco coming, scratchy noises rising from his throat. The girl, who was somewhere between 12 and 14 years old, had her arms laid out over her head, her eyes closed, her mouth opened—unconscious, but as if in a silent scream.

I made it to the field and saw Yuk Yuk kissing the other girl on a section of cinder-block wall while Fuzzy opened her legs with his hand to get a better feel.

Ernie looked at me and motioned me to come over. I didn't want any part of it. Something filled my throat and I puked around my shoes. Yuk Yuk by then had thrown the girl to the ground. I knew what they were going to do, and wandered off.

I walked up the slope, saw Paco pulling his pants up through the slightly-opened van doors. As before, I found myself ambling along a dirt road.

Wilo and Payasa moved to El Monte to live with an aunt, partly to remove themselves from the violence surrounding the barrio. Their older brothers stayed and continued to carry on the fight. Glad my friends were not to be in the line of fire, I went to say goodby on the day they were leaving.

They lived on Berne Street, a section of Lomas called "Little TJ," which consisted of a road which flowed in mud on rainy days, making it difficult to get in and out. Makeshift stucco, brick and clapboard shacks clawed the hills on either side of the road.

Payasa looked different, following several months in rehab hospitals and half-way homes. Her hair was back to its normal luster, short and combed straight down instead of teased. She had on no makeup and thus seemed a stranger, although we were so close at one time, sleeping together on park benches, sniffing and groping in the tunnel or in my garage room. I no longer knew this person in front of me.

Payasa didn't smile. Yet she acknowledged me rather sweetly.

"Oh my Chin—you'll miss me?" she asked, more a statement than a question.

"Depends," I replied. "Just keep in touch."

"I'll always remember you, homes," she said and placed her hand on my face; meandering scars across her arms. "We've seen things most people never see. We've seen death. And here we are, still able to say goodby. I don't know if we deserve this."

"*Orale*, sure we deserve it. Don't ever forget that."

"I mean, we haven't done anything really decent," she said, then paused.

"You know," she continued. "I've forgotten what it is to cry. I don't know why."

"Me neither, but I know one thing, we better find out."

Wilo came by with a medium-sized bag of his belongings, but then he wasn't one for possessions.

"Hey, *ése*, what's up?" he said.

"*Aquí nomás*. You got everything?"

"You pack for where you're going, and where I'm going there's nothing to pack for."

"Are you sure you want to do this?"

"I'm sure I don't want to do this," he answered, then looked back toward his former home. "But there's nothing I can do about it. Even my *carnales* want us to leave. And I do what they say."

I helped Payasa and Wilo put their things into their father's beat-up station wagon which had a side door held on by twine and good wishes. I would miss them but it was best they leave, maybe start fresh again if this were possible.

"I owe you man," I finally said, something I never told Wilo about his role in my near-death experience. "You saved my life."

"*Chale, ése* don't put that on me," he said. "You don't owe me nothing. Just pay yourself back."

I hugged them both and proceeded down Berne Street to the nearest fields. It would be the last time I ever saw them again.

Later I found out Payasa ended up pregnant and in a prison of matrimony somewhere. But 10 days after they moved, dudes from the Monte Flores barrio would shoot and run over Wilo several times; his body discovered wedged between metal trash bins in an obscure alley. Payasa called me one day to say she hadn't heard from Wilo for a day or so. Then she called back to tell me she heard of his death while listening to the radio. Wilo was 15 years old. Payasa didn't cry.

Everything lost its value for me: Love, Life and Women. Death seemed the only door worth opening, the only road toward a future. We tried to enter death and emerge from it. We sought it in heroin, which bears the peace of death in life. We craved it in our pursuit of Sangra and in battles with the police. We yelled: *You can't touch this!*, but *Come kill me!* was the inner cry. In death we sought what we were groping for, without knowing it until it caressed our cheeks. It was like an extra finger in the back of our heads, pressing, gnawing, scraping. This fever overtook us, weakening and enslaving us. Death in a bottle. In spray. In the fire-eyes of a woman, stripped of soul and squeezed into the shreds of her humanity.

Shirley: Navigating the Way Home from Prison

PATRICIA O'BRIEN

After a sleepless night waiting for the morning light, I finally heard, "pack out, time to go." By the time they finished all the processing her out and release of her "personals" it was after noon and after she got a ride to the bus station in the blue IDOC labeled van, she couldn't catch a bus until late afternoon. The trip home to Chicago from Decatur Correctional Center was the pits—180 miles and almost 4 hours long. You know you leave in the colors unless your family picks you up and brings you some street clothes? In my case, military-looking ugly prison whites that made me avoid anyone's eyes for what I might see in them: pity or more likely, disgust. I looked out the window and watched the sun set over the farms and fields of Central Illinois and wondered what it would have been like to grow up in a small rural town. The littered sidewalks, empty storefronts, cramped apartments, and, my biggest fear, drug dealers on seem like every corner, belonged to a different universe from these long stretches of space. I tried to think through some plans for starting a new life. But the fears got in my way. I wondered how I could avoid the pitfalls of the streets and the disaster my life had been in the last five years. As the bus turned up north, I swore I would not return to this place. My body had been locked down but prison had not sapped my spirit and if I could draw on that, I could manage the hard road ahead of me.

The first time she was arrested, Shirley had served six months on probation for possession. All she had to do was finish the drug treatment program and stay clean for three more months but she got bored with the everyday class sessions that no longer held her attention and frustrated with the lack of control over her everyday choices. No one at the center spent any one-on-one time with her to really know her or what she was dealing with and she got tired of resisting the high that would release her from the grief of Dwayne's death, when he was shot accidentally by another dealer in the 'hood. So, she turned up with a dirty drop and that slip got her a ride downstate for a three year prison sentence for violating conditions of her probation and for drug possession. She now says that prison "saved my life" because it gave her a time out from her chaotic life that she used to reestablish her priorities—and to escape from the guilt she felt every time she saw her teen-aged daughter's face—the silent reminder of her disappearance from her daughter's life over the last three or four years since Dwayne's death.

In prison, Shirley worked to stay clear of the games and the drugs that sometimes came in through the visitors' door. Unlike most other women in prison, she had several years of college. She had worked as an accountant for a company and had had a nice life at one time. At first, the drug dealing she and

Dwayne did was for the "extras"—the nice cars, the clothes, the trips. Dwayne's job as a mechanic paid the real bills. And the dealing at first was small stuff, but then the layoffs started and the bored men wanted more so they kept working to meet the demand. But from the first several times that Shirley used crack, it picked her up and didn't put her down and she knew (though in the early days denied it), she was addicted. She knew she needed help but didn't know how to get it without looking weak, without leaving Dwayne behind, without looking like the bad mother she was at that time. As she thought about it, she felt lucky—all told she only served about 15 months, and she was determined, just like other women she saw leaving Decatur and then returning through the revolving door, that she would be different, that she could "keep it real" and not get sucked back into that black hole that she had tripped into before.

In addition to staying clean while she was in prison, her time there was also about surviving the boredom and finding some way to do her time so it wouldn't "do" her. She participated in everything she could think of from playing volleyball to going to church. She also was one of the lucky inmates who got to enroll in the drug treatment program while she was incarcerated. Most of the women doing a short bit didn't become eligible for one of the slots in time before going back out the door and likely back to the life they had before they came in. Much to her surprise, she even made some friends. Learning from an early age that you just can't trust women, she hadn't bothered with them prior to entering prison. She found she even had something to talk about with Donna, a white woman from rural Illinois who at first meeting seemed different from her in most every way! They did however, share the commonality of a bunch of trouble related to using—but Donna's poison had been alcohol at the tap down the road from where she lived. She too had experienced the loss of a husband too soon.

Shirley had developed an attitude that had helped her cope with the days and nights behind the walls, and that was first of all to accept where she was and then to get a job in the facility where she could learn something and do the best job possible. She wanted to work in one of the offices, but of course those were the best jobs on the compound, and Shirley wouldn't be inside long enough to work up the ladder to be eligible for one of those. She had hated to cook before coming to the penitentiary but sure enough, as a new inmate, the job she got assigned to was in the kitchen—first three months as dishwasher, and then she "moved up" to food prep, and then actual cooking. She ultimately got a certificate in culinary arts, something her mother would likely laugh about when she saw it, given her aversion to the kitchen.

Shirley had held many jobs before she was arrested, and she desperately wanted to work again so she could have money for getting reestablished, and most of all so that she could be a mother again to Audrey. But she also knew she now had an "X" on her forehead, and it would be even harder to get a job. On this day of release, she repeated the phrases she learned in PreStart, Illinois' discharge planning program: "I've made some mistakes and I've paid for them. Being in prison has turned my life around. I'm going to work harder for you than anyone else you could hire." She laughed as she recalled another woman in the class saying, "I'm going to take my dope fiend mentality and apply it to my job search." Shirley hoped these lines and that attitude would work for her so she would be able to explain where she'd been and why, and her new goals, to a prospective employer who might give her a second chance. She was no longer young—certainly not as young as most of the women coming into prison—she had started her drug career relatively late—almost 42 now, would that work for her or against her? Would employers, that she once had felt were so easy to persuade of her value, believe that she was more than ready to put her old life behind her and create a new life for herself and her daughter? She tried not to think of all the people likely wanting a job who did not have that experience in the criminal justice system, courtesy of the state.

Shirley had received $50.00 gate money from the facility and had had to spend $28 on the bus ticket. She would have received more from her job pay but had spent it all on her last visit to the commissary so she could leave some things behind for her cellmates and several of the other girls who she knew had even less than she. But now she thought about her generosity—and the $20 more that might have helped her. Restarting her life on the outside wasn't going to be easy. "It's like they get you both ways—put you away, then when you get out, hand you a nickel and tell you to change your life." She was used to being told what to do, what to wear for how long, what to eat, when to sleep and get up, and where to go. She had to reassure herself that she could make good decisions, even though she recalled that she hadn't done so well over the last five years before she was incarcerated.

Shirley had done her time without too many problems. She had been written up for "trafficking and trading" a couple of times—a concept that in the free world is called "caring and sharing." She had had one cellie with whom she had almost constant conflict, but before it got too bad for either one of them the other woman was transferred to the mental health unit.

Luckily for Shirley, she had met Beth, the social worker from Grace House, the transitional residential shelter for women ex-offenders in Chicago, during one of the PreRelease sessions. She took an application when Beth talked to her awhile after her presentation about what it might be like for her to try something different. Beth didn't talk down to her, and somehow in their brief conversation she realized that Beth believed she could construct a new life, that she could find a job that would pay her enough so she could have her own place and car again, and that finally, especially since Audrey had been staying with her sister, it likely wasn't too late for her to reestablish her role as a mother. She took a deep breath and then she sat down and filled out the brief application right then and there and handed it to Beth. A few weeks later, she got the letter from Grace House saying she had been accepted! She knew this meant they had some faith in her and just the thought of it made her hold her head up a bit, knowing that her past did not seal her future.

Once she got to the bus terminal in Chicago, she remembered Beth telling her that they would pick her up at the bus station, but since it was late in the evening she thought it would be better to go to her sister's tonight. She knew that her parole officer would be contacting her at Grace House by tomorrow, but she desperately wanted to see her daughter who had stayed with her sister off and on since she was ten years old. Audrey was now 15, and Shirley worried about the separation they had had, even before she went to prison. Shirley had attended a parenting program, and as a result of that had started writing letters to Audrey, taking responsibility for what had happened and asking for her forgiveness. She hadn't heard anything back from her.

She caught a bus going to the west side and soon was knocking on her sister's door. Her younger sister Ramone was delighted to see her. Shirley was upset though when she saw that several old friends were gathered in the living room and sure enough, they had some blunts' with them. Though she was worried about being guilty by association, she was relieved to know that her daughter was spending the night with a friend so at least she wasn't there. Of course she imagined that it likely didn't matter to Ramone whether Audrey was there or not if her friends were going to use, and she felt the additional pressure that she had to get Audrey out of there as soon as she could get on her feet. The arrangement with Ramone to care for her daughter was all she could think of at the time of her arrest—Ramone had other kids and generally was a good mother to them. And she had heard from so many other women that leaving her child with a family member was about the best thing she could do to make sure she didn't disappear into the state system. She remembered learning in the parenting class about a new law that made the timeline even shorter for parents to prove they could take care of their children or lose their rights permanently. She thought that such a law might be okay for some people who never really wanted to parent their children, and maybe it meant those kids could get a safe and loving foster or adoptive home, but she sure wasn't one of those.

She said good-night quickly to the partiers and went to bed, praying she wouldn't hear a knock on the door from the police, as she knew by the increasing numbers who came into prison during her stint that "they're not building prisons just to look at them." And it no longer mattered if you were a parent either. They didn't seem to care that there was no other momma to watch the children. Her head swirled with all the things she would have to do: "No drug use, get and KEEP a job, random urine tests, don't hang out with the wrong people." How was she to avoid all these people when they were all around her? She hoped for a sound sleep and a quick ride to Grace House in the morning that would help her to stay clean and start down the unmarked path toward reconstructing her life after release from prison.

In the morning she got to see Audrey. She greeted her with wide-open arms, but the hug felt a little awkward. The girl had grown a foot it seemed in the last couple of years, and she kept her head down, didn't seem to have much to say to Shirley. But Shirley kept talking to her and touching her beautiful daughter. Finally, Audrey asked, "Are you going to stay here?" Reluctantly Shirley told Audrey she had to go away again for possibly six months, to a special house where she thought Audrey could visit her. Audrey looked both sad and curious about where her mother would be going. Shirley tried to tell her that "it was going to be different this time," and that she planned to be the mother Audrey deserved when she could support her. Meanwhile, Audrey would have to stay with her Auntie and continue to work hard in school. Shirley also had a conversation with Ramone about not having drugs at the house while her daughter stayed there. Shirley also reminded Ramone that the whole family could be evicted under new federal guidelines that provided for automatic eviction, and no possibility of receiving subsidized or public housing for up to 5 years, if caught with drugs. Ramone agreed to respect her wishes but also told Shirley that her time of caring for Audrey was coming to an end and that she needed some money for the necessities. Shirley gave her the remainder of her gate money as a down payment and promised she would give her more once she got a job.

By this time it was almost noon, and Shirley flew out of the door to catch a bus to Grace House—she had called and got the directions and found out that it wasn't too far from where Ramone lived, so maybe she would get to visit Audrey or maybe Audrey would be able to visit her at the house. She would have to check out the situation, but she knew it was time that she started being a momma to this young girl, almost woman, and hoped she could undo some of the harm her absence had caused. Audrey was a sweet girl, and she was still in school. Shirley hoped they could both be patient with the process of rebuilding their family.

She was nervous and at the same time excited about what the next several months would bring. While she was in prison, she hadn't been able to see clearly how she could make her life different. But that seemed to be what Grace House promised—a new start in a different neighborhood, and an opportunity to prove she could make different choices and even be successful again. She recalled that Beth made the program sound both tough and supportive at the same time. She just hoped she would be treated as an adult and helped to know what her options were. She wasn't sure what was ahead of her but she knew for sure where the dead-end road she had taken before led her!

As she walked the couple of blocks from the bus stop, she saw a pretty, two-story house that seemed to be connected to the house right next to it. On the front of the gate she saw a small, gold-embossed sign that said "Grace House," so she pushed the gate open and walked up the steps to the front porch and rang the bell. She was buzzed in and Beth came to the door to help her with her bags. The place seemed both huge and cozy. The bedrooms were mostly in the second house that was connected on the upper level. The rooms were small but not too crowded, and she was relieved to learn she would only have one roommate. At lunch in the cheery room on the first floor she met some of the other women who were living there and other staff people. Most of the other residents were also black and the staff was a mix of colors. Rev. Barbara was a Latina woman, Beth and the director were white, and Pamela, the case manager, was black. She found out from the residents at her table that Beth was a nun and that Carla, the receptionist she met at the desk by the front door, had once been a resident.

After lunch, Beth gave Shirley the run-down on the rules and helped her understand the program schedule. She was surprised and a little hurt to learn that she wouldn't be able to leave the House at all for two weeks, and then she would be on restricted movement for the next 30 days. It was harsh, thinking that she had to abide by these rules as soon as she walked in the door on her first full day of freedom. Beth's calm explanation about the need to teach structure helped her understand the reasons for the policy. And slowly she began to relax as she realized she didn't have to deal with the streets or worry about what people might be thinking about her. She didn't have to worry about finding a job right away or be tempted by an easy high. Her body had lost that addictive urge, but she wasn't sure that she was totally free of the desire for an escape, especially when she thought of all she had facing her. She also knew that ultimately the decision to stay at Grace House irrespective of the rules was hers. She couldn't make her life different if she didn't start by trying something different than what she had done before. Beth also reassured her that when she felt the worry, the pain, the grief, or the guilt, she would have someone she could talk to about whatever she felt. She recalled the euphoria she had felt yesterday as she rode the bus toward Chicago, remembering that if she could keep body and spirit together in prison, surely she could deal with the restrictions— week after week, because of what she had learned there.

And this place was nice—it seemed the people in charge had really taken some time with the furnishings and the décor. She didn't feel like it was a place for down-and-out women but rather for women who had some belief and hope for their future. There were pictures of all kinds of strong women on the walls and sayings that made her think. Beth assured her that all her needs would be taken care of while she was at Grace House and that there was no charge for anything! Beth would be working with her to develop her goals while she resided at the house. After the two weeks were up, Audrey would be welcome to visit the House during a designated family time. Although the house was filled to capacity now, there might also be an option for her to spend the night on a weekend. Shirley would be able to leave on the weekends for overnight stays after she had satisfactorily completed the first level of the programming that required her to participate in a lot of groups and individual sessions with Beth. Beth also explained that all the residents at Grace House had the same parole officer who came by to see the women there once a month and she would be meeting her at the House later that afternoon.

The P.O., Ronnie, is an educated black woman who took the time to talk with me. I didn't know what to expect from her. She explained that she would be meeting with me monthly for the first three months, and then I would be on a less frequent schedule of contacts, mostly by phone. She also told me she would be doing the random urine drops required by my parole. So I'll never know when she's coming to do that. She was cool with the house-imposed delay in going out for a job because she said she thought it gave me time to get "on my feet" and have a better sense of myself before going out competing for a job. I liked her because she treated me like a person, not just a case. She told me to feel free to call her if I need to but that's she's not going to be riding my back.

The next time Beth and I met I had been a week at the House and was beginning to feel more relaxed about the routine. At this meeting Beth told me that we would do an "assessment." This sure was different, as she asked me lots of questions, and they included things like what I did for fun. She seemed really interested in the dreams that I had once had about college and whether I thought about those plans anymore. It was sort of fun and more like a conversation with a friend. I kept thinking she would talk about all the things I had done to mess up my life and how I planned to stay clean. We did talk about my drug use but she helped me understand it better in the context of other things that had happened in my life. Finally, she helped me create a plan in different areas of my life including potential living arrangements, real world and legal income that I need to support myself and Audrey, health, going back to school, developing relationships both in and out of the house and social support. And oh, she even talked about developing a plan for fun because she thinks that having balance in all this will make it manageable and interesting. Whew—I've never thought about things in this way before.

Three months later

Maybe the best thing I've ever done for myself is making the decision to come here. It hasn't been easy but I didn't expect it would be. I've gone to lots of educational groups about everything from "dressing for success" to how to talk about my conviction. We've role-played and cried and laughed together as we heard about some of the girls' attempts. We've celebrated the new job or those who have had a good family visit. We've been sad about the ladies who have chosen to leave or been requested to leave. I have met one of the volunteers with Grace House who has agreed to be my mentor. It's sort of like having a AA/NA sponsor but broader than that. She says I can talk to her about anything and she takes me out for coffee, and has met Audrey a couple of times, too. It's almost time for me to start looking for a job. I've learned a lot more about the barriers I'll be facing. There's the stigma that comes to me just because I've been an addict and spent time in prison. But worse is that employers really can discriminate against me. Well, there's no law that says they can't discriminate against me and there's such a thing as "negligent hiring" that provides them the excuse. So I've learned some of the ways I can be ASSERTIVE and talk about the federal bonding program and also about some of the tax credits they may be eligible for. And I've grown to accept that it's not likely that I'll be able to work as an accountant again. That doesn't bother me, really. Some of the girls here at the house tell me that I'm a good listener, and sometimes I think I might like to counsel others—work with other addicts. But that's a long way off—another thing I will have to wait and see.

Patience is something I've been learning about everyday that I'm further beyond the prison gate. Beth has been a wonderful counselor. I never realized how much grief and hurt was bottled up inside of me. Sometimes it is just too much to talk about it. And in those times, I know I can take my time—Beth will wait to listen to me when I'm ready. All the staff at the House have been kind. Pamela has helped me get enrolled in a computer skills class at the community college not far from the House. She figures that if I get that certificate, it will help me with the job search. She's also told me about a program called Americorps, where I could work and get benefits and an education subsidy for when I return to college to finish my Bachelor's degree.

My biggest hurt and concern now comes from what is going on with Audrey. I have not been able to see her as often as I want since I've been here at Grace House because Ramone won't bring her over. And the last time I saw Audrey, she finally told me with lots of tears that she might be having a baby by some guy at her high school. She doesn't *know what to do and I feel overwhelmed as well. I thought I had learned some things about making decisions and choices, but the girl has no respect for me and I don't know how we can possibly manage with a new baby on the way. But one of the things I've learned from Beth is how to take a deep breath, check out my feelings, and think through my options before I act. That's been important because the way I feel right now is just jumbled up guilt, shame, and yes, even some anger at my daughter for both her bad choices and how the consequence might get in my way.*

When I met with Beth, she maintained a constant focus on my objectives. She used them to guide our discussion about even this possible crisis, and helped me understand how I could do better than react to this situation (as I had so often in the past). She helped me look at how far I've progressed over the last three months and reminded me that Grace House would still be a source of support and resources for as long as I needed it. I got to talk about my feelings about the situation with Audrey, and together we explored all the different options and scenarios. I still feel worried about what's going to happen, but I finally feel in control of my life.

When I saw Audrey the next day I was ready to really talk to her. First, we needed to find out if she really was pregnant and how far along she was, and get her involved in some regular prenatal care. Next, we needed to discuss the young man involved in this picture and maybe even plan a visit to meet with his family to see how he could be involved in care of this baby. I wanted to find out about whether there were any programs that could help her stay in school during her pregnancy, and maybe even have tutoring at home after the baby was born until she could return to school. As I sat back and looked at her, I realized that we were going to weather this storm. There would be many other decisions along the way, and getting some income to support my possibly growing family was still ahead of me, but despite the obstacles I had heard about and experienced, I knew that it was possible for me to make it and that I had both the courage on the inside and the supports on the outside to make it happen.

NOTES

"Blunts" is slang for a large marijuana cigarette.

Questions for Further Study

1. In "Black Eagle Child," from (Ray Young Bear's *Black Eagle Child: The Face Paint Narratives*), Lorna Bearcap and Claude Youthman are ostracized and relieved of their positions and responsibilities with the Weeping Willow School and advisory board. The reasons for this have a great deal to do with the desire of those in power to maintain the status quo. In what other ways does this story reflect this phenomenon? After thinking about this question, can you think of strategies for advocating for redress of the injustices at Weeping Willow?

2. The question facing African-American men of the most "righteous" way of resolving the Darden Dilemma is a potentially difficult one indeed. To best capture this difficulty, imagine yourself in Christopher Darden's shoes—as an African-American male, in Los Angeles, the site of the Rodney King riots, racial profiling and abuse, and documented police corruption in the arrest and prosecution of African-American men.[1] How might you have resolved this dilemma? Write an honest appraisal of your own thought processes from the perspective of this African-American man.

3. One of the features of an addict that Margaret (from *Workin' It: Women Living Through Drugs and Crime* by Leon Pettiway) has in common with other addicts is the time she spends on her addiction—thinking about the drugs, working the streets for drug money, buying them, using them, worrying about the quality, etc. What interpersonal conditions will have to be present for Margaret to think about changing her behavior and her life? What do you think are the environmental conditions that need to change as well?

4. This excerpt from Luis Rodriguez's *Always Running: La Vida Loca: Gang Days in LA* illustrates how difficult it is to escape the gang life, even if one clearly understands the need to do so. If you were a social worker working in the barrios with gang members, how might you approach this with someone like Chin, who clearly envisions a different future for himself but seems unable to take the necessary steps that would make that future more likely?

5. "Shirley: Navigating the Way Home from Prison," by Patricia O'Brien, tells the story of a woman who seeks to reestablish herself in her community following her release from prison. What does this case tell you, the reader, about what women are likely to need upon release from prison? How might women's needs be different from men's?

NOTE

[1]See the following news stories for more information on the corruption scandal within the Los Angeles Police Department:
www.cnn.com/2000/US/02/16/lapd.corruption

Invited Commentary

DIANE S. YOUNG

One area of great social importance that is often overlooked within social work education and preparation is practice and policies related to criminal justice. As the number of adults under correctional supervision (prison, jail, probation, parole) in the United States reaches six-and-a-half million (Bureau of Justice Statistics, 2001), more social workers will find themselves working with offenders and their families, even outside of traditional correctional settings. In addition, one of the most troublesome aspects of our current justice system (more accurately, multiple justice systems) is the tremendous racial and ethnic disparity among populations under correctional control throughout the United States. Efforts to obtain social justice for all must include addressing discriminatory criminal justice practices and policies.

My task is to examine the readings in this section from an ethical perspective. Keeping in mind the Social Work Code of Ethics, what does ethical practice require of social workers when it comes to interaction with the criminal justice system and those involved in it? The four narratives in this section present a disheartening picture of the circumstances of those involved in our criminal justice system and of the potential for meaningful structural changes to the system. The authors remind us of heinous acts committed against humanity, entrenched poverty, lack of opportunities for individuals and whole communities, and pervasive and established racism and sexism. The case study presents a more hopeful picture of the possibilities for change, but even so, it highlights some of the systemic and societal barriers to rehabilitative goals. How then, does one practice ethically within a system that is too often unethical or, at the very least, unfair?

Before addressing these questions, I briefly describe the lens from which I examine the readings in this section. My experiences and culture have shaped my perceptions and perspectives. Sharing this background allows the reader to understand something of the context within which my comments are made and evaluate my conclusions in that light. I am white, female, middle class, and Ph.D. educated. I worked as a social worker in a correctional setting with adult offenders for almost ten years. After that, I broadened my knowledge via the reading, study, and experiences that come with teaching and conducting research in corrections. I have never been incarcerated or personally involved in the criminal justice system as a defendant or as a victim. This composite of experiences shapes my comments (just as the various writers in Ellis Cose's book write from their own lenses and come to decidedly different conclusions in many cases). Thus, my comments are my own, and friends (some have been involved in the criminal justice system) and colleagues (of different races and genders) might understandably have different reflections were they to write this commentary.

The mission of the social work profession is built upon core values, including the dignity and worth of each person (National Association of Social Workers [NASW] 1996). Ethical social work practice, within criminal justice systems and elsewhere, begins with the recognition that the worth of all individuals must be upheld. Activity on behalf of offenders fits with the professional social work mission to "enhance human well-being and help meet the basic human needs of all people" described in the Code of Ethics (NASW p. 1). Indeed, a "historic and defining feature of social work is the profession's focus on individual well-being in a social context and the well-being of society" (NASW p. 1). The problems experienced by offenders (e.g., discrimination, incarceration, poverty, sense of powerlessness) touch not only their lives but also the lives of their families and communities, so vividly illustrated by Ray Young Bear and Luis Rodriguez in their narratives. For example, Youthman's incarceration removed him abruptly from the lives of his wife and children for five years, certainly without their say in the matter. The gang activity, described by Rodriguez, ravaged whole communities, as "everyone was fair game in barrio wars." Chin proceeded with the firebombing even though he knew that "somebody's mother, little sister or brother could be hurt or killed." His own 13-year-old sister was shot at in retaliation for his actions. Rodriguez also writes that rapes became a way of life, "a common circumstance," as young men attempted to demonstrate their power. In addition, when lampposts were shot out so that offenders were better hidden from agents of the law, the neighborhood experienced further physical deterioration. To address societal well-being, we must also address the factors that shape individuals' circumstances and choices.

Basic to social work is "attention to the environmental forces that create, contribute to, and address problems in living. Social workers promote social justice and social change" (NASW 1996, p. 1). An essential component of the social work mission is to promote societal changes that seek "to end discrimination, oppression, poverty, and other forms of social injustice" (NASW 1996, p. 1). Yet to advocate for desperately needed changes in criminal justice policies and practices, the social work profession needs to be informed and actively engaged in the debate. As Creasie Hairston (1997) aptly stated,

> Concerns about working with involuntary clients, the need for self-determination, and working in an oppressive system of social control have overshadowed parallel needs for the social work profession to be engaged in the debate about criminal justice policies, programs, and services. . . . While the nation builds more prisons to house more of a population that is predominantly poor and nonwhite, the social work profession has remained remarkably silent. (p. 151)

Social work needs to become an active voice in the criminal justice arena.

Cose's work highlights the disagreement about the best way to make the criminal justice system one of justice for all, regardless of color or class. Paul Butler disagrees with Christopher Darden and others who suggest that the way to improve the criminal justice system is by working with and supporting the system. Rather, subversion is called for; there is so much wrong with the system that it is better to fight it than to join it. Lynch and Mitchell (1995), in their editorial about the necessity for justice system advocacy, state that "social workers should not be passive collaborators in the system; social workers must be active, aggressive advocates for their clients" (p. 10). Oftentimes this advocacy, of necessity, must occur outside the system by those who have decided to pursue social change through aggressive political and/or legal action. After all, there are not many prosecutors, judges, police officers, wardens, corrections officers, and prison social workers who could retain their jobs while actively engaging in full scale political and legal action against the systems they work within. It is clear that there is need for such action, and Cose and Young Bear provide ample illustrations of severe injustices against persons of color brought about by agents of the criminal justice system. Why should anyone, as Young Bear illustrates, be charged with "serious assault and terrorism" for pitching cantaloupes and mistakenly walking out of the courthouse, and then be sent to prison for five years? Why are we, as Cose points out, content to jail blacks roughly eight times as often as whites? Advocacy is an ethical obligation, supported by the Code of Ethics, and we need social workers that work from outside the system (e.g., in legal advocacy organizations or political lobbies) to effect positive change on a macro level.

A social worker's ethical responsibility is inclusive, however, encompassing both clients and broader society (NASW 1996). Darden would certainly agree with this. In his view, it does not make sense to remove oneself from the system because it is unfair, and blacks should, through participation in the system, strive to improve it. Sometimes broader society *is* best served when individual offenders are encouraged, coaxed, and, yes, even coerced to change. Despite the failings of the criminal justice system, most of us would agree that many individual offenders' behaviors need to change and that personal rehabilitation is an important goal of criminal justice policies. Just as the problems of offenders affect their families and communities, so do positive results with offenders benefit society. Social workers within the criminal justice system and on the edges (e.g., working in drug and alcohol treatment facilities) are equally responsive to the profession's mission when they actively work to promote positive changes within individuals and enhance an individual's capacity to change.

These kinds of typically micro level social work activities can be utilized with those on the fringes of the law in almost every setting known to social workers. When Margaret, whose story appears in Pettiway's work, stayed in the hospital for five months, first because "the guy that was such good friends of mine" broke her jaw, and then because her continued drug usage hindered the healing process, there may have been a wonderful, but missed, opportunity for a hospital social worker to engage Margaret in a process of personal change. (The narrative does not actually tell us whether a social worker ever contacted Margaret during her hospital stay.) Too often we miss available opportunities because we are not present, we are distracted with other tasks, or because biases about certain types of people keep us from seeing evidence that indicates readiness for change.

In contrast to Margaret's experience, Patricia O'Brien's case study provides an excellent example of a seized opportunity and of a social worker who works alongside the criminal justice system to make a difference in the lives of individual offenders transitioning out of prison. Beth's contact with Shirley was made early, prior to her release from prison, and Beth skillfully found a way to nurture "the courage on the inside and the supports on the outside" that Shirley identified as critical to her successful re-integration. Ray Young Bear's transition experience was very different from Shirley's. Upon his release, there was no one to help him make the transition back to tribal life or figure out how to effectively use his newly gained knowledge and skills. Community re-integration after a term of incarceration is critical, for individual and societal well-being, and our relative lack of attention to its importance goes hand-in-hand with extremely high recidivism rates. Shirley is one of the fortunate ones.

What then does ethical practice require of social workers when interfacing with a system that adversely and unfairly impacts people of color (and low socioeconomic status)? How are we to proceed? First and foremost, we must be present in the debate about criminal justice policies and practices. We must be active participants in efforts to design interventions, services, and policies that promote social justice for all. Actively engaging communities of color in the discussion and planning efforts would likely help us to create non-discriminatory and culturally appropriate interventions and policies. As several of Cose's writers point out, communities of color have been hard hit not only by unjust law enforcement, judicial, and correctional practices but also by perpetrators of crime, as many within these communities are victims of criminal acts.

Problems related to crime, justice, and punishment as experienced by the tribal community in Young Bear's narrative, the Los Angeles ethnic communities infiltrated by gangs described by Rodriguez, and black communities highlighted in Cose's narrative will be difficult to resolve solely by "outside" efforts. The general distrust blacks have of whites, portrayed in Elijah Anderson's discussion of the "black tax" (Cose p. xi), illustrates the difficulty of merely imposing "solutions" designed by those in power on communities of color. Young Bear's narrative, in particular, although describing an incident over 35 years ago, poignantly reminds us that the majority view is often different from the minority one. When asked his opinion about Youthman by the judge, the mayor replied, "they [Indians] are no different than children who need strict supervision. . . . They need to be more appreciative of what they acquired from us." To these comments, the jury and courtroom audience (no doubt primarily white) applauded.

We could also learn much from ex-offenders and ex-addicts if we would include them in the discussion. O'Brien's case study illustrates this. Shirley shares with us what she needs, and what, most certainly, many others need as well: employment with enough income to get re-established, stable living arrangements away from former negative influences, assistance in working through past trauma, guidance on how to re-connect with one's children, and information about relevant policies (e.g., parole expectations, the federal bonding program and tax credits for potential employers). What better way to find out what individuals need than to ask them? More inclusive approaches to addressing community problems fit well with one of the standards for cultural competence in social work practice; empowerment and advocacy include "advocating for *and with* clients whenever appropriate" (NASW 2001, p. 1, emphasis added).

As we, as a profession, actively engage in the debate and invite others to participate, we would do well to remember that our ethical responsibility as social workers encompasses both efforts in harmony with the system and in opposition to the system. All of the narratives and the case study provide examples of individuals and families that potentially could have benefited or did benefit from direct interventions: work with individuals or families on a case-by-case basis to enhance well-being or the implementation of services to assist individuals at risk of violence, incarceration, or addiction. These activities can operate alongside the criminal justice system. At the same time, we must acknowledge that social and political action is typically required for significant large-scale change to occur. Cose is correct; prison is indeed a poor substitute for effective social policy. Our ethical responsibility as social workers includes addressing the problems on multiple fronts and with multiple methods. There is much to be done, and being engaged at all levels is responsive to our social work mission and our Code of Ethics.

REFERENCES

Bureau of Justice Statistics. (2001). *Probation and Parole in the United States, 2000—Press Release* (Publication No. NCJ 188208). Washington, DC: Author.

Hairston, C. F. (1997). "Family Programs in State Prisons." In *Policy and Practice in the Justice System*, eds., C. A. McNeece and A. R. Roberts, 143–157. Chicago: Nelson-Hall.

Lynch, R. S., and Mitchell, J. (1995). "Justice System Advocacy: A Must for NASW and the Social Work Community." *Social Work, 40*(1): 9–12.

National Association of Social Workers. (1996). *Code of Ethics*. Washington, DC: Author.

National Association of Social Workers. (2001). *NASW Standards for Cultural Competence in Social Work Practice*. Washington, DC: Author.

Unit 8 USING OUR SOCIAL WORK KNOWLEDGE BASE TO HELP CLIENTS ATTAIN HEALTH

Editors' Introduction

Dudes   2/2   Amanda

The knowledge base of social work practice is breathtaking in its scope. The National Association of Social Workers (NASW) has enumerated no fewer than twenty-five elements that form our knowledge base, and each of these elements is broadly defined (1996).[1] Additionally, the Council on Social Work Education (CSWE), the accrediting body for all Schools, Colleges, and Departments of Social Work in the United States, has conceived of the knowledge base necessary for effective practice as consisting of eight different content areas in its Educational Policy and Accreditation Standards (2001).[2] Clearly, the articulation of basic knowledge necessary for effective practice has been a priority for our profession.

This unit will help us examine how the knowledge base of social work practice is used to advance the health of clients. Health refers to the general condition of the mind, body, or spirit, and is considered synonymous with well-being. Social workers working in this field, then, need additional, specialized health knowledge in order to be effective. As one can see, the volume of information is likely to be unmanageable, unless one is able to adopt a framework, or lens through which to evaluate and apply these bodies of knowledge.

The *biopsychosocial* framework is one that has proven most useful for social workers. Applied to any phenomena that consists of biological, psychological, and social elements, this framework allows us to view health in all of its complexity. For example, the biopsychosocial framework places within our purview such diverse health-related phenomena as the impact of stress upon disease; the differential health outcomes of persons based upon race or sex; the larger meanings that people impute to health or illness; the role of biology in behavior; and the impact of culture upon our perceptions of health and disease, to name but a few. The literary selections and case study in this unit offer an opportunity to learn more about how such knowledge advances effective practice.

The excerpt from the chapter "Sioux and Elephants Never Forget," from Mary Crow Dog's *Lakota Woman*, is a first-person consideration of the underlying causes (and the cure) of a "love sickness" that gripped the author shortly after her marriage to Leonard Crow Dog. After reading this piece and learning about the history of the family from which the author sought acceptance, you may or may not agree that such an assessment is valid and plausible. Were a non-Native social worker to observe Mary, he or she might surmise that Mary suffered from depression. Such different assessments call for very different interventions: failing to consider the meaning of this illness to Mary and her extended family, some might be inclined to consider a prescription for Zoloft and intensive family therapy. However, given the cultural environment, such treatment would have been both inappropriate and ineffective. Instead, Mary is treated with peyote, coupled with social support and encouragement from an attentive Crow Dog family. She is cured within weeks, i.e., at a rate that conventional treatments could not effect. Thus, this selection illustrates the importance for helping professionals of knowing and assessing the multiple meanings that illness has for clients and their extended families and of incorporating this knowledge into the treatment.

"Thrall," from *Double Down: Reflections on Gambling and Loss*, also focuses upon addiction, a condition that still eludes consensus within the general public as to its underlying causes. In this case, the addiction is gambling, and the Barthelme brothers provide a classic portrait, replete with the denial of the seriousness of the problem, the minimization of the consequences ("So what ? . . . the disadvantages were felt only at the bank"), the thrill of the activity, and the generalized intensity of feeling that addictive behaviors bring to the rest of one's world. Additionally, the Barthelme brothers are knowing, perceptive, and funny about the ways in which their families have shaped their lives, and how this addiction paradoxically helps them feel normal. This cerebral piece presents addiction both as a disease with environmental triggers and as a lapse in personal responsibility. A biopsychosocial lens applied to addiction integrates these perspectives and allows us to see how biological, psychological, social, and spiritual elements contribute both to its etiology and to its recovery.

In "The Spirit Catches You and You Fall Down," from a book of the same title, Anne Fadiman uses her training as a social scientist to recount the ultimately tragic story of Lia Lee, the daughter of Hmong immigrants. Lee is diagnosed with epilepsy or *qaug dab peg* which, translated from Hmong, means "the spirit catches you and you fall down." In Hmong culture, *qaug dab peg* is understood as a condition that carries with it the aura of being "chosen" as the host of a healing spirit or, at the very least, of being special. Conversely, our western medical community views epilepsy as a potentially life-threatening brain disorder, to be controlled by medication. Recognition of this fundamental difference of opinion, and the ability to act on this knowledge to minimize the potential damage, is one of the most important contributions that a social worker can make to the client's ultimate well-being.

Carol Anne Douglas's "The Madwoman of 'Off Our Backs'," from *Restricted Access: Lesbians on Disability* examines the author's experience with mental illness. More importantly, Douglas provides us with a gateway for thinking about how homosexuality, which was not so long ago viewed as a mental illness in and of itself, may impact the treatment a person receives, as well as her response to it. She also notes the lack of understanding and dearth of research on menopause and its effect on mental health. Using a biopsychosocial perspective through which to examine this narrative allows us to see the importance of support and community to recovery, as well as the special vulnerabilities that women and lesbians (and gay men) may experience in a health care setting. Douglas advises psychiatrists to treat their clients with respect, to consult them regarding their treatment, and to tamper with them as little as possible.

The case study "The Application of Systems Theory to Chronic Illness and the Educational Environment" was co-written by Carolyn Banta and her mother Lisa. To remedy the lupus and other ailments that Carolyn suffers during her teen-aged years, Lisa aggressively seeks out the best physicians, treatment regimens, and rehabilitative supports for her daughter. At the same time, they are challenged by the teachers and administrators at Carolyn's school, who appear unwilling to accommodate Carolyn's special needs. We consider this study important because, ironically, this young woman has advantages that elude most of our clients. Her family is well-educated, and has access to many resources including the best doctors, and her social worker is actually her mother, working on her most important case. Yet, despite extremely aggressive advocacy on Lisa Banta's part, the inability of the school system to understand this young woman's illness, its resistance to change, and its seeming resentment of a family invoking their legal right to accommodation result in Carolyn's early exit from high school. At the end of this case, Carolyn reflects on the meaning of this disease in her life. Although she is still struggling, she is actively trying to transform her view of this disease;

instead of viewing it as an enemy, she wants to see it as a gift that she must reluctantly accept.

In our guest commentary, Gwat-Yong Lie discusses, among other things, how the gender of the provider *vis-a-vis* the gender of the client can affect the outcomes that clients attain. This insight has implications for the organization of health care services and falls within the biopsychosocial purview.

These pieces reflect the importance of knowledge to the social work enterprise. We must understand the medical dimensions of illness and the contemporary thinking about its origins, but we also must pay careful attention to the meanings of illness from the client's perspective and try to operate from that perspective. We must know about the relationship between the biological, the psychological, the social, and the spiritual. Not only does the client's health depend upon this, but the mandate within our Code of Ethics to practice with cultural competence requires it.

REFERENCE

National Association of Social Workers (1996). *Standards for the Classification of Social Work Practice*. Washington, D.C.: National Association of Social Workers.

NOTES

[1]The full listing of the elements of knowledge identified by NASW in the document cited above may be obtained, by request. Visit the NASW website at www.naswdc.org.

[2]The eight content areas that must be addressed in all social work curricula, as identified in the Educational Policy and Accreditation Standards, and developed by the Council on Social Work Education, are: values and ethics; diversity; populations-at-risk and social and economic justice; human behavior and the social environment; social welfare policy and services; social work practice; research; and field education. A full description of these content areas may be obtained from the Council's website at www.cswe.org.

Sioux and Elephants Never Forget

MARY CROW DOG

Beside being tumbled headfirst into this kind of situation, still in my teens, with a brand-new baby and totally unprepared for the role I was to play, I still had another problem. I was a half-blood, not traditionally raised, trying to hold my own inside the full-blood Crow Dog clan which does not take kindly to outsiders. At first, I was not well received. It was pretty bad. I could not speak Sioux and I could tell that all the many Crow Dogs and their relations from the famous old Orphan Band were constantly talking about me, watching me, watching whether I would measure up to their standards which go way back to the old buffalo days. I could tell from the way they were looking at me, and I could see the criticism in their eyes. The old man told me that, as far as he was concerned, Leonard was still married to his former wife, a woman, as he pointed out again and again, *who could talk Indian*. Once, when I went over to the old folks' house to borrow some eggs, Henry intercepted me and told me to leave, saying that I was not the right kind of wife for his son. Leonard heard about it and had a long argument with his father. After that there was no more talk of my leaving, but I was still treated as an intruder. I had to fight day by day to be accepted.

My own family was also against our marriage—for opposite reasons. Leonard was not the right kind of husband for me. I was going back to the blanket. Here my family had struggled so hard to be Christian, to make a proper red, white, and blue lady out of me, and I was turning myself back into a squaw. And Leonard was too old for me. I reminded them that grandpa had been twelve years older than grandma and that theirs had been a long and happy marriage. But that was really not the issue. The trouble was the cultural abyss between Leonard's family and mine. But the more our parents opposed our marriage, the closer became the bond between Leonard and myself.

I came to understand why the Crow Dogs made it hard for me to become one of them. Even among the traditional full-bloods out in the back country, the Crow Dogs are a tribe apart. They have built a wall around themselves against the outside world. For three generations they have lived as voluntary outcasts. To understand them, one must know the Crow Dog legend and the Crow Dog history.

Kangi-Shunka, the founder of the clan, had six names before he called himself Crow Dog. He was a famous and fearless warrior, a great hunter, a chief, a medicine man, a Ghost Dance leader, a head of the Indian police, and the first Sioux—maybe the first Indian—to win a case before the Supreme Court. As

Leonard describes him, "Old Kangi-Shunka, he was the lonely man of the prairie. He goes by the sun and moon, the stars and the winds. He harvests from the earth and the four-legged ones. He's a buffalo man, a weed man, a pejuta wichasha. He sees an herb and he hears the herb telling him, 'Take me for your medicine.' He has the kind of spirit and words out of which you create a nation."

For most people, what their ancestors did over a hundred years ago would be just ancient history, but for the Crow Dogs it is what happened only yesterday. What Kangi-Shunka did so long ago still colors the life-style and the actions of the Crow Dogs of today and of their relations, of the whole clan—the tiyospaye, which means "those who live together." Sioux and elephants never forget.

Some of the Crow Dogs trace their origin back to a certain Jumping Badger, a chief famous in the 1830s for having killed a dozen buffalo with a single arrow, for having counted fourteen coups in war, and for distinguishing himself in fifteen horse-stealing raids. It is certain that the first Crow Dog belonged to a small camp of about thirty tipis, calling themselves the Wazhazha or Orphan Band, which followed a chief called Mato-Iwa, Scattering Bear, or Brave Bear. Kangi-Shunka was born in 1834 and died in 1911. He was raised in the bow-and-arrow days when the prairie was covered with millions of buffalo and when many Sioux had still to meet their first white man. He died owning a Winchester .44 repeating rifle with not a single buffalo left to use it on. He lived long enough to ride in a car and make a telephone call. At one time he was a chief of the Orphan Band. He played his part in the proud history of our tribe.

As Old Man Henry tells it, Crow Dog got his name in this way: He was taking his people to Hante Paha Wakan, to Cedar Valley, to hunt. Before riding out he had a vision. He saw a white horse in the clouds giving him the horse power, and from then on his horse was Shunkaka-Luzahan, the swiftest horse in the band. And he heard the voice of Shunk-Manitu, the coyote, saying, "I am the one." Then his horse suddenly raised its two ears up and the wind got into the two eagle feathers Crow Dog was wearing, and the feathers were talking, the feathers were saying, "There is a wichasha, a man up ahead on that hill, between the two trees." Crow Dog and his companions saw the man clearly. The man raised his hands and suddenly was gone. Crow Dog sent out two scouts, one to the north and one to the south. They came back saying that they had seen no one. Had this man on the hill been a wanagi, a spirit, trying to warn Crow Dog?

Crow Dog told his men to make camp near a river. He said, "Put the tipis close to the bank, so that the enemy cannot surround us." They did this. During the night Crow Dog could hear the coyote howl four times. Shunk-Manitu was telling him, "Something bad is going to happen to you." Crow Dog understood what the coyote was saying. Crow Dog got the men of his warrior society together, the Kit Foxes. They were singing their song:

> I am a fox.
> I am not afraid to die.
> If there is a dangerous
> deed to perform,
> That is mine to do.

They painted their faces black. They prepared themselves for a fight, for death.

At dawn the enemy attacked—white settlers led by a white and many Crow scouts, with many Absaroka warriors helping them. With Crow Dog were many famous warriors. Numpa Kachpa was there, Two Strikes, who got his name when he shot down two white soldiers riding on the same horse with one bullet. Kills in Water was there, and Hollow Horn Bear's son, and Kills in Sight. Two Crows had wounded Kills in Sight and unhorsed him. Crow Dog came in on a run, killed the two Crows, and put Kills in Sight on his horse. He whipped the horse and it took off with Kills in Sight hanging on to it. The horse was fast and got Kills in Sight safely home.

Crow Dog was looking around, hoping to catch himself one of the riderless Crow horses, when he took two enemy arrows, one high on his chest right under the collarbone and the other in his side. He broke off the arrows with his hands. Hollow Horn Bear's son and two others of his men came to help him. They were wounded, and their horses all had at least one arrow stuck in them. Crow Dog told them, "I am hurt bad. I cannot live. No use bothering with me. Save yourselves."

They rode off. Crow Dog managed to get hold of a horse and got on it, but he weakened soon. He became so weak he fell off this pony. He was lying in the snow. He had hardly strength to sing his death song. Suddenly two coyotes came, hooping gently. They said, "We know you." They kept him warm during the night, one lying on one side and one on the other. They brought Crow Dog deer meat to make him strong, and they brought him a medicine. One of the coyotes said, "Put this on the arrow points." Crow Dog did what the coyote told him. The medicine made his flesh tender and caused it to open up so that he could take the arrowheads and what was left of the shafts out. They almost came out by themselves.

The medicine the coyotes gave him cured Crow Dog. The nourishment they brought him made him strong. The coyotes brought him home to his camp. A crow showed the way. Crow Dog said, "I was already walking on Ta-Chanku, on the Milky Way, on the road to the Spirit Land, but the coyotes led me back." And so he took on his seventh and last name, Kangi-Shunka, Crow Dog. Of course, it should have been Crow Coyote.

Years later, he was on his way to join Sitting Bull in Canada, and near the sacred Medicine Rocks he and his men were jumped by white soldiers. Crow Dog was hit by two bullets. His companions tied him to his horse and managed to get him home. This time a medicine man by the name of Sitting Hawk saved him. He told Crow Dog, "I will put my wound medicine into you. But I will not take the bullets out. One day you will die and go back to Mother Earth and the bullets will still be in you. Your human body will dissolve but the bullets will remain as evidence of what the wasičun have done to us."

This is the legend of Crow Dog, which Old Man Henry has told me many times. The first Crow Dog was a great warrior though he never took part in a big battle, such as the Little Big Horn. He preferred to do his fighting as a member of a small war party made up of warriors from his own Orphan Band. He fought the wasičun and Pawnee and Crow warriors.

Crow Dog had been a close friend of Crazy Horse. Together with Touch the Clouds, White Thunder, Four Horns, and Crow Good Voice, he accompanied Crazy Horse when this Great Warrior surrendered himself at Fort Robinson in 1877. After Crazy Horse was treacherously murdered, it was Crow Dog's cool head and bravery which prevented a general massacre. As the enraged Sioux faced the soldiers who were only waiting for a pretext to start the killing, Crow Dog rode back and forth between them, pushing back the over-eager warriors and soldiers with the butt end of his Winchester.

Crow Dog was most famous for his having shot and killed Spotted Tail, the paramount chief of the Brule Sioux. They were cousins and when they were young, they had been friends. Later, their paths diverged. Spotted Tail said, "It's no use trying to resist the wasičun." He cooperated with the whites in most things. Crow Dog was like Sitting Bull; he stuck to the old ways. The so-called "friendlies" gathered around Spotted Tail, and the so-called "hostiles" around Crow Dog. This led to rivalry and rivalry led to trouble, big trouble that was slowly building up between the two men.

On August 5, 1881, Crow Dog was hauling wood in his buckboard with his wife beside him when he saw Spotted Tail coming out of the council house and getting on his horse. Crow Dog handed his wife the reins, took his gun, which was hanging beside him out of its scabbard, got down from his seat, and faced the chief. Spotted Tail saw him. He said, "This is the day we settle this thing which is between us like men." Spotted Tail went for his six-shooter. Crow Dog knelt down and fired, beating Spotted Tail to the draw. He hit the chief in the chest. Spotted Tail tumbled from his horse and died, the unfired six-gun in his hand. Turning Bear shot at Crow Dog's wife, but missed. Crow Dog drove back to his home with his wife. A man called Black Crow prepared a sweat lodge to purify Crow Dog. He loaded up the Winchester and shot it into the sacred rocks four times, saying, "Now Spotted Tail's spirit won't bother you." They then purified themselves with water.

A judge in Deadwood sentenced Crow Dog to be hanged. He asked leave to go home to prepare himself. The judge asked, "How do we know that you will come back?" Crow Dog said, "Because I'm telling you." The judge let him go. For a month Crow Dog prepared for his death. He made up a death song and gave all his things away. What little he had, his horses, wagon, chickens, he gave to the poor. His wife prepared a white buckskin outfit for him, plain, without beads or quillwork. He wanted to be hanged in this. When all was ready he hitched up his last horse to an old buggy and with his wife drove the one hundred and fifty miles to Deadwood for his own execution.

When he arrived at Deadwood his lawyer was waiting for him with a big smile: "Crow Dog, you are a free man. I went to the Supreme Court for you and the Court ruled that the U.S. government has no jurisdiction over the reservation and that there is no law for punishing an Indian for killing another Indian." Crow Dog said, "You're a damn heap good man. I have driven a hundred and fifty miles for nothing." Then he went home with his wife.

Black Crow told Crow Dog: "Cousin, the blood guilt will be upon you for four generations. From now on you will not smoke the pipe with other men. You will smoke a small pipe of your own, and you will smoke alone. You will not eat from a common dish; you will eat alone from your own bowl. You will drink from your own cup. You will not drink water from the dipper when it is handed around. You cannot eat from other people's dishes and they will not eat from yours. You will live apart from the tribe. Cousin, yours will be a lonely life."

Kangi-Shunka paid blood money. He gave the Spotted Tail family many horses and white-man dollars. That made peace between the families, but not between the Crow Dogs and the spirits. They suffered their ostracism with a certain arrogance. They were weighed down by Crow Dog's deed, but at the same time they were proud of it. Theirs was a proud sort of shame. The first Crow Dog was an outcast but also something of a hero. The Crow Dogs wrapped themselves in their pride as in a blanket. They turned guilt into glory. They began speaking of the royalness of their bloodline. The first Crow Dog had shown them the way. As a chief he had the right to wear a war bonnet, but he never did. Instead he found somewhere an old, discarded white man's cloth cap with a visor and to the top of it he fastened an eagle feather. And that he wore at all times—the lowest and the highest. He used to say: "This white man's cap that I am wearing means that I must live in the wasičun's world, under his government. The eagle feather means that I, Crow Dog, do not let the wasičun's world get the better of me, that I remain an Indian until the day I die." In some mysterious way that old cap became in the people's mind a thing more splendid than any war bonnet. And it was into this clan that I married.

The shock of having to deal at the same time with the myth and the reality, with trying to break through the Crow Dog buckskin curtain, and having to take care of the needs of so many people as well, was too much for me. I broke down. I got sick. I was down to ninety pounds. My body just collapsed. I could no longer stand up. If I tried, my legs would cramp up and hurt. My joints ached. I told Leonard, "I don't feel good. I can't sleep, and if I do I dream about people who have died, my dead friends and relations. Every time I close my eyes I see those who have been killed. I am sad, always. I think I am going to die too."

Leonard said he would do a doctoring meeting for me. He put up the peyote tipi for me. Another road man, Estes Stuart, came to help him. I ate the sacred medicine. I kept eating and eating. I was so weak I could not sit up. They made me lie down on a blanket. Leonard gave me some peyote tea to drink. It was old tea and very strong. I drank two whole cups of it. At midnight Estes prayed, and he talked while the water was going around. He said that since he was a peyote man he had X-ray vision, X-ray eyes which could see into my body, and he could not detect any sickness in me except one—love sickness. I felt so bad that tears came to my eyes. I thought, "Here I am, sick unto death, and they are making fun of me." I think I was a little paranoid. Estes had not been making fun at all. He explained later that what he meant was that mine was not a sickness of the body, but of the mind. That I felt that nobody loved me, not Leonard, not his family, not the people I cooked and washed for. I was sickening for want of love.

Suddenly people were all around me, talking to me, comforting me. Old Man Henry was patting my cheek, calling me "daughter." All those present were praying for me. All through the night I ate peyote. And Grandfather Peyote was calling me daughter.

When the sun rose, I rose too. I suddenly could sit up, even walk. I stepped outside the tipi and all around me I could see strange tropical birds flying, birds of metallic, fluorescent rainbow colors leaving trails of gold and silver. I went inside the house to lie down. I went to my bed, drew aside the blanket, and my legs turned to water. In my bed lay a strange woman, her hands crossed over her breast, her face stiff and white, her eyes unseeing. She was dead!

I got very scared. All of a sudden my whole body stopped. My heart quit pumping. My blood froze. I could not breathe.

Then I saw that the strange woman lying dead in my bed was me. Myself. And a great weight was lifted from me. I could breathe again. My heart was beating. I felt good. What was dying, what had died, was my former self, but I would go on living. Leonard came in and asked how was I doing. He put his arm around me and kissed me. He told me to lie down in the bed. As I did, the dead woman disappeared. The peyote power got hold of me. I started laughing. I kept on giggling and giggling. My ribs were sticking out, I had grown so skinny. I was all bones. But I kept on laughing for an hour. I would be all right.

Reading   # Thrall

FREDERICK AND STEPHEN BARTHELME

We had heard about gambling and addiction, about people who had lost their jobs, their houses, their cars, their families, their lives. We'd heard about people who got crosswise with a bookie or other unconventional lender. We had seen the gambling movies, Karel Reisz's *The Gambler*, Robert Altman's *California Split*. We had read Dostoyevsky's novella. We had read *Under the Volcano*, seen *The Lost Weekend* and *Days of Wine and Roses*. We wondered if that was us. Decided that it was.

We discussed addiction on those long drives down Highway 49. We were analytical about it, examined it in excruciating detail. We knew that your average psychologist would have said we were addicts in a minute. We knew the threatening jargon, that we were "enabling" each other, that we were a codependency case, and in the normal course of things, had we seen ourselves flying to the coast every four or five days for eighteen hours of blackjack and slot machines, we might have said we were addicts. But in the car headed down there this characterization seemed insufficient.

There was a catch: So what? Being an addict didn't mean anything. One of the virtues of having gambling as your vice—as opposed to sex, drugs, or alcohol—was that the disadvantages were felt only at the bank. As long as you had the bankroll, these disadvantages were only superficial wounds. At worst, we were in an early stage of addiction, before the wounds amounted to much, and the customary assumption (which all of the movies, books, and hand-wringing newspaper articles made) that the later, catastrophic stages were inevitable was something we didn't buy. We doubted it. We had been trained to doubt the omnipotent sway of psychology.

Ours was not a family brought up on psychology. In our father's view, the great seething life of feelings could be a damn nuisance. Father had more than a teaspoon of the Frank Bunker Gilbreth about him. Although the family did recognize the psychological dimension, pragmatism—some kind of physical pragmatism—superseded psychology when explanations or remedies were wanted.

Being good sons of our father, we rode to the coast night after night, streaming through the sweltering Mississippi heat, clouds of grasshoppers popping off the highway like a plague of sparks, humidity as thick as gravy, and when we said to each other that we were addicts, when we talked about being addicts, it was a joke—a joke with a nasty twist, but still a joke. Later, after we became accused felons, we would call each other Lyle and Erik, with the idea that a joke needs a Menendezian edge.

You're a gambling addict, so what? Have you got money in the bank? Yes? Go on being an addict. A part of the pleasure was being able to go over the top, way over the top, without any of the mess or travail associated with doing drugs or becoming alcoholics or cheating on our wives, which is not to say the wives approved. They did not. But neither did they react the way they might have had we become enmeshed in other vices.

Sometimes, at first, they went with us. Later, not. But even then, during our long gambling nights, we would call in, advise our spouses how we were doing, how far ahead or behind we were, tell them that we loved them. And we did love them, somehow more fiercely when we were at the coast, when we were free to go to the coast. Something about the intensity of the experience of gambling, of risking the money, of risking loss, made the security and solidity of the home front much more important, much more sweet. More than that, it was a detachment, the anesthetic clarity with which you sometimes saw things in the middle of a drunk. Once Rick stood at the bank of telephones downstairs at the Grand, leaning his forehead against the chrome surface of a wall phone, standing there after hanging up from a conversation with Rie. They had exchanged I love yous and suddenly, after the call, he felt that love with crippling intensity.

An addict is someone who "surrenders" to something, the dictionary will tell you, "habitually or obsessively." Most people are at least a little addicted to something—work, food, exercise, sex, watching sports on television, cooking, reading, the stock market. Some people are addicted to washing their hands. Some people trim their hedges from dawn to dusk. Some people play too much golf. Almost anything can be the object of addiction.

Whatever his pleasure, an addict usually knows he is, or may be, an addict, but inside the warmth of his addiction, the label seems secondary, does not signify, as we like to say over at the college. It's like telling a horse he's a horse. Take President Clinton, for example. When he was involved in certain activities, he must have known he was addicted to something; he just didn't care. We felt just like the president. We didn't care. We supposed, in our conversations, both in Hattiesburg and en route to the coast, that when the time came we would bail. We knew that push would come to shove at some point, and at that point we would get out of the game.

Steve, wisely but very late in all of this, bought a house with some of his inheritance. Made a down payment, got a low mortgage, *invested* in a home. Buying houses didn't come easy to us, in part because the house in which we had grown up was as much a cultural declaration as a dwelling, embodying ideas about design always to be defended against Philistines. Since we had left that house, we had lived in more or less ordinary houses for many years, but we had always rented. Buying an undistinguished house seemed like giving in, disloyalty. There were other reasons, of course. We had led unstable lives, so the idea of settling in the same place for thirty years had seemed laughable. Until Steve started teaching, and for some time afterward, he had never had the steady income to envision buying a house. Buying a house seemed rash when half one's worldly goods were in cardboard boxes awaiting the next move.

We admitted having "addictive personalities," but we *liked* our addiction, the object of our addiction. It wasn't so different from all the other things, large and small, that we had intense attachments to—Diet Coke and Russian writers, springer spaniels and computers, box wrenches and movies. From childhood we had been taught that the object of an addiction was secondary. It was the way in which you cared about something, the quality of your interest rather than its object, that mattered. The first measure of the quality of an interest was its intensity, its thoroughgoingness. Best was to surrender oneself to something habitually or obsessively. We had done that all our lives.

Now the important thing was gambling. The care and feeding of our addiction, the pleasure of our addiction. Gambling was a very cerebral, almost slow-motion activity, which made it easy to savor. It was markedly more satisfying because we were doing it together. As brothers, we shared all the surprise and exhilaration of a new and consuming interest, like any new hobby—skydiving, methamphetamine. Codependency has its good side. Both doing it, we were each part performer and part audience. Every gambling session wrote its own swift, strange story, filled with highs and lows, finely calibrated details ("she flipped another five . . .") and compelling nuances ("and I thought, 'Fuck, ace, next one's an ace,' and then, sure as shit . . ."). Gamblers want to talk. For us, there was always someone to tell, someone who knew in his blood what you were talking about. After a trip, our conversations went on for days, full of lurid, taunting laughter. The kind that revealed just how completely we were hooked on risk, on gambling.

We weren't measuring ourselves against the real daredevils of the culture; we were measuring ourselves against other normal people, middle-class people, good solid stock, people with jobs, families, houses, cars, and responsibilities that they dispatched in a workmanlike way. People like us. We told ourselves that betting a thousand dollars on a hand of blackjack might be stupid, but it wasn't as stupid as shooting yourself full of heroin or, as various members of our family had done for years, drinking yourself into oblivion by five o'clock in the afternoon—or better yet, doing it by noon, waking up at three and doing it again by five, having dinner and doing it again by nine. Maybe we were just looking for a way to keep up with the rest of the family, members of which had had their troubles with various forms of conspicuous consumption, of obsession, of, well, for lack of a better word, addiction. Yes, it ran in the family. From our father on down, maybe even from *his* father on down.

The only time you really think of yourself as an addict is when you want to stop. When it's time to stop. When you're in so much trouble that stopping is the only thing left. But we never got there. We could afford it. It was fun. It was a way to blow off steam. It took us out of ourselves in a way that we hadn't been taken out of ourselves by anything else.

We had had good luck with addictions in the past. Both of us had been drinkers and smokers. Rick had been a drunk in his early twenties, but had stopped dead after he moved to New York and discovered that getting drunk and waking up at four A.M. on a Lower East Side street was not healthy. Steve had long since given up heavy drinking for steady drinking, three drinks a day, give or take a couple, for the past thirty years. Both of us had had smoking habits—two or three packs a day—and while we'd tried to curb them, following the path of declining tar and nicotine, going from regular cigarettes to pretend cigarettes like True and Carlton, we'd had no intention of quitting until, as mentioned, our two older brothers were diagnosed with throat cancer, one within a month of the other.

We quit smoking.

But gambling wasn't producing a downside for us. Gambling was only producing the release, the euphoria, and the opportunity to behave bizarrely, just like—we imagined—ordinary, everyday people. We didn't think we were wild and crazy; we thought gambling made us regular guys.

It was an aesthetic thing too. Everywhere around us were writers and artists and professors, hard at work at what Ishmael Reed describes as "all wearing the same funny hat." It had long seemed obvious that the best course was the other direction. Neither of us had the customary late-twentieth-century middle-class phobia for people who were deemed ordinary. In fact, ordinary was what we both liked best.

What we didn't like about the academy was the falseness: conservative people presenting themselves in Che Guevara suits, digging hard for career advantage while settling hearty congratulations all around for assigning radical authors to their students to read, thus threatening the established order. Soon they would take their SUVs into the mountains.

This put a little extra heat under the affection we had for the ordinary people we imagined existed somewhere and for whom we felt a special kinship. It was ordinariness that we were extending with our gambling, by being addicted to it, by doing it to excess, by risking more money than made any sense at all, by telling ourselves that we were going to win, or that we might win, when we knew as surely as anybody else that the likelihood of that was slim. Still, you'd be surprised at how much positive thinking goes on on the highway at midnight.

You'd be surprised by how dearly the heart holds the idea that tonight you might actually win, that this two thousand dollars, the last two thousand you have in your bank account, will be the basis of your big comeback. Even in the heat of battle, down five or fifteen thousand in a night, the not particularly well heeled but still liquid blackjack loser can imagine winning it all back in a flash.

And he would not imagine it had he not already done it once or twice or maybe more. Had he not experienced that thrill of the cards having run against him all night, run against him for five consecutive hours and having in that time lost an enormous amount of money, gone to the cashier's cage again and again, new resources, the thrill that comes when the cards turn, when they become your cards, when they became his cards, not the casino's, when in the space of forty-five minutes you recognize that you're going to win whatever you bet. And if you recognize it soon enough, and if you're secure enough in the recognition, you can turn around the whole night, turn around five thousand dollars in twenty minutes. You can turn around fifteen thousand dollars in an hour.

It's a rare, even amazing experience. It almost makes gambling worthwhile. Everything you touch turns to gold. You bet five hundred dollars and you bet a thousand. You double down and you win. Your stacks of chips grow. Pretty soon they are paying you in hundreds, then five hundreds—the purple chips. You've got a stack of those in front of you. Then, if the going is really good, they start paying you in orange—the thousand-dollar chips. The thousand-dollar chips are slightly larger, a sixteenth of an inch larger in diameter than all the other chips. You stack them separately.

Your stack grows, and maybe you bet one of them or two of them on a hand. Or you play two hands. And still you win. Sure, this isn't Monte Carlo, you're not some duke or some heiress, and so you're not betting hundreds of thousands of dollars a hand, but that fact makes your betting and your winning just that much sweeter, because you have no business in the world betting a thousand dollars on a hand of blackjack, and you know it. You have no business in the world betting five thousand dollars on a hand of blackjack, and you know it. So when you do, and when the cards are coming your way, and when your five thousand turns to ten, your ten to twenty, it's mesmerizing. Suddenly that business they always say about feeling like you'll live forever becomes a little bit true, because you've crossed over some line, gone into some other territory, become somebody else.

You're part of the table, part of the machine that plays blackjack, part of the casino, part of the system. Only you're not the part that gives your money to them anymore, you're not the part you usually play: the mark, the bozo. You've skidded out onto the ice in the middle of the Olympics in a huge stadium filled with cheering people and swaying, lime-colored spotlights and, suddenly, inexplicably, you can skate like an angel.

Reading

The Spirit Catches You and You Fall Down

ANNE FADIMAN

When Lia was about three months old, her older sister Yer slammed the front door of the Lees' apartment. A few moments later, Lia's eyes rolled up, her arms jerked over her head, and she fainted. The Lees had little doubt what had happened. Despite the careful installation of Lia's soul during the *hu plig* ceremony, the noise of the door had been so profoundly frightening that her soul had fled her body and become lost. They recognized the resulting symptoms as *qaug dab peg*, which means "the spirit catches you and you fall down." The spirit referred to in this phrase is a soul-stealing *dab*; *peg* means to catch or hit; and *qaug* means to fall over with one's roots still in the ground, as grain might be beaten down by wind or rain.

In Hmong-English dictionaries, *qaug dab peg* is generally translated as epilepsy. It is an illness well known to the Hmong, who regard it with ambivalence. On the one hand, it is acknowledged to be a serious and potentially dangerous condition. Tony Coelho, who was Merced's congressman from 1979 to 1989, is an epileptic. Coelho is a popular figure among the Hmong, and a few years ago, some local Hmong men were sufficiently concerned when they learned he suffered from *qaug dab peg* that they volunteered the services of a shaman, a *txiv neeb*, to perform a ceremony that would retrieve Coelho's errant soul. The Hmong leader to whom they made this proposition politely discouraged them, suspecting that Coelho, who is a Catholic of Portuguese descent, might not appreciate having chickens, and maybe a pig as well, sacrificed on his behalf.

On the other hand, the Hmong consider *qaug dab peg* to be an illness of some distinction. This fact might have surprised Tony Coelho no less than the dead chickens would have. Before he entered politics, Coelho planned to become a Jesuit priest, but was barred by a canon forbidding the ordination of epileptics. What was considered a disqualifying impairment by Coelho's church might have been seen by the Hmong as a sign that he was particularly fit for divine office. Hmong epileptics often become shamans. Their seizures are thought to be evidence that they have the power to perceive things other people cannot see, as well as facilitating their entry into trances, a prerequisite for their journeys into the realm of the unseen. The fact that they have been ill themselves gives them an intuitive sympathy for the suffering of others and lends them emotional credibility as healers. Becoming a *txiv neeb* is not a choice; it is a vocation. The calling is revealed when a person falls sick, either with *qaug dab peg* or with some other illness whose symptoms similarly include shivering and pain. An established *txiv neeb*, summoned to diagnose the problem, may conclude from these symptoms that the person (who is usually but not always male) has been chosen to be the host of a healing spirit, a *neeb*. (*Txiv neeb* means "person with a healing spirit.") It is an offer that the sick person cannot refuse, since if he rejects his vocation, he will die. In any case, few Hmong would choose to decline. Although shamanism is an arduous calling that requires years of training with a master in order to learn the ritual techniques and chants, it confers an enormous amount of social status in the community and publicly marks the *txiv neeb* as a person of high moral character, since a healing spirit would never choose a no-account host. Even if an epileptic turns out not to be elected to host a *neeb*, his illness, with its thrilling aura of the supramundane, singles him out as a person of consequence.

In their attitude toward Lia's seizures, the Lees reflected this mixture of concern and pride. The Hmong are known for the gentleness with which they treat their children. Hugo Adolf Bernatzik, a German ethnographer who lived with the Hmong of Thailand for several years during the 1930s, wrote that the Hmong he had studied regarded a child as "the most treasured possession a person can have." In Laos, a baby was never apart from its mother, sleeping in her arms all night and riding on her back all day. Small children were rarely abused; it was believed that a *dab* who witnessed mistreatment might take the child, assuming it was not wanted. The Hmong who live in the United States have continued to be unusually attentive parents. A study conducted at the University of Minnesota found Hmong infants in the first month of life to be less irritable and more securely attached to their mothers than Caucasian infants, a difference the researcher attributed to the fact that the Hmong mothers were, without exception, more sensitive, more accepting, and more responsive, as well as "exquisitely attuned" to their children's signals. Another study, conducted in Portland, Oregon, found that Hmong mothers held and touched their babies far more frequently than Caucasian mothers. In a third study, conducted at the Hennepin County Medical Center in Minnesota, a group of Hmong mothers of toddlers surpassed a group of Caucasian mothers of similar socio-economic status in every one of fourteen categories selected from the Egeland Mother-Child Rating Scale, ranging from "Speed of Responsiveness to Fussing and Crying" to "Delight."

Foua and Nao Kao had nurtured Lia in typical Hmong fashion (on the Egeland Scale, they would have scored especially high in Delight), and they were naturally distressed to think that anything might compromise her health and happiness. They therefore hoped, at least most of the time, that the *qaug dab peg* could be healed. Yet they also considered the illness an honor. Jeanine Hilt, a social worker who knew the Lees well, told me, "They felt Lia was kind of an anointed one, like a member of royalty. She was a very special person in their culture because she had these spirits in her and she might grow up to be a shaman, and so sometimes their thinking was that this was not so much a medical problem as it was a blessing." (Of the forty or so American doctors, nurses, and Merced County agency employees I spoke with who had dealt with Lia and her family, several had a vague idea that "spirits" were somehow involved, but Jeanine Hilt was the only one who had actually asked the Lees what they thought was the cause of their daughter's illness.)

Within the Lee family, in one of those unconscious processes of selection that are as mysterious as any other form of falling in love, it was obvious that Lia was her parents' favorite, the child they considered the most beautiful, the one who was most extravagantly hugged and kissed, the one who was dressed in the most exquisite garments (embroidered by Foua, wearing dime-store glasses to work her almost microscopic stitches). Whether Lia occupied this position from the moment of her birth, whether it was a result of her spiritually distinguished illness, or whether it came from the special tenderness any parent feels for a sick child, is not a matter Foua and Nao Kao wish, or are able, to analyze. One thing that is clear is that for many years the cost of that extra love was partially borne by her sister Yer. "They blamed Yer for slamming the door," said Jeanine Hilt. "I tried many times to explain that the door had nothing to do with it, but they didn't believe me. Lia's illness made them so sad that I think for a long time they treated Yer differently from their other children."

During the next few months of her life, Lia had at least twenty more seizures. On two occasions, Foua and Nao Kao were worried enough to carry her in their arms to the emergency room at Merced Community Medical Center, which was three blocks from their apartment. Like most Hmong refugees, they had their doubts about the efficacy of Western medical techniques. However, when they were living in the Mae Jarim refugee camp in Thailand, their only surviving son, Cheng, and three of their six surviving daughters, Ge, May, and True, had been seriously ill. Ge died. They took Cheng, May, and True to the camp hospital; Cheng and May recovered rapidly, and True was sent to another, larger hospital, where she eventually recovered as well. (The Lees also concurrently addressed the possible spiritual origins of their children's illnesses by moving to a new hut. A dead person had been buried beneath their old one, and his soul might have wished to harm the new residents.) This experience did nothing to shake their faith in traditional Hmong beliefs about the causes and cures of illness, but it did convince them that on some occasions Western doctors could be of additional help, and that it would do no harm to hedge their bets.

County hospitals have a reputation for being crowded, dilapidated, and dingy. Merced's county hospital, with which the Lees would become all too familiar over the next few years, is none of these. The MCMC complex includes a modern, 42,000-square-foot wing—it looks sort of like an art moderne ocean liner—that houses coronary care, intensive care, and transitional care units; 154 medical and surgical beds; medical and radiology laboratories outfitted with state-of-the-art diagnostic equipment; and a blood bank. The waiting rooms in the hospital and its attached clinic have unshredded magazines, unsmelly bathrooms, and floors that have been scrubbed to an aseptic gloss. MCMC is a teaching hospital, staffed in part by the faculty and residents of the Family Practice Residency, which is affiliated with the University of California at Davis. The residency program is nationally known, and receives at least 150 applications annually for its six first-year positions.

Like many other rural county hospitals, which were likely to feel the health care crunch before it reached urban hospitals, MCMC has been plagued with financial problems throughout the last twenty years. It accepts all patients, whether or not they can pay; only twenty percent are privately insured, with most of the rest receiving aid from California's Medi-Cal, Medicare, or Medically Indigent Adult programs, and a small (but to the hospital, costly) percentage neither insured nor covered by any federal or state program. The hospital receives reimbursements from the public programs, but many of those reimbursements have been lowered or restricted in recent years. Although the private patients are far more profitable, MCMC's efforts to attract what its administrator has called "an improved payer mix" have not been very successful. (Merced's wealthier residents often choose either a private Catholic hospital three miles north of MCMC or a larger hospital in a nearby city such as Fresno.) MCMC went through a particularly rough period during the late eighties, hitting bottom in 1988, when it had a $3.1 million deficit.

During this same period, MCMC also experienced an expensive change in its patient population. Starting in the late seventies, Southeast Asian refugees began to move to Merced in large numbers. The city of Merced, which has a population of about 61,000, now has just over 12,000 Hmong. That is to say, one in five residents of Merced is Hmong. Because many Hmong fear and shun the hospital, MCMC's patient rolls reflect a somewhat lower ratio, but on any given day there are still Hmong patients in almost every unit. Not only do the Hmong fail resoundingly to improve the payer mix—more than eighty percent are on Medi-Cal—but they have proved even more costly than other indigent patients, because they generally require more time and attention, and because there are so many of them that MCMC has had to hire bilingual staff members to mediate between patients and providers.

There are no funds in the hospital budget specifically earmarked for interpreters, so the administration has detoured around that technicality by hiring Hmong lab assistants, nurse's aides, and transporters, who are called upon to translate in the scarce interstices between analyzing blood, emptying bedpans, and rolling postoperative patients around on gurneys. In 1991, a short-term federal grant enabled MCMC to put skilled interpreters on call around the clock, but the program expired the following year. Except during that brief hiatus, there have often been no Hmong-speaking employees of any kind present in the hospital at night. Obstetricians have had to obtain consent for cesarean sections or episiotomies using embarrassed teenaged sons, who have learned English in school, as translators. Ten-year-old girls have had to translate discussions of whether or not a dying family member should be resuscitated. Sometimes not even a child is available. Doctors on the late shift in the emergency room have often had no way of taking a patient's medical history, or of asking such questions as Where do you hurt? How long have you been hurting? What does it feel like? Have you had an accident? Have you vomited? Have you had a fever? Have you lost consciousness? Are you pregnant? Have you taken any medications? Are you allergic to any medications? Have you recently eaten? (The last question is of great importance if emergency surgery is being contemplated, since anesthetized patients with full stomachs can aspirate the partially digested food into their lungs, and may die if they choke or if their bronchial linings are badly burned by stomach acid.) I asked one doctor what he did in such cases. He said, "Practice veterinary medicine."

On October 24, 1982, the first time that Foua and Nao Kao carried Lia to the emergency room, MCMC had not yet hired any interpreters, de jure or de facto, for any shift. At that time, the only hospital employee who sometimes translated for Hmong patients was a janitor, a Laotian immigrant fluent in his own language, Lao, which few Hmong understand; halting in Hmong; and even more halting in English. On that day either the janitor was unavailable or the emergency room staff didn't think of calling him. The resident on duty practiced veterinary medicine. Foua and Nao Kao had no way of explaining what had happened, since Lia's seizures had stopped by the time they reached the hospital. Her only obvious symptoms were a cough and a congested chest. The resident ordered an X ray, which led the radiologist to conclude that Lia had "early bronchiopneumonia or tracheobronchitis." As he had no way of knowing that the bronchial congestion was probably caused by aspiration of saliva or vomit during her seizure (a common problem for epileptics), she was routinely dismissed with a prescription for ampicillin, an antibiotic. Her emergency room Registration Record lists her father's last name as Yang, her mother's maiden name as Foua, and her "primary spoken language" as "Mong." When Lia was discharged, Nao Kao (who knows the alphabet but does not speak or read English) signed a piece of paper that said, "I hereby acknowledge receipt of the instructions indicated above," to wit: "Take ampicillin as directed. Vaporizer at cribside. Clinic reached as needed 383–7007 ten days." The "ten days" meant that Nao Kao was supposed to call the Family Practice Center in ten days for a follow-up appointment. Not surprisingly, since he had no idea what he had agreed to, he didn't. But when Lia had another bad seizure on November 11, he and Foua carried her to the emergency room again, where the same scene was repeated, and the same misdiagnosis made.

On March 3, 1983, Foua and Nao Kao carried Lia to the emergency room a third time. On this occasion, three circumstances were different: Lia was still seizing when they arrived, they were accompanied by a cousin who spoke some English, and one of the doctors on duty was a family practice resident named Dan Murphy. Of all the doctors who have worked at MCMC, Dan Murphy is generally acknowledged to be the one most interested in and knowledgeable about the Hmong. At that time, he had been living in Merced for only seven months, so his interest still exceeded his knowledge. When he and his wife, Cindy, moved to Merced, they had never heard the word "Hmong." Several years later, Cindy was teaching English to Hmong adults and Dan was inviting Hmong leaders to the hospital to tell the residents about their experiences as refugees. Most important, the Murphys counted a Hmong family, the Xiongs, among their closest friends. When one of the Xiong daughters wanted to spend the summer working in Yosemite National Park, Chaly Xiong, her father, initially refused because he was afraid she might get eaten by a lion. Dan personally escorted Chaly to Yosemite to verify the absence of lions, and persuaded him the job would do his daughter good. Four months later, Chaly was killed in an automobile accident. Cindy Murphy arranged the funeral, calling around until she found a funeral parlor that was willing to accommodate three days of incense burning, drum beating, and *qeej* playing. She also bought several live chickens, which were sacrificed in the parking lot of the funeral parlor, as well as a calf and a pig, which were sacrificed elsewhere. When Dan first saw the Lees, he instantly registered that they were Hmong, and he thought to himself: "This won't be boring."

Many years later, Dan, who is a short, genial man with an Amish-style beard and an incandescent smile, recalled the encounter. "I have this memory of Lia's parents standing just inside the door to the ER, holding a chubby little round-faced baby. She was having a generalized seizure. Her eyes were rolled back, she was unconscious, her arms and legs were kind of jerking back and forth, and she didn't breathe much—every once in a while, there would be no movement of the chest wall and you couldn't hear any breath sounds. That was definitely anxiety-producing. She was the youngest patient I had ever dealt with who was seizing. The parents seemed frightened, not terribly frightened though, not as frightened as I would have been if it was my kid. I thought it might be meningitis, so Lia had to have a spinal tap, and the parents were real resistant to that. I don't remember how I convinced them. I remember feeling very anxious because they had a real sick kid and I felt a big need to explain to these people, through their relative who was a not-very-good translator, what was going on, but I felt like I had no time, because we had to put an IV in her scalp with Valium to stop the seizures, but then Lia started seizing again and the IV went into the skin instead of the vein, and I had a hard time getting another one started. Later on, when I figured out what had happened, or not happened, on the earlier visits to the ER, I felt good. It's kind of a thrill to find something someone else has missed, especially when you're a resident and you are looking for excuses to make yourself feel smarter than the other physicians."

Among Dan's notes in Lia's History and Physical Examination record were:

History of Present Illness: The patient is an 8 month, Hmong female, whose family brought her to the emergency room after they had noticed her shaking and not breathing very well for a 20-minute period of time. According to the family the patient has had multiple like episodes in the past, but have never been able to communicate this to emergency room doctors on previous visits secondary to a language barrier. An english speaking relative available tonight, stated that the patient had had intermittent fever and cough for 2–3 days prior to being admitted.

Family & Social History: Unobtainable secondary to language difficulties.

Neurological: The child was unresponsive to pain or sound. The head was held to the left with intermittent tonic-clonic [first rigid, then jerking] movements of the upper extremities. Respirations were suppressed during these periods of clonic movement. Grunting respirations persisted until the patient was given 3 mg. of Valium I.V.

Dan had no way of knowing that Foua and Nao Kao had already diagnosed their daughter's problem as the illness where the spirit catches you and you fall down. Foua and Nao Kao had no way of knowing that Dan had diagnosed it as epilepsy, the most common of all neurological disorders. Each had accurately noted the same symptoms, but Dan would have been surprised to hear that they were caused by soul loss, and Lia's parents would have been surprised to hear that they were caused by an electrochemical storm inside their daughter's head that had been stirred up by the misfiring of aberrant brain cells.

Dan had learned in medical school that epilepsy is a sporadic malfunction of the brain, sometimes mild and sometimes severe, sometimes progressive and sometimes self-limiting, which can be traced to oxygen deprivation during gestation, labor, or birth; a head injury; a tumor; an infection; a high fever; a stroke; a metabolic disturbance; a drug allergy; a toxic reaction to a poison. Sometimes the source is obvious—the patient had a brain tumor or swallowed strychnine or crashed through a windshield—but in about seven out of ten cases, the cause is never determined. During an epileptic episode, instead of following their usual orderly protocol, the damaged cells in the cerebral cortex transmit neural impulses simultaneously and chaotically. When only a small area of the brain is involved—in a "focal" seizure—an epileptic may hallucinate or twitch or tingle but retain consciousness. When the electrical disturbance extends to a wide area—in a "generalized" seizure—consciousness is lost, either for the brief episodes called petit mal or "absence" seizures, or for the full-blown attacks known as grand mal. Except through surgery, whose risks consign it to the category of last resort, epilepsy cannot be cured, but it can be completely or partially controlled in most cases by anti-convulsant drugs.

The Hmong are not the only people who might have good reason to feel ambivalent about suppressing the symptoms. The Greeks called epilepsy "the sacred disease." Dan Murphy's diagnosis added Lia Lee to a distinguished line of epileptics that has included Søren Kierkegaard, Vincent van Gogh, Gustave Flaubert, Lewis Carroll, and Fyodor Dostoyevsky, all of whom, like many Hmong shamans, experienced powerful senses of grandeur and spiritual passion during their seizures, and powerful creative urges in their wake. As Dostoyevsky's Prince Myshkin asked, "What if it is a disease? What does it matter that it is an abnormal tension, if the result, if the moment of sensation, remembered and analysed in a state of health, turns out to be harmony and beauty brought to their highest point of perfection, and gives a feeling, undivined and undreamt of till then, of completeness, proportion, reconciliation, and an ecstatic and prayerful fusion in the highest synthesis of life?"

Although the inklings Dan had gathered of the transcendental Hmong worldview seemed to him to possess both power and beauty, his own view of medicine in general, and of epilepsy in particular, was, like that of his colleagues at MCMC, essentially rationalist. Hippocrates' skeptical commentary on the nature of epilepsy, made around 400 B.C., pretty much sums up Dan's own frame of reference: "It seems to me that the disease is no more divine than any other. It has a natural cause just as other diseases have. Men think it is divine merely because they don't understand it. But if they called everything divine which they do not understand, why, there would be no end of divine things."[*]

Lia's seizure was a grand mal episode, and Dan had no desire to do anything but stop it. He admitted her to MCMC as an inpatient. Among the tests she had during the three days she spent there were a spinal tap, a CT scan, an EEG, a chest X ray, and extensive blood work. Foua and Nao Kao signed "Authorization for and Consent to Surgery or Special Diagnostic or Therapeutic Procedures" forms, each several hundred words long, for the first two of these. It is not known whether anyone attempted to translate them, or, if so, how "Your physician has requested a brain scan utilizing computerized tomography" was rendered in Hmong. None of the tests revealed any apparent cause for the seizures. The doctors classified Lia's epilepsy as "idiopathic": cause unknown. Lia was found to have consolidation in her right lung, which this time was correctly diagnosed as aspiration pneumonia resulting from the seizure. Foua and Nao Kao alternated nights at the hospital, sleeping in a cot next to Lia's bed. Among the Nurse's Notes for Lia's last night at the hospital were: "0001. Skin cool and dry to touch, color good & pink. Mom is with babe at this time & is breastfeeding. Mom informed to keep babe covered with a blanket for the babe is a little cool." "0400. Babe resting quietly with no acute distress noted. Mom breast feeds off & on." "0600. Sleeping." "0730. Awake, color good. Mother fed." "1200. Held by mother."

Lia was discharged on March 11, 1983. Her parents were instructed, via an English-speaking relative, to give her 250 milligrams of ampicillin twice a day, to clear up her aspiration pneumonia, and twenty milligrams of Dilantin elixir, an anticonvulsant, twice a day, to suppress any further grand mal seizures.

---

[*]Despite this early attempt by Hippocrates (or perhaps by one of the anonymous physicians whose writings are attributed to Hippocrates) to remove the "divine" label, epilepsy continued, more than any other disease, to be ascribed to supernatural causes. The medical historian Owsei Temkin has noted that epilepsy has held a key position historically in "the struggle between magic and the scientific conception." Many treatments for epilepsy have had occult associations. Greek magicians forbade epileptics to eat mint, garlic, and onion, as well as the flesh of goats, pigs, deer, dogs, cocks, turtledoves, bustards, mullets, and eels; to wear black garments and goatskins; and to cross their hands and feet: taboos that were all connected, in various ways, with chthonic deities. Roman epileptics were advised to swallow morsels cut from the livers of stabbed gladiators. During the Middle Ages, when epilepsy was attributed to demonic possession, treatments included prayer, fasting, wearing amulets, lighting candles, visiting the graves of saints, and writing the names of the Three Wise Men with blood taken from the patient's little finger. These spiritual remedies were far safer than the "medical" therapies of the time—still practiced as late as the seventeenth century—which included cauterizing the head with a hot iron and boring a hole in the skull to release peccant vapors.

The Madwoman of *Off Our Backs*

CAROL ANNE DOUGLAS

Although I know that many women suffer from depression, psychoses and other mental illnesses, I never expected it to happen to me. I thought that if I ever had a mental illness, it would be Alzheimer's disease, which my mother had for ten years before she died; I fear that I may have inherited a predisposition to that terrible illness. But when madness struck, it was not Alzheimer's.

As a lesbian feminist living a double life—twenty-four years at the newspaper *off our backs*, which pays no salary, and twelve years at my paying job for a liberal nonprofit publisher (let's call it News Pubs)—I felt that my life was somewhat schizophrenic, but I didn't expect literal madness.

Looking back, it's hard to tell when the madness began. News Pubs was changing for the worse. Many people had been fired, including my dearest friend there. There had been a nasty power struggle, in which I supported Tom, my boss, who also is my friend. He won the power struggle, but the place was still full of tension.

I had seen the actual plots accurately, but then I began to see too many plots.

Bill, an editor who had been rude to me, cutting me out of conversations, became more so, no matter how polite I was to him. I was having a difficult time coping with his fierce competitiveness with me and his temper. One day he started talking about a prominent member of our advisory board, who had just left me a message on my voice mail. I was certain that Bill had bugged my telephone.

Terrified, I called a detective agency and asked if they could determine whether someone was bugging my phone. A handsome man who looked as if he were straight out of a TV detective series came to check out my office on Sunday when no one else was there. He said the phone was not bugged.

Then, I thought my home phone was bugged. Then my home and work computers were bugged, and someone was reading everything I typed.

When I told Tom I was afraid my phone had been bugged, he responded gently that my fears sounded paranoid, and he advised me to ignore them. Instead, in a panic, I called other coworkers and asked for their help in stopping the bugging of my phone.

Tom requested that I see a therapist and urged me to stop worrying. I agreed to see a therapist, but only the lesbian therapist I had seen several times over the years, Lorraine.

I began looking for another job, certain I could never forgive Tom for call-ing me paranoid and not believing me. I went to Lorraine, who listened to me and appeared to believe me.

I told my lover (let's call her Jane) only a little because I didn't want to alarm her. When I had the locks changed and gave her the new key, I said only that someone had been coming into my apartment and stealing things. I became terrified that if enemies did come into my apartment they would take my cat.

Soon there seemed to be more police in the streets and I became convinced the police were after me. Perhaps someone from work had framed me for a crime. The FBI was after me. I wanted to tell them I was not guilty. Why wouldn't they just arrest me and give me a chance to tell my side? But no, they were playing cat-and-mouse games with me, waiting for me to slip and commit a crime. They wanted more evidence. Well, no matter how much they pressured me, I wouldn't commit a crime.

After having my locks changed twice, I stopped. If it was the FBI after me, I thought, they could get in no matter what I did. I believed they had taken over the adjoining apartments and were looking into my apartment, seeing every-thing I did.

This was not the first time I had considered the FBI an enemy. My first month at *off our backs* in 1973, the Weather Underground (a leftist political dissi-dent group) left us a communiqué to publish. Not long afterwards, someone broke into our office; nothing was taken, but all of the papers were scattered. We were sure it was the government.

Political movements in the seventies were full of paranoia about the gov-ernment. At *off our backs* we believed our phones were tapped. Once someone claimed that an out-of-town collective member was a government agent. We published an article charging that Gloria Steinem was an agent, and I got a phone tip accusing another famous radical feminist of being an agent (I didn't believe it). Some collective members even insisted we use pseudonyms. When I said that my code name would be "Coca-Cola," I was criticized for lack of rev-olutionary seriousness.

Of course our fears weren't without some basis: The government *did* ques-tion women in feminist communities about the whereabouts of underground ac-tivists, and some were jailed for refusing to cooperate. It was not uncommon then to know people who had committed illegal political acts (and I don't mean just sit-ins), and *off our backs* published articles advising women not to talk to the FBI.

I hadn't worried about the FBI in many years, but it was not impossible to imagine that they were out to get me. My straight employer, News Pubs, cov-ered a lot of news about the Internal Revenue Service, and I thought that per-haps the government wanted to take over News Pubs secretly as well as take over the feminist movement via *off our backs*. I had been naive to imagine that I could hold both a straight editorial job and a position at *off our backs:* Now, the government would use me to get at both.

The news stories that came to my desk at News Pubs suddenly seemed so difficult that I found them impossible to edit. I went to Bill and another editor and demanded to know whether one story was fake; the next day my boss had the personnel manager tell me that I had to take medical leave and couldn't come back to News Pubs until a psychiatrist said I was fit to work. I was devastated.

I thought I had been framed and that what I really needed was a lawyer, not a psychiatrist. It seemed that my food and water were being drugged. If I ate or drank anything, I became incoherent or fell asleep, so I tried to eat and drink as little as possible. I thought the FBI knew I hated drugs, and I wanted to preserve my mind more than anything. After watching my mother's Alzheimer's disease, I couldn't bear to have that happen to me. I thought they were trying to force me to surrender and confess to something I hadn't done, but I never would.

Soon I began to fear that the new interns at *off our backs* were police plants out to get me—that a woman on the collective I had always liked before was really an FBI agent. They must have convinced her that I was a criminal and that it would destroy *off our backs* if I was arrested while on the staff, so she was trying to get me off.

My friend Tricia came from Georgia to Washington, D.C., on very short notice because I was so distraught and couldn't tell her over the phone what was happening. I begged her to share all my food and every beverage with me, because I believed they wouldn't drug anyone else; the whole point was to make *me* seem crazy. Tricia agreed, and we split all food and poured our drinks from the same bottles. I ate a little more.

Jane, my lover, looked at me with fear in her eyes. Some friends of hers from out of town had come to visit her, and I was afraid the FBI had told them to turn her against me. One morning I woke up with the terrible fear that Tricia was not Tricia, that someone was posing as her. I felt sick. That very morning, Jane told me she didn't want to make love for a while. I sobbed. I didn't want to, either, because I was afraid the FBI was watching us, but I didn't want her to distance herself from me. I went and sobbed in my bed. If the woman in the next room really had been Tricia, I would have cried with her.

During this time I had been calling psychiatrists, trying to get an evaluation from one saying that I could go back to work, but I couldn't get appointments soon enough with the few who had been recommended by feminists, and others said they didn't do such evaluations. I went to Lorraine, my therapist, and saw to my horror that she, too, had been replaced by someone who looked like her but wasn't really her. I was too frozen to talk and left the appointment early.

The next day, Jane, Tricia (I had decided she was really Tricia and apologized to her for thinking she wasn't) and my friends Jennie and Karla from *off our backs* said they had made an appointment with a psychiatrist at my HMO and would I please come with them right away. They were cheery, and I played along with them, although I was afraid to go to a psychiatrist who hadn't been recommended by feminists.

My friends said the only psychiatrist they could get an appointment with that day was a man. I had not been to a male doctor since I had become a feminist, and I didn't want to see one. I told them that I'd try him, but that I might walk out if I didn't like him and would wait until I could see a woman.

They insisted on going in with me to make sure I said what they thought I should. Jane even told the psychiatrist that I thought my food was drugged. I was very upset that they were making me tell him things I didn't want to tell him. He would believe I had a mental illness.

I didn't like the psychiatrist. He was cold, and when I asked him what his philosophy of therapy was, he didn't seem very forthcoming. He said he was a psychopharmacologist, which scared me. Jane had said that maybe I needed drugs, which had upset me. Being drugged was just what I was trying to avoid.

I told him very politely that I never saw male medical professionals, that it was nothing against him personally (which wasn't true), but I was going to wait until I could see a woman. I walked out.

My friends followed me, and all four of them huddled in the hall of the medical center. They were very upset and told me that because I wouldn't see him, I would have to go to the emergency room. I refused. "Why should I?" I asked. "I'm not shouting, I'm not hurting anyone. Why must you insist that I go to the emergency room?" I said I was willing to see any woman psychiatrist the next day (it was then five o'clock). I was telling them the truth.

My lover said she had reached the end of her rope and might break up with me if I didn't go to the emergency room. Terrified of losing her, I went, though I dreaded the emergency room above all things. I had taken my mother there for a broken arm years before and they had kept her waiting many hours and set her arm wrong, so that it was crooked for the rest of her life. I told my friends that, but they insisted that I go anyway.

The emergency room personnel showed me forms that required me to agree to accept their treatment and to stay until they signed me out. I was petrified. What if they kept me, or put me in a psychiatric ward? What if they never let me out? What if this was just what the FBI wanted? I was afraid they would let me rot there. They didn't have enough evidence to convict me, so they'd prefer to have me incarcerated in a mental institution. There were cops standing around outside the emergency room. Of course I thought it was because of me.

"You don't know what you're doing," I kept trying to tell my friends, but they kept insisting. Once I was in there, they might not be able to get me out, I explained. They said that under the law I couldn't be held without my consent for more than seventy-two hours, but I thought that a lot could be done to me in seventy-two hours.

I knew that lesbians had been abused in psychiatric wards. In the seventies, my first lesbian lover told me she had been given electric shocks at the sight of pictures of naked women by a doctor trying to force her to be straight. My friends didn't believe that she was telling the truth, but I did (and still do).

I didn't think this hospital would do that, but what kind of drugs would they give me? The nursing homes my mother had been in for Alzheimer's had given her drugs that sometimes made her dopey or made her body tremble. One drug made her aggressive and when she began hitting the other old women, the staff tied her to a chair, even though it was the drug, not her, at fault. I had had to fight with them often about overdrugging her. I had no trust in the medical profession—none.

I wouldn't go into the examination room without a friend. The nurse said that only a relative could go with me (heterosexual bias strikes again), so we said that Karla was my cousin.

I thought the doctors who examined me were police doctors. They made me keep repeating what had happened at my workplace again and again. They were trying to build a case that I was crazy. The main doctor was a woman, but she had no bedside manner at all. Karla made me tell her that I thought the police were after me. The doctor said I needed to have a CAT scan. I was wheeled off to a room where my head was stuck in a large tube with odd sounds. I was afraid that they might do something with the sound waves to make me deaf. A friend of mine had lost much of her hearing after improper hospital treatment for a case of the flu.

I clutched Karla and begged her to get in touch with famous feminists I thought might help me, such as Phyllis Chesler (author of *Women and Madness*), if my friends couldn't get me out. While I was between doctors, Karla said she thought I needed an antipsychotic drug. I screamed—I had wanted Karla to go in with me because she had written an antitherapy article.

The tough cookie doctor recommended that I be hospitalized. "No, no," I begged. She said that if my "cousin" would accept responsibility for me, she'd let me out, but only if friends would stay with me day and night. Karla hesitated. She said she would discuss it with my other friends in the waiting room. "Please, Karla, please," I begged. "Don't let them hospitalize me."

After what seemed like an eternity but was probably fifteen minutes, Karla and the doctor returned and the doctor said I was going to be released into the custody of my friends, who would take turns staying with me. I was released conditionally, and I had to sign a paper saying I was going back to the medical center to see a psychiatrist the next day. I also had to promise several other things that I can scarcely remember. Perhaps not to hurt myself? Perhaps to tell anyone if I had any delusions? I did promise to go back to the emergency room if I was in pain. I didn't know what signing the paper meant. Could I be hauled in off the street if I broke the conditions? Who could commit me?

The next morning, I went to see a psychiatrist, accompanied by Jane and Tricia. This time, I asked them not to talk, and they didn't, except to tell the psychiatrist that they loved me and that I was a wonderful person. This psychiatrist, Susan, was a woman with a gentle-seeming voice and face, but I thought she was a fake (or a police psychiatrist) because she sometimes said "um" and "er," and I thought she was mocking my speech patterns. She gave me a prescription for Risperdal, an antipsychotic drug she said would also help me sleep. I agreed to take it.

Friends spent nights on my sofa, supposedly to help me if I had any side effects from the medication, which made me afraid to take it, but I did. Since I believed that the psychiatrist was a cop, I had to take it. The cops might get me and take a blood test to find out whether I was taking the medication. If it made me unable to function, I could always stop, I told myself.

I began to think that these people weren't my friends, but other people substituted for them. I thought my lover wasn't my real lover. I sobbed and sobbed.

I believed that the FBI had taken them all away as part of the Federal Witness Protection Program and substituted other people. I wondered whether I would ever see my real friends and lover again. Perhaps not until and unless I went on trial. If only they would charge me and put me on the stand. It would be better to go to jail than to live like this.

I no longer thought of calling famous feminists to ask them to help me. I didn't want them to be "disappeared" by the FBI. Perhaps this was a bigger plot than I realized. Perhaps this was happening to feminists all over the country; they were being disappeared, they were being institutionalized. I wondered whether Mary Daly was safe. Was Catharine MacKinnon safe? Who was left?

Walking to *off our backs* one day, I saw several white cars back up. I thought it was a signal that someone would take away my little white cat. If I left *off our backs*, perhaps I could keep my cat. *off our backs* was my life, and I had thought I would never leave it until it died or I did, but I was afraid that someone was going to hurt my cat. Even if they didn't hurt her, she'd be terrified if she were taken away to a strange place. So I got on the phone and resigned from the collective, asking them to take my name off the masthead. It felt like the greatest defeat of my life. But it appeared that someone had taken my cat away anyway and substituted a cat that looked like her. It was a fairly nice cat, but I wanted my Chloe. I thought the FBI was so cruel, so determined to destroy me, that they wouldn't even leave me my own cat. They were determined to show me my utter helplessness.

I believed they were even trying to take away the satisfaction of reading from me. The *Washington Posts* I got in the morning were full of fake news: For example, I thought that John Denver hadn't really died or that he had been killed to scare me. And when I started to read a book, it seemed that someone had substituted a fake version for the real one.

One night Jane (or pseudo-Jane, as I thought of her) said she was going to bring me dinner, but instead she came with two other friends to tell me I should hospitalize myself because I was so depressed. She talked about my going on permanent disability. They kept me talking for hours. I was hungry and annoyed. It felt like a siege. No, I said, I won't hospitalize myself for anything in the world. Jane again threatened to leave if I wouldn't go, but I told her that tactic would never work again. I was still angry about the emergency room and would never go there again.

Jane responded she would have to take care of herself, then. She was worn out. Fine, I said, take care of yourself, and let me be. When they suggested I should take an antidepressant, I said fine, I was willing to take an antidepressant. I'd take anything that might make me feel even a little bit better. Taking an antidepressant wasn't strange like taking an antipsychotic; many women I knew did. Finally they left.

The next day I saw the psychiatrist, Susan, and she prescribed an antidepressant, Zoloft, and said I should go to a day-treatment program for people with mental illnesses. I asked her if that was the way to stay out of the hospital, and she said yes. Susan said that Jane had been calling her, and I felt I had to ask Susan not to listen to Jane, because she wanted me to be hospitalized. I asked that Jane not be considered my spokesperson and gave Susan the name of another friend, who didn't think I should be hospitalized, as my contact person. I realized the irony in my having championed for more than two decades the rights of lesbian partners in case of illness, but now I thought my doctors were paying too much attention to Jane.

I took the Zoloft, and within hours I felt better. I was able to write, which I hadn't been able to do in weeks. I wrote bitter poetry, disguised by being about Shakespearean characters, and read Shakespeare. I was determined to keep my mind functioning. I would read my books, even if they were fakes.

I was afraid to go to the day-treatment program, but I did. Everyone was fairly nice, though they were obviously trying to brainwash me into believing I had a mental illness. I told them, as I told my psychiatrist, that I didn't have any more delusions that policemen were trying to get me, that I didn't think anyone was trying to get me. I knew what I had to say to keep out of the hospital. I knew that I had to pretend to go along.

My psychiatrist diagnosed me as having severe depression with delusions. The staff at the day-treatment program diagnosed me as having delusional disorder with severe depression. They showed me an article on delusional disorder that described feelings so much like mine that I thought it was an article the FBI had written to convince me I was delusional. I still had no idea I was sick. I was sure that all the staff at the day-treatment center were cops. So were all the other patients. But that wasn't so terrible. I could cope with that and pretend that they were the real thing.

What was much harder was pseudo-Jane. I didn't want to touch her and thus betray the real Jane, even though the real Jane had abandoned me and let the FBI take her away. Sometimes pseudo-Jane said she loved me, and I'd respond, "I love Jane" instead of "I love you." I desperately missed my real friends, who I thought I'd never see again. No matter how nice people were to me, I didn't believe they were who they said they were. I saw them as subtly threatening me.

I felt I now understood how people survived losing everyone they loved in wars. There was still some part of me that wanted to go on though I had lost everyone and everything that was important to me. I felt suicidal at times, particularly the day after I was at the emergency room, but I was afraid to try killing myself because I knew I'd be hospitalized if I didn't succeed. Sometimes I thought I was a fool or a coward not to kill myself because something much more terrible, such as hospitalization or torture, might happen to me, but I didn't anyway. I told myself that it was all right to be a little cowardly about physical things. I was brave mentally.

I wondered how I could live an ethical life while I had to lie to everyone and could trust no one. I hated pretending that pseudo-friends were my real friends, but I felt I had to for self-protection, and I hoped that my real friends would understand. And how could I live a meaningful life without working for the women's movement?

After I had completed three weeks at the day-treatment program, my psychiatrist gave me a clean bill of health to go back to work at News Pubs. I was full of joy when I went back to work. I even believed my coworkers were their real selves. The coworker who had been rude to me before left me alone, and two others who had worked with me closely proved to be true friends and wanted me back at work. I managed to work without saying or doing anything strange, even though I silently believed the FBI still controlled my world. I knew what I had to do to fit in.

It seemed that the FBI had let me live. They had let me go back to work. Since I had started taking the antidepressant, eating didn't make me fall asleep, so I thought they had stopped drugging my food. Perhaps the FBI would even let me write for the movement. I wrote an article for *off our backs*. The collective agreed to publish it. Perhaps they would let me come to layout weekend and help with layout. I went. Everyone was nice to me. Perhaps they weren't all FBI agents after all. Perhaps none of them were.

Gradually, person by person, I began to realize people were their real selves. By that time I had been taking the antipsychotic drug for nearly two months. All along, I had been watching for signs that would tell me whether people were my real friends or substitutes, asking them questions that only my friends would know the answers to. But even when they knew the answers, I thought that they had been unbelievably well briefed. Nothing convinced me.

One day on a walk by the canal with Jane, she mentioned that on the first walk we had taken together we had seen three different species of grebes swimming there. How could she know something that specific, such a small detail, if she wasn't Jane? But the thought that she might be the real Jane was horrifying, not consoling. Perhaps Jane had been part of some plot against me all along, not a woman who had ever loved me. I suddenly thought that everything she had ever said to me and done with me had been false, that I had been a fool. How could I have believed, for instance, that anyone could think that my hair was beautiful, as she had told me, when I know it is stringy? Now I realized she had been too good to be true.

I can't remember the moment when I realized that my oldest friend, Ginny, was really herself, not an FBI substitute. She had gone out with me often to movies—always one of our favorite things to do together—during my illness. But nothing she said seemed out of character, and one day I realized that she really was Ginny.

The gentlest woman I know, Jackie, was one of the people I had most feared. I had stayed the night at her home and after eating the worst TV dinner I had ever tasted, I had believed she was trying to poison me. Because her cats were timid and hid, I believed that she was a right-wing, anti-abortion fanatic who had stolen pro-abortion people's cats, and that she would steal mine. (I had always been terrified after I heard about "right-to-lifers" killing the cats of an abortion clinic worker.) I had had difficulty finding her house, and I lay awake that night worrying that I had been kidnapped to the suburbs and would never be able to find my way back to the city. On my way home the next morning, I had heart palpitations (probably from the Risperdal) and was convinced she really had poisoned me.

One day I just knew that Jackie was really Jackie. And if she, who I had feared the most, was her real self, then I knew I must have been sick to think that she was not. She was warm and reassuring, so she was the first person I talked to about my illness, even though she was not one of my closest friends. We went out to brunch, and I told her I had been sick and hadn't believed she was her real self. She was astonished, and was very good to talk with. She had no idea that I hadn't known who she was (neither did anyone else, except Tricia, the only one I had told), but she responded with warmth and encouragement rather than fear. I felt so good after talking with her that I wanted to tell everyone else, too, about what an amazing thing had happened to me. But I proceeded cautiously, deciding which person to tell when, because I knew that some people might be more afraid than reassuring.

It was a great shock for me when I finally realized I had really been sick. For several months, everything I had thought was happening was not. I was used to trusting my own perceptions, so it was devastating to realize that I, who had always prided myself on my mind above everything, had been betrayed by it. I, who had rebelled against biological determinism, who said biology isn't destiny, had been controlled by my biology. I had a serious mental illness, probably delusional disorder. I, who had always opposed psychiatric medication, had been restored to my normal mental state by pills. Two pills a day kept my mind and body in balance.

I was stunned by my own frailty. I knew that many people had chemically caused mental illnesses and I had seen some of my friends improve their lives by taking antidepressants, but it can be hard to believe that it has happened to you. In the 1970s, most of my friends and I had believed that all mental illnesses were socially caused, that women came down with mental illnesses only because they were oppressed. We had been very skeptical of the idea that there could be a physiological cause for it and thought that people who focused on that aspect or gave women drugs were just trying to pacify women so that we wouldn't rebel.

Although I was shocked to find that I had been mentally ill, I was also delighted that the rest of the world had not changed. I had loved my life for years—loved my lover, my friends, *off our backs*, my straight job and my interests, like bird-watching. It was indescribably wonderful to know that that life had not somehow disappeared.

Throughout the illness, when people told me I was sick, I had thought, "If only I were. It would be great news if I really were just sick, and I still had my world." So it was a happy as well as sobering realization. Finally, I could say what had happened to me. Finally, I could tell the truth to my lesbian therapist, Lorraine, and my psychiatrist, Susan, letting them know that I hadn't believed in them or told them what I was really thinking. I told them that I had believed that everyone in my life was a substitute. I also told most of the people I had thought were fakes. It was wonderful to live in a world where I could tell the truth. I called all my friends, delighted that they were their real selves. Most of them wanted to talk about it, although a few were a little queasy. It was such a joy, knowing that I was with my real friends. And that my dear cat was my real cat after all. My books had always been my real books.

In recent years, I had become a little bored with writing for *off our backs*. After you have written hundreds of book reviews, it can become automatic. But after having believed I would be prevented from writing for the movement, I felt renewed excitement at realizing that I still could, and have written a flurry of articles since then.

I also began to want to be affectionate with my lover again. I hadn't liked everything Jane had done, but I also saw now that she had practically fallen apart from the strain. Jane had wanted me to be hospitalized because she was afraid I would kill myself; the truth, ironically, was that it was the thought of hospitalization that made me feel suicidal. We entered couple counseling with another lesbian therapist to help us cope with what we had been through.

Jane now understands more about what happened to my mother and why it made me distrust the medical profession and, I hope, how my passionate love for nature made confinement in a hospital seem particularly horrifying. I was used to spending every weekend taking long walks, and I continued that as much as possible when I was ill. Even at my sickest, I found some slight comfort in being outdoors. (Not as much as I had before, because I was afraid that the FBI would damage the parks I loved as a punishment for me.)

I now understand what Jane went through, for I have had the experience of seeing people I love have mental illness and know how frightening and agonizing that is. To my astonishment, I really was helped by psychiatrists. They had diagnosed me correctly and given me the right medication the first time, without experimentation, which everyone says is practically a miracle.

I am also pleased, but not surprised, that my friends stood by me and saw me even when I was ill. Only one woman, who I had not kept up with very well, was so put off by my apparent distrust of her when I was ill that she wants nothing more to do with me. None of my close friends reacted that way, nor did any other friends. Indeed, my friends were afraid I would never forgive them for trying to get me to a doctor and to take medication.

I do appreciate that intervention was needed to get me to a psychiatrist, and I am grateful that my lover pushed for it to be a psychiatrist at my HMO, where it was all paid for. Otherwise, I would have had terrible medical debts to face in addition to everything else. I know from experience what a burden medical debts can be; my family went from affluence to poverty as a result of my father's and mother's illnesses, my mother ending up with nothing but Medicaid and Social Security, which went to the nursing home to pay for her care.

I now realize that I desperately needed drug treatment and would have fallen completely apart and lost my job, my lover and most of the rest of my life without that treatment. I'm glad my friends and lover understood that. I'm also glad that my boss was understanding—in fact, he was the first person who understood what was happening to me—and that he didn't simply fire me but pressured me to get the help I needed.

However, I still think I should not have been forced to go to the emergency room, an experience that was terrifying for me and not helpful. My lesbian friends should have understood my refusal to see a male psychiatrist and believed me when I said I would see a female psychiatrist the next day without having to go to the emergency room. I'm glad they didn't leave me in the hospital when the emergency room doctor wanted to hospitalize me; it might have been hard to forgive them if they had left me. I still see no good reason for the doctor to hospitalize me. I had done nothing suicidal, nor threatened suicide; nor had I done anything even slightly threatening to anyone else. I don't believe that anyone should be hospitalized unless she is violent to others.

My friends now say that they didn't know what to do and shouldn't be judged harshly for trying to do their best and perhaps not always doing the right thing. I can appreciate that, but I would be less understanding if I had actually been hospitalized. My lesbian therapist, Lorraine, and some of my friends were determined to help me stay out of the hospital, and I appreciate that. Tricia came from Georgia especially to keep me from being hospitalized. Unlike the emergency room doctor, my psychiatrist, Susan, has treated me with respect, showing me my diagnosis and telling me what she was doing and what I needed to do to stay out of the hospital.

I believe I was very wise to do everything I could, including lying about what I was perceiving, to avoid hospitalization. As a lesbian feminist, I knew enough to have an intelligent fear of mental hospitals. I also spoke very strongly about being skeptical of drugs and of wanting to take the lowest possible dose, and, fortunately, Susan agreed. I have since spoken with a number of feminists, including those who have written very critically about the mental-health profession, who say that drugs now are very different from what they were twenty or even ten years ago, and that they can be helpful. Phyllis Chesler told me she believes failing to provide needed treatment, which can include drugs, can be as harmful as the mistreatment she has recorded in her writings about psychiatry.

Chesler asked me what age I was when I became ill. When I told her fifty-one, she responded, "Aha, menopause," and I agree. Nothing like this had ever happened to me before. I doubt this mental illness due to a chemical imbalance would have come about now unless it was connected to menopause. I was going through much stress at work, but I have gone through great stress before without becoming mentally ill. The doctors say that psychoses appearing at this late age are relatively rare. But are they just not diagnosed? I had been having hot flashes for about a year before the illness became obvious, but they became worse that spring, as I began to have irregular periods. I felt premenstrual all the time, with no relief. I became tense, more easily afraid and angry beginning in April; I started thinking people were bugging my phone in August. I am sure there is a connection. And interestingly, since I have been taking the medication, my hot flashes have almost disappeared, as has my heightened state of tension.

I am angry more research has not been done on menopause and mental illness, angry that not one of the books on menopause that I've seen says that there may be a connection between the onset of menopause and the onset of mental illness. Who knows how many women have gone through what I did. I want more women to be aware of the possibility in case they notice they or their friends are going through something similar at menopause. Susan and other psychiatrists at the medical center seem very interested and, with my active encouragement, are looking into the connection between mental illness and menopause.

It is no coincidence that my fears were of persecution by the FBI. It's not unreasonable to believe that radical feminists could be harassed by the government, nor, of course, is it unreasonable for a lesbian to fear mental hospitals. As Phyllis Chesler has demonstrated in her research, including a fall 1997 article in *On the Issues*, women still are being abused in some mental hospitals. In some cases, other patients and hospital staff have abused the women, and no one believes them because they are labeled mentally ill.

The strain of living a double life also no doubt contributed to my stress and eventual illness. Although I have always been out as a lesbian at work and have had good support from my boss and most coworkers, being the editor of a straight though nonprofit tax magazine and being on the staff of a radical feminist newspaper can feel like a schizophrenically double life. Trying to act like a feminist with some coworkers who are anything but is a particular strain.

Although I want to encourage other lesbians to get medical help and even drug treatment if all of the friends they usually trust say they should, I hope no one will construe this essay as suggesting that it's always safe for lesbians to see psychiatrists or to take psychiatric drugs. That's far from the case, though I now think they can be helpful in some cases, and I am grateful I had this help before my illness became even worse. But in the day-treatment program, I met women who shook constantly—and always will—because they had been given Haldol. The doctors at the treatment program were very critical of Haldol, but some doctors still prescribe it. Others patients said their sex lives had been ruined for years.

Even the small doses of Zoloft I am taking have a negative effect on sexual ability, which is infuriating given that I have fought so hard to live as a lesbian. I still feel as much desire for sex as ever, but my ability to have orgasms is impaired, a common side effect of Zoloft. If my sexual response doesn't improve, I shall change medications. Susan supports me in that and is suggesting Wellbutrin as a possible alternative. Drugs are much better than they used to be, but they could be still better, and such research should be an important priority.

Being in the psychiatric day-treatment program was, in retrospect, a powerful experience. I am ashamed to say that it was my first prolonged time (three weeks, all day) of intensely personal discussions in a predominately working-class, African-American setting (the other patients, not the staff, which was predominately white). Many of the patients were on Medicaid. I thought I was empathetic before, but now seeing homeless people feels much more personal to me. I always have given homeless women money, but now I give it to homeless men, too, and am friendlier to them. They could be me. Or they could be like one of the people I liked in the day-treatment program; one had been a homeless, alcoholic man.

I also have a more personal empathy for ill people like the man who shot up the U.S. Capitol (in 1998). True, I never had the least violent impulse when I was ill, but I know what it is to feel that the government is spying on and controlling every aspect of your life and you are helpless to prevent it. I am also more concerned than ever about being a good person. I feel that I have a second chance at life. I still want to do all the things I was doing before, but I want to do them better.

My therapist and several of my friends have told me that I am more emotionally available since my illness. And, as one friend put it, "You write better since you went crazy." I hold back less, because why the hell not be emotional? What more do I have to be afraid of? Actually, I'm very afraid of the possible recurrence of the illness. Intellectually, I can't quite believe it could happen to me again. Surely I was deceived before only because I had no idea that it was a mental illness. Now, if it happened, I would know very quickly and seek medication. People tell me that it isn't that simple, however. I hope never to find out. Certainly I think I would be readier to listen to my friends if they told me they thought I was becoming ill again. I know they would understand what was happening sooner than they did before.

It appears that I won't have a relapse as long as I am on the medications. My doctors say that I need to keep taking them at least through the menopause years, and then they'll try tapering the dose. If that doesn't work, I might need to be on them for the rest of my life. I have asked whether I might become addicted to the drugs, but they tell me that these drugs aren't addictive. I say that I could become addicted to sleeping well, because I now sleep much better than I ever have in my adult life.

After I gave a talk about my illness at the Cambridge, Massachusetts Women's Center, some kind feminists from Bloodroot Restaurant feared that I had become too comfortable with the idea of taking drugs and sent me information about naturopathic remedies, such as St. John's wort, which I may take someday when I am no longer on my present antidepressant.

Sadly, some friends are afraid that I may become ill again and, perhaps a little afraid of me as a result, watch to see whether I am doing anything unusual. I find that aggravating and frustrating. I need my friends to see that I am not ill now, as most of them do. The hardest part of my illness is not learning my own limitations, but learning other people's.

I've always been out before, so it's important to me to be out about my illness, too, with the hope I might help someone with a similar illness to recognize it. My psychiatrist asked me if I was willing to go before a group of psychiatrists to discuss my illness, and I readily agreed. After discussing my illness (apparently my cure is considered very quick and they are proud of it), they asked me what advice I would give psychiatrists. I said that they should allow people to stay in their own homes, treat them with respect, consult them as much as possible about their treatment and try low doses of medication.

I wrote about my illness in *off our backs* and received more letters in response than I have for anything I have ever written. I think lesbians and feminists are willing to try to understand mental illness because we see its political and social context as well as its biological aspects. We live in a violent, fiercely competitive society—a patriarchy—which isn't good for preserving our mental health.

Any of us can become mentally ill. Fortunately, psychiatry has changed considerably in recent years, at least in some places, and there may be a chance that we can get help for ourselves or our friends if we become ill. However, we should be cautious. I was helped by drugs, but not all drugs are benign. We should be as informed as possible about the policies of the medical practitioners we see and the side effects of the drugs that they prescribe.

Before this illness, I would have done anything I could to keep any of my friends out of the hands of psychiatrists, but now I see that some illnesses require medication. When I didn't believe that people were their real selves, there was no way anyone could reach me until the medication took effect.

Now I am horrified to think of the women and men who need the kind of medication I am taking but do not have adequate medical care to provide or pay for it, as my HMO does. I have always supported nationalized medical care, which all other prosperous nations have, and I do now more than ever.

But such treatment needs to happen in the context of a caring lesbian community that pays attention to the treatment their friend is getting and that gives as much support as possible, as my friends did. Even when one is mad, a warm, friendly tone conveys something, although one isn't sure whether to trust it.

I have just begun talking with other lesbians with disabilities as one of them. Through the Disability Caucus of the National Women's Studies Association, I have learned that there are places where we can get respectful attention for sharing our concerns. I used to report on the caucus from an outsider's perspective, but this year I attended its workshop as one of those affected. The women welcomed me, and now I have a new identity. Accustomed to being out in all my identities, I think it is important to be out in this one as well, to challenge stereotypes and speak up for our rights.

The Application of Systems Theory to Chronic Illness Issues and the Educational Environment

LISA AND CAROLYN BANTA

[Editor's note: This case study was written at the request of the co-editors of this book. Carolyn and Lisa Banta are actual people. They have given permission for their real names to be used. Lisa, Carolyn's mother, is a trained social worker. We appreciate their generosity and hard work, and believe this case underscores an important point: the Bantas are a family with considerable resources at their disposal. Lisa, by training a skilled advocate, is working on the most important case of her life. Even so, the difficulties of moving systems to respond to her "client" are obvious and enormous. Carolyn's description of her experience is interspersed with Lisa's professional presentation of their case and appears in italics. This case study, we think, brings the difficulty of aggressive advocacy—and its rewards—into the light.]

INTRODUCTION

A system is a set of interrelated elements that function to make a whole. Systems theory states that individuals are constantly interacting with their environment, and that change in any one part of the system will affect other aspects of the system. Systems may either resist or accommodate this change, but the impact is always the same: the system is constantly working to bring itself into homeostasis, or stability, even as it is buffeted by outside forces.

The following case study demonstrates how the medical, educational, and legal system interact on an individual's struggle with a chronic illness. When Carolyn Banta became ill with adolescent lupus, the medical system was attempting to diagnose and treat her symptoms, which were not definitive. Social workers may frequently counsel clients who have a cluster of symptoms, which do not lead to a clear diagnosis. Often the medical community will consider the illness to be psychogenic, particularly if they cannot find a clear physiological basis in the symptomatology. In the past, illnesses such as asthma, multiple sclerosis, mononucleosis, and migraines were considered to be "psychological" in origin. Today, we understand the physical process of these diseases.

As Carolyn and we, her family, struggled on the micro level with individual physicians, and on the macro level, with the general viewpoint of the medical community about Carolyn's early symptoms, we also needed the family, medical, and educational systems to interact with each other. Throughout our lives, particularly in times of distress, individuals and families are interacting with multiple systems on different levels. Large macro systems (e.g. the medical, educational, or social service community) may begin to exert pressure on other systems to instigate change or obtain accommodations or financial support for their patients. In Carolyn's case, the medical system supported her need for accommodations within the educational system. However, when the educational system failed to respond, we, her parents needed to involve the legal system to secure Carolyn's rights under state and federal law. The American Disabilities Act, a federal law, states that individuals may not be discriminated against because they are disabled and has guidelines and grievance and complaint procedures for people to utilize. This law governed Carolyn's original education plan. However, as you will see later in this case, the pressure exerted by the legal system to force accommodations for Carolyn resulted in a struggle by the educational system to maintain itself (homeostasis) and to make as few changes as possible.

LUPUS: AN ELUSIVE CONNECTIVE TISSUE DISEASE

Carolyn is a sixteen-year old girl diagnosed with mixed connective tissue disease (lupus) and fibromyalgia. At first glance, she appears to be your typical high school junior; however, if you look closely at her complexion, body language, and countenance, you would see a very different person. She lives with chronic swollen painful joints, muscle pain and fatigue; thus, her gait is slow and guarded. Her posture is frequently hunched over. She is pale, almost ghost-like, from anemia. She struggles with low-grade fevers and symptoms of hypoglycemia, in addition to the fatigue. She says that she feels daily as if she "has a severe case of the flu, and has been hit by a truck."

Carolyn's illness began with an unrelated incident: a severe elbow injury sustained in physical education class. After months of rest and physical therapy, she began to develop unexplained muscle pain in her shoulders, neck, and upper back.

The following April, Carolyn developed a flu-like illness consisting of severe muscle pain, mild vertigo, vision difficulties, muscle-tingling, numbness, and fatigue. Her blood work for numerous illnesses, e.g. Epstein-Barr virus and Lyme Disease, were normal. Testing continued for the next several months, until one specific test revealed low protein levels common in persons with lupus. Although further tests were needed to confirm this diagnosis, the physician suggested that Carolyn be referred to a psychiatrist, as the physician believed that Carolyn might be somaticizing other stressors in her life.

Doctors are nebulous. From one perspective, society puts them in a Christ-like stature and sees their Hippocratic oath to help humanity as a benefit for mankind. However, if one looks beyond the façade of superficiality, many of the practitioners devoted to health care are malevolent. If one cannot see, one does not believe. I felt like my disease was a ghost. Its presence lurked in my body, unable to be detected by modern technology. It was only when the ghost decided to no longer be invisible and the blood tests turned positive, that the doctors began to believe. If one can see, one can believe. For the health care system is strictly governed by analysis and science, which often leads to misdiagnoses of illnesses in the human body.

During this time, I had just completed my research internship for my Ph.D. in social work at Rutgers University. I took a leave of absence and began to devote my time to research on my daughter's illness. Research is one of my loves and fortes, so I spent numerous hours poring over journals, and online doing medical research about rheumatoid illnesses, pain disorders, and psychogenic illnesses. As a social worker, I have worked with adolescent clients who were motivated by secondary gain to exaggerate many different physical symptoms, and I truly did not see Carolyn as one of these girls. I felt, rather, that her life was full of primary losses. Carolyn spent the summer in bed, resting and trying desperately to overcome her pain and fatigue. Her social contacts became infrequent; she was unable to spend an evening at a dance, or go to a party, or a shopping mall. She spent many hours playing video games, watching TV, and sleeping.

It feels like twenty years have passed since I became ill. I felt shipwrecked, and the ways of my teenager years—dancing at the winter formal, shopping for a pair of jeans, and attending parties—had all been lost at sea. I was deserted on an island alone, with only a few keys to help me survive: my family, my boyfriend, and my one true childhood friend. I am still unable to fathom what secondary gain a patient can obtain alone in a bed, with only her cat and stuffed animals for company, constantly hearing and looking out on a world that she is unable to be a part of. True loss permeated me, as my adolescent life was carried out to sea.

My research led me to an eminent rheumatologist who had written extensively on an illness, fibromyalgia, whose patients exhibited most of the symptoms that Carolyn had. I was extremely lucky to gain an appointment in August, 2000.

[I wondered] how would he treat me? Did I look too sick? Too well? Maybe they would think that I looked depressed? A thousand questions lingered in my mind like a plague poisoning my body. Somewhere in the midst of it all, when I heard my name called, and met with the doctor, his office no longer seemed like a jail cell.

The doctor reviewed Carolyn's medical records and diagnosed her with fibromyalgia, a pain and fatigue disorder of unknown origin. He prescribed a pain medication that led to an improvement in her condition. However, this doctor only conducts annual reviews on cases, and stated that it was imperative that Carolyn find a local rheumatologist [a physician who specializes in inflammation, or pain, in muscles, joints, or fibrous tissue] or physiatrist [a physician who specializes in rehabilitation and treatment of musculoskeletal conditions] to monitor Carolyn's illness. At this point, we found Dr. Knee, who became a great advocate for Carolyn in her educational struggle, and has written many

letters to the school district in an attempt to help her secure needed accommodations. Dr. Knee's diagnosis, lupus (followed in the winter of 2001 with an additional diagnosis of Epstein-Barr syndrome) underscores the elusiveness of all
rheumatological disorders.

THE EDUCATIONAL AND LEGAL SYSTEM

Carolyn attends a public county magnet school for high achieving students. The
school year begins in mid August and continues until the end of June. The
school day lasts from 8:00 to 4:30. At the end of her freshman year, Carolyn was
ranked fifth in a class of 330 students. Carolyn was also very active in many social and school related activities. She took art classes one night each week,
played basketball, and worked out at the local gym several times a week. She
was active in and excelled at many social and school-related activities. Prior to
an injury, she set three of the high school's physical fitness records.

After Carolyn became ill, I became very concerned that this long school day
would be too fatiguing for her. As a result, I contacted the director of Special
Services in July 2000 and asked that a 504 Education Plan be written [this refers
to a plan for accommodating students with disabilities under the federal Rehabilitation Act]. Her physician recommended numerous accommodations that
were necessary for Carolyn to function in the school setting. Several school personnel met with Carolyn and me in August 2000 to discuss these accommodations. During our meeting, the school personnel were very disagreeable. The
Director of Special Services and Director of Guidance suggested that Carolyn return to her home district for the last three years of high school, where the school
day would be shorter and intensity of work would be easier. Since our local
school district did not offer the same educational opportunities, we refused. According to the American Disability Act (ADA) and the 504 Rehabilitation Act,
Carolyn was entitled to accommodations within the school setting. When I received Carolyn's written 504 educational plan, it contained minimal accommodations; I therefore could not sign the plan.

The dispute over her educational plan continued into the Fall, despite numerous notes sent by physicians. In November 2000, I asked for a Child Study
Team Evaluation of Carolyn so that she could be classified as "Other Health Impaired" and would receive an appropriate Individual Education Plan. New Jersey State law states that if a parent feels that her child needs special education
she may request a full child study team evaluation. Under state law, a school
has 90 days from the receipt of such a request to evaluate a student and implement a plan. Carolyn's educational rights would also be protected under the Individuals with Disabilities Education Act, (IDEA). The school agreed to conduct
a full child study team evaluation and to have a rheumatologist, physiatrist,
psychiatrist, physical and occupational therapist and assistive technology specialist evaluate Carolyn.

"What? Am I dreaming? I am one of your best students. The same child who you
congratulated last year for winning so many awards and honors, the same child who is

fifth in her class, the same child who you handpicked as the winner in the principal essay contest. And now that I need help, you refuse to acknowledge my needs? How could anyone possibly be so heartless? Why would you choose to become an educator when it is apparent that you do not recognize your responsibilities?"

The school's rheumatologist was a young doctor, who had been studying lupus at Yale's Medical School for the past ten years. He spent about three hours evaluating Carolyn and agreed with Dr. Knee's diagnosis and treatment. However, the school's physiatrist (a doctor of physical medicine) had a completely different perspective.

From the moment we walked into his office, he had a preconceived opinion that Carolyn's illness was psychogenic. He was abrupt, impatient, rude, and condescending. He dismissed Carolyn's laboratory tests as inconclusive and did not believe that fibromyalgia was a physical illness. When I questioned him about the current research about rheumatory illnesses, especially connective tissue diseases, it became apparent that he had not read any current research. He was inattentive and had a scattered memory, and on several occasions confused her current medication, a non-narcotic pain reliever, with a similarly named narcotic. Carolyn and I felt that he was viewing her as a mentally ill child who was creating her illness and had a substance abuse problem.

After his ten-minute examination of Carolyn, he asked to speak with me privately. He diagnosed Carolyn with a somatic pain disorder, which had no physical origin. His recommendation was to discontinue all medications, begin a vigorous exercise program, and consult with a psychiatrist, who could recommend treatment for her imagined illness and possible prescription narcotic addiction.

The intensity of my wrath was immeasurable. I felt like a balloon ready to burst from enormous pressure. I was ready to lash out and obliterate anyone in my path. After only ten minutes this fiend had determined that I was malingering? In the car ride home I felt inclined to run back into his office and flail repeatedly at the physician. I felt the need to scream in agony from the pain he caused. The balloon had been punctured and my innermost animosity had begun to seep out.

It is unfortunate that many physicians believe that they can look at a cluster of symptoms and assign a diagnosis without ever really looking at the person who is seeking help. I had watched numerous doctors superficially and cursorily assess and diagnose Carolyn without ever really trying to understand the true meaning and depth of her symptoms.

Fortunately, the psychiatrist who evaluated Carolyn was a competent professional. These are the words from his report: *"Carolyn seems to have appropriate access into her emotional life. . . In terms of 'gain' from her illness, I saw no indication of emotional dependency. Nor was there any indication that Carolyn has been experiencing adolescence, competition, school responsibilities, separation-individuation issues, or any other area as being unduly stressful in such a way as to lead to exaggeration of her symptoms.*

"Carolyn is a tenth grade student who, based on the material presented to me, suffers from fibromyalgia syndrome, chronic fatigue syndrome, and may be developing a collagen vascular disease. Although there are physical findings

associated with the above conditions, these are often vague and non-specific. In addition, pain is a subjective symptom, which can be influenced by a patient's emotional state. One must always be mindful of the possibility that a patient can (consciously or unconsciously,) gain some element of benefit from his or her symptoms. This could range from the frank avoidance of responsibilities to the subtle sense of security which results from being cared-for and worried-about.

"The above being said, I found no indication that Carolyn either suffers from a specific psychiatric condition or that she experiences any demonstrable gain or gratification from her symptoms. I do not feel that a psychiatric diagnosis is indicated. I cannot document that emotional factors significantly affect her physical condition.

"In my opinion, the reasonable course of action would be to provide accommodations as are medically necessary. The goal would be for Carolyn to participate in the academic and social programs to the greatest extent possible."

I carefully pondered each response to the psychiatrist's evaluation and examined the repercussions of my answers. He asked, "Did I ever cry?" Of course, I thought! What human would not cry at times, if she were dealing with such struggles? However, if I said yes, would he think I cried all the time? If I said no, would he think I was lying? He inquired, "Did I worry about succeeding academically?" Of course, I thought again. What good student doesn't feel apprehensive about her academics? If I said yes, he would assume I was creating undue stress that resulted in the symptoms of my illness. If I said no, he may think that I was depressed and was too downcast to achieve academically. Instead, I contemplated stolid answers, which would pacify his psychogenic intuitions of my illness.

The psychological evaluation was completed in March 2001, and it took more than a month for the school psychologist to write the report. The school social worker completed her evaluation in 15 minutes through a telephone call to Carolyn and me. Unfortunately, her final report contained numerous errors. Other delays served to prolong the evaluation process far beyond the 90 day period specified in the law.

The school held another meeting on April 23, 2001, though the evaluation was incomplete. A tentative verbal agreement was reached for the remainder of the 2001 school year; however, an additional meeting was held in May 2001 to clarify several points. At this meeting, the school presented us with two plans. The first one covered the remainder of the school year and contained several accommodations.

The second plan outlined Carolyn's education plan for her junior year of high school. New Jersey State law states that a school may not present parents with a new individual education plan unless a meeting with the parents has been held to discuss any changes. Without any prior discussion with my husband and I, the second plan stated that if Carolyn accumulated 60 days of home instruction, she would have to withdraw from her high school and return to her local school district. The school reasoned that she would be unable to benefit from her placement at this school if she were on home instruction for a duration longer than sixty days. Thus, if this situation arose, the school's decision was that Carolyn must withdraw and return to her home district.

"The school is the shining example of a system that hides under the façade of superficiality. At freshman orientation, I was amazed at the benevolence and amicability these educators avidly displayed. However, what I soon learned was that this altruism was only displayed towards those students who fit the ideal mold of perfection: silent and obedient students who did not question authority; healthy and strong students who could function on three hours sleep per night; students who were machines. And the machines that were controlled by the educators and programmed to achieve, achieve, achieve."

My husband and I refused to sign either plan and immediately consulted an attorney. One week after the May 2001 meeting, we were mailed a third plan for the 2001–2002 school year. This plan placed Carolyn in her home district and would not allow her to continue to attend her high school in her junior year. The attorney suggested that we sign the initial April 23, 2001 plan, which was outlined for Carolyn's sophomore year, and initiate a request for due process over her educational placement for next year. Although, the April 23, 2001 plan was incomplete, we decided to sign it in order to allow her to "stay put." The New Jersey law states that if there is dispute over a child's new IEP, then the "stay put" IEP is binding until the dispute is resolved. Therefore Carolyn could remain in this high school for her junior year, until the case was settled in court.

The legal system looks favorably upon the ability of both parties to compromise, so our attorney filed a petition for mediation through the Office of Administrative Law in June 2000. Mediation occurred at the Office of Administrative Law in July and was unsuccessful, because the school insisted that Carolyn would not benefit from their program. In addition, the school argued that her fatigue and loss of sensation in her hands posed a safety risk in the technical portion of her art class.

When mediation fails, the court system has forty-five days to hear and try a case that involves a child's educational plan. Since the office of administrative law is understaffed, most cases in New Jersey are not resolved in the forty-five day limit. Our judge could not begin to hear our case until September 24, 2001.

Carolyn began her junior school year with the agreed-upon accommodations. Carolyn began school in late August, but her teachers were not informed of any of these accommodations until September 18, 2001. Though her accommodations were minimal, we were confident that Carolyn would be able to function in the school setting. The school agreed to compress Carolyn's schedule so she could leave school early and access her related services (i.e. physical therapy and occupational therapy).

Two weeks before the September 24 court hearing, the judge decided that the official due process would not begin, but rather she would meet with both attorneys to determine if a settlement could be reached. The judge's attempt was futile, because the school again insisted that Carolyn had to return to her local school district. Due process dates were again rescheduled, but postponed repeatedly. New Jersey State law states that a due process educational case must be settled within forty-five days of a party's application for due process. Our case had been filed in late July 2001. It was now February 2002, more than six months later.

As a child, I have distinct memories of watching courtroom dramas. Such movies would often put on a miraculous display of disputing right from wrong and seeing that justice prevailed. My childhood notions of the justice system were immediately redefined as the court dates were continually postponed. I had earned the right to speak against my oppressors and be heard by the judicial system in a court of law. Nearly six months later, justice had not prevailed. New Jersey has very poor educational and legal services for children who are classified as disabled. The judges do not hear their cases within the legal time frame and the judicial system does not enforce the following of the time frame. So parents are caught in a very difficult predicament.

Carolyn was able to stay in school with minimal absences during the fall. During the winter months, Carolyn was absent more frequently and was on home instruction four times for about one week. However, Carolyn managed educationally with her "stay put" plan, even though school personnel made it very difficult for Carolyn to be successful: one teacher, for example, berated her in front of the class, and told her to "go see your psychiatrist."

Though Carolyn's IEP states that when she is absent for three consecutive days, home instruction will be implemented, the guidance counselor was unable or unwilling to find home instructors in physics and Spanish. Several months later we found out that physics and Spanish home instructors had been tutoring another student all year. On numerous occasions the guidance counselor stated that she did not receive the physician's faxes about Carolyn's illness and need for home instruction.

Since the school personnel did not meet the needs of Carolyn's disability, it became my responsibility to learn about education law and advocate for her. I wrote about sixty letters to the Director of Special Services, Carolyn's case manager, and the principal, who rarely answered my letters. The New Jersey law states that a parent's letter is to be responded to in twenty days. When my attorney would call the school's attorney, he was unavailable and took many days to return her phone call. This lack of response resulted in many missed opportunities for Carolyn, and constituted violations of the Americans with Disabilities Act.

Occasionally, when browsing through local newspapers, I heard about harassment and discrimination cases in which the plaintiff was awarded a substantial sum of money for "pain and suffering." Before my dealings with the school system, I believed this to be ludicrous. However, now that I have experienced harassment first hand, I realize that the emotional strain it causes is indescribable. It is often hard to understand one's pain when we have not experienced it first hand. However, as individuals we must widen our horizons and understand the anguish and torment that harassment and discrimination can cause.

While there is a pending due process case, parents cannot file a complaint with any other agency about issues that relate to their child's situation. Since our case had been open since July and had been postponed numerous times, we could not file a complaint with the State Department of Education for violations of educational laws. These issues were supposed to be handled by our judge.

However, each time the two attorneys had phone conferences with the judge, the judge just insisted that both parties must work harder at a compromise and settle this case. She did not want to hear any specific complaints. I was exasperated and I was caught in a never-ending bind by the legal and educational system.

I have been shipwrecked and confined to an academic institution that has thwarted my talents for the past three years. I am seventeen, unable to drive or vote, but maintain the virtues, values, and maturation of an adult. College life can provide my rescue from the stagnation of the deserted island of high school.

In mid February, our family decided that we did not have the strength to continue to fight the school for another year. Even though we were engaged in a tentative settlement, the school was not following their agreement. We felt that Carolyn's senior year of high school would be a continuing battle. Carolyn had enough credits to graduate high school if she took a health and English course in Summer 2002. New Jersey's requirements for high school graduation are 120 credits and four years of English, health, and physical education. Each individual high school, however, may add to this minimum requirement. Carolyn's high school does not allow students to graduate in three years; however, our local district will allow exceptional qualified students to graduate early. The home district agreed to issue a high school diploma to Carolyn upon her completion of 120 credits at her high school and an independent fourth year study of health and her passing of a literature class at a local college.

We informed Carolyn's school of her plan to graduate at the end of this school year and hoped that we could put our differences behind us and let Carolyn complete the last four months of high school in a fairly peaceful educational environment. However we were sadly mistaken. The harassment continued. When Carolyn handed in her request for her secondary school report to be sent to several colleges, the guidance office refused to write a recommendation for her though she had maintained an A average in school. The guidance office stated that it would only send her transcript and grade point average. It seemed that the school wanted to thwart Carolyn's college plans. Fortunately, one of Carolyn's home instructors was also a licensed guidance counselor, and he wrote her secondary school counselor's recommendation.

LIFE: ACCEPTING, NOT CONQUERING, DISEASE

Lupus breaks all the rules of living. The diagnosis changes the reality in which the rules apply. Most people are governed by an intrinsic desire to have control over many aspects of their lives. As each day commences, I live in the pursuit of one fundamental, to live with, and not die from, disease. People who live with chronic illness must accept the reality that those rules are extraneous to their lives; they must let go of their innate desire to control their illness. If I had been asked to outline the significant aspects of my life two years ago, I probably would have stated that I wanted to follow in my brother's footsteps, graduate from Princeton University, and become a high-powered advertising executive. I thought that these goals encompassed the aspirations of success. I was a teenager, amassed among a myriad of others, who contemplated the pursuit of attending an Ivy

League university, achieving high SAT scores, and participating in social activities. This was my life before Lupus.

When you experience tragedy so intense in magnitude, your heart transforms. It feels as if you are viewing the world through a new set of eyes. These eyes that were previously focused outward to the world are now looking inward and frequently assess the illness. At the pinnacle of my failing health, in May 2001, I rested awake in a hospital bed, tender from a spinal tap, nauseated from medication, and delusional from a fever of 104 degrees. I was awaiting the pending diagnosis of meningitis. When I closed my eyes in Intensive Care that night, I faced that this day could be the one that marked my demise. I realized that I would no longer be able to control the illness and that in order to live, I need to accept the course of the disease. When I awoke the next morning, the fever had broken. I began to embark then on a journey of acceptance. My emotional recovery truly began. I came to the realization that I could no longer conquer Lupus. I concluded that the connection between my mind, body, and spirit needed to learn to live with this debilitating chronic illness, instead of trying to surmount it. Lupus is a predator. It drains energy and inflicts pain upon its prey. You cannot escape it, nor can you outrun the intensity of its wrath. When I awoke that morning, I lost sight of all the superficialities that reside on the surface of each one of us. I no longer hid behind a façade, or envied the pursuit of monetary gain, career achievement, or eminence of status. Instead, I acknowledged that the most crucial ambition in my life was living itself.

Life is truly a gift. The disheartening fact is that most of us do not even realize it until it is too late. I have learned to embrace what is sacred by furthering my relationships with those nearest and dearest to my heart. I awaken each day with a renewed spirit that rejoices in the simplicity of living.

My goal for this year is the acceptance of my ailment and the ability to understand and accept the things that I cannot change: to know that Lupus is a part of me, but that it does not define me. For so long I have been asking myself the question, "Why me?" I know now that life is not a quest for the answers to the questions, but rather the acceptance to live with the questions. I want to be able to accept Lupus as a gift, rather than an illness to conquer. I need to embrace the suffering and understand that it is a call to do something precious for humankind. It does not need to be grand. It may be the opportunity to touch another through compassion by the simple touch of a hand or sound of a comforting voice. Perhaps my ultimate goal is to help another person live with the same acceptance.

Epilogue

In March 2002, Carolyn received word that she was accepted into Lehigh University for the Fall on the basis of her academic work to date. She was awarded a Dean's scholarship and a journalism scholarship. She plans to major in scientific journalism and to continue to write about chronic illness and to advocate for people with disabilities. The Office of Special Services at Lehigh has been extremely helpful in initial talks with Carolyn and her family regarding accommodations that might need to be made so that she can continue to achieve. Carolyn's success has empowered them to continue to fight, in court, so that other students with disabilities might achieve due process in the future.

Questions for Further Study

1. In *Lakota Woman*, by Mary Crow Dog and Richard Erdoes, how does the legend of the first Crow Dog continue to influence the Crow Dog family in the present? What are the implications of the importance of family and tribal lore to First Nations peoples for social workers working with such clients?

2. In "The Spirit Catches You and You Fall Down," by Anne Fadiman, the difficulties associated with diagnosing and treating Lia are seen primarily as the result of a clash of world views, as well as a significant language barrier. These difficulties, however, are compounded by conditions that exist at the organizational level. How did those conditions directly impact the care that Lia and her family received? Also, the social worker at Merced Hospital is reported to be the only person associated with this case who asked the Lees what Lia's illness meant to them. Why is this important? What other questions might she have asked that would have helped the team in their ongoing efforts to care for Lia?

3. Addiction is said to have biological, psychological, social, and spiritual components. The Barthelme brothers seem to capture all of these in "Thrall," from *Double Down: Reflections on Gambling and Loss*. Can you identify where, throughout the text, each of these components are reflected?

4. Carol Anne Douglas, in "The Madwoman of 'Off Our Backs'," from *Restricted Access: Lesbians and Disability*, demonstrates how her status as a lesbian complicated her treatment for acute mental illness. However, some of her difficulty also arose because she is female. What is the relative contribution of each of these statuses to the responses made to illness by the medical system?

5. The case study here, Lisa and Carolyn Banta's "The Application of Systems Theory to Chronic Illness Issues and the Educational Environment," demonstrates that, even for families with a great deal of resources and will, instigating system change is extraordinarily difficult. Given the outcome, were the Bantas successful? What might you have done differently, had you been working with them towards this goal? Why do you think the school system was so resistant (if, in fact, you believe it was)? What sorts of biopsychosocial knowledge might have enabled the educational system to accommodate Carolyn?

Invited Commentary

GWAT-YONG LIE

The four excerpts and one essay on which this commentary is based are "Sioux and Elephants Never Forget" (from *Lakota Woman* by Mary Crow Dog), "Thrall" (from *Double Down* by Frederick and Steven Barthelme), "The Spirit Catches You and You Fall Down" (from the book of the same name, by Anne Fadiman), "The Madwoman of 'Off Our Backs'" (from *Restricted Access*) by Carol Anne Douglas; and *"The Application of Systems Theory to Chronic Illness Issues and the Educational Environment"* by Lisa and Carolyn Banta. The assignment was to adopt a biopsychosocial framework as the analytical lens with which to understand and assess the plight of individuals presented in the excerpts and case study, and to apply biopsychosocial knowledge to practice. Observations and insights gained about the intersection of socioeconomic and cultural factors; mental health, health or behavioral health challenges, and individual strengths, are described and explained. Rounding off the essay is a discussion of the social work practice implications that emerge in connection with sensitivity to such factors and to their shaping influence, as evidenced in the readings, on individual realities and on coping/response strategies.

In "Sioux and Elephants Never Forget," Mary Crow Dog endured tasks and responsibilities commensurate with being a young mother, wife of a *wicasha wakan*, daughter-in-law of the chief, a non-traditionally raised half-blood, non-Sioux speaking woman, and new resident, with an estranged presence in the Crow Dog clan. Both sets of parents objected to the marriage, and instead of breaking up the relationship, parental opposition simply served to cement the bond. She "tumbled headfirst" into a complex and overwhelming situation; still, she did not turn tail and head back to where she came from. She struggled and managed. But her body caved in under the stress, strain and tension; "I broke down." She lost weight, she could not stand up, her joints ached, she could not sleep, she felt "sad, always," and thought that she was at death's door—"I dream about people who have died. . . . Every time I close my eyes I see those who have been killed" (referring to the belief that dead people visit those about to die to allay fears of dying, and to keep them company on their journey to the nether world upon death).

Estes, a "road man," diagnosed the condition as "not a sickness of the body, but of the mind." The sickness was "love sickness," not feeling loved by any one, even Leonard. The holy man's prescription was peyote, "a sacred medicine." The effect of the peyote was to bring about the death of the former self, and the emergence of a recharged self; "I would be alright." She recovered.

Mary Crow Dog's experience underscores the need to appreciate and work *with* (as opposed to working *against*) *other* worldviews, traditions, values and beliefs. Careful "listening" to her telling of interactions with key members of the clan and of the history and legends that "still colors the life-style and the actions of Crow Dogs today" (and by implication, Mary herself) offered rich material for a biopsychosocial assessment. The potential for misunderstanding metaphors and symbolisms, actions and intents, is ever present when the person making the assessment and the person being assessed subscribe to different worldviews, traditions, values and beliefs. The likelihood of mis-assessments can be reduced significantly when the yardstick for assessment is founded on the worldviews, traditions, values and beliefs of the person being assessed—viewing the other's reality through their eyes and not your own.

Like Mary Crow Dog, Carol Anne Douglas experienced a mental illness: severe depression. Like Mary Crow Dog, a space in which she spent a significant portion of her time was a space of hostilities, fraught with stress, strain, and tension. In addition, she was, in her own words, a "lesbian feminist leading a double life." Like Mary Crow Dog her body and mind gave in to the stress and strain. Her story is one of gradual descent into "madness." Unlike Mary Crow Dog who was alienated from her own family and estranged from the one she married into, her lifeline to sanity was her "family," her lover and a few close friends.

Carol Anne Douglas was given an accurate diagnosis and received the appropriate treatment, which in turn alleviated the depression. Carol Anne Douglas was diagnosed and treated by a psychiatrist. Zoloft was prescribed to address the depression, and the cost of the treatment was underwritten by an HMO. Unlike Mary Crow Dog, who eased into a course of treatment and recovery that was familiar and comfortable, Carol Anne Douglas' visit to a psychiatrist and decision to ingest a psychotropic medication was not a natural and conflict-free course of action for her; "I, who rebelled against biological determinism, who said biology isn't destiny, had been controlled by my biology." Further, "I, who had always opposed psychiatric medication, had been restored to my normal mental state by pills."

Mary Crow Dog was comfortable with a male healer and his helper; she lived in a male dominated world, and her healer was the holy man who was also her husband. Although Carol Anne Douglas shuttled daily between a male-dominated, paid, job world; a feminist volunteer work environment, and a private personal world of mainly women, she was not comfortable at being seen by a male psychiatrist, especially one whom she never met before. Her lover and women friends were instrumental in getting her into care. She did not want to be hospitalized even though it was a medical referral, and her friends were willing to take turns to stay with her so that she could be released into their custody.

Insights she gained from her slide into madness and subsequent recovery have instigated her to push for research on the connection between menopause and mental illness. Through her writings in *off our backs,* she was also able to generate discussion among readers about the social construction versus biological determinism perspectives on mental illness. Further, the day treatment program was also a consciousness-raising experience for her. It opened up her world to people most unlike her in socioeconomic and racial attributes, and plight; "my first prolonged time . . . of intensely personal discussions in a predominantly working class, African American setting . . .," and homeless alcoholic men.

One of the many implications for social work practice gleaned from Carol Anne Douglas' experience include the ability to honor and respect sociopolitical objections to psychiatric intervention and psychotropic medication yet to still be able to persuade the individual to consider the merits of such treatment so that an informed choice could be made. Another enlightening point is the importance of social supports to serve as custodial agents and to advocate in one's best interests, especially in cases where the individual's mental capacity is suspect. A final example of another practice/advocacy/social policy implication is, that in a fee-for-service world, access to good mental health care is contingent on availability of either out-of-pocket, or more commonly third party, payment resources, or philanthropic dollars to underwrite the cost of mental health care. Certain health care insurance policies do not include provisions for mental health care, or where allowed, offer restrictive and limited coverage. Still another alternative, and one espoused by Carol Anne Douglas, is health care reform—nationalized medical and mental health care.

Anne Fadiman tells the story of a Hmong family who, in spite of their reservations about the efficacy or appropriateness of Western medicine for *qaug dab peg*, or epilepsy, were sufficiently worried to seek it for their daughter. Similar to Mary Crow Dog, they had turned to traditional healing for resolution of Lia's symptoms. However, unlike Mary Crow Dog whose symptoms were alleviated, Lia's persisted. Further, Foua's and Nao Kao's experience with hospital emergency room services were as alienating and confusing to them as Carol Anne Douglas' had been to her.

Carol Anne Douglas was fortunate to have her lover and friends with her in the emergency room. They were there to ensure that she got the services that she needed, to interpret medical directives, and to advocate on her behalf against hospitalization. Foua and Nao Kao did not even have the benefit of the services of a language interpreter, let alone support persons vested in seeing to it that their medical needs were appropriately met. They were unable to communicate to the resident on duty that they were seeking attention for Lia's seizures, which had stopped by the time they saw the resident. Predictably, Lia was misdiagnosed.

The same experience repeated itself on another occasion with the same end result. It would have repeated itself for a third time if not for a family practice resident, "most interested in and knowledgeable about the Hmong," the fact that Lia was actively seizing, and the presence of an English-speaking relative. This time around, Lia's parents knew to bring someone who could communicate their concerns to emergency room staff.

In this case, it is hard not to recognize that the language barrier served to exacerbate frustrations felt by staff as well as the family, and to culminate in misdiagnosis and mistreatment of the patient. Hospital administration was not ignorant of the need for interpreters, because in 1991 a short-term grant had enabled the hospital to "put skilled interpreters on call around the clock." But the program expired when funding ran out, and there was no commitment or investment on the part of the hospital to specifically earmark funds for interpreters. Instead, it relied on bilingual staff, Hmong families, and even children—anyone whom they were able to corral off the hospital floor—to interpret, for free.

It follows then that practice implications include advocating for skilled interpreters to be available around the clock. This need is especially critical given the sociodemographic profile of residents of the hospital's environs, and the fact that "on any given day there are still Hmong patients in almost every unit." Even though "more than eighty percent [of Hmong patients] are on Medi-Cal," it would be less costly in the long run for the hospital to diagnose and treat correctly on the first visit with the help of interpreters than to support a revolving door of repeatedly misdiagnosed and mistreated patients. More importantly, language barriers cannot, and must never be the excuse for the practice of "veterinary medicine" on human beings.

Hospital staff would benefit from in-service initiatives aimed at educating them about the history and background of the Hmong people, their traditions, healing rituals and practices, values and beliefs. It might even be of benefit to them to be aware of cross-cultural parallels (e.g., ancient Greeks) in conceptualizations of epilepsy, to dispel likely notions that Hmong perspectives on the condition were unique to the group, and simply primitive. Instead of being dismissive of other perspectives and realities, hospital staff, as other service providers in the community, need to be respectful of differences in outlook and worldviews.

The well-being of the family—of Foua, Nao Kao and the other children—needs to be assessed. Where indicated, the family should be alerted to culturally competent services to alleviate the stress and strain associated with caring full-time for a special needs child. The family may choose not to draw on those non-family/non-clan services (e.g., for respite purposes); however, they do need to be informed of their availability, and of ways to access them if they so choose. Brain-storming with the family on familial or clan resources for support and for respite may be more productive, as these are resources that the family is more disposed to using.

The welfare of Yer, the sibling who slammed the door that caused Lia's soul to flee her body, needed to be assessed. Given the report that the family blamed Yer for Lia's plight, and that as a result have "treated her differently from their other children," the need for a prompt response with an assessment was clearly indicated.

Carolyn Banta's experience with the health care system was also frustrating. Yet both Carolyn and her mother are native speakers of English, and assertive enough to make their needs known and to see to having those needs receive expert attention. And, because Carolyn Banta's condition was "invisible," as was Lia's (the seizures had stopped by the time she arrived at the emergency room), both their illnesses were misdiagnosed. Carol Anne Douglas' paranoia and delusions were not evident in the emergency room. But she had her lover and close friends present to attest to behaviors that they considered abnormal for their friend. As Carolyn Banta noted, only when "one can see, one can believe," did both Lia and Carolyn Banta begin to receive the appropriate tests and evaluations for their respective illnesses.

Carolyn Banta had to endure insinuations that her condition was psychogenic in origin when a referral for psychiatric evaluation was made because no physical basis for her illness could be detected. The same rush to judgment dogged Carol Anne Douglas. She was diagnosed as having severe depression with delusions, and the assumption was made that she was likely to be a danger to herself even though there were reportedly no signs or indications to support this. The medical directive was to have her hospitalized just in case she was suicidal, thus avoiding any liability in the event that she did harm herself.

It was only with Lisa Banta's research and persistence that they found a rheumatologist skilled in dealing with fibromyalgia, symptoms that Lisa Banta had observed in Carolyn. It was also through Lisa Banta's skillful presentation of Carolyn's plight that they avoided having to wait a long 9 months for an appointment with this specialist. It was also because of the financial resources that the family had that they were able to travel to and take advantage of the best known (to them) medical resources available. It is not difficult to imagine/speculate about the nature and extent of Carolyn Banta's plight had her mother not persevered in looking for alternative help; or, if they had simply accepted the 9 month wait for an appointment; or, if they were on Medicaid, or were simply unable to afford medical care.

In all three cases, the cure for their respective conditions remained elusive. Carol Anne Douglas' depression was managed with Zoloft, but not without side effects. The prognosis was that the illness might resolve itself after menopause; otherwise she might need to be on medications for the rest of her life. In Lia's case, epilepsy cannot be completely cured, but it could be partially controlled by anticonvulsant drugs. As for Carolyn Banta, indefinite use of medications to manage her illness appeared to be her fate.

Denial and rationalizations about the toll that gambling has on family life and other relationships, contradictions, and delusions about winning mark behaviors attributed to the gambling addiction afflicting brothers Frederick and Steven Barthelme. They wax eloquent about the "virtues" of gambling as a vice, and rationalize that "it is not like we were cheating on our wives or boozing or doing drugs." They were emphatic that "when the time came, we would bail." They would not only recognize when they should bail, but they would not hesitate to do so. But therein lay a contradiction.

They have also described the heady and seductive power of the prospect of winning, "you recognize that you're going to win no matter what." Fueled by the rare occasions when they did win, and remembering the exhilaration and excited anticipation of winning, they became obsessed with the idea of recouping their losses. When the "cards turn," and "you recognize that you're going to win whatever you bet," it becomes a "rare, even amazing experience. It almost makes gambling worthwhile. Everything you touch turns to gold." Because the gambling addict is forever focused on having one of these moments, and because it is impossible to predict or know exactly when these moments will strike, the addict keeps waging his bets, hoping that the next round will be the one that will turn the tide for him. Contrary to what the Barthelmes contend, the addict does not know when to bail; "[t]he only time you really think of yourself as an addict is when you want to stop."

Gambling addiction is neither gender- or socioeconomic-specific. By the time addicts seek help, they are likely to have alienated family and friends, amassed a mountain of debts, and even run afoul of the law to feed their habit. Without professional intervention, and a deliberate commitment at working on the addiction, recovery would be impossible to achieve. The work is even more complex when a brother is similarly addicted, for each serves to enable the other and in so doing they continually feed each other's habit out of self interest.

In closing, the authors of the four excerpts and one case study have been extremely articulate in describing human phenomena, its complexities, frailties and strengths. The challenge for all helping professionals is to continually upgrade and refine their awareness and knowledge of the wrinkles and subtle nuances imposed by race, culture, class, gender, and illness or differing abilities. Even more important than having the awareness that different realities exist, and the knowledge as to ways in which the realities differ, is the ability to respond to the differences in customized ways, and with compassion, competence, and skill.

Unit 9   ADVOCATING ON BEHALF OF CLIENTS IN POVERTY

Editors' Introduction

One of the most crucial roles a social worker can play is that of advocate, in which we work alongside clients, amplifying their voices in the quest for social change. It is through the advocacy role that the potential exists not only to enable our client(s) to improve their lives, but also to improve the lives of persons faced with the same circumstances. We have paired our readings on the lives of the poor with the skill of advocacy because economically disenfranchised people stand to benefit the most from both case and class advocacy.

Advocacy refers to the act of defending the interests of other persons, and it is considered a basic obligation of professional social workers (NASW Code of Ethics 1996). Generally, social workers are called upon to advocate on behalf of their clients (or all those in the same situation) when an abrogation of rights is imminent or has occurred, or when social policies with potential impacts upon clients are being developed or debated. In every city and state, as well as at the federal level, new policies and executive decisions are being made that will impact the poor in our communities.

For example, as we write this essay, new data analyses on poverty are emerging, and new policy developments aimed at moving the poor into "self-sufficiency" are being discussed. New census statistics reveal that the prosperity of the last decade of the twentieth century was enjoyed mostly by affluent Americans, modestly by the middle class, and very little by persons below the poverty line. In 2001, about 11.7 percent of our population was living in poverty, up from the previous year's 11.3 percent (U.S. Census 2002). By 1999, two years after welfare reform began to be implemented, our welfare rolls had decreased nationally, by more than half in many states (DHHS 2000), but the rate of poverty did not drop proportionally. Clearly, assistance for the poor is not as accessible as it once was. At the same time, President Bush has proposed two controversial changes to existing welfare laws: the first is to increase the federal work requirement for welfare recipients to 40 hours per week (see below); the second is to use federal money to implement programs aimed at encouraging marriage for single welfare mothers.

We make no judgments here about the efficacy or the "rightness" of these proposals, particularly the latter, except to say that it seems an astonishing departure from traditional conservatism to suggest that intrusion into the private lives of our citizenry at this profound level is permissible. We encourage you to discuss with your classmates, fellow community members, politicians, and others, this discrepancy between our current governmental philosophy and its application to programs designed to assist the poor. Part of being an effective advocate is developing a deep understanding of the issues, and the means for effecting change, if change is called for. Assuming that you have decided that change is necessary, you can then consciously and purposefully add your voice to those who, without organization and alliances, cannot make their own voices heard in the public arena, even at the level of a whisper. The purpose of this unit, and the others in this volume, is to ground us in that more profound understanding.

"Dumpster Diving," is a selection from *Travels with Lizbeth*, by Lars Eighner. Like many other people with limited means, Eighner chose to live without a home, in part because he was unwilling to abandon his dog Lizbeth, who was unwelcome at the places he might otherwise have made his home. In this selection, the author explains the unwritten rules, ethics, and indeed the art of scavenging for food, a practice he had begun even before he became homeless. Eighner comes across as an enlightened instructor who wants us to fully understand and accept a phenomenon prevalent among persons in dire circumstances. His is a sharply observed self-study that reveals a mode of life that is not simply distressed but also thoughtful and deliberate. Furthermore, he observes the peculiarity of a society that is capable of supporting others not through charity but through waste. Like the very wealthy, Eighner notes, he is detached from the acquisitive spirit that drives consumer society. While Eighner's essay offers us insight into the life of a single dumpster diver living without a home, it should be noted that his experience is not generalizable to that of a family with children. Children are far more susceptible to illness from food-borne contaminants and more vulnerable to harsh weather conditions. According to Bread for the World, one in four children in the United States suffers from hunger or is at risk.[1]

Gregory Howard Williams' *Life on the Color Line: The True Story of a White Boy Who Discovered He Was Black* is a rich and provocative narrative about two brothers, uprooted from their relatively affluent lives in northern Virginia and taken to live in poverty with their father's relatives in Indiana. Only at this point, when he is ten years old, does Williams discover that his father had been "passing" as white. Now that he lives with his father's black family, he and his brother find themselves suddenly black instead of white. In the chapter offered here, "Learning How to be Niggers," the author recounts his recollections of the deprivation he and his brother suffered due to a reversal of his family's fortunes. Despite the deep resentment and meager resources of their father's extended family, the boys are taken in, clothed, and fed. We raise this point because resource sharing is a necessity in very poor communities, yet it is almost never seen or acknowledged by others.[2]

In addition to revealing the difficulties of children in poverty, this reading offers an opportunity to consider and discuss the realities of whiteness and white privilege and the absurdities that flow from the social construction of race. Although Williams' story takes place in the 1950s, our country has not yet resolved difficult questions regarding race and poverty. Issues such as Affirmative Action, the apparent discrepancy between whites and blacks in the adjudication of criminal cases, and continuing income disparities between these two groups are concerns within the social work community and are continuing targets of advocacy efforts.[3]

In three short sections ("Throughput," "Stroking," and "Detecting Lies") from *Fast Food Nation: The Dark Side of the All-American Meal*, Eric Schlosser considers the social and economic reverberations of the rapid growth of the fast-food industry. With an employment force made up largely of teens and those who have emigrated from other countries, this industry has been able to keep wages low and benefits almost non-existent. At the same time, efforts by employees to unionize or fight for fair working conditions (including pay for overtime) are met with fierce resistance. As we noted in the beginning paragraphs of this introduction, President Bush recently introduced in the welfare reform reauthorization bill a mandate that seventy percent of welfare recipients be employed in full-time (40-hour/week) jobs (Reuters January 13, 2003). He called it "the key to helping families lift themselves out of poverty." We include these pieces because they offer us a macro-level perspective on the difficulty of escaping poverty in a full-time, minimum wage job, due to an array of social arrangements that cannot be mitigated entirely by the worker's motivation to succeed. At the present time, many communities around the country are engaged in living wage campaigns, spearheaded by the Association of Community Organizations for Reform Now (ACORN). Social workers in such communities are often participants in these campaigns.[4]

The excerpt from Michael Patrick MacDonald's "All Souls," about a working-class family from South Boston, takes place in a bygone era, when "social workers" were employed largely as instruments of control of the poor. As shown here, social workers and clients played cat-and-mouse games, in which the consequences of being "caught" by appearing too prosperous, or by having a man in the house, would result in a loss of benefits for the entire family. As can be seen from many of the selections in this book, as well as this one, the biography-memoir canon is replete with such descriptions. Although social workers have long been out of the business of income investigation, the reputation of the profession remains sullied. For this and other reasons, it is important to educate others about what social workers do, in other words, to advocate on behalf of the profession. We want you to be social workers who change the way the public views the profession, through your understanding of the populations you are trying to help and through your ability to fight with, for, and alongside those you serve.

The case study by Richard Lange, "Design and Development of a Parenting Training Group for Low-Income African American Parents" provides an exemplar of a program designed to teach parenting skills to families referred for suspected or substantiated child abuse and neglect. Serving populations suffering from racism requires an acknowledgment of social structures not easily or quickly reformed, such as racial profiling. Lange's training program helps clients recognize such social structures and build a repertoire of responses directed at coping with them responsibly. At its best, a program aimed at helping parents understand the impact of racism on their daily lives can place them in a position to become advocates for themselves.

Note that Lange's group failed several times before he and his associates learned what they needed to make it work: highly trained professionals, combining therapeutic and skill-based elements, and a clear understanding of the role that race played in the entry of these parents into the system. We bring this up because failure is inevitable: if failure were not part of our work, we would not call it social work "practice," but rather social work "perfect"!

This brings us to our final point, and one that Scott Harding raises in his guest commentary: advocacy practice requires a variety of skills. The ability to explain complex information; to be persuasive; to organize groups of people, often with competing motivations, into a coalition focused on a common purpose; and to learn from the mistakes we make, are but a few. Difficult as it may be, these skills can be acquired, with experience. We encourage you to develop your skills by getting involved.[5]

REFERENCES

Department of Health and Human Services (2000). www.os.dhhs.gov/news/press/2000pres/20000822.html

Ehrenreich, B. (2001). *Nickel and Dimed: On (Not) Getting by in America.* New York: Metropolitan Books.

Reuters News Service (January 14, 2003, 4:29 PM ET). Bush calls for stricter welfare work rules.

U.S. Census (2001). www.census.gov/hhes/poverty/poverty01/table1.pdf

Stack, C. (1997). *All Our Kin: Strategies for Survival in Black Community.* Boulder, CO: Westview Press; New York: Harper and Row, 1974.

NOTES

[1]To learn more about this problem and what you can do about it, in the United States and worldwide, visit Bread for the World at www.bread.org/howtohelp/activist/index.html.

[2]Two books that describe the necessity of resource-sharing among the poor—and its invisibility in affluent communities are Ehrenreich (2001) and Stack (1997).

[3]Visit the National Association of Social Workers website www.naswdc.org/advocacy/default.asp to learn more about the advocacy efforts of our profession's largest member organization.

[4]To learn more about such efforts and whether a campaign is already underway in your community, visit www.livingwagecampaign.org.

[5]To find out about other issues of interest to social workers, visit The New Social Worker at www.socialworker.com/websites.htm.

Reading   # On Dumpster Diving

LARS EIGHNER

Long before I began Dumpster diving I was impressed with Dumpsters, enough so that I wrote the Merriam-Webster research service to discover what I could about the word *Dumpster*. I learned from them that it is a proprietary word belonging to the Dempster Dumpster company. Since then I have dutifully capitalized the word, although it was lowercased in almost all the citations Merriam-Webster photocopied for me. Dempster's word is too apt. I have never heard these things called anything but Dumpsters. I do not know anyone who knows the generic name for these objects. From time to time I have heard a wino or hobo give some corrupted credit to the original and call them Dipsy Dumpsters.

I began Dumpster diving about a year before I became homeless.

I prefer the word *scavenging* and use the word *scrounging* when I mean to be obscure. I have heard people, evidently meaning to be polite, use the word *foraging*, but I prefer to reserve that word for gathering nuts and berries and such, which I do also according to the season and the opportunity. *Dumpster diving* seems to me to be a little too cute and, in my case, inaccurate because I lack the athletic ability to lower myself into the Dumpsters as the true divers do, much to their increased profit.

I like the frankness of the word *scavenging*, which I can hardly think of without picturing a big black snail on an aquarium wall. I live from the refuse of others. I am a scavenger. I think it a sound and honorable niche, although if I could I would naturally prefer to live the comfortable consumer life, perhaps—and only perhaps—as a slightly less wasteful consumer, owing to what I have learned as a scavenger.

While Lizbeth and I were still living in the shack on Avenue B as my savings ran out, I put almost all my sporadic income into rent. The necessities of daily life I began to extract from Dumpsters. Yes, we ate from them. Except for jeans, all my clothes came from Dumpsters. Boom boxes, candles, bedding, toilet paper, a virgin male love doll, medicine, books, a typewriter, dishes, furnishings, and change, sometimes amounting to many dollars—I acquired many things from the Dumpsters.

I have learned much as a scavenger. I mean to put some of what I have learned down here, beginning with the practical art of Dumpster diving and proceeding to the abstract.

What is safe to eat?

After all, the finding of objects is becoming something of an urban art. Even respectable employed people will sometimes find something tempting sticking out of a Dumpster or standing beside one. Quite a number of people, not all of them of the bohemian type, are willing to brag that they found this or that piece in the trash. But eating from Dumpsters is what separates the dilettanti from the professionals. Eating safely from the Dumpsters involves three principles: using the senses and common sense to evaluate the condition of the found materials, knowing the Dumpsters of a given area and checking them regularly, and seeking always to answer the question "Why was this discarded?"

Perhaps everyone who has a kitchen and a regular supply of groceries has, at one time or another, made a sandwich and eaten half of it before discovering mold on the bread or got a mouthful of milk before realizing the milk had turned. Nothing of the sort is likely to happen to a Dumpster diver because he is constantly reminded that most food is discarded for a reason. Yet a lot of perfectly good food can be found in Dumpsters.

Canned goods, for example, turn up fairly often in the Dumpsters I frequent. All except the most phobic people would be willing to eat from a can, even if it came from a Dumpster. Canned goods are among the safest of foods to be found in Dumpsters but are not utterly foolproof.

Although very rare with modern canning methods, botulism is a possibility. Most other forms of food poisoning seldom do lasting harm to a healthy person, but botulism is almost certainly fatal and often the first symptom is death. Except for carbonated beverages, all canned goods should contain a slight vacuum and suck air when first punctured. Bulging, rusty, and dented cans and cans that spew when punctured should be avoided, especially when the contents are not very acidic or syrupy.

Heat can break down the botulin, but this requires much more cooking than most people do to canned goods. To the extent that botulism occurs at all, of course, it can occur in cans on pantry shelves as well as in cans from Dumpsters. Need I say that home-canned goods are simply too risky to be recommended.

From time to time one of my companions, aware of the source of my provisions, will ask, "Do you think these crackers are really safe to eat?" For some reason it is most often the crackers they ask about.

This question has always made me angry. Of course I would not offer my companion anything I had doubts about. But more than that, I wonder why he cannot evaluate the condition of the crackers for himself. I have no special knowledge and I have been wrong before. Since he knows where the food comes from, it seems to me he ought to assume some of the responsibility for deciding what he will put in his mouth. For myself I have few qualms about dry foods such as crackers, cookies, cereal, chips, and pasta if they are free of visible contaminates and still dry and crisp. Most often such things are found in the original packaging, which is not so much a positive sign as it is the absence of a negative one.

Raw fruits and vegetables with intact skins seem perfectly safe to me, excluding of course the obviously rotten. Many are discarded for minor imperfections that can be pared away. Leafy vegetables, grapes, cauliflower, broccoli, and similar things may be contaminated by liquids and may be impractical to wash.

Candy, especially hard candy, is usually safe if it has not drawn ants. Chocolate is often discarded only because it has become discolored as the cocoa butter de-emulsified. Candying, after all, is one method of food preservation because pathogens do not like very sugary substances.

All of these foods might be found in any Dumpster and can be evaluated with some confidence largely on the basis of appearance. Beyond these are foods that cannot be correctly evaluated without additional information.

I began scavenging by pulling pizzas out of the Dumpster behind a pizza delivery shop. In general, prepared food requires caution, but in this case I knew when the shop closed and went to the Dumpster as soon as the last of the help left.

Such shops often get prank orders; both the orders and the products made to fill them are called *bogus.* Because help seldom stays long at these places, pizzas are often made with the wrong topping, refused on delivery for being cold, or baked incorrectly. The products to be discarded are boxed up because inventory is kept by counting boxes: A boxed pizza can be written off; an unboxed pizza does not exist.

I never placed a bogus order to increase the supply of pizzas and I believe no one else was scavenging in this Dumpster. But the people in the shop became suspicious and began to retain their garbage in the shop overnight. While it lasted I had a steady supply of fresh, sometimes warm pizza. Because I knew the Dumpster I knew the source of the pizza, and because I visited the Dumpster regularly I knew what was fresh and what was yesterday's.

The area I frequent is inhabited by many affluent college students. I am not here by chance; the Dumpsters in this area are very rich. Students throw out many good things, including food. In particular they tend to throw everything out when they move at the end of a semester, before and after breaks, and around midterm, when many of them despair of college. So I find it advantageous to keep an eye on the academic calendar.

Students throw food away around breaks because they do not know whether it has spoiled or will spoil before they return. A typical discard is a half jar of peanut butter. In fact, nonorganic peanut butter does not require refrigeration and is unlikely to spoil in any reasonable time. The student does not know that, and since it is Daddy's money, the student decides not to take a chance. Opened containers require caution and some attention to the question. "Why was this discarded?" But in the case of discards from student apartments, the answer may be that the item was thrown out through carelessness, ignorance, or wastefulness. This can sometimes be deduced when the item is found with many others, including some that are obviously perfectly good.

Some students, and others, approach defrosting a freezer by chucking out the whole lot. Not only do the circumstances of such a find tell the story, but also the mass of frozen goods stays cold for a long time and items may be found still frozen or freshly thawed.

Yogurt, cheese, and sour cream are items that are often thrown out while they are still good. Occasionally I find a cheese with a spot of mold, which of course I just pare off, and because it is obvious why such a cheese was discarded, I treat it with less suspicion than an apparently perfect cheese found in similar circumstances. Yogurt is often discarded, still sealed, only because the expiration date on the carton had passed. This is one of my favorite finds because yogurt will keep for several days, even in warm weather.

Students throw out canned goods and staples at the end of semesters and when they give up college at midterm. Drugs, pornography, spirits, and the like are often discarded when parents are expected—Dad's Day, for example. And spirits also turn up after big party weekends, presumably discarded by the newly reformed. Wine and spirits, of course, keep perfectly well even once opened, but the same cannot be said of beer.

My test for carbonated soft drinks is whether they still fizz vigorously. Many juices or other beverages are too acidic or too syrupy to cause much concern, provided they are not visibly contaminated. I have discovered nasty molds in vegetable juices, even when the product was found under its original seal; I recommend that such products be decanted slowly into a clear glass. Liquids always require some care. One hot day I found a large jug of Pat O'Brien's Hurricane mix. The jug had been opened but was still ice cold. I drank three large glasses before it became apparent to me that someone had added the rum to the mix, and not a little rum. I never tasted the rum, and by the time I began to feel the effects I had already ingested a very large quantity of the beverage. Some divers would have considered this a boon, but being suddenly intoxicated in a public place in the early afternoon is not my idea of a good time.

I have heard of people maliciously contaminating discarded food and even handouts, but mostly I have heard of this from people with vivid imaginations who have had no experience with the Dumpsters themselves. Just before the pizza shop stopped discarding its garbage at night, jalapeños began showing up on most of the thrown-out pizzas. If indeed this was meant to discourage me, it was a wasted effort because I am a native Texan.

For myself, I avoid game, poultry, pork, and egg-based foods, whether I find them raw or cooked. I seldom have the means to cook what I find, but when I do I avail myself of plentiful supplies of beef, which is often in very good condition. I suppose fish becomes disagreeable before it becomes dangerous. Lizbeth is happy to have any such thing that is past its prime and, in fact, does not recognize fish as food until it is quite strong.

Home leftovers, as opposed to surpluses from restaurants, are very often bad. Evidently, especially among students, there is a common type of personality that carefully wraps up even the smallest leftover and shoves it into the back of the refrigerator for six months or so before discarding it. Characteristic of this type are the reused jars and margarine tubs to which the remains are committed. I avoid ethnic foods I am unfamiliar with. If I do not know what it is supposed to look like when it is good, I cannot be certain I will be able to tell if it is bad.

No matter how careful I am I still get dysentery at least once a month, oftener in warm weather. I do not want to paint too romantic a picture. Dumpster diving has serious drawbacks as a way of life.

I learned to scavenge gradually, on my own. Since then I have initiated several companions into the trade. I have learned that there is a predictable series of stages a person goes through in learning to scavenge.

At first the new scavenger is filled with disgust and self-loathing. He is ashamed of being seen and may lurk around, trying to duck behind things, or he may try to dive at night. (In fact, most people instinctively look away from a scavenger. By skulking around, the novice calls attention to himself and arouses suspicion. Diving at night is ineffective and needlessly messy.)

Every grain of rice seems to be a maggot. Everything seems to stink. He can wipe the egg yolk off the found can, but he cannot erase from his mind the stigma of eating garbage.

That stage passes with experience. The scavenger finds a pair of running shoes that fit and look and smell brand-new. He finds a pocket calculator in perfect working order. He finds pristine ice cream, still frozen, more than he can eat or keep. He begins to understand: People throw away perfectly good stuff, a lot of perfectly good stuff.

At this stage, Dumpster shyness begins to dissipate. The diver, after all, has the last laugh. He is finding all manner of good things that are his for the taking. Those who disparage his profession are the fools, not he.

He may begin to hang on to some perfectly good things for which he has neither a use nor a market. Then he begins to take note of the things that are not perfectly good but are nearly so. He mates a Walkman with broken earphones and one that is missing a battery cover. He picks up things that he can repair.

At this stage he may become lost and never recover. Dumpsters are full of things of some potential value to someone and also of things that never have much intrinsic value but are interesting. All the Dumpster divers I have known come to the point of trying to acquire everything they touch. Why not take it, they reason, since it is all free? This is, of course, hopeless. Most divers come to realize that they must restrict themselves to items of relatively immediate utility. But in some cases the diver simply cannot control himself. I have met several of these pack-rat types. Their ideas of the values of various pieces of junk verge on the psychotic. Every bit of glass may be a diamond, they think, and all that glisters, gold.

I tend to gain weight when I am scavenging. Partly this is because I always find far more pizza and doughnuts than water-packed tuna, nonfat yogurt, and fresh vegetables. Also I have not developed much faith in the reliability of Dumpsters as a food source, although it has been proven to me many times. I tend to eat as if I have no idea where my next meal is coming from. But mostly I just hate to see food go to waste and so I eat much more than I should. Something like this drives the obsession to collect junk.

As for collecting objects, I usually restrict myself to collecting one kind of small object at a time, such as pocket calculators, sunglasses, or campaign buttons. To live on the street I must anticipate my needs to a certain extent: I must pick up and save warm bedding I find in August because it will not be found in Dumpsters in November. As I have no access to health care, I often hoard essential drugs, such as antibiotics and antihistamines. (This course can be recommended only to those with some grounding in pharmacology. Antibiotics, for example, even when indicated are worse than useless if taken in insufficient amounts.) But even if I had a home with extensive storage space, I could not save everything that might be valuable in some contingency.

I have proprietary feelings about my Dumpsters. As I have mentioned, it is no accident that I scavenge from ones where good finds are common. But my limited experience with Dumpsters in other areas suggests to me that even in poorer areas, Dumpsters, if attended with sufficient diligence, can be made to yield a livelihood. The rich students discard perfectly good kiwifruit; poorer people discard perfectly good apples. Slacks and Polo shirts are found in the one place; jeans and T-shirts in the other. The population of competitors rather than the affluence of the dumpers most affects the feasibility of survival by scavenging. The large number of competitors is what puts me off the idea of trying to scavenge in places like Los Angeles.

Curiously, I do not mind my direct competition, other scavengers, so much as I hate the can scroungers.

People scrounge cans because they have to have a little cash. I have tried scrounging cans with an able-bodied companion. Afoot a can scrounger simply cannot make more than a few dollars a day. One can extract the necessities of life from the Dumpsters directly with far less effort than would be required to accumulate the equivalent value in cans. (These observations may not hold in places with container redemption laws.)

Can scroungers, then, are people who must have small amounts of cash. These are drug addicts and winos, mostly the latter because the amounts of cash are so small. Spirits and drugs do, like all other commodities, turn up in Dumpsters and the scavenger will from time to time have a half bottle of a rather good wine with his dinner. But the wino cannot survive on these occasional finds; he must have his daily dose to stave off the DTs. All the cans he can carry will buy about three bottles of Wild Irish Rose.

I do not begrudge them the cans, but can scroungers tend to tear up the Dumpsters, mixing the contents and littering the area. They become so specialized that they can see only cans. They earn my contempt by passing up change, canned goods, and readily hockable items.

There are precious few courtesies among scavengers. But it is common practice to set aside surplus items: pairs of shoes, clothing, canned goods, and such. A true scavenger hates to see good stuff go to waste, and what he cannot use he leaves in good condition in plain sight.

Can scroungers lay waste to everything in their path and will stir one of a pair of good shoes to the bottom of a Dumpster, to be lost or ruined in the muck. Can scroungers will even go through individual garbage cans, something I have never seen a scavenger do.

Individual garbage cans are set out on the public easement only on garbage days. On other days going through them requires trespassing close to a dwelling. Going through individual garbage cans without scattering litter is almost impossible. Litter is likely to reduce the public's tolerance of scavenging. Individual cans are simply not as productive as Dumpsters; people in houses and duplexes do not move so often and for some reason do not tend to discard as much useful material. Moreover, the time required to go through one garbage can that serves one household is not much less than the time required to go through a Dumpster that contains the refuse of twenty apartments.

But my strongest reservation about going through individual garbage cans is that this seems to me a very personal kind of invasion to which I would object if I were a householder. Although many things in Dumpsters are obviously meant never to come to light, a Dumpster is somehow less personal.

I avoid trying to draw conclusions about the people who dump in the Dumpsters I frequent. I think it would be unethical to do so, although I know many people will find the idea of scavenger ethics too funny for words.

Dumpsters contain bank statements, correspondence, and other documents, just as anyone might expect. But there are also less obvious sources of information. Pill bottles, for example. The labels bear the name of the patient, the name of the doctor, and the name of the drug. AIDS drugs and anti-psychotic medicines, to name but two groups, are specific and are seldom prescribed for any other disorders. The plastic compacts for birth-control pills usually have complete label information.

Despite all of this sensitive information, I have had only one apartment resident object to my going through the Dumpster. In that case it turned out the resident was a university athlete who was taking bets and who was afraid I would turn up his wager slips.

Occasionally a find tells a story. I once found a small paper bag containing some unused condoms, several partial tubes of flavored sexual lubricants, a partially used compact of birth-control pills, and the torn pieces of a picture of a young man. Clearly she was through with him and planning to give up sex altogether.

Dumpster things are often sad—abandoned teddy bears, shredded wedding books, despaired-of sales kits. I find many pets lying in state in Dumpsters. Although I hope to get off the streets so that Lizbeth can have a long and comfortable old age, I know this hope is not very realistic. So I suppose when her time comes she too will go into a Dumpster. I will have no better place for her. And after all, it is fitting, since for most of her life her livelihood has come from the Dumpster. When she finds something I think is safe that has been spilled from a Dumpster, I let her have it. She already knows the route around the best ones. I like to think that if she survives me she will have a chance of evading the dog catcher and of finding her sustenance on the route.

Silly vanities also come to rest in the Dumpsters. I am a rather accomplished needleworker. I get a lot of material from the Dumpsters. Evidently sorority girls, hoping to impress someone, perhaps themselves, with their mastery of a womanly art, buy a lot of embroider-by-number kits, work a few stitches horribly, and eventually discard the whole mess. I pull out their stitches, turn the canvas over, and work an original design. Do not think I refrain from chuckling as I make gifts from these kits.

I find diaries and journals. I have often thought of compiling a book of literary found objects. And perhaps I will one day. But what I find is hopelessly commonplace and bad without being, even unconsciously, camp. College students also discard their papers. I am horrified to discover the kind of paper that now merits an A in an undergraduate course. I am grateful, however, for the number of good books and magazines the students throw out.

In the area I know best I have never discovered vermin in the Dumpsters, but there are two kinds of kitty surprise. One is alley cats whom I meet as they leap, claws first, out of Dumpsters. This is especially thrilling when I have Lizbeth in tow. The other kind of kitty surprise is a plastic garbage bag filled with some ponderous, amorphous mass. This always proves to be used cat litter.

City bees harvest doughnut glaze and this makes the Dumpster at the doughnut shop more interesting. My faith in the instinctive wisdom of animals is always shaken whenever I see Lizbeth attempt to catch a bee in her mouth, which she does whenever bees are present. Evidently some birds find Dumpsters profitable, for birdie surprise is almost as common as kitty surprise of the first kind. In hunting season all kinds of small game turn up in Dumpsters, some of it, sadly, not entirely dead. Curiously, summer and winter, maggots are uncommon.

The worse of the living and near-living hazards of the Dumpsters are the fire ants. The food they claim is not much of a loss, but they are vicious and aggressive. It is very easy to brush against some surface of the Dumpster and pick up half a dozen or more fire ants, usually in some sensitive area such as the underarm. One advantage of bringing Lizbeth along as I make Dumpster rounds is that, for obvious reasons, she is very alert to ground-based fire ants. When Lizbeth recognizes a fire-ant infestation around our feet, she does the Dance of the Zillion Fire Ants. I have learned not to ignore this warning from Lizbeth, whether I perceive the tiny ants or not, but to remove ourselves at Lizbeth's first pas de bourée. All the more so because the ants are the worst in the summer months when I wear flip-flops if I have them. (Perhaps someone will misunderstand this. Lizbeth does the Dance of the Zillion Fire Ants when she recognizes more fire ants than she cares to eat, not when she is being bitten. Since I have learned to react promptly, she does not get bitten at all. It is the isolated patrol of fire ants that falls in Lizbeth's range that deserves pity. She finds them quite tasty.)

By far the best way to go through a Dumpster is to lower yourself into it. Most of the good stuff tends to settle at the bottom because it is usually weightier than the rubbish. My more athletic companions have often demonstrated to me that they can extract much good material from a Dumpster I have already been over.

To those psychologically or physically unprepared to enter a Dumpster, I recommend a stout stick, preferably with some barb or hook at one end. The hook can be used to grab plastic garbage bags. When I find canned goods or other objects loose at the bottom of a Dumpster, I lower a bag into it, roll the desired object into the bag, and then hoist the bag out—a procedure more easily described than executed. Much Dumpster diving is a matter of experience for which nothing will do except practice.

Dumpster diving is outdoor work, often surprisingly pleasant. It is not entirely predictable; things of interest turn up every day and some days there are finds of great value. I am always very pleased when I can turn up exactly the thing I most wanted to find. Yet in spite of the element of chance, scavenging more than most other pursuits tends to yield returns in some proportion to the effort and intelligence brought to bear. It is very sweet to turn up a few dollars in change from a Dumpster that has just been gone over by a wino.

The land is now covered with cities. The cities are full of Dumpsters. If a member of the canine race is ever able to know what it is doing, then Lizbeth knows that when we go around to the Dumpsters, we are hunting. I think of scavenging as a modern form of self-reliance. In any event, after having survived nearly ten years of government service, where everything is geared to the lowest common denominator, I find it refreshing to have work that rewards initiative and effort. Certainly I would be happy to have a sinecure again, but I am no longer heartbroken that I left one.

I find from the experience of scavenging two rather deep lessons. The first is to take what you can use and let the rest go by. I have come to think that there is no value in the abstract. A thing I cannot use or make useful, perhaps by trading, has no value however rare or fine it may be. I mean useful in a broad sense—some art I would find useful and some otherwise.

I was shocked to realize that some things are not worth acquiring, but now I think it is so. Some material things are white elephants that eat up the possessor's substance. The second lesson is the transience of material being. This has not quite converted me to a dualist, but it has made some headway in that direction. I do not suppose that ideas are immortal, but certainly mental things are longer lived than other material things.

Once I was the sort of person who invests objects with sentimental value. Now I no longer have those objects, but I have the sentiments yet.

Many times in our travels I have lost everything but the clothes I was wearing and Lizbeth. The things I find in Dumpsters, the love letters and rag dolls of so many lives, remind me of this lesson. Now I hardly pick up a thing without envisioning the time I will cast it aside. This I think is a healthy state of mind. Almost everything I have now has already been cast out at least once, proving that what I own is valueless to someone.

Anyway, I find my desire to grab for the gaudy bauble has been largely sated. I think this is an attitude I share with the very wealthy—we both know there is plenty more where what we have came from. Between us are the rat-race millions who nightly scavenge the cable channels looking for they know not what.

I am sorry for them.

Learning How to Be Niggers

GREGORY HOWARD WILLIAMS

January 26, 1954, Dad roused us for our first trip to Garfield Elementary School. My biggest worry was that it would be a "colored" school. I did not fear being in classes with black children, but I couldn't shake the memories of the ramshackle school buildings and ancient playground equipment I had seen when accompanying Raymond to collect his nieces and nephews from the all-black Fairfax County schools. It was a great relief to see a new bright-red brick building, and both white and black children milling about the schoolyard.

In the office I peered over Dad's shoulder while he laboriously printed "J. Anthony Williams" in the enrollment form box for "Father." In the blank for occupation he listed "U.S. Army." When he scrawled a "W" in the space for race, I nudged him. He frowned sharply. Rebuked, I joined Mike, who slouched at the door.

The secretary ushered us into the principal's office. A slightly balding man rose from behind a desk stacked high with folders. With little more than a curt "Good morning," he led us from the office. Just down the hall we stopped at Mike's new room. "Lehman," the principal said sternly, "come along." Mike hesitated, hiding behind Dad, his wide brown eyes on the verge of tears. "Go ahead, Mike," Dad said gently, and nudged him forward. As the principal guided Mike through the door, Dad whispered, "Good luck, son. Billy will be waiting on you after school." Mike returned a forlorn nod.

School had been difficult for Mike. He failed the first grade in Virginia, and he was struggling in the second. I knew he wasn't dumb, but I didn't know what was wrong. None of us did. As we stood in the hallway that morning, I hoped Indiana would be better for him. But I worried as he followed the principal to the front of the room, and giggles filtered out to the hallway when his classmates saw the small holes in the seat of his threadbare trousers.

Dad and I were hustled down green concrete steps to the basement. A tall, overweight man with horn-rimmed glasses huffed as he climbed the stairway toward us. His suit nearly burst at the seams. Mr. Hunt, my new fourth grade teacher, perhaps noticing I was tall for my age, asked eagerly, "Do you like basketball?" I searched my mind for something called basketball. In Virginia I played baseball, football, and even volleyball. Suddenly, I remembered a game called "medicine ball." Maybe that was it. The heavy ball was impossible to lift. No one in my gym class enjoyed it. You couldn't throw it, kick it, or run with it. No, I don't like it, I thought. Yet three adults stared intently waiting for an answer. I gulped and muttered, "Yes."

We entered a basement classroom reminiscent of a World War II bunker. Everything was solid concrete except for two small rectangular windows at the very top of the outside wall. From my assigned seat near the back I surveyed my new classmates. A fat boy spilled over the seat in front of me. Two rows over, a girl with horn-rimmed glasses was perfecting the studious look of one in pursuit of the "teacher's pet" prize. I counted five black children around the classroom. Though I had many black playmates in Gum Springs, we never attended school together. I wondered what it would be like. Then I remembered Dad on the bus: "Billy, you're part colored." I wondered if I looked any different. I wondered if anyone else could tell. I wondered if I would have any friends . . . black or white.

Two aisles away near the wall I spied bouncing blond curls and the twinkle of blue eyes gazing at me.

"Get to work!" the teacher shouted from the front of the room. I lowered my head, desperate to appear busy even though I had no assignment. He lumbered down the aisle toward me. I cringed. Mr. Hunt paused three seats in front of me, beside a brown-haired boy with thick glasses.

"Are you going to take all day, Donald?" He glared.

Silence.

"You've got the right name, Donald, because Donald Dolittle does little." He smiled, congratulating himself on his wit, reached across two students, and thrust a mimeographed math assignment toward me. His sharp tongue made me glad I lied about basketball. Though I solved the long division problems in less than two minutes, I continued to hover over my paper to avoid calling attention to myself. At recess we filed out the rear of the building onto a large shiny blacktop play area complete with swing sets, a jungle gym, monkey bars, and even a sandbox. Students from other classes filled the playground, and I searched for Mike among them. Unable to find him, I drifted toward my new classmates.

"Where you from?" asked Dolittle as we stood in line for a swing. Classmates gathered around as I talked about Virginia and seeing President Eisenhower once when Dad drove us by the White House. Dolittle's eyes glazed as I rambled on about Mount Vernon, but the girl with the blond curls edged closer. Her name was Molly. A head shorter than I, she had the rosiest cheeks I had ever seen. I could hardly take my eyes off her as she introduced her friend, Sally. Tall for a girl, Sally looked me straight in the eye. Her bobbed brown hair swished back and forth as her eyes flitted between Molly and me. For the first time since we stepped off the bus on South Walnut Street twenty four-hours earlier, I dared to smile.

Schoolwork was much easier than it had been in Virginia. That first week I received the teacher's praise several times. What I valued more was the friendship of Molly and Sally. The three of us soon became inseparable. They quizzed me endlessly about Washington. I described the Cherry Blossom Festival and the Lincoln and Jefferson memorials in elaborate detail. They only appeared to lose interest when I babbled at length about seeing the wreckage of the first airplane collision over National Airport.

One afternoon during our second week in Muncie my cousin Mary Lou ran to catch up with Mike and me as we walked to Aunt Bess's. That day was the first time I had seen her on the playground. She skipped back and forth in front of me as we made our way down Monroe Street, her toothy smile inches from my face, chanting, "Billy likes a white peck! Billy likes a white peck!"

"No, I don't." I spat. "She's just in my class. I can talk to white kids."

She put her hands on her hips and blocked my way.

"I bet she wouldn't talk to you if she knew you was colored."

"Yes she would. Color don't have nothing to do with it!" I protested.

"That's what you think, Mr. Bigshot!"

Ever since we arrived at Garfield, Mary Lou had told anyone who would listen that we were her cousins. I really didn't like it, but when black children asked, "Are you related to Mary Lou?" I didn't deny it. It was only when I saw the revulsion it produced in white kids that I became very nervous.

The next day after lunch at Aunt Bess's, I pulled on my tattered fatigue jacket and headed to school. Opening the gate, I glanced down the hill toward the busy Monroe and Willard Street intersection. No white families lived north of Willard, so normally only various shades of black and brown faces were on the corner. That day was different. Two white faces stood out from the crowd— Molly and Sally. Even from a distance I saw shock register on their faces. They turned toward each other. Molly stared up the hill once more. A final glance, then she darted from the intersection, her blond curls disappearing behind the corner grocery store.

That afternoon Molly and Sally sat in their seats on the far side of the room. As I walked through the door, their heads snapped toward the small window. I slumped at my desk for an endless hour of math problems. When it was time for recess I kept my head down. Mr. Hunt had to order me outside.

On the playground I took a deep breath and moved haltingly toward Molly and Sally, desperately concocting a story about being at Aunt Bess's. I decided to say she was our maid and that Mike and I just ate lunch there. I never had a chance to lie. When the girls saw me approach, they turned their backs to me. I retreated to the safety of the fire escape, feigning indifference. Heads bobbed up and down as they chattered animatedly with other white girls. Some of them stole glances in my direction. I hunched over and hid my face.

After school that afternoon I caught their burning stares once more as I stood alone outside the school door waiting for Mike. The disgust on their faces made me feel like I had committed some grievous wrong. Mike never came out of the building, and I trudged home forlorn, feeling the weight of the world on my shoulders. Mike lay on Aunt Bess's couch with a large white cotton bandage taped to his forehead. He raised himself up on his elbows and thrust his oily face toward me.

"I fell off the fire escape during the fire drill. The principal took me to get stitches. Then he drove me home. He didn't believe we lived here. He was gonna drive off till Aunt Bess waved him down and told him we was colored boys."

A month dragged by and Dad did not return from Virginia. I was furious with him and felt abandoned, and I wasn't alone in my anger. The mere mention of his name caused Uncle Osco to snarl, and his bad humor spilled over into the household. When Mike tracked mud in from the backyard, Aunt Bess gave him a switching. When I sloshed water while carrying it from the outdoor faucet, she swatted me with the "rooster" broom. Every day after school I withdrew into my private corner of the sitting room and played with a small bag of clay. Hours passed while I molded imaginary soldiers who killed, maimed, bombed, and demolished everything in their path. Men, women, and children all died; ships sank; towns were leveled—everything was destroyed.

One afternoon Aunt Bess tired of me being underfoot and ordered me outside. I sat at the edge of the playground. Mike was playing football with boys from the Projects. I smiled as he streaked across the gravel field with the ball tucked under his arm. A chocolate-skinned boy in a blue cotton cowboy suit complete with fringed pant legs gave chase. He grabbed Mike's arm and jerked him to the ground. Mike slid across the gravel as the ball bounced crazily into the street. I leaped to my feet. Mike lay motionless for several seconds, then finally pushed himself up from the hard ground.

"What'd you knock me down for?" he demanded.

"This is tackle. We get you down any way we can," the boy growled in response. "It ain't two-handed touch like you crackers play."

"Tell him, Reggie," crowed a boy I recognized from Garfield School.

Mike brushed the gravel from his clothes and nodded. From then on, every time Reggie's team ran in Mike's direction, he fiercely blocked Mike. Even when runners headed in the opposite direction, Reggie swung at Mike. Finally, red-faced and exasperated, Mike lunged at his attacker. Reggie punched him in the face. Mike fell backward. The other boys surrounded them, shouting, "Whip him! Kick his butt, Reggie! Kill that cracker!" I raced to Aunt Bess's for help.

"Aunt Bess, Aunt Bess, some colored boys is beatin' up Mike!" She sauntered to the window overlooking the playground. "Come on! Come on! Mike needs help!" I shouted, tugging at her apron.

"Let go, boy." She pushed me away. "You better get on over there and help him. He's your brother. You the one gotta take care of him."

I hesitated.

"Whatcha waitin' for, boy? Do you wanna fight me or them? Git!" she shouted one final time, and reached for the buggy whip in the corner near the stove.

Tears filled my eyes as I realized no one was going to help Mike. Not Mom, not Dad, not Aunt Bess. We were on our own. I ran through the house and leaped off the porch. As I reached the crowd, Mike lay on the ground shielding his face. Blood seeped between his fingers as he twisted and turned, trying to dodge the hail of fists. Reggie grinned at the laughing crowd. "Guess I showed that cracker. . . ." I pushed through the boys and grabbed him by the neck, pulling him off Mike. He tumbled backward on the gravel. I kneed him in the stomach. A fist to the mouth. Then all over his head, the same way he hit Mike.

Soon his nose bled. The crowd fell silent. "That white mothafucka's kicking Reggie's ass," I heard. "Let's get him."

The sound of shoes shuffling across the gravel distracted me. Then a crack filled the air. With my hands gripped around Reggie's neck, I looked over my shoulder. Aunt Bess was lashing her buggy whip.

"Don't you all bother him!" she shouted. "If you do, I'm gonna put this here whip across your little black butts!"

"Miss Bessie, that white boy's gonna kill Reggie!" protested one boy.

"They ain't no white boys," responded Aunt Bess. "They niggers just like you. They got the same right to be here! Come on, Billy, git Mike and let's go on back to the house."

I left Reggie holding his nose and pulled Mike to his feet. There was yet another long rip in the sleeve of his army fire sale jacket. We followed Aunt Bess across the gravel playground. Maybe, I thought, there is somebody in the world who cares about us.

The next Saturday morning a tall, golden-skinned boy of sixteen arrived at the house. Aunt Bess called Mike and me into the living room and said, "Boys, this is your brother Jimmy."

As I surveyed the young stranger, I tried to absorb Aunt Bess's startling pronouncement. Neither Mom nor Dad had ever mentioned him. Yet his prominent nose and dark brown eyes bore a remarkable resemblance to Dad. He also had Dad's lanky build. In fact, he looked more like our father than either Mike or I. I wondered why we had never heard of him before. But if Jimmy had been forgotten he was not unfriendly.

"Glad to meet you, brother Billy," Jimmy said, cheerfully extending his hand.

Jimmy, a drummer for the Muncie Central High School Bearcats band, wore black pants, a long wool coat with brass buttons, and a purple-and-white cape. He was on the way to a high school pep rally and invited us along. As a result of my teacher's obsession with basketball, I learned a lot about it. In fact, our class spent more time discussing Muncie basketball teams than any other subject. Although there were two high schools in Muncie, only Central counted when it came to basketball. Central had won four state championships and was the odds-on favorite to capture a fifth in March 1954. The Muncie Fieldhouse, where the Bearcats played, seated over seven thousand people and was packed for every game. Folks waited years to buy season tickets. The Bearcats were ultimately derailed that year by a team from a tiny Indiana town called Milan. Later, the saga of Milan's march to the state championship and final victory over Muncie Central was the basis for the popular movie *Hoosiers*.

That morning Jimmy urged us to go to the rally and then "to Whitely and see Uncle Sam and Aunt Ceola."

The new names and places were strange and unfamiliar, but Mike and I eagerly followed Jimmy downtown. Purple-and-white team posters were prominently displayed in every window, and purple-and-white banners stretched high across South Walnut Street. Names of Bearcat team members like Jimmy Barnes, "Big John" Casterlow, and George Burks were whispered as if they were gods. In spite of the huge crowd gathered at the fieldhouse, and a boisterous pep rally, basketball still held little interest for me, and I was glad when we left the gathering.

Broadway curved northeast away from downtown Muncie to McCulloch Park. Directly east of the park was Whitely, the home of Muncie's second-largest concentration of blacks. Bounded on the north by Centennial Road, on the south by the White River, and on the east by the Nickel Plate Railroad tracks, it was isolated from the rest of Muncie. The tracks edged along the eastern border of Whitely for almost twenty blocks without one street connecting it with the adjacent white areas.

Jimmy led us to a small grocery store at the corner of Lowell and Penn. The sign over the door said SAM WHEELER'S GROCERIES, THE COUNTRY STORE THAT'S GOING TO TOWN. The store shelves were crammed with canned goods, breads, cookies, and potato chips. A near empty glass meat case stretched across the rear of the wooden-floored room. Behind it stood two large glass-doored freezers. A light golden-skinned woman in her mid-forties stood at the checkout counter. Jimmy introduced her as Aunt Ceola.

"Hi, boys," she said in a cheerful voice. "I'm so glad to see you. Jimmy's been talking about you all week." She reached under the counter and handed Mike and me each a candy bar.

We gushed thanks and ripped off the wrappers. She turned behind the counter and drew back a cloth curtain that opened onto a small living area. I heard a television from within.

"Boys, you all come on out here. I got somebody I want you to meet."

Two dark-brown-skinned boys our age walked from the room. Though the older boy and I were the same height, he outweighed me by at least thirty pounds. His thick shoulders and full, square face resembled those of a boxer. The younger boy was about the same size and weight as Mike.

Aunt Ceola explained that the boys were related to her and to Jimmy and, therefore, probably to us. It all sounded so complicated, but the boys seemed to accept our relationship without question.

"Why don't you run up to Longfellow and play some ball?" said Aunt Ceola. "Boys, show Mike and Billy the playground."

Recalling my last playground fight, I mumbled softly, "I don't wanna go."

Jimmy, no doubt sensing my fear, accompanied us.

Longfellow School playground was almost a mirror image of Madison Street—mostly sand and gravel. All of the children were black. That is, none of them were white. There was every imaginable hue of brown, ranging from deep chocolate to the color of the speckled light brown eggs we found in Aunt Bess's henhouse. And now two palefaces—Mike and me.

As we stood at the edge of the basketball court, an unusually short light-brown-skinned boy approached us. Though his skin color fit in with the rest of the boys, he seemed a bit out of place. All at once I realized that his hair was different. It was the same as Mike's and mine—long, dark, and straight. I towered over him by at least six inches, but he stood squarely in front of me and demanded, "What you white boys doing here?"

I was ready to quip, "None of your business, Shorty," when Jimmy interjected.

"They're my brothers, Pancho! Don't mess with them or I'll kick your little Mexican butt back across the street. Anyway, what you bothering them for? They're your cousins, too."

I tried to conceal my amazement, wondering how many more surprises the day would hold.

"No way," protested Pancho. "I'm Mexican John Vargas's boy. We don't have no crackers."

"Yeah, but Ruth Vargas used to be a Williams, which makes us cousins with all the Vargases."

Pancho shrugged his shoulders, tapped the basketball, and said, "Let's play ball!"

With the growing list of honey, brown, and chocolate relatives, it was becoming harder and harder to perceive myself as white. Yet I knew I also had two white grandparents, three white uncles, two white aunts and a houseful of white cousins. They were less than one mile away, just across the Nickel Plate Railroad steel barrier that separated Whitely from white Muncie. Not one of them had come for us.

That evening while I was doing homework, I overheard Aunt Bess and Uncle Osco arguing in the kitchen.

"Them boys gonna eat me out of house and home if Buster don't get here soon," Osco complained. "And they fight with Mary Lou all the time. I don't care what you say. I'm gonna get shed of them 'fore they drive us to the poorhouse." I held my breath, wondering what he meant.

"Osco," replied Aunt Bess, "them boys is family. We can't just turn 'em out."

"Well, we ain't the only family they got. Sallie Ann's they grandmother, and she ain't even been up here to see after 'em. They got white folks, too. If'n they still here by next weekend, you gonna give 'em to the orphanage."

I couldn't sleep that night, and my stomach ached all the next day. That afternoon as Mike and I sat alone on the concrete ledge surrounding the playground, I told him what I'd overheard.

In a weak voice he said, "Billy, I'm scared. We won't know anybody at the orphanage. Do you think we'd stay together?"

"Not if one of us got adopted. We might never see each other again, and we'd never find Mom and Dad."

A miserable week followed. Mike came down with a cold, and my stomach continued to ache. We hoped for Mom or Dad, or our white aunts or uncles, or even Jimmy to appear, but we had no visitors. The dreaded Sunday of Uncle Osco's ultimatum arrived. Miss Sallie was summoned. There was no warm greeting for us from the woman we now called Grandma Sallie. She remained the stern, angry woman we remembered from our past life in Virginia. She huddled with Aunt Bess and Uncle Osco in the living room. Mike and I listened intently from the kitchen door.

"Osco, I ain't got no room for them little peckawoods in my shack."

"I ain't got no room up here either. We too crowded."

"How am I supposed to take care of 'em? I work all day at the drive-in. I can't cook. I only got a hot plate."

"Look, Sallie Ann, these your grandchildren. You either take 'em or Bessie's gonna give 'em to the welfare people tomorrow morning."

"Damn that Buster," said Grandma. "I'm always cleaning up his shit. Why don't he grow up? You'd think a Howard University nigger be smarter."

She paused, and then exhaled. "All right. I'll come and get 'em next Saturday."

"No, Sallie!" Osco shouted. The rocker slid across the floor as he stood abruptly. "You gotta take 'em now."

She started to argue, then sighed. "All right. Pack their bags, Bessie."

Aunt Bess walked into the kitchen, her eyes downcast. We looked at her, hoping for a reprieve. She shook her head. Stretching to a shelf above the sink, she grabbed two brown paper sacks and handed one to each of us. Uncle Osco fled to his bedroom, Aunt Bess and Mary Lou stayed in the refuge of the kitchen. We moved silently to the sitting room and stuffed all our worldly belongings into the bags. Grandma Sallie stood in the doorway, crossing and uncrossing her arms impatiently. We followed Grandma through the now-vacant living room. There were no good-byes. Clutching the grocery sacks, we walked the four blocks through the Projects to 601½ Railroad Street.

What I had mistaken for a tool shed in January was now our home. Three tiny rooms. Crammed into the narrow kitchen were a two-person table and an ancient potbellied stove. A two-burner hot plate was on a counter next to a cold water faucet. There was no sink or drain. Dirty water was tossed into the yard. Squeezed into the room next to the kitchen were Grandma's bed, a couch, and a dresser. Her house did have one advantage over Aunt Bess's—an indoor toilet in the tiny, windowless back room—but there was no sink, tub, or shower. Crammed next to the toilet was a wooden army folding cot—our bed. Mike curled up at one end, with me at the other.

We soon discovered that Grandma, like Dad, was an alcoholic. She had no appetite. Whatever food she needed she nibbled while cooking at the Madison and Kirby drive-in. Every evening after school we lingered at the kitchen window overlooking the alley, waiting for her to trudge up the hill behind the service station. To keep warm we turned on the hot plate and rubbed our hands over it. We had to make sure it was off and the burner was cool when she arrived so she wouldn't complain about her electric bill. Once I tried to start a fire in the potbellied stove, but only succeeded in filling the shack with smoke. Most evenings Mike and I huddled together for warmth until she arrived.

There was little to do at Grandma's. We spent countless hours pouring over the contents of an old shoebox that contained the memorabilia of our father. It was full of photographs and love letters to him. I was disappointed not to find any pictures of my mother. Dad's youthful face beamed from photos taken in exciting places like the Boardwalk of Atlantic City and Times Square, New York. He sported stylish clothes, and invariably had a beautiful woman on his arm.

I read and reread the letters to him. A judge's daughter from Arkansas explained how she would love him forever, but marriage was out of the question. She had discovered he was colored. Dr. Alain Locke of Howard University expressed profound sorrow that Dad felt he must pass into the "white world." I poured over and over the mementos of Dad's past for clues, hoping to understand what had happened to my father and to our family.

As I touched and searched the photographs, a multitude of feelings were evoked by them. Mike, Sissy, the baby, and I had been let down. More than let down, we had been betrayed . . . why? The handsome smiling face staring back at me showed so much promise. What had gone wrong? Every day I looked at the photos and letters. If I'd had a bad day on the playground or at school I felt hatred for both Mom and Dad. Then I'd feel remorse for my feelings and just beg God to let me see them again.

When Grandma appeared at the crest of the hill, Mike and I raced from the cold shack to rummage through her purse for the two frozen hamburger patties and the handful of french fries she stole while alone in the drive-in's basement kitchen. Grandma Sallie was a woman of few words. She had unique ways of conveying the rules of the house. She had absolutely no tolerance for complaints. Once when she placed our hamburger patties and fries before us, Mike clamored, "Greg has more french fries than me." My grandmother swiftly and silently picked up Mike's plate and scraped half his fries onto mine. Mike's mouth dropped open in bewilderment. As I wolfed down our evening meal, I was grateful my grandmother was willing to steal to feed us. I felt shame when I recalled how much I had hated her in Virginia.

Every day after school we stopped at Aunt Bess's. If Uncle Osco wasn't there she quickly whisked us to the kitchen, where we gobbled the remains of navy beans and biscuits left over from breakfast, rushing to finish before Osco returned. If he was home, she shook her head no when answering the door. Even as she put her finger to her lips, she slipped us a piece of corn bread or some cold biscuits in a bag. We stepped quietly off the porch and gulped the food down on the sidewalk, making sure we didn't have anything in our hands as we passed the kitchen window and waved to Uncle Osco on our way to the playground. On Saturdays, Aunt Bess bought groceries at the Park & Shop Supermarket on South Walnut Street. On the way home, she paused near the playground ledge where Mike and I often played by ourselves. After a quick glance to the house to make sure Uncle Osco wasn't peeking out the kitchen window, she reached into the bag and handed us a loaf of bread or a quart of milk and ordered us to take it straight to Grandma's. We scurried through the Projects with our bounty.

Grandma complained bitterly about how much Mike and I ate, and about what we cost her in heat and electricity. If I forgot to turn off the kitchen light after studying, she grumbled about it for over an hour. If I threw a piece of coal in the potbellied stove without permission, her shrill voice filled the room until we were asleep.

Late one evening while I finished my homework, Grandma and Mike left the house together. When they returned later, Mike averted his eyes, and his whole body quivered. That night as we lay on the cot, I asked Mike where they had been.

"Grandma made me steal coal from Dague's."

"You're lying. They got fences all around the place."

"I crawled under the fence."

"Mike, if the police caught you they'd send you to reform school."

"She's gonna make you steal next time, Billy. She said so."

"I ain't gonna," I said, lying back on the hard canvas cot.

Later that week Grandma took me to the coal yard after dinner. We picked up coal that had fallen off the railroad cars. When I balked at crawling under the fence, she said, "You little peckawood! Get your butt under there and get that coal. We gonna freeze if you don't."

"I don't care, Grandma," I said, shivering in the late winter night. "I ain't gonna go to jail. You can beat me if you want to, but I just can't steal."

"Don't nobody want to beat your narrow behind," she said in exasperation. She glared at me for a moment and then sniffed, "Get on the other side of this bucket. Help me carry it back to the house."

Luckily, the weather soon turned warmer and our late-night trips to the coal yard ended. However, the spring brought little change in our daily routine.

Night after night I lay on the cot, consoling myself with the belief that my parents were just testing us. They wanted to give us a taste of how hard life could be. Relentlessly, I clung to the dream that one day Mom, Dad, Sissy, and the baby would arrive in our Cadillac. Mike and I would step into it and return to the good days we knew in Virginia.

Late the Friday night before Easter 1954, Grandma Sallie shook us awake.

"Wake up boys, your daddy's here! 'Bout time he gave his poor old mother some relief! Thinks I don't have anything better to do than take care of his little peckawoods."

Dad stood silhouetted in the doorway.

"Where you been, Buster? I been lookin' after these boys for almost two months."

"Momma, you know I've been in Virginia trying to salvage the business. Aunt Bess promised she'd keep the boys until I returned. I didn't even ask you because I didn't want to impose."

"You may not of asked me, but I had to take your boys before Bessie and Osco gave them to the orphanage. And don't be giving me no words like *savage* and *impose*. Tell that to your white friends. Just because you went to colleg don't mean you a big shot nigger 'round here."

Sitting up in bed, I rubbed my eyes.

"Get dressed, boys," Dad said grimly. "Let's go outside and talk."

Sullenly, I pulled on my pants and shoes, glad to see him after his le absence, but angry that he had deserted us for so long. I moved silently th the shack past Grandma, now back under the covers beside her boyfrie I could just make out the green luminous dial of the clock on her dress a.m. We walked through the alley to Kirby and Monroe. Dad dropp curb and motioned for us to join him. Mike scooted as close as poss tating, I moved to the far side of Mike.

The street lamp cast a sharp cold light on our hunched fi clothes were different from those he'd bought in Washingtor stores. His gabardine suit was dull and oil stained. Buttons were missing, and there was a small tear on the shoulder. His white shirt had a frayed collar. Only a dark brown fedora angled across his forehead was a reminder of better days.

Dazed and uncertain, Mike and I slouched over the curb, elbows resting on our knees. The fatigue pants we'd bought so long ago in Washington were completely tattered and stained. Our shoes were too small for us and had worn-down heels and holes in the bottoms. Perhaps embarrassed by his long absence, Dad delivered an order like a drill sergeant.

"Sit up straight, boys! Don't hunch over, it's bad for your posture." We straightened our backs and turned expectantly toward him.

"Didn't think I'd see you boys tonight. Aunt Bess told me she'd keep you till I came back. Were you bad?"

"No, Daddy, we weren't bad," answered Mike.

"What in the hell happened, Billy?" he said, challenging me again as if I were to blame for everything that had occurred in our lives. Still, for some reason I felt a strong sense of responsibility for the family, and tried to explain what I really couldn't understand.

"When you didn't come back like you said, Uncle Osco got mad. He told Aunt Bess he wasn't gonna take care of a no-'count nigger's half-breed boys. He said that the best thing to do was to send us to an orphanage, and that was what he was gonna do if you didn't come back within a week, so Grandma Sallie took us."

The chill of the concrete penetrated my thin pants and gave me goose bumps. I began to fidget and moved closer to Mike. Dad began again. "I just don't understand it. Aunt Bess knows Momma doesn't have any place fit to eep you. And Momma doesn't have any sense either. Look at her, in there lay- up in bed with Joe Turnipseed. . . ."

Dad reached into his pocket and drew out a bottle of Wild Irish Rose. He screwed the cap off the bottle and took a long swallow of wine. We re- s he exhaled a pungent breath.

s, I thought I was going to work out something with the business, but oreclosed and we lost everything, the tavern, the Pitt Street house, the e don't have shit."

g the bottle straight up and guzzled down the contents. Then he le across the sidewalk into the night shadows.

our momma, though. She's living in Washington with that black ff with. I found out where she was and called to see the chil- t over there, him and two other mothafuckers acted like they hit, if it had been my Golden Glove days I would have them by myself."

see us?"

e. She didn't say anything about it. She asked how you w what I told her?"

dy?" asked Mike, leaning forward, full of hope.

Muncie, learning how to be niggers!"

Behind the Counter

ERIC SCHLOSSER

THROUGHPUT

Every Saturday Elisa Zamot gets up at 5:15 in the morning. It's a struggle, and her head feels groggy as she steps into the shower. Her little sisters, Cookie and Sabrina, are fast asleep in their beds. By 5:30, Elisa's showered, done her hair, and put on her McDonald's uniform. She's sixteen, bright-eyed and olive-skinned, pretty and petite, ready for another day of work. Elisa's mother usually drives her the half-mile or so to the restaurant, but sometimes Elisa walks, leaving home before the sun rises. Her family's modest townhouse sits beside a busy highway on the south side of Colorado Springs, in a largely poor and working-class neighborhood. Throughout the day, sounds of traffic fill the house, the steady whoosh of passing cars. But when Elisa heads for work, the streets are quiet, the sky's still dark, and the lights are out in the small houses and rental apartments along the road.

When Elisa arrives at McDonald's, the manager unlocks the door and lets her in. Sometimes the husband-and-wife cleaning crew are just finishing up. More often, it's just Elisa and the manager in the restaurant, surrounded by an empty parking lot. For the next hour or so, the two of them get everything ready. They turn on the ovens and grills. They go downstairs into the basement and get food and supplies for the morning shift. They get the paper cups, wrappers, cardboard containers, and packets of condiments. They step into the big freezer and get the frozen bacon, the frozen pancakes, and the frozen cinnamon rolls. They get the frozen hash browns, the frozen biscuits, the frozen McMuffins. They get the cartons of scrambled egg mix and orange juice mix. They bring the food upstairs and start preparing it before any customers appear, thawing some things in the microwave and cooking other things on the grill. They put the cooked food in special cabinets to keep it warm.

The restaurant opens for business at seven o'clock, and for the next hour or so, Elisa and the manager hold down the fort, handling all the orders. As the place starts to get busy, other employees arrive. Elisa works behind the counter. She takes orders and hands food to customers from breakfast through lunch. When she finally walks home, after seven hours of standing at a cash register, her feet hurt. She's wiped out. She comes through the front door, flops onto the living room couch, and turns on the TV. And the next morning she gets up at 5:15 again and starts the same routine.

Up and down Academy Boulevard, along South Nevada, Circle Drive, and Woodman Road, teenagers like Elisa run the fast food restaurants of Colorado Springs. Fast food kitchens often seem like a scene from *Bugsy Malone*, a film in which all the actors are children pretending to be adults. No other industry in the United States has a workforce so dominated by adolescents. About two-thirds of the nation's fast food workers are under the age of twenty. Teenagers open the fast food outlets in the morning, close them at night, and keep them going at all hours in between. Even the managers and assistant managers are sometimes in their late teens. Unlike Olympic gymnastics—an activity in which teenagers consistently perform at a higher level than adults—there's nothing about the work in a fast food kitchen that requires young employees. Instead of relying upon a small, stable, well-paid, and well-trained workforce, the fast food industry seeks out part-time, unskilled workers who are willing to accept low pay. Teenagers have been the perfect candidates for these jobs, not only because they are less expensive to hire than adults, but also because their youthful inexperience makes them easier to control.

The labor practices of the fast food industry have their origins in the assembly line systems adopted by American manufacturers in the early twentieth century. Business historian Alfred D. Chandler has argued that a high rate of "throughput" was the most important aspect of these mass production systems. A factory's throughput is the speed and volume of its flow—a much more crucial measurement, according to Chandler, than the number of workers it employs or the value of its machinery. With innovative technology and the proper organization, a small number of workers can produce an enormous amount of goods cheaply. Throughput is all about increasing the speed of assembly, about doing things faster in order to make more.

Although the McDonald brothers had never encountered the term "throughput" or studied "scientific management," they instinctively grasped the underlying principles and applied them in the Speedee Service System. The restaurant operating scheme they developed has been widely adopted and refined over the past half century. The ethos of the assembly line remains at its core. The fast food industry's obsession with throughput has altered the way millions of Americans work, turned commercial kitchens into small factories, and changed familiar foods into commodities that are manufactured.

At Burger King restaurants, frozen hamburger patties are placed on a conveyer belt and emerge from a broiler ninety seconds later fully cooked. The ovens at Pizza Hut and at Domino's also use conveyer belts to ensure standardized cooking times. The ovens at McDonald's look like commercial laundry presses, with big steel hoods that swing down and grill hamburgers on both sides at once. The burgers, chicken, french fries, and buns are all frozen when they arrive at a McDonald's. The shakes and sodas begin as syrup. At Taco Bell restaurants the food is "assembled," not prepared. The guacamole isn't made by workers in the kitchen; it's made at a factory in Michoacán, Mexico, then frozen and shipped north. The chain's taco meat arrives frozen and precooked in vacuum-sealed plastic bags. The beans are dehydrated and look like brownish corn flakes. The cooking process is fairly simple. "Everything's add water," a Taco Bell employee told me. "Just add hot water."

Although Richard and Mac McDonald introduced the division of labor to the restaurant business, it was a McDonald's executive named Fred Turner who created a production system of unusual thoroughness and attention to detail. In 1958, Turner put together an operations and training manual for the company that was seventy-five pages long, specifying how almost everything should be done. Hamburgers were always to be placed on the grill in six neat rows; french fries had to be exactly 0.28 inches thick. The McDonald's operations manual today has ten times the number of pages and weighs about four pounds. Known within the company as "the Bible," it contains precise instructions on how various appliances should be used, how each item on the menu should look, and how employees should greet customers. Operators who disobey these rules can lose their franchises. Cooking instructions are not only printed in the manual, they are often designed into the machines. A McDonald's kitchen is full of buzzers and flashing lights that tell employees what to do.

At the front counter, computerized cash registers issue their own commands. Once an order has been placed, buttons light up and suggest other menu items that can be added. Workers at the counter are told to increase the size of an order by recommending special promotions, pushing dessert, pointing out the financial logic behind the purchase of a larger drink. While doing so, they are instructed to be upbeat and friendly. "Smile with a greeting and make a positive first impression," a Burger King training manual suggests. "Show them you are GLAD TO SEE THEM. Include eye contact with the cheerful greeting."

The strict regimentation at fast food restaurants creates standardized products. It increases the throughput. And it gives fast food companies an enormous amount of power over their employees. "When management determines exactly how every task is to be done . . . and can impose its own rules about pace, output, quality, and technique," the sociologist Robin Leidner has noted, "[it] makes workers increasingly interchangeable." The management no longer depends upon the talents or skills of its workers—those things are built into the operating system and machines. Jobs that have been "de-skilled" can be filled cheaply. The need to retain any individual worker is greatly reduced by the ease with which he or she can be replaced.

Teenagers have long provided the fast food industry with the bulk of its workforce. The industry's rapid growth coincided with the baby-boom expansion of that age group. Teenagers were in many ways the ideal candidates for these low-paying jobs. Since most teenagers still lived at home, they could afford to work for wages too low to support an adult, and until recently, their limited skills attracted few other employers. A job at a fast food restaurant became an American rite of passage, a first job soon left behind for better things. The flexible terms of employment in the fast food industry also attracted housewives who needed extra income. As the number of baby-boom teenagers declined, the fast food chains began to hire other marginalized workers: recent immigrants, the elderly, and the handicapped.

English is now the second language of at least one-sixth of the nation's restaurant workers, and about one-third of that group speaks no English at all. The proportion of fast food workers who cannot speak English is even higher. Many know only the names of the items on the menu; they speak "McDonald's English."

The fast food industry now employs some of the most disadvantaged members of American society. It often teaches basic job skills—such as getting to work on time—to people who can barely read, whose lives have been chaotic or shut off from the mainstream. Many individual franchisees are genuinely concerned about the well-being of their workers. But the stance of the fast food industry on issues involving employee training, the minimum wage, labor unions, and overtime pay strongly suggests that its motives in hiring the young, the poor, and the handicapped are hardly altruistic.

STROKING

At a 1999 conference on foodservice equipment, top American executives from Burger King, McDonald's, and Tricon Global Restaurants, Inc. (the owner of Taco Bell, Pizza Hut, and KFC) appeared together on a panel to discuss labor shortages, employee training, computerization, and the latest kitchen technology. The three corporations now employ about 3.7 million people worldwide, operate about 60,000 restaurants, and open a new fast food restaurant every two hours. Putting aside their intense rivalry for customers, the executives had realized at a gathering the previous evening that when it came to labor issues, they were in complete agreement. "We've come to the conclusion that we're in support of each other," Dave Brewer, the vice president of engineering at KFC, explained. "We are aligned as a team to support this industry." One of the most important goals they held in common was the redesign of kitchen equipment so that less money needed to be spent training workers. "Make the equipment intuitive, make it so that the job is easier to do right than to do wrong," advised Jerry Sus, the leading equipment systems engineer at McDonald's. "The easier it is for him [the worker] to use, the easier it is for us not to have to train him." John Reckert—director of strategic operations and of research and development at Burger King—felt optimistic about the benefits that new technology would bring the industry. "We can develop equipment that only works one way," Reckert said. "There are many different ways today that employees can abuse our product, mess up the flow . . . If the equipment only allows one process, there's very little to train." Instead of giving written instructions to crew members, another panelist suggested, rely as much as possible on photographs of menu items, and "if there are instructions, make them very simple, write them at a fifth-grade level, and write them in Spanish and English." All of the executives agreed that "zero training" was the fast food industry's ideal, though it might not ever be attained.

While quietly spending enormous sums on research and technology to eliminate employee training, the fast food chains have accepted hundreds of millions of dollars in government subsidies for "training" their workers. Through federal programs such as the Targeted Jobs Tax Credit and its successor, the Work Opportunity Tax Credit, the chains have for years claimed tax credits of up to $2,400 for each new low-income worker they hired. In 1996 an investigation by the U.S. Department of Labor concluded that 92 percent of these workers would have been hired by the companies anyway—and that their new jobs were part-time, provided little training, and came with no benefits. These federal subsidy programs were created to reward American companies that gave job training to the poor.

Attempts to end these federal subsidies have been strenuously opposed by the National Council of Chain Restaurants and its allies in Congress. The Work Opportunity Tax Credit program was renewed in 1996. It offered as much as $385 million in subsidies the following year. Fast food restaurants had to employ a worker for only four hundred hours to receive the federal money—and then could get more money as soon as that worker quit and was replaced. American taxpayers have in effect subsidized the industry's high turnover rate, providing company tax breaks for workers who are employed for just a few months and receive no training. The industry front group formed to defend these government subsidies is called the "Committee for Employment Opportunities." Its chief lobbyist, Bill Signer, told the *Houston Chronicle* there was nothing wrong with the use of federal subsidies to create low-paying, low-skilled, short-term jobs for the poor. Trying to justify the minimal amount of training given to these workers, Signer said, "They've got to crawl before they can walk."

The employees whom the fast food industry expects to crawl are by far the biggest group of low-wage workers in the United States today. The nation has about 1 million migrant farm workers and about 3.5 million fast food workers. Although picking strawberries is orders of magnitude more difficult than cooking hamburgers, both jobs are now filled by people who are generally young, unskilled, and willing to work long hours for low pay. Moreover, the turnover rates for both jobs are among the highest in the American economy. The annual turnover rate in the fast food industry is now about 300 to 400 percent. The typical fast food worker quits or is fired every three to four months.

The fast food industry pays the minimum wage to a higher proportion of its workers than any other American industry. Consequently, a low minimum wage has long been a crucial part of the fast food industry's business plan. Between 1968 and 1990, the years when the fast food chains expanded at their fastest rate, the real value of the U.S. minimum wage fell by almost 40 percent. In the late 1990s, the real value of the U.S. minimum wage still remained about 27 percent lower than it was in the late 1960s. Nevertheless, the National Restaurant Association (NRA) has vehemently opposed any rise in the minimum wage at the federal, state, or local level. About sixty large food-service companies—including Jack in the Box, Wendy's, Chevy's, and Red Lobster—have backed congressional legislation that would essentially eliminate the federal minimum wage by allowing states to disregard it. Pete Meersman, the president of the Colorado Restaurant Association, advocates creating a federal guest worker program to import low-wage foodservice workers from overseas.

While the real value of the wages paid to restaurant workers has declined for the past three decades, the earnings of restaurant company executives have risen considerably. According to a 1997 survey in *Nation's Restaurant News*, the average corporate executive bonus was $131,000, an increase of 20 percent over the previous year. Increasing the federal minimum wage by a dollar would add about two cents to the cost of a fast food hamburger.

In 1938, at the height of the Great Depression, Congress passed legislation to prevent employers from exploiting the nation's most vulnerable workers. The Fair Labor Standards Act established the first federal minimum wage. It also imposed limitations on child labor. And it mandated that employees who work more than forty hours a week be paid overtime wages for each additional hour. The overtime wage was set at a minimum of one and a half times the regular wage.

Today few employees in the fast food industry qualify for overtime— and even fewer are paid it. Roughly 90 percent of the nation's fast food workers are paid an hourly wage, provided no benefits, and scheduled to work only as needed. Crew members are employed "at will." If the restaurant's busy, they're kept longer than usual. If business is slow, they're sent home early. Managers try to make sure that each worker is employed less than forty hours a week, thereby avoiding any overtime payments. A typical McDonald's or Burger King restaurant has about fifty crew members. They work an average of thirty hours a week. By hiring a large number of crew members for each restaurant, sending them home as soon as possible, and employing them for fewer than forty hours a week whenever possible, the chains keep their labor costs to a bare minimum.

A handful of fast food workers are paid regular salaries. A fast food restaurant that employs fifty crew members has four or five managers and assistant managers. They earn about $23,000 a year and usually receive medical benefits, as well as some form of bonus or profit sharing. They have an opportunity to rise up the corporate ladder. But they also work long hours without overtime— fifty, sixty, seventy hours a week. The turnover rate among assistant managers is extremely high. The job offers little opportunity for independent decision-making. Computer programs, training manuals, and the machines in the kitchen determine how just about everything must be done.

Fast food managers do have the power to hire, fire, and schedule workers. Much of their time is spent motivating their crew members. In the absence of good wages and secure employment, the chains try to inculcate "team spirit" in their young crews. Workers who fail to work hard, who arrive late, or who are reluctant to stay extra hours are made to feel that they're making life harder for everyone else, letting their friends and coworkers down. For years the McDonald's Corporation has provided its managers with training in "transactional analysis," a set of psychological techniques popularized in the book *I'm OK— You're OK* (1969). One of these techniques is called "stroking"—a form of positive reinforcement, deliberate praise, and recognition that many teenagers don't get at home. Stroking can make a worker feel that his or her contribution is sincerely valued. And it's much less expensive than raising wages or paying overtime.

The fast food chains often reward managers who keep their labor costs low, a practice that often leads to abuses. In 1997 a jury in Washington State found that Taco Bell had systematically coerced its crew members into working off the clock in order to avoid paying them overtime. The bonuses of Taco Bell restaurant managers were tied to their success at cutting labor costs. The managers had devised a number of creative ways to do so. Workers were forced to wait until things got busy at a restaurant before officially starting their shifts. They were forced to work without pay after their shifts ended. They were forced to clean restaurants on their own time. And they were sometimes compensated with food, not wages. Many of the workers involved were minors and recent immigrants. Before the penalty phase of the Washington lawsuit, the two sides reached a settlement; Taco Bell agreed to pay millions of dollars in back wages, but admitted no wrongdoing. As many as 16,000 current and former employees were owed money by the company. One employee, a high school dropout named Regina Jones, regularly worked seventy to eighty hours a week but was paid for only forty. In 2001, Taco Bell settled a class-action lawsuit in California, agreeing to pay $9 million in back wages for overtime and an Oregon jury found that Taco Bell managers had falsified the time cards of thousands of workers in order to get productivity bonuses.

DETECTING LIES

After working at Burger King restaurants for about a year, the sociologist Ester Reiter concluded that the trait most valued in fast food workers is "obedience." In other mass production industries ruled by the assembly line, labor unions have gained workers higher wages, formal grievance procedures, and a voice in how the work is performed. The high turnover rates at fast food restaurants, the part-time nature of the jobs, and the marginal social status of the crew members have made it difficult to organize their workers. And the fast food chains have fought against unions with the same zeal they've displayed fighting hikes in the minimum wage.

The McDonald's Corporation insists that its franchise operators follow directives on food preparation, purchasing, store design, and countless other minute details. Company specifications cover everything from the size of the pickle slices to the circumference of the paper cups. When it comes to wage rates, however, the company is remarkably silent and laissez-faire. This policy allows operators to set their wages according to local labor markets—and it absolves the McDonald's Corporation of any formal responsibility for roughly three-quarters of the company's workforce. McDonald's decentralized hiring practices have helped thwart efforts to organize the company's workers. But whenever a union gains support at a particular restaurant, the McDonald's Corporation suddenly shows tremendous interest in the emotional and financial well-being of the workers there.

During the late 1960s and early 1970s, McDonald's workers across the country attempted to join unions. In response the company developed sophisticated methods for keeping unions out of its restaurants. A "flying squad" of experienced managers and corporate executives was sent to a restaurant the moment union activity was suspected. Seemingly informal "rap sessions" were held with disgruntled employees. The workers were encouraged to share their feelings. They were flattered and stroked. And more importantly, they were encouraged to share information about the union's plans and the names of union sympathizers. If the rap sessions failed to provide adequate information, the stroking was abandoned for a more direct approach.

In 1973, amid a bitter organizing drive in San Francisco, a group of young McDonald's employees claimed that managers had forced them to take lie detector tests, interrogated them about union activities, and threatened them with dismissal if they refused to answer. Spokesmen for McDonald's admitted that polygraph tests had been administered, but denied that any coercion was involved. Bryan Seale, San Francisco's labor commissioner, closely studied some of McDonald's old job applications and found a revealing paragraph in small print near the bottom. It said that employees who wouldn't submit to lie detector tests could face dismissal. The labor commissioner ordered McDonald's to halt the practice, which was a violation of state law. He also ordered the company to stop accepting tips at its restaurants, since customers were being misled: the tips being left for crew members were actually being kept by the company.

The San Francisco union drive failed, as did every other McDonald's union drive—with one exception. Workers at a McDonald's in Mason City, Iowa, voted to join the United Food and Commercial Workers union in 1971. The union lasted just four years. The McDonald's Corporation no longer asks crew members to take lie detector tests and advises its franchisees to obey local labor laws. Nevertheless, top McDonald's executives still travel from Oak Brook, Illinois, to the site of a suspected union drive, even when the restaurant is overseas. Rap sessions and high-priced attorneys have proved to be effective tools for ending labor disputes. The company's guidance has helped McDonald's franchisees defeat literally hundreds of efforts to unionize.

Despite more than three decades of failure, every now and then another group of teenagers tries to unionize a McDonald's. In February of 1997 workers at a McDonald's restaurant in St. Hubert, a suburb of Montreal, applied to join the Teamsters union. More than three-quarters of the crew members signed union cards, hoping to create the only unionized McDonald's in North America. Tom and Mike Cappelli, the operators of the restaurant, employed fifteen attorneys—roughly one lawyer for every four crew members—and filed a series of legal motions to stall the union certification process. Union leaders argued that any delay would serve McDonald's interests, because turnover in the restaurant's workforce would allow the Cappellis to hire anti-union employees. After a year of litigation, a majority of the McDonald's workers still supported the Teamsters. The Quebec labor commissioner scheduled a final certification hearing for the union on March 10, 1998.

Tom and Mike Cappelli closed the St. Hubert McDonald's on February 12, just weeks before the union was certified. Workers were given notice on a Thursday; the McDonald's shut down for good the following day, Friday the thirteenth. Local union officials were outraged. Clement Godbout, head of the Quebec Federation of Labour, accused the McDonald's Corporation of shutting down the restaurant in order to send an unmistakable warning to its other workers in Canada. Godbout called McDonald's "one of the most anti-union companies on the planet." The McDonald's Corporation denied that it had anything to do with the decision. Tom and Mike Cappelli claimed that the St. Hubert restaurant was a money-loser, though it had operated continuously at the same location for seventeen years.

McDonald's has roughly a thousand restaurants in Canada. The odds against a McDonald's restaurant in Canada going out of business—based on the chain's failure rate since the early 1990s—is about 300 to 1. "Did somebody say McUnion?" a Canadian editorial later asked. "Not if they want to keep their McJob."

This was not the first time that a McDonald's restaurant suddenly closed in the middle of a union drive. During the early 1970s, workers were successfully organizing a McDonald's in Lansing, Michigan. All the crew members were fired, the restaurant was shut down, a new McDonald's was built down the block—and the workers who'd signed union cards were not rehired. Such tactics have proven remarkably successful. As of this writing, none of the workers at the roughly fifteen thousand McDonald's in North America is represented by a union.

Reading   # All Souls: A Family Story from Southie

MICHAEL PATRICK MACDONALD

Jamaica Street was my only experience living with families who had a father going off to work every day. We were probably the only family on welfare. Looking back I realize our Irish neighbors had some American middle-class pretensions that were at odds with the ways of my mother and us kids. And if we ever did anything considered lower class—like go to the corner store barefoot—in front of someone from Ireland, they might call us "fookin' tinkers." This was the worst you could be, according to Irish immigrants, especially once you'd already made it to the Promised Land.

While we were happy not to be living in the project for once, my family still spent a lot of time visiting the one nearby and hanging out with the other families on welfare. It was a pretty equally mixed project racially, and as a result the tensions weren't as bad as in Columbia Point. This all changed when the Jamaica Plain development shifted toward a black majority and poor whites started to flee. That's when the fights broke out. That's when the chanting started:

Beep beep beep beep,
Walkin' down the street,
Ten times a week.
Ungawa ungawa,
This is black power,
White boy destroyed.
I said it, I meant it,
I really represent it.
Takes a cool cool whitey from a cool cool town,
It takes a cool cool whitey to knock me down.
Don't shake my apples, don't shake my tree,
I'm a J.P. nigga, don't mess with me.

The white kids started to say the same chant, switching "whitey" and "nigga." But for a while, my older brothers and sisters hung out with mixed groups. Especially Mary, who by the mid-seventies had adopted a style that my grandfather criticized in a thick Irish brogue as an "African hairdo." She was dressing too in platform shoes and doing the dances that only the black girls knew. She could do "the robot" like the dancers on "Soul Train." Later, when Mary had two children "out of wedlock" in her late teens before finally marrying the father, my grandfather traced her alleged downfall back to the African hairdo.

There was never much traffic, so we were able to take over Jamaica Street with games of tag, dodgeball, and red rover. All the kids from the other Irish families would join in. Then they'd disappear, called in to dinner. But we stayed outside because we could eat whenever we wanted to. They'd come out again after dinner, but a couple of hours later we were again on our own, as all the other kids on the street had strict curfews, usually before dark.

The kids from the projects could stay out late too, so it was better to hang out with them. Sometimes we'd stay out really late telling ghost stories on the porch. Stories like the one about the hatchet lady, who carried a shopping bag full of little boys' heads. As her bag was very heavy and she was very old, a polite youngster would offer to carry it for her. Before he got to her door with the heavy bag, he'd get curious and ask what was in it. The hatchet lady would let him look into the bag, and while he was bent over, she'd cut his head off with a hatchet, adding another head to her collection. I believed every word of these stories and was horrified when I saw Frankie or Kevin helping an older woman with groceries to her door. But they always got a quarter for their courtesy and still had their heads.

Kids from all over Jamaica Plain started to hang out with us, because they liked our house and could do what they wanted there. My older brothers and sisters set up a clubhouse in the basement, inviting friends over to smoke cigarettes and play spin the bottle. Friends would stay overnight in the cellar, especially when they weren't getting along with their parents, or were running away from home. Most of them started calling my mother "Ma."

On hot summer nights, we'd all sleep on mattresses on the front porch. The house was stifling and we didn't have the air conditioners that others on the street had. Most families in the neighborhood seemed perplexed by our ways. Mrs. Schultz, an older woman from Germany who lived upstairs from us, used to wake us all up to send us inside the house. She was bothered by the idea of having to climb over loads of kids in their underwear, all wrapped in sheets like mummies. She seemed mean, speaking in German and shooing us into the house before we'd had a good night's sleep. Our makeshift way of living seemed normal to us, but it opened us to harsh judgment, like gypsies.

Any time any programs about gypsies were on, Ma would call us all to the TV to watch. She had a great fascination with gypsies, and especially with the tinkers in Ireland. When she'd traveled to Ireland as a teenager, she'd run away from her relatives and hung out with caravans of tinkers, playing the accordion for them. Her aunts wrote back to my grandparents telling them that she was shaming them all over Ireland by joining up with "the tribes." I grew up with a romantic picture of the tinkers from my mother's stories and always wondered if we had tinker blood in us, blood that my grandparents would never mention.

Looking back, it seems that early on I took over the job of trying to keep things looking whatever way they were supposed to look. I worried both about keeping up with the other families and their ways and about making sure that we looked poor enough for surprise visits by the social workers from welfare.

Ma would get an unexpected call early in the morning saying that the social worker was on her way. She'd wake us all up in a panic about the state of the house. The problem wasn't that the house was a mess, but rather that it looked like we owned too many modern conveniences for our own good. Poor people weren't supposed to have a color TV. We'd all have to get up right away on those days to pull a fast one. I actually loved devising strategies for outwitting the inspectors. In no time flat, we'd be running in all directions, getting rid of anything of any value. Out went the toaster. It didn't work without using a steak knife to pull the bread out, at the risk of electrocution. But a toaster might mean that there's a man living in the house, giving gifts or money to my mother. Welfare wouldn't allow for that; God knows a woman with eight kids shouldn't have a man living in the house! But who needs a man in the home, I always thought, when you have the welfare office? A man would only be abusive, tear at Ma's self worth, and limit her mobility in life. Welfare could do all that *and* pay for the groceries. No man ever did that in our home. But our interrogators seemed to be obsessed with the notion of some phantom man sneaking in during the night and buying us appliances. So out went the blender too. Really poor people have no time for exotic milkshakes. We thought it would be enough to put things in the cabinets under the sink, but the social workers got keen to that hiding place. They were shameless about going through cabinets and drawers. We had to resort to the crawl space under the front porch.

But the new color TV was too big to hide. It was one of those huge wooden-cased televisions with fancy-looking cabinets on either side. So we pulled down a heavy green velvet drape from one of the windows and threw it over the television, turning it into a lovely table to serve the social worker a cup of tea on. We had to look as if we had *some* television-watching in a house with so many kids, so we pulled out the contraption we'd been using before we finally entered the modern age of Technicolor. It was two sets actually, one sitting on top of the other. One had only sound, and the other had a black-and-white picture that would get scrambled from time to time. You'd have to get someone to hold a butter knife to the place where the antenna used to be, in order to keep the picture straight. Usually that someone was me; everyone raved that I had some kind of magic power to set that TV straight. Ma said that I was the seventh son, and therefore had special powers that the others didn't have. I was so proud of myself that I would sit for hours holding the butter knife to the back of the TV, forming a human antenna while my family watched its shows: cartoons, "Soul Train," or stories about gypsies and gangsters. For a while this was all we had, and I often felt helpless when "The Brady Bunch" would proudly advertise "in color" at the beginning of the show, knowing there was no way that that butter knife would help on that score.

By the time the social worker arrived, everyone would've left for school except me, as I wasn't yet school age. I got to walk through the house with her and my mother, proud that we looked like we owned nothing at all. Just a few mattresses and an awkward-looking table with an ugly green velvet tablecloth that reached well beyond the floor. And of course while the social worker had her tea on top of our well-draped color television, I sat holding the butter knife to the back of the other TV contraption, reaching my head around to the front to watch morning cartoons. I used to guess at what colors the characters on the set would be if I were watching the TV that the social worker was sitting at. And I couldn't wait for her to leave so I could find out if I was right.

The interrogation lasted about an hour, and it usually focused on men. The social worker would take time out to ask if we had heard from "the father." Ma always said she had no idea where he was. Of course she knew exactly where Mac lived, but didn't want to let on, reminded as she was of the days of abuse with no groceries at all.

There had been times when "the father" had tried to come back. I'd always heard the story of the time he came over drunk, smashed the front door window, and started beating on my mother once he got inside. I was less than two years old, standing in a crib. Ma had stored her accordion on a shelf near the crib, and she always loved telling me how I picked it up and smashed it over Mac's head. She said he was knocked for a loop, and quieted down after that. Of course I don't remember any of it, but I was proud of the way Ma told the story of me putting up a fight.

But Ma didn't tell the social worker any of that. There were a few things Ma didn't mention. She never told the social worker that there were men living in our house from time to time. She never had a problem meeting men as she was very beautiful and played it up with her long red hair, spike heels, fishnet stockings, and penciled-on beauty mark on her right cheekbone. Whenever we passed construction sites in town, all the workers would stop everything and come running to the fence to gawk and catcall. Ma ignored them, strutting through the streets singing her country-western songs and holding my hand. She could have got us a father with a job on the construction site, but she didn't, and I thought it was just as well because I was horrified to see them looking at Ma that way, like animals in a cage.

The trouble was, Ma was drawn to men who would end up living off us, rather than providing for us. Ma was always trying to save someone from the gutter, and that's literally where she met some of her boyfriends. They were usually Irish or Irish American and often alcoholic and jobless. But before long she'd have them sober and scrubbed up, with hair slicked back, a clean collared shirt, and shiny shoes from the thrift shop on their feet. Off they'd go to get a day's pay from Casey and Hayes Moving Company or some other job. But by then she'd be fed up with them and would send them off into the world to fend for themselves. Just when they were primed to bring some money into the home as an able-bodied working father figure. Within weeks we'd all wake up to some new scruffy soul off the street, lying on our legless couch watching the color TV that the social worker didn't know we had. The men were always startled to see eight kids climbing out of the woodwork bright and early to inspect their new dad. We just gathered around and stared. And they stared back.

But these were not stories for the social worker's docket. Before long Ma would offer to play the social worker a few tunes on the accordion. Of course she knew that would help to hurry our visitor off to the next inspection in her caseload, since most social workers had no hint of fun in them. So off each one went with Ma's threats of jigs and reels. Finally I could get on with my day, eating toast, blending shakes, and watching TV programs in full color.

Design and Development of a Parenting Training Group for Low-income African American Parents

RICHARD LANGE

As a social worker supervising and attending therapeutic home visits in a poor urban community of minority residents, I consistently find parents lack adequate skills to manage the behavior of their children. Frequently, I observe common disciplinary techniques incorrectly applied. I have seen parents apply the techniques of "time out" by sending their children to their rooms for hours at a time. Many parents have no positive interactions with their children, and only attend to them when there is a problem. I see parents who attempt to use behavioral bribes such as "if you sit down I'll give you some cookies" become frustrated when their child, not hungry, refuses to sit down. And worst, I hear about parents who use force: slapping, punching, belts, and paddles.

Over time I have come to the conclusion that much of this parent abuse stems from ignorance, not malice. I thought that our not-for-profit agency could have a positive effect by developing a method of disseminating information about the basics of parenting to such families. This case study is the story of how that program came about—a ten year odyssey to develop a parenting group to meet the needs of a culturally diverse and economically poor community—a story with ideas, failures, and ultimately success.

The nonprofit organization (where I work) provides services for families and children in Camden, New Jersey. Camden, located just across the river from Philadelphia, was a prosperous economic center until the 1960s, when industries, lured by the cheapness of land in the suburbs, moved out, leaving Camden residents with no source of employment. Camden by the 1990s was the fifth poorest city in the nation. With industry gone, a massive "white flight" occurred, leaving a city of predominantly African American and Hispanic residents. Drug trafficking moved in and with it came a host of other problems. The combination of poverty and drugs led to an increase in violence and Camden rose to the rank of second most violent city in the nation.

Urban families in poor communities face a multitude of problems. Unemployment forces families to rely on welfare and other community services for basic living needs. Family life is strained by limited resources. Parents who find employment outside of the city need to rely on their parents, relatives, or others for childcare. So much time is spent on day-to-day survival that it is understandable that many families never develop effective parenting skills. Often it is only when a family comes to the attention of child protection service workers that parents realize that they lack necessary parenting skills and are given an opportunity to develop them.

In New Jersey, families under the care of the state's child protection services (The Division of Youth and Family Services—DYFS) for substantiated or suspected abuse are required to receive supportive services to stabilize their family. These services include psychotherapy, counseling, drug treatment, home visits, case management, and other services deemed appropriate. Services are purchased through subcontracts between DYFS and local nonprofit organizations.

As a subcontracted service, my staff and I were providing in-home counseling for DYFS-referred families. Realizing the need for additional parenting training, I approached DYFS with the idea of setting up a Parenting Resource Center (PRC), a place where parents could get information on parenting issues. DYFS, also recognizing the need, was agreeable. An initial meeting was set up with DYFS and (at my suggestion) an advisory committee was created to develop a curriculum.

After two advisory committee meetings consisting of DYFS, a nurse, a foster care representative, and my staff, the curriculum focus of the PRC was established. The committee felt the best approach would be for the parenting groups to teach "hands on" skills such as how to bathe a baby. The curriculum included: infant care, housekeeping, discipline for children, personal hygiene, budgeting (including finding employment), and anger management. Working every day for a month with a newly assigned MSW parenting coordinator, I was able to oversee the development of the curriculum. Each topic was defined by a behavioral objective for which we developed a measurement instrument. Parents were pre-tested by asking them very concrete, practical questions such as, "How do you know your child has a fever?" Groups consisted of one-hour sessions, held once a week, during which the group leader demonstrated skills. Each topic consisted of four sessions. At the end of the last session, the parents were administered a post-test that allowed us to measure the effectiveness of the group training. The first groups were run by paraprofessional African American women who lived in the community and had experience as life-skill counselors in our home visiting program. The advisory committee thought that parents might be more responsive to instruction from community members.

Our first year was not a success. Parents did not score significantly better on the post-test than they did on the pre-test. The dropout rate was high after the second session. The paraprofessionals complained that running the groups was "too difficult" for them.

One issue that unexpectedly emerged was that many parents had significant unmet therapeutic needs. Parents presented with serious clinical issues that required skills that were beyond the training of the paraprofessionals. Some paraprofessionals tried to help by listening to stories of depression, fear, anxiety, and low self-esteem. However, without the necessary clinical training, the paraprofessionals did not know how to respond, and when they tried the group lost its focus. Other paraprofessionals, not knowing how to help, ignored the parent's clinical problems and returned the group's focus to the skill topic. Not responding to the parent's clinical need had the result that many parents felt unheard, then responded by dropping out of the group. It is understandable that the paraprofessionals found the group work unrewarding and "too difficult."

After a careful analysis of the first year, my PRC coordinator and I made the decision to hire only masters-level group leaders. (We were able to hire two African American group leaders.) Once re-established, we refocused on a therapeutic curriculum. We expanded contact time to eight sessions of one hour and thirty minutes weekly. We divided the program into two general topics: discipline and communication. We revamped the curriculum to better suit the needs of the community.

The major dilemma was deciding whether the parenting group should be a therapy group or a skills-based training group. In operating the groups, we frequently had to deal with parents arriving at group in crisis, for example, in tears because of a fight with a boyfriend. What should we do? Ask the parent in crisis not to discuss her problem in group because it is unrelated to the parenting issue scheduled for discussion? Doing so risks alienating the parent by making her feel that she is not valued. Or should we devote group time to helping the parent in crisis and thereby reduce the time available to teaching parenting skills?

Evaluating the success and failures of the first year led to the conclusion that the group really needs to be both. So we developed a combination approach that allows us to address our young parent's dilemma while simultaneously teaching parenting skills. The dual-program approach involves extracting from the parent's crisis a lesson that is universally applicable to the whole group. The leader listens to the parent's story, e.g., a fight with her boyfriend, and then uses the situation for a group discussion on anger, fighting, and conflict resolution. The leader in the course of discussion skillfully refocuses the topic to fighting between children or arguments between parents and children. Thus a link is made between the problems confronting the parent in crisis and the curriculum of the group.

Once we realized that we were going to focus on therapeutic issues we needed to choose a general therapeutic approach. We adopted a humanistic approach based on the work of Carl Rogers. We wanted our group leaders to be non-judgmental, empathic and reflective.

Early on we began to understand the long history of disappointment our parents had faced. Most parents had been through failed relationships, and were single parents or living in chaotic living situations. Often estranged from their mothers and other relatives, they were devoid of any social support system. The city provided no neighborhood or community support. The only source of emotional support for many parents was their children. And frequently, by the time they came to group, even that source of support was gone, since DYFS had removed their children to foster care. We recognized that part of our mission was to help these parents feel (at least for the time in group) supported and valued. We found we needed to be non-judgmental and provide the parents with a sense that they were not "bad parents."

It is our belief that parents (with a few exceptions) do not intentionally harm their children. Most parents try to do what they think is the right thing to do; their knowledge of alternatives is limited. Limited knowledge of choices can cause parents to abuse their children unintentionally. Often the reason why parents beat their children is because they know no other strategy of discipline. Take for example a child who misbehaves in school. The parent, Ms. J., spanks her child with the intention of "teaching the child a lesson." Next day the child's teacher sees marks on the child's legs, reports the parent to DYFS, and an investigation follows during which the parent admits she spanked her child. Suddenly the parent is labeled a "child abuser." It does not take a profound clinical judgment to see why the parent is angry when she arrives at group. "I don't need parenting group. What can you tell me that I don't know? Why am I here?" Ms. J. would become even angrier if the leader began by discussing what was wrong with the way she handled the situation.

Our leaders will reflect and engage Ms. J. before any attempt is made to teach parenting skills. "Ms. J, it sounds like you are angry. And you have every right to be angry. You were only trying to do your best." Once engaged, the work can begin, "Ms. J., remember when you hit little J. for talking in school? Can you think of other ways now that might have worked more effectively?"

Many humanistic skills come to play in engaging parents. Empathic and reflective listening are two of the more effective techniques. "I know how you feel when your son cries all night." "That makes me sad to think that your teenage son runs away from home for days at times." Empathy connects the group leader with the parents. Once joined, they can search together for solutions to the problems of the parents. Reflective listening provides the groundwork for the empathic responses. "What I hear you saying, Ms. B., is that it upsets you when your son refuses to do his homework." "It sounds like you are confused about what to do with your son who is always fighting in school."

It is important that parents learn to accept themselves. One means of encouraging self-acceptance is to explore the punishments inflicted on the parents when they were children. We help the parents see that they were punished harshly as children not because they were especially bad, but because their parents, like themselves, knew no other techniques of discipline, or believed in archaic notions like "spare the rod and spoil the child." Parents often express relief when they come to realize that they were not responsible for the beatings they received as children. While there is not enough time to fully analyze a parent's past life, we have found that these issues need to be addressed or the parent will be blocked from learning new skills. "Why can't I hit my kids? I was hit and I turned out fine." "So what if I scream at my kids, my parents screamed at me!"

We found we could improve the effectiveness of group by departing from the way groups are normally run. Typical groups begin with an introduction and group rules. Since many of the parents who come to parenting group are frightened and worried about being exposed, we eliminated introductions and dispensed with ground rules to make the group more congenial. We attempted to reduce anxiety by delaying the time when parents first had to address the group. For some, just introducing themselves can be frightening. When a parent arrives at group, we ask him or her to sign in. While there are no introductions, the leader knows the names of the parents and uses them frequently to help acquaint the members with each other.

Elimination of group rules also helps parents to relate quickly to each other and the group leader. Parents who come to group have been through a series of degrading experiences. They have had their homes inspected, their personal lives reviewed by therapists, and if they were charged with substance abuse, they have been exposed to a multitude of humiliating experiences such as urine tests. One parent told me what it was like when DYFS came to her house:

> DYFS started looking around the house as if I was hiding something. They wanted to know if I had a bed for my child. I have a cot that I put away for my boy to sleep on. They wanted me to pull out the cot. I did and then they asked "where do I sleep?" I told them on the sofa. What else did they want to know?

Our parents do not need someone else "laying down rules." So we begin group by introducing the leaders and starting right into the topic of the day.

We tailored the teaching style to the traditions and culture of the community. Acknowledging something as mundane as the different speaking styles of cultural groups affects group interactions and the likelihood that an individual will become part of the group process. For example, African Americans are not offended if another person begins talking before they finish. Known as "call and response," this verbal tradition has roots in the languages of Africa. Leaders acknowledge this speaking style and do not attempt to modify it in group.

Since oral traditions play such a strong part in African-American culture, many of the skill building exercises are presented as stories. The stories often tell how the leader faced with a difficult situation responded. We found that these stories encourage group members to place themselves in situations analogous to those in which children "get into trouble," so that they can more easily understand the motivation and feelings of their children. Here is an example of a story that helps parents cope with children who lie:

> Let's say you are driving home from work. It is late at night and you want to get home. You know that there is a stop sign by your house, but you don't see any cars coming and you kinda tap the breaks and coast through. Two blocks later, you see the cop car lights. You're pulled over, you roll down the window and you say . . . Here responses from the group are solicited. OK now let's think about your children. It's raining, they are bored, and they know they are not allowed to play ball in the house, but they do so anyway—CRASH, down goes a picture. You walk into the room. What do your kids say? Here the leader points out the similarities between what the parents said to the police officer and what the child says to the parents.

An issue with many parents is that their children lie. If the story of children playing ball in the house had been presented without the car story, most parents would predict that their child would lie about breaking the picture. The parent's response would be to become angry with the child. The first part of the story helps the parents see the story from the child's point of view. Able to empathize with the child, the parent does not become so angry.

Another technique that leaders find especially effective is role-play. The role-plays help minority parents to build skills and express their feelings. Role-playing gives the parent a chance to describe confrontational situations. Before we introduced role-playing into the group, parents accused us of "not knowing what it is like." We now respond that "maybe we don't know, but I would like you to show me. Why don't you play your daughter and I'll play you." The role-play enables parents to demonstrate situations that they would have had difficulty articulating because of poor communication skills or their inability to understand the emotional content of an interaction.

Role-playing also allows individual group members to tell their stories to the group as a whole. By having the parent play the role of the child, the parent is put in a position to understand, from a perspective closer to that of the child, how the child perceives when the parent becomes angry or abusive.

We soon realized that we had to change the curriculum from what was used in most parenting groups. It became apparent that most parenting programs were designed for middle-class families, and that they addressed problems unrelated to the problems faced by our parents.

Sadly, we found that we needed to include a section on violence. During group time we encourage parents to discuss violence in their lives: violence on the streets, in the homes, at school, or even on television. Parents describe techniques they have developed to survive the everyday life of the street. The purpose of this section is to help parents teach children how to avoid potentially violent situations. We encourage our parents to talk to their children about violence. One of the skills emphasized is the need for children to understand that it is not cowardly to leave a situation if it looks unsafe.

Group leaders talk frankly about the racial tension experienced by African Americans in our society. One experience I had with a parent will serve as an illustration.

> An African American parent complained to me that her fourteen-year-old son was "never home." He spent his time in the streets. She worked long hours and when she came home he was never there. She was ready to have him arrested as a runaway. When I met with the boy he told me that he liked to go out. "I get bored with television, I don't like it. I want to meet people. I go out, play cards, and hang with my friends. I'm a social person. I don't like to be stuck in the house." I pointed out to the mother that if they were white living in a suburban community, he would be considered an outgoing and sociable young man. However, because they lived in the city, the mother was worried that he would become a street kid or a runaway.

Stores participate in their own form of racial profiling—especially of low-income families: a poor African American family is watched closely from the minute they enter a store. African American children, even at a young age, realize they can use this discrimination to their advantage by threatening their parents with misbehavior if they do not buy them what they want. Some African American parents admit that they do not take their children to stores because they do not want to be manipulated by their children and risk expulsion from the store.

In group we address this issue by teaching parents that, because of the extra attention paid to African American families, they have be especially thorough in teaching their children how to behave in stores. We recommend that parents rehearse store behaviors with children. Children tend to act out when they know their mother has to have something at the store and cannot leave without it. We recommend that parents practice store behavior with their children on trips to the store when it does not matter if the parent leaves empty-handed. On these trips, the child is told clearly that if he or she acts out they will leave immediately. After a few times, the child will learn that acting out is not rewarded, and that only if they behave will they be allowed to accompany their mother on future trips to the stores.

One of our goals has been to make our parenting groups culturally responsive. With regard to this objective we see two tasks: 1) include in our teaching effective techniques that are already part of African American culture, and 2) explain to African American families cultural differences that might impact them.

One effective African American parenting technique is "the look." "The look" is a facial expression that signals to the child that they have done or might do something wrong. "My mother could give me 'the look' from across the room and I knew I was in trouble." "My kids were acting up so I gave them 'the look.'" As leaders we found this was a non-violent way of correcting a child's behavior. "When Thomas was acting up in the store, did you give him 'the look'?"

An example of a cultural difference that can lead to misunderstanding is the different way in which whites and African Americans give directives. African American families speak in a direct manner to their children; "Sit down." "Put away the crayons." "Pick up your coat." White families tend speak in a non-directive way: "Wouldn't you like to sit here?" "Don't you think that it's time to pick up your crayons?" "Is that your coat on the floor?" What happens to African American children in school is that many of the teachers are white. The non-directive way of talking to children makes the African American child confused. So when the teacher says; "Don't you think it's time we put away our reading books?" The African American child hears this as a question and not as a command and responds with a "No." The teacher sees the child as "defiant." In group, we discuss these differences and help parents understand the language of the teacher.

The parenting program has been operational for nearly a decade. Judging from the positive evaluation given the program by exiting parents and the low recidivism rate, we conclude that the program has been mostly successful. Our humanistic approach has been well received by parents. In the exit surveys parents have expressed the following: "I felt that I was listened to." "I liked hearing from others in the group." "I learned that I was not alone with my problems." "I liked learning to deal with feelings." We continue to tune the curriculum to the needs of our parents, and as we do, we frequently get positive growth. Exit statements such as: "Learned how to discipline without hitting," "Learned better ways to communicate," "Learned to control my temper and talk to the children in a calmer way," encourage us to continue our work.

Our program continues to struggle every session with the problems of developing appropriate techniques to teach skills to inner-city parents. This case study presents the story of our program's efforts to identify the parenting skills needed by a low-income, predominantly African American, inner-city community and implement techniques to teach them in an eight-week course. Our objective in relating the history of this program is to inspire others to develop programs to help teach parenting skills to other needy populations.

Questions for Further Study

1. Two of the themes of Lars Eighner's essay "On Dumpster Diving," from his book *Travels with Lizbeth* are respect and accountability. How are these themes reflected in his words about the dumpster diving enterprise and in his behavior as a diver?

2. In the excerpt from *All Souls: A Family Story from Southie*, MacDonald describes an incident in which the family outwits the social worker through deception and cleverness. Their activities allow the family to continue to collect income support. Of course, this incident takes place in a time when social work was less professionalized, and certainly long before the advent of welfare reform. How might the MacDonald family's situation be different in the present? Would those differences be positive or negative (or neither) for the children?

3. In "Learning How to be Niggers," from Gregory Williams' *Life on the Color Line: The True Story of a White Boy Who Discovered He Was Black*, young Billy and his brother Mike are transformed literally overnight from white children from a middle-class family to low-income black children. As can be seen from this excerpt, the boys quickly learn the limitations imposed by membership in these two groups. What do you think were the differential effects of these limitations? In other words, how might life have changed if only their race or only their class status had changed in this way?

4. The excerpts from *Fast Food Nation* reprinted here depict some of the forces that determine the wages and working conditions of lower-level employees in the fast food industry. As a social worker with an obligation to advocate for social justice, what do you think would be the most effective action you (in concert with others) could take on behalf of this work force? Would it be union organizing? Advocating for employment training? Educating yourself and others in the complexities of the industry? Working with living wage campaigns in your community? Organizing boycotts, or other more public expressions of desire for change? These are but a few of the many forms that your advocacy could take. Discuss what you would do, and explain why.

5. Richard Lange's case study, "Design and Development of a Parenting Training Group for Low-Income African American Parents," details the design and implementation of an ultimately successful parenting group. What were some of the elements that made this group successful? What did you learn from this, and the other readings, that might change your practice with low-income African American clients? Do you think Lange had any opportunities to practice class advocacy? Where?

Invited Commentary

SCOTT HARDING

THE REALITIES OF POVERTY

Though poverty has been gradually erased from public debate and the media as a significant social problem, it nevertheless remains a fundamental reality for millions of Americans. Despite the most prolonged period of economic growth in U.S. history, the recent decline in the rate of impoverishment only reduced levels of poverty to those that existed almost thirty years ago (Census Bureau 2001), and preliminary additional data for 2002 suggest that poverty (and inequality) is worsening. The pervasiveness of this problem, and its relative disappearance from the public policy agenda, suggests that those promoting victim blaming—whereby poor people are themselves to blame for their plight—have succeeded. Thus "harsh and racist representations of the poor" have been replaced, in the age of the so-called "new economy," by the creation of an "invisible poor" removed from our lives and public discussion (Goode and Maskovsky 2001). One significant impact is that this lack of connection to how poor people are forced to live their lives facilitates a retreat from a larger social responsibility to address poverty.

The essays in this section provide a range of views about the daily realities facing those in poverty. Of note, most offer a non-traditional examination of economic destitution. This topic, abundant in the social science and social work literature, is often made abstract by focusing on demographic data about poverty. While the use of statistics is a practical approach, these essays offer a perspective that numbers alone cannot present: the human aspect of poverty and economic inequality. Though several of these "stories" are set in a prior time period, they nevertheless present a timeless truth. Their strength is that they allow us to experience this issue in a manner that truly befits social work by examining life in poverty as lived by real people. As such, these essays make it much harder for us to ignore the reality of "the other America," where some dreams don't come true.

The selection from *All Souls*, by Michael Patrick MacDonald, highlights some of the ways that people in poverty are expected to live and act. In order to meet the approval of an invasive welfare state, the poor must prove (by their clothing, by their household furnishings) that they own nothing of worth, and operate from different values and norms than mainstream society. Aside from describing long-discredited home visitation practices by social workers, MacDonald provides an unsparing glimpse of how one poor family perseveres. The value of his memoir is that in spite of deplorable and often dangerous conditions, his family demonstrates a remarkable spirit of resiliency. Rather than despair at their plight, they find joy in the company of neighbors, the ability to survive (and even thrive) in the face of oppressive conditions, and by outwitting "the system."

None of these articles is more dramatic than Lars Eighner's seemingly benign tale of rooting around in trash dumpsters, *On Dumpster Diving*. If he were making observations about some "foreign" culture, Eighner might be hailed as an astute anthropologist, drawing meaning from the refuse of a gluttonous society. As it is, he introduces us to a facet of American society few can imagine: the reality of being homeless and surviving on the endless waste of others. His depiction of how to subsist by "dumpster diving" (he prefers the term "scavenging") highlights in stark terms the extremes of inequality that exist in American capitalism. After an unrivaled period of economic growth and low unemployment, at a time when wealth has reached unprecedented levels, Eighner reminds us that a rising tide clearly fails to lift all boats.

While on one level we can be grateful for the ingenuity of Eighner and countless others living on the streets, his essay, though at times absurd and humorous, is ultimately tragic and shameful. What kind of society would force their fellow citizens to resort to scavenging in trash dumpsters for their daily existence? What kind of society facilitates a level of excess and waste that even makes it possible for people to eat and live out of garbage cans? At some point, Eighner notes, he came to the realization that "people throw away perfectly good stuff, a lot of perfectly good stuff." While it would be easy to make harsh judgments of those who do scavenge for a "living," a temptation apparently irresistible to much of society, Eighner forces us to recognize a larger reality: those who "dumpster dive" are still people, and in fact they *are* earning a living:

> I think of scavenging as a modern form of self-reliance. In any event, after having survived nearly ten years of government service, where everything is geared to the lowest common denominator, I find it refreshing to have work that rewards initiative and effort.

The idea that poverty is not something that only happens to "bad" people due to poor habits or moral failure, but instead may be caused by key social structures like the economy is emphasized in the selection from *Fast Food Nation*. Eric Schlosser demonstrates how workers in the fast food industry, one of the nation's largest occupational sectors, are routinely set up for economic failure by receiving little or no useful job skills training and low wages, and are often prevented from working full time. Schlosser describes the relatively hidden world of mostly low-paid, part-time, unskilled teenage employees who comprise the bulk of the labor force at fast food restaurants. He makes clear that most fast food workers are mere cogs in a regimented and exceptionally profitable industry. These firms target marginalized workers who are easily replaced—the industry has one of the highest turnover rates of any occupational category—and relatively powerless. Not surprisingly, these same workers do not benefit from the enormous profits generated by the likes of Burger King, Taco Bell, and

McDonalds. Fast food employees comprise "the biggest group of low-wage workers in the United States today" (p. 72).

Life on the Color Line presents a childhood memoir of poverty and race in the 1950s, a bleak glimpse into an era when racial segregation and destitution were more overt. Despite being bi-racial, Williams describes how he feared that his new school would be "black," and thus have inferior facilities. In painful detail, he recounts how he and his brother tried to avoid standing out from the other students, both for their racial identity, and their low socioeconomic status—his fear of looking "different." In a scene powerful for its symbolism of society's response to difference, Williams describes how his two best friends from school, Molly and Sally, turn their backs when they learn his true identity.

> *Even from a distance I saw shock register on their faces. They turned toward each other. Molly stared up the hill once more. A final glance, then she darted from the intersection, her blond curls disappearing behind the corner grocery store.*

What his two white schoolmates saw was color; what they failed to see was how Williams and his family struggled to overcome the accompanying poverty still common to African American households.

Combined, these essays provide an unmistakable challenge to acknowledge and confront the oppressive conditions of poverty in America. For the social work profession, these essays raise a fundamental question: should social workers use the skill of advocacy for people in situations like those depicted here? If so, how and when can they best use this approach?

LINKS TO ADVOCACY

What is advocacy? Broadly defined it represents change efforts focused on policy and practices with and on behalf of clients, usually as a way to empower communities and individuals. Advocacy is about *changing* social situations, for example, eliminating the conditions (and causes) of poverty. In this respect, advocacy demands the involvement of social workers to create change. Similarly, social work clients can and should be engaged as often as possible as partners in the process of improving their social and economic status.

There are different types of advocacy, using different strategies, tools, and tactics. Case versus class advocacy is the most common example.

> *Case advocacy refers to working with the client's interaction with the environment. Class advocacy refers to intervention to change the environment through social policy (Mickelson 1995, p. 96).*

Advocacy is goal seeking, a process involving multiple activities (Ezell 2000). Advocacy should thus be seen as appropriate and accessible to social workers and clients in a range of practice settings. For educators, teaching advocacy skills is a form of advocacy training, and should also be viewed as a vital aspect of social work education and consistent with CSWE curriculum mandates.

Jansson (1999) highlights a range of policy practice (or advocacy) tasks and skills that social work students should master. Among these, getting an issue "on the table"—creating the context for advocacy on a particular issue or political initiative—is central to advocacy practice. Thus problem definition is often seen as a critical first stage in advocacy. Jansson and others suggest that the initial definition of a social issue shapes public perceptions and potential choices during policy deliberations. In this respect, Jansson describes a key *analytic challenge* facing social work advocates: the need to provide factual and technical information to convince others of the seriousness of a given social problem. This can illuminate the reality of a crisis and demonstrate that a problem is so serious as to warrant new policies or programs. However, social workers are often noticeably absent in this process, letting those with power and influence shape social policy agendas. In this respect, social workers are more often reactive to the policy preferences of elites, rather than wielding their own (often untapped) power to advocate for policy and program change.

Haynes and Mickelson (2000) also stress the need for social workers to engage in policy analysis, policy making and other advocacy to improve services and policies affecting oppressed populations. They claim that social work practitioners are experts on both what policies and programs work, and on identifying existing problems, needs and gaps in service delivery. To be more effective policy advocates—to be community change agents—they claim the effective use of *information* is the critical resource common to social work.

They highlight the crucial role of information in advocacy, suggesting that information links various practice interventions. Haynes and Mickelson find that *documentation* is a key advocacy task, for example, documenting social problems and service needs/gaps. Thus documentation is a key requirement of policy change—"a primary step in any problem solving process in social work." As such, data and research are critical to policy practice and change. Again, this highlights the special role of social workers as insiders with expert knowledge: social workers have a special understanding of practice knowledge, and should serve as conduits of vital information throughout the advocacy process.

Jansson (1999) also describes four skills (*policy competencies*) as a way to think of different styles of policy (advocacy) practice. He notes that no one style is more or less effective in all settings, but that different situations require the use of different skills and practices. *Analytic Skills* refer to the ability to evaluate social problems and their severity, and to develop policy proposals in response to identified problems utilizing knowledge of what does/doesn't work. *Political Skills* can be used to develop and implement political strategy, or to develop and lend support to policy initiatives. *Interactional Skills* require policy practitioners to participate in task/work groups, a process to gain access to networks of people with information and power, and to build organizational support and resources. *Value-Clarifying Skills* allow for the identification and ranking of relevant principles when engaging in policy practice. Most of these are common (core) social work skills, making advocacy practice a natural "fit" for social work students, educators, and practitioners.

The utility of advocacy skills is made apparent in the previous readings. For example, Richard Lange recounts how the staff at a community non-profit agency and at the state Department of Youth and Family Services advocated for and created community-based programs for parents in a poor urban neighborhood receiving family services. These efforts started after staff members identified a lack of adequate parenting skills among many community members, which led to other family and community problems. What began as a parenting-skills-based training group evolved into a program that included therapy to address the range of issues confronting low-income parents, *and* a parenting skills course. Of note, the initial attempt to establish these services largely excluded the input of neighborhood residents, the same families who were to receive the proposed services. However, by responding to the range of problems and concerns raised by those living in a poor and largely isolated community, group leaders were better able to address key parenting issues that emerged. Using a non-traditional group format, with a teaching style geared toward the culture and customs of community members, social workers developed a curriculum and new services targeting the unique needs of local low-income parents.

Schlosser's tale of the world of fast food highlights how acting on *documentation* would be a crucial step toward expanding the life options of these low-wage workers. With a primary industry goal of maximizing output and profit by designing equipment that requires minimal or no training of workers, most fast food employees have little opportunity to improve their skills for future and better-paid jobs. This scenario is all the more striking when one factors in the multitude of corporate tax subsidies and credits available to these already profitable firms for job "training" that in fact rarely occurs. Further, some of the largest fast food corporations in the United States have been among the most active industry opponents of *the existence of* the minimum wage, while companies like McDonalds appear to have perfected a range of tactics in order to prevent their employees from organizing into labor unions to improve their economic status.

REFERENCES

Ezell, M. (2001). *Advocacy in the Human Services*. Belmont, CA: Brooks/Cole Publishing Company.

Haynes, K. S. and Mickelson, J. S. (2000). *Affecting Change: Social Workers in the Political Arena*. Boston: Allyn & Bacon.

Goode, J. & Maskovsky, J. (2001). *The New Poverty Studies: The Ethnography of Power, Politics, and Impoverished People in the United States*. New York: New York University Press.

Jansson, B. S. (1999). *Becoming an Effective Policy Advocate: From Policy Practice to Social Justice*. Pacific Grove, CA: Brooks/Cole Publishing Company.

Mickelson, J. S. (1995). Advocacy. *Encyclopedia of Social Work* (19th ed.). Washington, D.C.: NASW Press (pp. 95–100).

U.S. Bureau of the Census (2001). *Poverty in the United States: 2000*, Current Population Reports, Consumer Income, P-60-214. Washington, D.C.: U.S. Department of Commerce.

About the Editors

ALICE LIEBERMAN (Ph.D.—University of Wisconsin, Madison) is Associate Professor of Social Work and former Director of the Undergraduate Program at the University of Kansas. She is the author of *The Social WorkOut Book* (Pine Forge Press, 1998). She has also conducted research and written in the fields of child welfare, mental health, and reproductive rights. Lieberman received the HOPE Award (Honor for the Outstanding Progressive Educator) in 1999. She was Co-Founder (with the late Liane Davis) of Options for Women, Inc., Co-Founder (with Sylvie Rueff) of the Second Chance Fund, is currently a member of the Board of Directors of the Council on Social Work Education, and was formerly on the board of the National Association of Social Workers, Kansas chapter.

CHERYL LESTER (Ph.D.—SUNY, Buffalo) is Associate Professor of English and American Studies, Graduate Director of the American Studies Program, chair of the Jewish Studies Steering Committee, and Courtesy Faculty Member of African and African American Studies at the University of Kansas. Lester is the author of articles on American literature and critical and cultural theory. In 1995 she was an NEH fellow, in 1997 she was a visiting professor at the University of Hong Kong, and in 1998 she was a visiting professor at the University of Gaston-Bérgère in St. Louis, Senegal. At the University of Kansas, Lester received a Kemper Teaching Award in 1998 and Center for Teaching Excellence Awards in Undergraduate and Graduate Teaching in 1998 and 2000. She attended the Postgraduate Program in Bowen Family Systems Theory and its applications at the Georgetown Family Center in Washington, D.C., from 1997 to 2001.

Contributors

Gloria **Anzaldua,** a self-described "chicana dyke-feminist, tejana patlache poet, writer, and cultural theorist," was born to sharecropper/field-worker parents on September 26th, 1942 in South Texas' Rio Grande Valley. In 1969 Anzaldua received her B.A. in English, Art, and Secondary Education from Pan American University. She then earned an M.A. in English and Education from the University of Texas. Anzaldua has won numerous awards for her works, such as the Lambda Lesbian Small Book Press Award for Haciendo Cara, an NEA Fiction Award, the Before Columbus Foundation American Book Award for *This Bridge Called My Back*, and the Sappho Award of Distinction.

Lisa **Banta** is currently a Ph.D. candidate in social work at Rutgers University, and an adjunct faculty member in the Ramapo College undergraduate psychology program. She has worked with families, children, and adolescents as a teacher and mental health social worker, and holds three bachelor's degrees in elementary, preschool, and special education.

Carolyn **Banta** graduated from high school in the Summer, 2002, and currently attends Lehigh University, in Bethlehem, PA.

Frederick **Barthelme** heads the writing program at the University of Southern Mississippi. He is author of fourteen books including *Moon Deluxe, Second Marriage, Tracer, Two Against One, Natural Selection, The Brothers, Painted Desert,* and *Bob the Gambler.* He is an occasional contributor to *The New Yorker* and has published in *GQ, Kansas Quarterly, Epoch, Playboy, Esquire, TriQuarterly, North American Review, Frank,* and other places. His memoir, *Double Down: Reflections on Gambling and Loss,* released in November 1999, was co-authored with his brother Steve. A retrospective collection of stories, *The Law of Averages,* was published by Counterpoint in November 2000 and released in paperback in August 2001.

Steven **Barthelme** publishes widely in literary magazines; he has a story collection, *And He Tells the Little Horse the Whole Story,* and he won a Pushcart Prize in 1993; his nonfiction appears in the *New York Times Magazine, Los Angeles Times, Washington Post, Texas Observer, Elle Decor,* and elsewhere. His memoir, *Double Down: Reflections on Gambling and Loss,* released by Houghton Mifflin in November 1999, was co-authored with his brother.

Sheida **Bates** was born in Tehran, Iran in April of 1964. She emigrated to the United States in 1982. Bates is currently a graduate student in the Department of English at the University of Kansas. She is married and lives in Prairie Village, KS.

Kathleen **Belanger,** LMSW, is a faculty member in the School of Social Work at Stephen F. Austin State University, Nacogdoches, Texas. She is also Director of the Child Welfare Professional Development Program, a Title IV-E program. She has a B.A. from Catholic University and an M.M.S.W. from the University of Texas at Austin.

Nancy **Boyd-Franklin,** Ph.D. is an African American family therapist, psychologist, and Professor, Graduate School of Applied and Professional Psychology, Rutgers University. She is the author of *Black Families in Therapy: A Multisystems Approach* and an editor of *Children, Families and HIV/AIDS: Psychosocial and Psychotherapeutic Issues.* Dr. Boyd-Franklin is an internationally recognized lecturer and author of articles on issues such as the treatment of African American families, extended family issues, spirituality and religion, home-based family therapy, group therapy for black women, parent and family support groups, community empowerment, and the multisystems model. She is the recipient of numerous awards, including the Psychotherapy with Women Award from Division 35 of APA, the Carolyn Attneave Award for Contributions to Cultural Diversity Training from Division 43 of APA, and the 1994 Distinguished Psychologist of the Year Award from the New York Chapter of the Association of Black Psychologists.

Ona **Bregman** teaches in the Family Mental Health Concentration in the MSW program, Syracuse University. She provides supervision and consultation to social work clinicians and human service organizations, conducts training workshops, and maintains a small clinical practice. Professor Bregman was selected teacher of the year by the faculty of the School of Social Work, Syracuse University, in 1995. As a member of NASW, she has served on the board and as a delegate to the national delegate assembly. She is a fellow of the American Orthopsychiatric Association and the

Society of Clinical Social Workers. Professor Bregman serves on community boards and advisory committees. Her research interests are in the areas of the impact of loss on a family system and the development of systems theories.

Jean-Robert **Cadet** has done more to expose the system of child slavery in Haiti than any other human being. His book, *Restavec: From Haitian Slave Child to Middle Class American*, begins with his descent into the restavec system following the death of his mother, a poor black. His wealthy white father places him with one of his other mistresses, and so begins a life of torment that is to last for years, until his father finds the resources to bring him and the family to the United States. There, he finishes high school, enters the army, enters school on the GI Bill, and ultimately achieves his dream of entry in to the American middle class. In 2000, Cadet resigned from his position teaching in a high school, and started the Restavec Foundation, dedicated to educating US citizens about the restavec system and raising money to help children enslaved within it.

Maxine **Clair** is the author of *Rattlebone*, a collection of short stories, which won the Chicago Tribune's Heartland Prize for fiction; a collection of poems, *Coping With Gravity*; and a novel, *October Brown*, which won Baltimore's Artscape Prize. Born and raised in Kansas City, Kansas, she worked for many years as chief medical technologist at the Children's Medical Center in Washington, D.C. She is now an associate professor of English at George Washington University.

Ellis **Cose,** author, columnist and contributing editor (since 1993) for *Newsweek* magazine and former chairman of the editorial board and editorial page editor of the *New York Daily News*, began his journalism career as a weekly columnist for the *Chicago Sun-Times*—becoming, at the age of 19, the youngest editorial page columnist ever employed by a major Chicago daily. He is author of *The Rage of a Privileged Class*, a book-length essay on race in America (HarperCollins, 1994), *A Man's World* (HarperCollins, 1995), *A Nation of Strangers*, a history of American immigration (William Morrow and Co., 1992), and *The Press* (Morrow, 1989). Cose's new book, *The Envy of the World*, an in-depth essay on the state of black men in America was published by Washington Square Press, an imprint of Simon and Schuster, in 2002.

Mary **Crow Dog** was born in 1955 on a South Dakota reservation, and endured great hardship during her childhood and adolescence. Raised in a one-room cabin without running water or electricity, Mary was sent to a Catholic missionary boarding school for Native children, where she endured the cruelty and prejudice so common in these environments at the time. Discouraged from living according to Native traditions by her mother as well as boarding school teachers, Mary became a disaffected adolescent, living a marginal life of urban shoplifting, barhopping, and drug use.

Her initiation into the ways of First Nations peoples came during the occupation of Wounded Knee in 1973 by American Indian Movement activists, and there, at 17, Mary gave birth to a daughter in the midst of flying bullets and death threats. Later, as the wife of Leonard Crow Dog, a descendent of Sitting Bull and a revered medicine man, she learned a great deal about Native rites and beliefs. The excerpt we offer here, taken from her book, *Lakota Woman* (Harper Trade, 1991) offers the reader insights into that experience. Now divorced from Leonard Crow Dog, the author goes by the name of Mary Brave Bird. Her follow-up book, *Ohitika Woman* (Harper Perennial, 1994) recounts her continuing struggle to live a rich, rewarding life, free from the struggles with alcohol that have continually plagued her. Both books, although recounting a life that has been difficult and, at times, bleak, offer the reader a sense of the hopefulness, pride, and rich cultural life of the American Indian.

Carol Anne **Douglas** joined the staff of the ground-breaking radical feminist monthly *off our backs* in 1973, and has worked and written prolifically for the paper ever since. She earned her master's degree in political science at UCLA, studying international affairs. She has taught women's studies and feminist theory courses in the Washington, DC area.

Joel **Dreyfuss** is a Senior Editor at Fortune Magazine. He was also the Editor-in-Chief and Associate Publisher/Editorial Director of Information Week. Prior to this, he was the Editor of *PC Magazine* for three years. Dreyfuss has written freelance articles for *The New York Times Magazine and Book Review*, the *Los Angeles Times*, the *Washington Post*, and the online magazine *Salon*. He received his BS degree in sociology from the City College of the City of New York.

Lars **Eighner** was born in Corpus Christi, Texas, November 25, 1948, the grandson of Texas poet and author of *The Big Thicket* Alice Ewing Vail. Eighner was surrounded by literary influences throughout his childhood. He was the subject of light verse by New England poet Robert P. Tristram Coffin, and at the age of eleven he was permitted to attend a three-week workshop on creative writing by George Williams of Rice University. Following a loss of employment in 1987, Eighner found himself on the streets. His 1993 book about his experience, *Travels with Lizbeth*, was a critical success and was as commercially successful as many literary books, and his essay "On Dumpster Diving" has been reprinted numerous times.

Louise **Erdrich** was born in 1954, in Little Falls, Minnesota and grew up in Wahpeton, North Dakota where her parents worked for the Bureau of Indian Affairs. She received an M.A. degree from the John Hopkins University in 1979. Erdrich's fiction and poetry draws on her Chippewa heritage to examine complex familial and sexual relationships among full and mixed blood Native Americans as they struggle with questions of identity in white European American culture. She is a novelist, poet, short story writer, essayist and a critic.

Anne **Fadiman** is the editor of *The American Scholar*, a literary quarterly that has been published since 1932 by the Phi Beta Kappa Society. Her journal received this year's National Magazine Award for the best American magazine with a circulation under 100,000. Fadiman is the author of *The Spirit Catches You and You Fall Down: A Hmong Child, Her American Doctors, and the Collision of Two Cultures* (Farrar, Straus & Giroux, 1997), which won the National Book Critics Circle Award for general nonfiction, the Salon Book Award for nonfiction, the Los Angeles Times Book Prize for current interest nonfiction, and the Boston Book Review Ann Rea Jewell Award for nonfiction. *The Spirit Catches You and You Fall Down* tells the story of a refugee family from Laos and its tragic encounters with the American medical system. Fadiman's second book, *Ex Libris: Confessions of a Common Reader* (Farrar, Straus and Giroux, 1998), is a collection of essays about her lifelong love affair with books and language. Fadiman's essays and articles have appeared in *Harper's, The New Yorker, The New York Times*, and *The Washington Post*, among other publications. While she was a staff writer at *Life*, she won a National Magazine Award for Reporting for her reportage on suicide among the elderly. In 1997, Fadiman delivered the Phi Beta Kappa orations at both Harvard (of which she is a 1975 graduate) and Yale. She was a 1991–92 recipient of a John S. Knight Fellowship at Stanford.

Dr. Temple **Grandin** is a designer of livestock handling facilities and an Assistant Professor of Animal Science at Colorado State University. Facilities she has designed are located in the United States, Canada, Europe, Mexico, Australia, New Zealand, and other countries. In North America, almost half of the cattle are handled in a center track restrainer system that she designed for meat plants. She obtained her B.A. at Franklin Pierce College and her M.S. in Animal Science at Arizona State University. Dr. Grandin received her Ph.D. in Animal Science from the University of Illinois in 1989. Today she teaches courses on livestock behavior and facility design at Colorado State University and consults with the livestock industry on facility design, livestock handling, and animal welfare. She has appeared on television shows such as *20/20, 48 Hours*, and *CNN Larry King Live*, and has been featured in *People Magazine*, the *New York Times, Forbes*, and *U.S. News and World Report*. She has also authored over 300 articles in both scientific journals and livestock periodicals on animal handling, welfare, and facility design. Her story of living with the diagnosis of autism, and using her condition as a mechanism for better relating to the animals she works with, have provided both fascination and inspiration to countless families of children with autism and similar conditions.

Ben **Hamper**'s "Impressions of a Rivethead" column was the most widely read page in the alternative biweekly, the *Flint Voice*. When that paper became the *Michigan Voice*, his popularity soared, and his irreverent neo-gonzo prose was brought to the masses by publications like the *Wall Street Journal, Harpers* and (briefly) *Mother Jones*. In 1990, Ben published the book *Rivethead*, a compilation of his best columns throughout the years. *Rivethead* became a national best-seller and received critical acclaim throughout the country. His *Directions to Nowhere* column may be accessed at: www.michaelmoore.com/hamper.

Scott **Harding** is Assistant Professor, Social Welfare, University of Kansas, where he teaches social welfare policy, and writes about poverty policy.

Vanessa **Hodges** is Associate Dean, School of Social Work, the University of North Carolina, Chapel Hill, NC. Her research and teaching interests center on child welfare and cultural diversity issues.

Barbara "Pua" **Iuli** of Kapi'olani Medical Center at Pali Momi was named Hawaii Medical Social Worker of the Year by the National Association of Social Workers. In addition to being director of social services at Kapi`olani Medical Center at Pali Momi, using specifically Hawaiian markings, Iuli mentors students from local universities who are training to become social workers. Over the past eight years, Iuli has mentored over 50 interns at Pali Momi.

Elisabeth **Kenny**, LMSW, is the Field Instruction Specialist with the Child Welfare Professional Development Program, the Title IV-E program in the School of Social Work, Nacogdoches, Texas, where she works with field students in child welfare. She has a B.A. from Vassar College and an M.S.S.W. from the University of Texas at Arlington.

Leonard **Kriegel** was left without the use of his legs due to childhood polio. It is a loss he has transmuted into art from the moment he became a writer. Kriegel brings a lyrical, uncompromising voice to the interlaced themes of courage and masculinity, in a context where something has been taken away. Recalling his coming of age in the 1950s, he portrays an interior life partly sustained by traditional visions of manhood, partly raging at the impossibility of fully living them out. Kriegel's work has appeared frequently in *Harper's, The Nation, The New York Times Magazine, Best American Essays*, and many other publications. He is author of six books and lives in New York City with his wife.

Richard **Lange** has been working in direct practice for twenty years. He has earned a Master's Degree in Counseling Psychology from Antioch University, a Master's of Social Work from the University of Pennsylvania, and is currently a Social Work Ph.D. student at Rutgers University. Richard's direct practice work is with community organizations. In Philadelphia he worked with adults with mental illness and developmental disabilities for the Community Organization for Mental Health and Mental Retardation. For the past eleven years he had been with Family Counseling Services in Camden, New Jersey, a non-profit community organization. Ten years ago he founded the Parenting Resources Center for which he continues to consult and run groups.

Michael Patrick **MacDonald** grew up in "the best place in the world"—the Old Colony projects of South Boston—where 85 percent of the residents collect welfare in an area with the highest concentration of impoverished whites in the United States. He organized a popular gun buy-back program in the Boston area, and continues to be an activist in the local community.

Nancy **Mairs,** though born by accident of war in Long Beach, California, grew up north of Boston. In 1964, she received an A.B. *cum laude* from Wheaton College (Norton, Massachusetts), which made her a Doctor of Humane Letters thirty years later. She did editorial work at the Smithsonian Astrophysical Observatory and the Harvard Law School before moving to Tucson, Arizona, where she earned an M.F.A. in creative writing (poetry) in 1975 and a Ph.D. in English literature (with a minor in English education) in 1984 from the University of Arizona. She has taught writing and literature at Salpointe Catholic High School, the University of Arizona, and the University of California at Los Angeles. A poet and an essayist, she was awarded the 1984 Western States Book Award in poetry for *In All the Rooms of the Yellow House* (Confluence Press, 1984) and a National Endowment for the Arts Fellowship in 1991. Her first work of nonfiction, a collection of essays entitled *Plaintext: Deciphering a Woman's Life*, was published by the University of Arizona Press in 1986. Since then, she has written a memoir, *Remembering the Bone House*, a spiritual autobiography, *Ordinary Time: Cycles in Marriage, Faith, and Renewal*, and three more books of essays, *Carnal Acts, Voice Lessons: On Becoming a (Woman) Writer,* and *Waist-High in the World: A Life Among the Nondisabled*, all available from Beacon Press. Her most recent work is entitled *A Troubled Guest: Life and Death Stories*. She and her husband, George, a retired high-school English teacher, continue to live in Tucson, though they make public appearances throughout the country. A Research Associate with the Southwest Institute for Research on Women, she also serves on the Committee on Disability Issues of the Modern Languages Association, the Commission on the New Aging of the Pima Council on Aging, and the board of the Arizona Center for Disability Law.

Wilma (Pearl) **Mankiller,** former Principal Chief of the Cherokee Nation of Oklahoma, lives on the land which was allotted to her paternal grandfather, John Mankiller, just after Oklahoma became a state in 1907. Surrounded by the Cherokee Hills and the Cookson Hills, she lives in a historically rich area where a person's worth is not determined by the size of their bank account or portfolio. Her family name "Mankiller," as far as they can determine, is an old military title that was given to the person in charge of protecting the village. As the leader of the Cherokee people, she represented the second largest tribe in the United States, the largest being the Dine (Navajo) Tribe. Mankiller was the first female in modern history to lead a major Native American tribe. With an enrolled population of over 140,000, and an annual budget of more than $75 million, and more than 1,200 employees spread over 7,000 square miles, her task may have been equalled to that of a chief executive officer of a major corporation. Initially, Wilma's candidacy was opposed by those not wishing to be led by a woman. Her tires were slashed and there were death threats during her campaign. But now as Wilma shares her home with her husband, Charlie Soap, and Winterhawk, his son from a previous marriage, things are very different. She has won the respect of the Cherokee Nation, and made an impact on the culture as she has focused on her mission—to bring self-sufficiency to her people.

Jeanne **Matich-Maroney** is currently an Assistant Professor of social work at Iona College in New Rochelle, New York. She comes to her academic appointment with 15 years of experience in the field of developmental disabilities, and she has served as an administrator, clinical supervisor and direct service clinician. Dr. Matich-Maroney holds a special interest and expertise in mental health and sexuality related issues for people with mental retardation/developmental disabilities and was instrumental in designing and implementing innovative clinical programs in this area. She has conducted numerous professional training sessions and conference presentations on the topic of sexuality and developmental disabilities. As a full-time faculty member at Iona, Dr. Matich-Maroney strives to infuse information about people with developmental disabilities into the social work curriculum. She is a member of the college's Diversity Collaborative. Dr. Matich-Maroney earned her Ph.D. (clinical social work), MSW and B.S. (social work) at New York University's Ehrenkranz School of Social Work.

Noreen **Mokuau** is Professor of Social Work at the School of Social Work at the University of Hawaii at Manoa. She is a Native Hawaiian interested in multicultural issues in social work practice and is specifically concerned about groups of individuals from the Pacific Islands. Author of several journal articles and book chapters, she has edited a book titled *Handbook of Social Services for Asian and Pacific Islanders* (Greenwood Publishing Group, 1991).

Shani **Mootoo** was born in Ireland in 1958 and raised in Trinidad. She moved to Canada at the age of 19, where she began a career as a visual artist. A skilled multimedia artist and videomaker, she has had exhibitions in the United States and Canada, and her videos have been shown at a number of film festivals. Mootoo has said that she has gravitated to the visual most of her life, because as a child, when she told her grandmother of the sexual abuse she suffered at the hands of an uncle, she was told never to say those words again. So, in different ways, she found it safer not to use words and started making pictures. Finally acknowledging and naming her experience of abuse prompted Mootoo to return to words, and write her first collection of short stories, *Out on Main Street*, published in 1993. Her second book, *Cereus Blooms at Night*, published in 1996, is her first novel.

Bharati **Mukherjee** has published widely on the field of diasporic Indian literature. Born in Calcutta, India, in 1940, she grew up in a wealthy traditional family. She studied in a Bengali school in her early years, and learned English when she traveled with her family for three years in Europe. She attended the universities of Calcutta and Baroda, where she earned a master's degree in English and Ancient Indian Culture. She came to America in 1961 to attend the Iowa Writers Workshop and earned her master of fine arts and Ph.D. in English from the University of Iowa. She married Canadian author Clark Blaise in 1963, immigrated to Canada in the mid-1960s and became a naturalized citizen in 1972. She was teaching English at McGill University in Montreal when she began writing fiction. After fourteen years in Canada, she found life as a "dark-skinned, non-European immigrant to Canada" very hard, so she moved with her husband to the United States and took US citizenship. She won the National Book Critics' Circle Award for best fiction for *The Middleman and Other Stories*. She has taught creative writing at Columbia University, New York University, and Queens College and is currently professor of English at the University of California at Berkeley. She has two sons.

Patricia **O'Brien** is Assistant Professor, Jane Addams School of Social Welfare, University of Illinois, Chicago Circle, Chicago, IL. She is the author of *Making It in the 'Free World': Women in Transition from Prison* (Suny Series in Women, Crime, and Criminology), State University of New York Press, 2001.

Debora **Ortega** is Assistant Professor, School of Social Welfare, University of Kansas, Lawrence, KS. She is the Principal Investigator, IV-E Short-Term Training, in cooperation with the Kansas Department of Social and Rehabilitation Services, and has written primarily in the area of child welfare. She received her doctorate from the University of Washington.

Leon **Pettiway** holds a doctoral degree in urban geography. One of his primary research interests is the integration of geographical and criminological theories to explain patterns of crime in urban areas. He has published a series of articles on the impact of ghettoization on patterns of arson and the roles of environmental and individual factors in arson for revenge. Another focus of Professor Pettiway's work has been the relationship between an individual's drug use, criminal participation, and the formation of crime partnerships. He is completing a large-scale, three-year project funded by the National Institute on Drug Abuse (NIDA) on the criminal behavior of adult opiate and cocaine users. In this study, he has investigated the criminal decision-making of addicts and nonusers in light of various environmental cues, including environmental crime prevention strategies, to determine whether offenders who are deterred in one setting seek other locations for crime. His first book, *Honey, Honey, Miss Thang: Being Black, Gay, and on the Streets* (Temple University Press, 1996), is an examination of the lives of gay transvestites who were drug addicted and committed acts of prostitution. His second book, *Workin' It: Women Living Through Drugs and Crime* (Temple University Press, 1997), is an examination of drug use and crime participation among a group of inner-city women. Professor Pettiway teaches courses on urban crime patterns, drug use and criminal behavior, theories of crime and deviance, and quantitative methods.

Nocona **Pewewardy** is a doctoral student, University of Kansas, Lawrence, KS, where her research interests center on practice and pedagogy about white privilege. Upon receiving her MSW from the University of Oklahoma, she worked in public child welfare for the State of Oklahoma.

Colleen J. **Reed** is currently a doctoral student at the School of Social Welfare, University of Kansas, and a researcher in the School's Office of Aging and Long-Term Care. Her practice experience has focused largely on persons living with AIDS and HIV.

Carter **Revard** was born in Oklahoma and raised on the Osage reservation. After earning his undergraduate degree from the University of Tulsa he went to England as a Rhodes scholar to study at Oxford University, where he received his Masters degree. Revard received his doctorate in English in 1959 at Yale. He is currently a professor of English at Washington University in St. Louis, Missouri. Revard is also a Gourd Dancer, and has served on the Board of the American Indian Center in St. Louis. His Osage name is Nompehwahteh which means "Fear-inspiring."

Luis **Rodriguez** is a recipient of a Lila Wallace–Reader's Digest Writers' Award, a Lannan Foundation Literary Fellowship, a Hispanic Heritage Award in Literature, a Dorothea Lang/Paul Taylor Prize from the Center for Documentary Studies at Duke University (with Donna DeCesare), and a National Association for Poetry Therapy Public Service Award and fellowships from the Illinois Arts Council. He is founder-director of Tia Chucha Press, a Chicago-based poetry press; a founder of Rock A Mole (rhymes with *guacamole*), which produces Hip Hop Jazz, and Rap artists, and urban youth arts festivals in Los Angeles. In 1996, he was featured in the CD compilation "In Their Own Voices: A Century of Recorded Poetry," issued by Rhino Records. He is a founder/board member of Youth Struggling for Survival, featured in the 1997 PBS-TV series "Making Peace" (Moira Productions for the Independent Television Service). He is also a founding member of the League of Revolutionaries for a New America. He has visited juvenile facilities, prisons, public schools, community centers, Indian reservations, and youth programs throughout the country. Since 1994, he has helped facilitate events concerning violence, youth, and elders for the Mosaic Multicultural Foundation as well as in El Salvador and Mexico.

Mary **Romero** is currently Professor, School of Justice Studies, Arizona State University. She received her Ph.D. in sociology in 1980 from the University of Colorado. In 2000, she became a Carnegie Scholar in the Pew National Fellowship Program and Carnegie Academy of the Scholarship of Teaching and Learning. She is the author of numerous books and articles whose focus has been on women and work, and the intersection of sex and gender, with particular attention to how these phenomena are expressed in Mexican and Mexican-American communities.

Esmeralda **Santiago** is the eldest of eleven children. She spent her childhood in Puerto Rico, moving back and forth between a tiny village and Santurce, a suburb of San Juan. With her mother and siblings she moved to New York in 1961, at the age of thirteen. She attended junior high school in Brooklyn and Performing Arts High School in Manhattan. After the extraordinary years described in her two memoirs, *When I Was Puerto Rican* and *Almost a Woman*, she graduated from Harvard University and received a master's degree from Sarah Lawrence College. Santiago is also the author of *Amèrica's Dream* and is coeditor, with Joie Davidow, of *Las Christmas: Favorite Latino Authors Share Their Holiday Memories*. Santiago lives in Westchester County, New York, with her husband and two children.

Eric **Schlosser** is a correspondent for the *Atlantic Monthly*. He has received a number of journalistic honors, including a National Magazine Award for an *Atlantic* article he wrote about marijuana. *Fast Food Nation* is his first book.

Vicki L. **Sears** is a writer, storyteller, and psychotherapist. Currently, she resides in Seattle.

Uma A. **Segal** is professor and director of the undergraduate social work program at the University of Missouri, St. Louis. She holds research fellow positions in the University's Public Policy Research Center and its Center for International Studies. She has written extensively about child welfare from an international perspective, with special interest in India and Japan, and a book on the immigrant experience of Asian Americans. An immigrant herself, she came from India at age 13. Uma Segal received her Ph.D. from Washington University, St. Louis, MO.

Leslie Marmon **Silko** was born in Albuquerque, New Mexico and grew up on the Laguna Pueblo Reservation. Silko received her B.A. (with honors) from the University of New Mexico in 1969. In addition to writing, her career includes an association with the University of New Mexico, Albuquerque; Navajo Community College in Tsaile, Arizona; and professor of English at the University of Arizona, Tucson, where she is currently employed. Her works in progress include a screenplay for public television.

Gloria **Steinem** is one of the leading activists in the modern feminist movement. A journalist and author by trade, Steinem is best known for founding (along with women's rights activist Dorothy Pitman Hughes) *MS* Magazine in 1972, and contributing numerous articles in the intervening years. Her books include *Outrageous Acts and Everyday Rebellions* (1983); *Marilyn: Norma Jean* (1986); and *Revolution from Within: A Book of Self-Esteem* (1992). In addition, Steinem has spoken out about feminist issues and is credited with coining the phrase, "reproductive choice," to signify that women are entitled to the right to decide whether or not to have a child. Steinem's early life was anything but conventional, particularly for the times. In 1944, Gloria's parents, Ruth and Leo Steinem, split up. Ruth had a history of mental instability, which necessitated Gloria's taking on the role of caring for her mother. The narrative Gloria constructed about her mother's life was intertwined with her expanding world view of the role of women in the United States and the wider world.

James **Wahlberg** was, until his death, Professor, Social Work, East Tennessee State University, Johnson City, TN. Prior to that, he served as Associate Professor and Director of Social Work and Criminal Justice Studies at Minot State University. His areas of expertise included clinical social work practice with Native Americans.

Stevan **Weine** directs the Kosovo Professional Training Collaborative, a partnership between CCFH, the University of Illinois, the American Family Therapy Academy, and the University of Pristina. This program sends teams of U.S. family therapists to Kosovo to conduct tri-monthly weeklong training sessions in collaboration with local mental health professionals. The program provides resilience-based services for family recovery from war-related trauma and loss. Dr. Weine is an associate professor of psychiatry, as well as the co-founder and co-director of the Project on Genocide, Psychiatry and Witnessing at the University of Illinois at Chicago. He is the principal investigator of the NIMH funded project, Family Education and Support for Bosnian Families.

Gregory Howard **Williams** is currently the President of the City University of New York. Prior to his appointment in 2001, Dr. Williams was the Carter C. Kissell Professor of Law and Political Science and Dean, School of Law, at the Ohio State University. Dr. Williams began his career in higher education at George Washington University. He served as Coordinator of the GW-Washington Project, an all University office designed to serve as the liaison between the University and District of Columbia communities with special needs. His work in developing University-sponsored programs in Anacostia, an area of significant poverty, and the Adams Morgan community, the District of Columbia's largest concentration of Latinos, was recognized as one of the most outstanding outreach projects in the nation.

Patricia J. **Williams** is a Professor of Law at Columbia University School of Law. A graduate of Wellesley College and Harvard Law School, she has served on faculties of the University of Wisconsin School of Law, Harvard University's Women's Studies Program, and the City University of New York Law School at Queen's College. She has held fellowships at the School of Criticism and Theory at Dartmouth College, the Humanities Research Institute of the University of California at Irvine, and the Center for Advanced Study in the Behavioral Sciences at Stanford University. Before entering academia, she practiced law, as a consumer advocate and Deputy City Attorney for the City of Los Angeles, and as a staff attorney for the Western Center on Law and Poverty. At present, she serves on the boards of the Center for Constitutional Rights, NOW Legal Defense and Education Fund, and the Society of American Law Teachers. She has authored numerous articles for scholarly journals and popular magazines and newspapers including *USA Today, Harvard Law Review, Tikkun, The New York Times Book Review, The Nation, Ms. Magazine* and the *Village Voice.* Her book, *The Alchemy of Race and Rights,* was named one of the twenty-five best books of 1991 by the *Voice Literary Supplement* and one of the "feminist classics of the last twenty years" that "literally changed women's lives," by *Ms. Magazine's* Twentieth Anniversary Edition.

Karl **Woelz** is a recipient of both the Lambda Literary Award and the National Gay & Lesbian Press Award. He is the editor of the forthcoming *M2m: New Gay Fiction,* and co-editor of *Men On Men 2000.* His writing has appeared in more than a dozen books and journals, including *Best American Gay Fiction 2, Men On Men 6, The Harvard Gay & Lesbian Review, Lambda Book Report, The James White Review, Cottonwood, Bento, Asspants,* and *The Baltimore Alternative.* He holds degrees in English from Columbia University, The University of Texas at San Antonio, and The University of Kansas. He lives among a small community of Amish in rural Pennsylvania.

Shanlon **Wu** has served as an Assistant U.S. Attorney in the District of Columbia since 1990. He also served as Counsel to former Attorney General Janet Reno from November 2000 to January 2001. He holds a J.D. from the Georgetown University Law Center, a Master in Fine Arts from Sarah Lawrence College, and a B.A. from Vassar College. Following law school, he clerked for two federal judges before joining the Department where he has served as both a line prosecutor and supervisor. While on detail he served as Senior Associate Independent Counsel in the independent counsel investigation concerning former Secretary of the Interior Bruce Babbitt. His community service includes participation on the Washington, D.C. Circuit's Task Force on Gender, Race & Ethnic Bias and membership in the D.C. Coalition Against Drugs & Violence. He is a past president of the Asian Pacific American Bar Association.

Michael **Yellow Bird** is a citizen of the Sahnish (Arikara) and Hidatsa First Nations, and Professor, School of Social Work, at Arizona State University, Tempe, AZ. He is active in the struggle to free Indian activist Leonard Peltier from prison (where he is currently serving a life sentence), and in the effort to rename professional and college athletic teams who use Native symbols and people as mascots.

Gwat **Yong-Lie** is Associate Professor, Helen Bader School of Social Work, University of Wisconsin-Milwaukee, where she teaches, researches, and writes about mental health issues, sex abuse, and cultural diversity issues.

Diane S. **Young** is Assistant Professor, Syracuse University, Syracuse, NY. She received her Ph.D. and MSW degrees from the University of Washington, Seattle, WA. Her research interests include social work with incarcerated individuals, health promotion among disadvantaged populations, program planning, and research methodology.

Ray Anthony **Young Bear** was born in Iowa in 1950 and grew up at the Mesquakie Tribal Settlement. His poetry has been influenced by his maternal grandmother Ada Kapayou Old Bear and his wife, Stella L. Young Bear. Young Bear attended Claremont College in California, as well as Grinnell, University of Iowa, Iowa State and the University of Northern Iowa. He has been a visiting faculty member at Eastern Washington University and the University of Iowa. Young Bear and his wife co-founded the Woodland Song and Dance Troupe of Arts Midwest in 1983. Young Bear's group has performed traditional Mesquakie music in this country and the Netherlands.

Credits

Unit 1

Mary Romero, "Intersection of Biography and History: My Intellectual Journey," from *Maid in the USA* by Mary Romero. Copyright © 1992 by Routledge, Chapman, and Hall, Inc. Reprinted by permission of Routledge, Inc. part of The Taylor & Francis Group.

Jean-Robert Cadet, from *Restavec: From Haitian Slave Child to Middle-Class American*, University of Texas Press. Copyright © 1998 by the University of Texas Press. Reprinted by permission of University of Texas Press.

Joel Dreyfuss, "The Invisible Immigrants: Haitians in America Are Industrious, Upwardly Mobile and Vastly Misunderstood," *Critical Issues in Contemporary Culture*, New York Times Magazine, May 23, 1992. Copyright © 1992 by The New York Times Company. Reprinted with permission.

Ben Hamper, from *Rivethead: Tales from the Assembly Line*. Copyright © 1986, 1987, 1988, 1991 by Ben Hamper. Reprinted by permission of Warner Books, Inc.

Nancy Boyd Franklin, "Therapy With African American Inner-City Families," *Integrating Family Therapy: Handook of Family Psychology and Systems Theory*, Richard Mikesell, Don-David Lusterman and Susan McDaniel, eds. Copyright © 1995 by American Psychological Association. Reprinted with permission.

Unit 2

Maxine Clair, "The Creation," from *Rattlebone* by Maxine Clair. Copyright © 1994 by Maxine Clair. Reprinted by permission of Farrar, Strauss and Giroux, LLC.

Patricia J. Williams, Reprinted by permission of the publisher from "The Death of the Profane" in *The Alchemy of Race and Rights: Diary of a Law Professor* by Patricia J. Williams, Cambridge, Mass.: Harvard University Press. Copyright © 1991 by the President and Fellows of Harvard College.

Esmeralda Santiago, "The American Invasion of Macún" in *When I Was Puerto Rican* by Esmeralda Santiago. Copyright © 1993 by Esmeralda Santiago. Reprinted by permission of Perseus Books, publishers, a member of Perseus Books, L.L.C.

Wilma Mankiller, "Child of the Sixties" in *Mankiller: A Chief and Her People* by Wilma Mankiller and Michael Wallis. Copyright © 1993 by Wilma Mankiller. Reprinted by permission of St. Martin's Press, LLC.

James Wahlberg, "Personal Growth and Self-Esteem through Cultural Spiritualism: A Native American Experience" in *Case Studies in Generalist Practice* by Robert Rivas and Grafton Hull, International Thomson Publishing, 1996.

Unit 3

Temple Grandin, from *Thinking in Pictures* by Temple Grandin. Copyright © 1995 by Temple Grandin. Used by permission of Doubleday, a division of Random House, Inc.

Unit 4

Unit 5

Unit 6

Name Index

I

Subject Index